About the Managing Editor

Nicolás Kanellos has been professor at the University of Houston since 1980. He is founding publisher of the noted Hispanic literary journal *The Americas Review* (formerly *Revista Chicano-Riqueña*) and the nation's oldest Hispanic publishing house, Arte Público Press.

Recognized for his scholarly achievements, Dr. Kanellos is the recipient of a 1990 American Book Award, a 1989 award from the Texas Association of Chicanos in Higher Education, the 1988 Hispanic Heritage Award for Literature presented by the White House, as well as various fellowships and other recognitions. His monograph, *A History of Hispanic Theater in the United States: Origins to 1940* (1990), received three book awards, including that of the Southwest Council on Latin American Studies.

Among his other books are the *Biographical Dictionary of Hispanic Literature of the United States* (1989) and *Mexican American Theater Legacy and Reality* (1987).

Dr. Kanellos is the director of a major national research program, Recovering the Hispanic Literary Heritage of the United States, whose objective is to identify, preserve, study, and make accessible tens of thousands of literary documents of those regions that have become the United States from the colonial period to 1960.

Reference Library of
HISPANIC
AMERICA

Advisors

Dr. Edna Acosta-Belén, *Director, Center for Caribbean and Latin American Studies, University of Albany*

Dr. Rodolfo Cortina, *Director, Bibliographic Database, Recovering the U.S. Hispanic Literary Heritage Project, and Professor of Spanish, Florida International University*

Dr. Rodolfo de la Garza, *Professor of Political Science, The University of Texas at Austin*

Dr. Ricardo Fernández, *President, Lehman College, City University of New York*

Dr. Arturo Madrid, *Director, the Tomás Rivera Center, Claremont, California*

Dr. Michael Olivas, *Associate Dean of Law and Director of the Institute for Higher Education Law and Governance, University of Houston*

Contributors

Roberto Alvarez, *Department of Anthropology, Arizona State University*

Gilbert Paul Carrasco, *School of Law, Villanova University*

José Fernández, *Department of Foreign Languages, University of Central Florida*

María González, *English Department, University of Houston*

Gary Keller, *Bilingual Review Press, Arizona State University*

Thomas M. Leonard, *Department of History, Philosophy & Religious Studies, University of North Florida*

John Lipski, *Department of Modern Languages, University of Florida*

Tatcho Mindiola, *Mexican American Studies Program, University of Houston*

Silvia Novo Pena, *Department of English and Foreign Languages, Texas Southern University*

Manuel Peña, *Foreign Languages, California State University, Fresno*

Jacinto Quirarte, *College of Fine and Applied Arts, University of Texas, San Antonio*

Arturo Rosales, *Department of History, Arizona State University*

Guadalupe San Miguel, *History Department, University of Houston*

Federico Subervi, *Department of Radio-Television-Film, University of Texas, Austin*

Dennis Valdez, *Chicano Studies Program, University of Minnesota*

Jude Valdez, *College of Business, University of Texas, San Antonio*

Reference Library of

HISPANIC AMERICA

VOLUME

II

Nicolás Kanellos,
EDITOR

Distributed by Educational Guidance Service

Reference Library of Hispanic America is based upon *The Hispanic-American Almanac*, published by Gale Research Inc. It has been published in this 3-volume set to facilitate wider usage among students.

Nicolás Kanellos, *Editor*

Gale Research Inc. Staff: ───────────────────

Lawrence W. Baker,
Christine B. Hammes,
    Senior Developmental Editors
Rebecca Nelson, *Developmental Editor*
Peg Bessette, Kevin S. Hile,
Neil R. Schlager,
    Contributing Editors

Mary Beth Trimper, *Production Director*
Evi Seoud, *Assistant Production Manager*
Mary Kelley, *Production Assistant*

Cynthia Baldwin, *Art Director*
Barbara J. Yarrow,
    Graphic Services Supervisor
Mark C. Howell, *Cover Designer*
Arthur Chartow, *Page Designer*
Willie F. Mathis, *Camera Operator*
Nicholas Jakubiak, *Keyliner*

Benita L. Spight, *Data Entry Supervisor*
Gwendolyn S. Tucker,
    Data Entry Group Leader
Tara Y. McKissack, Nancy K. Sheridan,
    Data Entry Associates

∞™ This book is printed on acid-free paper that meets the minimum requirements of American National Standard for Information Sciences Permanent Paper for Printed Library Materials. ANSI Z39.48-1984.

ISBN 0-8103-9621-1

Printed in 1994
Printed in the United States of America
for distribution by
Educational Guidance Service

Ofrezco esta labor a mi hijo adorado, Miguel José Pérez Kanellos, con la esperanza de que él, su generación y las que siguen puedan tener plena consciencia de su historia, sus artes, sus tradiciones y acceso a información básica acerca de su gente. Que el pueblo hispano y, particularmente los estudiantes, jamás vuelvan a carecer de básicos recursos informativos en sus bibliotecas y en sus escuelas. Que el pueblo americano en general tenga también acceso y plena conciencia de una parte importante—la contribución hispana—de la identidad nacional estadounidense y la abrace como suya.

I offer this labor of love to my adored son, Miguel José Pérez Kanellos, in hope that he, his generation, and those that follow will be able to possess a complete awareness of their history, arts and traditions and have access to basic information about their people. May Hispanic Americans of the United States, and especially Hispanic students, never again be impoverished of basic informational resources in their libraries and schools. May the American people in general have access to and a full awareness of an important part—the Hispanic contribution— of the national identity of the United States and embrace it as theirs.

N.K.

Contents

VOLUME I

VOLUME II

VOLUME III

Acknowledgments

My most sincere thanks to all the scholars who have contributed to this volume, for indulging me in my obsession and for producing such wonderfully researched and written chapters, despite the pressure I exerted on you for making deadlines and supplying illustrations and other materials. My thanks as well to my editors at Gale Research Inc., especially Christine Nasso, Christine Hammes, and Rebecca Nelson, whose guiding hand was always characterized by a gentle touch, whose advice was always offered with compassion and understanding. I feel very fortunate to have become part of the Gale family.

Thanks also to my scholarly advisors, especially Dr. Michael Olivas, who assisted me greatly in contacting contributors for this volume. My deepest appreciation and thanks to my assistant, Hilda Hinojosa, who helped organize, type, and maintain oral and written communications with the contributing scholars and with my editors. This, the largest project of my career as a scholar, was brought to press, with her able, efficient, and enthusiastic support.

And from my wife Cristelia Pérez and my son Miguel, I beg their forgiveness for the months that I spent communicating more with my computer screen than with them. Without Crissy's love, support, and understanding this project would never have gotten off the ground, much less seen the light of day. Thank you; I love you.

Nicolás Kanellos

Preface

Reference Library of Hispanic America is the research product of a national team of outstanding scholars who unanimously have invested their time, energy, and genius to create the first one-stop source for information about a broad range of important aspects of Hispanic life and culture in the United States. In their labors for *Reference Library of Hispanic America,* as well as in their day-to-day academic work, these scholars have actively engaged in the difficult task of working with original documentary sources, oral interviews, and field work to create a written record of Hispanic life where none existed before. These scholars are among the first in our country's academic history to research, analyze, and preserve much of the information offered here. The scholars, and this work, are dedicated to filling an informational void relating to the history and culture of Hispanics of the United States—a void that has existed for too long in libraries, classrooms, and homes.

Prior to this publication, the scant information that has been available has quite often resulted from prejudice, propaganda, and folklore (quite often created to support the political and economic exploitation of Hispanics) covering a people conquered through war or imported for their labor, but who were never fully incorporated into the national psyche, the national identity, or the national storehouse of educational, economic, and political opportunities.

The vast majority of Hispanics in the United States are working-class citizens. Even those Hispanics in the professional class often share working-class backgrounds. The majority of Hispanics in the United States are *mestizos*—the product of mixed races and cultures, for the American Indian and African heritages have blended in every aspect of everyday life to produce today's Hispanic peoples of the Americas. The Spanish language, which introduced and reinforced a common culture and religion for these peoples for centuries, serves as a unifying factor for Hispanics, regardless of whether or not the individual speaks Spanish in daily life. These central factors—social class, ethnicity, linguistic-cultural background—unify the people and the information presented in *Reference Library of Hispanic America,* while also respecting the tremendous diversity in racial, ethnic, geographic, and historical backgrounds that exists among Hispanics today.

The final result of this endeavor, we hope, is an easy-to-use compendium that presents an up-to-date overview of each subject, summarizing the known data and presenting new, original research. Moreover, *Reference Library of Hispanic America* has been written in a language and style that make it accessible to students and lay people. Illustrations—photographs, drawings, maps, and tables—bring the data to life. For further reading, subject-specific bibliographies (at the end of each chapter) as well as a general bibliography (on pages A-13 and A-14 of each volume) provide ready reference to other important sources. A complete index (on pages A-15 through A-40 of each volume) assists the reader in locating specific information. A glossary of Spanish terms (on pages A-9 through A-11 of each volume) has also been included to facilitate the reading of *Reference Library of Hispanic America*.

As this is the first edition of a very new type of resource, we are aware there may be some gaps in information, resulting from incomplete data or unavailable resources (be they documentary, informational, or human). However, great pains have been taken to ensure the accuracy of the data and the representativeness of the scholarly interpretation and opinion presented in each chapter. Research is ongoing and future editions of *Reference Library of Hispanic America* will update the present volume.

Nicolás Kanellos
University of Houston

Introduction

The Hispanic Population

With a Hispanic population of more than 22 million, the United States is among the largest Spanish-speaking countries in the world. According to the U.S. Census Bureau, the number of Hispanics in this country has grew by 53 percent from 1980 to 1990. It is projected that by the year 2000, there will be almost 33 million Hispanics living in the United States.

Reference Library of Hispanic America, based on *The Hispanic-American Almanac*, is a one-stop source for information on people of the United States whose ancestors—or they themselves—originated in Spain, the Spanish-speaking countries of South and Central America, Mexico, Puerto Rico, or Cuba.

While the Spanish language is a unifying factor among Hispanics, the diversity that exists within the Hispanic community continues to profoundly influence the collective American experience.

Scope and Contents

Reference Library of Hispanic America covers the range of Hispanic civilization and culture in the United States—providing a chronology and Historical Overview, presenting the facts and figures in such chapters as Law and Politics and Population Growth and Distribution, and discussing the arts, including Theater, Music, and Film.

Twenty-five subject chapters were written by scholars in the field of Hispanic studies. These experts have drawn upon the body of their works and new research to compile their chapters, ending each with a list of references that can be used for further research into any of the subjects covered in *Reference Library of Hispanic America*. A bibliography at the back of each volume of *Reference Library of Hispanic America* provides sources for general information on Hispanics.

Concise biographical profiles in many chapters highlight Hispanics who have excelled in their fields of endeavor.

A glossary of Spanish terms, found in each of the three volumes, facilitates the reading of the material.

The keyword index, also found in each volume, provides quick access to the contents of *Reference Library of Hispanic America*.

More than 400 illustrations—including photographs, drawings, tables, and figures—punctuate the discussion in each chapter.

Suggestions Are Welcome

The managing editor and publisher of *Reference Library of Hispanic America* will appreciate suggestions for additions or changes that will make future editions of this book as useful as possible. Please send comments to:

Reference Library of Hispanic America
Gale Research Inc.
835 Penobscot Bldg.
Detroit, MI 48226

Chronology

50,000-10,000 B.C. Asian peoples migrate to North and South America.

ca. 1000 B.C. Celts move into the Iberian Peninsula.

ca. 500 B.C. Carthagenians establish themselves on the south coast of Spain.

200 B.C. The Iberian Peninsula becomes part of the Roman Empire.

350-850 A.D. Teotihuacan civilization flourishes in the central plateau of Mexico.

500 A.D. Vandals and Goths invade and conquer the peoples of the Iberian Peninsula.

700-900 A.D. Nahua peoples gain ascendancy in Mexico's central plateau.

711 A.D. The Moors invade and conquer the Visigothic kingdoms of the Iberian peninsula.

718-1492. The Reconquest of the Iberian peninsula takes place. Queen Isabella and King Ferdinand unify Spain through their marriage in 1469, and culminate the Reconquest by defeating the last Moorish stronghold—Granada.

1000 Mayan civilization flourishes in the Yucatán peninsula and Guatemala.

1492. The native American population of the Western Hemisphere may have reached between thirty-five to forty-five million.

August 3, 1492. Christopher Columbus sails from the Spanish port of Palos de Moguer with three ships: the Pinta, the Niña, and the Santa María, his flagship.

October 12, 1492. The Spaniards land on an island called San Salvador—either present-day Watling Island or Samana Cay in the eastern Bahamas.

October 27, 1492. Columbus and his crews land on the northeastern shore of Cuba. Convinced that it is either Cipango or Cathay (in Asia), Columbus sends representatives to the Great Khan and his gold-domed cities, only to find impoverished Arawak living in *bohíos* (huts).

November 1493. On his second voyage Columbus discovers the Virgin Islands and Puerto Rico.

1494. After establishing Isabela on La Española (Hispaniola), the first permanent European settlement in the New World, Columbus sets sail and encounters Jamaica in the summer of 1494.

1508. Juan Ponce de León sails in a small caravel for Puerto Rico, where he establishes friendly relations with the native chieftain, Agueibana, who presents him with gold.

1509. Ponce de León is appointed governor of Puerto Rico.

1510. Diego Velázquez de Cuéllar departs with more than three hundred men to conquer Cuba, and lands at Puerto Escondido. He is successful in defeating Arawak chieftain Hatuey's guerrilla raids.

1511. Velázquez is commissioned governor of Cuba. That same year the Cuban Indians are subjected to the *encomienda*.

1512. The Jeronymite Fathers in La Española decide to save the decimated Arawak population by gathering them into missions. Soon, missions spread like wildfire throughout the Spanish Empire.

1512. The Laws of Burgos: Promulgated by the Crown, the regulations are in response to the extremely harsh treatment that desperate colonists in the Caribbean imposed on natives through the deplorable *encomienda* system.

1513. Juan Ponce de León lands on the shores of Florida, exploring most of the coastal regions and some of the interior. At the time, there were an estimated 100,000 native Americans living there.

September 27, 1514. Ponce de León is granted a patent, empowering him to colonize the island of Bimini and the "island" of Florida.

1515. Diego Velázquez becomes a virtual feudal lord of Cuba, and establishes what are to become Cuba's two largest cities, Santiago and Havana. He also directs the explorations of the Mexican Gulf Coast by Francisco Hernández de Córdoba and his nephew Juan de Grijalva. These expeditions betray the existence of civilizations in the interior of Mexico.

1518. Hernán Cortés sets out from Cuba to explore the mainland of Mexico in order to confirm reports of the existence of large, native civilizations in the interior.

1519. Alonso Alvarez de Pineda claims Texas for Spain.

1519. Hernán Cortés lands on the coast of Veracruz, Mexico.

1520. Explorer Alvarez de Pineda settles the question of Florida's geography: He proves it is not an island, but part of a vast continent.

1520s. Continuing their maritime adventures, the Spanish explorers cruise along the northern shore of the Gulf of Mexico, seeing Alabama, Mississippi, and Texas, and also sailing up the Atlantic coast to the Carolinas.

July 1, 1520. Under the leadership of Cuitlahuac, Moctezuma's brother, the Aztecs force the Spaniards out of Veracruz, just a year after the Spaniards had come into the city. The Spaniards called this *La noche triste* (The Sad Night). Moctezuma was stoned to death by his own people during this debacle.

1521. Cortés and his fellow Spaniards level the Aztec empire's city of Tenochtitlán, and begin building Mexico City on the same site.

1524. King Charles establishes the Council of the Indies, designed to oversee the administration of the colonies of the New World.

1536. Álvar Núñez Cabeza de Vaca returns to Mexico, indirectly involving Spain in exploring and colonizing what becomes the American Southwest: In Mexico City rumors were that Cabeza de Vaca and his companions had discovered cities laden with gold and silver, reviving the legend of the Seven Cities, which dated from the Moorish invasion of the Iberian Peninsula.

1537. Àlvar Núñez Cabeza de Vaca returns to Spain and spends some three years writing *La relación*, an account of his wanderings in the North American continent. Published in 1542, *La relación* is a document of inestimable value because of the many first descriptions about the flora, fauna, and inhabitants of what was to become part of the United States.

May 18, 1539. From Havana, Cuba, Hernando de Soto sets sail for Florida; he eventually reaches as far north as present-day Georgia and South Carolina. His expedition later crosses the Great Smoky Mountains into Tennessee. From the mountains, the expedition heads southwest through present-day Georgia and Alabama.

1540. There are an estimated sixty-six Pueblo villages in the area of New Mexico, growing such crops as corn, beans, squash, and cotton. On April 23, 1541, Coronado sets out to reach Quivira—thought to be the legendary Cities of Gold—near present-day Great Bend, Kansas.

1542. The New Laws are proclaimed. They are designed to end the feudal *encomienda*.

July 1542. Coronado returns to Mexico City with fewer than one hundred of the three hundred Spaniards that once formed part of his company.

September 28, 1542. Juan Rodríguez de Cabrillo, a Portuguese sailor commissioned by the viceroy to sail north of Mexico's west coast in search of treasures, enters what he describes as an excellent port—present-day San Diego, California.

1563. Saint Augustine, Florida, the earliest settlement in North America, is founded. It remains a possession of Spain until 1819.

1573. The Franciscan order arrives in Florida to establish missions, which a century later would extend along the east coast of North America, from Saint Augustine, Florida, to North Carolina. The Franciscans also establish a string of missions from Saint Augustine westward to present-day Tallahassee.

1580s. Diseases have all but wiped out the Indians of Puerto Rico. The flourishing of sugar production will now have to await the importation of large numbers of African slaves.

1598. Juan de Oñate begins the colonization of New Mexico.

1610. Santa Fe, New Mexico is founded.

1680. A Pueblo Indian named Popé leads a rebellion that forces the Spaniards and Christianized Indians out of northern New Mexico southward toward El Paso, Texas; they found Ysleta just north of El Paso.

1689. In part due to the need to provide foodstuffs and livestock to the rich mining regions in southern Mexico, the first royal *mercedes* (land grants) are granted to Spaniards in the fertile valleys of Monclova, in northern Mexico, just south of the present border.

May 1690. The first permanent Spanish settlement in Texas, San Francisco de los Tejas, near the Neches River, is established.

1691. Father Eusebio Kino, an untiring Jesuit missionary, makes the first inroads into Arizona. By 1700, Kino establishes a mission at San Xavier del Bac, near present-day Tucson; he later establishes other missions in Arizona: Nuestra Señora de los Dolores, Santa Gertrudis de Saric, San José de Imuris, Nuestra Señora de los Remedios, and San Cayetano de Tumacácori.

1693. Despite the fact that Texas is made a separate Spanish province with Don Domingo de Terán as its governor, the Spanish Crown orders its abandonment. Fear of Indian uprisings is the reason given by the Spanish authorities.

1716. Concerns about possible French encroachment prompt the Spaniards to reoccupy Texas in 1716 by establishing a series of missions, serving to both ward off the French and convert the natives to Catholicism. Of these missions, San Antonio, founded in 1718, is the most important and most prosperous.

1718. The San Antonio de Béjar and de Valero churches are built where the city of San Antonio is located today.

1760. After the Seven Years' War, which united France and Spain against Britain, France cedes claims to all lands west of the Mississippi in order not to give them to the victorious British. Overnight, New Spain's territory expands dramatically.

September 17, 1766. The presidio of San Francisco is founded, becoming Spain's northernmost frontier outpost.

1767. King Charles III expels the Jesuits from the Spanish Empire. This event opens the door for the Franciscan conquest of California. This conquest would never have been accomplished without Fray Junípero de Serra.

July 3, 1769. Fray Junípero de Serra establishes the first mission of Alta California in what would become San Diego. Serra eventually founds ten missions, travels more than ten thousand miles, and converts close to sixty-eight hundred natives.

1770-1790. At least 50,000 African slaves are brought to Cuba to work in sugar production.

1774. Pedro de Garcés, a Spanish Franciscan missionary, founds the first overland route to California.

1776. In the American Revolution, because of their alliance with France, the Spaniards are able to obtain lands all the way to Florida.

1776. Anglo-Americans declare their independence from England, and thirty-four years later Hispanics proclaim their independence from Spain. The thirteen former British colonies come to be known as the United States of America in 1781, and the newly independent people of New Spain name their nation the Republic of Mexico.

1783. Spain regains Florida. In July 1821, the sun finally sets on Spanish Florida when the peninsula is purchased by the United States for $5 million.

1790s-1820s. The Apache threat subsides because of successful military tactics and negotiations on the part of local Spanish leaders, and Hispanic settlements begin to thrive in Pimería Alta (California). At one point as many as one thousand Hispanics live in the Santa Cruz Valley.

1798. The Alien Act of 1798 grants the U.S. president the authority to expel any alien deemed dangerous. Opposed by President Thomas Jefferson, the Alien Act expires under its own terms in 1800.

1798. The Naturalization Act of 1798 raises the number of years—from 5 to 14—that an immigrant has to live in the United States before becoming eligible for citizenship.

1800. Large, sprawling haciendas with huge herds of cattle and sheep characterize the economy and society of northeast New Spain.

1803. A powerful France under Napoleon Bonaparte acquires the Louisiana Territory, from Spain which was ceded during the Seven Years' War in the previous century. Napoleon, vying for dominance in Europe and in need of quick revenue, sells the vast territory to the United States, thus expanding the borders of the infant nation to connect directly with New Spain.

1804. To the consternation of Spain, President Thomas Jefferson funds the historical expedition of Lewis and Clark. Spain is obviously worried that the exploration is a prelude to the settlement of the territory by Anglos.

1810. In Mexico, Father Miguel Hidalgo y Castilla leads the revolt against Spain.

September 16, 1810. With the insurrection of Father Miguel Hidalgo y Castilla, the Spaniards withdraw their troops from the frontier presidios.

1819. When Andrew Jackson leads a U.S. military force into Florida, capturing two Spanish forts, Spain sells Florida to the United States for $5 million under the Onís Treaty.

1820. Stephen Long leads a revolt, ostensibly as part of the Texas independence movement against the Spanish, but obviously he is acting as a filibuster for his countrymen. Spain finally enters into delibera-tions with Moses Austin, a Catholic from Missouri, to settle Anglo-Catholic families in Texas.

1821. Mexico acquires its independence from Spain. By this time permanent colonies exist in coastal California, southern Arizona, south Texas, and in most of New Mexico and southern Colorado. The imprint of evolving Mexican culture is stamped on today's Southwest. Soon after Mexico gains independence, Anglo-American settlers begin to move into the Mexican territories of the present-day U.S. Southwest, especially Texas.

1823. Erasmo Seguín, a delegate to the national congress from Texas, persuades a willing U.S. Congress to pass a colonization act designed to bring even more Anglo settlers to Texas. Between 1824 and 1830, thousands of Anglo families enter east Texas, acquiring hundreds of thousands of free acres and buying land much cheaper than they could have in the United States. By 1830, Texas has eighteen thousand Anglo inhabitants and their African slaves, who number more than two thousand.

1823. Fray Junípero de Serra's death does not stop missionary activity in California. His fellow Franciscans establish another twelve missions. The famous mission trail of California includes the missions San Diego de Alcalá (1769), San Carlos de Monterey (1770), San Antonio de Padua (1771), San Gabriel Arcángel (1771), San Luis Obispo de Tolosa (1772), San Francisco de Asís (1776), San Juan Capistrano (1776), Santa Clara de Asís (1777), San Buenaventura (1782), Santa Bárbara (1786), La Purísima Concepción (1787), Santa Cruz (1791), San José de Guadalupe (1797), San Juan Bautista (1797), San Miguel Arcángel (1797), San Fernando Rey (1797), San Luis Rey (1798), Santa Inés (1804), San Rafael Arcángel (1817), and San Francisco Solano (1823).

1829. Slavery in Mexico is abolished by the new republican government that emerges after independence.

1836. The Anglo settlers declare the Republic of Texas independent of Mexico.

1836. The Texas constitution stipulates that all residents living in Texas at the time of the rebellion will acquire all the rights of citizens of the new republic, but if they had been disloyal, these rights are forfeited. Numerically superior Anglos force Mexicans off their property, and many cross the border to Mexico.

1840. To meet the wage-labor demands, 125,000 Chinese are brought to Cuba between 1840 and 1870 to work as cane cutters, build railroads in rural areas, and serve as domestics in the cities. Also, the influx of European immigrants, primarily from Spain, increases during that period. Newly arrived Spaniards become concentrated in the retail trades and operate small general stores called *bodegas.*

1845. Texas is officially annexed to the United States.

1846. The United States invades Mexico under the banner of Manifest Destiny. The treaty of Guadalupe Hidalgo ends the Mexican War that same year. Under the treaty, half the land area of Mexico, including Texas, California, most of Arizona and New Mexico, and parts of Colorado, Utah, and Nevada, is ceded to the United States. The treaty gives Mexican nationals one year to choose U.S. or Mexican citizenship. Seventy-five thousand Hispanic people choose to remain in the United States and become citizens by conquest.

1848. The gold rush lures a flood of Anglo settlers to California, which becomes a state in 1850. Settlement in Arizona and New Mexico occurs at a slower pace, and they both become states in 1912.

1850. The Foreign Miners Tax, which levies a charge for anyone who is not a U.S. citizen, is enacted.

1851. Congress passes the California Land Act of 1851 to facilitate legalization of land belonging to Californios prior to the U.S. takeover.

1853. General Santa Anna returns to power as president of Mexico and, through the Gadsden Treaty, sells to the United States the region from Yuma (Arizona) along the Gila River to the Mesilla Valley (New Mexico).

1855. Vagrancy laws and so-called "greaser laws" prohibiting bear-baiting, bullfights, and cockfights are passed, clearly aimed at prohibiting the presence and customs of Californios.

1855. The Supreme Court rules that the Treaty of Guadalupe Hidalgo did not apply to Texas.

1857. Anglo businessmen attempt to run off Mexican teamsters in south Texas, violating the guarantees offered by the Treaty of Guadalupe Hidalgo.

1862. Homestead Act is passed in Congress, allowing squatters in the West to settle and claim vacant lands, often those owned by Mexicans.

April 27, 1867. Spanish troops stationed on Puerto Rico mutiny, and are executed by the colonial governor.

1868. Cubans leave for Europe and the United States in sizable numbers during Cuba's first major attempt at independence.

1868. Fourteenth Amendment to the U.S. Constitution is adopted, declaring all people of Hispanic origin born in the United States are U.S. citizens.

September 17, 1868. A decree in Puerto Rico frees all children born of slaves after this date. In 1870, all slaves who are state property are freed, as are various other classes of slaves.

September 23, 1868. El Grito de Lares, the shout for Puerto Rican independence, takes place, with its disorganized insurrectionists easily defeated by the Spanish.

October 1868. Cuban rebels led by Carlos Manuel de Céspedes declare independence at Yara, in the eastern portion of the island.

1872. Puerto Rican representatives in Spain win equal civil rights for the colony.

1873. Slavery is finally abolished in Puerto Rico.

1875. The U.S. Supreme Court in *Henderson v. Mayor of New York* rules that power to regulate immigration is held solely by the federal government.

1878. The Ten Years' War, in which Spanish attempts to evict rebels from the eastern half of Cuba were unsuccessful, comes to an end with the signing of the Pact of El Zajón. The document promises amnesty for the insurgents and home rule, and provides freedom for the slaves that fought on the side of the rebels.

1880s. In Cuba, slavery is abolished by Spain in a gradual program that takes eight years. The influx of new European immigrants has made Cuba more heterogeneous, leading to the social diversity that is still apparent today.

1880s. Mexican immigration to the United States is stimulated by the advent of the railroad.

1892. The Partido Revolucionario Cubano is created to organize the Cuban and Puerto Rican independence movement.

1894. The Alianza Hispano Americana is founded in Tucson, Arizona, and quickly spreads throughout the Southwest.

1895. José Martí and his Cuban Revolutionary Party (PRC) open the final battle for independence.

1896. A Revolutionary Junta is formed in New York to lead the Puerto Rican independence movement.

1897. Spain grants Cuba and Puerto Rico autonomy and home rule.

April 1898. The *USS Maine* mysteriously blows up in Havana Harbor. And on April 28, President William McKinley declares war against Spain.

May 1898. The U.S. military invades San Juan in pursuit of Spaniards, and is welcomed by the cheering crowds, longing for independence.

December 10, 1898. Spain signs the Treaty of Paris, transferring Cuba, Puerto Rico, and the Philippines to the United States.

1900s. Brutality against Mexican Americans in the Southwest territories is commonplace. Lynchings and murders of Mexican Americans become so common in California and Texas that, in 1912, the Mexican ambassador formally protests the mistreatment and cites several brutal incidents that had recently taken place.

1900. The Foraker Act establishes a civilian government in Puerto Rico under U.S. dominance. The law allows for islanders to elect their own House of Representatives, but does not allow Puerto Rico a vote in Washington.

1901. The Federación Libre de los Trabajadores (Workers Labor Federation) becomes affiliated with the American Federation of Labor, which breaks from its policy of excluding non-whites.

1902. The Reclamation Act is passed, dispossessing many Hispanic Americans of their land.

1902. Cuba declares its independence from the United States.

1910. The Mexican Revolution begins, with hundreds of thousands of people fleeing north from Mexico and settling in the Southwest.

1911. In Mexico, the long dictatorship of Porfirio Díaz comes to an end when he is forced to resign in a revolt led by Francisco Madero.

1913. Victoriano Huerta deposes Francisco Madero, becoming provisional president of Mexico.

1914. President Woodrow Wilson orders the invasion of Veracruz in an effort to depose Victoriano Huerta, who soon resigns.

1917. During World War I, "temporary" Mexican farm workers, railroad laborers, and miners are permitted to enter the United States to work.

1917. The Jones Act is passed, extending U.S. citizenship to all Puerto Ricans and creating two Puerto Rican houses of legislature whose representatives are elected by the people. English is decreed the official language of Puerto Rico.

February 1917. Congress passes the Immigration Act, imposing a literacy requirement on all immigrants, aimed at curbing the influx from southern and eastern Europe, but ultimately inhibiting immigration from Mexico.

May 1917. The Selective Service Act becomes law, obligating non-citizen Mexicans in the United States to register with their local draft boards, even though they are not eligible for the draft.

1921. Limits on the number of immigrants allowed to enter the United States during a single year are imposed for the first time in the country's history.

1921. As the first of two national origin quota acts designed to curtail immigration from eastern and southern Europe and Asia is passed, Mexico and Puerto Rico become major sources of workers.

1921. A depression in Mexico causes severe destitution among Mexicans who suddenly find themselves unemployed.

1925. The Border Patrol is created by Congress.

July 1926. Rioting Puerto Ricans in Harlem are attacked by non-Hispanics as the number of Puerto Ricans becomes larger in Manhattan neighborhoods (by 1930 they will reach fifty-three thousand).

1929. With the onset of the Great Depression, Mexican immigration to the United States virtually ceases and return migration increases sharply.

1929. The League of United Latin American Citizens is founded in Texas by frustrated Mexican Americans who find avenues for opportunity in the United States blocked.

1930s-1940s. With the onset of the Great Depression, many Mexican workers are displaced by the dominant southern whites and blacks of the migrant agricultural labor force.

1930. The United States controls 44 percent of the cultivated land in Puerto Rico; U.S. capitalists control 60 percent of the banks and public services, and all of the maritime lines.

1930. Within the next four years, approximately 20 percent of the Puerto Ricans living in the United States will return to the island.

1933. The Roosevelt Administration reverses the policy of English as the official language in Puerto Rico.

1933. Mexican farm workers strike the Central Valley, California, cotton industry, supported by several groups of independent Mexican union organizers and radicals.

1933. Cuban dictator Gerardo Machado is overthrown.

September 1933. Fulgencio Batista leads a barracks revolt to overthrow Cuban provisional President Carlos Manuel de Céspedes y Quesada, becoming the dictator of the Cuban provisional government.

1934. The Platt Amendment is annulled.

1938. Young Mexican and Mexican-American pecan shellers strike in San Antonio.

1940s-1950s. Unionization among Hispanic workers increases rapidly, as Hispanic workers and union sympathizers struggle for reform.

1940. The independent union Confederación de Trabajadores Generales is formed and soon replaces the FLT as the major labor organization in Puerto Rico.

1940. Batista is elected president of Cuba.

1941. The Fair Employment Practices Act is passed, eliminating discrimination in employment.

1941. With the U.S. declaration of war in 1941, Hispanics throughout the country enthusiastically respond to the war effort.

1943. Prompted by the labor shortage of World War II, the U.S. government makes an agreement with the Mexican government to supply temporary workers, known as "braceros," for American agricultural work.

1943. The so-called "Zoot Suit" riots take place in southern California.

1944. Batista retires as president of Cuba.

1944. Operation Bootstrap, a program initiated by the Puerto Rican government to meet U.S. labor demands of World War II and encourage industrialization on the island, stimulates a major wave of migration of workers to the United States.

1946. The first Puerto Rican governor, Jesús T. Piñero, is appointed by President Harry Truman.

1947. More than twenty airlines provide service between San Juan and Miami, and San Juan and New York.

1947. The American G.I. Forum is organized by Mexican-American veterans in response to a Three Rivers, Texas, funeral home's denial to bury a Mexican American killed in the Pacific during World War II.

1950s. Through the early 1960s, segregation is abolished in Texas, Arizona, and other regions, largely through the efforts of the League of United Latin American Citizens (LULAC) and the Alianza Hispano Americana.

1950s. Immigration from Mexico doubles from 5.9 percent to 11.9 percent, and in the 1960s rises to 13.3 percent of the total number of immigrants to the United States.

1950s-1960s. Black workers continue to be the most numerous migrants along the eastern seaboard states, while Mexican and Mexican-American workers soon dominate the migrant paths between Texas and the Great Lakes, the Rocky Mountain region, and the area from California to the Pacific Northwest.

1950s-1960s. As more and more Puerto Ricans commit to remaining on the U.S. mainland, they encounter a great deal of rejection, but at the same time demonstrate a growing concern for social and economic mobility. Their early employment pattern consists of menial jobs in the service sector and in light factory work—in essence low-paying jobs.

1950. In spite of the resurgence of Mexican immigration and the persistence of Mexican cultural modes, Mexican Americans cannot help but become Americanized in the milieu of the 1950s and 1960s, when more and more acquire educations in Anglo systems, live in integrated suburbs, and are subjected to Anglo-American mass media—especially television.

July 3, 1950. The U.S. Congress upgrades Puerto Rico's political status from protectorate to commonwealth.

1951. The Bracero Program is formalized as the Mexican Farm Labor Supply Program and the Mexican Labor Agreement, and will bring an annual average of 350,000 Mexican workers to the United States until its end in 1964.

1952. Congress passes the Immigration and Nationality Act of 1952, also known as the McCarran-Walter Act, reaffirming the basic features of the 1924 quota law by maintaining a restrictive limit on immigration from particular countries. Immigration from the Western Hemisphere remains exempt, except that applicants must clear a long list of barriers devised to exclude homosexuals, Communists, and others.

1952. Batista seizes power of Cuba again, this time as dictator, taking Cuba to new heights of repression and corruption.

1954. In the landmark case of *Hernández v. Texas* the nation's highest court acknowledges that Hispanic Americans are not being treated as "whites." The Supreme Court recognizes Hispanics as a separate class of people suffering profound discrimination, paving the way for Hispanic Americans to use legal means to attack all types of discrimination throughout the United States. It is also the first U.S. Supreme Court case to be argued and briefed by Mexican-American attorneys.

1954-1958. Operation Wetback deports 3.8 million persons of Mexican descent. Only a small fraction of that amount are allowed deportation hearings. Thousands more legitimate U.S. citizens of Mexican descent are also arrested and detained.

1959. The Cuban Revolution succeeds in overthrowing the repressive regime of Batista; Fidel Castro takes power. The vast majority of Cuban Americans immigrate to the United States after this date: between 1959 and 1962, 25,000 Cubans are "paroled" to the United States using a special immigration rule. Large-scale Cuban immigration to the United States occurs much more quickly than that from either Puerto Rico or Mexico, with more than one million Cubans entering the country since 1959.

1959. Most of the two million Puerto Ricans who have trekked to the U.S. mainland in this century are World War II or postwar-era entries. Unlike the immigrant experience of Mexicans, or Cubans before 1959, the vast majority of Puerto Ricans enter with little or no red tape.

1960s. A third phase of labor migration to the United States begins when the established patterns of movement from Mexico and Puerto Rico to the United States are modified, and migration from other countries increases. The Bracero Program ends in 1964, and, after a brief decline in immigration, workers from Mexico increasingly arrive to work under the auspices of the H-2 Program of the Immigration and Nationality Act of 1952, as well as for family unification purposes, or as undocumented workers.

1960s-1970s. The migrant agricultural work force is changing rapidly. With the rise of the black power and Chicano movements, the appearance of modest protective legislation, and the increasingly successful unionization efforts of farm workers, employers seek to recruit and hire foreign workers to replace the citizens.

1961. Aspira (Aspire) is founded to promote the education of Hispanic youth by raising public and private sector funds. Aspira acquires a national following, serving Puerto Ricans wherever they live in large numbers.

April 1961. Anti-Communist Cuban exiles who are trained and armed by the United States, attempt a foray into Cuba that is doomed from the beginning. The failure of the infamous Bay of Pigs invasion embitters thousands of exiled Cubans, while strengthening Castro's position at home. Many observers throughout the world criticize the Kennedy administration for the attempt to overthrow a legitimately based government.

1962. The United Farm Workers Organizing Committee in California, begun as an independent organization, is led by César Chávez. In 1965 it organizes its successful Delano grape strike and first national boy-cott. It becomes part of the AFL-CIO in 1966. Today the union is known as the United Farmworkers of America.

October 1962. Kennedy redeems himself from the Bay of Pigs disgrace by blocking a Soviet plan to establish missile bases in Cuba. Soviet Premier Khru-shchev agrees to withdraw the missiles with the pro-viso that the United States declare publicly that it will not invade Cuba.

1964. Congress enacts the first comprehensive civil rights law since the Reconstruction period when it passes the Civil Rights Act of 1964. One result of the act is the establishment of affirmative action pro-grams. Title VII of the Act prohibits discrimination on the basis of gender, creed, race, or ethnic back-ground, "to achieve equality of employment opportu-nities and remove barriers that have operated in the past." Discrimination is prohibited in advertising, recruitment, hiring, job classification, promotion, discharge, wages and salaries, and other terms and conditions of employment. Title VII also establishes the Equal Employment Opportunity Commission (EEOC) as a monitoring device to prevent job dis-crimination.

1964. The Economic Opportunity Act (EOA) is the centerpiece of President Lyndon B. Johnson's War on Poverty. The EOA also creates the Office of Economic Opportunity (OEO) to administer a number of pro-grams on behalf of the nation's poor. These include the Job Corps, the Community Action Program (CAP), and the Volunteers in Service to America (VISTA).

1965. The experienced *braceros* (manual laborers) inspire other Mexicans to immigrate to the United States. Many of these contract laborers work primar-ily in agricultural communities and in railroad camps until the program ends in 1965.

1965. A border industrialization program, the *maquiladora* (assembly plant), is initiated. Mexico hopes to raise the standard of living in its northern border region, while the United States hopes to avoid the possible negative political and economic conse-quences of leaving hundreds of thousands of Mexican workers stranded without employment as the Bracero Program is ended.

1965. Although the single aim of the Voting Rights Act of 1965 is African-American enfranchisement in the South, obstacles to registration and voting are faced by all minorities. The act's potential as a tool

for Hispanic Americans, however, is not fully real-ized for nearly a decade.

1965. For the first time, the United States enacts a law placing a cap on immigration from the Western Hemisphere, becoming effective in 1968.

1965. Fidel Castro announces that Cubans can leave the island nation if they have relatives in the United States. He stipulates, however, that Cubans already in Florida have to come and get their relatives. Nauti-cal crafts of all types systematically leave Miami, returning laden with anxious Cubans eager to rejoin their families on the mainland.

1965. A major revision of immigration law results when Congress amends the Immigration and Nation-ality Act of 1952. The national origin quota system is abolished.

Late 1960s-early 1970s. Intellectual foment and rebel-lion reign in the United States. Caught up in the mood, young Mexican Americans throughout the country seek a new identity while struggling for the same civil rights objectives of previous generations. This struggle becomes known as the Chicano move-ment. The word "Chicano" is elevated from its pejora-tive usage in the 1920s when it denoted lower-class Mexican immigrants, and from its slang usage of the 1940s and 1950s, to substitute for "Mexicano."

1966. Hundreds of Chicago Puerto Rican youths go on a rampage, breaking windows and burning down many of the businesses in their neighborhoods. Os-tensibly, the riots are in response to an incident of police brutality, but the underlying causes are broader, linked to the urban blight that characterizes their life in Chicago.

1966. A program is initiated to airlift Cubans to the United States. More than 250,000 Cubans are airlifted to the United States before the program is halted by Castro in 1973. About 10 percent of the island's population immigrates to the United States between 1966 and 1973.

1968. Chicano student organizations spring up throughout the nation, as do barrio groups such as the Brown Berets. Thousands of young Chicanos pledge their loyalty and time to such groups as the United Farmworkers Organizing Committee, which, under César Chávez, has been a great inspiration for Chicanos throughout the nation. An offshoot of both the farm worker and the student movements, is La Raza Unida party in Texas, an organization formed in

1968 to obtain control of community governments where Chicanos are the majority.

1969. After the establishment of the Central American Common Market in the 1960s led to economic growth and improved conditions in the region, the border war between Honduras and El Salvador leads to the collapse of the common market and the rapid decline of economic conditions in Central America.

1970s. Immigration and Naturalization Service (INS) Commissioner Leonard Chapman seeks to increase funding and expand the power of his organization, claiming that there are as many as 12 million undocumented workers in the country. Other observers most commonly place the number in the range of 3.5 million to 5 million people.

1970s-early 1980s. The rise in politically motivated violence in Central America spurs a massive increase in undocumented immigration to the United States.

1970. Eighty-two percent of the Hispanic population of the nation lives in nine states, with the proportion rising to 86 percent in 1990. The major recipients of Hispanic immigrants are California, Texas, and New York, and to a lesser degree Florida, Illinois, and New Jersey.

1970. A Chicano Moratorium to the Vietnam War is organized in Los Angeles. Journalist Rubén Salazar is accidentally killed by police.

1970. The struggle over affirmative action continues when opponents coin the term "reverse discrimination," suggesting that white males are victims of discrimination as a result of affirmative action on behalf of women, blacks, Hispanics, and other underrepresented groups.

1970. Brutality against Mexican Americans continues. In *López v. Harlow*, a case filed in an attempt to bring the violence under control, a police officer shoots and kills López, a Mexican American, allegedly in self-defense, because he thought López was about to throw a dish at him.

1970. The amendments constituting the landmark Voting Rights Act of 1970 add a provision that is designed to guard against inventive new barriers to political participation. It requires federal approval of all changes in voting procedures in certain jurisdictions, primarily southern states. This act prevents minority votes from being diluted in gerrymandered districts or through at-large elections.

1971. La Raza Unida Party wins the city elections in Crystal City, Texas.

1972. Ramona Acosta Bañuelos becomes the first Hispanic treasurer of the United States.

1973. The right of the Puerto Rican people to decide their own future as a nation is approved by the United Nations. In 1978, the United Nations recognizes Puerto Rico as a colony of the United States.

1973. An employment discrimination case, *Espinoza v. Farah Manufacturing Company*, argues discrimination toward an employee, Espinoza, on the basis of his citizenship status under the Civil Rights Act. However, the Supreme Court holds that there is nothing in Title VII, the equal employment opportunities provisions of the Civil Rights Act of 1964, that makes it illegal to discriminate on the basis of citizenship or alienage.

1973. The Labor Council of Latin American Advancement (LCLAA) forms to promote the interests of Hispanics within organized labor.

1974. Congress passes the Equal Educational Opportunity Act to create equality in public schools by making bilingual education available to Hispanic youth. According to the framers of the act, equal education means more than equal facilities and equal access to teachers. Students who have trouble with the English language must be given programs to help them learn English.

1975. The Voting Rights Act Amendments of 1975 extend the provisions of the original Voting Rights Act and makes permanent the national ban on literacy tests. Critical for Hispanic Americans, the amendments make bilingual ballots a requirement in certain areas.

1977. The INS apprehends more than one million undocumented workers each year.

1977. A group of young Cuban exiles called the Antonio Maceo Brigade travels to Cuba to participate in service work and to achieve a degree of rapprochement with the Cuban government.

1978. The median income of Hispanic families below the poverty level falls from $7,238 in 1978 to $6,557 in 1987, controlling for inflation.

1978-1988. Hispanic female participation in the work force more than doubles, from 1.7 million to 3.6 million. In 1988, 56.6 percent of Hispanic women are in the work force, compared with 66.2 percent of white women and 63.8 percent of blacks.

1978-1988. The proportion of Hispanic children living in poverty rises more than 45 percent, and by 1989, 38 percent of Hispanic children are living in poverty.

1979. Political upheaval and civil wars in Nicaragua, El Salvador, and Guatemala contribute to large migrations of refugees to the United States.

1980s. Japanese industrialists take advantage of the maquiladoras by sending greater amounts of raw materials to Mexico where they are finished and shipped duty-free to the United States.

1980s. The rates of immigration approach the levels of the early 1900s: legal immigration during the first decade of the century reached 8.8 million, while during the 1980s, 6.3 million immigrants are granted permanent residence. The immigrants are overwhelmingly young and in search of employment, and Hispanic immigrants continue to account for more than 40 percent of the total.

1980s. Programs to apprehend undocumented immigrants are implemented, and reports of violations of civil rights are reported.

1980. A flotilla converges at Cuba's Mariel Harbor to pick up refugees. By year end, more than 125,000 "Marielitos" migrate to the United States. Castro charges that the exiles he allowed to return on visits had contaminated Cubans with the glitter of consumerism.

1980. The Refugee Act of 1980 removes the ideological definition of refugee as one who flees from a Communist regime, thus allowing thousands to enter the United States as refugees.

April 1980. A bus carrying a load of discontented Cubans crashes through the gates of the Peruvian embassy in Havana and the passengers receive political asylum from Peru. Castro begins to revise his policy of gradually allowing Cubans to leave.

1980-1988. The Reagan administration maintains that affirmative action programs entail quotas, constituting a form of reverse discrimination.

1980-1988. The number of Hispanics in the work force increases by 48 percent, representing 20 percent of U.S. employment growth.

1986. After more than a decade of debate, Congress enacts The Immigration Reform and Control Act (IRCA), creating an alien legalization program: legal status is given to applicants who held illegal status in the United States from before January 1, 1982, until the time of application. The program brings legal status to a large number of undocumented Hispanics.

1987. 70.1 percent of Hispanic female-headed households with children are living in poverty.

1988. Ronald Reagan appoints the first Hispanic Secretary of Education: Dr. Lauro F. Cavazos.

1989. Median family income for white families is $35,210; for blacks, $20,210; and for Hispanics, $23,450. Per capita income is $14,060 for whites, $8,750 for blacks, and $8,390 for Hispanics.

1989. Immigration from the Americas rises from 44.3 percent in 1964 to 61.4 percent. Of the major countries, Mexico accounts for 37.1 percent of total documented immigration to the United States, the next highest number of immigrants being from El Salvador, 5.3 percent.

1990. George Bush appoints the first woman and first Hispanic surgeon general of the United States: Antonia C. Novello.

1990. The erosion of past civil rights legislation by the Supreme Court during the Reagan and Bush administrations results in efforts by representatives of civil rights, black, and Hispanic organizations to initiate a push for a new Civil Rights Act. A series of compromises produces a watered-down Civil Rights Act in 1991.

1991. The proposed North American Free Trade Agreement between Mexico, the United States, and Canada expands even further the *maquiladora* concept, offering potentially greater tax abatements for U.S. businesses.

March 1991. Unemployment among U.S. Hispanics reaches 10.3 percent, roughly double the rate for whites.

Law and Politics

✹ Origins of Hispanics in the United States ✹ The Development of U.S. Immigration Law
✹ The Current Debate over U.S. Immigration Law ✹ The Legalization Program
✹ Employment Discrimination ✹ Police Brutality
✹ Federal Legislation Affecting Hispanic Americans
✹ Important Cases Affecting Hispanic Americans ✹ Hispanics in the Legal Profession
✹ Hispanics in the U.S. Judiciary ✹ Presidential Appointment of Hispanics to the Courts
✹ Hispanics in the Political Process ✹ Hispanic Voting and the Voting Rights Act of 1965
✹ Congressional Hispanic Caucus ✹ Hispanics in Congress
✹ Selected Prominent Hispanic Federal Officials
✹ Prominent Hispanic Politicians in State Government
✹ Prominent Hispanic Metropolitan Leaders ✹ Legal and Political Organizations

The Hispanic experience is unique in U.S. history. U.S. Hispanics are at once the oldest and the newest immigrants to the United States. In a nation of immigrants from all over the world, Hispanic immigrants have endured a long history of obstacles.

To understand the problems facing many Hispanics, how they arose, and why they still exist today, we must first examine the Hispanic-American experience in history. Unique historical milestones have colored the collective experience of Hispanics and have influenced American attitudes and decisions throughout the past. Unlike any other ethnic group in the United States, Hispanics are the only people to become citizens by conquest, with the exception of certain native Americans.

✹ORIGINS OF HISPANICS IN THE UNITED STATES

From the landing of Christopher Columbus on October 12, 1492, until the early nineteenth century, the entire Spanish-speaking world was controlled by Spain. The Spanish settled in North America long before the American Revolution, with the earliest settlement established at Saint Augustine, Florida, in 1563. Spanish settlers then began immigrating to the Southwest and founded El Paso, Texas, in 1598

and Santa Fe, New Mexico, in 1609. By 1760, there were an estimated twenty thousand settlers in New Mexico and twenty-five hundred in Texas. In 1769, the mission at San Diego, California, was established and the colonization of California began.

In 1810 in Mexico, Father Miguel Hidalgo y Castilla led the revolt against Spain, and Mexico gained its independence in 1821. Soon after Mexico became independent, Anglo-American settlers began to move into the Mexican territories of the present-day U.S. Southwest, especially Texas. In 1836, the Anglo settlers declared the Republic of Texas independent of Mexico. In 1846, the United States invaded Mexico under the banner of Manifest Destiny. The treaty of Guadalupe Hidalgo ended the Mexican War that same year. Under the treaty, half the land area of Mexico, including Texas, California, most of Arizona and New Mexico, and parts of Colorado, Utah, and Nevada, was ceded to the United States. The treaty gave Mexican nationals one year to choose U.S. or Mexican citizenship. Seventy-five thousand Hispanic people chose to remain in the United States and become citizens by conquest. James Gadsden was later sent to Mexico to complete the U.S. acquisition of the Southwest and negotiated the purchase of an additional 45,532 square miles, which became parts of Arizona and New Mexico. As more Anglos settled in the newly acquired lands, the new Hispanic Americans gradually became a minority population in the Southwest. The 1848 gold rush lured a flood of Anglo settlers to California, which became a state in 1850. Settlement in Arizona and New Mexico occurred at a slower pace, and they both became states in 1912.

The Treaty of Guadalupe Hidalgo guaranteed the property rights of the new Hispanic-American landowners by reaffirming land grants that had been made by Spain and Mexico prior to 1846. However, the treaty did not explicitly protect the language or cultural rights of these new U.S. citizens. Over the next fifty years, most Southwestern states enacted language laws inhibiting Hispanic participation in voting, judicial processes, and education. More devastating, the Reclamation Act of 1902 dispossessed many of these same Hispanic Americans of their land. Only in New Mexico were the civil rights of the descendants of the original Spanish-speaking settlers protected.

Such conditions of discrimination discouraged immigration to the United States for most of the late nineteenth century, even though the United States had no immigration statutes relating to the admission of foreign nationals until 1875. In fact, entering the country without a visa was not a punishable offense until 1929. However, in the 1890s there was a demand for low-wage laborers to construct American railroads, and Mexican immigration was encouraged, especially after 1882, when Congress passed the Chinese Exclusion Act of 1882, which virtually ended immigration from China to the United States.

By 1910, conditions in Mexico deteriorated under the considerable political repression of the dictatorship of President Porfirio Díaz, who ruled Mexico for thirty-four years, from 1876 to 1910. Dispossession of property, widespread poverty, and runaway inflation forced many Mexicans to join forces in revolt. After the Mexican Revolution began in 1910, hundreds of thousands of people fled north from Mexico and settled in the Southwest. Between 1910 and 1930, about 10 percent of the entire population of Mexico immigrated to the United States, including 685,000 legal immigrants. They were welcomed during this period because of the labor needs of the expanding U.S. economy. Special rules were developed in 1917, during World War I, to permit "temporary" Mexican farm workers, railroad laborers, and miners to enter the United States to work. By the late 1920s, as much as 80 percent of the farm workers in southern California were of Mexican descent.

The Great Depression of the 1930s brought rapid change to Mexican immigration. From 1929 to 1934, more than 400,000 persons were "repatriated" to Mexico without any formal deportation proceedings. Thousands of U.S. citizens were illegally deported because they were of Mexican descent.

During World War II, the United States again needed workers and immigration was encouraged. In 1942, an arrangement was made with the Mexican government to supply temporary workers, known as "braceros," for American agriculture. Formalized by legislation in 1951, the Bracero Program brought an annual average of 350,000 Mexican workers to the United States until its end in 1964.

Mexican Americans again faced economic difficulties and discrimination because of competition for jobs during the late 1950s. This led to Operation Wetback, in which 3.8 million persons of Mexican descent were deported between 1954 and 1958. Only a small fraction of that amount were allowed deportation hearings prior to being deported. Thousands more legitimate U.S. citizens of Mexican descent were also arrested and detained.

In 1965, the United States enacted a law placing a cap on immigration from the Western Hemisphere for the first time, which became effective in 1968. Immediate family members of U.S. citizens were not subject to the cap and could legally immigrate. Legal immigration from Mexico averaged about sixty thousand persons per year from 1971 to 1980. A substantial number of undocumented persons entered the United States from Mexico during those years, and that number has increased dramatically since. Estimates of the number of undocumented immigrants in the United States often range from three to five million people. In the early 1980s, programs to apprehend undocumented immigrants were again implemented, and once more there were reports of violations of civil rights of U.S. citizens and lawful permanent residents of Mexican descent.

Mexican Americans are only a part of the entire U.S. Hispanic population. Many other Spanish-speaking peoples became U.S. citizens under different circumstances. For example, Florida, Puerto Rico, and Cuba were possessions of Spain until the nineteenth century. Florida was claimed for Spain after its discovery by Juan Ponce de León in 1513. Saint Augustine in Florida was the earliest settlement established in North America, founded in 1563. It remained a possession of Spain until 1819. After Andrew Jackson led a U.S. military force into Florida, capturing two Spanish forts, Spain sold Florida to the United States for $5 million under the Onís Treaty.

Puerto Ricans, like the first Mexican Americans, became U.S. citizens through conquest. In 1898, following the brief Spanish-American War, Puerto Rico became a possession U.S. through the Treaty of Paris.

Many Puerto Ricans assumed that annexation meant that all Puerto Ricans were U.S. citizens, thus entitling them to all the rights and privileges of citizenship. However, that was not the case. Many Puerto Ricans were denied the right to vote, and many were prevented from moving to the U.S. mainland.

Nearly twenty years later, the Jones Act of 1917 finally resolved this problem, making all Puerto Ricans U.S. citizens. Since then, Puerto Ricans have had the unrestricted right to travel between the island and the mainland. By the early 1920s, there were significant Puerto Rican communities in U.S. cities, most notably New York.

Cuba also became a U.S. possession in 1898 through the Treaty of Paris, which ended 387 years of Spanish rule. However, Cuba was a possession only for a brief time and became independent in 1902. In the late nineteenth century, a small number of Cubans migrated to the United States, mainly to Florida and New York. By 1930, only about 20,000 Cubans lived in the United States, and by 1950, only about 35,000.

The vast majority of Cuban Americans immigrated to the United States after 1959, when Fidel Castro took power in Cuba. Between 1959 and 1962, 25,000 Cubans were "paroled" to the United States using a special immigration rule. The immigration laws did not provide for special refugee status without proof of physical persecution until 1965. In 1966, a program was initiated to airlift Cubans to the United States, but it was halted by Castro in 1973. Over 250,000 Cubans were airlifted to the United States during that period. About 10 percent of the island's population immigrated to the United States between 1966 and 1973.

Throughout the remainder of the 1970s, many Cubans immigrated to the United States by routes through other Latin American countries. In 1980, a "boat-lift" of Cubans from Mariel Harbor was permitted by Castro, and about 130,000 refugees arrived in the United States. Controversy surrounded this boat-lift because a small percentage of the refugees were from Cuban prisons and institutions for the mentally ill.

Today, about one million Cuban Americans live in the United States, with the majority residing in Florida, although there are increasing numbers in California, Illinois, Massachusetts, New York, and New Jersey. While many early Cuban refugees expected to return to Cuba, the continuation of the Communist regime under Castro has led many to conclude that they will not be able to return. They have become naturalized citizens at a much higher rate than any other Hispanic immigrant group.

At different times in U.S. history, waves of immigrants have arrived from other Latin American countries, such as Nicaragua, Colombia, the Dominican Republic, Guatemala, Honduras, and El Salvador, as well as many others. More than half of these immigrants have come to the United States since 1970. Often they have entered the United States through Mexico. Some have entered legally under established immigration quotas, others have come as students or tourists and stayed in this country after their temporary legal status expired. Many immigrants from the Caribbean and Central and South America have come through circuitous and difficult routes to escape civil war, poverty, and repression.

More recent Central American immigration can be traced largely to economic and political conditions in the source countries, especially during the past two decades. During the 1960s, the establishment of the Central American Common Market led to economic growth and improved conditions in the region. In 1969, however, the border war between Honduras and El Salvador led to the collapse of the common market and the rapid decline of economic conditions in Central America.

Since 1979, political upheaval and civil wars in Nicaragua, El Salvador, and Guatemala have contributed to large migrations of refugees to the United States. The number of Central and South Americans in the United States in 1950 was about 57,000. Estimates in 1985 ranged from 1.4 million to 1.7 million, but these figures may be low because of difficulties in accurately counting large numbers of undocumented emigrants from Central and South America.

❋THE DEVELOPMENT OF U.S. IMMIGRATION LAW

Americans have always taken pride in their immigrant heritage but ironically have feared new immigration at the same time. Since the United States declared its independence from Great Britain in 1776, protectionism has had its place in the population's subconscious. In later years it was often used as justification for restricting immigration.

Article I of the U.S. Constitution entrusted Congress with the power to regulate immigration and "to establish an uniform Rule of Naturalization." During the first one hundred years following the American Revolution, the United States had an open-door policy with regard to immigration, which meant that immigrants from any country in the world were allowed to enter the United States unimpeded.

The first legislation to limit immigration to the United States came during the administration of President John Adams; it did not, however, limit the

numbers or the origin of immigrants. The Naturalization Act of 1798 raised the number of years an immigrant had to live in the United States to be eligible for citizenship from five years to fourteen. The Alien Act of 1798 granted the president the authority to expel any alien he deemed dangerous. Opposed by President Thomas Jefferson, the Alien Act expired under its own terms in 1800, during his presidency.

Although the United States had a neutral immigration policy with few restrictions, some state legislatures enacted laws restricting immigration, most notably denying entry to Catholic immigrants in the early 1800s owing to fear of being dominated by the pope. These fears were used in 1854 by the American party, better known as the Know-Nothing party, which mounted successful local campaigns by denouncing immigration and Catholics and other groups. The Know-Nothing party won forty seats in the Congress that year. In 1856 the party launched a national campaign and nominated former president Millard Fillmore for the presidency. Fillmore suffered defeat and won only 8 of 296 electoral votes.

In 1875, the U.S. Supreme Court in *Henderson v. Mayor of New York*, 92 U.S. 259, ruled that all power to regulate immigration was held solely by the federal government and struck down state restrictions as unconstitutional. However, Congress passed the first major federal immigration restrictions during the ensuing years.

The first statutes aimed at excluding certain persons from immigrating to the United States denied admission to convicts and prostitutes. In 1882, the first general federal immigration law was enacted, which included an entry tax of fifty cents per person and denied entry to the United States to "idiots, lunatics, convicts and persons likely to become public charges." But the first major legislation to reverse the century-old tradition of free and open immigration to the United States was the Chinese Exclusion Act of 1882. By its terms, the Exclusion Act put an end to Chinese immigration to the United States for ten years; later laws extended the ban indefinitely and prohibited the naturalization of Chinese persons already in the United States. It was not repealed until 1943.

The first literacy test law to restrict immigration was enacted in 1917, over the veto of President Woodrow Wilson. The literacy test acted to limit immigration from areas outside northern Europe, requiring literacy in some language for immigrants over age 16. Ironically, that same year the Jones Act of 1917 was passed, which extended U.S. citizenship to all Puerto Ricans.

By 1920, Congress had passed about a dozen major immigration laws that restricted certain kinds of individuals from immigrating to the United States, such as criminals, persons with chronic diseases, and persons with unacceptable moral or political beliefs. In 1921, limits on the number of immigrants allowed to enter the United States during a single year were imposed for the first time in the country's history. This legislation limited immigration from Europe to 3 percent of each European nationality present in the United States in 1910, a sharp reduction from previous immigration levels. The National Origins Quota Law of 1924 restricted the immigration of southern and eastern Europeans even more, and immigration from Asia was banned.

Immigration from Latin American countries was exempt from the quota restrictions that Congress created for two reasons. The first, and most important, was that farmers and manufacturers in the southwestern states had become dependent on cheap, plentiful labor from Mexico. The second reason was that the United States was attempting to emerge as a leader of cooperative spirit among its neighbors in the Western Hemisphere under the banner of Pan-Americanism. Even without the quota restrictions, immigration from Latin America, excluding Mexico, remained low from the 1930s through the 1950s.

Following World War II, President Harry Truman allowed large numbers of displaced persons from Europe to enter the United States far in excess of the countries" quotas. In response to Truman's action, Congress passed the Immigration and Nationality Act of 1952, also known as the McCarran-Walter Act. The act reaffirmed the basic features of the 1924 quota law by maintaining a restrictive limit on immigration from particular countries. Immigration from Asia was legalized, but only at very low levels. England, Ireland, and Germany represented two-thirds of the yearly quota for the entire world. Immigration from the Western Hemisphere remained exempt, except that applicants had to clear a long list of barriers devised to exclude homosexuals, Communists, and others.

Immigration from Latin America increased following the enactment of the McCarran-Walter Act. During the 1950s, immigration from Mexico doubled from 5.9 percent to 11.9 percent, and in the 1960s it rose to 13.3 percent of the total number of immigrants to the United States. Immigration from Cuba during this same period was 7.75 percent of the total. The total number of immigrants from Latin American countries during this time, including Mexico and Cuba, was 39 percent of all immigrants entering the U.S.

In 1965, a major revision of immigration law resulted when Congress amended the Immigration and Nationality Act of 1952. The national origin quota system was abolished. A complex seven-category preference system for granting visas was created in its place. The 1965 amendments gave preference to family reunification. Spouses, parents, and children of U.S. citizens were given preference in awarding visas and were not bound by a quota. The amendments maintained limits on immigration through the seven-category preference system, providing for immigration from each country of no more than 20,000 immigrants per year. Race or national origin was no longer a consideration. More important, the 1965 amendments imposed a quota ceiling on immigration from countries in the Western Hemisphere as well. This marked the first time in U.S. history that such a numerical restriction was placed on immigration from these countries.

Amendments to the law passed in 1978 removed the ceilings for each hemisphere and established a worldwide competition for 290,000 visas granted each year. Every country in the world was subject to the seven-category preference system and to the 20,000-per-year limit. The 1965 and 1978 amendments led to a dramatic shift in immigration. No longer were Europeans, formerly favored by law, the largest group of immigrants. They now represented only 13 percent of the total. Asians benefited most, representing 21 percent of the total number of immigrants entering the United States per year. Immigration from Latin American countries and the Caribbean remained at about 40 percent of the total.

The Immigration Act of 1990 continues to permit immigration of immediate relatives of U.S. citizens without numerical limitation but sets a "pierceable" overall cap on worldwide immigration of 700,000 for fiscal years 1992 through 1994, and of 675,000 for fiscal year 1995. The seven-category preference system has been replaced by one based on family relationships, employment, and diversity. The per-country limit is 25,000.

The 1970s and early 1980s brought a different kind of immigration problem to the attention of the American public. The rise in politically motivated violence in Central America spurred a massive increase in undocumented immigration to the United States. The flight of "boat people" from Indochina following the Vietnam War created an enormous refugee settlement challenge for the United States. In a six-month period alone in 1980, some 125,000 Cubans arrived in Florida in an uncontrolled sea migration to the United States. At about the same time, over 10,000 Haitians fled the repressive regime of dictator Jean Claude Duvalier and sailed to the United States in overcrowded fishing boats.

These immigrants, or more appropriately, refugees, created a problem for U.S. immigration authorities. They were not eligible to enter the United States under established quotas without visas, nor could many of them meet the requirements to enter the United States under an exemption to the quota system as "refugees." Previous U.S. law provided for the admission of persons fleeing persecution or having a well-founded fear of persecution from Middle Eastern Communist-dominated countries. This was advantageous to the Cubans fleeing Communist dictator Fidel Castro and the Vietnamese fleeing the Communist regime in Vietnam but was no help to the thousands of Central Americans who were fleeing political violence. The Refugee Act of 1980 removed the ideological definition of refugee as one who flees from a Communist regime, thus allowing thousands to enter the United States as refugees who otherwise would have been excluded.

✳ THE CURRENT DEBATE OVER U.S. IMMIGRATION LAW

The high level of illegal immigration from Mexico and other Latin American countries has fueled continuing debate about U.S. immigration policies. Beginning in the early 1970s, Congress, along with Presidents Nixon and Ford, assembled high-level commissions to study the problem, with no tangible results.

President Jimmy Carter appointed the bipartisan Select Commission on Immigration and Refugee Policy to forge a consensus in Congress and to propose solutions. The commission went through hundreds of reports on trends in immigration and their effects on the nation and held a long series of hearings throughout the country. The commission's final report was issued in 1981 and is entitled *U.S. Immigration Policy in the National Interest*. The report states, "The United States is disturbed by immigration. The very fact that so many come outside of the law or abuse their nonimmigrant visas is troubling in a nation which prides itself on respect for law generally, and for its legal immigration system specifically."

Once separated from the fear and deception of racist sentiments, the current immigration policy debate involves three key issues: control of U.S. borders, economic interests of the United States, and enforcement of U.S. immigration law. There is genuine concern over the nation's ability to humanely control immigration at its borders. As the number of undocumented immigrants apprehended at the southern border rises, so does concern over regaining control of the rate of immigration. There is also illegal immigration from the north, but the numbers are smaller, and there is a higher proportion of native English-speakers who look American in appearance.

If the United States is to maintain an immigration

policy consistent with the American notion of an open society, while at the same time limiting immigration to serve the national interest, most national policymakers believe that immigration must be controlled. But border enforcement must also be equitable and must maintain an open society. Limits imposed because of color, race, nationality, or religion are not fair. Moreover, those who are admitted must be allowed the full rights of participation in U.S. society.

The U.S. economy is a key force behind illegal immigration as well as a major cause for American concern about it. In much of Mexico, especially in rural areas, finding employment is extremely difficult, and a job pays only a small fraction of the minimum wage in the United States. Similar economic pressures encourage immigration from other countries, but illegal immigration is most practical for Mexicans and Central Americans, who can reach the United States by land. In southwestern states, certain U.S. industries depend on undocumented laborers, who work hard for very low pay and who seldom complain. Thus, illegal immigration is welcomed by many employers. As history demonstrates, the United States typically welcomes immigrants in times of economic growth and labor shortages, and repels them during economic hard times.

The economic effects of illegal immigration are intensely argued today. Some argue that undocumented laborers steal jobs from American workers and that undocumented aliens abuse the welfare and social services system. However, others argue and several studies demonstrate that undocumented laborers actually create jobs and thereby bolster the national economy. Furthermore, the data show that undocumented aliens rarely use any form of public assistance and, for the most part, are ineligible for government assistance because of their immigration status. Immigration policy should take into account the economic impact on the national economy, but it must first carefully examine labor needs and the actual effects of illegal immigration.

Enforcement of U.S. immigration law is a key issue in the immigration debate. Once policy is set and law is enacted, it should be enforced fairly. Our immigration laws should reestablish and maintain a consistent, practicable and humane rule of law.

❋THE LEGALIZATION PROGRAM

The Immigration Reform and Control Act of 1986 created a major alien legalization program. Under the act, legal status was given to applicants who had held illegal status in the United States from before January 1, 1982, until the time of application. The act also offered legal status to Special Agricultural Workers (SAW) who could prove they had spent at least ninety days during a qualifying period doing agricultural work in specific crops. The Immigration and Naturalization Service (INS) accepted legalization applications between May 5, 1987, and May 4, 1988, and SAW applications from June 1, 1987, to November 30, 1988.

It is estimated that approximately three to five million undocumented immigrants lived in the United States at the time the legalization program began. On a case-by-case basis, the program has allowed those undocumented immigrants who could demonstrate continuous residence in the United States since 1982 and who would otherwise be admissible as immigrants to become legal residents. The program dealt with a complex statute and was often the subject of intense controversy, particularly over who was eligible and what documentation was needed. Disputes with the INS over the regulations led many applicants to the courtroom, where the INS usually lost.

Despite these problems, the program was successful and brought major benefits to a large number of Hispanics. More than three million applicants applied for legal status under the program, and over 90 percent of such applicants received at least temporary legal status. The largest number of applicants, about 69 percent, was from Mexico. Approximately 11 percent were from Central America, 2 percent from Caribbean countries, and about 1.5 percent from South America. The remaining applicants were from various countries around the world.

Among the most obvious and immediate benefits is the ability of applicants who receive legal status to cross borders legally. Additionally, the massive number of applicants has been vital in unscrambling close to two million Social Security accounts that were incorrect or fraudulent. Applicants who had acquired a false or incorrect Social Security card had the opportunity to correct their Social Security account. One subtle change has been in the behavior of the newly legalized. Many are showing an increased willingness to use public health facilities and to assert legal rights they always had but were afraid to invoke for fear that it would lead to questions about their immigration status. Many have left the very worst jobs and are now able to seek higher-paying employment.

The legalization program might not have been without its difficulties, but the program has made a necessary difference for a powerless class of individuals. It has improved the lives of millions of Hispanics and provided them with the opportunity to obtain full U.S. citizenship.

✳EMPLOYMENT DISCRIMINATION

As demonstrated by the history of U.S. immigration law, employment has always been closely related to patterns of immigration by Hispanics. Mexican-American workers suffered widespread abuses after the Southwest was ceded to the United States by Mexico. Mexican-American workers endured various forms of mistreatment, including intolerable working conditions, substandard pay, and extended work hours.

Following the conquest of the Southwest, Hispanic Americans, deprived of virtually any means of building a decent economic base, were forced to work in the employ of newly arrived Anglo-Americans. During the 1800s, many Mexican Americans worked twelve-hour days, six days a week, in mines, yet they were paid only half the wages paid to white miners. Mexican-American workers were denigrated and were always the most poorly paid.

Mexican-American farm workers in Texas were described as subhuman by historian Pauline Kibbe in 1946. She referred to this population of laborers as "but a species of farm implement that comes mysteriously into being coincident with the maturing of the cotton, that requires no upkeep or special consideration during the period of usefulness, needs no protection from the elements, and when the crop has been harvested, vanishes into the limbo of forgotten things, until the next harvest season rolls around."

Hispanic-American citizens historically have always faced employment discrimination on the basis of their national origin. Such discrimination is comparable to that experienced by members of other minority groups. It was not until the landmark case of *Hernández v. Texas* (1954) that the nation's highest court acknowledged that Hispanic Americans were not being treated as "whites." The Supreme Court recognized Hispanics as a separate class of people suffering profound discrimination. The 1954 decision paved the way for Hispanic Americans to use legal means to attack all types of discrimination throughout the United States.

Among the most important legislation enacted to end employment discrimination against all minorities was the Civil Rights Act of 1964, which made it illegal for an employer to discriminate on the basis of race, color, religion, sex, or national origin. The statute was designed to protect Hispanic Americans and other minorities. It is still often used to challenge unlawful denial of jobs to Hispanic Americans.

Today, the law of employment discrimination is complex, and there are many relevant federal statutes. An important development regarding employment discrimination against immigrants was the enactment of antidiscrimination provisions in the Immigration Reform and Control Act of 1986. As noted earlier, the immigration laws were amended in 1986, making it unlawful for employers to hire undocumented persons. However, Congress believed, when passing this legislation, that the threat of sanctions created the risk that employers might refuse to hire or might discriminate against persons who appear to be foreign, have foreign-sounding names, or speak in a foreign language or with a foreign accent. Consequently, Congress included the antidiscrimination provisions in the act as a counterbalance to employer sanctions. These provisions created a new legal tool for Hispanic Americans who have experienced discrimination on the basis of national origin. The law states that it is an unfair immigration-related employment practice to discriminate in hiring, recruitment, or discharge because of a person's national origin or citizenship status. Protection against discrimination arising from citizenship status extends to all citizens, as well as to other classifications of immigrants who are legally in the United States.

✳POLICE BRUTALITY

In the 1800s, brutality against Mexican Americans in the Southwest territories was commonplace. In fact, lynchings and murders of Mexican Americans became so common in California and Texas that, in 1912, the Mexican ambassador formally protested the mistreatment of Mexicans and cited several brutal incidents that had recently taken place.

The prevailing conditions in the 1920s along the Texas-Mexico border were intolerable. Texas Rangers killed Mexicans along the border without fear of penalty. No jury along the border would ever convict a white man for shooting a Mexican. Abuse of Mexican Americans by rangers and police continued unchecked in the 1930s.

In 1943 *Time* magazine reported that two hundred navy men, angered by scuffles with Hispanic youth, commandeered taxicabs and began attacking Mexican Americans in East Los Angeles. The Los Angeles police followed the caravan of navy men and watched them beat the Hispanics and did nothing to stop them. Mexican-American boys were dragged from movie theaters, stripped of their clothing, beaten, and left naked in the streets. Police did nothing to stop the attacks.

Courts of law were rarely a source of justice for Mexican-American victims of such abuse. In 1947, for example, a nineteen-year-old Mexican American was convicted of murder in Hudspeth County, Texas. He was blind and mentally retarded, and had retaliated to an attack on his elderly father. He was not proved to have the legally necessary intent to kill to justify first-degree murder, but an all-white jury found him guilty of first-degree murder anyway. He was sentenced to death. The ruling was appealed on the grounds that some Mexican Americans should have been on the jury because the population of Hudspeth County was 50 percent Hispanic. The appellate court held that the Fourteenth Amendment, which prohibits discrimination on the basis of race or color, did not protect Mexican Americans, and the young man was executed.

As late as 1970, brutality against Mexican Americans continued. In *López v. Harlow*, a case filed in an attempt to bring the violence under control, a police officer shot and killed López, a Mexican American, allegedly in self-defense, because he thought López was about to throw a dish at him. Since the 1970s, Hispanics have come forward in greater numbers and have documented abuses by police, abuses that include unreasonable seizures, physical brutality, and incarceration without cause. Ammunition against police abuse is growing, but the fight on this issue is destined to be a long one.

✳FEDERAL LEGISLATION AFFECTING HISPANIC AMERICANS

Reclamation Act of 1902

From a Hispanic perspective, the Reclamation Act of 1902 is among the most devastating pieces of legislation in history. This law dispossessed Hispanic Americans of their land in the Southwestern territories fifty years after the Treaty of Guadalupe Hidalgo ceded these lands to the United States in 1846. Only in New Mexico were the civil rights of the descendants of the original Spanish-speaking settlers protected.

Jones Act of 1917

The Jones Act of 1917 gave residents of Puerto Rico full U.S. citizenship. Puerto Rico had been annexed by the United States in 1898 following the Spanish-American War. With the enactment of this law, Puerto Ricans were granted the unrestricted right to travel between the island and the U.S. mainland.

Civil Rights Act of 1964

Among the most important laws enacted to end discrimination against all minorities, the Civil Rights Act of 1964 made it illegal to discriminate on the basis of race, color, religion, sex, or national origin. The statute was designed to protect Hispanic Americans and other minorities, and it is often used to challenge unlawful denial of jobs for Hispanic Americans.

Immigration and Nationality Act of 1965

In 1965, Congress, for the first time in history, placed a limitation on the number of persons allowed to immigrate to the United States from Western Hemisphere countries, which had always been exempt from quotas until the enactment of this law. The abolition of the national origins system brought greater equality to the American immigration system.

Voting Rights Act of 1965

Although the single aim of the Voting Rights Act of 1965 was African-American enfranchisement in the South, obstacles to registration and voting faced by all minorities were affected. Its potential as a tool for Hispanic Americans, however, was not fully realized for nearly a decade.

Voting Rights Act of 1970

The 1970 amendments constituting the landmark Voting Rights Act of 1970 added a provision that was designed to guard against inventive new barriers to political participation. It requires federal approval of all changes in voting procedures in certain jurisdictions, primarily southern states. This act prevents minority votes from being diluted in gerrymandered districts or through at-large elections.

Equal Educational Opportunity Act of 1974

Congress passed the Equal Educational Opportunity Act of 1974 to create equality in public schools by making bilingual education available to Hispanic youth. According to the framers of the act, equal education means more than equal facilities and equal access to teachers. Students who have trouble with the English language must be given programs to help them overcome their difficulties with English.

Voting Rights Act Amendments of 1975

The Voting Rights Act Amendments of 1975 extended the provisions of the original Voting Rights Act and made permanent the national ban on literacy tests. Critical for Hispanic Americans, the amendments made bilingual ballots a requirement in certain areas.

Refugee Act of 1980

Under previous U.S. law, persons fleeing persecution or having a well-founded fear of persecution in Middle Eastern or Communist-dominated countries could be admitted to the United States despite any applicable restrictions. This was advantageous to

Cubans fleeing Communist dictator Fidel Castro and the Vietnamese fleeing the Communist regime in Vietnam, but it was no help to the thousands of Central Americans who were fleeing political violence. The Refugee Act of 1980 removed the ideological definition of refugee as one who flees from a Communist regime, thus allowing thousands who otherwise would have been excluded to enter the United States as refugees.

Voting Rights Act Amendments of 1982

The Voting Rights Act Amendments of 1982 prohibit any voting law or practice created by a state or political subdivision that "results" in denial of the right of any citizen of the United States to vote on account of race, color, or language minority status. This amendment also eliminates the need to prove that the state or political subdivision created a voting law with the "intention" of discriminating against minority voters.

Immigration Reform and Control Act of 1986

The Immigration Reform and Control Act of 1986 created a major alien legalization program. Lawful resident status was extended to applicants who had held illegal status in the United States from before 1982 until the time of application. The Immigration and Naturalization Service (INS) accepted applications for one year, from May 1987 until May 1988. The program was successful and brought legal status to a large number of undocumented Hispanics. More than three million applicants applied for lawful residence under the program, and over 90 percent of them received at least temporary legal resident status.

Additionally, the act made it unlawful for employers to hire undocumented workers. However, because of the threat that sanctions might deter employers from hiring or cause them to discriminate against persons appearing to be foreign, Congress included antidiscrimination provisions in the Immigration Reform and Control Act.

Immigration Act of 1990

The Immigration Act of 1990 continues to permit immigration of immediate relatives of U.S. citizens without numerical limitation but sets a "pierceable" overall cap on worldwide immigration to the United States of 700,000 for fiscal years 1992 through 1994, and 675,000 for fiscal year 1995. The seven-category preference system has been replaced by allocation of visas based on family relationships, employment, and diversity. The per-country limit is now 25,000.

✻IMPORTANT CASES AFFECTING HISPANIC AMERICANS

Hernández v. Texas
347 U.S. 475 (1954)

A crucial case argued in 1954, *Hernandez v. Texas* was the first Mexican-American discrimination case to reach the nation's highest court. It was also the first U.S. Supreme Court case to be argued and briefed by Mexican-American attorneys. The case was brought by lawyers Carlos Cadena and Gus García. It was an important victory.

The defendant, Pete Hernández, had been tried and convicted for murder in Jackson County, Texas. Jackson County was 14 percent Hispanic, but the jury panel that found Hernández guilty did not include any Hispanics. In fact, no Spanish-surnamed person had served on any jury of any sort in Jackson County for twenty-five years prior to the trial.

Chief Justice Earl Warren, speaking for the Supreme Court, held that the Texas court was in error by "limiting the scope of the equal protection clause to the white and negro classes" and that Mexican Americans were entitled to the protection of the Fourteenth Amendment of the U.S. Constitution. The Court had acknowledged that Mexican Americans were not being treated as "whites" in the Southwest. Mexican Americans were recognized as a separate class of people who were suffering profound discrimination. The 1954 decision paved the way for Hispanic Americans to use legal means to attack discrimination throughout the country.

Allen v. State Board of Elections
393 U.S. 544 (1969)

In *Allen v. State Board of Elections*, the U.S. Supreme Court extended federal authority to object to discriminatory alterations in voting districts, the introduction of at-large voting, and other such changes, in addition to reaffirming the original power to object to discriminatory innovations involving registration and voting.

Graham v. Richardson
403 U.S. 365 (1971)

Graham v. Richardson was a decision involving application of the equal protection clause of the U.S. Constitution to state welfare laws discriminating against aliens in Arizona and Pennsylvania. The Supreme Court held that provisions of state welfare laws conditioning benefits on citizenship and imposing durational residency requirements on aliens violated the equal protection clause.

San Antonio Independent School District v. Rodríguez
411 U.S. 1 (1973)

A suit brought on behalf of poor schoolchildren, *San Antonio Independent School District v. Rodríguez,* challenged the Texas system of financing its school system based on local property taxation. The Supreme Court held that the system did not violate the constitutional right of the children to equal protection under the Fourteenth Amendment. By a 5-4 majority, the Court ruled that education is not a fundamental right and poverty is not a reason to hold otherwise.

Espinoza v. Farah Manufacturing Company
414 U.S. 86 (1973)

An employment discrimination case, *Espinoza v. Farah Manufacturing Company* was brought against Farah for discrimination toward an employee, Espinoza, on the basis of his citizenship status under the Civil Rights Act. However, the Supreme Court held that there was nothing in Title VII, the equal employment opportunities provisions of the Civil Rights Act of 1964, that makes it illegal to discriminate on the basis of citizenship or alienage.

Lau v. Nichols
414 U.S. 563 (1974)

Lau v. Nichols was brought before the Supreme Court by students who did not speak English. The Court held that the California school system's failure to provide English-language instruction to the students denied meaningful opportunity to participate in public educational programs and was in violation of Title VI of the Civil Rights Act of 1964.

Matthews v. Díaz
426 U.S. 67 (1976)

Resident alien Díaz, age 65, brought suit challenging the constitutionality of the Social Security Act provision requiring resident aliens to have resided in the United States for five years before they are eligible for Medicare. The U.S. district court in Florida held that it was an unconstitutional requirement, but the Supreme Court reversed, holding that Congress may condition aliens" eligibility for participation in Medicare, or any other federal program, on citizenship or continuous residence in the United States.

Plyler v. Doe
457 U.S. 202 (1982)

Plyler v. Doe was brought on behalf of Mexican children who had entered the United States illegally and resided in Texas. The suit challenged a Texas statute excluding the children from attending public schools. The Supreme Court struck down the Texas statute as unconstitutional and in violation of the equal protection clause, which provides that no state shall deny to any person the equal protection of the laws.

League of United Latin American Citizens v. Pasadena Independent School District
662 F. Supp. 443 (S.D. Tex. 1987)

In the *League of United Latin American Citizens v. Pasadena Independent School District,* the League of United Latin American Citizens (LULAC), on behalf of undocumented aliens who were terminated from their employment as Pasadena school district custodial workers because they provided false Social Security numbers, brought suit against the school district. The U.S. District Court for the Southern District of Texas held that the aliens were entitled to their jobs because the termination violated the antidiscrimination provision of the Immigration Reform and Control Act of 1986.

Hernández v. New York
111 S. Ct. 1859 (1991)

In *Hernández v. New York* Hernández appealed a conviction by a New York State court on the basis that the prosecutor had discriminated against him by dismissing two prospective Spanish-speaking jurors. The prosecutor argued that he doubted the jurors" ability to defer to the official translation of anticipated Spanish-language testimony. The Supreme Court held that the state trial court was justified in concluding that the prosecutor did not discriminate on the basis of race.

✸HISPANICS IN THE LEGAL PROFESSION

As early as the 1730s, with the formation of the Society of Gentlemen Practisers in the Courts of Law and Equity, attorneys have established organizations for the purpose of improving standards in the American legal profession. Historically, however, such professionals have established an elite class of lawyers who are able to maintain control over the legal profession and its development. These lawyers came to represent the bar and established the rules and guidelines affecting the entire legal community.

In particular, they were able to limit participation by defining the qualifications for admission to the bar, thereby maintaining the status quo. The early legal profession was designed to promote certain political views and to resist change. Such standards were effectively, if not intentionally, racist and served to restrict access to the powerful bar. The American Bar Association, established in 1878, itself has recognized its unenviable history of inaction in reaching out to minorities.

Adoption of the Fourteenth Amendment to the U.S. Constitution in 1868 marked a turning point. This constitutional amendment, along with civil rights legislation, helped the United States move toward equality. The road was difficult, and even after a century had passed, discrimination and inequality still existed.

Congress enacted the first comprehensive civil rights law since the Reconstruction period when it passed the Civil Rights Act of 1964. One result of the act was the establishment of affirmative action programs. During the early years of affirmative action, equal opportunity plans were an effective way of ending employment discrimination. The U.S. Supreme Court supported this view, in many cases striking down employment and hiring practices that discriminated on the basis of race, color, gender, or national origin. As a result, civil rights legislation and affirmative action programs were pivotal in providing minorities with equal opportunities in professions from which they were previously barred.

Despite these legislative advances, Hispanic Americans continue to be underrepresented in the legal profession, especially in the nation's largest law firms. To increase Hispanic representation, large law firms must recognize that a greater, more concerted effort is needed to assist Hispanic Americans in getting through the subtle acculturation process found within law firms.

The number of Hispanic attorneys working for U.S. corporations is 50 percent greater than the number of Hispanic attorneys in the nation's largest law firms. A survey conducted by the *National Law Journal* reported that Hispanics represent 1.2 percent of all the attorneys in the 251 largest law firms in the United States. In large part, the reason for underrepresentation of Hispanic Americans in the legal profession, especially in large law firms, is that Hispanics are not attending law schools in numbers proportionate to the Hispanic population in the United States.

Hispanics and Legal Education

Despite many advances, Hispanic-American representation in the legal profession, as in most prestigious fields, is still not proportionate to the number of Hispanics in the general population. The low number of Hispanics admitted to U.S. law schools is the major barrier.

The American Bar Association (ABA) reported that Hispanic-American enrollment in ABA-approved law schools was 1.5 percent of all law students in 1975. About ten years later, the ABA reported that the number had increased slightly to 2 percent. Although this is an improvement, it is far from representative of the Hispanic presence in the general population. Hispanic-American law school enrollment is also adversely affected by a high attrition rate, much higher than that of law students overall. Even more devastating is the high dropout rate among Hispanic youth in high school and college; almost half of all Hispanic college students drop out during their first two years, which has prevented large numbers of them from reaching law school or other professional schools.

Another commonly noted problem of Hispanic students is a deficiency in academic background. This often requires a long academic adjustment period, private tutoring, or some other form of academic support to assist the student in completing law school. This may often be the case for Hispanic students who speak Spanish as their native language. Many Hispanic students also experience pressure from peers who attempt to dissuade them from pursuing higher education. These academic problems are often accompanied by financial difficulties. Unfortunately, many, if not most, law schools do little to accommodate Hispanic students" needs.

Obstacles to financing the high costs of a legal education may be a significant reason for the high number of law school dropouts. Many of the resources that helped Hispanic Americans to attain higher education in the 1970s are becoming more and more scarce. Financial aid has been decreasing because of government cutbacks, and the political climate has become less receptive to affirmative action and other programs that had previously facilitated the higher education of Hispanics and other minorities.

Hispanic Americans who do graduate from law school may face additional obstacles before entering law firms. Perhaps the most significant one is the bar examination, which all attorneys must pass to practice law. The bar is a hurdle for all would-be attorneys, but is a more significant impediment for Hispanics. In California, which has a large Hispanic population, scores for the California Bar Examination in July 1985 showed that while 61.5 percent of whites passed, only 33.5 percent of Hispanics did. Whether the bar examination is discriminatory against minorities is a volatile issue that is hotly debated.

Hispanics in Large Law Firms

Even once Hispanics pass the bar examination, as attorneys they face formidable obstacles in joining

TRENDS IN LAW SCHOOL ENROLLMENT

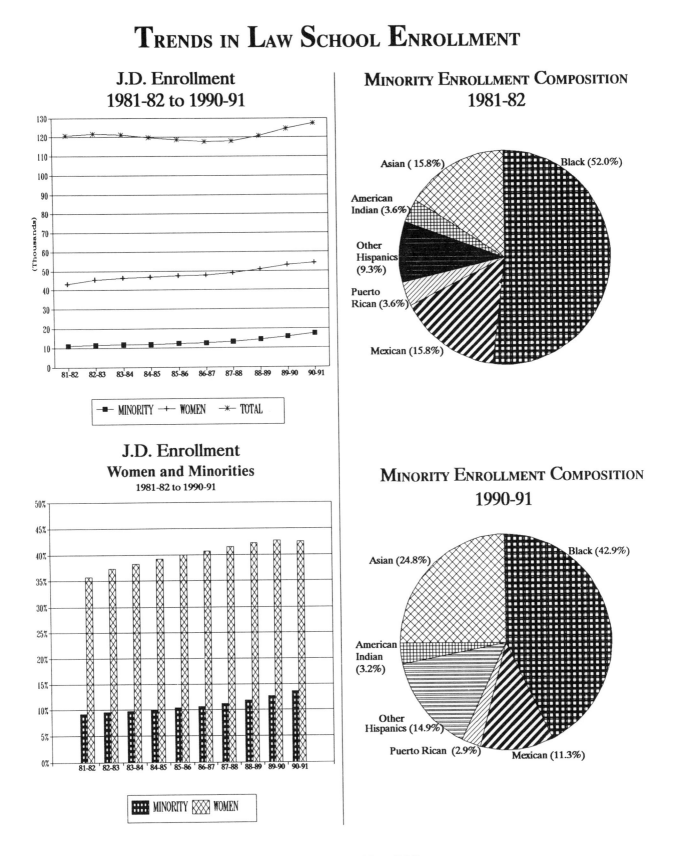

J.D. Enrollment
1981-82 to 1990-91

MINORITY ENROLLMENT COMPOSITION
1981-82

J.D. Enrollment
Women and Minorities
1981-82 to 1990-91

MINORITY ENROLLMENT COMPOSITION
1990-91

Four charts on law school enrollment (*Consultant's Digest*, May 1991).

law firms. According to a survey conducted by Stanford Law School in 1987, Hispanic-American graduates reported they felt they had to overcome barriers when joining law firms that nonminorities do not face. At the interviewing stage of the hiring process, Hispanics must confront the preconceptions many interviewers will have of them, preconceptions that large law firm interviewers may not even be aware of. Hispanic students are often stereotyped as being oriented more to public service careers than to careers with large law firms. In the past, Hispanic law school graduates have generally gravitated toward government jobs, poverty law, or legal services. This phenomenon is largely the result of greater opportunity in those types of law practice. Today, however, many Hispanics are pursuing careers in large law firms more aggressively.

Overcoming preconceptions about the kind of law Hispanics want to practice is not the only problem facing Hispanic American law graduates. Although major law firms are gradually opening up opportunities for minorities, they usually hire only attorneys, including minorities, with outstanding academic records who have attended top law schools.

The problems Hispanics face in getting jobs at the country's major law firms do not end with the first job after law school. Having been barred from entry-level positions at large law firms, Hispanics are effectively prevented from joining firms later as lateral hires, because few Hispanics have substantial legal experience in corporate law or in other fields of law in which many large firms specialize. As long as Hispanics have difficulty joining these firms at entry level, the number gaining experience at large law firms will continue to be minimal. Because the firms tend not to hire lawyers without that required experience, Hispanic representation in large law firms is not likely to be improved through lateral hiring.

Increasingly, however, Hispanic attorneys are overcoming the entry barriers and joining large law firms. Even for some of these attorneys, disadvantages may appear within the law firm in the form of additional barriers or added pressures. Breaking the racial barriers of a firm by being the first or only Hispanic attorney is not an easy task. Culture shock for Hispanics entering corporate law firms may not be an uncommon experience. A feeling of isolation may result and is often enhanced by the lack of Hispanic mentors within the law firm. Mentors serve as role models and advisers, and many attorneys think not having a minority mentor hurts their progress within the firm.

Hispanics in the Public Interest

A great number of Hispanic attorneys have chosen a career in the public interest. Many serve at government posts or with nonprofit legal organizations established to aid underprivileged and disenfranchised clients. Many attorneys who enter service in the public interest do so because they have a desire to aid other Hispanic Americans with legal, social, and cultural problems.

In public interest service, Hispanic attorneys have the opportunity to make gains for not only themselves and their community but also all Americans. They take pride in the victories made in the struggle for equal rights at a time when the tide is running against civil rights efforts of minorities. Public interest firms often act as watchdogs that monitor government action to see that public resources are effectively channeled into the Hispanic community. By monitoring these agencies, they can ensure that programs they devise realistically account for the needs of Hispanics. However, public interest firms and organizations are plagued by insufficient funding and staff. Despite these limitations, those people who join the public interest have achieved a great deal in this country.

Issues often monitored by public interest groups include immigration, employment, education, housing, voter registration and elections, public funding, discrimination, and civil rights. In the past two decades, there has been dramatic growth in the number of public interest organizations specifically created to assist Hispanics with legal problems and to advocate political involvement. Some of the most well known and effective national public interest groups in the United States include local offices funded by the Legal Services Corporation; Migrant Legal Action Program; Mexican-American Legal Defense and Educational Fund; Puerto Rican Legal Defense and Education Fund; and the National Immigration Law Center.

Selected Prominent Hispanic Attorneys and Law Professors

James E. Blancarte (1953-)

Litigation Attorney

Blancarte was born in 1953 in Pomona, California, and graduated from Pomona College. He received his law degree from the University of California School of Law and was admitted to the bar in 1979. Blancarte's current areas of practice are litigation and entertainment and business law.

Blancarte was president of the Mexican American Bar Association of Los Angeles in 1983 and was president of the western region of the Hispanic National

Bar Association in 1988. He is currently a partner with the firm of Mitchell, Silberberg & Knupp in Los Angeles.

Wilfredo Caraballo (1947-)

Public Advocate/Public Defender, State of New Jersey

Caraballo was born in Yabucoa, Puerto Rico, in 1947 and grew up in a tough neighborhood of New York City. Caraballo attended St. Joseph's University and went on to New York University Law School and received his law degree in 1974. He then worked the streets of New York City as a community activist and a legal aid lawyer. Caraballo was also active in the Puerto Rican Legal Defense and Education Fund.

In 1975, he joined Seton Hall Law School in Newark, New Jersey, as a clinical professor. During his fifteen years at Seton Hall, Caraballo specialized in teaching contract, commercial, and bankruptcy law. He was a visiting professor at New York University, the City University of New York, and Pace College law schools. In 1982 he was named associate dean of Seton Hall Law School. Caraballo took a leave of absence from his post as associate dean in 1990.

Governor James Florio appointed Caraballo to the Office of Public Advocate and Public Defender, a cabinet post, in 1990, where he served until 1992. Caraballo states that one of the reasons he was so enthusiastic about becoming New Jersey's fourth public advocate is that the post gives him an opportunity to deal with the same kinds of public interest problems he faced firsthand as a young man growing up on the streets of Brooklyn and the South Bronx.

Daniel P. García (1947-)

Attorney

Daniel García was born in Los Angeles in 1947. He was educated in Los Angeles and attended Loyola University, where he received a degree in business in 1970. He went on to the University of Southern California and earned his M.B.A. in 1971. García then attended U.C.L.A. School of Law and was awarded a law degree in 1974.

In 1974, García joined the prestigious firm of Munger, Tolles & Olson in Los Angeles where he is now a partner. He is a member of the board of the Mexican-American Legal Defense and Education Fund and has been active in Los Angeles politics. García was a member of the Los Angeles Planning Commission from 1976 to 1988 and was its president from 1978 to 1988.

Of Hispanic participation in the legal profession, García believes that in recent years Hispanic attorneys have done much better in breaking barriers to

Wilfredo Caraballo.

join the nation's largest firms. García himself is among that group.

Antonia Hernández

President and General Counsel, Mexican-American Legal Defense and Educational Fund (MALDEF)

Born in Coahuila, Mexico, Hernández earned her B.A. at UCLA, om 2948, a teaching credential at the university's School of Education, and her law degree at the UCLA School of Law in 1974. Hernández began her legal career as a staff attorney with the Los Angeles Center for Law and Justice that same year. In 1977, she became the directing attorney for the Legal Aid Foundation office in Lincoln Heights.

An expert in civil rights and immigration issues, Hernández worked with Senator Edward M. Kennedy and the U.S. Senate Committee on the Judiciary in 1979 and 1980. She was also the Southwest regional political coordinator of the Kennedy for President campaign in 1980. Active in community affairs, she presently serves on the board of directors of several organizations, including the National Hispanic Leadership Conference, the Latino Museum of History, Art & Culture, and the Independent Sector.

Antonia Hernández.

Hernández has been the president and general counsel of MALDEF since 1985, served as its vice president from 1984 to 1985, as employment program director from 1983 to 1984, and as an associate counsel from 1981 to 1983. As president of MALDEF, she directs all litigation and advocacy programs, manages a $4.5 million budget and a 65-person staff, and is responsible for the organization's long-range plans and goals.

Gerald P. López (1948-)

Law Professor

López attended the University of Southern California. He received his law degree from Harvard Law School in 1974. López then served as law clerk to U.S. District Court Judge Edward Schwartz from 1974 to 1975 in San Diego. López has taught at California Western School of Law, UCLA Law School, and Harvard Law School. He has been a professor at Stanford School of Law since 1985.

Vilma S. Martínez (1943-)

Former General Counsel, Mexican American Legal Defense and Educational Fund (MALDEF)

Martínez is a partner in the firm of Munger, Tolles & Olson in Los Angeles. Martínez was born in San Antonio, Texas, in 1943. She attended the University of Texas and went on to Columbia University Law School, where she received her law degree in 1967.

As general counsel of MALDEF from 1973 to 1982, Martínez was an influential advocate during the congressional hearings for the Voting Rights Act of 1975, which opened the door to greater access to political participation by Hispanics. Martínez also served as a consultant to the U.S. Commission on Civil Rights from 1969 to 1973.

Miguel Angel Méndez-Longoria (1942-)

Professor

Méndez-Longoria attended Texas Southmost College and received his law degree from George Washington University Law School in 1968. He was admitted to the Texas bar that same year.

Méndez-Longoria served as a law clerk for the U.S. Court of Claims in Washington, D.C., from 1968 to 1969. He then was legal assistant to U.S. Senator Alan Cranston (D-CA) from 1969 to 1971. Méndez-Longoria was a staff attorney for the Mexican American Legal Defense and Educational Fund (MALDEF) in San Francisco from 1971 to 1972 and was deputy director of California Rural Legal Assistance in San Francisco from 1972 to 1974. Méndez-Longoria served as deputy public defender for Monterey County, California, from 1975 to 1976.

Since 1976, Méndez-Longoria has taught law at the University of Santa Clara Law School, University of California at Berkeley Law School (Boalt Hall), Vermont Law School, University of San Diego Law School, and Stanford University Law School. He has been a professor at Stanford University Law School since 1984.

Mario G. Obledo (1932-)

Cofounder, Hispanic National Bar Association (HNBA) and Mexican-American Legal Defense and Educational Fund (MALDEF); Past President, the League of United Latin American Citizens (LULAC)

Born in San Antonio, Texas, Obledo attended the University of Texas, where he was awarded a degree in pharmacy. After serving in the Korean War, he returned to Texas and received his law degree from St. Mary's University Law School in 1961.

Obledo has been active in Hispanic affairs for over thirty years. In LULAC he has held local, district,

Mario G. Obledo.

League of United Latin American Citizens (LULAC) Education Resource Center in Washington, D.C., from 1979 to 1982. In 1982, he began teaching law at the University of Houston Law School. He is director of the Institute for Higher Education Law and Governance there and was named associate dean in 1990.

Andrea S. Ordin (1940-)

Former U.S. Attorney, District of California

Ordin attended the University of California, where she received her B.A. degree and her law degree. She was admitted to the bar in 1966.

Leo M. Romero (1943-)

Dean, University of New Mexico Law School

Romero is the only Hispanic dean in the United States. He attended Oberlin College and received his J.D. degree from Washington University Law School in St. Louis, Missouri, and his LL.M. degree from Georgetown University Law School in Washington, D.C. Romero was associate editor of the *Washington University Law Quarterly* and was editor-in-chief of the *Urban Law Review* at Washington University.

Romero has taught law at Dickinson University Law School, the University of Oregon Law School, and the University of New Mexico Law School. He became associate dean at the University of New Mexico Law School in 1989 and was named dean in 1991.

state, and national offices, including the presidency. He was also active in the Southwest Voter Registration Project.

Obledo has been active in government and is a former Secretary of the California Health and Welfare Agency, where he was instrumental in bringing thousands of Hispanics into state government. Obledo was also assistant attorney general for the state of Texas and has lectured at Harvard Law School.

Currently, Obledo is chairman of the National Rainbow Coalition. He has offices in Austin, Texas, Sacramento, California, and Washington, D.C., where he remains active in national politics.

Michael A. Olivas (1951-)

Professor

Olivas attended Pontifical College in Columbus, Ohio, where he was awarded a B.A. degree in 1972 and an M.A. degree in 1974. He then went on to Ohio State University to receive his Ph.D. degree in 1977. Olivas received his law degree from Georgetown University Law School in 1981.

Olivas served as director of resources for the

Gerald Torres (1952-)

Professor

Torres was born in Victorville, California. He attended Stanford University, where he received his B.A. in 1974. He received his J.D. degree from Yale Law School in 1977 and his LL.M. degree from the University of Michigan Law School in 1980. He was admitted to the bar in 1978.

Torres was staff attorney for the Children's Defense Fund in Washington, D.C., from 1977 to 1978. He began teaching law in 1980 and has taught at the University of Pittsburgh Law School, the University of Minnesota Law School, and Harvard Law School. He now teaches jurisprudence, environmental law, property law, and agricultural law, at the University of Texas School of Law.

Abelardo López Valdez (1942-)

Attorney, Former Presidential Aide, and Government Official

Valdez was born in Floresville, Texas, and attended Texas A&M University. He received a J.D. degree from Baylor University Law School and an

LL.M. degree from Harvard Law School. He was admitted to the bar in 1970.

Valdez served as an aide to President Lyndon Johnson from 1965 to 1967. He was an attorney for the Overseas Private Investment Corporation from 1971 to 1973 and was general counsel for the Inter-American Foundation from 1973 to 1975.

Under President Carter, Valdez was assistant administrator of the Latin American and Caribbean region for the U.S. Agency for International Development from 1977 to 1979. He served as U.S. ambassador and chief of protocol for the White House from 1979 to 1981. In 1981, Valdez joined the law firm of Laxalt, Washington, Perito & Dubuc in Washington, D.C., where he is a partner. Valdez's areas of law are administrative, regulatory, and international law.

✹HISPANICS IN THE U.S. JUDICIARY

The U.S. federal court system was created by the Constitution of the United States. Article III of the Constitution states that the "judicial Power of the United States, shall be vested in one supreme Court" and authorizes the Congress to create lower federal courts, which the first Congress did in 1789. Congress created federal trial courts, which are known as district courts and, later, intermediate appellate courts, which are called circuit courts. Article II provided that all federal judges, including Supreme Court justices, are to be appointed by the president and confirmed by the U.S. Senate. Article III provides that federal judges hold their offices for life terms. The American judiciary has great independence, yet its judges are carefully selected through the process of presidential nomination and Senate confirmation.

Almost all of the nation's judicial business was handled by state courts in the early years of the country, partly because there were few federal judges and their jurisdiction was limited. Each state system differed, but nearly all had lower courts to hear trials and appellate courts to hear appeals. Even today, most of the nation's judicial business is handled by state rather than federal courts.

The federal government expanded significantly after the Civil War ended in 1865, and the federal courts grew along with it. In 1891, Congress created the tier of regional appellate courts called courts of appeals, to which appeals of the decisions of the federal trial courts could be taken. These appellate courts, more commonly known as circuit courts, were so named from the days when a judge used to ride a "circuit" on horseback.

The growth of the federal courts was gradual but accelerated after 1958, when the number of cases filed in federal court increased at a rapid pace. Between 1958 and 1988 Congress responded by doubling the number of judges serving in the district courts and courts of appeals. Additionally, Congress created a host of diverse judicial adjuncts, such as magistrates and administrative law judges, to which some of the caseload is delegated.

The Supreme Court, the nation's highest court, consists of the chief justice and eight associate justices. The Supreme Court has original jurisdiction in all cases involving "ambassadors, other public Ministers and Consuls" and those arising from disputes between the states. The Supreme Court can also hear appeals of decisions of the courts of appeals, the intermediate court, and the final decisions of the highest courts of each state if they involve federal questions. The Supreme Court may choose which cases it wants to hear and generally limits its review to cases involving national questions or to issues on which different courts of appeals have reached conflicting results.

There are currently thirteen courts of appeals, or circuit courts. The United States is divided into twelve geographical circuits. In addition to these, there is a U.S. Court of Appeals for the Federal Circuit, a specialized court that hears appeals from the Court of Claims and the Court of Customs and Patent Appeals. Each circuit court of appeals is headed by a chief judge and has between six and twenty-six judges. They usually sit in three-judge panels to review decisions of lower courts, but occasionally meet in greater numbers in important cases. In rare cases, all the judges of the circuit will preside en banc to hear an appeal.

U.S. district courts have been established in every state, the District of Columbia, and the U.S. territories. Each state has at least one U.S. district court, and states with large populations are divided into two or more subdistricts. For example, the heavily populated states of California, New York, and Texas are each divided into four subdistricts, while the states of Alaska, Arizona, Montana, and New Mexico each contain one district despite their enormous size.

Hispanic Judges in Federal Courts

Almost all Hispanic judges currently sitting on the bench at all levels of the judiciary received their appointments in the last three decades. Hispanics now sit on both the U.S. district courts and the U.S. courts of appeals. However, no Hispanic has yet sat on the U.S. Supreme Court.

In 1985, the Fund for Modern Courts conducted a study identifying minority judges in all fifty states, excluding Puerto Rico and the District of Columbia. According to that study, there was a total of 24 Hispanic judges in the federal courts at all levels, representing 3.2 percent of the 753 federal judges

TABLE 9.1
HISPANIC JUDGES IN STATE COURTS

COURT	HIGHEST (A)	INTERM. (B)	TRIAL (C)	MUNICIPAL (D)	MAGISTRATE/JOP (E)	OTHER (F)
AL	0	0	1	0	0	0
AK	0	0	1	0	0	0
AZ	0	2	42	18	19	0
CA	0	3	86	41	0	9
CO	1	1	14	3	0	1
DC	0	0	3	0	0	0
FL	0	0	25	0	0	0
HI	0	0	1	0	0	0
IL	0	0	16	0	0	0
IN	0	0	2	0	0	0
KS	0	0	1	0	0	0
LA	0	0	4	0	0	0
MD	0	0	1	0	0	0
MI	1	0	2	0	0	1
MN	0	0	2	0	0	0
MO	0	0	1	0	0	0
MT	0	0	1	0	1	0
NV	0	0	7	0	2	0
NJ	0	0	13	5	0	0
NM	1	4	86	35	18	1
NY	0	1	25	11	0	0
OH	0	0	2	0	0	0
OR	0	0	1	0	0	0
PA	0	0	2	0	0	0
TX	2	3	280	93	114	0
UT	0	0	1	0	0	0
VA	0	0	1	0	0	0
WA	0	0	4	0	0	0
TOTAL	5	14	625	206	154	12

Source: Hispanic National Bar Association Nationwide Summary of Hispanics in the State Judiciary (1992). This summary excludes judges sitting in Puerto Rico courts.

A. Judges in state courts of last resort; in most states, such courts are called supreme courts

B. State appellate or intermediate court judges

C. State judges in trial courts of general jurisdiction

D. Municipal or metropolitan court judges

E. Local magistrates, or justices of the peace

nationwide in 1985. Two of the 24 Hispanic judges were court of appeals judges and 22 were district court judges.

According to the *Directory of Hispanic Judges of the United States*, there were 85 Hispanic members of federal tribunals in 1991, but this includes judges in the District of Columbia and Puerto Rico as well as U.S. magistrates and administrative law judges.

Today, five Hispanic judges sit on the court of appeals, the second-highest federal court in the United States. The Honorable Juan R. Torruella sits on the U.S. Court of Appeals for the First Circuit, which has jurisdiction over Massachusetts, Rhode Island, Maine, New Hampshire, Puerto Rico, and the Virgin Islands. The Honorable Reynaldo G. Garza and the Honorable Emilio M. Garza sit on the U.S. Court of Appeals for the Fifth Circuit, which has jurisdiction over Texas, Louisiana, and Mississippi. The Honorable Arthur L. Alarcón and the Honorable Ferdinand Francis Fernández sit on the U.S. Court of Appeals for the Ninth Circuit, which has jurisdiction over California, Arizona, Nevada, Washington, Oregon, Idaho, Montana, Alaska, Hawaii, Guam, and the Northern Mariana Islands.

Twenty-five Hispanic judges have been appointed to U.S. district courts across the country. They sit on district courts in Arizona, California, Connecticut, Florida, Indiana, Michigan, Missouri, New Jersey, New Mexico, New York, Rhode Island, Texas, and Puerto Rico.

Additionally, eight Hispanic judges serve as U.S. magistrates, four serve on the U.S. Bankruptcy Court, and forty-three currently serve as administrative law judges for various federal agencies, such as the Executive Office for Immigration Review (special inquiry officers), the Social Security Administration, and the Federal Communications Commission (FCC).

Hispanic Judges in State Courts

Ninety percent of the nation's judicial business is currently handled by state rather than federal courts. Each state system differs, but nearly all have trial courts, intermediate courts, and a court of last resort. Those states that mirror the federal three-tier court system generally have district or superior courts in each county, intermediate courts of appeals to review decisions of the trial courts, and state supreme courts, which provide the ultimate review of decisions of the lower courts.

Hispanic Americans have made the greatest inroads at the state, county, and municipal court levels, where hundreds have been appointed or elected to these courts. Hispanic judges have served on state courts throughout the history of the United States, but almost always at the lowest levels. In recent years this trend has changed, as large numbers of Hispanics have been both appointed and elected to all levels of state courts.

In its 1985 study, the Fund for Modern Courts found that there were approximately 163 Hispanic state court judges across the country, representing 1.3 percent of the 12,093 full-time judges of state courts. In 1992, the Hispanic National Bar Association found that over 600 Hispanic Americans are judges on state tribunals of all kinds, including state supreme courts, state appeals courts, and state trial courts.

The growing number of Hispanic judges can be attributed to the increasing Hispanic population as well as to favorable legislation such as the Civil Rights Act of 1964 and the Voting Rights Act of 1965, which have enabled Hispanics to become full participants in the U.S. political and judicial process.

Today, Hispanics serve on some of the highest state courts in the nation. Five Hispanics are state supreme court justices, in Colorado, Michigan, New Mexico, and Texas. Fourteen Hispanics serve as state appeals court judges in the states of Arizona, California, Colorado, New Mexico, New York, and Texas.

Most dramatic are the large numbers of Hispanic Americans serving in lower state courts. Six hundred twenty-five Hispanics serve on various state trial courts. Table 9.1 lists the number of Hispanic judges in each state.

Critics of the process of selecting judges charge that the system is subject to a wide range of problems and abuses, including discrimination against minorities. The appointment process, critics charge, is also subject to political interference from special interest groups, influence peddling, and highly inflammatory campaigning by opposition groups. The nominee's qualifications are rarely the test of whether he or she should be a judge. For example, a 1988 analysis of U.S. Supreme Court appointments published in *Texas Lawyer* found that of twenty-seven failed nominations to the Court, only five were denied because of qualifications or ethical concerns. Political concerns were the primary reasons the other nominees were not confirmed.

Discrimination is a serious problem in the appointive system. The Mexican American Legal Defense

Judge Reynaldo G. Garza.

and Educational Fund (MALDEF) recently concluded that the appointive system is discriminatory. According to MALDEF, approximately 97 percent of all individuals making judicial appointments are white, which consequently tends to limit the opportunities for minority nominees. (MALDEF states that the elective system is of the greatest benefit to Hispanics and other minorities.) Instead of taking politics out of the system, the appointive process takes the voter out of the system.

Fortunately, today the majority of states select judges through the election process. Eight states choose all their judges in partisan elections; twelve use nonpartisan elections. One state, Virginia, uses legislative election exclusively to select its judges. Another thirteen states have variable procedures, appointing judges to certain courts and electing them to others.

The elective franchise is a fundamental and cherished right for all Americans. Advocates of the election process state that judicial officeholders should be held accountable to voters in the same manner as legislators. Proponents of an appointive system often state that areas of the country with small Hispanic populations would be better served by the appointment process. Election advocates charge that the underlying assumption of those who promote an appointive system is that the voters cannot be trusted to select good judges. Regardless of which method is used, if the courts of the United States are to reflect the population they serve, Hispanic lawyers must be included in greater numbers among those who become members of the judiciary.

✳PRESIDENTIAL APPOINTMENT OF HISPANICS TO THE COURTS

The president appoints federal judges, with the advice and consent of the U.S. Senate. The presidential appointment process has had varied success in elevating Hispanics to the federal courts during the last three decades. The most significant progress for Hispanic Americans was seen during the administration of President Jimmy Carter.

Presidents generally receive district court recommendations for nominations from the senior home-state senator of the president's party, or if there is no such senator, from the state's governor, senior member of Congress of the president's party, or party leader. President Lyndon B. Johnson, whose presidency was from 1963 to 1968, appointed three Hispanic Americans to the district court. President Richard M. Nixon appointed two Hispanics to the court during his presidency, from 1968 to 1974. President Gerald R. Ford appointed one Hispanic American to

the district court during his brief presidency, from 1974 to 1977.

The years of the presidency of Jimmy Carter, from 1977 to 1981, were years of change in the judicial selection process. Carter issued an executive order creating a U.S. Circuit Judge Nomination Commission in 1977, modeled after the merit selection system he established while governor of Georgia. The president's order resulted in the appointment of sixteen Hispanic Americans to federal courts, nearly thrice the total appointed by Presidents Johnson, Nixon, and Ford combined and more than all previous presidents of the United States combined throughout the history of the country. Fourteen of these were appointed to the district court and two to the court of appeals.

President Ronald Reagan did not continue the nomination commission begun by President Carter and reverted to the old system used by earlier presidents. During the Reagan years, from 1981 to 1989, ten Hispanic Americans were appointed to the district court and one to the court of appeals. President George Bush has not changed the old system used by President Reagan.

From the time Bush became president in 1989 through December of 1991, he had appointed only two Hispanic Americans to the district court and two to the court of appeals. After Supreme Court Justice Thurgood Marshall announced his retirement in mid-1991, there was intense speculation that Bush might nominate the first Hispanic to the Supreme Court. Speculation ended when he nominated Judge Clarence Thomas, an Afro-American, to the Court.

Prominent Hispanics at the Federal and State Judicial Levels

Raymond L. Acosta (1925-)

Raymond Acosta was born in New York City and grew up in Teaneck, New Jersey. After graduating from high school in 1943, Acosta joined the U.S. Navy during World War II and took part in the Normandy invasion. He returned to New Jersey after the war and graduated from Princeton University in 1948. Acosta received his law degree in 1951 from Rutgers University Law School in Newark, New Jersey. From 1951 to 1954, he was in private practice in Hackensack, New Jersey, and worked for the Federal Bureau of Investigation in Washington, D.C., from 1954 to 1958. In 1958, he moved to Puerto Rico to serve as assistant U.S. attorney there. From 1962 to 1980, he was in the private sector, practicing law in San Juan, Puerto Rico, with the firm of Igaravídez & Acosta, and held posts with various real estate and banking interests. From 1980 to 1982, Acosta was the U.S.

Judge Raymond L. Acosta.

attorney for Puerto Rico. In 1982, President Reagan appointed Acosta to the U.S. District Court for the District of Puerto Rico.

Robert P. Aguilar (1931-)

Former judge of the U.S. District Court for the Northern District of California, Robert Aguilar attended the University of California, Berkeley, where he received his B.A. degree in 1954. He then went on to receive his law degree from the University of California Hastings College of Law. He practiced law with the firms of Mezzetti & Aguilar, Aguilar & Aguilar, and Aguilar & Edwards from 1960 to 1979.

In 1979 Aguilar was appointed a California Superior Court judge for Santa Clara County. He was later appointed to the U.S. District Court for the Northern District of California by President Jimmy Carter in 1980, where he remained until his resignation in 1991.

Arthur L. Alarcón (1925-)

Arthur Alarcón received his B.A. degree in 1949 and his LL.B. degree in 1951, both from the University of Southern California. President Carter appointed

him to the U.S. Court of Appeals for the Ninth Circuit in 1979.

John Argüelles (1927-)

Former supreme court justice for the state of California, John Argüelles was born in Los Angeles, California, to Arturo Argüelles, a Mexican American who graduated from Columbia University with an accounting degree, and Eva Powers, the daughter of an Oklahoma judge.

Argüelles was educated in public schools in Los Angeles and went on to UCLA where he received a degree in economics in 1950. He continued his education at the UCLA law school and received his degree in 1954. Argüelles practiced law in East Los Angeles and Montebello, California, from 1955 to 1963. During that time he was president of the local bar association and was elected to the Montebello City Council with the largest vote in that city's history.

In 1963 Governor Edmund G. Brown, Sr. appointed Argüelles municipal court judge for the East Los Angeles Municipal Court. He was then elevated to the Los Angeles Superior Court by Governor Ronald Reagan in 1969. Argüelles was appointed to the California Court of Appeal for the Second District in 1984

Justice Joseph F. Baca.

by Governor George Deukmejian. Three years later, Deukmejian named Argüelles to the California Supreme Court, where he served until his retirement in 1989.

At the end of 1989, Argüelles joined the law firm of Gibson, Dunn & Crutcher.

Joseph Francis Baca (1936-)

New Mexico Supreme Court Justice Baca was born in Albuquerque, New Mexico, in 1936 to Mexican-American parents. He graduated from the Uni-

Justice John A. Argüelles.

versity of New Mexico in 1960 with a degree in education. He studied law at George Washington University in Washington, D.C., and received his degree in 1964.

Baca served as assistant district attorney in Santa Fe from 1965 to 1966, then as special assistant to the attorney general of New Mexico from 1966 to 1972. He also established a private law practice in Albuquerque during this time.

In 1972 Baca was appointed by Governor Bruce King to fill a vacancy in the New Mexico District Court for the Second District in Albuquerque. Baca was elected to six-year terms in 1972, 1978, and 1984. In 1988, Baca was elected to an eight-year term as justice of the New Mexico Supreme Court, and has served there since 1989.

Juan C. Burciaga (1929-)

Juan Burciaga attended the U.S. Military Academy at West Point, where he received his B.S. degree in 1952. He then served in the U.S. Air Force from 1952 to 1960. He received his law degree from the University of New Mexico School of Law in 1963. Burciaga was in private practice from 1964 to 1979 with the firm of Ussery, Burciaga & Parrish.

In 1979, President Jimmy Carter appointed Burciaga to the U.S. District Court for the District of New Mexico. Burciaga became chief judge of that court.

José A. Cabranés (1940-)

Born in Mayagüez, Puerto Rico, José Cabranés is the first native Puerto Rican appointed to the federal court within the continental United States. Cabranés moved with his family to New York from Puerto Rico when he was only five. After attending public schools in the Bronx and Flushing, Queens, he graduated from Columbia College in 1961. He received his law degree from Yale University Law School in 1965, and an LL.M. degree in international law from the University of Cambridge in Cambridge, England, in 1967.

Cabranés served as general counsel of Yale University from 1975 to 1979. Previously he had practiced law at the firm of Casey, Lane & Mittendorf in New York City from 1967 to 1971; taught law at Rutgers University School of Law in New Jersey from 1971 to 1973; and served as special counsel to the governor of Puerto Rico and as administrator, Office of the Commonwealth of Puerto Rico, Washington, D.C.

He also served in the administration of President Jimmy Carter as a member of the President's Commission on Mental Health from 1977 to 1978; as a member of the U.S. delegation to the Belgrade Conference on Security and Cooperation in Europe from 1977 to 1978; and as consultant to U.S. Secretary of State

Judge José A. Cabranes.

Cyrus Vance in 1978. In 1979, Carter appointed Cabranés to the U.S. District Court for the District of Connecticut.

In December 1988 U.S. Supreme Court Chief Justice William H. Rehnquist named Judge Cabranés as one of five federal judges for the fifteen-member Federal Courts Study Committee, created by an act of Congress "to examine problems facing the federal courts and develop a long-range plan for the future of the federal judiciary."

Santiago E. Campos (1926-)

Santiago Campos served in the U.S. Navy during World War II. He attended Central College in Fayette, Missouri, and received his law degree from the University of New Mexico in 1953. Campos was assistant attorney general for the state of New Mexico from 1954 to 1957. He was a New Mexico district judge from 1971 to 1978. President Carter appointed Judge Campos to the U.S. District Court for the District of New Mexico in 1978.

John M. Cannella (1908-)

Cannella is a Colombian American and played professional football for the New York Giants from 1933 to 1935. He attended Fordham University, where he received his B.A. degree in 1930 and his law degree in 1933. Cannella was assistant U.S. attorney for the Southern District of New York from 1940 to 1942. In 1963 President Kennedy appointed him to the U.S. District Court for the southern district of New York.

Carmen C. Cerezo (1940-)

Carmen Cerezo attended the University of Puerto Rico, where he received his B.A. degree in 1963 and his LL.B. degree in 1966. He was a judge on the Puerto Rico Court of Inter Appeals from 1976 to 1980, and was on the Superior Court of Puerto Rico from 1972 to 1976. President Carter appointed Judge Cerezo to the U.S. District Court for the District of Puerto Rico in 1980.

James DeAnda (1925-)

Born in Houston, James DeAnda received his B.A. degree from Texas A&M University and his J.D. degree from the University of Texas in 1950. He was in private practice from 1951 until 1979. In 1979, Judge DeAnda was appointed to the U.S. District Court for the Southern District of Texas where he subsequently became chief judge.

Ferdinand Francis Fernández (1937-)

Ferdinand Fernández attended the University of Southern California and was awarded his B.A. degree in 1958 and his J.D. degree in 1962. He was in private practice from 1964 to 1980 with the law firm of Allard, Shelton & O'Connor in Pomona, California. Fernández was on the U.S. District Court for the Central District of California from 1985 to 1989. In 1989, Judge Fernández was appointed to the U.S. Court of Appeals for the Ninth Circuit by President Bush. Judge Fernández was reportedly considered as a potential replacement for retiring U.S. Supreme Court Justice Thurgood Marshall.

José Antonio Fuste (1943-)

José Fuste attended the University of Puerto Rico, where he received his B.A. degree in 1965 and his LL.B. degree in 1968. He was in private practice from 1968 to 1985 with the law firm of Jiménez and Fuste. Fuste was appointed to the U.S. District Court for the District of Puerto Rico by President Reagan in 1985.

Fernando J. Gaitán, Jr. President Bush appointed Gaitán to the U.S. District Court for the Western District of Missouri in 1991.

Edward J. García (1928-)

Edward García attended the Sacramento City College and graduated in 1951. He received his law degree from the McGeorge School of Law in 1958. García was deputy district attorney for Sacramento County from 1959 to 1964, supervising deputy district attorney from 1964 to 1969, and chief deputy district attorney from 1969 to 1972. He was a Sacramento Municipal Court judge from 1972 until 1984. President Reagan appointed Judge García to the U.S. District Court for the Eastern District of California in 1984.

Hipolito Frank García (1925-)

Frank García served in the U.S. Army during World War II. He then attended St. Mary's University, where he received his B.A. degree in 1949 and his LL.B. degree in 1951. He was a Texas county court judge from 1964 to 1980. In 1980 President Carter appointed García to the U.S. District Court for the Western District of Texas.

Emilio M. Garza (1947-)

Emilio Garza attended the University of Notre Dame and was awarded his B.A. degree in 1969 and M.A. degree in 1970. He received his law degree from the University of Texas in 1976. He was in private practice from 1976 to 1987 with the law firm of Clemens, Spencer, Welmaker & Finck. Garza was a judge for the U.S. District Court for the Western District of Texas from 1988 to 1991. President Bush appointed Judge Garza to the U.S. Court of Appeals for the Fifth Circuit in 1991.

Reynaldo G. Garza (1915-)

Reynaldo Garza was born in Brownsville, Texas. His parents were both born in Mexico and had immigrated to the United States in 1901. Garza attended the University of Texas, where he received his law degree in 1939. He practiced law in Brownsville as a solo practitioner until he joined the air force during World War II. After the war, he resumed his private practice until 1950, when he joined the firm of Sharpe, Cunningham & Garza.

President Kennedy in 1961 appointed Garza to the U.S. District Court for the Southern District of Texas; in 1974 he became chief judge of that court. In 1979, Garza was appointed to the U.S. Court of Appeals for the Fifth Circuit by President Jimmy Carter. In 1987, U.S. Supreme Court Chief Justice William H. Rehnquist appointed Garza to the Temporary Emergency Court of Appeals of the United States. He was later named by Rehnquist as chief judge of that court.

Garza has often been recognized for his active role in education, community affairs, and the law. He was honored when a small law school opened its doors in Edinburg, Texas, and was named the Reynaldo G. Garza School of Law. Pope Pius XII twice decorated Garza for his work with the Knights of Columbus, conferring on him the Medal Pro Ecclesia et Pontifice in 1953 and recognizing him as a Knight of the Order of St. Gregory the Great in 1954. Garza received the American Association of Community and Junior Colleges Alumnus of the Year Award in 1984, and in 1989 he was given the Distinguished Alumnus Award of the University of Texas.

President Carter offered the position of attorney general of the United States to Judge Garza. Garza declined the cabinet post because he would have had to resign from his position as a federal judge, which is a lifetime appointment.

Gilberto Gierbolini (1926-)

Gierbolini attended the University of Puerto Rico, where he received his B.A. degree in 1951 and his LL.B. degree in 1961. He was a captain in the U.S. Army and served during the Korean War from 1951 to 1957.

Gierbolini served as assistant U.S. attorney for Puerto Rico from 1961 to 1966, as a superior court judge from 1966 to 1969, as assistant secretary of justice for Puerto Rico from 1969 to 1972, and as solicitor general of Puerto Rico from 1970 to 1972. Gierbolini was in the private practice of law between 1972 and 1980. In 1980, President Carter appointed Judge Gierbolini to the U.S. District Court for the District of Puerto Rico.

Ricardo H. Hinojosa (1950-)

Ricardo Hinojosa attended the University of Texas, where he received his B.A. degree in 1972. He received his law degree from Harvard University Law School in 1975. He was in private practice as a partner in the law firm of Ewers & Toothaker in McAllen, Texas, from 1976 until 1983. In 1983, Hinojosa was appointed by President Reagan to the U.S. District Court for the Southern District of Texas.

Héctor M. Laffitte (1934-)

Judge Laffitte was born in Ponce, Puerto Rico. Laffitte received his B.A. from the Interamerican University in 1955, his law degree from the University of Puerto Rico in 1958 and his LL.M. degree from Georgetown University in 1960.

Laffitte was the Civil Rights Commissioner for the commonwealth of Puerto Rico from 1969 to 1972. He was in private practice from 1972 to 1983 with the firm of Laffitte, Domínguez & Totti. President Reagan appointed Laffitte to the U.S. District Court for the District of Puerto Rico in 1983.

George La Plata (1924-)

George La Plata was born in Detroit to Mexican-American parents. He attended Wayne State University, where he received his B.A. degree in 1951. He received his law degree from the Detroit College of Law in 1956. La Plata also served in the U.S. Marine Corps during World War II, reaching the rank of colonel.

La Plata, in conjunction with George Menéndez, adviser to the Republic of Mexico, helped pioneer the representation of migrant workers in Michigan, Ohio, and Indiana during the 1950s. From 1956 to 1979, La Plata was in private practice. La Plata served as a Michigan county judge from 1979 to 1985. When appointed to that position in 1979, he became the first Hispanic judge in Michigan history. President Reagan appointed Judge La Plata to the U.S. District Court for the Eastern District of Michigan in 1985. He remains active in providing pro bono services to Hispanics in his community.

Rudolpho Lozano (1942-)

Rudolpho Lozano attended Indiana University, where he received his B.A. degree in 1963 and his law degree in 1966. He was in private practice with the law firm of Spangler, Jennings, Spangler, & Dougherty in Merrillville, Indiana, from 1966 to 1988. In 1988 President Reagan appointed Lozano to the U.S. District Court for the Northern District of Indiana.

Alfredo C. Márquez (1922-)

Alfredo Márquez served in World War II as an ensign in the U.S. Navy. After the war, he attended the University of Arizona, where he received his B.S. degree in 1948 and his law degree in 1950. Márquez served as assistant attorney general for the state of Arizona from 1951 to 1952, as prosecutor for the city of Tucson and assistant county attorney for Pima County from 1953 to 1954, and as an aide to Congressman Stewart Udall (D-AZ) in 1955.

Márquez was in private practice with the firm of Mesch, Márquez & Rothschild from 1957 until 1980. Márquez was appointed by President Carter in 1980 to the U.S. District Court for the District of Arizona.

Harold R. Medina, Sr. (1888-1991)

Former U.S. circuit court judge, Harold Medina was born in Brooklyn, New York, of Mexican-American and Dutch-American parents. His father, Joaquín Medina, came to the United States as a

Judge George La Plata.

refugee from a bitter civil and race war in the Yucatan Peninsula. Harold Medina attended Princeton University, where he graduated with honors in 1909. He went on to Columbia University Law School and received his law degree in 1912. Medina began practicing law and also lectured at Columbia Law School at the invitation of Dean Harlan Fiske Stone.

In 1918, Medina formed his own law firm and specialized in appeals. The most famous case argued by Medina was the Cramer treason case during World War II. Anthony Cramer, of Brooklyn, was accused of helping two Nazi spies who had landed from a submarine. Medina initially lost the case in the lower courts but won it on appeal to the U.S. Supreme Court.

After World War II ended, Medina was appointed to the U.S. District Court for the District of New York by President Harry Truman. In 1951 President Truman appointed Judge Medina to the U.S. Court of Appeals for the Second Circuit.

Federico A. Moreno, Sr. (1952-)

Federico Moreno was born in Caracas, Venezuela, and immigrated to the United States with his family in 1963. In 1974, Moreno graduated from the Univer-

Judge Federico A. Moreno.

sity of Notre Dame, where he received his B.A. degree in government. He worked as a janitor and in restaurants to pay his way through college. After graduating, he taught at the Atlantic Community College in Mays Landing, New Jersey, and at Stockton State College in Pomona, New Jersey, in 1975 and 1976. In 1978, Moreno received his law degree from the University of Miami School of law.

Moreno was an associate with the law firm of Rollins, Peeples & Meadows in 1978 and 1979, and served as an assistant federal public defender from 1979 to 1981. He was a partner in the law firm of Thornton, Rothman & Moreno from 1982 to 1986. He served as Dade County judge in 1986 and 1987. Moreno was a Florida Circuit Court judge from 1987 until 1990. President Bush appointed Judge Moreno to the U.S. District Court for the Southern District of Florida in 1990.

Philip Newman (1916-)

The first Mexican-born U.S. judge, Newman was born in Mexico City to a German-American father and a Mexican mother. His family fled Mexico in the 1920s during the Mexican civil war and settled in California. Arriving destitute in the United States, Newman's father put himself through law school at night and became an attorney. Newman also became an attorney in 1941. He won landmark cases protecting the rights of individuals against unwarranted searches and seizures and leading to changes in immigration law. He was the founder of the Community Services Organization in Los Angeles. In 1964, Newman was appointed by Governor Edmund G. Brown to a Los Angeles municipal judgeship, where he remained until his retirement in 1982.

Juan M. Pérez-Giménez (1941-)

Juan Pérez-Giménez received his B.A. degree in 1963 and his LL.B. degree in 1968 from the University of Puerto Rico; his M.B.A. degree was conferred by George Washington University in 1965. He was an assistant U.S. attorney for Puerto Rico from 1971 to 1975. President Carter appointed Pérez-Giménez to the U.S. District Court for the District of Puerto Rico in 1979.

Jaime Pieras, Jr. (1924-)

Jaime Pieras served in the U.S. Army during World War II. He received his B.A. degree from Catholic University in 1945 and his J.D. degree from Georgetown University in 1948. Pieras was in private practice from 1949 until 1982. In 1982, Judge Pieras was appointed to the U.S. District Court for the District of Puerto Rico by President Reagan.

Edward C. Prado (1947-)

Edward Prado attended the University of Texas, where he received his B.A. degree in 1969 and his J.D. degree in 1972. In 1984, President Reagan appointed Prado to the U.S. District Court for the Western District of Texas.

Raul Anthony Ramírez (1944-)

After receiving his law degree from the University of the Pacific, McGeorge School of Law, Ramírez went into private practice. He served as a municipal court judge in Sacramento from 1977 until 1980. In 1980, he was appointed by President Carter to the U.S. District Court for the Eastern District of California.

Manuel L. Real (1924-)

Manuel Real's parents immigrated to the United States from Spain. His mother was born in Albunol, Granada, Spain, and his father was born in Sierra de Yegas, Malaga, Spain. Real was educated in California and received his B.S. degree from the University

Chief Judge Manuel L. Real.

of California in 1944 and his LL.B. degree from Loyola University in 1951. Real also served as assistant U.S. attorney from 1952 to 1955 for the Southern District of California. He was in private practice from 1955 to 1964 in San Pedro, California, and was assistant U.S. attorney for the Southern District of California from 1964 to 1966.

In 1966, Real was appointed to the U.S. District Court for the Central District of California by President Johnson. He was named chief judge of that court in 1982.

Cruz Reynoso (1931-)

Former state supreme court justice for California, Cruz Reynoso was born on May 2, 1931, of farm worker parents in the small town of Brea, California, where he was raised and received his early education. He attended Fullerton Junior College and Pomona College, where he earned his B.A. degree in 1953. From 1953 to 1955, he served in the U.S. Army. After his discharge, Reynoso entered the study of law at the University of California, Berkeley, and was awarded his degree in 1958. That same year he began the private practice of law in El Centro, California.

During the 1960s, Reynoso acted as assistant chief of the Division of Fair Employment Practices for California. From 1967 to 1968, he was associate general counsel to the Equal Employment Opportunity Commission in Washington, D.C., returning to California to become the first deputy director and then director of California Rural Legal Assistance. In 1972, he accepted a position at the University of New Mexico Law School, where he served for four years.

In 1976, Reynoso was appointed to the California Court of Appeal in Sacramento as an associate justice. Governor Jerry Brown then appointed him to the California Supreme Court in 1982. Reynoso became the first Hispanic on the court and served until 1986. In 1987, he entered private practice with the firm of O'Donnell & Gordon in Los Angeles and subsequently was of counsel to Kaye, Scholer, Fierman, Hays & Handler in Sacramento.

Reynoso has been honored by appointment to four presidential commissions, including the Select Commission on Immigration and Refugee Policy and the UN Commission on Human Rights. He was appointed to the law faculty of the University of California, Los Angeles, in 1990.

Dorothy Comstock Riley (1924-)

Supreme court justice for the state of Michigan, Dorothy Riley was born to Hispanic parents in Detroit. She attended Wayne State University, where she received both her B.A. degree in politics and her law degree. She went into private practice in 1950 and established the firm of Riley and Roumell in 1968.

Riley sat on the Michigan Court of Appeals from 1976 until 1982, when she was elevated to the Michigan Supreme Court as an associate justice. Judge Riley was named chief justice in 1987 and remains in that position.

Joseph H. Rodríguez (1930-)

Rodriguez received his B.A. degree from LaSalle University in 1955 and his J.D. degree from Rutgers University in 1958. He was in private practice from 1959 to 1982 with the firm of Brown, Connery, Kulp, Wille, Purcell, & Greene and was also an instructor at Rutgers University School of Law from 1972 to 1982.

In 1982, Rodriguez was appointed New Jersey public advocate, a state cabinet position, and served until 1985. He litigated landmark cases in the areas of education and housing. President Reagan appointed Judge Rodriguez to the U.S. District Court for the District of New Jersey in 1985. Judge Rodriguez has always been involved in community affairs and continues to be active today.

Luis D. Rovirá (1923-)

Supreme court justice for the state of Colorado, Luis Rovirá was born in San Juan, Puerto Rico. His family moved to Colorado, where he was educated. Rovirá attended the University of Colorado and received both B.A. and law degrees. He was in private practice with the firm of Rovirá, DeMuth & Eiberger until 1976.

In 1976, Rovirá was appointed to the Colorado District Court for the second district. In 1979, he was elevated to the Colorado Supreme Court as an associate justice and became chief justice in 1990.

Ernest C. Torres (1941-)

Ernest Torres graduated from Dartmouth College in 1963 and received his law degree from Duke University School of Law in 1968. He was in private practice from 1968 to 1974. In 1975, Torres was elected to the Rhode Island House of Representatives, where he served until 1980. After leaving the state house, he went into private practice. Torres was appointed by President Reagan in 1988 to the U.S. District Court for the District of Rhode Island.

Justice Dorothy Comstock Riley.

Judge Joseph H. Rodríguez.

Chief Justice Luis D. Rovirá.

Juan R. Torruella (1933-)

Juan Torruella received his B.A. degree from the University of Pennsylvania in 1954 and his LL.B. degree from Boston University in 1957. He was appointed by President Ford to the U.S. District Court for the District of Puerto Rico in 1974 and was chief judge of that court from 1982 to 1984. In 1984, President Reagan appointed Judge Torruella to the U.S. Court of Appeals for the First Circuit.

Filemón B. Vela (1935-)

Vela graduated from the University of Texas and received a J.D. degree from St. Mary's University in 1962. He was in private practice from 1962 to 1975 and also served as an attorney for the Mexican American Legal Defense and Educational Fund (MALDEF) from 1962 to 1975. He was a Texas district court judge from 1975 to 1980. President Carter appointed Vela to the U.S. District Court for the Southern District of Texas in 1980.

✳HISPANICS IN THE POLITICAL PROCESS

Widespread political activity at the national level by Hispanic Americans has been intermittent since the first Hispanic was elected to Congress. Joseph Marion Hernández was elected to Congress representing Florida in 1822 as a member of the Whig party. No other Hispanic held national office for thirty years. A total of eleven Hispanics were elected to the U.S. Congress in the entire nineteenth century, all from New Mexico, except for one from California and Congressman Hernández from Florida. From the turn of the century until the 1950s, there were a total of fifteen, five from New Mexico, two from Louisiana, and eight resident commissioners from Puerto Rico, which became a U.S. possession in 1898. Since the 1960s, the number of Hispanic Americans elected to Congress has been steadily increasing. In 1991, there were thirteen Hispanics serving in the 102d U.S. Congress, representing constituents from California (Hispanic population 26 percent), Florida (Hispanic population 12 percent), New Mexico (Hispanic population 38 percent), New York (Hispanic population 12 percent), Texas (Hispanic population 26 percent), Puerto Rico, Guam, and the U.S. Virgin Islands.

For a century, the majority of Hispanic Americans holding political office at the local level was limited to southwestern states, southern Florida, and New York City. Since the 1960s, growth in the population of Hispanics and favorable civil rights legislation, such as the Voting Rights Act of 1965, have combined to create opportunity for Hispanic candidates to win public office in other areas of the country. Hispanic Americans have made the greatest inroads at the municipal level. In 1991, Hispanics held elected office at the local level in thirty-five of the fifty states.

Harry P. Pachón, national director of the National Association of Latino Elected and Appointed Officials (NALEO), stated that in 1990 NALEO identified "4,004 Hispanic Americans holding publicly elected offices throughout the country." Pachón stated that "although this number is only a small fraction of the nation's 504,404 elected officials, less than one percent, the number of Hispanic elected officials for various states is quite large."

In the past thirty years, Hispanic Americans have become one of the largest and fastest-growing groups of elected officials in the United States. Congressman Bill Richardson (D-NM) states, "National candidates and both major political parties are undertaking major campaigns to woo Hispanic American support. We are recognized as the nation's fastest growing minority group and are being courted as such. This attention will only increase our political strength."

✳HISPANIC VOTING AND THE VOTING RIGHTS ACT OF 1965

The primary aim of the Voting Rights Act of 1965 was African-American enfranchisement in the South. Specifically, obstacles to registration and voting faced by African Americans were the major concern of those who framed the statute in the 1960s. Its potential as a tool for Hispanic Americans was not fully realized until the act was extended and amended in 1970.

The 1970 amendments to this landmark legislation added a provision that was designed to guard against inventive new barriers to political participation by requiring federal approval of all changes in voting procedure in certain jurisdictions, primarily southern states. Disgruntled officials in Mississippi and other southern states embarked on schemes to dilute African-American voter impact in elections by eliminating single-member districts and creating at-large voting.

The U.S. Supreme Court responded, in *Allen v. State Board of Elections*, 393 U.S. 544 (1969), by extending federal authority to object to proposed discriminatory alterations in voting districts, the intro-

duction of at-large voting, and other such changes, in addition to reaffirming the original power to object to discriminatory innovations involving registration and voting.

Until 1980, the U.S. Census Bureau had historically classified Hispanic Americans as "white," with the single exception of the 1930 census, and many argued that to extend coverage of the Voting Rights Act to a class of people who considered themselves white was unjustifiable. The Fifteenth Amendment rights secured by the statute protected against denial of the right to vote only on account of "race, color or previous condition of servitude." If Hispanic Americans were white, they were ineligible for the special protection of the Voting Rights Act.

During congressional hearings to extend the Voting Rights Act in 1975, J. Stanley Pottinger, assistant attorney general of the U.S. Justice Department's Civil Rights Division, saw the labeling problem as inconsequential and told Congress that the Justice Department's practice "has been to treat Indians, Puerto Ricans, and Mexican-Americans as racial groups." His argument hardly settled the matter for everyone, but Congress agreed to amend the act to include "language minorities," which specifically included Spanish-speakers.

Vilma S. Martínez, president of the Mexican American Legal Defense and Educational Fund (MALDEF), testified before Congress in 1975 about voting districts in Texas where assistance to non-English-speaking voters was being denied. She testified further that Texas had been gerrymandering voting districts to give unfair advantage to English-speaking residents. State action creating at-large voting, annexations to voting districts, and redistricting plans fragmented Hispanic voting strength. Additionally, majority vote requirements, numbered posts, and other confusing procedural rules diminished the likelihood that a Hispanic American would gain an elected office.

Congress acted decisively. The Voting Rights Act Amendments of 1975, which extended the provisions of the Voting Rights Act of 1965, made permanent the national ban on literacy tests. The amendments condemned any action by states, which was no longer limited to southern states, to realign voting districts to dilute the impact of minority voters who resided within the district. Any redistricting plan would have to be approved by the federal government.

In 1980, the U.S. Supreme Court, in *City of Mobile v. Bolden*, 446 U.S. 55, rejected a challenge to at-large elections in Mobile, Alabama, because the Court was not convinced that the city had acted with the purpose of discriminating against minority voters. The

Court, in its sharply divided decision, found that the city had not violated the Voting Rights Act.

Congress reacted to the Supreme Court decision with the important Voting Rights Act Amendments of 1982. The amendments, under Section 2, prohibit any voting law or practice created by a state or political subdivision that "results" in denial of the right of any citizen of the United States to vote on account of race, color, or language-minority status. The amendments eliminated the need to prove that the state or political subdivision created a voting law with the "intention" of discriminating against minority voters.

In one of the first cases to be tried under Section 2 of the 1982 amendments, *Velásquez v. City of Abilene*, 725 F.2d 1017 (5th Cir. 1983), prominent judge Reynaldo G. Garza delivered the opinion of the U.S. Court of Appeals for the Fifth Circuit. Garza stated for the court that the intention of Congress was clear in cases of vote dilution, referring to the 1982 amendments. Garza stated that the city of Abilene's use of at-large voting, bloc voting, and other voting mechanisms resulted in vote dilution and had a discriminatory effect on Hispanic American voters in the city.

A year later, the Fifth Circuit Court made a similar ruling in *Jones v. City of Lubbock*, 727 F.2d 364 (5th Cir. 1984). The city of Lubbock, Texas, a medium-sized city with a diverse population, had a clear white majority. Under an at-large voting scheme, the majority uniformly elected an all-white city council. The court found that the voting method used by the city polarized voting between the white majority and minority voters, and the result was discrimination against minority voters.

In the last decade, holdouts of racially discriminatory electoral patterns have been coming under intense pressure from the courts to end discrimination against minority voters. The success in the courts has contributed to the growing numbers of Hispanic Americans holding elected offices across the United States. In 1991, for the first time in history, the city of Abilene had two Hispanics on its city council; the city of Lubbock had one Hispanic on its city council, as well as a Hispanic county commissioner.

The 1982 amendments to the Voting Rights Act are due to expire in 1992, and friends and foes are already preparing their cases for congressional hearings. Hispanic Americans owe much to the act for making political participation a reality and must take advantage of the right to vote to elect people who will address their concerns as well as those of society at large.

✳CONGRESSIONAL HISPANIC CAUCUS

The Congressional Hispanic Caucus, organized in December 1976, is a bipartisan group of twelve members of Congress of Hispanic descent. The caucus is dedicated to voicing and advancing, through the legislative process, issues affecting Hispanic Americans in the United States and its territories.

Organized as a legislative service organization under the rules of Congress, the caucus is composed solely of members of the U.S. Congress. Under these rules, associate membership is offered to dues-paying members of Congress who are not of Hispanic descent. With its associate members, caucus membership represents twenty states, Puerto Rico, Guam, and the U.S. Virgin Islands.

Although every issue that affects the quality of life of all U.S. citizens is a Congressional Hispanic Caucus concern, there are national and international issues that have a particular impact on the Hispanic community. The caucus monitors legislative action as well as policies and practices of the executive and judicial branches of government that affect these issues.

✳HISPANICS IN CONGRESS

The growing Hispanic population remains significantly underrepresented in the U.S. Congress today. Hispanic-American voting levels have traditionally fallen well below the national average. In spite of favorable legislation, advocates actively seeking to increase Hispanic-American voter registration still cite poverty, inadequate education, language barriers, and alienage as critical obstacles that have discouraged voting. Despite these problems, Hispanic Americans have been going to the polls in increasing numbers. This is evident at the national level, where, in 1991, thirteen Hispanic Americans were serving in the U.S. House of Representatives.

Ten of the thirteen Hispanic representatives currently holding office in the 102d Congress have full voting privileges and represent districts in the states of California, Florida, New Mexico, New York, and Texas. The three nonvoting members are the resident commissioner of Puerto Rico and the delegates from Guam and the Virgin Islands. Eleven of the Hispanic members are Democrats, and several occupy powerful positions in the Democratic hierarchy of the House. Congressman Henry B. González of Texas is the chairman of the powerful House Banking, Finance and Urban Affairs Committee; Congressman E. (Kika) de la Garza of Texas is the chairman of the House Agriculture Committee; and Congressman Edward R. Roybal of California is the chairman of the House Select Committee on Aging. Two Hispanic members are Republicans: Congresswoman Ileana Ros-Lehtinen of Florida and the nonvoting delegate, Ron de Lugo, from the Virgin Islands.

No Hispanic-American candidate has been elected to the U.S. Senate since 1970, when New Mexico Democrat Joseph Manuel Montoya won his second and last election. Senator Montoya served in the Senate from 1964 to 1977. The only other Hispanic American to be elected to the Senate was New Mexico Democrat Dennis Chávez, who served with great distinction from 1935 to 1962. Both Senators Chávez and Montoya served as members of the U.S. House of Representatives prior to being elected to the Senate.

Hispanic Members of the 102d U.S. Congress

Ben Blaz (R-Guam)

Ben Blaz was born on February 14, 1928, and resides in Ordot, Guam. Blaz lived in Guam during the two-year Japanese occupation of that island during World War II. He regards the liberation of Guam by the U.S. Marines as the most exciting experience of his life. Blaz attended college at the University of Notre Dame and received a master's degree in busi-

Ben Blaz. Delegate to the U.S. Congress from Guam.

ness administration at George Washington University. Blaz also attended the Naval War College and served in the U.S. Marine Corps in both Korea and Vietnam. He reached the rank of brigadier general before retiring from the service.

Blaz was first elected to Congress as a Republican delegate representing the island of Guam in 1984. As a delegate, Blaz is a nonvoting member of Congress. However, he represents the citizens of Guam before the Congress and the executive branch of the federal government through his involvement in numerous congressional committees. He is a member of the House Armed Services Committee, the House Foreign Affairs Committee, the House Interior and Insular Affairs Committee, and the House Select Committee on Aging. Blaz is also a member of the Congressional Hispanic Caucus.

Albert G. Bustamante (D-Texas)

Albert Bustamante was born on April 8, 1935, and resides in San Antonio, Texas. Bustamante attended college at Sul Ross State University. Bustamante was first elected to Congress as a Democrat representing the 23rd district of Texas in 1984. He is a member of the House Armed Services Committee, the House Government Operations Committee, and the House Select Committee on Hunger. Congressman Bustamante is also a member of the Congressional Hispanic Caucus.

E. (Kika) de la Garza (D-Texas)

Congressman Kika de la Garza was born on September 22, 1927, in the Mexican border town of Mercedes, Texas. He comes from a family with roots in the Rio Grande Valley that go back to the 1700's. After graduating from high school, de la Garza, by struggle and perseverance, obtained his education at Edinburg Junior College and St. Mary's University in San Antonio. His education was interrupted by the Korean War, in which he served as an artillery officer from 1950 to 1952. He then earned his B.A. degree from St. Mary's in 1952 and later received his law degree from St. Mary's Law School.

With heavily Mexican-American Hidalgo County as his base of support, de la Garza was elected to the Texas House of Representatives in 1952. He was re-elected for another five terms. De la Garza was first elected to Congress in 1964 as a Democrat from the Rio Grande Valley's Fifteenth District. His election was a milestone for Texas Mexican Americans.

De la Garza is chairman of the House Agriculture Committee and an ex officio member of all its subcommittees. He is also a member and former chairman of the Congressional Hispanic Caucus. He is an active member of the League of United Latin American

Ron de Lugo. Delegate to the U.S. Congress from the U.S. Virgin Islands.

E. (Kika) de la Garza, U.S. Congressman. (D-Texas)

Citizens (LULAC) and a host of other organizations. In 1978 Mexican President José López Portillo awarded de la Garza Mexico's highest award to a foreigner, the order of the Aztec Eagle.

Ron de Lugo (D-Virgin Islands)

The de Lugo family migrated from Puerto Rico to the Virgin Islands in 1879. Ron de Lugo was born on August 2, 1930, in Saint Thomas. He attended school in the Virgin Islands and Puerto Rico.

In 1968, De Lugo was elected at-large as the first representative from the Virgin Islands and was re-elected to that post in 1970. In 1972, he was elected as the Virgin Islands" first seated Delegate in the U.S. Congress. Now in his ninth term as the Virgin Islands" delegate to Congress, De Lugo is chairman of the House Subcommittee on Insular and International Affairs, with jurisdiction over the Caribbean and Pacific island areas associated with the United States. De Lugo is also a member of the House Interior and Insular Affairs Committee and the House Public Works and Transportation Committee. De Lugo is also a member of the Congressional Hispanic Caucus.

Jaime B. Fuster (D-Puerto Rico)

Jaime Fuster was born on January 12, 1941, in Guayama, Puerto Rico. He graduated from the University of Notre Dame in 1962 and received his law degree from the University of Puerto Rico in 1965. During 1980 and 1981, Fuster was U.S. deputy assistant attorney general, U.S. Department of Justice, in Washington, D.C. He later served as president of Catholic University of Puerto Rico.

Fuster was first elected to Congress as the resident commissioner of Puerto Rico in 1984. As resident commissioner, Fuster is a nonvoting member of Congress. However, he represents the 3.6 million citizens of Puerto Rico before Congress and the executive branch of the federal government through his involvement in numerous congressional committees. Fuster sits on the Foreign Affairs Committee, the influential Education and Labor Committee, and the Interior and Insular Affairs Committee. He is also a member and former chairman of the Congressional Hispanic Caucus.

Henry Barbosa González (D-Texas)

Henry González was born on May 3, 1916, in San Antonio, Texas, to Mexican refugees. He grew up in a family that stressed education and intellectual pursuits. González received his early education in San Antonio public schools. He went on to attend San Antonio Junior College and the University of Texas at Austin, where he received his bachelor's degree. He then attended St. Mary's University Law School, where he received his law degree in 1943. After graduation, González worked at a variety of jobs, including teaching and social services.

In 1950, González entered the political arena and ran for San Antonio City Council. He lost narrowly, but won in his second bid three years later. González fought for a city ordinance ending segregation in city facilities. In 1956, he was elected to the Texas Senate. González was the first Mexican-American Texas state senator in 110 years. He attracted national attention as an outspoken advocate of equal rights for minorities and as an opponent of racist legislation.

In 1960 González was elected to Congress for the first time, as a Democrat representing the Twentieth District of Texas. He has been overwhelmingly reelected to Congress for each subsequent term. Congressman González is currently the chairman of the influential House Banking, Finance and Urban Affairs Committee and is also chairman of the Housing and Community Development Subcommittee.

The first Texan of Mexican descent to serve in the U.S. House of Representatives, he has fervently defended civil rights, distinguishing himself nationally as a liberal Democrat during the 1960s and 1970s. He was chairman of the Viva Kennedy campaign in 1960 and the Viva Johnson campaign in 1964. In 1964, he contributed significantly to the termination of the infamous Mexican Bracero Program.

Matthew G. Martínez (D-California)

Matthew Martinez was born on February 14, 1929, and resides in Monterey Park, California. Martinez

Matthew G. Martínez, U.S. Congressman. (D-California)

attended the Los Angeles Trade Technical School and was involved in small business prior to his election to the U.S. Congress. He is also a veteran of the U.S. Marine Corps.

Martínez was Mayor of Monterey Park, California, in 1974-75. He was a member of the California legislature from 1980 to 1982. Martinez was first elected to Congress as a Democrat in 1981, representing the Thirtieth District of California. He is a member of the important House Education and Labor Committee and is chairman of its Human Resources Subcommittee. Martinez is also a member of the House Government Operations Committee and the House Select Committee on Children, Youth, and Families. In January 1991, Congressman Martinez was elected vicechairman of the Congressional Hispanic Caucus.

Solomon P. Ortiz (D-Texas)

Solomon Ortiz was born on June 3, 1937, in Robstown, Texas. He attended Del Mar College in Texas. Ortiz was first elected to office in 1964 as Nueces County constable. Four years later he was elected Nueces County commissioner and was re-

William B. Richardson (D-New Mexico)

William Richardson was born on November 15, 1947, and lives in Santa Fe, New Mexico. Richardson attended Tufts University and received a master's degree from the Fletcher School of Law and Diplomacy.

Richardson was first elected to Congress in 1982 to represent New Mexico's newly created Third Congressional District, one of the largest in square miles and one of the most ethnically diverse in the country: 40 percent Anglo, 40 percent Hispanic, and 20 percent native American. He won reelection with over 70 percent of the vote in 1986 and 1988. Congressman Richardson rose relatively quickly to become a member of the House leadership and serves as majority whip at-large. He is a member of the House Energy and Commerce Committee, the House Interior and Insular Affairs Committee, the House Select Committee on Aging, and the House Select Committee on Intelligence.

Ileana Ros-Lehtinen (R-Florida)

Ileana Ros-Lehtinen was born on July 15, 1952, and resides in Miami, Florida. She attended Florida Inter-

Solomon P. Ortiz, U.S. Congressman. (D-Texas)

elected to that post in 1972. In 1976, Ortiz was elected Nueces County sheriff and was reelected in 1980.

In 1982, Ortiz first ran for national office as a Democrat for a seat in the 98th Congress. He was elected and has been reelected to each subsequent session to date. Congressman Ortiz is a member of the Congressional Hispanic Caucus and was elected chairman of the caucus in January 1991. He sits on the powerful House Armed Services Committee, the Merchant Marine and Fisheries Committee, and the Select Committee on Narcotics Abuse and Control.

Bill Richardson, U.S. Congressman. (D-New Mexico)

Ileana Ros-Lehtinen, U.S. Congresswoman. (R-Florida)

Roybal began his education there in public schools. He graduated from high school in 1934 during the depths of the Great Depression and began working for the Civilian Conservation Corps. Later he continued his education at the University of California and Southwestern University. Roybal took a position as a health care educator beginning in the late 1930s. He served in World War II during 1944 and 1945, and returned to Los Angeles to continue to work in health care.

Following World War II, a group of concerned Mexican Americans formed a group to elect a Mexican American to the Los Angeles City Council, and Roybal was their choice for candidate. In 1947, he ran and was defeated. Instead of giving up, Roybal and the group intensified their efforts to get out the vote in East Los Angeles, and in his second bid for city council in 1949, Roybal was elected. He was the first Mexican American on the council since 1881. Roybal was reelected several times and served on the council for thirteen years.

Roybal was first elected to Congress in 1962 as a Democrat from the Twenty-fifth District of California. He is a member of the powerful House Appropriations Committee and is chairman of the House

national University, where she received both a bachelor's and a master's degree. After graduating from college, Ros-Lehtinen taught at a private school in Miami that she owned and operated.

In 1982, Ros-Lehtinen was elected as a Republican to the Florida legislature. In 1986, she was elected to the Florida state senate, where she served until 1989.

Congresswoman Ros-Lehtinen was elected in 1989 as a Republican to the U.S. Congress for the Eighteenth District in Florida. She is a member of the critical House Foreign Affairs Committee and the House Government Operations Committee and serves as the ranking minority member of the House Employment and Housing Subcommittee. Ros-Lehtinen has also been elected twice to the post of secretary-treasurer of the Congressional Hispanic Caucus, of which she is the only woman and the only Cuban-American member.

Edward R. Roybal (D-California)

Edward Roybal was born on February 10, 1916, in Albuquerque, New Mexico, into a middle-class Mexican-American family. When he was four, his family moved to the Boyle Heights area of Los Angeles.

Edward R. Roybal, U.S. Congressman, (D-California)

Select Committee on Aging. Roybal is also a member and former chairman of the Congressional Hispanic Caucus.

During his three decades in Congress, Roybal has worked for social and economic reforms. In 1967, he introduced legislation that became the first federal bilingual education act. In 1982, as chairman of the Congressional Hispanic Caucus, he led the opposition to employer sanctions for hiring the undocumented, which ultimately was enacted as the Immigration Reform and Control Act of 1986. Throughout his tenure, Congressman Roybal has consistently advocated greater citizen participation in party politics and in the federal and local government.

José E. Serrano (D-New York)

Jose Serrano was born in Mayaguez, Puerto Rico, on October 24, 1943. His family moved to the South Bronx in 1950. Serrano attended public schools and went to the City University of New York.

He was a New York state assemblyman from 1974 until he was elected to Congress as a Democrat in 1990. He represents the Eighteenth District in New York. Congressman Serrano is a member of the influential House Education and Labor Committee and

José E. Serrano, U.S. Congressman. (D-New York)

the House Small Business Committee. He is also a member of the Congressional Hispanic Caucus.

Esteban Edward Torres (D-California)

Esteban Edward Torres was born on January 27, 1930, in Miami, Arizona, where his Mexican-born father was a miner. When his father was deported in 1936 as a result of his union-organizing activities, the family moved to East Los Angeles, where Torres received his early education. After graduating from high school in 1949, he joined the army and served during the Korean War. After being discharged in 1954, Torres took a job on an assembly line at Chrysler and attended California State University at night, receiving his B.A. degree in 1963. Torres was a supporter of the United Auto Workers Union.

In 1974, Torres narrowly lost his first bid for the Democratic nomination for the U.S. House of Representatives. In 1977, President Jimmy Carter appointed Torres as the U.S. representative to UNESCO, with diplomatic rank. President Carter also appointed Torres as his special assistant for programs and policies concerning Mexican Americans.

After President Reagan took office in 1981, Torres returned to California. The next year, he was elected to Congress as a Democrat representing the Thirty-fourth District in California. He is a member of the House Banking, Finance and Urban Affairs Committee and is chairman of its Consumer Affairs Subcommittee. Torres is also a member of the House Small Business Committee and a member of the Congressional Hispanic Caucus.

Hispanic Members of Congress, 1822-1991

As of 1991, forty-six Hispanic Americans had served in the U.S. House of Representatives and represented constituents in California, Florida, Louisiana, New Mexico, New York, and Texas. This includes fifteen nonvoting members from Puerto Rico, Guam, and the Virgin Islands.

Two members of the House of Representatives, Dennis Chavez and Joseph Manuel Montoya, both of New Mexico, became the only Hispanics to serve in the U.S. Senate.

Following is a selected list of the Hispanic members, their parties and states, and the years in which they served.

Herman Badillo (1929-)

The first Puerto Rican ever elected as a voting Member of Congress, Herman Badillo was born in Caguas, Puerto Rico. Orphaned at age 5, he was eventually sent to the United States in 1940 to live with

Esteban E. Torres, U.S. Congressman. (D-California)

relatives in New York City. He attended the City College of New York, where he graduated with honors, then attended the Brooklyn Law School at night.

In 1961, Badillo entered politics, narrowly losing a race for the state assembly. After serving in several local appointed positions, he ran unsuccessfully for mayor of New York. Badillo gained popularity as a result of his strong showing in the mayoral election and later won election to Congress in 1970. Badillo served as a U.S. congressman from New York for four terms, representing the Twenty-first District.

After serving in Congress for seven years, Badillo resigned in 1978 to accept an appointment as deputy mayor of New York City under Mayor Edward Koch. Badillo went into the practice of law in New York after leaving the deputy mayor's office. In 1986, he ran for the post of New York state comptroller. He lost the statewide race, but carried 61 percent of the New York City vote. Many in the New York Hispanic community suggest that Badillo may again run for mayor.

HOUSE OF REPRESENTATIVES		
NAME	PARTY AND STATE	YEARS SERVED
Joseph Marion Hernández	W-Florida	1822-1823
Jose Manuel Gallegos	D-New Mexico	1871-1873
Miguel Antonio Otero, Sr.	D-New Mexico	1856-1861
Francisco Perea	R-New Mexico	1863-1865
Jose Francisco Chaves	R-New Mexico	1865-1867
Trinidad Romero	R-New Mexico	1877-1879
Mariano Sabino Otero	R-New Mexico	1879-1881
Romualdo Pacheco	R-California	1879-1883
Tranquillino Luna	R-New Mexico	1881-1884
Francisco Manzanares	D-New Mexico	1884-1885
Pedro Perea	R-New Mexico	1899-1901
Julio Larringa	U-Puerto Rico*	1905-1911
Luis Muñoz Rivera	U-Puerto Rico*	1911-1916
Ládislas Lázaro	D-Louisiana	1913-1927
Benigno Cárdenas Hernández	R-New Mexico	1919-1921
Felix Córdova Dávila	U-Puerto Rico*	1917-1932
Nestor Montoya	R-New Mexico	1921-1923
Dennis Chávez	D-New Mexico	1931-1935
Joachim Octave Fernández	D-Louisiana	1931-1941
José Lorenzo Pesquera	NP-Puerto Rico*	1932-1933
Santiago Iglesias	C-Puerto Rico*	1933-1939
Bolívar Pagán	C-Puerto Rico*	1939-1945
Antonio Manuel Fernández	D-New Mexico	1943-1956
Jesús T. Piñero	PD-Puerto Rico*	1945-1948
Antonio Fernós-Isern	PD-Puerto Rico*	1949-1965
Joseph Manuel Montoya	D-New Mexico	1957-1964
Henry B. González	D-Texas	1961-present
Edward R. Roybal	D-California	1962-present
E. (Kika) de la Garza	D-Texas	1965-present
Santiago Polanco-Abreu	PD-Puerto Rico*	1965-1969
Manuel Luján, Jr.	R-New Mexico	1969-1988
Jorge Luis Córdova	NP-Puerto Rico*	1969-1973
Herman Badillo	D-New York	1971-1977
Ron de Lugo	D-Virgin Islands	1981-present
Jaime Benítez	PD-Puerto Rico*	1973-1977
Baltasar Corrada	NP-Puerto Rico*	1977-1984
Robert García	D-New York	1978-1989
Matthew G. Martínez	D-California	1982-present
Solomon P. Ortiz	D-Texas	1983-present
William B. Richardson	D-California	1983-present
Esteban Edward Torres	D-California	1983-present
Ben Blaz	R-Guam*	1985-present
Albert G. Bustamante	D-Texas	1985-present
Jaime B. Fuster	D-Puerto Rico*	1985-present
Ileana Ros-Lehtinen	R-Florida	1989-present
José E. Serrano	D-New York	1990-present
SENATE		
Dennis Chávez	D-New Mexico	1935-1962
Joseph Montoya	D-New Mexico	1964-1977

Source: Congressional Hispanic Caucus. *Nonvoting member of Congress.
Party Affiliation: D=Democrat; R=Republican; C=Congress; PD=Popular Democratico; NP=Nuevo Progresista; U=Unida; W=Whig.

Herman Badillo, Former U.S. Congressman. (D-New York)

José Francisco Chaves (1833-1904)

José Chaves was born in what is today Bernalillo County, near Albuquerque, New Mexico. His father, Mariano Chaves, was an important political figure in the Mexican government in the late 1830s. After his early education in New Mexico and Chihuahua, Chaves was sent to school in Saint Louis by his father so that he might better cope with the westward flood tide of American frontiersmen. After returning to New Mexico during the U.S. war with Mexico, Chaves went to New York to complete his education.

When his father died, Chaves returned to New Mexico to manage the family ranch. During the 1850s, he was involved in various Indian campaigns to preserve cattle ranges. His participation in the Indian campaigns proved useful in the Civil War, in which he reached the rank of lieutenant colonel in the New Mexico infantry.

After the war, Chaves studied law and entered the

New Mexico political arena. He was elected New Mexico territorial delegate in several bitter, brawling campaigns and served three terms between 1865 and 1871 as a Republican. In 1875, he was elected to the New Mexico territorial legislature and reelected until his death thirty years later. Chaves was a dynamic political leader, fighting the Sante Fe Ring and strongly supporting New Mexico Governor Miguel Otero, Jr.

On the night of November 26, 1904, Chaves was assassinated by an unknown assailant at Pinos Wells, New Mexico. The murder was rumored to be politically motivated and connected to his opposition to the infamous Santa Fe Ring. Despite a $2,500 reward offered by the legislature, his murderer was never identified.

Dennis Chávez (1888-1962)

Dennis Chavez was a member of the U.S. House of Representatives and the first Hispanic U.S. senator. Chávez was born as the third of eight children in a village west of Albuquerque, New Mexico, to a poor family. The family moved to Albuquerque seven years later and Chávez attended school there, but family poverty forced him to drop out of school in the eighth grade to work delivering groceries for the next five years. He continued to educate himself in the evenings at the public library.

From 1906 to 1915, he worked for the Albuquerque city engineering department. In 1912, Chávez worked as a Spanish interpreter for the successful Democratic candidate for U.S. Senate, Andrieus Jones. Jones obtained a clerkship in the Senate for Chávez, who entered law school at Georgetown University in Washington, D.C. In 1920, Chávez was awarded a law degree.

Chávez then returned to New Mexico, where he began a successful law practice and ran for public office in the classic pattern of American political advancement. As Chávez rose in Democratic party ranks, he successfully ran for a seat in the New Mexico legislature. In 1930, Chávez defeated the incumbent Republican and won a seat in the U.S. House of Representatives. He was reelected to the House in 1932.

In the 1934 elections, Chávez ran for the U.S. Senate seat held by the powerful Republican Bronson Cutting and was defeated by a narrow margin. Chávez challenged the validity of Cutting's reelection, charging vote fraud, and took the challenge to the floor of the U.S. Senate. While the challenge was pending, Cutting was killed in an airplane crash. Chávez was appointed by the governor of New Mexico to the U.S. Senate. Chávez was reelected easily in the 1936 elections.

As a Democratic senator, Chávez was a staunch supporter of President Roosevelt's New Deal. As chairman of the Public Works Committee, Chávez obtained federal funding for irrigation and flood control projects in New Mexico. As a Western isolationist, he opposed U.S. entry into World War II and argued that the country should follow a policy of strict neutrality. Serious attempts to unseat him at home were halted by the loyalty of New Mexico supporters who sustained him politically.

During the years after the war, Chávez did some of his best work in the Senate. Perhaps his greatest contribution to Hispanic Americans, and to the nation, was his support of education and civil rights. Cháavez drafted a bill to create the federal Fair Employment Practices Commission and fought tirelessly for its enactment.

In all, Senator Chávez was elected to the Senate five times. A champion of civil rights and full equality for all Americans to the last, the long and distinguished national career of this son of New Mexico was ended by a heart attack in mid-November 1962.

José Manuel Gallegos (1815-1875)

Jose Gallegos was a territorial delegate to the U.S. Congress for New Mexico. Gallegos was born in northwest New Mexico in present-day Rio Arriba County, in the town of Abiquiu. He hailed from a prominent family and was educated in Taos and later went to the College of Durango, Mexico to study for the priesthood. Upon graduation in 1840, he was ordained a priest. He first went to southwestern New Mexico to work among the people of San Juan, and later to Albuquerque and Santa Fe.

While in Santa Fe, Gallegos began to get involved with politics. In 1843, he was elected to the New Mexico provincial legislature on the eve of the American conquest and served until 1846 in that assembly. After New Mexico became part of the United States by the Treaty of Guadalupe Hidalgo, he was elected to the first territorial council in 1851.

In 1853, Gallegos was elected territorial delegate to the U.S. Congress as a Democrat. He lost his bid at reelection in 1855 to Miguel Otero, Sr., in a hotly disputed campaign. He returned to service in the territorial legislature in 1860 and was named Speaker of the House. He again made a bid for territorial delegate two years later but lost.

Meanwhile, the Civil War broke out, and Gallegos, a staunch Unionist, was imprisoned in 1862 by invading Texan Confederate forces. At the end of the war, he was appointed territorial treasurer, where he served from 1865 to 1866. At the end of his term, he again won election to the territorial legislature.

In 1870, Gallegos again ran for territorial delegate to the U.S. Congress and won. His bid for reelection two years later was unsuccessful. He returned to Santa Fe and after a short illness died in April 1875.

Benigno Cárdenas Hernández (1862-1954)

Benigno Hernández was born in Taos, New Mexico, during the Civil War and was educated there in public schools. He began his business career as a store clerk in the 1880s. Ten years later he began a stock-raising business and in 1896 opened his own general store in Lumberton in Rio Arriba County.

Hernandez entered politics in 1900 and served as Rio Arriba County's probate clerk, recorder, sheriff, treasurer, and tax collector over the following ten years. Very active in Republican politics, Hernandez was elected to the U.S. House of Representatives in 1914 and was reelected in 1918. His bid for a third term was unsuccessful.

After the end of his second term in 1921, President Warren G. Harding appointed Hernández collector of Internal Revenue for the state of New Mexico. Hernández held that post until 1933, when President Franklin D. Roosevelt took office. He was then age 71. He later served on the Selective Service Board of New Mexico during World War II. In the 1950s, Hernández moved to Los Angeles, where he died at age 92.

Joseph M. Montoya (1915-1978)

Joseph Montoya was born in the small village of Pena Blanca, New Mexico, where his father was county sheriff. Montoya's parents were descendants of eighteenth-century Spanish immigrants to New Mexico. After graduating from high school in 1931, he attended Regis College in Denver, Colorado. In 1934, he entered Georgetown University Law School in Washington, D.C.

In 1936, during his second year of law school, Montoya was elected as a Democrat to the New Mexico House of Representatives at age twenty-one, the youngest representative in the state's history. Two years later, he received his LL.B. degree from Georgetown University and was reelected to the state legislature. In 1940, Montoya was elected to the state senate; at age twenty-five, he was the youngest senator in the state's history. He served a total of twelve years in the state legislature. He then served four terms as lieutenant governor of New Mexico, from 1946 to 1950 and from 1954 to 1957.

In 1957, at age 42, Montoya was elected as a Democrat to the first of four consecutive terms in the U.S. House of Representatives. He established a reputation as a hardworking legislator and loyal party man. He followed a moderate political course and was regularly returned to Congress with well over 60 percent of the vote.

When Senator Dennis Chavez (D-NM) died in 1962

leaving a Senate seat vacant, Montoya won election to the Senate. He also won a second term to the Senate in 1970. One of the most influential senators in Washington, he was a member of the Appropriations Committee and the Public Works Committee. However, in the early 1970s Montoya's popularity at home waned, and he was defeated in his bid for reelection in 1976 by former astronaut Harrison Schmitt.

Montoya's health declined rapidly following the 1976 election. After undergoing surgery for cancer, he died of complications in June 1978.

Nestor Montoya (1862-1923)

Nestor Montoya was born in Albuquerque, New Mexico, on April 14, 1862. He was educated in Albuquerque public schools and then graduated from St. Michael's College in Santa Fe. After college, he worked in the Santa Fe post office and the U.S. Treasury office there. In 1889, Montoya founded *La voz del pueblo*, a Spanish-language newspaper. Montoya founded a second paper in 1900 called *La bandera americana*.

In addition to his journalistic activities, Montoya was also involved in New Mexico politics. In 1892, he was elected to the New Mexico territorial legislature's lower house and was repeatedly reelected, serving until 1903. The following year Montoya was elected to the legislature's upper house and in 1910 was elected a delegate to the New Mexico Constitutional Convention. He worked hard for the rights of Hispanics at the convention and gained the respect of many across the state.

In 1920, Nestor Montoya was elected as New Mexico's representative to the U.S. Congress. He died in 1923 before his term ended.

Mariano S. Otero (1844-1904)

Mariano Otero was born in the tiny town of Peralta, New Mexico, on August 29, 1844, during the last years of Mexican control. As a member of the powerful Otero clan, he attended local parochial and private schools and later studied at Saint Louis University in Missouri. After college, Otero became a banker.

In the early 1870s, he was appointed probate judge of Bernalillo County. In 1874, he turned down the Democratic nomination for congressional delegate. In 1878, however, he accepted the Republican nomination for congressional delegate and won. He declined to run for reelection in 1882 and returned to his banking business. Between 1884 and 1886, Otero twice ran for Congress but was defeated.

In the 1890s, Otero moved to Albuquerque to continue his banking activities. He died there in 1904 at age 59.

Miguel A. Otero, Sr. (1829-1882)

Born in Valencia, New Mexico, on June 21, 1829, Miguel Otero was the son of Vicente Otero, an important local leader during both the Spanish and Mexican eras. After completing his early education in Valencia, Otero was sent to Missouri in 1841 to attend Saint Louis University. Six years later, he went to Pingree's College in New York. He later taught there and then began the study of law. In 1851, he returned to Saint Louis, where he continued his legal studies and was admitted to the bar.

Returning to New Mexico in 1852 to practice law in Albuquerque, Otero became private secretary to territorial Governor William C. Lane and immediately plunged into politics. That same year, Otero was elected to the territorial legislature. Two years later, he was appointed New Mexico attorney general. Otero's political experience and wide family connections (his older brother Antonio Jose Otero was chief justice at the time) worked to his advantage, and in 1855 he was nominated by the Democratic party for the office of territorial delegate to Congress. Otero won the election and went on to win reelection to Congress, serving a total of six terms.

In Congress, Otero's efforts ensured that the transcontinental railroad would cross through New Mexico, giving great promise to the state's future. By doing so, he aligned himself with other Southern states that also favored a southern route for the railroad. As a result of Otero's influence, New Mexico legislated a slave code in 1859. The following year he supported a compromise to avoid civil war by extending slavery to the territories south of the 36th parallel, including New Mexico. The outbreak of the Civil War greatly reduced Otero's political influence. He did not support the Confederacy, but he did support a separate confederation of western states.

President Lincoln offered the post of minister to Spain to Otero, but he declined it in favor of the nomination of secretary of the Territory of New Mexico. The U.S. Senate did not confirm him because of his political views.

After the Civil War ended, Otero pursued banking and land business interests with the coming of the railroad. He founded and was the first president of the San Miguel National Bank. He was also part of the business group that purchased the immense Maxwell Land Grant in 1870. He was a director of the Maxwell Land Grant and Railroad Company and was also a director of the Atchinson, Topeka, and Santa Fe Railroad. The first terminal of the Santa Fe Railroad was named Otero in his honor.

In 1880, despite his failing health, Otero made a last bid for territorial delegate to Congress but was defeated. His health continued to deteriorate rapidly, and in 1882 he died at the age of 53.

Romualdo Pacheco (1831-1899)

Romualdo Pacheco was born in Santa Barbara, California, on October 31, 1831. He was the son of an aide to the Mexican governor of California, Manuel Victoria. Pacheco's father was killed in battle shortly after his birth. His mother remarried and Pacheco's stepfather sent him to Honolulu to be educated at an English missionary school. When he returned to California at age 15, Pacheco began working on his stepfather's ships.

After the U.S. takeover of California, Pacheco left the sea to manage the family's large estate and began to show an interest in politics. During the 1850s, Pacheco was successively elected county judge and state senator as a Democrat. Having switched from the Democratic party to the Union party (and later to the Republican party) at the outbreak of the Civil War, Pacheco was reelected to the state senate, and from 1863 to 1867 he served as state treasurer. In 1871 he was elected lieutenant governor and became governor of California in 1875 when then-Governor Newton Booth was appointed to the U.S. Senate. In the next election he failed to secure the Republican nomination for Governor.

In 1876, Pacheco was elected to the U.S. House of Representatives, and was reelected in 1879 and 1881. He was not known as an aggressive congressman, but did serve on the influential Public Expenditures Committee and the Committee on Private Land Claims. In 1883, he did not seek reelection and returned to his family business interests in California.

In 1890, he was named minister plenipotentiary to Central America by President Benjamin Harrison. He remained at that post until Democratic President Grover Cleveland took office in 1893. Pacheco then returned to his California home and died in 1899.

Francisco Perea (1830-1913)

Francisco Perea was born in the small New Mexico town of Los Padillas, near Albuquerque, to Juan Perea and Josefa Chavez, descendants of two important families. Having completed his early education in Los Padillas and Santa Fe, he was sent to study with the Jesuits at Saint Louis University in Missouri from 1843 to 1845. After the U.S. takeover of New Mexico, he went to New York and studied at the Bank Street Academy between 1847 and 1849.

In 1850, Perea returned to New Mexico to engage in stock trading. He became a commercial success by transporting sheep to California to sell to meat-hungry miners. His family and his commercial success helped him in 1858 to be elected to the New Mexico territorial legislature's upper house. After the Civil War broke out, he was twice reelected as an active supporter of the North.

Perea was also active in the military and formed "Perea's Battalion," which he commanded as lieutenant colonel. The battalion took part in the defeat of Confederate invaders of New Mexico at Glorieta Pass in 1862.

After the victory at Glorieta Pass, Perea was elected to the U.S. Congress as territorial delegate for New Mexico. His bid for reelection two years later was unsuccessful. He returned to New Mexico and opened a resort hotel at Jemez Springs, which he owned and operated until 1905. Perea then moved to Albuquerque,where he remained until his death in 1913.

Pedro Perea (1852-1906)

Pedro Perea was born April 22, 1852, in the central New Mexico town of Bernalillo in Sandoval County. After his early education there, he was sent to Saint Michael's College in Santa Fe, then to Georgetown University in Washington, D.C. In 1871 he graduated from Saint Louis University in Missouri.

Like many sons of prominent New Mexican families of the era, he returned to New Mexico to engage in stock raising and business. From 1890 to 1894, he was president of the First National Bank of Santa Fe. He also began to take an interest in New Mexico politics at this time.

Between 1889 and 1897, he served three terms in the New Mexico territorial legislature's upper house as a Republican. In 1898, he was elected territorial delegate to the U.S. Congress. He chose not to run for reelection and returned to New Mexico at the end of his term in 1900 to resume his banking activities. He died in 1906.

✳SELECTED PROMINENT HISPANIC FEDERAL OFFICIALS

Tirso del Junco, M.D. (19?-)

A member of the board of governors of the U.S. Postal Service in Washington, D.C., del Junco was born in Havana, Cuba, received a medical degree in 1949 from the Havana School of Medicine, and became a U.S. citizen in 1963.

He is a member of the board of regents of the University of California and was a delegate to the Republican National Conventions for the past six presidential elections. In 1983 he was a U.S. delegate to the Twenty-second conference of UNESCO in Paris. Del Junco is the founder and former chairman of the Los Angeles National Bank and is a member of the Queen of Angels Hospital Clinic and Research Foundation.

Del Junco was a captain in the U.S. Army and chief of surgery at the Camp Howland Army Hospital from 1955 to 1957. In 1948, del Junco was a member of the Cuban Olympic team and participated in the crew competition.

Cari M. Domínguez (1949-)

Director of the Office of Federal Contract Compliance Programs, U.S. Department of Labor, Cari Domínguez was born in Havana, Cuba, in 1949. Her family immigrated to the United States and she was raised in Takoma Park, Maryland. She holds a bachelor's degree and a master's degree from American University in Washington, D.C.

In 1974, Domínguez joined the Office of Federal Contract Compliance Programs, where she held a variety of positions until 1983. In 1984, she left the Department of Labor and began working for the Bank of America in San Francisco, where she served as corporate manager of equal opportunity programs. In 1986, she was promoted to vice president and director of executive programs, in charge of executive compensation and benefits programs, succession planning, development, and staffing services.

In 1989, President Bush appointed Domínguez director of the Office of Federal Contract Compliance Programs of the U.S. Department of Labor. As director, she is responsible for the enforcement of federal mandates prohibiting discrimination and requiring affirmative action in the employment and advancement of the disabled, women, minorities, and veterans.

Jimmy Gurulé (19?-)

U.S. assistant attorney general, Jimmy Gurulé grew up in Utah. He received both his bachelor's degree and his law degree from the University of Utah. Prior to joining the Department of Justice, Gurulé was an associate professor of law at the University of Notre Dame Law School. He is a former president of the Hispanic National Bar Association.

Gurulé was appointed assistant attorney general by President George Bush and was sworn in on August 3, 1990. He is the highest-ranking Hispanic in the history of the Department of Justice. As assistant attorney general for the Office of Justice Programs, Gurulé is responsible for coordinating policy, management, and priorities within the Office of Justice Programs in Washington, D.C., and its five program bureaus and field offices. He works to form partnerships among federal, state, and local government officials to improve administration of justice, combat violent crime and drug abuse, meet the needs of crime

Cari M. Domínguez, Director, Office of Federal Contract Compliance Programs.

Manuel Luján, Jr. (19?-)

Secretary of the Department of the Interior, Luján grew up in Santa Fe, New Mexico, and earned his B.A. degree from the College of Santa Fe. After college, Luján was a partner in a family insurance and real estate business.

Luján served as a Republican congressman and represented the First District of New Mexico in the U.S. House of Representatives from 1969 to 1989. In Congress, Luján was the ranking minority member of the House Interior Committee.

In 1989, President Bush appointed Luján as the forty-sixth secretary of the interior. Luján believes that the United States can have both the resource development needed for economic security and the environmental protection required to ensure quality of life. Luján has implemented a "no net loss of wetlands" goal through actions to enlarge the Everglades National Park in Florida and a proposal to repair environmental damage at Kesterson Reservoir in California.

victims, and find innovative ways to address problems such as narcotics trafficking, gang-related crime, white-collar crime, and corruption. Gurulé was awarded the Attorney General's Distinguished Service Award in 1990 for his excellence as an assistant U.S. attorney in prosecuting the killers of Drug Enforcement Administration Special Agent Enrique Camarena, who had been working in Guadalajara, Mexico.

Manuel Luján, Jr., Secretary of the Interior.

Robert Martínez, Director, Office of National Drug Control Policy, and Former Governor of Florida.

Robert Martínez (1934-)

Director of the Office of National Drug Control Policy, Robert Martínez was born in Tampa, Florida, on December 25, 1934. He received his bachelor's degree in education from the University of Tampa in 1957 and a master's degree in labor and industrial relations from the University of Illinois in 1964.

Martínez went into business following college and owned and operated a restaurant in Tampa until 1983. He became involved in local politics in the late 1970s and was elected to two terms as a Republican mayor of Tampa from 1979 to 1987.

In 1988, Martínez was elected governor of Florida and served one term. During his tenure as governor, President Reagan named Martínez to the White House Conference on a Drug-Free America.

Martínez was appointed by President Bush as director of the Office of National Drug Control Policy in 1991. As director, he is responsible for developing a national strategy to combat illicit drugs. He is charged by law to coordinate and oversee both the international and domestic anti-drug abuse functions of all executive branch agencies, and to ensure that such functions sustain and complement state and local anti-drug abuse efforts.

Antonia C. Novello (1944-)

The first woman and first Hispanic surgeon general of the United States, Antonia Novello was born in Fajardo, Puerto Rico, on August 23, 1944. She received a B.A. degree in 1965 and an M.D. degree in 1970 from the University of Puerto Rico. Novello was awarded her master's degree in public health from Johns Hopkins University in 1982.

Novello joined the U.S. Public Health Service in 1978 after working in the private practice of pediatrics and nephrology. She served in various capacities at the National Institutes of Health (NIH) beginning in 1978, including serving as deputy director of the National Institute of Child Health and Human Development.

In 1990, President Bush appointed Novello as the fourteenth surgeon general. Among her duties as surgeon general, she is responsible for recommending precautions necessary to protect public health and safety.

Catalina Vásquez Villalpando (1940-)

Treasurer of the United States, Villalpando was born April 1, 1940, in San Marcos, Texas, and is a graduate of Southwest Texas State University. Villalpando joined Communications International, a multinational telecommunications systems integrator, and became a senior vice president. From 1985 until her executive appointment, Villalpando directed all public relations and marketing for the company's northeast region, based in Washington, D.C.

Villalpando served as White House special assistant for public liaison to President Ronald Reagan from 1983 to 1985. Prior to assuming her duties at the White House she served as liaison director for the Republican party of Texas.

Antonia C. Novello, M.D., M.P.H., Surgeon General, United States Public Health Service.

Catalina Vásquez Villalpando, Treasurer of the United States.

Selected Prominent Hispanic Former Federal Officials

Everett Alvarez, Jr. (1937-)

Former deputy administrator of the U.S. Veterans Administration, Everett Alvarez was born in Salinas, California, of farm worker parents from Mexico. His parents emphasized hard work and education as the way to succeed. Alvarez was awarded an engineering degree from the University of Santa Clara in 1960. Alvarez was a navy pilot during the Vietnam War and was shot down over the Gulf of Tonkin. He was held prisoner by the Viet Cong for over eight years. After his release in 1973, Alvarez went back to school and received a law degree from George Washington University and practiced law as a patent attorney.

In 1981, President Reagan appointed Alvarez deputy director of the Peace Corps. In 1982, the president appointed Alvarez deputy administrator of the Veterans Administration.

Diego Archuleta (1814-1884)

U.S. Indian agent under President Abraham Lincoln. Archuleta was born of a prominent family in the

In 1989, President Bush appointed Villalpando as the thirty-ninth treasurer of the United States. As treasurer, Villalpando oversees the operation of the U.S. Mint, the Bureau of Engraving and Printing, and the U.S. Savings Bond Division. Villalpando also advises the secretary of the treasury on matters relating to coinage, currency, and production of other negotiable instruments.

Rio Arriba country of New Mexico during the Mexican war for independence and was educated at the Seminary at Durango, Mexico. In 1840, he returned to New Mexico and from 1843 to 1845 served as representative from New Mexico at the National Congress in Mexico City. When American forces invaded New Mexico in 1846, Archuleta gave no resistance to General Stephen Kearny's army. Disappointed at not being made part of the new American government in New Mexico, Archuleta took a leading role in two unsuccessful Taos rebellions in 1846 and 1847. After his passions had cooled, Archuleta took the oath of allegiance to the United States and sought to use American institutions to his advantage. During the 1850s, he was repeatedly elected to the New Mexico state assembly, and in 1857 he was named U.S. Indian agent to the Utes and Apaches, in which capacity he served until the Civil War broke out. He became a brigadier general in the New Mexico militia during the war and was reappointed U.S. Indian agent by President Abraham Lincoln. After the war Archuleta returned to service in the New Mexico state assembly, where he served until his death in 1884.

Romana Acosta Bañuelos (1925-)

The first Mexican American and the sixth woman to hold the post of treasurer of the United States, Bañuelos was born in Miami, Arizona, of undocumented Mexican parents. During the Great Depression, she was forced at age 6 to accompany her parents when they were repatriated to Mexico in 1931. She grew up in Mexico and at age 19 moved back to the United States and settled in Los Angeles.

In 1949, she started a small tortilla factory with $400. Over the following twenty years, she developed it into a $12-million-a-year business, Romana's Mexican Food Products, employing hundreds of workers and producing dozens of food items. She also helped to establish the Pan American National Bank in Los Angeles, of which she was a director and chairwoman.

In 1971, President Nixon appointed Bañuelos treasurer of the United States. She served as treasurer from December 1971 until February 1974. While retaining some interest in politics, she has since devoted herself principally to her business activities.

Arturo Morales Carrión (1913-1989)

Former deputy assistant secretary of state under President John F. Kennedy, and the first Puerto Rican to be appointed to such a high State Department position, Arturo Carrión was born in Havana, Cuba, on November 16, 1913. He earned a B.A. degree from the University of Puerto Rico in 1935, an M.A.

degree from the University of Texas in 1936, and a Ph.D. degree from Columbia University in 1950.

Carrión taught at the University of Puerto Rico and became chairman of the history department. He then went into politics and served as undersecretary of Puerto Rico's State Department, in charge of external affairs.

He joined the Kennedy administration in 1961 as deputy assistant secretary of state for inter-American affairs. He remained at that post until the assassination of President Kennedy in 1963. Carrión was a member of the Kennedy administration's Latin American Study Group, which warned of a Communist threat to Latin America.

After leaving the State Department, Carrión became special assistant to the secretary general of the Organization of American States. He later returned to Puerto Rico to become president of the University of Puerto Rico. Carrión died in San Juan in 1989 at age 75.

Leonel J. Castillo (1939-)

Former director of the U.S. Immigration and Naturalization Service (INS), Leonel Castillo was born in Victoria, Texas, where he grew up and attended school. He graduated from St. Mary's University in San Antonio, Texas, in 1961. Castillo joined the Peace Corps after graduation and served in the Philippines from 1961 to 1965. Upon his return to the United States, he attended the University of Pittsburgh, where he received his master's degree in social work in 1967.

Castillo then returned to Texas and lived in Houston, where he took an active role in local politics. In 1970, he won a surprise victory in his election as Houston city comptroller against a twenty-five-year incumbent. In 1974, he was named treasurer of the Texas Democratic party.

President Jimmy Carter appointed Castillo to head the INS in 1977. After thirty months of trying to modernize the INS, to reduce violence on the border, and to emphasize service rather than enforcement, he resigned in 1979. Castillo then returned to Houston to head Castillo Enterprises.

Fernando E. Cabeza de Baca (1937-)

Former special assistant to President Gerald Ford and a direct descendant of the famous Spanish explorer Alvar Núñez Cabeza de Baca (often spelled "Vaca"), Fernando Cabeza de Baca was born in Albuquerque, New Mexico. He received his early education in New Mexico, and at the end of the 1950s he received a degree in public administration from the University of New Mexico in Albuquerque. He also studied at the University of New Mexico School of

Law. During the Vietnam War, he served in the U.S. Army and returned from the war disabled and decorated.

In the late 1960s and early 1970s, de Baca held high-ranking positions with the New Mexico Department of Transportation, the Civil Service Commission, and the Department of Health, Education and Welfare. He then became chairman of the Federal Regional Council for the Western United States.

In 1974, President Gerald Ford appointed de Baca as special assistant to the president. In this role, at age 37, he became both the youngest and the highest-ranking federal executive of Hispanic descent.

De Baca returned to New Mexico to pursue business activities after Ford left the presidency in 1976. He remains deeply involved in veterans affairs and is active in the New Mexico Republican party.

Lauro F. Cavazos (1927-)

Former U.S. secretary of education and the first Hispanic named to a cabinet-level position, Lauro Cavazos left a distinguished career as the president of Texas Tech University in Lubbock, Texas, to join President Reagan's cabinet in 1988. Previously, Cavazos had been the dean of Tufts University School of Medicine.

Appointed secretary of education by President Reagan in 1988 and reappointed by President Bush in 1989, Cavazos was instrumental in persuading President Bush to sign the executive order creating the President's Council on Educational Excellence for Hispanic Americans. Cavazos's leadership and sensitivity raised the awareness of Congress regarding the educational needs of Hispanics in the United States. Secretary Cavazos resigned in December 1990, and Lamar Alexander was appointed to replace him.

Edward Hidalgo (1912-)

Former secretary of the navy, Edward Hidalgo was born in Mexico City. His family immigrated to the United States. in 1918 and he was naturalized in 1936. He holds law degrees from both countries, a J.D. degree from Columbia University, which he received in 1936, and a similar degree from the University of Mexico, which was conferred in 1959.

During World War II, Hidalgo was special assistant to Secretary of the Navy James Forrestal in 1945-46 and was a member of the Eberstadt Commission on the Unification of the Military Services in 1945. After the war, he returned to private practice as an attorney. In 1965, Hidalgo was named special assistant to Secretary of the Navy Paul Nitze. From 1977-79 he served as assistant secretary of the navy. Hidalgo was appointed secretary of the navy by President Carter in 1979 and remained there until 1981.

Katherine D. Ortega (1934-)

Former treasurer of the United States, Katherine Ortega was born in rural south-central New Mexico. She received her early education in Tularosa, New Mexico. From her early years, she excelled in mathematics and accounting. After high school, Ortega worked at the Otero County Bank for two years until she saved enough money to go to college. She graduated from the Eastern New Mexico State University at Portales in 1957, with honors. After college, she began her own accounting firm in New Mexico.

In 1969, she moved to Los Angeles to work as a tax supervisor and later became a vice president of the Pan American National Bank. She then became the first woman president of a California bank when she was named president of the Santa Ana State Bank in 1975.

In 1978, she returned to New Mexico with her family and became active in the Republican party. In 1983, President Reagan appointed Ortega as U.S. treasurer. She remained at that post throughout the Reagan presidency. Ortega then returned to New Mexico and is still active in politics.

✳ PROMINENT HISPANIC POLITICIANS IN STATE GOVERNMENT

Toney Anaya (1941-)

Former Democratic governor of New Mexico from 1983 to 1986, Toney Anaya was one of ten children born to New Mexican parents in Moriarty, New Mexico. He spent his childhood in an adobe house with a dirt floor and no electricity or plumbing. Although his parents had no more than a couple of years of schooling, they encouraged their children to get a good education. Anaya attended the New Mexico Highlands University, on a Sears Foundation scholarship.

Anaya moved to Washington, D.C., where he graduated from Georgetown University. In 1967, he received his law degree from American University. While he was attending American University, he worked for Senator Dennis Chavez, and following graduation worked for Senator Joseph Montoya.

In 1970, Anaya returned to New Mexico. He ran for attorney general of New Mexico in 1974 and won, serving until 1978. Anaya then ran for the Senate, but lost a close election to incumbent Pete Domenici. In 1982, Anaya was elected governor of New Mexico, where he served until 1986.

Jerry Apodaca (1934-)

Former governor of New Mexico, Jerry Apodaca was born and raised in Las Cruces, New Mexico, where his family had lived for over one hundred years. He graduated from the University of New Mexico in 1957 and worked as a teacher and businessman. In 1966, Apodaca entered politics and was elected to the New Mexico state senate as a Democrat. After eight years in the state legislature, Apodaca, at age 40, was elected in 1974 as the first Hispanic governor of New Mexico in over fifty years (Governor Octaviano Larrazolo had served from 1918 to 1920). After Apodaca's term as governor ended, President Carter appointed him as chairman of the President's Council on Physical Fitness and Sports. Apodaca has since resumed his business interests and is currently on the board of directors of the Philip Morris Company.

Polly Baca-Barragán (1941-)

The first Hispanic woman to be elected state senator to the Colorado legislature, Polly Baca-Barragán was born in La Salle, Colorado. In 1963 she graduated from Colorado State University. During the 1960's, she was active in the Democratic party and worked on the Presidential campaigns of President John F. Kennedy, President Johnson and Senator Robert F. Kennedy. From 1971 to 1972 she was Director of Spanish Speaking Affairs for the Democratic National Committee. In 1974 Baca-Barragán made a successful bid for State Representative to the Colorado legislature. In 1978 she became the first Hispanic woman to be elected to the Colorado State Senate and was reelected in 1982.

Casimiro Barela (1847-1920)

A delegate to the Colorado State Constitutional Convention and a Colorado state senator, Casimiro Barela was born in Embudo, New Mexico, and was educated in Mora by Archbishop Jean B. Salpointe. Barela's family moved to Colorado in 1867, where they raised cattle. In 1869, Barela was elected justice of the peace and over the next six years held several elected posts, including county assessor and sheriff.

In 1875, Barela was elected as a delegate to the state constitutional convention, in which he took a leadership role. He secured a provision in the constitution protecting the civil rights of Spanish-speaking citizens as well as publication of laws in both Spanish and English, but this provision was limited to twenty-five years. Barela was elected to the first Colorado senate in 1876 and served until 1916. He was twice elected president of the Colorado senate.

Stephanie Gonzales (1950-)

Secretary of state for New Mexico, Stephanie Gonzales was born in Santa Fe, New Mexico. She is a graduate of Loretto Academy for Girls in Santa Fe. From 1987 to 1990, Gonzales was the deputy secretary of state under then-secretary Rebecca Vigil-Giron. In 1990, Gonzales, a Democrat, was elected secretary of state of New Mexico.

Art Torres (1941-)

State senator for California, Art Torres was born and raised in East Los Angeles. He received his B.A. degree from the University of California, Santa Cruz, and a J.D. degree from the University of California,

Stephanie Gonzales, Secretary of State, New Mexico.

Davis, Law School. He later served as a John F. Kennedy teaching fellow at Harvard University.

In 1976, Torres was first elected to the California Senate and has been reelected for each subsequent term. As state senator, Torres has worked to improve education at all levels, particularly through legislation to prevent attrition of high school students.

Torres was recently elected to the Council on Foreign Relations of New York. He also participates on the National Commission on International Migration and Economic Development, which recommends to Congress and the president the economic policies the United States should implement in Latin America.

✳ PROMINENT HISPANIC METROPOLITAN LEADERS

Henry G. Cisneros (1947-)

Former Mayor of San Antonio, Texas, Cisneros was born in a west-side Mexican barrio of San Antonio to a civil servant. He was educated in the city's parochial schools and attended Texas A&M University, where he received a B.A. degree and a master's degree in urban planning in 1970.

Ygnacio D. Garza, Mayor, Brownsville, Texas.

In 1971, Cisneros moved to Washington, D.C., where he worked for the National League of Cities and began full-time graduate studies in public administration at George Washington University. During 1971, at age 22, Cisneros became the youngest White House fellow in U.S. history. When his fellowship ended, he earned a second master's degree, in public administration, at Harvard University. He then went on to complete his work at George Washington University and received a Ph.D. degree in public administration. He then returned to San Antonio and taught government at the University of Texas.

Cisneros ran for the city council on the Good Government League ticket in 1975 and won. He gained a reputation as a bright, young politician, and in 1977 he was reelected in a landslide. In 1981, Cisneros ran for mayor of San Antonio, the ninth-largest city in the United States and won 62 percent of the vote. In 1983, he was reelected with 94 percent of the vote, again reelected in 1985 with 72 percent, and reelected in 1987 with twice as many votes as his closest opponent.

Cisneros did not thereafter seek reelection as mayor. Still popular in San Antonio, he is often mentioned as a possible candidate for the Texas governorship or the U.S. Senate.

Ygnacio D. Garza (1953 -)

Mayor of Brownsville, Texas, Ygnacio Garza, the son of U.S. Federal Court of Appeals Judge Reynaldo G. Garza, was elected mayor of the city of Brownsville in 1987 and served in that capacity until 1991. By law, the mayor of Brownsville is nonpartisan, and Garza is not affiliated with any political party. Brownsville's population is 85 percent Hispanic, and Garza believes that Hispanics are adequately represented in this border town: the mayor, all the city council members, and the majority of the school board members are Hispanic. However, Garza believes that the Hispanic population is not adequately represented nationally, and that the United States still has a long way to go in equalizing the balance of political power.

Ana Sol Gutiérrez (19-)

A member of the Montgomery County, Maryland, Board of Education and the first Hispanic to be elected to any office in Maryland history, Ana Gutiérrez was born in El Salvador in 1942. Her father, Jorge Sol Castellanos, was El Salvador's first finance minister. Her family moved to Montgomery County, Maryland, in 1945. She attended the University of Geneva in Switzerland and lived in South America briefly following graduation. She then returned to Maryland and became active in local politics.

In 1990, Gutierrez ran successfully for a seat on the Board of Education of Montgomery County, one of Maryland's most affluent counties. Gutierrez was named by U.S. Senator Barbara Mikulski (D-MD) to serve on the senator's Academic Review Board, which advises her on national and state educational issues. Many in the Hispanic community regard Gutierrez as someone to watch and a possible contender for a seat in the U.S. Congress.

Gloria Molina (1948-)

County supervisor of Los Angeles, Gloria Molina was born in Los Angeles on May 13, 1948 to Mexican parents who had immigrated to the United States the year before. She grew up and received her early education in the small town of Pico Rivera, California, and then attended East Los Angeles College. In 1967, an accident suffered by her father forced her to become the full-time provider for the family at age 19. Her job as a legal assistant did not prevent her from continuing her education, and she received a bachelor's degree from California State University in Los Angeles.

Taking a vigorous role in community affairs, Molina served on the board of United Way of Los Angeles and was active in the Latin American Law Enforcement Association. In 1973, she was the founding president of the Comision Femenil de Los Angeles and served as national president from 1974 to 1976. She is also a founding member of Hispanic American Democrats, the National Association of Latino Elected and Appointed Officials, and Centro de Ninos.

Molina was first elected to office in 1982 as state assemblywoman for the Fifty-sixth District of California. In 1987, she was elected to the Los Angeles City Council, on which she served as councilwoman of the First District until 1991. In 1991, she was elected to the Los Angeles County Board of Supervisors. Molina is the first Hispanic American in history elected to the California state legislature, the Los Angeles City Council, and the Los Angeles County Board of Supervisors.

Prior to being elected to public office, Molina served in the Carter White House as a deputy for presidential personnel. After leaving the White House, she served as deputy director for the U.S. Department of Health and Human Services in San Francisco. With a reputation for candor and independence, Molina is known for her strong, issue-oriented style and her commitment to community empowerment.

Gloria Molina, Los Angeles County Supervisor.

Federico Peña (1947-)

Former mayor of Denver, Colorado, Federico Peña was born in Laredo, Texas. Pena was raised in Brownsville, Texas, and received his early education there. He attended the University of Texas at Austin, where he received both an undergraduate degree and a law degree. Peña follows in a tradition of public service in his family. One of his great grandfathers served as mayor of Laredo during the Civil War and another was a member of that city's first school board. Peña's grandfather held the office of alderman in Laredo for almost a quarter of a century.

At age 36 Peña was elected Denver's thirty-seventh mayor in 1983 and was reelected to a second term in 1987. At the time he entered office, he was among the youngest chief executives in Denver history. Mayor Peña's efforts to strengthen Denver's economy have placed the city in the national spotlight. The U.S. Conference of Mayors recently selected Denver over one hundred other cities as the winner of its prestigious City Liveability Award.

Mayor Peña did not seek a third term as mayor in

Prior to the Civil War, Requena switched from the Democratic to the Republican party and openly supported the candidacy of Abraham Lincoln. At the time, Los Angeles was heavily Democratic and Requena did not win election to the city council again until 1864, when he was elected to a seventh term; subsequently he was reelected to an eighth term. During the 1860s, he continued his business interests, served on the school board, and founded an orphanage.

Louis E. Saavedra (1933-)

Mayor of Albuquerque, New Mexico, Louis Saavedra was born in Socorro, New Mexico. Saavedra's family has lived within thirty miles of Albuquerque since the 1600s. Saavedra received a B.A. degree and an M.A. degree from Eastern New Mexico University in Portales.

Saavedra is the former president of the Albuquerque Technical Vocational Institute, a community college with an enrollment of fifteen thousand. He has held high-ranking positions with the institute since 1965. Saavedra also served on the Albuquerque City Commission between 1967 and 1974. From 1973 to 1974, he was chairman of the city commission.

Federico Peña, Mayor, Denver. (Photo by Larry Lazlo)

1991. Still very popular in Denver, Pena has gone into private business.

Manuel Requena (1802-1876)

Mayor of Los Angeles in 1856, Manuel Requena was born and raised in Mexico and moved to Los Angeles in 1834. Active in the shipping business, he quickly became an important business and political figure.

Avoiding conflict when U.S. forces invaded California during the Mexican-American War, Requena was elected to the Los Angeles City Council in 1850 as a member of the Democratic party. He was reelected to four more terms, serving most of the time as president of the council. In 1852, he was elected to the first Los Angeles County Board of Supervisors. Losing his 1855 bid for reelection to the city council, he ran again in 1856 and was reelected to a sixth term, and was again elected president.

When the Los Angeles mayor resigned that year, Manuel Requena became mayor until an election was held eleven days later. He thus was briefly the only Mexican American to serve as mayor of Los Angeles during the American period.

Louis E. Saavedra, Mayor, Albuquerque.

In 1989, Louis Saavedra was elected mayor of Albuquerque, a post he still holds. Saavedra has been active in Latin American politics and has worked in eleven Latin American countries and seven countries in the West Indies.

Xavier L. Suárez (1949-)

Mayor of Miami, Florida, Xavier Suarez attended Villanova University, studying engineering, and graduated first in his class. Suárez went on to Harvard Law School and the John F. Kennedy School of Government at Harvard, where he obtained the joint degrees of J.D. and master of public policy in 1975. He also holds an honorary law degree from Villanova University School of Law. After graduation, Suárez moved to Miami and began to practice law with the firm of Shutts & Bowen.

In 1985, Suárez was elected mayor of Miami, and was reelected to second and third terms in 1987 and 1989. President Bush appointed Suárez to the board of directors of the Legal Services Corporation.

Suárez states that Hispanic American voters have made a significant impact on Miami politics, but remaining impediments are large electoral districts for county commission and school board elections.

Xavier L. Suárez, Mayor, Miami.

✸LEGAL AND POLITICAL ORGANIZATIONS

Selected Public Interest Law Organizations

Cuban-American Legal Defense and Education Fund

2119 South Webster Street
Fort Wayne, IN 46804
(219) 745-5421
Chairperson: Graciela Beecher.

The Cuban-American Legal Defense and Education Fund (CALDEF) was established in 1980 and is a national nonprofit organization funded by corporate and public contributions. CALDEF was created to assist Cuban Americans and other Hispanics in gaining equal treatment and equal opportunity in the fields of education, employment, housing, politics, and justice. CALDEF strives to end negative stereotyping of Hispanics and to educate the American public about the problems faced by Hispanics.

The Hispanic National Bar Association

One Farragut Square S.
1634 Eye Street, NW, Ste. 901
Washington D.C. 20006
(303)771-6200.

The Hispanic National Bar Association (HNBA) was originally established in 1972 as La Raza National Lawyers Association and is a professional association dedicated to the advancement of Hispanic Americans in the legal profession. Its membership includes Hispanic attorneys, judges, and law professors from around the United States. Members of the HNBA have joined together to open doors for Hispanic attorneys in the legal profession so that future lawyers may have greater opportunities. The HNBA also has been actively involved in providing testimony to congressional committees and national commissions, in litigation pertaining to issues of concern to the Hispanic community, and in advocacy regarding legislation and executive nominations.

In addition, the HNBA created a Law Student Division to unite Hispanics in law schools across the country. The Law Student Division has affiliate memberships from more than eighty-five law schools and individual membership has risen from forty to over three hundred.

Both the HNBA and the Law Student Division sponsor an annual convention open to all members. It has become a forum for Hispanics in the legal profession to discuss barriers openly and to propose solutions.

Legal Services Corporation

400 Virginia Avenue, SW
Washington D.C., 20024-2751
(202)863-1820.

The Legal Services Corporation Act created the Legal Services Corporation (LSC) in 1974. The LSC currently funds sixteen national support centers providing a variety of services that promote representation of the poor on issues of substantial complexity as well as thousands of local offices throughout the country that represent indigents in a wide variety of civil legal matters.

In 1989, the LSC funded representation in 232,198 cases involving Hispanic clients. That represents 16.88 percent of the total number of clients assisted by offices funded by the LSC.

Mexican American Legal Defense and Educational Fund

634 South Spring Street, Eleventh Floor
Los Angeles, CA 90014
(213) 629-2512
President: Antonia Hernández; Vice President for Legal Affairs: E. Richard Larson.

The Mexican-American Legal Defense and Educational Fund (MALDEF) was established in 1968, and over the past twenty years has been at the forefront of promoting and protecting the civil rights of Hispanic Americans throughout the United States. MALDEF recognized the need for removing barriers preventing Hispanic Americans from fully participating in American society. Those efforts have allowed the organization to work within the legal system to create beneficial solutions through class action litigation, community education, and leadership training.

With a national office in Los Angeles and regional offices in Chicago, San Antonio, San Francisco, and Washington, D.C., MALDEF concentrates on building awareness among Hispanic Americans regarding their heritage and issues affecting their lives. MALDEF's specific program areas are education, employment, political access, immigration, and leadership. MALDEF also administers the Law School Scholarship Program for Mexican-Americans.

Migrant Legal Action Program, Inc.

2001 S Street, NW
Washington, D.C. 20009
(202) 462-7744.
Chairperson: Gail McCarthy;
President: Roger C. Rosenthal

The Migrant Legal Action Program (MLAP) was established in 1970 to protect and further the rights and interests of migrant and seasonal farm workers, the poorest group of working people in America. MLAP is not a membership organization and is funded by the Legal Services Corporation (LSC). MLAP provides assistance to migrant legal services programs funded by LSC, as well as to basic LSC-funded field programs and private practitioners in their representation of eligible clients. There are about seventy migrant attorney field offices and many private attorneys and groups for which MLAP provides services. Such services include resource materials, policy development, litigation support, public education and training on farm worker housing, labor conditions, and education.

National Immigration Law Center (formerly, National Center for Immigrants'' Rights)

1636 West Eighth Street, Suite 215
Los Angeles, CA 90017
(213) 487-2531
Directing Attorney: Charles H. Wheeler; Senior Attorneys: Susan Drake, and Linton Joaquín.

The National Immigration Law Center (NILC) provides backup assistance to legal services programs and other nonprofit agencies on issues involving immigration law and aliens'' rights. NILC specializes in areas relating to visa processing, legalization, defenses to deportation, and aliens'' eligibility for public benefit programs. Other areas of litigation include constitutional challenges to actions of the Immigration and Naturalization Service (INS) and specific responses to INS unlawful conduct.

Puerto Rican Legal Defense and Education Fund

99 Hudson Street, Fourteenth Floor
New York, NY 10013
(212) 219-3360
President: Rubén Franco.

The Puerto Rican Legal Defense and Education Fund (PRLDEF) was established in 1972. It was created to protect and further the legal rights of Puerto Ricans and other Hispanics. PRLDEF is a nonprofit organization that challenges discrimination in housing, education, employment, health, and political participation. PRLDEF maintains a placement service for Hispanic lawyers and offers advice and financial assistance to Hispanics considering entering the legal field.

Other National Hispanic American Political Organizations

Democratic National Committee Hispanic Caucus
430 South Capitol Street, SE
Washington, DC 20003
(202) 863-8000

Hispanic Elected Local Officials Caucus
1301 Pennsylvania Avenue, NW
Washington, DC 20004
(202) 626-3180

Hispanic Political Action Committee
246 O'Connor Street
Providence, RI 02905
(401) 941-6831

League of United Latin American Citizens (LULAC)
400 First Street, NW
Washington, DC 20001
(202) 628-8516

Mexican-American Democrats of Texas (MAD)
302 Stokes Building
Austin, TX 78701
(512) 585-4509

Mexican-American Political Association (MAPA)
5613 Forty-second Street
Sacramento, CA 95824
(916) 429-9462

Mexican-American Women's National Association (MANA)
1201 Sixteenth Street, NW
Washington, DC 20036
(202) 822-7888

National Association of Cuban-American Women (NACAW)
2119 South Webster Street
Fort Wayne, IN 46804
(219) 745-5421

National Association of Latino Elected and Appointed Officials (NALEO)
708 G Street, SE
Washington, DC 20003
(202) 546-2536

National Conference of Puerto Rican Women (NACOPRW)
5 Thomas Circle, NW
Washington, DC 20005
(202) 387-4716

National Hispanic Democrats, Inc.
11011 Fourteenth Street, NW
Washington, DC 20005
(202) 371-1555

National Hispanic Leadership Conference (NHLC)
2590 Morgan Avenue
Corpus Christi, TX 78405
(512) 882-8284

National Latinas Caucus (NLC)
853 Broadway, Fifth Floor
New York, NY 10003
(212) 673-7320

National Puerto Rican Coalition, Inc. (NPRC)
1700 K Street, NW
Washington, DC 20006
(703) 223-3915

National Puerto Rican Forum, Inc.
31 East Thirty-second Street, Fourth Floor
New York, NY 10016
(212) 685-2311

Republican National Hispanic Assembly of the U.S. (RNHA)
440 First Street, NW
Washington, DC 20001
(202) 662-1355

Southwest Voter Registration Education Project
403 East Commerce Street
San Antonio, TX 78205
(512) 222-0224

Directory of State-Level Advocacy Programs

Arizona Association of Chicanos for Higher Education (AACHE)
P.O. Box 2426
Tempe, AZ 85285
(602) 423-6163

Cafe de California (Chicano Advocates for Employment)
1012 J Street, Second Floor
Sacramento, CA 95814
(916) 448-9016

Colorado Institute for Hispanic Education and Economic Development
1006 Eleventh Street
Box 220
Denver, CO 80204
(303) 556-4436

Comite Hispano de Virginia
6031 Leesburg Pike
Falls Church, VA 22041
(703) 671-5666

**Connecticut Association for United Spanish Action
(CAUSA)**
3580 Main Street
Hartford, CT 06120
(203) 549-4046

**District of Columbia Commission on Latino
Community Development (CLCD)**
1801 Belmont Road, NW
Washington, DC 20009
(202) 673-6772

Florida Commission on Hispanic Affairs
Office of the Governor
The Capitol
Tallahassee, FL 32399-0001
(904) 579-9000

Hispanic Women's Council of California
5803 East Beverly Boulevard
Los Angeles, CA 90022
(213) 725-1657

Iowa Spanish-Speaking Peoples Commission
Lucas State Office Building
Des Moines, IA 50319
(515) 281-4080

**Kansas Advisory Committee on Hispanic Affairs
(KACHA)**
1309 Southwest Topeka Boulevard
Topeka, KS 66612-1894
(913) 296-3465

Maryland Commission on Hispanic Affairs
311 West Saratoga Street, Room 254
Baltimore, MD 21201
(301) 333-2532

Spanish-Speaking Community of Maryland, Inc.
8519 Piney Branch Road
Silver Spring, MD 20901
(301) 587-7217

Michigan Commission on Spanish-speaking Affairs
Post Office Box 30026
Lansing, MI 48909
(517) 373-8339

Minnesota Spanish-Speaking Affairs Council
506 Rice Street
Saint Paul, MN 55103
(612) 296-9587

Nebraska Mexican-American Commission
Post Office Box 94965
Lincoln, NE 68509-4965
(402) 471-2791

Nevada Association of Latin Americans
323 North Maryland Parkway
Las Vegas, NV 89101-3134
(702) 382-6252

Nevada Hispanic Services, Inc.
190 East Liberty Street
Post Office Box 11735
Reno, NV 89501
(702) 786-6003

New Jersey Office of Hispanic Affairs
Department of Community Affairs
101 South Broad Street
Trenton, NJ 08625
(609) 984-3223

New Jersey Puerto Rican Congress
515 South Broad Street
Trenton, NJ 08611
(609) 989-8888

**New York State Governor's Office for Hispanic
Affairs**
2 World Trade Center, Suite 5777
New York, NY 10047
(212) 587-2266

Ohio Commission on Spanish-Speaking Affairs
77 South High Street, 18th Floor
Columbus, OH 43266
(614) 466-8333

Oregon Commission on Hispanic Affairs
695 Summer Street
NE, Salem, OR 97310
(503) 373-7397

Oregon Council for Hispanic Advancement (OCHA)
621 Southwest Morrison, Suite 729
Portland, OR 97205
(503) 228-4131

Pennsylvania Governor's Advisory Commission on Latino Affairs
Forum Building, Room 379-80
Harrisburg, PA 17120
(717) 783-3877

Texas Assn. of Mexican-American Chambers of Commerce (TAMACC)
2211 South IH-35, Suite 103
Austin, TX 78741
(512) 447-9821

Utah Governor's Office on Hispanic Affairs
Department of Community Development, Room 6234
Salt Lake City, UT 84114
(801) 538-3045

Washington Commission on Hispanic Affairs
1515 South Cherry Street
Olympia, WA 98504
(206) 753-3159

Wisconsin Governor's Council on Hispanic Affairs
819 North Sixth Street, Room 270
Milwaukee, WI 53203
(414) 227-4344

References

Alpert, Thomas M. "The Inherent Power of the Courts to Regulate the Practice of Law—An Historical Analysis." *Buffalo Law Review* 32 (1983): 525.

Aranda, Benjamin III. *Directory of Hispanic Judges of the United States*, Unpublished (1991).

Boswell, Richard A., with Gilbert P. Carrasco. *Immigration and Nationality Law*, 2d ed. Durham, N.C.: Carolina Academic Press, 1992.

Brunelli, Richard. "Study on the Task Force on Minorities in the Legal Profession of the American Bar Association." *Chicago Daily Law Bulletin* 132, no. 7 (November 1986): 1.

Camarillo, Albert. *Latinos in the United States*. Santa Barbara, Calif.: ABC-CLIO, 1986.

Davila, Lind E., "The Underrepresentation of Hispanic Attorneys in Corporate Law Firms," *Stanford Law Review* 39 (July 1987): 1403.

Fund for Modern Courts. *The Success of Women and Minorities in Achieving Judicial Office: The Selection Process*. New York: Fund for Modern Courts, 1985.

Garcia, Bernardo M. "The Hispanic Lawyer: Equal Access to the Legal Profession," Hispanic National Bar Association-Law Student Division HNBA-LSD *Legal Briefs*, 1, no. 3 (1991).

Kurzban, Ira J. *Immigration Law Sourcebook,* 2d ed. Washington, D.C.: American Immigration Law Foundation, 1991.

League of United Latin American Citizens. "Immigration in the United States from Latin America, Past and Present," Washington, D.C., 1, no. 4 (July 1986).

MacLachlen, Claudia, & Rita Henley Jensen. "Progress Glacial for Women, Minorities; But the Recession Hits White Male Associates the Hardest." *National Law Journal* (January 27, 1992).

Marquis. *Who Was Who in America*, Chicago, Ill.: The A.N. Marquis Company (1967).

Martinez, John. "Fighting Minority Underrepresentation in Law." Hispanic National Bar Association-Law Student Division HNBA-LSD Legal Briefs 1, no. 3 (1991).

Meier, Matt S. *Mexican-American Biographies*, Westport, Conn.: Greenwood Press (1988).

Oliveira, Annette. *MALDEF: Diez Anos*. San Francisco: Mexican-American Legal Defense and Educational Fund, 1978.

Pachon, Harry P. *1990 National Roster of Hispanic Elected Officials*. Washington, D.C: NALEO Educational Fund, 1990.

Powers, William B., and Susan A. Weimer. "Trends in Law School Enrollment." *Consultant's Digest* 1, no. 1 (May 1991).

Roberts, Maurice A., and Stephen Yale-Loehr. *Understanding the 1986 Immigration Law*. Washington, D.C.: Federal Publications, 1987.

Select Commission on Immigration and Refugee Policy. *U.S. Immigration Policy and the National Interest*. 1981.

Silas, Faye A. "Minority Judges: More Appointed Than Elected." *American Bar Association Journal* 72, (March 1986): 19.

Spears, Franklin S. "Selection of Appellate Judges." *Baylor Law Review* 40 (1988): 501.

Thernstrom, Abigail M. *Whose Votes Count?* Cambridge, Mass.: Harvard University Press, 1987.

U.S. Bureau of the Census, *Statistical Abstract of the United States: 1991*. 111th ed. Washington, D.C.: U.S. Government Printing Office, 1991.

Wagman, Robert. *World Almanac of U.S. Politics*. New York: Pharos Books, 1991.

West, *Almanac of the Federal Judiciary*. St. Paul, Minn.: West Publishing, 1991.

West, *Association of American Law Schools Directory of Law Teachers*. St. Paul, Minn.: West Publishing, 1991.

Gilbert Paul Carrasco

Education

The roots and patterns of contemporary Hispanic education can be found in the Spanish, Mexican, and Anglo conquests of North America. The original Spanish influence extended from the Carolinas and Florida on the East Coast, down through the Gulf Coast and on to the western part of the United States. By the end of the Spanish period in the early 1800s, the vast majority of Spanish subjects were concentrated in Indian-controlled lands of what we know today as the American Southwest: California, Arizona, New Mexico, and Texas. Informal rather than formal learning was the norm during the first three hundred years of Spanish rule.

Formal learning, or schooling as it is more commonly known in today's world, began to emerge during the nineteenth century to meet the increasing needs of the Hispanic population for literacy and socialization. A variety of public, parochial, and private secular schools were established during this period. The schools provided, however, were limited in many respects. They were segregated, assimilationist, nonacademic in orientation, and inferior to those provided for other children. No higher education facilities were provided for Hispanic children. In the early twentieth century and until 1965, public education became the dominant form of learning in the Hispanic community. Private forms of schooling existed, but the community, augmented by an influx of Puerto Ricans from the island, began to increasingly support public education over other types of schooling. Due to their subordinate status in the society where they were concentrated, Mexican Americans and Puerto Ricans were provided with segregated and inferior forms of public education.

During the contemporary period, from 1965 to the present, public education continues to be the domi-

Children during recess at the Guadalupe Aztlán alternative school in Houston 1981. (Photo by Curtis Dowell. Courtesy of the *Texas Catholic Herald*.)

nant form of schooling for the Hispanic population. As a result of various pressures, the schools have become more sensitive to the academic, cultural, and

287

linguistic needs of the Hispanic population during this period. However, the patterns of inequality have continued. Unequal access to unequal schools continues to characterize the schooling of Hispanics. Unlike the past, the Hispanic community is now more diverse and includes a significant number of immigrants from all areas of the Spanish-speaking world, including Mexico, Puerto Rico, the Caribbean, Central America, and the rest of Spanish America. This chapter documents the particular manner in which Hispanic education has evolved in the United States over the last five hundred years.

✳EDUCATION OF HISPANICS IN THE SPANISH PERIOD, 1540-1821

During the years from 1540 to 1821 education in Spain's far northern frontier was a function of the Crown, the church, and, to some extent, the settlers. As in most agricultural societies, education was broadly conceived as an informal aspect of institutional life and included at least three elements: knowledge, skills, and behaviors needed in making a living, in maintaining a household, and in satisfying personal wants. Education, however, was not conducted in schools. Schools were available in the far northern region of the Spanish regime but they were rare. The missions at times established schools, but only sporadically. The missions in California and especially in New Mexico made reference to formal instruction in them. There is no mention of schooling in any of the Texas missions. The primary reason given was that Texas Indians were more nomadic than those in other parts of the Southwest. Sedentary groups such as those found in New Mexico were easier to teach than nomadic ones. Schooling in the missions was for the benefit of the Indians. Basic literacy skills were taught in them. Schools outside the mission were rarely found. The sons and daughters of the Spanish settlers, including the military personnel, rarely received formal instruction on the frontier.

The diverse population that came to comprise the Hispanics, that is, the indigenous groups, the Spaniards, and the mestizoes or other racially mixed groups, acquired basic literacy skills and knowledge or behaviors necessary for adult life not from schools per se but from other institutions. Education was an informal process that occurred in the three major institutions established in the far northern frontier: the missions, the settlements, and the presidios. The primary purposes of these institutions were to conquer, civilize, and control the Indian population in this part of the Americas in order to exploit their resources for the benefit of Spain. These institutions,

however, served an educational purpose. This is especially the case with the missions. They provided informal instruction on political culture, moral, and religious values, and attitudes and skills needed for adult life in Spanish America.

Missions, presidios, and pueblos in the far northern frontiers were established decades after Spaniards in search of gold, glory, and new trade routes explored the area. Spaniards, for instance, explored Florida and the Atlantic coast from 1513 to the 1540s and both New Mexico and Arizona in the late 1530s. But after finding no gold or precious minerals, they left. Although Spain decided to withdraw from the area once it realized that there were no precious minerals to be found, the Jesuits and other religious orders stayed to convert the Indians. They made religious arguments for colonization, but their pleas went unheeded for nearly half a century.

Serious colonization of the far northern frontier began in the seventeenth century. These efforts were led by the missionaries who established a large number of missions to convert the Indians to Christianity, that is, to a Spanish way of life. The missions were initially financed by the state, but eventually became self-supporting. Most missionaries were scholarly and literate "men of high calibre" who wrote many historical tracts, scientific documents, ethnographically rich reports and translations of Indian languages. Unlike those in central Mexico, the missionaries in this far northern frontier, comprised of both Jesuit and Franciscans, requested the presence of soldiers in their colonization efforts. Fear for their lives because of hostile Indians provided the rationale for such actions. Some of the soldiers assigned to protect them, however, were a hindrance to their educational endeavors, since they mistreated the Indians.

Settlement efforts were first initiated in New Mexico during the 1590s. In 1595, a large force of missionaries, soldiers, and settlers set off to colonize New Mexico. The first permanent settlement was in 1598. However, by 1601 there was no missionary work done; it was mostly military. Missionary work and the construction of missions began in earnest between 1605 and 1608. By 1626, there were over twenty-five missions, forty-three churches, and more than thirty-six thousand new converts.

Between 1659 and 1665, the new civil governors established a reign of tyranny and alienated all groups in the far northern frontier. They also did irreparable harm to the missions. Eventually these actions led to the 1680 Pueblo revolt and to the killing of the missionaries. The area was reconquered by Spain between 1695 and 1698. Continuing conflict and tensions for the next decade, including a second rebellion involving at least fifteen pueblos, slowed down but did not stop the Franciscans from doing their missionary work. However, the success of the past was not equaled. By 1774, some success in conversion, mission and church establishment, and in teaching the practical arts and education was made. The missions continued to decline after 1775 owing to insufficient number of missionaries and to friction between missionaries and local Spanish officials.

Arizona was the second area settled by the Spanish government. As in New Mexico, the missionaries led the way. Because to Indian resistance, this area was not settled until the late 1600s, although it had been explored in the 1630s. By 1680, there were six Franciscan missions in northeast Arizona. After the Pueblo revolt of 1680, these missions were abandoned and never rebuilt. In the south, the Jesuits founded several missions in 1700. During the next sixty-seven years two missions and eleven visitas (substations) were founded. The Jesuits were expelled in 1767 and the missions were assigned to the Franciscans, but the hostility of Indians forced them to close five visitas. Two additional ones were established under them. Despite this activity, the missionaries were unable to establish more missions because of the Indian raids and the area's lack of strategic value. Few settlers went to Arizona. By the end of the colonial period, it contained a sparse Mexican population centered in the Santa Cruz Valley.

Defense against foreign powers rather than economic considerations was the major reason for settling California and Texas. Religious conversion, however, was still a primary goal of the missionaries. Successful missions were established in the El Paso region between 1659 and 1684. Missionaries explored east Texas in the 1670s but no missions were established until 1690, and then largely due to fears of French activity in that area. But Indian raids slowed the growth of a Spanish presence. For this reason missionary activity in Texas was more uneven and at times less successful than in New Mexico. By 1690, the missions were abandoned because of Indian resistance to missionary activity and agriculture. Some scholars have reported the founding of many more missions than originally suspected in other parts of the state. Sister Mary Stanislaus Van Well, in her *The Educational Aspects of the Missions of the Southwest* (1942), says as many as fifty of them were founded during the late 1600s and early 1700s. In San Antonio, more than five missions were founded. The first and longest-lasting one, San Antonio Mission, was founded in 1718.

Spain colonized California for defensive reasons, too, but missions came to dominate the life of the province. Fear of Russian traders in the north in 1769 encouraged Spanish authorities in Mexico to settle California. Between 1769 and 1823, for instance, twenty-one missions and a large number of presidios were constructed. Despite the large number of missions and the excellent climate, few individuals settled in California. Those who did settled in widely scattered pueblos throughout California. By 1821, the non-native population was located in pueblos scattered along the coast.

During this entire period, education occurred in the missions and in the pueblos. The mission community was considered a school of civilization. In a San Antonio mission founded in 1718, for instance, the missionaries taught Indian children and adults Catholic religious and moral instruction, adherence to Spanish custom and law, and training in agriculture and the domestic arts. All the Indians knew the Christian doctrine (prayers, beliefs, and so on) and spoke Spanish, and most played musical instruments or sang. They also dressed with "decency," assisted in making furniture, raised their own food, and went to school. The missionaries likewise taught the Indians family living, stock raising, European farming techniques, church construction, and furniture making.

Education also occurred in the Spanish settlements and to some extent in the presidios. As in most agricultural societies, the family and the community were the primary vehicles for teaching non-Indian youths in the pueblos and presidios the values and skills needed to survive. People also learned from other sources of nonformal education, including textbooks, folklore, oral history, drama, traveling puppet shows, and the Spanish mail service.

By the end of the Spanish period, several patterns of educational development were discernible. First, formal instruction was not an integral aspect of community development. If present, it was peripheral to other community institutions. Second, the primary goal of education in the mission was to assimilate, forcefully if need be. Education was for the purpose of teaching Indians the dominant political and religious values of Spanish culture. In the process of teaching Christianity and Spanish ways, the missionaries either showed contempt or else disregarded the population's native language and culture. Under the Spaniards, most of the indigenous institutions, including the educational traditions and native languages, were trampled and destroyed. The government's official policy toward language, for instance, called for the abolition of the native language in instruction and the sole use of Spanish in religious conversion. In 1793, King Carlos IV decreed that schools in the American empire should replace the Indian languages with Castilian. This did not occur because of the special linguistic circumstances faced by the missionaries. Third, the informal curriculum that was provided, especially in the mission, emphasized vocational or industrial education at the expense of academic instruction. Fourth, there was disagreement among the missionaries over the role that the native language would play in Christianization. Most of the Franciscans, for instance, strongly believed in Spanish and failed to learn the native languages of the Indians. The Jesuits, on the other hand, were supportive of native languages in conversion. They used Spanish whenever possible and learned the languages of those whom they sought to convert. But, the Jesuits, for the most part, were not in support of native language maintenance. They, similarly to the Spanish Crown, believed that Spanish should replace the Indian languages. The use of the Indians'' native language in instruction was a temporary measure aimed at more easily assimilating them into Spanish culture. Fifth, a distinct pattern of community distrust of educators and educational institutions emerged during this period. Owing to the foreign teachings and the mistreatment by soldiers and some missionaries, the Indian community began to distrust Spanish institutions and leaders. In New Mexico, especially, missionaries destroyed native religious objects, built the church away from the Indian community, utilized soldiers to ensure compliance with their rules, and imposed harsh discipline on Indians for failing to adhere to Spanish religious and work practices. These teachings and mistreatment were for the most part rejected or resisted by the native populations. These incipient patterns of educational development in the Spanish period were modified and eventually strengthened in the decades to come, especially with the emergence of schooling as an important socialization agency in the nineteenth and twentieth centuries.

✳EDUCATION OF HISPANICS IN THE MEXICAN PERIOD, 1821-1848

During the latter part of the eighteenth and early nineteenth centuries, the family and the parish church replaced the missions as the key educational institutions in the northern provinces. The focus and objectives of instruction also shifted from teaching Indians to teaching non-Indian children, from propagating Spanish political, economic, and cultural values to preserving them, and from teaching religious values to teaching basic literacy skills. The decline in the number of missionaries and in the Indian population, as well as the increase in the non-Indian population (for instance, it nearly trebled in New Mexico from 1750 to 1800), led to increasing pressure to better serve the spiritual needs of the colonists who were concentrated in certain parts of the northern frontier. This period also led to the emergence of schools as important frontier institutions.

The Decline, Collapse, and Weakening of Frontier Institutions

The missions and pueblos began to decline in significance in the late eighteenth century. Their complete collapse occurred under independent Mexico. The lack of federal funds, the shortage of priests, ideological opposition to missions, and various local conditions led to their eventual decline.

The order to secularize the missions led to their eventual demise. This order, issued originally in 1813 but resurrected in 1821 once Mexico gained its independence, was based on the notion that all men, including Indians, were equal before the law. These sentiments were embodied in the government's Plan of Iguala in 1821. It called for the elimination of all distinctions on the basis of race or class. The missions were antiquated institutions that oppressed Indians and had to be eliminated. The missions also aided the church in amassing immense wealth and property and in maintaining its influence in secular affairs. The need to undercut the church's power, both economic and political, thus served as a rationale for secularization.

Within a decade and a half after Mexico declared its independence, the missions of the far northern provinces fell to pieces. After secularization, Indians deserted the missions, the buildings began to decay, the fields lay bare, and the Franciscans disappeared from sight. With secularization, the colonizers became parishioners. This led to the emergence of the Catholic parish church as one of the most significant institutions involved in educating the population, composed now primarily of mestizo settlers.

The secularization of the missions brought an end to the influence of missionaries on the frontier and to the weakening of the Catholic church. The church remained strong in central Mexico, but weak in the frontier during the period of Mexican independence. It failed to fill the void created by the dismantling of the missions and the departing of the Franciscans for several reasons. First, its leadership decreased due to the expulsion of all Spaniards from Mexico during the 1830s. Second, there was a shortage of priests and funds. Mexico did not train its own priests and the Vatican forbade sending any new ones to Mexico. The church also abolished all tithes and service fees, for example for marriages, births, and deaths. The major result of the church's weakened leadership and lack of funds or priests was the neglect of the spiritual welfare of the mestizos and the decline in the morale and morality of frontier clerics.

In addition to the church's collapse, the military supremacy over the frontier also slipped away. In many areas of the frontier, the decades following independence saw relations worsen with the Indians, who rejected Christianity and much of Hispanic culture. The Indians increased their attacks on Mexican settlements for various reasons. According to David J. Weber, in *The Mexican Frontier, 1821-1846* (1982), missionaries had forcibly recruited Indian neophytes for missions or for slavery and settlers sought their land after secularization in 1830. But most important, Indian resistance to the Spanish/Mexican presence increased due to the influx of Anglos who upset the balance of power in the frontier, while the Mexican government failed to strengthen its military and economic posture. Anglo traders as well as some Mexican ones, in some cases, provided firepower to Indians in return for stolen goods and encouraged them to attack Mexican settlements and missions. Firepower upset the balance of power on the frontier. Anglo settlers also pushed Indians out of traditional areas in their westward expansion, especially in Texas.

The new resistance by Indians led to discussions of how best to deal with them. Mexicans for the most part were in disagreement whether Indians should be assimilated and provided with gifts to maintain the peace or whether they should be annihilated or removed, as in the United States. The former view prevailed, although it was perceived to be a failure.

The decline of these frontier institutions led to a disruption in the education of the population in the northern provinces. Other frontier institutions, especially the family, the Catholic parish church, and the state-sponsored public schools, began to replace the missions as key educational institutions. The emergence of these institutions accompanied the secularization of the missions and the growth of ranches and pueblos in the far northern provinces.

The Emergence of New Frontier Institutions and the Education of Hispanics in the Early Eighteenth Century

Ranches and pueblos emerged in California during the period of Spanish control. In addition to land provided for the establishment of the missions, the Spanish government also allotted land to private individuals. Independent Mexico confirmed these grants and distributed many more. The numbered ranches increased after the secularization of the missions in 1834. Similar to the missions, the ranches provided most of the daily needs of their owners and workers. They raised sheep and hogs and cultivated grapes, fruit, wheat, and other grains.

Towns also were established during the Spanish period, but did not expand until the latter part of the 1700s, when Indian raids were halted and local economies began to expand. Pueblo life revolved around the plaza, a parklike square that formed the center of town. On one side of the plaza stood the church. Opposite the church was the town government building, known as the *cabildo*, and on the remaining two sides local ranchers built their town houses on lots referred to as *solares*.

In both the ranch and pueblo the extended family pattern was the norm. A typical household included parents, children, grandchildren, in-laws, other relatives, occasionally orphans, and Indian servants all living together. The children learned obedience, respect, political values, religious beliefs, and cultural traditions. The families in the ranches likewise taught routine household tasks such as cooking, washing, and the making of candles, soap, cloth, and wine. They also taught the planting of crops, the raising of cattle and sheep, and the making of clothing and other goods needed for survival on these ranches.

The church was another important institution that taught the knowledge, skills, and attitudes necessary for Christian living in these areas. It served an educational function through such activities as mass, religious rituals, weddings, christenings, wakes, and celebrations of town saints. The education of Indians decreased but learning among non-Indians increased.

In addition to the informal education provided by the church and the family residing in the ranches and pueblos, the state, especially in the form of the federal and provincial governments, began to express an interest in the formal instruction of the population. The declining influence of the church, as well as pressure from the settlers, encouraged the federal government late in the colonial period and in the Mexican era to support the establishment of public schools.

The Emergence of Schooling in the Far Northern Provinces

The initial interest for public education was expressed by the King of Spain in 1793 when he mandated the establishment of public schools in the colonies. High illiteracy among soldiers prompted the king to pass this mandate. However, nothing concrete was done to promote schooling in the far northern provinces until the early part of the 1800s. In 1802, for instance, Governor Juan Bautista Elguezábal of Texas issued a compulsory school attendance law for children up to age 12. This law however could not be enforced. As a result, no new schools were produced and existing ones were eradicated. Social and economic factors, compounded by political unrest, during these years ended the period of Spanish rule without a semblance of an educational system.

In California, two governors—Governor Diego de Borica and Pablo Vicente de Solá—promoted schooling in the latter part of the Spanish period. During Governor Borica's administration, from 1794 to 1800, approximately ten schools in five different cities were established. Under Governor Solá's administration, from 1815 to 1822, nine schools in two different cities were established. These schools, however, did not last long and had a negligible effect on the population. Public officials were unsuccessful in establishing a viable public school system in California during the Spanish period for many reasons, including the lack of public education tradition among the settlers, the isolation and sparseness of the population, general indifference, financial problems, shortage of funds, poor quality of teachers, external threats from foreign powers and rivalries, and internal bickering among state and local officials. No publicly sponsored schools were established in New Mexico during this same period.

Government leaders continued to support the establishment of public schools after Mexican independence. In Texas, for instance, state officials prodded local authorities and provided them with some financial assistance for the establishment of schools. In 1827, the state of Coahuila-Texas formulated a state constitution that required all municipalities to establish primary schools. Between 1828 and 1833, state officials issued several decrees attempting to encourage local authorities, usually known as *ayuntamientos*, to establish schools. Local officials, however, faced many obstacles in establishing schools, including individual and municipal poverty, lack of qualified teachers and lack of commitment to the importance of education among "ordinary" folks. In 1833, the state issued land grants for the support of local schools, but political unrest in central Mexico once again ended all efforts at establishing public schools. As in prior years, then a variety of social, political, and economic factors deflected government interest in formal education and prevented officials from establishing public schools.

In New Mexico, government officials were temporarily successful in establishing schools during the Mexican period. Between 1825 and 1827, for instance, eighteen schools were established in New Mexico. Efforts by Mexican government officials to establish more schools were thwarted by indifference, political turmoil, and poverty.

Government officials were not the only ones interested in the establishment of schools in the far northern provinces of the Mexican nation. There was also a fluctuating interest in schooling on the part of religious leaders and private individuals. Anglo settlers in Texas, for instance, established some private schools. These private schools started by American settlers in Texas during the Mexican period fared better than public ones.

Formal education for the most part was not an important component of learning for the majority of the population during the latter part of the eighteenth and the first half of the nineteenth centuries. It nevertheless assumed an increasingly important part in the lives of Hispanics and other school children with the coming of Anglos and American rule after 1848.

✸EDUCATION OF HISPANICS: THE AMERICAN PERIOD IN THE NINETEENTH CENTURY, 1850-1900

During the first half-century of American rule in the "Southwest," Hispanic traditions and institutions were trampled upon, modified to meet new needs, or gradually replaced by American ones. After the signing of the Treaty of Guadalupe Hidalgo in 1848, Americans introduced new political, economic, cultural, and social institutions and organized the society on the basis of certain Protestant, capitalist, republican, gender, and racial ideals. They sought to create a world in their own image, but encountered passive or active resistance by significant numbers of Hispanics. A few wealthy Hispanics initially supported these efforts, but by the turn of the century they had been dispossessed of their fortunes, had been relegated to wage earners in seasonal or low-paying jobs, and had lost any semblance of political influence and social status. Many of the Hispanic elite then joined the majority of the population as members of a cheap labor force, a politically powerless group, and the victims of social and cultural discrimination.

The family during this period continued to be the central agency for educating Hispanic children. The family assumed greater importance in many respects because of the rapid changes occurring in the society, for example, immigration and the transformation of the pueblos into barrios, the Americanization of the Catholic church, the emergence of Protestantism in the Southwest, and the decline of the ranches and the emergence of farming in the rural areas. Of primary importance to Hispanic education was the emergence of the institution of schooling. Schools were established during this period by private individuals, the Catholic church, Protestant groups, and public officials to meet the increasing needs of developing an American social order.

By the middle of the 1800s, schools had undergone

a significant transition from transmitter of basic literacy skills to the agency of socialization. This change was due to the desires of one group to assert control over others and to improve the lives of those viewed as racially or culturally inferior. The changed mission of the school touched off a debate between Hispanics and school-based reformers over who would decide the education of these children and what role would be assigned to the native languages and cultures.

Reformers believed that the school was to shape desirable behaviors for functioning in American society. More specifically, its purpose was to promote uniformity and eliminate all differences, including regional, class, and ethnic. Hispanics disagreed with this view and argued that the role of the schools was to teach these youngsters, but not at the expense of their cultural identity. Hispanics generally opposed school reforms if they were aimed at the elimination of their cultural and linguistic heritage.

During the first half-century of American rule, then, schools became increasingly important to Hispanics, but unlike in earlier decades, they were not viewed as supplementary to education or as part of community life. For most Hispanics, the schools became alien institutions aimed at controlling them. This was especially the case with public forms of schooling, which were vehement in their insistence on cultural assimilation. In many respects, the school became the setting for a struggle for the loyalties of the next generation as reflected in important controversies, such as English-language school laws and sectarian influences in public schools.

Schools established by individuals from the community and by the Catholic church were very much a part of Hispanic culture and continued in the United States after 1848. The number of Catholic schools expanded significantly during the second half of the nineteenth century. Ironically, increased Catholic education among Hispanics came to be associated with cultural tolerance at a time in which the Catholic church was undergoing its own transformation and becoming an instrument of Americanization. This apparent association of an Americanizing Catholic church with cultural toleration was due to the large number of Spanish-speaking parishioners and the willingness by individual priests, nuns, and religious orders to accommodate to these differences. Demography and individual initiative rather than policy were the driving forces behind this apparent contradiction in church behavior. It is important to note that the Catholic church did not specifically create schools for Hispanic children. It founded schools that turned out to be attended primarily by Hispanics. Quite often it was residential segregation, not policy, that accounted for the development of "Hispanic" Catholic schools throughout the Southwest.

Reasons for the transformation of the Catholic church and for the expansion of its school system were varied. The emergence of secular institutions, especially public school systems, the growing educational needs of an increasing Catholic population, the anti-Catholic sentiments prevalent during the second quarter of the nineteenth century, and the proselytizing efforts made by various Protestant denominations acted as catalysts for the extension of Catholic parochial schooling in the Southwest. In response to these various forces, the Catholic church encouraged ecclesiastical authorities to promote the construction of additional parishes and schools by which an American Catholicism could be propagated.

Catholic education for Mexican children developed at uneven rates in the different states of the Southwest. In New Mexico, four religious orders came to dominate Catholic schooling during the period from 1851 to 1874: the Sisters of Loretto, the Christian Brothers, the Sisters of Charity, and the Jesuits. The Sisters of Loretto first came to the New Mexico territory in 1853. The Christian Brothers came from France to New Mexico in 1859. The other two religious orders, the Sisters of Charity and the Jesuits, arrived in New Mexico in 1865 and 1870, respectively. Together they established between fifteen and twenty schools in as many cities.

In California, beginning in 1854 and continuing into 1889, ecclesiastical authorities encouraged the construction of additional parishes and schools by which an American Catholicism could be propagated. In order to staff these new parochial schools, at least nine religious orders were recruited. They established parochial schools for Catholic children in Santa Barbara, Ventura, Los Angeles, and throughout other parts of the state where the majority of the Mexican population was concentrated.

In Texas, religious orders also were requested to assist in the establishment of parochial schools. In some cases, Catholic parishes initially established these schools with the support of their parishioners. Carlos E. Castañeda, in his massive study of the Catholic heritage in Texas, identified more than twenty important religious orders that came to this state to establish missions, convents, and schools during the second half of the nineteenth century. The Catholic church, with the assistance of these religious orders, established some of the more well-known Catholic parochial schools attended by Mexican children in cities such as El Paso, Brownsville, Corpus Christi, and San Antonio.

Protestant denominations also established schools for Hispanic children during the first half-century of American rule. Unlike the Catholic church, Protestant denomination acknowledged the presence of racially and ethnically distinct Hispanic children and took specific actions to encourage the establishment of schools for them.

Protestant schools varied tremendously within regions and across time, but they shared the common goals of Christianization and Americanization. The primary purpose of their elementary schools was, in the words of Melinda Rankin (1881), a prominent lay missionary of the 1850s, to "give them the Gospel, which is the antidote for all moral evils." In addition to these goals, the Protestant schools also promoted community leadership development. This task was assigned to the secondary schools established throughout the Southwest. One of the major goals of these schools was to train a Spanish-speaking Christian leadership that would propagate the Protestant faith and American ideals in their own communities. For this reason, some Protestant schools allowed for the use of the Spanish-language and Mexican cultural instruction in them. However, cultural and language diversity were viewed as means to an end, that is, as instruments for the more effective evangelization of the Mexican-American population. Despite this end, ethnicity in education became one of the major distinguishing characteristics of Protestant secondary schooling.

The Protestants have a long history of involvement with Spanish-speaking individuals in the Southwest. In the New Mexico territory, for instance, Protestant groups, including Presbyterians, Congregationalists, Baptists, and Methodists, all sponsored ambitious evangelization and educational programs during the second half of the nineteenth century. Presbyterian ministers began to conduct missionary work and organize schools in their missions in various cities as early as 1860. But they were unsuccessful in these early efforts because of lack of funds and support among the population. Despite these early setbacks, Presbyterian and other Protestant missionaries continued to evangelize and to establish schools. During the entire territorial period, from 1850 to 1912, they succeeded in establishing five major boarding schools and more than forty mission day schools. The latter were commonly known as plaza schools. Most of this growth was spurred by favorable church policies and financial assistance from national lay and religious organizations, as well as by the determination of individual missionaries. Catholic opposition to Protestant schools, as well as Mexican-American distrust of non-Catholic missionaries, acted as barriers to the establishment and growth of some of these schools.

While the Presbyterians were the most active Protestant sect, important educational institutions were also founded by other denominations. The Baptists, for instance, preceded the Presbyterians and began to establish churches and schools as early as 1849. Several efforts were made to establish Baptist schools in Santa Fe during the 1850s and early 1860s. Other New Mexico Baptist schools operated briefly at Alcalde (1851), Albuquerque (1851, 1855), Peralta (1852), Cubero (1854), and Socorro (1857). Since few Anglos were located in the New Mexico territory, one can assume that all of these schools were for the conversion of Mexican children to Protestantism. These schools were vigorously opposed by the Catholic clergy and rapidly were forced to close their doors because of the lack of students.

The Congregationalists in 1880 started several rural schools and academies. According to Jerry L. Williams, in *New Mexico in Maps* (1986), the Congregationalists opened more than a dozen schools between 1878 and 1891. Four of these were still in operation by 1911. The Methodists also conducted missionary work and educational development in New Mexico. They worked in New Mexico in the late 1840s and even established two mission schools in 1854. But these were not permanent ventures. In total, the Methodists opened approximately eleven schools during the second half of the nineteenth century. Three of them were still in operation by 1911.

In Texas, the Presbyterians dominated, but occasionally a group such as the Methodists established lasting schools. During the period from 1845 to the early decades of the twentieth century, individual Protestant missionaries led the way in providing educational opportunities for native Mexican children. Of primary importance were the Presbyterians. In total, individual missionaries sponsored by Presbyterians established seven major schools.

The Methodists also conducted "Spanish work" in Texas. Their major achievements were in the area of church development. Between 1874 and 1884, for instance, they organized four Mexican-American districts in west Texas. To complement their ministry to Mexican Americans, the Methodists established several schools. Three major educational institutions for Mexican children were founded between 1880 and 1914: the Holding Institute, the Lydia Patterson Institute for Boys, and the Effie Eddington School for Girls. The former was founded in Laredo in 1880. The latter two were founded in El Paso in 1914. In addition, there was also a school called the Anglo-Mexican Mission Institute founded in El Paso in 1907. This school was built by the Baptists in the heart of "Mexican El Paso."

Probably owing to the presence of public schools at an early period and to the dominance of the Catholic church, few Protestant groups other than the Methodists established schools in California during the nineteenth century. The Methodists were the most prominent group in this state. They did not begin to minister to Spanish-speaking Catholics until 1879. In this year the Southern California Conference of the Methodist Episcopal Church appointed a committee to investigate the possibility of starting "Spanish work." This work began in Los Angeles in 1880 and had spread by 1900 to include missions in all three of the conference's districts. During this period of growth, the Methodist church established the Forsythe Presbyterian Memorial School in 1884. Several years later, in 1900, the Francis de Pauw Methodist School for Mexican Girls was founded. Eleven years later, The Spanish American Institute for Boys was founded by the Presbyterians.

Public officials began to establish schools in the second half of the nineteenth century. Unlike the religious groups or private individuals, public officials sought to develop a public school system that would eventually enroll all children residing in each state. Racial discrimination, ideological differences, and political tensions based on conflicts of heterogeneous values and differential power relations, however, affected the development of Hispanic public education so much that by the end of the nineteenth century several distinct patterns had emerged. By 1900, Hispanic education was characterized by the following patterns: (1) denial of equal access to public schools, (2) the establishment of segregated facilities, (3) an absence of Hispanic individuals in decision-making positions, and (4) an assimilationist goal aimed at replacing Hispanic socioeconomic, political, moral, cultural, and linguistic ideologies with Anglo ones.

Denial of Equal Access to Public Schools

Local educators for the most part did not provide Mexican children with access to public school facilities until the post-Civil War period and usually years or decades after schools for white children had been established. During the period from 1836 to the late 1860s, they established a system of public education for the school-age population, but limited it only to white or Anglo students. Increasing financial ability and willingness, new state mandates, and local demands for education led to the establishment of public school facilities for the population. Political pressures from powerful economic interests and biased Anglo parents, local official indifference, and racial discrimination served to deny Hispanics full access to the emerging public school system. Some local communities, such as those in Santa Barbara and Los Angeles, California, did provide public school facilities for Hispanics during the 1850s and 1860s. But whenever enrollment occurred it was on Anglo terms. That is, access was based on the understanding that the Hispanic children's language and culture would be excluded from the schools.

Various means were used to deny Hispanics equal access to public schooling during these early years. Local officials either built public schools in Anglo communities and away from the Hispanic community or else allowed only members of the elite to enroll in the schools that were established. Once large numbers of working-class Hispanics were present and both the commitment and the resources were available, local officials began to provide Hispanics with their own school facilities.

The variety of conditions thus led to differential rates of public school access by Hispanics living in different parts of the Southwest. In California, Hispanics were allowed access to the public schools in the 1850s. Schools for Mexican children in Arizona were established in 1872, ten years after it became a territory. In Texas, public schools for Hispanic children in the urban areas were provided in the 1860s; rural school children were provided access to the schools in the 1880s. New Mexico officials failed to provide any significant access to public education until after 1872. The lack of finances, legal authority, and controversies over the issues of language, religion, and politics slowed educational developments in that territory.

Segregation

Although Hispanics were provided with increased access to public schools, the facilities provided in most cases were segregated owing to a combination of both race and residence. In most areas, residence played a large role in the establishment of segregated facilities. But in some districts race became a determining factor in the establishment of segregated schools for Mexican children. These segregated facilities were expanded over the years as the number of Hispanic children in the districts increased. Local officials expanded segregation through the use of containment and dispersal policies. In many cases, local officials prohibited the growing numbers of Hispanic children from enrolling in non-Mexican schools and kept assigning them to segregated facilities. If more Hispanic children enrolled, they usually added rooms to the existing school or purchased portables. Anglos on the other hand were provided with a greater number of school facilities that were dispersed throughout the local districts.

Absence of Hispanics in Decision-Making Positions

During the early years of American rule, Hispanics, especially members of the elite, were allowed to participate in the development of public education policy and in the establishment and operation of these schools. These individuals ran for political office and assumed important decision-making positions at various levels of government, including state or territorial legislatures, county boards of education, and local city councils and boards of education. In California, for instance, nine Hispanics were elected to the state senate and twelve to the state assembly during the years from 1849 to 1864. In the New Mexico territory, Hispanics were more fortunate, due to their numerical superiority and to the presence of a social and economic elite that was granted some political power. From 1850 to 1912, 177 Hispanics served in the territorial council and 531 served in the territorial house of representatives. Hispanics in the New Mexico territory also held other important legislative positions. Several of them were elected to the presidency of the upper chamber and nine were chosen to be Speaker of the House.

During the territorial period, from 1850 to 1912, Mexican Americans likewise assumed a few positions in the other branches of state government as well as in the federal government. Two Hispanics served as governor of the territory, one in the beginning of American rule and the other one at the turn of the century. Only one individual, Antonio José Otero, sat on the supreme court during the period from 1850 to 1912. Eleven of the eighteen individuals who were elected territorial delegates to the United States Congress from 1851 to 1908 were Hispanics, including José M. Gallegos, Mariano A. Otero, Francisco Perea, J. Francisco Chávez, Mariano S. Otero, Tranquilino Luna, F. A. Manzanares, Antonio Joseph, and Pedro Perea.

Hispanics for a short period of time during the 1850s and 1860s also occupied on occasion a few important regional decision-making positions, including those of county superintendent and positions on county school boards and local boards of education. In California, for instance, approximately 6 out of 293 county superintendents serving between 1852 and 1865 were Hispanics. In New Mexico, the native Mexican population in the early decades of American rule made up a significant proportion of those elected to the office of county superintendent and county school boards. For example, in the 1873-74 school year, Mexican Americans comprised slightly over 75

percent of the total number of county superintendents in the territory. Out of 13 county superintendents, 10 of these then were Hispanics.

By the latter part of the nineteenth century, however, Hispanics were relatively absent from the schools. Their involvement, for all intents and purposes, ceased to exist largely due to the relative increase of Anglo immigration, racial gerrymandering, vote-diluting policies and practices, structural changes in institutional life, and changing school policies and practices on governance and hiring. California legislators, for example, established citizenship and residency requirements for voting, used English-only ballots and voting procedures, and constantly changed registration procedures. They also enacted English literacy requirements for voting and holding office in the 1870s. This culminated in a constitutional amendment making English the official language of the state in 1890. Texas legislators voted to charge a poll tax for voting in the state beginning in the 1840s. They also established citizenship and literacy requirements for participation in the governmental process. Other forces, including the declining status of the Mexican population, the increasing proportions of non-Chicano immigrants to the areas, poverty, nonfamiliarity with the English language, and the legacy of distrust, acted to discourage any further participation and contributed to the decline of Mexican-American officeholders.

The actions taken by school officials also played an important role in the decline in leadership positions by Hispanics. Local and state officials, for the most part, made no serious efforts to encourage the continuation of Hispanic participation in the shaping of public educational structures, policies, or practices. They did little to encourage the election, selection, or hiring of Hispanics to important positions of authority in the school structure. With one minor exception at the turn of the century, no Hispanics, for instance, were appointed to important statewide positions in education. Few if any Hispanics were hired to be administrators or teachers in the public schools during this period. In the case of New Mexico, where Hispanics played important roles in local and county government, their numbers decreased appreciably over time so that by 1912, when the territory became a state, the vast majority of the teachers, administrators, and school board members were Anglos. This was true even in areas that were predominantly Hispanic.

The decreasing political influence and voting power of Hispanics in general made it nearly impossible for them to elect their own members to important state positions, such as those of the superintendency or the board of education. No Hispanic, for instance, was elected to a state superintendent position during the second half of the nineteenth century in any of the southwestern states or territories. With the exception of New Mexico, no Hispanics served in the state boards of education either.

Assimilationism and School Content

The schools provided for Hispanics became rigidly assimilationist over the years and highly intolerant of cultural differences. They inculcated the dominant political, social, and moral ideologies through the use of English; they also devalued and excluded the Hispanic heritage from the curriculum. Between 1848 and 1900, three key aspects of Hispanic heritage were excluded from the schools—the Catholic heritage, the Hispanic cultural traditions, and the Spanish language.

Public policy toward Hispanic education was based on a developing and strengthening notion of the American national cultural identity that evaluated the religious, cultural, and linguistic heritage of Hispanics and rejected it from the schools. In its place, educators and political authorities proposed an "essentially American" identity that was comprised of Pan-Protestantism, republican values, and core British values, especially the ability to speak English. The schools were to embody and reproduce these ideological notions of American culture. Alternative forms of cultural identity, especially those based on Catholicism, non-English languages, Mexican cultural traditions, and racially distinct individuals who embraced these cultural traits, were to be replaced with American ideals, traditions, and individuals. Political leaders thus developed educational policies that promoted and transmitted the essential elements of an American cultural identity to the multitude of culturally diverse children, including Hispanics.

These assimilationist ideals, nevertheless, were internally inconsistent and at times in conflict with each other. Various groups of political authorities and educators in the Southwest supported different strands of these ideals with varying intensities. In the early decades of American rule, most Anglo rulers in the Southwest supported cultural pluralist policies and practices, primarily out of political expediency. But toward the latter part of the nineteenth century, officials began to support more assimilationist policies in the schools and to devalue cultural diversity in education. The stated purpose of these assimilationist policies was to facilitate the entry and success of Mexican immigrant children into mainstream society. However, the underlying reason was to structurally exclude them from participating in the society and to reproduce the dominant cultural ideology.

The process of cultural intolerance in the schools is reflected in the history of Catholic exclusion from the schools in the New Mexico territory and other areas, of cultural exclusion in the textbooks, and of school language policies in the Southwest.

School Language Policies

School officials at the state level at first tolerated Spanish in the schools, as stated above, primarily out of political expediency. During the early years of American rule, political leaders enacted educational policies in the Southwest that were tolerant of language differences and accepted Spanish as an appropriate medium for conducting public affairs. For example, Texas legislators in the late 1830s tolerated Spanish and encouraged the printing of the republic's laws in that language. In California, legislators included in the 1849 constitution a provision requiring that all laws be printed both in English and Spanish. Prominent school leaders such as State Superintendent of Public Instruction John G. Marvin and San Francisco educator John Pelton also supported the teaching of Spanish and other modern languages in the public schools. Los Angeles city officials, as early as 1851, enacted a school ordinance supportive of bilingualism. It provided that "all the rudiments of the English and Spanish languages should be taught" in all the schools subsidized by public funds. In the Colorado territory, a school law of 1867 mandated the establishment of bilingual schools with at least twenty-five non-English-language children present.

The language policies developed during this early period of American rule were, in the words of H. Kloss in his *The Bilingual Tradition*, (1977, 25), "designed to serve certain ends of the government rather than the concerns of the minority." The use of Spanish in the conduct of local government agencies ensured their operation during a period in which many individuals lacked knowledge of English. It was in the interests of the state itself therefore to accommodate the first generation of non-English-speakers with respect to the language of public affairs. Publicly sponsored bilingualism also served to facilitate and accelerate the assimilation of culturally distinct groups.

The basis of this initial accommodation was power. Expediency-based language policies were based on the political balance of power between Anglos and Mexican Americans. Once Anglos consolidated their political control of state institutions, educational authorities began to enact subtractive school language policies (that is, policies that strengthened the use of English while weakening the use of Spanish). The primary purpose of these policies was to reproduce the dominant ideological and cultural order in the schools, not, as Arnold Leibowitz in his *Educational Policy and Political Acceptance* (1971) has argued, to deny Mexican children access to them or to their content. School language policies sought to reproduce the dominant cultural order by promoting English and simultaneously eliminating the use of Spanish in the schools. By the end of the century, nearly all the southwestern states that had at one time provided for the use of Spanish in public institutions, such as schools, had effectively converted to using English only. At the turn of the century, only New Mexico still formally recognized Spanish as a medium of communication in the schools and in other public institutions.

But within a decade after assuming political control of state institutions, educational authorities began to develop policies and practices that were subtractive. The policies strengthened the use of English by at first prescribing, then mandating it. They weakened Spanish by neglecting to use it in public life or by prohibiting its use in public and private institutions.

The establishment of subtractive policies and the shift to English in the Southwest began as early as 1841, when the Texas legislature adopted a resolution that suspended the printing of the laws in the Spanish language, and continued into the 1920s. During this period, policymakers eliminated Spanish-language use in the courts, the legislature, and the public schools and strengthened the use of English in public affairs. This is most apparent in the area of education, as school authorities enacted subtractive language policies that prescribed English as the language of instruction in education while simultaneously rejecting Spanish and other "foreign languages" in the schools. In some cases, Spanish and other non-English languages were rejected as academic subjects.

Policy decisions favoring the elimination rather than the preservation of the Spanish language in the Southwest were part of a larger national campaign against cultural and linguistic pluralism initiated at midcentury. The annexation of the Southwest in the late 1840s coincided with and probably facilitated the emergence of this campaign for conformity to American cultural and linguistic mores. This campaign deemphasized diversity of cultures and languages while it promoted the understanding of idealized American customs and the speaking of English. Strong assimilationist views motivated school leaders to seek the reduction or elimination of Spanish in public life. For the most part, Anglo officials and laypersons viewed non-English-language use among culturally different groups as a strong indicator of their "foreignness" and their unwillingness to adopt "American" ways over time. Elimination of non-English languages from all public institutions such as the schools was a sure way of encouraging the cultural incorporation of a group perceived to be "foreign" and un-American. It also served to maintain the cultural hegemony of white America while the diversity of this nation was increasing significantly during the second half of the nineteenth century.

These subtractive language policies, enacted in response to political pressure from groups with varying intensities of nationalist and racialist ideologies, did not go unchallenged. Hispanics and other groups supportive of cultural diversity sought to challenge, resist, and modify them over the years. At certain historical moments, changing political and economic circumstances created conditions that led to increasing degrees of tolerance and further modifications of these types of exclusionary policies. In most cases, however, these policies were ignored by the masses of Hispanics. The majority did not attend public or private schools during the nineteenth century and thus paid no attention to them. Those enrolled in the public schools also initially ignored the English-language policies and the culturally biased textbooks. They continued to speak their language in the schools, to overlook the demeaning comments made about their heritage in the curriculum, and to participate in the governance and administration of the public schools. But over the years, however, the exclusionary and assimilationist measures were strengthened. The increasing loss of wealth, political clout, and prestige made Hispanics unable to mount an effective challenge to them.

✳EDUCATION OF HISPANICS IN THE TWENTIETH CENTURY

In the twentieth century, Hispanic education underwent many significant transformations. In many ways it reflected the tremendous social, economic, political, and cultural changes underway in American life and both affected and was affected by these developments. Despite these changes, the patterns of Hispanic education formed in the latter part of the nineteenth century did not change significantly. The schools continued to be exclusionary, discriminatory, and assimilationist.

During this century, Hispanics continued to be educated by a variety of formal and informal institutions. Parochial, Protestant, and private secular schools provided essential knowledge, values, and skills for Hispanic achievement. Hispanics also were "taught" by new institutions, such as radio, TV, industry, the armed forces, the federal government, and their peers. Schooling, especially public education, assumed a new importance as it became the

Mexican fourth-graders at Drachman School (circa 1913). (Courtesy of the Arizona Historical Society.)

dominant form of education for all groups, including Hispanics. Increased state support for public schooling, as well as pressures from industry and from Hispanics, made this institution the dominant form of education in the twentieth century.

As did most institutions during the twentieth century, public education changed dramatically. So did the composition, status, and ideological orientation of the Hispanic population.

Between 1900 and 1980, the goals, structure, and content of public education were transformed as a result of pressures from various sources. Education was extended to individuals from all racial, national, gender, and age groups. Governance structures were altered to benefit middle-class individuals. New innovations in educational administration, such as standardized testing, were introduced. The curriculum was diversified to meet the varied needs of the heterogeneous student population. Educational programs were standardized. Instructional methodology was revolutionized through the introduction of a new psychology and more sophisticated learning theories. One-room schools in rural areas were consolidated into larger units for efficiency, and schools

became articulated from elementary to the postsecondary grades.

The Hispanic population also changed and became more diversified during the twentieth century. Between 1900 and 1980, the composition, social class status, and ideological orientation of the Hispanic population underwent dramatic transformation. The Hispanic population became more heterogeneous and included multiple groups with a range of views and experiences with education.

Between 1848 and 1940, Mexican-descent individuals were the predominant and, in some areas, the only group of Hispanics in the United States. Most of these individuals were concentrated in the Southwest. During the 1920s, Mexican-descent individuals began to migrate to other parts of the United States, especially the Midwest. During the 1940s, the United States experienced a tremendous influx of Hispanics from Puerto Rico. Beginning in 1959, the United States again experienced another tremendous influx of Hispanics. This time it was from Cuba. Beginning in the mid-1960s and spurred by political conflict and economic instability in their homelands during the 1970s, there was a tremendous influx of immigrants from Central and South American countries, such as

Guatemala, Nicaragua, and Peru. Despite the tremendous growth of this group in the last three decades, Mexicans, both citizen and noncitizen, continued to be the largest and oldest residing group of Hispanics in the United States.

The Hispanic population, with the exception of Cubans, is composed of a large poor and working-class sector and a small but increasing group of middle-class individuals. As a group, Hispanics are politically powerless, economically impoverished, and socially alienated. Most of them live in highly segregated communities, tend to speak Spanish as a group, and live in dismal housing conditions. Hispanics are predominantly a cheap source of labor for American industry.

Despite their "common lot," the Hispanic population has a range of views and experiences with education that has affected their schooling in this country. Some, such as the first wave of Cuban immigrants in 1959, were middle class in status and had benefited from education in their country. They embraced all forms of education and actively sought schooling in the United States. Others, such as Mexicans and Puerto Ricans, have more diverse experiences that range from no schooling of any sort to college degrees. They, unlike the Cubans, are more ambivalent about education in general and public schools in particular. A large proportion of those who migrated from poor rural areas in Mexico have no formal school traditions and tend to be indifferent or distrustful of education in this country. Still others, including the small but growing middle class and the more stable sectors of the working class, actively seek educational opportunities and take whatever measures are needed to obtain them.

The range of views and experiences with education, as well as the diversity of Hispanic groups, posed significant challenges for public schools over the decades. They, however, did not meet these challenges. For the most part, schools and those who shaped them ignored the special needs of the heterogeneous Hispanic student population or else interpreted them in such a way that the differences brought by these children had to be eliminated. In many cases, the schools responded not to the genuine needs of this diverse group of children but to those of other stronger political and economic interests. As a result of these contextual realities, the nineteenth-century pattern of inequitable, segregated, and inferior schooling was extended and strengthened over time. Hispanic students were provided with access to schools but it was inequitable. The schools they were provided with also were segregated and inferior, discriminating, assimilationist, and academically weak.

School Access in the Twentieth Century, 1900-1990

In the twentieth century, Hispanics were provided with increasing albeit inequitable access to the elementary, secondary, and postsecondary grades of the public schools. In the first half of the century, Mexican-American school-age children gained access to public education in large part owing to the increasing availability of school facilities, their migration to urban areas, greater economic stability, and, especially, their resolve and desire to educate their young.

Increased access to public education became apparent by 1930. In 1900, for example, slightly less than 50 percent of the Hispanic scholastics, that is, school-age children between five and seventeen in New Mexico were enrolled in the public schools. By 1930, Hispanic enrollment in the public schools had increased to 74 percent in New Mexico. Data from other parts of the Southwest, although incomplete, show that the proportion of Hispanic children enrolled in school also increased during these thirty years. In Texas at the turn of the century, for instance, less than 18 percent of the Hispanic scholastics were enrolled in

A poster encouraging Hispanics to register to vote, which shows education to be the top priority.

any type of school, much less public ones. By 1930, close to 50 percent of Hispanic school-age children in Texas were enrolled. In that same year, the proportion of Hispanic scholastics enrolled in public schools of California stood at 58 percent.

Access to public education stemmed from a variety of forces, including increased district ability to finance the establishment of schools, local willingness to expand educational opportunities to all levels of society, and political support for the enactment and enforcement of child-labor and school-attendance laws. Community resolve was also an important factor in increased school enrollment. Hispanics had, as did most other groups, diverse views toward education. Some Hispanics, especially those from the poorer classes and recent immigrants from Mexico, were unaware of the importance of education as an instrument of mobility. They were distrustful of the assimilationist role of public education. They were unable to send their children to school for economic reasons. But there were other Hispanic individuals and groups within the community who were supportive of education and took whatever actions they could to enroll their children in the schools. Although the majority of those in support of education came from the wealthier sector of the community, there were also working-class individuals. The number of working-class Hispanic individuals and groups who, despite their dire circumstances, made great sacrifices to educate their children increased over time. During the latter part of the nineteenth and early twentieth centuries, a larger number of them began to send their children to the public schools. An increasing stability in employment, migration to urban areas within the Southwest, and a slight increase in their ability to send their children to school encouraged these trends.

Despite the increasing access to education, a large proportion of Hispanic students continued to be out of school, largely because of poverty, mobility associated with rural employment, and discrimination on the part of educational policymakers. Three major groups of students were denied full access to public education during the first half of the twentieth century: agricultural migrants, secondary school-age students, and postsecondary school-age students. School officials excluded these children from the public schools or else took little positive action to encourage their enrollment. In the 1920s and early 1930s, for instance, local officials refused migrant and rural children admission to the elementary grades. Although special laws were passed in areas such as California and New Mexico for the education of migrant children, no significant action was taken by

public officials to ensure their enrollment. During the second quarter of the twentieth century, largely from 1925 to 1950, local officials also excluded older Hispanic students from gaining access to the secondary and postsecondary grades. Local officials refused to allow Hispanic students admission into Anglo high schools or failed to establish sufficient secondary schools for them. Higher-education officials also failed to recruit or allow Hispanics entry to postsecondary educational institutions.

After World War II, Hispanic access to the public schools increased so significantly that by the third quarter of the twentieth century this group gained parity in elementary and secondary school enrollment. Data from Texas, for instance, indicate that between 1942 and 1960 the proportion of Hispanic school-age children enrolled in public schools skyrocketed from 53 percent to 79 percent. Hispanic enrollment in the other states also became significant and ranged between 84 percent in Arizona to 91 percent in California.

Enrollment continued to increase so that by 1980 the overwhelming majority of Hispanic scholastics in the Southwest were enrolled in the elementary and secondary grades. By 1980, the proportion of Hispanic school-age children enrolled in the public schools increased to slightly over 91 percent.

Increased educational access during this period was spurred by a variety of forces, including the continued expansion and extension of public educational opportunities to all levels of society, the vigorous enforcement of child-labor and school-attendance laws, and the addition of new curricula aimed at working-class children. Added vigor in Hispanic resolve was also an important factor in increased school enrollment. The increased support by Hispanics for public education as well as their greater involvement in challenging the exclusionary and discriminatory character of public education likewise led to increased access.

Despite the increased access by Hispanics during the post-World War II period, there was still a significant proportion of these children who were not enrolled in the public schools. Two major groups of students continued to be excluded or denied full admission to the schools: noncitizens and college students. In the early 1970s, local officials, led by the state of Texas, excluded the children of undocumented workers from enrolling in public schools. Although this exclusionary practice was challenged and overturned by the courts, there were still thousands of children, both citizens and noncitizens, who were not allowed in the schools.

As noted earlier, by the 1970s, notwithstanding lingering inequities, Hispanics had reached parity

Children at the Guadalupe Aztlán alternative school in Houston in 1981, when public school education was denied to children of undocumented workers. (Photo by Curtis Dowell. Courtesy of the *Texas Catholic Herald*.)

with the total school-age population in the elementary and secondary grades, but not in postsecondary school enrollment. For this reason, the central issue by the 1970s was no longer access to the elementary and secondary grades but rather access to quality educational services within the public schools and access to higher education.

The Quality of School Facilities in the Twentieth Century: Separate and Unequal

Access to public schools for Hispanic children increased over time, but owing to their subordinate status, they were provided with segregated and unequal facilities. Although segregation originated in the mid-nineteenth century, it expanded significantly between 1890 and 1980. Segregation grew in existing communities in the Southwest in the first quarter of the twentieth century and expanded to the rest of the country by midcentury. Because of the high withdrawal rates of Hispanic children from the public schools in the early decades of the twentieth century, segregation was confined to the elementary grades. But once Hispanic children began to seek access to

secondary schooling, local officials established segregated facilities in these grades. The number of segregated secondary schools increased significantly after World War II. Today, Hispanics are now the largest single racial group in five of the fifty largest school districts in the country and more segregated than Afro-Americans.

Politics and prejudice were key in establishing segregated facilities, but culture and class became crucial in maintaining and extending this practice over time. State officials played an important role in the expansion of school segregation by sanctioning its presence and by funding local requests for increased Hispanic segregation. Residential segregation, demographic shifts in the population, and economic conditions likewise greatly affected the expansion of segregation in the twentieth century.

In addition to being separate, these schools were unequal in many respects to those provided for Anglo children. The facilities, for the most part, were older and more dilapidated than those for Anglos. Recreation space was usually minimal and substandard in comparison to Anglo schools. The school equipment was generally less adequate for the students'' needs.

A sixth-grade classroom in the Huelga School, an alternative school set up in St. Patrick's Chapel, Houston, when public education was denied to children of undocumented workers. (Photo by Curtis Dowell. Courtesy of the *Texas Catholic Herald*.)

Per pupil expenditures in the Hispanic schools was extremely low. Finally, the staff of these schools were less appropriately trained, qualified, and experienced than those in Anglo schools. In many cases, the teachers were sent to the Mexican schools as a form of punishment or to introduce them to the teaching profession.

Discrimination in School Administration in the Twentieth Century

The third major pattern of Hispanic education was in school administration. Local officials developed administrative measures that were discriminatory toward these children. This can be seen in the evolution of assessment and placement practices and in the pattern of interaction between Hispanic students, their peers, and the teaching staff.

Hispanic children, similarly to other working-class, immigrant, and racially different children, were consistently diagnosed as inferior, retarded, or learning-disabled, channeled into low-track classes, and deprived of opportunities for success. Their men-

tal, emotional, and language abilities were assessed on the basis of biased instruments and used to classify Hispanic children as intellectually inferior, culturally backward, and linguistically deprived. These assessments were shaped by class and racial biases and economic imperatives. Once classified as inferior, Hispanic children were systematically placed in "developmentally appropriate" instructional groups, classes, or curricular tracks. At the elementary level, Hispanics were assigned to mostly slow-learning or nonacademic classes. At the secondary level, administrators assigned these culturally different children to vocational or general education courses (tracks) and discouraged them from taking academic classes. Tracking of Hispanics originated in the late 1920s and expanded after World War II. The policies, procedures, and practices utilized by school administrators to assess and classify students, place them in classes, or promote them through the grades served to stratify the student population according to various categories and to reproduce the existing relations of social and economic domination in the classroom.

The discriminatory treatment of Hispanic children was also apparent in the interaction between them, the instructional staff, and their peers. Generally speaking, local educators provided Hispanic children with schools that were staffed by instructors who were insensitive or oblivious to the cultural and special educational needs of these children. Although some of these teachers were caring instructors, the majority had low expectations of the children's learning abilities, and they discouraged, at times unwittingly, Hispanics from achieving. They also ridiculed them for their culturally distinctive traits. Many a Hispanic child was punished simply for speaking Spanish at school or in the classroom. Teachers also interacted with Anglo students more and had less praise for Hispanic children.

The peers of Hispanic students likewise mistreated and ostracized them over time. Paul Taylor quoted, in *An American Mexican Frontier: Nueces County, Texas* (1934), Mexican students in the 1920s to illustrate what he called their severe "hazing" by Anglo children: "Some Americans don't like to talk to me," said one Hispanic youth in 1929. "I sat by one in high school auditorium and he moved away. Oh my god, it made me feel ashamed. I felt like walking out of school." Another student commented, "In grammar school they used to call us 'dirty Mexicans,' 'pelados' and greasers. A few times they moved away from me."

A poster encouraging affirmative action and equal opportunity in education in California.

Curricular Policies

During the twentieth century, public officials continued to provide Hispanic children with a curriculum that was culturally partial toward Anglos and linguistically subtractive, despite minority efforts to reintroduce language and culture into the schools. Local educators also provided these children with a curriculum that was academically imbalanced.

The curriculum for Hispanic schoolchildren originally was comprised of the three Rs and some socialization, but in the early decades of the twentieth century it began to change. Sometime between 1880 and 1930, the Hispanic curriculum began to emphasize socialization and nonacademic concerns at the expense of academic ones. At the elementary level, it shifted its emphasis from the three Rs to the three Cs, that is, it focused more on the teaching of common cultural norms, civics instruction, and command of the English mother tongue than on reading, writing, and arithmetic. At the secondary grades, the emphasis was shifted to vocational and general education. Although composed of some elements of the three Rs, the curriculum for Hispanics in the secondary grades came to have larger doses of more practical instruction.

In addition to becoming academically imbalanced, the curriculum also was assimilationist. More particularly, it was linguistically and culturally intolerant. The latter was reflected in instructional materials and school textbooks, which, for the most part, either omitted or distorted the Hispanic cultural heritage. Linguistic intolerance was reflected in the English-only policies and anti-Spanish practices found in most public school systems throughout the country. Both cultural and language exclusion were opposed by Hispanics and other groups and at times challenged by them. The history of language policy in the United States illustrates this process of Hispanic challenges to assimilationism in the schools.

The curriculum for Hispanics, as noted earlier, was by the second decade of the twentieth century increasingly intolerant of diversity. It had negatively evaluated and rejected the Spanish language and the Hispanic cultural background of these children. This form of intolerance was reflected in curricular language policies and in the passage of English-only laws. English-language policies, however, were consistently questioned or challenged over the years by various groups, including Hispanics. The repeal of prescriptive laws by the Supreme Court in the 1920s, the modification of prescriptive English-only laws in the Southwest during the 1930s and 1940s, and the introduction of foreign languages into the elementary schools during the 1950s illustrate the result of these new pressures in support of language diversity in American public life. The most significant attempt to confront the ideology of assimilationism in the schools and in American life was initiated by various groups, especially Hispanics, during the period from 1965 to 1980. These groups viewed political empowerment and cultural resurgence as the key to academic and socioeconomic success. As a result of their resurgent awareness and their growing political strength, these new forces began to challenge the cultural and political hegemony of the dominant groups by promoting significant educational reforms and by supporting the reintroduction of language, culture, and community into the public schools. Specific language reforms were proposed by activists, including the elimination of the English-only laws and the enactment of federal and state legislation supporting the use of non-English languages in the conduct and operation of public institutions, especially the schools.

Hispanics and their allies were quite successful in accomplishing these goals and in promoting increased tolerance toward Spanish and other non-English languages in the schools, as well as in other aspects of government. Their efforts more particularly led to the repeal of subtractive language policies and to the enactment of more tolerant ones. Federal policies, for instance, began to recognize and urge the utilization of non-English languages in the schools. The United States Congress enacted bilingual education legislation, the Supreme Court forbade English-only instruction and sanctioned the use of native-language instruction in the schools, and the executive branch of government issued various documents supporting the use of non-English languages in educational services.

These actions served as catalysts for the increased support of bilingualism in the schools at the state and local levels. Between 1967 and 1980, for instance, more than twenty-four states passed some form of legislation either permitting or requiring the use of a language other than English in its public institutions, especially the public schools.

The increased use of non-English languages in the public schools led to much confusion over the goals of bilingual education and whether this program should be aimed at promoting bilingualism or English fluency. Although prominent educators and government officials argued that the ultimate goal of bilingual education was to promote bilingualism and

biculturalism among schoolchildren, formal policy was geared toward the learning of English. The first piece of federal legislation, in 1968, for instance, said nothing about bilingualism. The reauthorized bills of 1974 and 1978 allowed for the use of two languages in instruction but underscored the importance of becoming proficient in English. The latter, especially, deemphasized the use of the primary language or of the minority culture in the instructional program. It also limited funding to accomplish this goal of English fluency. Even the Supreme Court decision *Lau v. Nichols*, as well as a variety of executive pronouncements, were aimed at promoting English fluency, not bilingualism.

In practice, English became the dominant language used in bilingual education programs. During the last two decades, various reports found empirical evidence of this fact. According to these reports, the vast majority of bilingual programs in the United States, usually over 80 percent of them, discouraged the use of minority children's native language and helped to facilitate language shift among them. Non-English languages then were rarely used in bilingual programs.

Dr. Manuel Pacheco, President of the University of Arizona.

Despite the dominance of English in bilingual policy and practice, even during its heyday in the 1970s, individuals and groups began to oppose the idea of non-English-language use in public life. In the 1980s, assimilationism once again, as in the 1920s, resurfaced with a vengeance, owing to, in many respects, the growing number of individuals and groups, such as the U.S. English and English First, who are opposed to pluralist and egalitarian ideologies. They have successfully led efforts to repeal bilingual policies and have enacted English-only laws. Although Hispanics continue to support bilingualism in American institutional life, the forces of assimilation have become once again dominant in today's world, including the public schools.

The Pattern of School Performance in the Twentieth Century

In the twentieth century, the major educational consequence of inferior schooling as well as unfavorable socioeconomic circumstances was the establishment of a pattern of skewed academic performance characterized by a dominant tradition of underachievement and a minor one of success.

The pattern of poor school performance has been documented over the decades by social scientists and scholars in general. The dimensions of the pattern of poor school performance can be documented by analyzing various measures, such as achievement test scores, withdrawal rates from school, and the median number of school years for the population age 25 years and older. For the most part, Hispanics have had lower test scores, higher withdrawal rates, and lower median number of school years than Anglos or the general population. Although there has been some improvement in these scores over the decades, the gap between these two groups has not changed significantly over time and continues into the contemporary period.

The case of Hispanics in Texas illustrates this continuing pattern of poor school performance. In the 1920s, an overwhelming majority of Hispanics in Texas, approximately 75 percent of them, withdrew from school by the third grade. During the 1940s, half of the Hispanic student population withdrew from the public schools before reaching the secondary grades. Withdrawal rates were still abysmally high in the 1960s and 1970s, ranging anywhere from 40 percent to 80 percent, depending on local and state circumstances.

Not all Hispanic students have done poorly in school. Contrary to popular and scholarly opinion, a small proportion of them have done extremely well in achievement test scores, received a high school diploma, and continued into postsecondary education. This small group, of which we know little, experienced a pattern of school success, not academic failure. This group is composed of those individuals who completed secondary school during the interwar years, from 1917 to 1940, and of those who completed postsecondary education during the 1960s and 1970s. Considering that the overwhelming majority of Hispanic students dropped out between the third and sixth grades prior to the 1950s, completion of secondary school can be viewed as one aspect of academic achievement. The emergence of a professional and intellectual group of Hispanics likewise indicates scholastic achievement that has gone unrecorded. The existence of high school graduates in the past and college graduates in the contemporary period refutes the myth of unprecedented underachievement and suggests a more diverse pattern of school performance in the Hispanic community.

Hispanics, then, have had a checkered pattern of academic performance, not merely one of underachievement. The pattern of success should be explored further in order to better understand how these students overcame what were obviously tremendous odds.

References

Carter, Thomas P., and Roberto Segura. *Mexican Americans in the Public Schools: A History of Neglect*. Princeton, N.J.: College Entrance Examination Board, 1979.

Castañeda, Carlos. *Our Catholic Heritage in Texas, 1519-1936*. New York: Arno Press, 1976.

Crawford, James. *Bilingual Education: History, Policy, Theory and Practice*. Trenton, N.J.: Crane Publishing, 1989.

De León, Arnoldo. *The Tejano Community*. Albuquerque: University of New Mexico Press, 1982.

Gallegos, Bernardo P. *Literacy, Society and Education in New Mexico, 1693-1821*. Albuquerque: University of New Mexico Press, 1991.

Kloss, Heinz. *The Bilingual Tradition*. Rowley, Mass.: Newberry House, 1977.

Leibowitz, Arnold. *Education Policy and Political Acceptance*. Washington, D.C.: ERIC, 1971.

Meier, Kenneth J., and Joseph Stewart. *The Politics of Hispanic Education*. New York: Russell Sage Foundation, 1987.

Manuel, Herschel T. *Spanish-Speaking Children of the Southwest*. Austin: University of Texas Press, 1965.

Rankin, Melinda. *Twenty Years Among the Mexicans: A Narrative of Missionary Labor*. Cincinnati, Ohio: Central Book Concerns, 1881.

San Miguel, Guadalupe Jr. *Desegregation of Black and Hispanic Students from 1968 to 1980*. Washington, D.C.: Joint Center for Political Studies, 1981.

"From a Dual to a Tri-partite School System." *Integrated Education* 17 (1979): 27-38.

Schneider, Susan G. *Reform, Revolution, or Reaction.* New York: Las Americas Publishing Company, 1976.

Taylor, Paul S. *An American Mexican Frontier: Nueces County, Texas.* Chapel Hill: University of North Carolina Press, 1934.

The Comptroller General of the United States. *Bilingual Education: An Unmet Need.* Washington, D.C.: GPO, 1978.

Weber, David J. *The Mexican Frontier, 1821-1846: The American Southwest under Mexico.* Albuquerque: University of New Mexico Press, 1982.

Williams, Jerry L., ed. *New Mexico in Maps.* Albuquerque: University of New Mexico, 1986.

Van Well, Sister Mary Stanislaus. *The Educational Aspects of the Missions of the Southwest.* Milwaukee: Marquette University Press, 1942.

Weinberg, Meyer. *A Chance to Learn.* New York: Cambridge University Press, 1977.

Guadalupe San Miguel, Jr.

Business

❋ Growth, Origins, and Facts and Figures ❋ Prominent Hispanics in Business

❋GROWTH, ORIGINS, AND FACTS AND FIGURES

Hispanic-owned businesses form a dynamic and complex sector of commerce in the United States. During the 1980s, Hispanic-owned businesses made impressive and important advances. In 1977, there were approximately 219,000 Hispanic-owned businesses, according to the U.S. Bureau of the Census. By 1982, there were slightly over 248,000 Hispanic-owned businesses, a 13 percent increase. According to the United States Census Bureau (1991, 1), in 1987 there were 422,000 Hispanic-owned businesses in the United States, an increase of 70 percent over the 1982 census. By comparison, during the same period of time, the number of nonminority businesses grew 18 percent from 1977 to 1982 and 14 percent from 1982 to 1987. Table 11.1 charts the growth of Hispanic-owned and nonminority-owned businesses for three census periods. (The U.S. Congress has authorized economic censuses to be taken at five-year intervals.)

Caution needs to be exercised in interpreting Hispanic business growth over the three periods. The data collected in each of the census periods are not entirely compatible. Changes in survey methodology,

for example, account for some of this incompatibility. However, there is no doubt that significant growth of Hispanic-owned businesses has occurred.

While the number of Hispanic-owned businesses is growing, at present they make up only 3 percent of the total number of companies in the country. If all His-

Poster for the 1985 United States Hispanic Chamber of Commerce convention showing the U.S. Hispanic business people are the bridge for commerce in the Americas.

TABLE 11.1
HISPANIC AND NONMINORITY BUSINESSES

YEAR	HISPANIC	NONMINORITY
1977	219,355	10,210,000
1982	248,141	12,059,950
1987	422,373	13,695,480

Sources: United States Bureau of the Census, 1980, 5; 1986, 4; 1991, 1.

309

panic-owned firms in the United States were merged into a single business, that "business" would have gross sales in excess of $24.7 billion. This new, merged Hispanic company would be equivalent in sales to Boeing, which ranks fifteenth on *Fortune* magazine's list of the five hundred largest U.S. companies.

Although 54 percent of all Hispanic businesses are owned by Mexican Americans, other ethnic groups within the U.S. Hispanic community have significant business interests. For example, 15 percent of all Hispanic businesses are owned by Cuban Americans, and 7 percent are owned by Puerto Ricans. Figure 11.1 provides information on business ownership by Hispanic origin.

Many Hispanic businesses have no employees and are staffed by a single individual who is typically the owner. Approximately 83,000 of the 422,000 U.S. Hispanic-owned companies have one or more employees. Nationally, these businesses employ close to 265,000 individuals, have an annual payroll of $3.2 billion, and have sales in excess of $17 billion. Table 11.2 includes a breakdown by Hispanic origin of the number of companies, sales generated, number of employees, and annual payroll.

The majority of Hispanic-owned companies are concentrated in services and retail trade. These two categories made up 60 percent of all Hispanic busi-

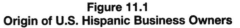

Figure 11.1
Origin of U.S. Hispanic Business Owners

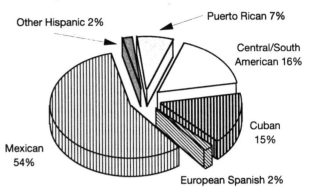

nesses and accounted for 55 percent of gross sales. Table 11.3 presents the number of companies and volume of sales for Hispanic businesses by industry category.

Hispanic-owned businesses exist in virtually every state. However, 78 percent of Hispanic companies, with 80 percent of the gross sales, are concentrated in California, Texas, Florida, New York, and New Mexico. Most of the Hispanic businesses in these states are located in large urban areas. Table 11.4 shows the ten metropolitan statistical areas (MSAs) with the largest number of Hispanic companies and their sales. These ten MSAs account for close to 50 percent

TABLE 11.2
NUMBER OF BUSINESSES, SALES VOLUME, NUMBER OF EMPLOYEES, AND PAYROLL BY HISPANIC ORIGIN OF OWNERS

HISPANIC ORIGIN	ALL BUSINESSES		BUSINESSES WITH PAID EMPLOYEES			
	FIRMS	SALES (THOUSAND $)	FIRMS	EMPLOYEES	ANNUAL PAYROLL (THOUSAND $)	SALES (THOUSAND $)
Mexican	229,706	11,835,080	49,078	148,008	1,687,401	8,403,796
Puerto Rican	27,697	1,447,680	4,629	13,231	179,379	903,848
Cuban	61,470	5,481,974	10,768	47,266	638,459	4,227,065
Other Central or South American	66,356	3,202,238	10,793	27,386	343,039	2,031,768
European Spanish	24,755	2,054,537	5,299	21,196	293,976	1,628,133
Other Hispanic	12,389	710,091	2,341	7,759	101,088	534,822
Total	422,373	24,731,600	82,908	264,846	3,243,342	17,729,432

Source: United States Bureau of the Census, 1991, 12.

TABLE 11.3
HISPANIC BUSINESSES BY MAJOR INDUSTRY CATEGORY

INDUSTRY CATEGORY	NUMBER OF COMPANIES	SALES (MILLION $)
Agricultural services	16,365	694
Mining	829	29
Construction	55,516	3,438
Manufacturing	11,090	1,449
Transportation and public utilities	26,955	1,380
Wholesale trade	10,154	2,445
Retail trade	69,911	7,643
Finance, insurance, and real estate	22,106	864
Services	184,372	6,031
Industries not Classified	25,075	758
Total	422,373	24,731

Source: United States Bureau of the Census, 1991.

TABLE 11.4
NUMBER AND SALES VOLUME OF HISPANIC BUSINESSES IN THE TEN LARGEST MSAS* VS. THOSE IN THE ENTIRE STATE

MSA	MSA		STATE	
MSA	BUSINESSES	SALES (THOUSAND $)	BUSINESSES	SALES (THOUSAND $)
Los Angeles-Long Beach, CA	56,679	3,346,076	132,212	8,119,853
Miami-Hialeah, FL	47,725	3,771,247	64,413	4,949,151
New York, NY	23,014	1,239,513	28,254	1,555,801
Houston, TX	15,967	584,356	94,754	4,108,076
San Antonio, TX	15,241	657,174	94,754	4,108,076
San Diego, CA	10,373	559,444	132,212	8,119,853
Riverside-San Bernardino, CA	10,195	576,537	132,212	8,119,853
Anaheim-Santa Ana, CA	9,683	650,604	132,212	8,119,853
El Paso, TX	8,214	450,840	94,754	4,108,076
Chicago, IL	7,848	506,393	9,636	588,646

*MSA=Metropolitan Statistical Area.
Source: United States Bureau of the Census, 1991, 4.

of the total number of Hispanic businesses in the United States and 50 percent of the gross sales.

Hispanic-owned businesses for the most part are small businesses. Hispanic businesses with employees total 82,908. Fully 72 percent of these businesses had one to four employees in 1990. In addition, 17 percent had five to nine employees, and .2 percent had one hundred employees or more (see Table 11.5). In terms of sales generated by Hispanic businesses, 70 percent of them generated less than $25,000 in annual sales (see Table 11.6). This would lead one to conclude that there is a large proportion of Hispanic business owners with part-time operations. This conclusion is supported by evidence that 55 percent of all Hispanic business owners spend fewer than forty hours per week working with their businesses (see Table 11.4).

There is a growing number of large Hispanic businesses. In 1991, *Hispanic Business* published its list of the five hundred largest Hispanic companies in the nation. Table 11.7 includes the top thirty Hispanic businesses from the "500 Directory." The list demonstrates the broad diversity of large Hispanic companies.

Hispanic business owners tend to be dynamic individuals who in some ways are very much like their nonminority counterparts and in other ways quite different. Hispanic business owners are likely to be younger than their nonminority counterparts. In Table 11.8 the owner's age for both groups is compared. In all, 80 percent of all Hispanic business owners are married, while a comparable 79 percent of nonminority business owners are married.

Hispanic business owners have less formal education than their nonminority counterparts. Approximately 7 percent of all Hispanic business owners possess an undergraduate college degree, compared with 15 percent for nonminority business owners. On the other hand, 27 percent of all Hispanic business owners possess a high school diploma or equivalent, as opposed to 32 percent of their nonminority counterparts. In Table 11.9 the formal education of Hispanic business owners is compared with their nonminority counterparts.

Generally, a larger percentage of Hispanic business owners are first-time entrepreneurs compared with their nonminority counterparts. Approximately 15 percent of Hispanic business owners have previously owned a business, while 21 percent of their nonminority counterparts have. In addition, only 28 percent of Hispanic business owners have close relatives who own a business, while 40 percent of nonminority business owners do. Hispanic business owners as a group also possess less managerial experience than their nonminority counterparts; approxi-

TABLE 11.5
NUMBER OF EMPLOYEES IN HISPANIC BUSINESSES

PERCENTAGE OF BUSINESSES	NUMBER OF EMPLOYEES
72	1-4
17	5-9
7	10-19
3	20-49
0.8	50-99
0.2	100+

Source: United States Bureau of the Census, 1991, 86.

TABLE 11.6
SALES VOLUME OF HISPANIC BUSINESSES

PERCENTAGE OF BUSINESSES	SALES ($)
34	Less than 5,000
35	5,000-24,999
20	25,000-99,999
7	100,000-249,999
3	250,000-999,999
1	1,000,000 or more

Source: United States Bureau of the Census, 1987, 140.

TABLE 11.7
THE THIRTY LARGEST HISPANIC BUSINESSES

RANK	COMPANY AND LOCATION	CHIEF EXECUTIVE	TYPE OF BUSINESS	NUMBER OF EMPLOYEES	YEAR STARTED	1990 SALES
1	Bacardi Imports, Miami, FL	Juan Grau	Rum/wine import distribution	280	1944	$602.09
2	Goya Foods, Secaucus, NJ	Joseph Unanue	Food manufacturing/marketing	1,500	1936	330.00
3	Sedano's Supermarkets, Miami, FL	Manuel A. Herran	Supermarket chain	1,450	1962	207.00
4	Galeana Van Dyke Dodge, Warren, MI	Frank Galeana	Auto dealerships	269	1969	165.22
5	Handy Andy Supermarkets, San Antonio, TX	A. Jimmy Jimenez	Supermarket chain	1,700	1983	154.00
6	Int'l. Bancshares Corp., Laredo, TX	Dennis E. Nixon	Financial services Institution	300	1966	141.49
7	Ancira Enterprises, San Antonio, TX	Ernesto Ancira, Jr.	Automotive sales/service	270	1983	138.37
8	Pizza Management, San Antonio, TX	Arturo G. Torres	Restaurant chain	4,600	1976	133.44
9	Capital Bank, Miami, FL	Abel Holtz	Financial services Institution	650	1982	120.01
10	Frank Parra Chevrolet, Irving, TX	Tim and Mike Parra	Automotive sales/service	265	1971	120.00
11	Gaseteria Oil Corp., Long Island City, NY	Oscar Porcelli	Gasoline stations	440	1973	105.00
12	Cal-State Lumber Sales, San Diego, CA	Benjamin Acevedo	Wood product sales	77	1984	104.01
13	Lloyd A. Wise, Oakland, CA	Anthony A. Batarse, Jr.	Automotive sales/service	191	1914	98.00
14	Precision Trading Corp., Miami, FL	Israel Lapciuc	Consumer electronics	35	1979	95.60
15	Condal Distributors, Bronx, NY	Nelson Fernandez	Wholesale food distribution	250	1968	95.00
16	TELACU, Los Angeles, CA	David C. Lizarraga	Economic development	630	1968	86.22
17	Northwestern Meat, Miami, FL	Elpidio Nunez	Wholesale beef/seafood dist.	118	1961	85.12
18	American Int'l. Container, Miami, FL	Remedios Diaz–Oliver	Glass container distributor	172	1976	83.70
19	Mexalloy Int'l., Theodore, AL	Enrique Gomez Palacio	Ferroalloys distribution	9	1984	82.65
20	Eagle Brands, Miami, FL	Carlos M. de la Cruz, Sr.	Wholesale beer distributor	187	1984	81.80
21	Gus Machado Enterprises, Hialeah, FL	Gus Machado	Automotive sales/service	100	1982	78.48
22	D.J. Sekin & Co., Dallas/Ft. Worth, TX	Peter Gilbert	Customs broker/freight fowarding	160	1984	78.00
23	Rosendin Electric, San Jose, CA	Raymond J. Rosendin	Electrical contracting	600	1919	78.00
24	Ruiz Food Products, Dinuba, CA	Frederick R. Ruiz	Food manufaturing	800	1964	70.64
25	H & H Meat Products Co., Mercedes, TX	Liborio Hinojosa	Meat packing/distribution	350	1947	67.00
26	Vega Enterprises, Las Vegas, NV	Rafael E. Vega	Variety store products	159	1983	64.02
27	Ramos Oil Co., West Sacramento, CA	William Ramos	Petroleum products dist.	120	1952	60.13
28	CareFlorida, Miami, FL	Paul L. Cejas	Health insurance	120	1973	60.00
29	RJO Enterprises, Lanham, MD	Richard J. Otero	Government res. & dev.	600	1979	59.71
30	Gator Industries, Hialeah, FL	Guillermo Miranda, Jr.	Shoe manufacturing	1200	1969	56.30

Source: "The 500," 1991, 42.

TABLE 11.8

HISPANIC AND NONMINORITY BUSINESS OWNERS BY AGE

	UNDER 25	25-34	35-44	45-54	55-64	OVER 65
Hispanic business owners	4%	22%	28%	24%	14%	4%
Nonminority business owners	3%	20%	25%	22%	18%	9%

***Source:** United States Bureau of the Census, 1987, 10.
Note: 4 percent of Hispanic business owners and 3 percent of nonminority business owners did not report age.

TABLE 11.10

HISPANIC AND NONMINORITY BUSINESS OWNERS ACROSS FOUR CHARACTERISTICS

	HISPANIC BUSINESS OWNERS (%)	NONMINORITY BUSINESS OWNERS (%)
College education	7	15
First-time entrepreneur	85	79
Management experience of 10 years or more	10	21
45 years of age or older	42	49

Source: United States Bureau of the Census,1987, 10, 18, 37, 74.

mately 10 percent have ten or more year's experience as managers prior to establishing their business, while 21 percent of nonminority business owners possess such experience. Finally, 30 percent of Hispanic businesses were established prior to 1976, compared with 42 percent of nonminority businesses. These data confirm that Hispanic business owners as a group tend to have less business experience and tend to be more recent entrants into the world of business than their nonminority counterparts. Variations between Hispanic and nonminority business owners across several dimensions are shown in Table 11.10.

There are other interesting similarities and contrasts between the groups. Slightly over 76 percent of Hispanic business owners used $10,000 or less in capital to start or acquire their business, while 72 percent of nonminority business owners required $10,000 or less. Start-up capital requirements for Hispanic and nonminority businesses are illustrated in Table 11.11.

The sources of start-up capital for Hispanic and nonminority business owners are varied. The major portion for both groups has come from personal savings. However, 19 percent of nonminority business owners borrowed the capital from commercial banks,

TABLE 11.9

HISPANIC AND NONMINORITY BUSINESS OWNERS BY YEARS OF EDUCATION

	LESS THAN 9 YEARS	9-11 YEARS	HIGH SCHOOL DIPLOMA	1-3 YEARS OF COLLEGE	COLLEGE DEGREE	MORE THAN 5 YEARS OF COLLEGE
Hispanic business owners	19%	11%	27%	20%	7%	12%
Nonminority business owners	5%	8%	32%	20%	15%	18%

Source: United States Bureau of the Census, 1987, 18.
Note: 4 percent of Hispanic business owners and 2 percent of nonminority business owners did not report education.

TABLE 11.11
START-UP CAPITAL REQUIRED FOR HISPANIC AND NONMINORITY BUSINESS OWNERS

	NONE	$1 – 4,999	$5,000 – 9,999	$10,000 – 24,999	$25,000 – 49,999	$50,000 – 99,999	$100,000 – 249,000	$250,000 OR MORE
Hispanic Businesses	27%	37%	12%	11%	4%	2%	6%	4%
Nonminority Businesses	27%	34%	10%	11%	6%	3%	2%	6%

Source: United States Bureau of the Census, 1987, 82.
Note: 6 percent of Hispanic business owners and 6.4 percent of nonminority business owners did not respond.

while 15 percent of Hispanic business owners did so. Approximately 8 percent of nonminority business owners obtained the capital from family and friends, compared with 13 percent of Hispanic business owners. Sources of start-up capital for Hispanic and nonminority business owners are illustrated in Figure 11.2.

Some indication of business productivity can be obtained by examining net profit or loss of Hispanic businesses and comparing them to nonminority businesses. More than 4 percent of Hispanic-owned businesses generated net profits of $50,000 or more, Compared with 6 percent of for nonminority businesses.

Approximately 14 percent of Hispanic businesses reported a loss, while 16 percent of nonminority businesses did. In terms of productivity when measured by profit or loss, it can be concluded that minority businesses are as productive as nonminority ones. Profit and loss for Hispanic and nonminority businesses are compared in Table 11.12.

The dominant form of Hispanic-owned businesses is the sole proprietorship; this is also the dominant form of all U.S. businesses. Sole proprietorship requires no legal documentation. Anyone who merely begins a business is automatically a sole proprietor unless he or she applies for incorporation. If two or

Figure 11.2
Sources of Start-up Capital for Hispanic and Nonminority Business Owners

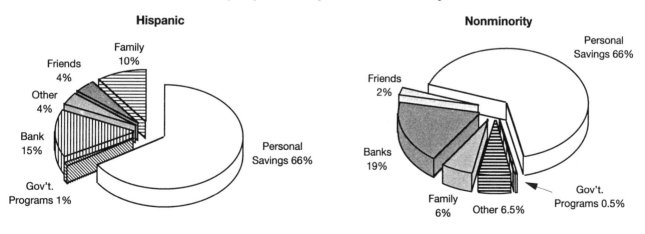

TABLE 11.12
PROFIT AND LOSS FOR HISPANIC AND NONMINORITY BUSINESSES

PROFIT

	LESS THAN $5,000	$5,000 – 9,999	$10,000 –19,999	$20,000 – 24,999	$25,000 – 29,999	$30,000 – 49,999	$50,000 – 74,999	$75,000 – 99,999	$100,000 – 249,000	$250,000 OR MORE
Hispanic	26%	14%	12%	4%	2%	4%	2%	1%	1%	0.5%
Non-minority	27%	11%	11%	4%	3%	5%	2%	1%	2%	1%

LOSS

	LESS THAN $5,000	$5,000 – $9,999	$10,000 – 24,999	$25,000 OR MORE
Hispanic-Owned Businesses	11%	2%	1%	0.6%
Nonminority-Owned Businesses	12%	2%	1%	1%

Source: United States Bureau of the Census, 1987, 114.
Note: 18.9 percent of Hispanic businesses and 17 percent of nonminority businesses did not respond.

TABLE 11.13
MINORITY EMPLOYEES IN HISPANIC AND NONMINORITY BUSINESSES

	NO MINORITY EMPLOYEES	1-9%	10-24%	25-49%	50-74%	75-100%
Hispanic Businesses	11	2	4	5	11	67
Nonminority Businesses	65	6	6	5	4	14

Source: United States Bureau of the Census, 1987, 130.

more individuals join in a business venture, they are a partnership.

The majority of Hispanic companies—94 percent—are operated as proprietorships (United States Bureau of the Census, 1991, 90: 1987, 62)). This is comparable to nonminority owned businesses, 92 percent of which are proprietorships. Hispanic-owned corporations account for 2 percent of the total number of Hispanic companies, while 3 percent of nonminority firms are corporations. Approximately 4 percent of Hispanic businesses are partnerships, compared with 5 percent of nonminority businesses.

Hispanic-owned businesses differ significantly from their nonminority counterparts in at least one area. Hispanic businesses tend to hire other Hispanics or minorities. Approximately 67 percent of Hispanic businesses report that their work force consists of 75 to 100 percent minority employees. This is quite a contrast to the 14 percent of nonminority businesses that reported their work force consist of 75 to 100 percent minority employees. The percentage of minority employees in both Hispanic and nonminority businesses is summarized in Table 11.13.

A very limited amount of information is available on the failure rate of Hispanic-owned businesses. Unfortunately, it is difficult to identify exactly when and if a business terminates. Business termination, of course, does not necessarily mean business failure. Some companies terminate voluntarily, without owner or creditor losses. Some research of Hispanic companies indicates that these businesses fail at a rate slightly higher than those of similar nonminority firms (Stevens, 1984, 10; Minority Businesses Development Agency, 1982). However, more research needs to be undertaken to determine rates and causes of failures. There is some evidence that minority firms are burdened by higher debt structure, resulting in more problems, especially during recessions or tight money periods.

Hispanic-owned businesses make up a sector of the U.S. economy that will continue to increase in number and productivity. Business ownership will continue to be avaliable career option for growing numbers of Hispanics.

✹PROMINENT HISPANICS IN BUSINESS

Deborah Aguiar-Vélez (1955-)
Computers

Born on December 18, 1955, in New York City, Aguiar received a B.S. degree in chemical engineering from the University of Puerto Rico in 1977 and a certificate from the University of Virginia Entrepreneurial Executive Institute in 1989. In her early career, she was a systems analyst for Exxon and then worked in the small-business division of the New Jersey Department of Commerce. After that she founded and was president of her own business, Sistemas Corporation. Her honors include selection in 1990 as the Outstanding Women Entrepreneur Advocate by American Women in Economic Development and selection for Coca-Cola commercials as a Hispanic woman entrepreneurial role model. Aguiar has served on the boards of the Hispanic Women's Task Force, the Hispanic Leadership Opportunity Program, and the New Jersey Women's Business Advisory Council, which she chaired from 1987 to 1988.

Gabriel Eloy Aguirre (1935-)
Sanitation

Born on January 12, 1935, in Akron, Ohio, Aguirre worked for SaniServ in Indianapolis in the service and sales divisions from 1957 to 1977; in 1977, he became the owner of the company. For his outstanding success with the company, he was named the 1987 Minority Entrepreneur of the Year by the president of the United States. Aguirre has been very active in the community, serving on numerous boards and as president of school boards and police commissions. Since 1988, he has been a member of the board of the U.S. Senate Task Force on Hispanic Affairs.

Carlos José Arboleya (1929-)
Banking

Born on February 1, 1929, in Havana, Cuba, Arboleya is a graduate of the University of Havana who developed his early career in banking as the Havana manager of the First National City Bank of New York. After the Cuban Revolution of 1959, he immigrated to the United States and worked at a number of banks in Miami, moving up the ranks from clerk to bank administrator. By 1966, he was executive vice president of the Fidelity National Bank of South Miami; by 1973, the co-owner, president, and director of the Flagler Bank; and by 1977, president and CEO of the Barnett Banks of Miami. Since 1983, he has been vice chairman of the Barnett Bank of South Florida. Arboleya has remained active in the profession and the community, serving as vice president of the American Institute of Banking and on the boards of such organizations as the Inter-American Affairs Action Committee, the National Advisory Council for Economic Opportunity, the American Arbitration Association, and the Cuban American Foundation. Among his many honors are the American Academy of Achievement Gold Plate Award in 1974, the Horatio Alger Award of the American Schools and Colleges Association in 1976, and the American Red Cross Man of the Year Award in 1988.

Humberto Cabañas (1947-)
Hotel Management

Born on September 3, 1947, in Havana, Cuba, Cabañas received a B.S. degree in hotel and restaurant management from Florida International University in 1974 and went on to rise through the ranks at Sheraton, Doral, and Stouffer hotels until becoming the founding president and CEO of the Benchmark Hospitality Group in the Woodlands, Texas, in 1979. Benchmark properties include the Woodlands Executive Conference Center and resort, the Woodlands Country Club, the Exxon Conference Center, the Tournament Players Golf Course, and the San Luis Resort Hotel on Galveston Island. He has been a president of the International Association of Conference Centers, from which he received a Distinguished Service Award in 1988. Cabañas serves on the industry advisory committee for the Conrad Hilton School of Hotel and Restaurant Management of the University of Houston and is a past president of the International Association of Conference Centers.

Gilbert Cuéllar, Jr.
Restaurant Chain Executive

Cuéllar is the chairman and CEO of the fifty-year-old restaurant chain founded by his family. Formerly

Gilbert Cuéllar, Jr.

known as El Chico Corporation, the Dallas-based chain is now Southwest Cafes and has, under Cuéllar's direction, expanded to various states under such local names as Cantina Laredo, Cuéllar's Cafe, Casa Rosa, and El Chico Restaurants. First becoming associated with the corporation in 1970, he served in various capacities, including manager of quality control, product research and development, and director of marketing research. In 1977, Campbell Taggart acquired the restaurant chain, and Cuéllar enrolled at North Texas State University and received an M.B.A. degree. After founding various restaurants of his own, he and his father were able to repurchase El Chico Corporation in 1982. In 1986, Cuéllar was named chairman of the corporation.

Roberto C. Goizueta (1931-)
Beverage Company Executive

Born on November 18, 1931, in Havana, Cuba, Goizueta received a B.S. degree in chemical engineering in 1953 from Yale University. He began at the Coca-Cola Company as an assistant vice president of research in 1964; by 1981, he had become the chairman of the board and CEO of Coca-Cola, one of the world's largest corporations. Goizueta has been active in service nationally and internationally. He is the founding director of the Points of Light Initiative and sits on the boards of the Ford Motor Company and Eastman Kodak, among others. Since 1980, he has been a trustee of Emory University. Among his many honors are being chosen a Gordon Grand Fellow of Yale University in 1984, the 1984 Herbert Hoover Humanitarian Award of the Boys Clubs of America, and the 1986 Ellis Island Medal of Honor.

Fredrick J. González (1949-)
Design Engineering Executive

Born on June 28, 1949, in Detroit, Michigan, González received a B.S. degree in engineering and an M.S. degree in architecture and urban planning from Princeton University in 1971 and 1972, respectively. After working for three years as an architect for Smith Hinchman Grylls Associates, in 1975 he and his father founded their own firm, González Design Engineering, in Madison Heights, Michigan, for which he has served as CEO since 1977, when his father died. In 1979, he also became the president of Semi-Kinetics, a printed circuit board assembly line in Laguna Hills, California. Since a 1968 automobile accident, González, who had been a high school football star, has been paralyzed from the waist down. Despite this and business barriers, González has become an outstanding businessman. Among his and his company's honors are being named by the White House as the National Minority Service Firm of the Year in 1975, selection as the 1989 Minority Businessman of the Year, and selection as the 1989 Minority

Roberto C. Goizueta.

Frederick J. González

Supplier of the Year by the National Minority Business Development Council. González participates on many boards, including the board of directors of the U.S. Hispanic Chamber of Commerce. González and his brother-partner, Gary, have been featured in full-page ads by General Motors as successful suppliers to the car company.

Frank A. Lorenzo (1940-)
Former Airline Company Executive

Born on May 19, 1940, in New York City, Lorenzo received a B.S. degree from Columbia University in

1961 and an M.B.A. degree from Harvard University in 1963. He began his career in air transportation as a financial analyst for Trans World Airlines from 1963 to 1965 and by 1966 had founded and become chairman of his own company, Lorenzo Carney and Company. From 1972 to 1980 he served as president and chairman of Texas International Airlines, which eventually became a major national and international holding company for Continental Airlines, for which he served as president from 1980 to 1985 and then as chairman and CEO from 1986 to 1990. After developing the company into the world's largest carrier through the purchase of various other carriers, Lorenzo was embattled by strikes, rising costs, and competition and the problems of deregulation, and he was eventually forced to resign.

Edgar J. Milán (1934-)
Controller

Born on November 23, 1934, in New York City, Milán received a B.S. degree in accounting from Hunter College in 1957 and pursued additional courses towards the M.S. degree at the City College of New York. He rose through the ranks as a career accountant in oil companies, serving in the United

Edgar J. Milán.

States, Canada, England, Peru, and Nicaragua. After serving in a number of vice presidential positions in the financial divisions of Tenneco Oil, one of the largest U.S. corporations, Milán was named vice president and controller in 1989. Milán serves on a number of advisory boards, including those of Arte Publico Press and the accounting programs for Texas Tech and Texas A&M Universities. Milán was also an outstanding college basketball player; and in 1957, he was selected Hunter College Athlete of the Year, and in 1991, he was inducted into the Hunter College Athletic Hall of Fame.

Robert Ortega, Jr. (1947-)
Construction Company Executive

Born on February 1, 1947, in El Paso, Texas, Ortega received B.S. and M.S. degrees in civil engineering from the University of Texas at El Paso in 1970 and 1980, respectively. He worked as an engineer in the U.S. Public Health Service, the U.S. Bureau of Reclamation, and the El Paso Housing Department before founding Construction Management Associates in 1983. In 1988, his company was rated the fifth-fastest-growing Hispanic company in the United States by *Hispanic Business Magazine*. In 1989, the company was named the Outstanding Small Business for the City of El Paso by the Small Business Administration. In 1980, Ortega was named Young Engineer of the Year and, in 1989, Engineer of the Year by the Texas Society of Professional Engineers. He is a past president of the Texas Society of Civil Engineers and of the Associated Builders and Contractors.

Carlos D. Ramírez (1946-)
Publishing

See Chapter 25.

Emyré Barrios Robinson (1926-)
Aerospace Company Executive

See Chapter 13.

John Rodríguez (1958-)
Advertising and Public Relations

Born on August 9, 1958, in New York City, John Rodríguez is cofounder and president of AD One, an advertising and public relations firm in Rochester, New York. Rodríguez completed his bachelor's degree at the Rochester Institute of Technology, where he majored in advertising and photography. He continues his education by attending classes at local universities and is currently working toward a master's degree in communications. As a young entrepreneur, he has built his company, AD One, into a successful firm that specializes in international sales promotion, recruitment, and the Hispanic market. AD One has successfully completed projects for many clients across the region, including Eastman Kodak Company, Bausch and Lomb, Preferred Care, The University of Rochester, the Girl Scouts, Rochester City School District, and Mobil Chemical.

Rodríguez has a strong sense of responsibility toward the community in which he lives and works. His commitment to his community and to Hispanic people is expressed in many ways. He brings issues to the surface by talking about them and then taking appropriate action. Rodríguez translates his thoughts into action in his involvement with the Rochester Hispanic Business Association and memberships with the Monroe County Human Relations Commission, the United Way of Greater Rochester, the Puerto Rican Youth Development and Resource Center, as well as many other organizations in the area. He is also quite active as a member of the Citizens'' Advisory Committee to Vision 2000, a major project to revitalize downtown Rochester. Rodríguez has also ventured into politics. He served as campaign director for his sister-in-law, Nancy Padilla, the first Hispanic elected to the Rochester City Council. For Rodríguez, having individuals sensitive to the Hispanic community in key policy-making positions is critical.

Oscar Rodríguez
Computers

Oscar Rodríguez was born and raised in San Antonio, Texas. He spent seventeen years as a very successful entrepreneur in Boston, Massachusetts. During his "exile" in Boston he obtained his master's of business administration degree at Harvard and then proceeded to start and sell three successful computer-oriented companies.

In 1985, after a highly successful business career, Rodríguez returned to his native San Antonio and joined forces with Héctor Dávila to buy out a failing computer services company. The new company, Antares Development Corporation, assumed the computer support responsibility for sixty of San Antonio's most respected firms. By the end of 1988, Antares Development Corporation had become one of the premier suppliers of computer services in San Antonio.

During the downturn in the computer industry in the late 1980s, Antares reexamined its mission as well as the future of the computing industry. This analysis led to a whole new outlook for the company. Specifically, Antares identified three new technologies that it saw as the future of computing: networking, data base management systems, and UNIX operating systems. Antares, under the guidance of Oscar Rodríguez, put into place a corporate strategy that was aimed at building a respected institution.

Vendors—"Once you have defined your market place, think of it as a closed system of symbiotic relationships where companies buy and sell from each other creating wealth for citizens. To the extent that it is consistent with your quality objectives, only buy from within this closed system. The extent that you buy from outside the system, you weaken your market place. Be concerned with vendor costs, but understand that the value of consistent quality and long term relationships can be measured in economic terms."

The Corporate Citizen—"Being a good corporate citizen is good business. It is naive to believe that governments alone can solve the great social problems of our time. The long term liability of your market place is directly contingent on an educated populace, a healthy environmental infrastructure and a government committed to improving these."

By early 1990, Antares had retrained its staff in new technologies and was well on the way to developing a set of new products and services based on its new direction. In 1990, the company increased sales by 50 percent.

Oscar Rodríguez has defined the goals of his company through the year 2000. First, he wants to have 1000 corporate clients with whom Antares has an ongoing support relationship. A second goal for the firm is to earn the Malcolm Baldridge National Award for Quality in the service sector. There is every reason to believe that these goals will be accomplished.

Eduardo G. Santiago (1949-)
Controller

Born on September 26, 1949, in Ponce, Puerto Rico, Santiago received a B.S. degree in accounting from Baruch College in 1975 and an M.B.A. degree in finance from Pace University in 1979. He began his career as an accounting clerk for Guy Carpenter & Co. in 1969. He worked for American International Marine and for MacMillan until 1975, when he became the controller of Philip Morris International.

Lionel Sosa (1939-)
Advertising

Born on May 27, 1939, in San Antonio, Texas, Sosa became a graphic artist who developed a career in advertising, founding his own company, Sosart, in 1966. In 1974, he became a partner of Ed Yardang and Associates. In 1984, he founded Sosa and Associates, for which he serves as chairman and CEO. Sosa and

Lionel Sosa.

Associates is the leading firm in handling national accounts targeted at Hispanic consumers. In 1990, *Adweek* magazine named Sosa and Associates the Agency of the Year and the Hottest Agency in the Southwest, with 1989 billings of $54.8 million. Sosa's clients include American Airlines, Anheuser-Busch, Burger King, Coca-Cola USA, Montgomery Ward, and Western Union. Among his many awards are the 1990 Entrepreneur of the Year, the 1989 Marketing Person of the Year Award, the 1989 Silver Award from the Public Relations Society of America, and the Gold ADDY from the American Advertising Founda-

tion in 1988. Sosa is active in the community, participating on many local and national boards.

Clifford Lane Whitehill (1931-)
Corporate Attorney

Born on April 14, 1931, the son of Catalina Yarza and Clifford Whitehill, Whitehill received a B.A. degree from Rice University in 1954, an LL.B. from the University of Texas, and an LL.M. from Harvard University in 1957 and 1958, respectively. He became a corporate attorney, working for various companies

Clifford L. Whitehill.

the American Arbitration Society. Among the many boards and directorates on which Whitehill serves are the National Hispanic Scholarship Fund and the United Nations Association of the USA, both of which he directs.

Independently owned businesses are the foundation of economic activity in the United States. They embody the American dream of financial independence and self-determination. Even in the relatively mediocre economy of the past decade, Hispanic businesses have continued to grow and prosper. The impressive gains made by Hispanic-owned businesses in the past decade will most assuredly continue into the next decade as younger and better educated Hispanics are attracted to self-employment. Business ownership will become an increasingly attractive career option for growing numbers of Hispanics.

References

The "500." *Hispanic Business* (June 1991).

Enterprises—Spanish Origin. Washington, D.C., 1980.

Minority Business Development Agency. *Minority Business Enterprise Today: Problems & Their Causes.* Washington, D.C., 1982.

Political Economy (Spring 1984).

United States Bureau of the Census. *1982 Survey of Minority-Owned Business Enterprises—Hispanic.* Washington, D.C., 1986.

United States Bureau of the Census. *1982 Characteristics of Business Owners.* Washington, D.C., 1987.

United States Bureau of the Census. *1987 Survey of Minority-Owned Business Enterprises—Hispanic.* Washington, D.C., 1991.

Unterberger, Amy L., ed. *Who's Who among Hispanic Americans. 1991-1992.* Detroit: Gale Research Inc., 1991.

Jude Valdez and Nicolás Kanellos

in Houston and New York until joining General Mills in Minneapolis as an attorney in 1962. He moved up the ranks to vice presidential positions. He attained his present position of senior vice president, general counsel and secretary in 1981. Among his honors is the 1988 Whitney North Seymour, Sr., Award from

Labor and Employment

✳ Hispanics in Organized Labor ✳ Immigration and Migration
✳ Hispanic Employment in Industry ✳ Federal Employment Programs and Laws
✳ Youth Employment ✳ Women's Employment ✳ Income, Poverty and Unemployment
✳ Selected Labor Facts

Hispanics are the fastest-growing major group in the labor force of the United States. Between 1980 and 1988, the number of Hispanics in the work force increased by 48 percent, representing 20 percent of U.S. employment growth. The employment of Hispanic women during this period increased by 56 percent, or more than two and one-half times the rate of other women.

Between 1980 and 1990, Hispanics increased from 6.1 percent to slightly more than 9 percent of the nation's work force. Their youth relative to other groups in the work force and continued high rates of immigration indicate that Hispanics will continue to increase their representation in the nation's work force in the foreseeable future.

Although the numbers have increased rapidly, conditions of employment for Hispanics have deteriorated during the 1980s. Many worker protections and benefits have been lost, incomes have declined in absolute terms, and the gap between Hispanics and whites has widened sharply.

In the final quarter of 1990, the median weekly earnings of Hispanic men were $331, compared with $370 for black men and $502 for white men. Hispanic women's weekly earnings were $283, compared with $313 for black women and $363 for white women. This means that white women and black men earned 74 percent, black women 62 percent, Hispanic men 66 percent, and Hispanic women 56 percent of that earned by white men. By March 1991, unemployment among Hispanics had reached 10.3 percent, roughly double the rate for whites.

Federal policy is partly responsible for the declining conditions, as the strategies of the Reagan-Bush era have resulted in the government's altering its priorities and shirking its earlier responsibilities. It

César Chávez exhorting people to start a new grape boycott in 1986. (Courtesy of the *Texas Catholic Herald*.)

has consciously adopted employment policies favoring large employers and higher income groups at the expense of the poor, particularly blacks and Hispanics. Employer abuses have even extended to child labor. In the four-year period from 1986 to 1990, child labor violations increased by 128 percent.

Brief History of Hispanics in the Labor Force

Between the late 1500s and the incorporation of northern Mexico into the United States at the end of the Mexican-American War in 1848, workers of Mexican birth who resided in the present-day Southwest worked largely in agricultural tasks. Most of them held land on which they grew and raised most of their sustenance, which they often supplemented by working for others. As they lost their lands after the war, a majority of them became wage laborers. They were employed as field hands, cowboys, railroad maintenance workers, ditchdiggers, and miners.

The movement of Mexican-American workers out of rural and agricultural tasks was relatively slow. As their numbers gradually increased in cities and towns, they found employment in service and manufacturing occupations. Yet, in contrast to the overall trend among whites, they experienced a marked

Mexican women working at a commercial tortilla factory in the 1930's. (Courtesy of the Library of Congress.)

downward mobility during the last half of the nineteenth century.

Another Hispanic group also appeared in the late nineteenth century. A small Cuban population migrated to Florida, partly in response to the independence movement against Spain, as exiles, revolutionaries, and workers. Applying skills they learned in Cuba, they were engaged largely in the tobacco industry, as field owners and workers, and in cigar factories of the State.

A new phase of the labor history of Hispanics in the United States began around the turn of the twentieth century, when employers in the Southwest, and soon afterward in the Midwest, began to recruit workers from the Mexican border. Their efforts set in motion a movement that has shaped migration patterns from Mexico throughout the twentieth century. Using labor contractors and other recruiters, they brought in workers from Mexico to perform largely unskilled, low-paying tasks. This planned labor migration quickly stimulated another pattern of individual migration that took on an independent character of its own and outpaced the rate of migration by labor recruitment. During the early twentieth century, a majority of Hispanic workers in the United States were Mexican immigrants and their children. In sheer numbers, the new arrivals soon overwhelmed the older Mexican-descent residents in most parts of the Southwest and Midwest, except New Mexico.

Mexico offered employers a reservoir of workers because of its high level of unemployment and very low incomes. The wage differential between Mexico and the United States throughout the century has always been very sharp. At present, an unskilled wage worker in the United States can earn approximately ten times as much as in Mexico, although the differences are largely offset by much higher prices for food, rent, and other living expenses in the United States.

In the early twentieth century, Mexicans were recruited largely for agricultural, railroad maintenance, and mining enterprises. Smaller numbers found employment in domestic and other service occupations, and in manufacturing. Mexican immigrant families often worked as a single unit in cotton, sugar beet, and fruit and vegetable planting, cultivation, and harvesting operations, especially in the Southwest. In other occupations, including mining, manufacturing, and most service occupations, adult workers were the rule, as child labor laws were harder to evade, restricting the employment of children.

As a result of the patterns of labor recruitment that evolved in the early twentieth century, cities and towns on and near the Mexican border, and eventu-

A cotton picker in 1933. (Photo by Dorothea Lange. Courtesy of the Library of Congress.)

ally throughout the Southwest and in many Midwestern settings, developed large labor pools of Mexican workers who were available to perform unskilled, low-paying jobs throughout the year. Characteristically, the Mexican workers found employment largely in seasonal tasks and experienced high rates of unemployment and frequent changes in employers. Although many of them brought skills from Mexico, few of the tasks they performed in the United States required high levels of training or English-language proficiency to perform.

The Spanish-American War in 1898 resulted in the incorporation of Puerto Ricans into the work force of the United States. As continental-based corporations quickly gained control of the best agricultural lands in Puerto Rico, they displaced many small landholders, offering them the alternatives of wage work in the fields or unemployment. By 1930, four U.S. corporations controlled about three-fifths of sugar production in Puerto Rico, and the sugar industry was responsible for more than two-thirds of all employment on the Island.

Because of World War I, Puerto Ricans were made citizens of the United States in 1917. The war also stimulated a modest migration from the island to New York City and environs, where the new arrivals worked in textiles and other low-wage industrial and service occupations.

Conditions of employment for all workers, but Mexicans in particular, deteriorated rapidly with the onset of the Great Depression in 1929. Immigration to the United States virtually ceased, and return migration to Mexico increased sharply. Mexican workers were singled out by employers and quickly fired or laid off, particularly in and near urban centers in both the Southwest and the Midwest.

In many cities, government agencies and employer groups collaborated to conduct organized repatriation drives that involved publicity and propaganda campaigns intent on convincing the English-speaking public that Mexicans were taking jobs away from U.S. citizens. Although the propagandists argued that repatriation would provide employment to unemployed citizens, most Mexicans had already lost their jobs. The underlying motive in the campaigns was to remove unemployed Mexicans from public welfare rolls. The intensity of the drives varied in different locations, but they were partly responsible for the reduction of the Mexican-descent population in the United States by about 25 percent during the early years of the Great Depression. Almost all the formal repatriation drives ended with the election victory of President Franklin D. Roosevelt and the ascendancy of the Democratic party in Congress in 1933. Unlike the Republicans, they did not consider Mexican workers a major cause of the depression.

In 1940 and 1941, the war in Europe stimulated production, and the demand for labor in the United States rose sharply. Employers wanted even more workers from Mexico, but the Mexican government opposed their efforts, concerned that another humiliating repatriation campaign might again occur at the time of the first economic downturn after the war. A compromise was reached in 1942 when employers convinced the U.S. government to make an agreement with the Mexican government to initiate a formal program of recruitment of contract laborers from Mexico for agricultural and railroad work. This new program included guaranteed minimum wages, worker protection, and an organized procedure for workers to return to Mexico on termination of the contract. The Mexican Labor Agreement was popularly called the Bracero Program. The war also stimulated labor migration from Mexico and the Caribbean to the United States via other formal programs and informal recruitment mechanisms.

World War II hastened changes in the employment

Mexican mine workers in the early 1900s. (Courtesy of the Arizona Historical Society.)

profile of Hispanic workers in the United States. The agricultural industry, which was the major single employer prior to the Great Depression, had been declining in relative terms throughout the century. It peaked in absolute numbers shortly after the end of World War II. With the onset of the war, employment for Hispanics expanded more rapidly in several areas of manufacturing and in the services. Hispanic workers continued to concentrate in unskilled and semi-skilled employment, largely in extractive agriculture, mining, and unskilled production tasks, especially as operatives, and in services.

The labor demands of World War II also stimulated a major wave of migration of Puerto Rican workers to the United States, largely through the auspices of Operation Bootstrap, a program initiated by the Puerto Rican government in 1944. Its major concern was to encourage industrialization in Puerto Rico and thereby diminish unemployment on the island. To further accomplish its goal of reducing the number of unemployed, it promoted a program of labor migration to the United States that involved arranging for labor recruiters to visit the island and also entailed working with airline companies to arrange

for cheap flights from Puerto Rico to New York City. The labor migration program was aimed mostly at securing employment in urban locations, but as part of the plan the Puerto Rican Department of Labor also devised arrangements with agricultural employers to hire seasonal agricultural workers under contract. Most of the agricultural workers went to eastern seaboard locations between Florida and New England to work in fruit and vegetable harvesting and canning operations. During the heyday of Operation Bootstrap, a net migration of at least 100,000 workers came to the United States from Puerto Rico each year, seeking permanent residence and employment principally in manufacturing and service industries.

A third phase of labor migration to the United States began in the 1960s, when the established patterns of movement from Mexico and Puerto Rico to the United States were modified, and migration from other countries increased. The Bracero Program ended in 1964, and after a brief decline in immigration, workers from Mexico increasingly arrived to work under the auspices of the H-2 Program of the Immigration and Nationality Act of 1952, as well as for family unification purposes or as undocumented workers. Workers from Puerto Rico continued to migrate to the United States, most often without promises of employment, but their migration at this time was increasingly offset by a massive return migration to Puerto Rico.

Another feature of this later labor migration has been the inclusion of people from a much wider range of countries in Latin America, and with a greater diversity of working backgrounds. Whereas Mexicans and Puerto Ricans continue to migrate for the most part as unskilled, semiskilled, or skilled workers, immigrants from other parts of the Caribbean and Central and South America have a wide range of backgrounds, including business and professional. This is particularly true of Cubans, the third most numerous Hispanic group in the United States. Their major wave of immigration occurred following the victory of the Cuban Revolution in 1959, and it included many prominent professionals and business-people. Later waves of Cuban immigrants were not as prosperous. The highly publicized Mariel boatlift in 1980 included many individuals from very poor, unskilled backgrounds, and with a lack of adequate job

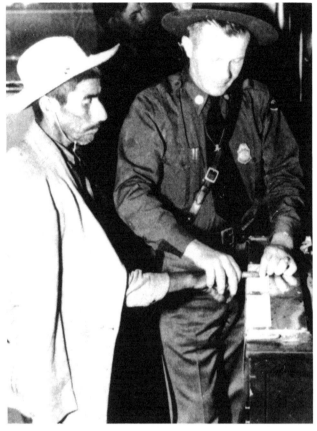

A Mexican worker being finger-printed for deportation. (Courtesy of the Library of Congress.)

training. Many of them have had great difficulty becoming incorporated into the work regimen of the United States.

✳HISPANICS IN ORGANIZED LABOR

As a predominantly working people, Hispanics have long been involved in efforts to organize as workers. One of their earliest groups, the Caballeros de Labor (Knights of Labor), was active in the Southwest in the late nineteenth century. Modeled after the American organization by the same name, Knights of Labor, its major stronghold was in New Mexico. It was never formally chartered, and it was more interested in land loss to recently arriving whites than labor issues. Other important cases of labor organizing in the late nineteenth century included Mexican cowboys in Texas and Cuban cigar workers in Florida.

During the late nineteenth and early twentieth centuries, a much greater number of Hispanic workers organized their own *mutualistas*, or mutual aid societies. These organizations engaged in social ac-

Puerto Rican garment workers in New York City.

Southern Pacific railroad workers during World War II in Tucson, Arizona. (Courtesy of the Arizona Historical Society.)

tivities and provided for basic needs of workers, including insurance and death benefits for members. Mutualistas functioned largely as self-help organizations and did not threaten employers, which helps explain their greater success than unions. In the early twentieth century, a plethora of mutualistas appeared, especially among groups of recent immigrants, who were encouraged by the local Mexican consular officials. They continued to represent the most widespread form of worker organization.

Apart from the mutualistas, labor organizing among Hispanics in the late nineteenth and early twentieth centuries was hindered by several factors. Hispanics were concentrated geographically in largely antiunion settings in the South and Southwest. They also faced hostility and discrimination because of societal attitudes, which often portrayed them as taking jobs away from white workers. The major labor organization in the nation, the American Federation of Labor (AFL), tended to be craft-exclusive and structurally not interested in the participation of largely unskilled Hispanic workers. More important, the AFL itself could not resolve internally the nativism and racism pervasive in American society that often led it and its local unions to adopt exclusionary policies. These problems severely reduced Hispanic participation in organized labor and resulted in significant organizing efforts outside the mainstream labor federation.

In the early twentieth century, union organizing among Hispanic workers increased in many areas. The most notable efforts took place in agriculture, which was still the most important single occupation. Most organizing took place under the auspices of independent Mexican unions, while in some cases there were either independent interethnic unions or multiethnic organizations, often with support from the radical Industrial Workers of the World. Railroad and other urban workers joined together for brief periods under the leadership of independent or Socialist organizations and, occasionally, the AFL. Many miners formed union organizations with the support and encouragement of the Western Federation of Miners in the early years of the twentieth century.

The most concentrated labor activity among the Spanish-speaking under the flag of the United States took place in Puerto Rico, led by the Federación Libre de los Trabajadores (Workers Labor Federation), or FLT, formed shortly before the turn of the century. In 1901, it affiliated with the American Federation of Labor, which broke from its more common policy of exclusivism toward non-whites. It accepted Puerto Rican workers because of its concern that they could enter freely into the United States and compete in the labor market and because of its fear of being overshadowed by rival organizations that also appeared in Puerto Rico. Important and widespread strikes in the sugar cane fields occurred in 1905 and 1906, and even larger ones took place in 1915 and 1916. After the early years of the century, however, the FLT organizing efforts turned more from the fields to the political arena.

Following a low point during the 1920s, labor organizing among Hispanic workers reached new peaks during the Great Depression. Independent organizations not affiliated with mainstream organized labor were most active and more typically composed of independent Mexican groups, Socialists, and members of the Communist party. In the later 1930s, leaders in the newly formed Congress of Industrial Organizations (CIO) also exhibited interest in organizing unskilled workers, and the CIO participated in the famous pecan shellers" strike in San Antonio in 1938, involving mostly young Mexican and Mexican-Amer-

ican women. Organizers Emma Tennayuca and Manuela Solis Seger gained attention in Texas at that time and remained active in labor for many years afterward.

Organizing and strikes in the 1930s also occurred among mining, industrial, and agricultural workers throughout the country. Mexican farm workers in California were particularly active throughout the decade. Their efforts were highlighted by the Central Valley cotton srike of 1933, in which several groups of independent Mexican union organizers and radicals offered support. The AFL considered these activities a serious challenge to its dominance, and in many occupations it permitted the formation of local unions for the first time to attract Mexican workers into its fold.

In Puerto Rico, workers upset with what they considered a sellout agreement between the FLT and U.S. owners who belonged to the Association of Sugar Producers staged a massive but unsuccessful spontaneous strike in 1933-34 to protest the arrangement. Their strike was the beginning of a long and protracted struggle against traditional FLT leadership that led to a sharp decline in the AFL-affiliated organization.

The turbulence of the 1930s reflected a sharp increase in expressions of sympathy toward unionism and unions among Hispanic workers. Much of the support had been latent but untapped until that time. Immigrants from Mexico frequently had strong union sympathies because of their earlier experiences before they arrived in the United States. Yet, traditional unions made only partial inroads into the Hispanic working population during the decade, hindered by continued employment discrimination, the success of employer efforts to pit workers against each other, and divisions within organized labor.

World War II served as a partial brake to direct labor organizing among Hispanic workers. But progressive elements within organized labor remained active, particularly in the struggle to eliminate many of the statutory forms of employment discrimination that Hispanics and other workers continually faced. Their efforts contributed to the formation of the Fair Employment Practices Committee (FEPC) in 1941. The FEPC investigated discrimination throughout the country by private companies with government contracts. Over a third of its cases in the Southwest involved Mexicans. Despite the efforts of President Truman, the FEPC was terminated at the end of World War II. It stands as an important predecessor to the corrective legislation and administrative bodies formed in the 1960s, particularly the Equal Employment Opportunity Commission.

Unionization among Hispanic workers increased

rapidly in the 1940s and 1950s, as Hispanic workers and sympathizers within both the AFL and CIO struggled for reforms that permitted them equal access and fair treatment. In many local unions they formed their own caucuses to demand representation and changes in discriminatory procedures by the union hierarchy and to encourage the union to challenge discriminatory practices by employers. They demonstrated union loyalty, sympathy, and a class-consciousness reinforced by their work experiences and treatment in the workplace. During this period they participated in many notable strikes, perhaps the best known of which was the "salt of the earth" strike by miners in Silver City, New Mexico, led by the International Mine, Mill and Smelter Workers Union between 1950 and 1953. The efforts of the National Farm Labor Union, later called the National Agricultural Workers Union, to organize in California during the 1940s and 1950s were also noteworthy. Union leader Ernesto Galarza demonstrated keen insight as a union leader, scholar, and role model for a later generation of Chicano activists.

In Puerto Rico, the independent Confederación de Trabajadores Generales, or CGT, formed in 1940, but it quickly affiliated with the CIO. It soon replaced the FLT as the major labor organization on the island. Through its close links to the government, it attained its greatest influence and membership during the 1940s and 1950s.

Among Hispanics, a number of independent unions again began to form in both Puerto Rico and in the continental United States. The most notable was the National Farm Workers Association in California, led by César Chávez. It began as an independent organization in 1962 and became part of the AFL-CIO in 1966. It is now known as the United Farmworkers of America. During its numerous strikes and boycotts of table grapes, wines, and lettuce, it popularized many tactics involving ethnic alliances, community organizing, and a focus on protecting the environment that suggest alternative organizing strategies for organized labor in the future. Another creative venture, The East Los Angeles Community Union (TELACU), was formed in 1971 as the result of cooperative efforts between the United Auto Workers and community organizers in East Los Angeles to build a "community" union.

Unemployed workers waiting in line at a relief office during the Depression. (Courtesy of the Library of Congress.)

A fruit picker in California. (Courtesy of the *Texas Catholic Herald*.)

A parade ending National Farm Workers Week in Union Square, New York in 1975. (Courtesy of the *Texas Catholic Herald*.)

Union-organizing activity in the United States peaked in the 1950s. From the early 1960s through the 1970s, the number of union members in the nation increased, though at a much slower rate than overall employment. The decrease in the rate of unionization during this period resulted from the reduction of jobs in highly unionized sectors, the growth of employment in traditionally nonunion occupations, the lack of vigilance of union leadership, increasingly sophisticated antiunion activities among employers and hostile government policy not enforcing protective labor legislation.

From the beginning of the Reagan Presidency in 1981 until 1985, union membership fell rapidly while total employment rose. Between 1985 and 1990, union membership declined more slowly, while total employment continued to rise. The decline in the 1980s is due to factors unfavorable to unions during the past generation, coupled with the most hostile federal government policy toward labor organizing and unions since the 1920s.

Unionization levels vary according to geography and occupation. Rates are highest in the Northeast and Midwest, and lowest in the South and Southwest, where Hispanic workers are most concentrated. In 1989, unionization in the public sector stood at 37 percent of workers, compared with 12 percent in private industry. It seems that private employers had a greater ability than the government to thwart worker organization despite the more rigid laws restricting labor organizing in the public sector. In the private arena, the more highly unionized sectors include transportation and public utilities at 32 percent, construction and manufacturing at 22 percent, and mining at 18 percent. In other major areas of private employment, union membership ranged from only 1 to 6 percent.

Union membership in 1990 was 16.1 percent of the working population over age 15, reflecting the continued decline over the past three decades. Unionization stood at 20 percent for men and 13 percent for women. By ethnicity, it was 22 percent among blacks, 16 among whites, and 15 percent among Hispanics. Among Hispanic men, 18 percent belonged to

A United Farm Workers picket line in Coachella, California in 1973. (Courtesy of the *Texas Catholic Herald*.)

unions, compared to 20.8 percent of white men and 27.5 percent of black men. Among women, 14.2 percent of Hispanics, compared with 14 percent of whites and 21.2 percent of blacks, were union members.

Union benefits typically include better working conditions; a greater range of such benefits as health care, vacation, and leave policy; worker protection; and higher wages. In 1990, union members earned an average of $420 per week, compared with $276 for nonunion members.

At present, there are 1.3 million Hispanic union members. Although there are many union officers, vice presidents, and directors, the only Hispanic president among the eighty-eight unions in the AFL-CIO is César Chávez of the United Farm Workers. In 1973, the Labor Council of Latin American Advancement (LCLAA) formed to promote the interests of Hispanics within organized labor.

✳ IMMIGRATION AND MIGRATION

Since the late 1960s, two major factors affecting immigration to the United States have become clear: an increase in the rate of undocumented immigration and a shift from Europe to Asia as the predominant source of immigration. Despite annual fluctuations, Latin America, dominated by Mexico, has maintained its proportionate contribution, while it has increased its total contribution of immigrants to the United States substantially, both in legal and undocumented immigration.

In the period from 1955 to 1964, 50.2 percent of all legal immigrants to the United States were from Europe, with rates declining to 10.1 percent in 1988. Immigration from Asia, meanwhile, increased from 7.7 percent during 1955-64 to 41.1 percent in 1988. Immigration from the Americas during this period increased from 41.1 percent to 44.3 percent. In 1989, immigration from the Americas rose to 61.4 percent. Of the major countries, Mexico accounted for 37.1 percent of total documented immigration to the United States, the next highest number of immigrants being from El Salvador, 5.3 percent, the Philippines, 5.2 percent, Vietnam, 3.5 percent, Korea, 3.1 percent, and China, 3.0 percent.

Between 1985 and 1989, immigration accounted for 2.7 percent of the nation's net population growth, with rates varying from 1.8 percent of whites, 2.1

percent of blacks, 15.5 percent of Hispanics, and 29.7 percent of the increase for other races.

Several formal and informal programs have been established to encourage immigration of workers to the United States. The best-known forms of organized labor recruitment have involved agricultural workers from Mexico and Puerto Rico. These include the mechanisms in the Bracero Program and Operation Bootstrap. Labor recruitment by the U.S. Farm Placement Service to encourage labor migration for temporary seasonal employment has also influenced permanent settlement patterns. The H-2 Program within the Immigration and Nationality Act of 1952, as amended by the 1986 Immigration Reform and Control Act of 1986 (IRCA), continues to guide immigration patterns to the United States.

Immigration from Mexico, Central and South America, and the Caribbean has also been encouraged by labor recruiters and by informal networks that link individual families and communities in Latin America and the United States together.

Internal migration has also affected the population patterns of Hispanics within the United States. The most general patterns of migration include the dispersal of Mexicans from their historic concentrations in the Southwest to the Midwest, the Pacific Northwest, and recently to Florida and the East Coast; the spread of Puerto Ricans beyond New York to other areas of the country; and the relocation of Cubans to places other than Miami. Most of this migration has been through informal mechanisms, established at the level of individuals and families, and by word of mouth.

The major net flows of Hispanics within the United States are from the Northeast and Midwest to Florida, Texas, and California; from New York to neighboring states in the Northeast; and from California to neighboring states in the West. Cuban Americans are becoming increasingly concentrated at somewhat higher levels in Florida, while Central and South Americans are becoming more concentrated in California and New York. People of Mexican origin are tending to disperse from the Southwest, while Puerto Ricans are moving away from their center of concentration in New York City. The total impact of migration and immigration in the 1970s and 1980s has been twofold. In absolute numbers, Hispanics have dispersed to a greater number of states and in wider areas within those states. In proportionate terms, they have concentrated at somewhat higher rates in the states already having large Hispanic populations. In 1970, 82 percent of the Hispanic population of the nation lived in nine states, with the proportion rising to 86 percent in 1990. The major recipients of Hispanic immigrants are California, Texas, and New York, and to a lesser degree Florida, Illinois, and New Jersey.

Hispanics born in the United States or residing in the country many years are more likely to migrate than are recent immigrants, who typically know less about the country, are less familiar with English, and generally of lower socioeconomic status. The recent immigrants are more likely to concentrate in ethnic enclaves for social and economic support.

Immigration remains an important factor accounting for the expansion of the labor force in the United States. The rates of immigration in the 1980s approached the levels of the early 1900s. Legal immigration during the first decade of the century reached 8.8 million, while during the 1980s 6.3 million immigrants were granted permanent residence. The immigrants are overwhelmingly young and in search of employment, and Hispanic immigrants continue to account for more than 40 percent of the total.

The Bracero Program

The term *bracero*, (from the Spanish *brazo*, meaning arm) applied to day laborers, generally; is sometimes used to refer to any Mexican worker in the United States under legal auspices. In this sense it includes workers entering the country under the H-2 Program of the Immigration and Nationality Act of 1952 and the H-2A Program of the Immigration Reform and Control Act of 1986, as well as to Mexican commuters often referred to as "green carders." "*Bracero*" is also occasionally used to refer to any unskilled Mexican workers brought into the United States.

The most popular use of "*bracero*" applies to the temporary Mexican agricultural and railroad workers first brought into the United States under contract in 1942 as an emergency measure to meet the temporary labor shortage of World War II. These braceros were an important part of the nation's agricultural labor force for almost a generation afterward. They dominated the harvest labor force in many parts of the Southwest and Midwest, particularly in sugar beets, cotton, pickles, tomatoes, and several other vegetable crops.

The Bracero Program, also referred to as the Mexican Farm Labor Supply Program and the Mexican Labor Agreement, began as a bilateral agreement between the governments of Mexico and the United States. It was given congressional sanction in 1943 as Public Law 45. Both governments considered it an important part of the Mexican contribution to the war effort.

The program was very popular among agricultural employers, who quickly organized and lobbied Congress to ensure its continuation beyond the end of the

A scene from the Bracero Program. (Courtesy of the Library of Congress.)

war. They were able to extend it temporarily several times, claiming a shortage of able and willing workers in the United States. Opponents of the Bracero Program, however, were able to reduce the scale of bracero employment in the late 1940s by demonstrating sufficient domestic worker availability. The outbreak of the Korean War in 1950, nevertheless, thwarted their efforts. In response to labor demands stemming from the war, agricultural employers convinced Congress in 1951 to pass Public Law 78, which renewed and expanded the program. On behalf of organized farm employers, the legislature passed several temporary extensions until 1964.

At the peak of the program in the late 1950s, the United States admitted more than 400,000 contract workers each season, almost twice as many as the number entering the country during the entire wartime emergency from 1942 to 1947.

The program was anathema to Mexican Americans and labor groups, who eventually gathered convincing evidence that, despite contract guarantees, braceros were not protected against abuses by employers and labor contractors, their working condi-

tions were not adequate, and they frequently were not paid the wages guaranteed them by contract. The opposition also demonstrated the program had an adverse effect on wages and working conditions of domestic workers and stifled unionization efforts not only in agriculture, but also in southwestern industry. The struggle against the program in the 1950s focused largely on its adverse effects, seeking reforms requiring employer compliance with contract guarantees and permitting braceros joining unions. This effort, nevertheless, failed, convincing opposition later in the decade to conduct an all-out attack on the program. Ultimately a combined group of labor union representatives, Mexican-American groups, religious and civic organizations, and their allies gained the support of a more pro-labor Democratic administration and obtained Congressional termination of the temporary program in 1964.

Since 1964 employer groups in agriculture have initiated several efforts in Congress to pass new and modified versions of the Bracero Program by hiring temporary seasonal contract workers from Mexico. As of 1991 none of their efforts had succeeded.

Termination of Public Law 78 was an important victory for Mexican-American and labor groups and helped pave the way for a flurry of labor organizing efforts in agriculture in the late 1960s.

The Maquiladoras

The abolition of the Bracero Program also demanded greater efforts by the Mexican government to relieve its own unemployment via industrialization. The most important element of its border industrialization program is the *maquiladora* (assembly plant) program, initiated in 1965. Mexico found industrialists and politicians in the United States very interested in the industrialization program. Mexico hoped that it could raise the standard of living in the northern border region, while both the U.S. and Mexican governments were concerned about the possible negative political and economic consequences of leaving hundreds of thousands of Mexican workers stranded on the border without employment when the Bracero Program was ended. Industrialists were eager to reap the benefits offered by tax and tariff breaks and by the availability of unemployed and underemployed workers in Mexico.

The central feature of the plan established "twin plants" on both sides of the Mexico-U.S. border. It also set up a duty-free zone which permits industrialists in the United States to ship unfinished goods to Mexico under bond for partial assembly or completion. The goods are then returned duty free to the "twin plant" on the U.S. side, to complete the manufacturing process. In the early years of the program,

A field worker in the Bracero Program. (Courtesy of the Library of Congress.)

about two-thirds of the products involved in the program were electric and electronic goods. As the program expanded in the 1970s and 1980s, the range of products expanded rapidly. By 1987, electric and electronic goods represented only about 35 percent of the total; textiles, clothing, and shoes, 18 percent; furniture, 10 percent; transportation equipment (including car motors), 9 percent; and a range of other goods, 28 percent.

The scale of production in the maquiladora industry also grew impressively. In 1966, it comprised 57 plants with about 4,000 workers. By 1979, it had about 540 plants hiring 120,000 workers, and by 1986 there were 844 plants employing 242,000 workers. By 1990, there were more than 1,000 plants employing about 450,000 workers. It is estimated that by 1995 there will be at least 1,500 plants with more than one million workers engaged in the program.

The maquiladora program in its actual operation is not at all as it was initially conceived. Its original intent was to alleviate the unemployment of male workers stranded at the end of the Bracero Program. Yet, the work force in the maquiladoras from the beginning has been approximately 85 percent female,

mostly teenage women with very high rates of turnover. In sum, the program does not offer steady employment or work to unemployed men.

Another discrepancy is that the program was initially restricted to a 12.5-mile-wide strip along the Mexican-U.S. border. A 1972 amendment, however, permitted its expansion into the Mexican interior. As a result, plants are now located throughout northern and central Mexico.

Still yet another flaw in the original plan is that the "twin plant" concept never became operational. While the production phase was conducted in the Mexican plants, the "plants" on the U.S. side were essentially warehouses. Like their counterparts in Mexico, the operations in the United States offered low-wage, unskilled employment. The maquiladora program in effect, thus, became a runaway shop taking advantage of cheap Mexican labor and exemption from tariffs.

U.S. companies involved in maquiladora operations assert that the program enables them to produce in Mexico rather than transfer their operations to Asia. Yet, during the 1980s Japanese industrialists took advantage of the maquiladoras to send greater amounts of raw materials to Mexico to have them finished, then shipped duty free into the United States. This led to a storm of protest in the United States, because, as Representative Duncan Hunter complained, "the Japanese can essentially use the program simply as a conduit into American markets without conferring benefits on American businessmen." In their discussion of the maquiladora program, very few politicians have considered the adverse impact on the much larger group of workers in the United States continuously displaced by the program.

The 1991 proposed Free Trade Agreement between Mexico and the United States expands even further the maquiladora concept in scale offering potentially greater tax abatements for U.S. businessmen. It will increase the number of runaway shops already relocated from the South and Southwest to across the border, where labor costs are lower, and worker and environmental protection, very weak. Furthermore, in Mexico it is difficult for organized labor and environmental and public interest groups from the United States to challenge corporations that are rooted in the United States and produce almost exclusively for the domestic market. Although advocates of the free trade agreement maintain that it will expand the size of markets in both Mexico and the United States, the sharp wage differential between Mexico and the United States makes it very difficult for Mexicans to afford to purchase the goods produced for export to the United States. In terms of worker protection, environmental damage, and the threat to the unity of Hispanic and Latin American workers on both sides of the border, the maquiladora program and the free trade agreement pose even greater threats than the Bracero Program.

Migrant Farm Labor

A migrant worker is a person employed at a job temporarily or seasonally and who may or may not have a permanent residence in another community, state, or nation. It is a misconception to portray farm workers solely as migrants or Hispanics, or to portray all migrant workers as farm workers. Migrants comprise only a small portion of the total of the ethnically diverse farm labor force of the United States. Seasonal migrant workers are employed in a wide range of occupations, including mining, forestry, and fishing, in addition to agriculture, which is the best-known form of migrant labor in the United States.

Most people who work on farms are either families who own or rent them or residents of nearby farms and communities who travel to work and return home at the end of the workday. Migrant farm workers are concentrated in the harvest operations of fruit and vegetable crops in several locations throughout the

United States. At other times of the year, they seek employment in agricultural or other occupations, often where they are permanently settled.

The number of agricultural migrant laborers has declined sharply since the late 1930s, when about four million people worked each season. Because of the problems of keeping track of them, it is very difficult to make an accurate estimate of their numbers. It is likely that about one million people were employed as migrant farm workers in the United States annually during the 1980s.

In the late nineteenth and early twentieth centuries, the size of the migrant labor force expanded rapidly owing to the introduction of large-scale commercial agriculture that was linked to the industrialization and urbanization of the nation's population. Millions of people left the farms and joined immigrants in the cities, augmenting the demand for foods they could not produce themselves.

Agricultural migrants at the turn of the century frequently were foreign immigrants who worked on farms temporarily while saving money to buy farms or seeking more permanent employment in nearby cities. On the West Coast, a large portion of the migrant farm workers at the end of the nineteenth and early twentieth centuries were Asians, while in other parts of the country most were Europeans and their children. With the expansion of the sugar beet, vegetable, and cotton industries in the early twentieth century, Mexican migrant workers increasingly took over seasonal farm labor, frequently returning to the Mexican border or nearby cities at the end of work in a crop or at the end of the season.

With the onset of the Great Depression, many Mexican migrant workers were displaced by southern whites and blacks, who dominated the migrant agricultural labor force in the 1930s and 1940s. In the 1950s and 1960s, black workers continued as the most numerous migrants along the eastern seaboard states, while Mexican and Mexican-American workers soon dominated the migrant paths between Texas and the Great Lakes, the Rocky Mountain region, and the area from California to the Pacific Northwest. Some observers noted very rough patterns of movement referred to as "migrant streams" that went northward from Florida, Texas, and Southern California each season in the 1940s and 1950s; but these became increasingly blurred over time.

A very large portion of the migrant agricultural labor force that traveled long distances eventually settled permanently wherever they could find higher-paying and more steady employment, especially in nearby towns and cities. Sometimes they continued to work in agricultural or food-packing or food-processing activities, but more often they left agricul-

A migrant work camp. (Courtesy of the Library of Congress.)

ture entirely. As a result of this unstable movement, there was a very rapid movement into and out of agriculture. Migrant workers who left agriculture were constantly replaced by new workers.

In spite of more sophisticated government programs on behalf of farm workers and governmental efforts to coordinate the needs of workers with the demands of employers since the 1950s, the movement of migrant workers between jobs remains very haphazard. Migrant and seasonal farm workers continue to experience long periods of unemployment, and are among the worst-paid and least-protected workers in the nation. They suffer high rates of illness, retain low levels of education, and they find few advocates within political circles. As outsiders to local communities, often separated by language and ethnic barriers, they seldom participate in decisions affecting the communities where they are employed.

In the 1960s and 1970s, the migrant agricultural work force changed rapidly. With the rise of the black power and Chicano movements, the appearance of modest protective legislation, and the increasingly successful unionization efforts of farm workers, employers increasingly sought to recruit and hire foreign workers to replace the citizens. Along the East Coast, they recruited increasingly from the Caribbean, and supplemented with workers from Mexico and Central America. In other parts of the country, they recruited mostly from Mexico and Central America. In the 1980s and 1990s, the vast majority of migrant farm workers in the United States have been foreign-born. Many of them migrate seasonally from Mexico and the Caribbean to the United States through the H-2 Program, which became an important mechanism of labor recruitment following the termination of the Bracero Program. In recent decades, undocumented workers from Latin America

have become the most important part of this labor force in many locations.

✴HISPANIC EMPLOYMENT IN INDUSTRY

Service Industries

The employment profile of workers in the U.S. has changed sharply in recent decades. The major category of service is increasing, while that of manufacturing is declining.

The service industries include a wide range of activities, from private household work, restaurant, hotel, and food services, and health and personal service occupations. Employment in service industries, which nearly doubled between 1970 and 1990, is high among females in most areas. The rate of Hispanic employment in service occupations is about double that of the non-Hispanic population for males, and about 40 percent higher for females.

In March 1989, 17.7 percent of employed Hispanic men worked in service industries, compared with 9 percent for non-Hispanic men. The rates were 24.1 percent for Hispanic women and 17.1 percent for non-Hispanic women.

Manufacturing and Basic Industries

Manufacturing and basic industries, traditionally the mainstay of the U.S. economy and historically the indicator of the leading economic nations in the world, are declining rapidly. Manufacturing occupations include precision production workers, craft and repair people, as well as operators, fabricators, and laborers. Both Hispanic males and females are highly overrepresented in this category, males by almost 25 percent and females at rates roughly double those of non-Hispanic females.

In 1989, about 47.9 percent of Hispanic males were employed in the broad category of manufacturing, compared with 39.8 percent of non-Hispanic males. Among females, 21.3 percent of Hispanics worked in manufacturing, compared with 10.5 percent of non-Hispanics.

✴FEDERAL EMPLOYMENT PROGRAMS AND LAWS

Title VII and the Equal Employment Opportunity Commission

The Economic Opportunity Act (EOA) of 1964 was the centerpiece of President Lyndon B. Johnson's War on Poverty. The philosophy behind the War on Poverty espoused private initiative and local efforts had not resolved longstanding problems of discrimi-

The interior of a migrant labor shack. (Courtesy of the *Texas Catholic Herald*.)

nation and poverty during the postwar boom in the United States. Furthermore, the government believed efforts to improve conditions were consistently thwarted by private interests, often in conjunction with local and state governmental authorities, where the poor, blacks and Hispanics were seldom represented. The federal government, thus, decided to initiate a program to provide training for workers to encourage recruitment, and to monitor hiring practices of public and private employers across the nation.

The EOA also created the Office of Economic Opportunity (OEO) to administer a number of programs on behalf of the nation's poor. These included the Job Corps, the Community Action Program (CAP), and the Volunteers in Service to America (VISTA).

The Job Corps is a job-training program whose goal seeks to help disadvantaged youths aged 16-21 find employment. In 1990, the typical Job Corps enrollee was eighteen years old, 83.5 percent were high school dropouts, 75 percent were minorities, 75 percent had never had a prior full-time job, 67 percent were male, and almost 40 percent came from families on public assistance.

VISTA, conceived as a domestic equivalent to the Peace Corps, worked with the poor in urban and rural locations. CAP was the primary OEO program, in which local groups combined the efforts of local government, business, labor, civic, and religious organizations and the poor to mobilize local resources to alleviate poverty.

Title VII of the Civil Rights Act of 1964 comprised the most important statute of the War on Poverty addressing employment discrimination. It prohibits discrimination on the basis of gender, creed, race, or ethnic background, "to achieve equality of employment opportunities and remove barriers that have operated in the past." Discrimination is prohibited in advertising, recruitment, hiring, job classification, promotion, discharge, wages and salaries, and other terms and conditions of employment. Title VII also established the Equal Employment Opportunity Commission (EEOC) as a monitoring device to prevent job discrimination. In effect, it renewed and expanded the Fair Employment Practices Committee, which had been dismantled at the end of World War II. The EEOC works in conjunction with state agencies in investigating charges of discrimination.

The issue of employment discrimination led to a great deal of litigation. Many important cases defined the scope of discrimination and employee protection under Title VII. In the key case of *Griggs v. Duke Power Company* (1971), Chief Justice Warren Burger, speaking for a unanimous Supreme Court, ruled that employers could not create screening devices in employment that operated as "built-in headwinds" for minority groups. The Court required employers to initiate practices that considered their impact on minorities. The ruling encouraged many employers in public and private sectors to devise programs encouraging the hiring of women and non-Euro-Americans.

Several of the important employment lawsuits directly involved Hispanics. *Espinoza v. Farah Manufacturing Company* (1973) held that Title VII does not protect discrimination against aliens. The Court also held, however, that Title VII prohibits practices that have "the purpose or effect of discriminating on the basis of national origin." In *Carino v. University of Oklahoma* (1984), the Court held that an employer cannot refuse to hire an individual "because the individual has the physical, cultural or linguistic characteristics of a particular national origin group," or discriminate "because of the individual's accent or manner of speaking."

In reaction to equal employment legislation and the increasing presence of Hispanics and other non-English-speaking people in the workplace, some states in the past several years have enacted so-called English-only amendments to their constitutions. Collectively they imposed English as the official language of their state.

Following the spirit of this legislation, many employers attempted to restrict the use of foreign languages by imposing "English-only" rules in the workplace. Such actions are prohibited under Title VII, which prohibits discrimination on the basis of national origin. EEOC policy provides that rules "which require employees to speak English only at all times are presumptively unlawful because they unduly burden individuals whose primary language is one other than English, and tends to create a hostile or discriminatory environment based on national origin."

Language rights have thus become an important employment issue challenging Hispanic workers in the 1990s, particularly where their numbers are high. Public and private employers commonly engage in hiring Hispanic employees because of their special skills as translators, but seldom grant them compensation or consider such skills as important factors in job promotion. In *Pérez et al. v. Federal Bureau of Investigation* (1988), Hispanic FBI agents offered their special skills to the FBI more than Anglo Spanish-speakers and non-Spanish-speakers, but did not receive compensation. The federal district court held that by being concentrated in interpreting tasks, the Hispanic agents were treated differently from and denied promotional opportunities offered to Euro-American agents.

As a result of positive legislation and court interpretations, conditions of employment for Hispanics registered significant improvements in several areas during the 1960s and much of the 1970s.

The EEOC and CETA under Nixon and Carter

During the Nixon presidency, the first efforts to dismantle the War on Poverty began. The Nixon administration did not overtly attack the concept of equal opportunity, nor did it challenge the theories or actual programs already established to deal with the chronically unemployed. Rather, its desire for changes focused on attempts to realign political relationships involving federal, state, and local governments and community organizations.

Its remedies were part of its "New Federalism" program. The Great Society programs in the Office of Economic Opportunity (OEO) were centralized, with training programs and a strong oversight mechanism headed by the federal government. Local involvement was conceived largely through participation in the organizations where citizens were directly involved, especially through the Community Action Program (CAP). The New Federalism sought to reduce federal involvement and place the programs in the hands of state and local governments.

While in theory local control should be superior in meeting local needs, the creators of the New Federalism conceived the change in political terms. The political problem they perceived was that under the War on Poverty programs, there was a modest shift in local power away from the old elites, particularly white politicians, in the direction of the poor, particularly Hispanics and blacks. They believed they could return power to the old elites by removing the presence of the federal government and eliminating the community organizations.

The poor were justifiably dubious of Nixon's argument that local officials were most responsive to those most in need, having recent memories of breaking down local barriers to education and employment, with the assistance of federal government intervention.

The Nixon administration placed all employment and training programs, previously in the OEO, into the new Comprehensive Employment and Training Administration (CETA), created in 1973. The major difference between the old and the new poverty efforts was that the earlier employment and training programs were clearly targeted to specific population groups and allocated as "categorical" grants, on the basis of national and local considerations. Under CETA, allocations were granted directly to local politicians in the form of "bloc" grants to state and local governments, which could then make decisions on the kinds of programs to establish. Another change was that the CETA plan reduced the power of the federal government's regulations, standards, and other monitoring mechanisms created to ensure the efficacy of the local programs. Furthermore, although the new plan intended to allow local people to determine needs locally, no affirmative action guidelines were established to ensure that the poor and, especially, women, blacks, and Hispanics, the people for whom the programs were intended, would be represented in the decision-making process. This was particularly evident as CAP was severely weakened. The success of CETA rested on the goodwill of federal and local authorities. During the Nixon administration, many of the community leaders were removed and CETA programs were made increasingly the province of local politicians.

During the Carter presidency, the federal government expressed an increased commitment to equal opportunity, and CETA was strengthened. It is no coincidence that at this time the economic well-being of Hispanics and other non-whites peaked and the gap with the white population narrowed.

Furthermore, CETA was considered a success by most of its Hispanic participants. In fiscal year 1978, 142,000 youths, or slightly more than one-tenth of those enrolled in CETA programs, were Hispanics. Overall, approximately 5 percent of the country's white youth, 19 percent of blacks, and 13 percent of Hispanic youth participated in CETA programs that year. Hispanic participation ranged from 23 percent of Puerto Ricans, 13 percent of Mexican Americans, and 7 percent of Cubans. Interviews conducted that year indicated that more than 87 percent were satisfied with the program, and more than 70 percent believed that it improved their job chances. Nevertheless, CETA and government training programs for the unemployed were being more strongly criticized than ever before by their nonparticipant detractors, who found their own opportunity when Reagan was elected president.

The Job Training Partnership Act

The Reagan administration philosophy led to a profound change in government policy on job training programs based on both political and economic thought. Politically, the Reagan administration

adopted the position that although it must still provide a "safety net" to assist the needy poor, such assistance should be distinguished from support, and that support is not a federal government responsibility. It also carried the New Federalism concept much further politically and economically than Nixon by reducing the amount of federal assistance for job creation and other social service programs.

The federal government also reduced its direct involvement by operating more in "partnership" with private as well as state and local government bodies. The impact of government philosophy and policy is clearly evident in the Job Training Partnership Act (JTPA) of 1983, the central employment training program of the Reagan and Bush years. The JTPA, like its predecessor, CETA, delivers employment and training services to the economically disadvantaged in need. Compared with CETA, the JTPA depends much more on the private sector to deliver these services.

The new program departs sharply from earlier direct job creation strategies that were central to projects of the 1960s and the 1970s. Federally funded jobs created by the Public Service Employment, offering employment to both the cyclically and structurally unemployed, were eliminated under the JTPA. Part of the concept of less government support for the poor, it represented a 60 percent reduction in subsidies for youth employment. It severely reduced employment prospects for many disadvantaged youth whose first full-time employment had come from CETA and its predecessors.

In effect, the JTPA is designed to serve the demands of employers rather than the needs of unemployed workers. It is performance-driven and is structured to reward programs with high placement rates and low costs. In practice however, its standards are ignored. Futhermore, government monitoring devices established by earlier programs have been virtually dismantled.

The JTPA, as an example of the New Federalism, has failed to meet its mandate of providing for the training needs of the unemployed. Its structure is flawed, does not meet the interests of society generally, and is riddled with corruption.

Several structural problems in the Job Training Partnership Act specifically hinder Hispanic participation. A high proportion of Hispanics are needy, in part because of a nearly 50 percent high school dropout rate and because over one-fourth are not fully proficient in English but they are vastly underserved. The JTPA penalizes these people more than any other among the poor by not including precisely those who are most disadvantaged and hrder to place. In addition, the JTPA has income-based eligibility stipulations requiring that people must either be receiving food stamps or not have more than a specific level of income. Many Hispanics who are eligible for JTPA, however, are imbued with a work ethic and are unwilling to accept food stamps. Still others are not eligible because they are willing to accept jobs that place them in an income level slightly above the sharply increased level of eligibility requirements. Another problem is that the JTPA has increased requirements for documentation of eligibility beyond those of CETA—a policy that has been criticized as unduly burdensome. Furthermore, Mexican Americans, in particular, lack familiarity with government programs, and the means of informing them about JTPA programs are woefully lacking. Finally, Hispanics lack a presence in most JTPA policy-making forums, and thus lack consistent advocates to set policies.

Beyond their structural problems, the cutbacks in job training efforts caused by the JTPA program have even broader negative consequences for the society at large. The reduction in training has been criticized by proponents of human capital, who argue that the reduced investment in training workers will have a costly long-term impact by reducing federal revenues and entitlement expenditures in the future. The disinvestment will also contribute to high unemployment and an inadequately trained work force. Society benefits, such as income tax and revenues for programs like Social Security, will decline, while costs for public assistance will increase.

The impact of Reagan job training policy, continued under the Bush administration, is further evident in the case of the Job Corps, created under the EEOC, and presently part of the JTPA. The Job Corps has residential and nonresidential centers where enrollees take intensive programs in education, vocational training, work experience, and counseling. It is popular in both parties of Congress, and the U.S. Department of Labor (USDL) has acknowledged its success. A 1985 USDL study determined that the Job Corps returns $1.38 to the U.S. Treasury in only three years for each $1 invested by the federal government. The funds come from continuing taxes paid by former Job Corps trainees once they begin employment and from reduced welfare payments. The Job Corps, serving the most disadvantaged, nonetheless, was among the programs cut most sharply by the JTPA.

Even the inadequate funds for the program are not being utilized effectively. Congress established specific levels of spending to ensure sufficient funding establishing adequate programs for the needy; yet in many areas the funds are not being spent.

Congressional hearings in 1990 found that corruption abounds in the training process itself.

Many private schools, so-called "proprietary schools," replaced government-trained OEO and CETA workers providing training. The proprietary schools are for-profit institutions set up specifically to receive government grants, and are paid to train workers. The recipients of the funds seldom have competent training in operating educational institutions. Many of the courses their schools teach lack rigor, are taught by untrained and uncertified teachers, prepare the workers for nonexistent jobs and are not placement driven.

The structural design of the incentives process created by the JTPA reveals severe difficulties in the program. Local JTPA offices are motivated by incentives based on the actual number of people hired by private employers. This has led to the process of "creaming" in client selection. Creaming selects the least-disadvantaged individuals because they are the easiest to place. The programs have targeted services primarily to in-school youth or high school graduates; thus, service to high school dropouts has declined sharply.

Furthermore, local employers are paid by JTPA funds to hire employees. This leads to widespread abuse, for it allows employers to receive government funds to "hire" individuals they would have otherwise hired without JTPA "incentives" of several weeks" or months" pay. The JTPA has become a major government subsidy for private employers, not a training program for those most in need.

The "New Federalism" originally was designed to transfer power from the federal government to local agencies and employers. In effect, it has taken away power from the poor and from community organizations, remaining largely pushed out of the decision-making process. In the past, community organizations worked in conjunction with federal government administrators. Under the JTPA, however, funding is granted directly to governmental agencies and private proprietors as rewards for their support. Because the monitoring system is so lax and community participation dismantled, efforts to expose the JTPA have been long delayed. As a result, the JTPA has shortchanged the needs of Hispanics, blacks, and others most in need of training, as well as society at large, while serving the narrow interests of employers in the private sector and their allies.

Employment Rights

During the 1980s, the Reagan and Bush administrations also launched an attack on civil rights legislation as it extended to the workplace. The new Supreme Court justices appointed by Reagan and Bush helped change the direction of court protection of employees. In effect, its rulings have relaxed the duties of employers and have made it much more difficult for women and non-whites to convince the courts that violations of civil rights laws have taken place. The attack peaked in a series of 1989 Supreme Court decisions relating to employment law. In *Patterson v. McLean Credit Union* (1989), the Supreme Court ruled that an individual could no longer sue for racial harassment at work under a 1966 civil rights statute: "A practice of racial harassment adopted after an employee was hired does not by itself violate that employee's rights under the statute." In effect, it permitted the employer to hound Ms. Patterson out of her job because of race.

In *Wards Cove Packing Co. v. Antonio* (1989), the Court ruled that a group of employees who were able to demonstrate that an Alaska cannery that hired whites for well-paid and skilled jobs and minorities for low-paid, unskilled jobs, and even segregated employees by race in mess halls and dormitories, did not offer sufficient evidence of employment discrimination. It reversed twenty-eight years of well-established law in its holding by imposing a heavier burden on employees in proving its employer did not have legitimate business reasons for engaging in such practices.

During the same period, other Supreme Court cases severely limited the filing of discrimination charges, and further ruled that a civil rights statute could not be used to sue local governments for damages for acts of discrimination. These and other cases successfully narrowed the coverage of civil rights statutes, making it extremely difficult for women and minorities to prove discrimination simultaneously making it easier for those opposed to civil rights to post challenges.

The erosion of past civil rights legislation by the Supreme Court during the Reagan and Bush administrations resulted in efforts by representatives of civil rights, black, and Hispanic organizations to initiate a push for a new Civil Rights Act in 1990 to return to previous standards. The legislation sought to redress the discriminatory impact of recent Supreme Court decisions that in sum eliminated much of the thrust of equal employment opportunity law established in the previous generation. Although the 1990 bill had overwhelming support in both houses of Congress, the Bush administration vetoed the legislation on the grounds that it promoted quotas. A series of compromises produced a watered-down Civil Rights Act in 1991.

Affirmative Action

Affirmative action, centering on the Civil Rights Act of 1964, was a central concept of the Great Society programs of the Johnson administration. It accepted the premise that the high levels of unemployment and ongoing discrimination that women and many non-white groups encountered were impediments to the vision of the Great Society. The federal government accepted the responsibility to devise "affirmative action" programs to remedy such discriminatory practices and their consequences.

Affirmative action is designed to counter the effects of practices that exclude individuals from the workplace and other settings because of race, color, creed, gender, and national origin. It accepts the assumption that because of their background, many highly qualified people have been passed over in hiring and promotion practices and that steps should be taken to rectify exclusionary practices. The federal mandate was to encourage employers to voluntarily increase the presence of underrepresented minorities in the work force to levels commensurate with their presence in the local community. Compliance officers in the Equal Employment Opportunity Commission (EEOC) and the Department of Labor set goals, targets, and timetables for employers. For example, Executive Order 11246 in 1972 established two requirements: nondiscrimination, or "the elimination of all existing discriminatory conditions whether purposeful or inadvertent," and affirmative action, whereby employers are to take positive efforts "to recruit, employ and promote qualified members or groups formerly excluded." It also encourages individual employers to voluntarily adopt affirmative action programs.

Affirmative action programs were immediately criticized by some conservative elements in the country who argued that affirmative action favored minorities over more "qualified" Whites. The struggle over affirmative action continued into the 1970s, when opponents coined the term "reverse discrimination," by which they suggested that white males were victims of discrimination as a result of affirmative action on behalf of women, blacks, Hispanics, and other underrepresented groups.

Within the federal government, the Reagan and Bush administrations in the 1980s intensified the attack and engaged in a systematic dismantling of affirmative action programs. The Reagan administration promoted the argument that affirmative action programs entailed quotas, constituting a form of reverse discrimination. The Justice Department under Reagan also spearheaded opposition to affirmative action, claiming that the administration "has profound doubts whether the Constitution permits governments to adopt remedies involving racial quotas to benefit persons who are not themselves the victims of discrimination." In essence it denied that broad discrimination against a group of people as a class could in theory exist. A highlight of the Reagan-Bush administration success was the Supreme Court decision in *City of Richmond v. Croson* (1989), which struck down an ordinance that set aside 30 percent of Richmond Virginia's construction contracts for minority businesses.

The attacks on affirmative action have had a profound impact on hiring policies in many sectors of private and public employment. They have contributed to the overall decline of the economic position of Hispanics and other ethnic minorities during the 1980s, both in absolute levels and in comparison with whites. It is most telling in top management positions in large corporations, where most surveys indicate that at least 95 percent of positions are still held by white males.

The federal government has failed not only to abide by its responsibility to serve as watchdog over affirmative action policies in the private sector but also to take affirmative steps itself. Although the Reagan administration could point to an increase in Hispanic representation in the federal work force from 4.3 percent to 4.8 percent between 1980 and 1988, the Hispanic population during that period increased from 6.4 percent to 8.1 percent. Thus, Hispanic underrepresentation in federal employment during the Reagan administration increased sharply, from 50 percent to 69 percent. The underrepresentation was most stark in the highest levels. At the top scale of government, senior executive service, Hispanics accounted for only 1 percent of the employees.

Undocumented Workers

Use of the term "undocumented" to refer to people who are in the United States without proper immigrant papers was established by the International Labor Organization in 1974. It was meant to be descriptive and neutral, in contrast to the term "illegal," which has negative connotations and implies criminality. The presence of undocumented aliens in the United States violates civil statutes but does not violate criminal laws. Some undocumented workers enter the country without legal authorization, while others enter under temporary permits but then extend their stay.

Immigration and Naturalization Service

The number of undocumented aliens cannot be precisely determined, and is the subject of intense debate. In the 1970s, Immigration and Naturalization Service (INS) Commissioner Leonard Chapman, seeking to increase funding and expand the power of his organization, claimed that there were as many as 12 million undocumented workers in the country.

Other observers most commonly place the number in the range of 3.5 million to 5 million people.

Popular perceptions and the press portray almost all undocumented workers as Mexicans. This is further bolstered by the policies of the INS, whose enforcement efforts are concentrated along the land border between Mexico and the United States, rather than at seaports and airports, or along the United States'' northern border. About 95 percent of INS apprehensions are Mexicans, yet it is likely that only about half of all undocumented workers in the United States are Hispanics, the remainder being mostly natives of Europe and Asia.

In addition to their numerical importance, undocumented workers have been at the center of several political battles. On several occasions in recent decades, a national hysteria among citizens developed over their presence, typically during periods of economic recession and depression. Debates intensified during those periods over whether the undocumented take jobs away from U.S. citizens.

Operation Wetback, which occurred during a time of recession in 1954, involved a concerted campaign by the federal government that successfully apprehended more than one million undocumented Mexican workers. The frenzy subsided when the government and private employers expanded the scale of the bracero program, reducing the demand of agricultural employers for undocumented workers.

Following abolition of the bracero program in the mid-1960s, the number of undocumented workers again began to increase, and a new hysteria appeared in public circles, accompanied by increased activity by the border patrol. By 1977, the INS was again apprehending more than one million undocumented workers each year.

The hysteria over the undocumented intensified during the 1980s. Several ultraconservative and nativist groups attempted to stir up the nation. In 1986, for example, the Ku Klux Klan announced that the influx of "illegal aliens" was responsible for Texas's economic problems, including its high level of unemployment, and vowed to hunt down illegal aliens and turn them over to the border patrol.

The effect of undocumented workers on the economy has stirred a wide-ranging debate in the nation. One side of the argument is that they are a major drain on public services and that they displace U.S. citizens by accepting low-paying jobs. These arguments frequently are based on stereotypes and ethnic biases, and they seldom address the related issue of why employers are permitted to disregard protective labor statutes and immigration law.

An opposing position is that the undocumented pay taxes, and because they seldom use available social services, they make a very positive contribution to the nation's economy. Further, the jobs in which they are employed typically are those that others are unwilling to perform.

Undocumented workers enter the United States for various reasons. The most important are to escape political and social turmoil in their native country, to escape poverty and poor living conditions, and to achieve a better life in the United States. These are combined with active and aggressive recruitment by employers, often with the implied consent of the U.S.government.

Undocumented Hispanic immigrants are concentrated geographically in the South and Southwest and employed largely in service occupations, manufacturing, and agriculture. While their average earnings exceed the minimum wage, their wages are significantly lower than legal residents and citizens in the same occupations. Furthermore, they are commonly hired at wages below the legal minimum, working in unsafe conditions and facing inhumane and discriminatory treatment. Politically they are vulnerable, and either unaware of their rights, or because of fear of deportation and loss of jobs, apprehensive about exerting the rights to which they are entitled under protective labor legislation.

Undocumented workers retain most employment rights of citizens, including those of minimum wage, joining and participating in union activities, the right to sue over contracts, and other protection under federal labor law. They are also deemed "employees" within the meaning of the National Labor Relations Act, and are protected under its provisions. Legal cases have also recognized the right to worker's compensation and protection under the Fair Labor Standards Act. Yet, employers frequently use the INS to escape their responsibilities under these laws and report for deportation workers who attempt to organize unions or assert other employment rights.

The anti-immigrant sentiments are often used by INS officials to increase their own power and that of the organization beyond its constituted civil authority. In its increasing exercise of violence, clearly in opposition to statutes that govern its operation, it is becoming a paramilitary organization. The tactic of INS workplace raids to apprehend undocumented workers has enabled the agency to violate workers" rights. In the 1984 INS Operation Jobs campaign, INS agents even raided businesses without valid search warrants or the consent of the employer.

In *Immigration and Naturalization Service v. Delgado* (1984), the Supreme Court ruled that workers were not subject to seizures as a result of INS raids on the workplace because the workers were "free to leave." Yet the raids occurred in the "presence of agents blocking each exit, armed with badges, walkie-talkies and guns and roving agents in open view questioning workers and taking some of them away." The INS has also intensified its border activities, increasing the use of force, intimidation, and other forms of violence.

Several observers, including the American Friends Service Committee, have reported widespread harassment and cases of assault by INS officers. They have documented "sexual abuse of undocumented immigrants, particularly refugee women," "beating undocumented immigrants, or those suspected of being undocumented immigrants," and the "deliberate destruction of immigrants" property or documents." Several tragedies occurred in the 1980s because of violent tactics of INS officials, including the deaths of at least fourteen farm workers seeking to escape apprehension by the Border Patrol during field operations. Civil rights and other organizations have exposed cases of inhumane treatment, including strip searches, beatings, unprotected exposure to the direct sun for several hours, lack of medical attention, denial of visitation by family members, and denial of counsel. In defense of their tactics, INS officials have criticized individuals and groups seeking to educate undocumented immigrants about their rights as "incredible" and "against America."

Hostility directed against foreign workers, particularly the undocumented, surfaced again in the 1970s and 1980s in congressional circles, and demands for a change in the nation's immigration laws intensified.

The Immigration Reform and Control Act of 1986

Sensitive to the increased immigration that began in the 1960s and the economic uncertainty of the 1970s, the Ford administration appointed several task forces to address the issue of undocumented entry into the United States. It encouraged several congressional representatives to introduce new legislation to control immigration to the United States. After more than a decade of debate, Congress enacted the Immigration Reform and Control Act of 1986, popularly referred to as IRCA.

The proponents of IRCA argued that the legislation was necessary to reverse the perceived accelerated immigration of the undocumented, to "save jobs for Americans," and to halt the perceived drain on social services. Numerous careful studies produced since that time have demonstrated that none of the above perceptions was accurate.

IRCA contains three major provisions. First, it establishes civil and criminal penalties, referred to as employer sanctions, on employers who fail to verify the documentation of employees hired since 1986 whether they are eligible to work. This marks the first time in the history of the United States that employers have been prohibited by law from hiring undocumented workers. Second, IRCA provided a one-time provision to legalize undocumented workers in the United States. The legalization process included a separate program to legalize seasonal agricultural workers (SAWs) in the United States. Third, the law specifically prohibits several forms of employment discrimination. In response to the concerns of Hispanic and civil rights groups that the employer sanctions would result in discrimination, the law mandated that the General Accounting Office (GAO) conduct in an ongoing investigation of the impact of IRCA for three years. IRCA specifically provides Congress with the statutory authority to repeal employer sanctions if the GAO's final report were to conclude that widespread discrimination existed. To facilitate the provisions of the law, Congress also strengthened the power and personnel of the INS.

The GAO made its final report on IRCA to Congress on March 29, 1990. It observed that the implementation and enforcement of employer verification and sanctions provisions were not carried out satisfactorily, that they had caused a widespread pattern of discrimination against members of minority groups, and that they caused unnecessary regulatory burdens on employers. Many employers were confused about the law and its application and initiated illegal discriminatory hiring practices against Hispanics, Asians, and other people who appeared "foreign." Even white workers experienced discriminatory practices. The GAO concluded that there was a "widespread pattern" of discrimination based on national origin, practiced by 19 percent of the employers surveyed, that included not hiring foreign-appearing or foreign-sounding job applicants for fear of noncompliance with the law. In a "sting" operation involving pairs of Hispanic and Anglo "testers," it found that "Anglo testers received 52 percent more job offers than the Hispanic testers with whom they were paired."

The GAO investigation was narrow in its view of what constituted "widespread discrimination" and did not support repealing employer sanctions. Other agencies and civil rights activists documented cases of discrimination, such as employers" firing applicants for legalization along with undocumented workers, depriving them of seniority and other benefits, imposing English-only rules, withholding paychecks, failing to pay overtime, harassing them sexually, assaulting them physically, and violating other civil and constitutional rights. In effect, IRCA pushed undocumented workers into even less regulated and more exploitative jobs.

Employers have also suffered the impact of employer sanctions. Estimates of total costs to businesses to perform record-keeping required by employer sanctions vary from $182 million to $675 million per year. Furthermore, businesses are paying millions of additional dollars in fines and otherwise suffering financially because of loss of workers and INS intrusions into the workplace.

In meeting one of its original goals, preventing the entry of undocumented workers into the United States, IRCA appears to have been successful in its first two years. Since that time, the entry of undocumented workers has increased sharply. In the early 1990s, it appears that the prohibitions of IRCA have not had a long-term impact on rates of undocumented entry into the country. They have proved to be a nuisance to employers and an additional burden to all workers—undocumented, legal residents, and citizens alike.

Thus, the GAO report and other evidence confirmed the fears of Hispanic groups before its enactment—that the law would intensify discrimination against Hispanics. On the basis of the GAO report and other evidence, employer sanctions are causing widespread discrimination. Hispanic activists are trying to convince Congress to comply with its own mandate and repeal employer sanctions.

✳YOUTH EMPLOYMENT

The Hispanic work force is younger than other major work force groups, and in the future it will represent an even greater portion of the work force. Hispanics have lower levels of schooling than other groups. Among youths ages 16-21 not attending college, more than two-fifths of employed blacks and whites are high school graduates, compared with less than one-third of Hispanics. Because government job training programs are being cut back, the nation's future work force may be inadequate.

Hispanic youths are more likely to work full time and year round than either white or black youths. Employed Hispanic male youths are also more likely to be married than black and white males. As with other groups, Hispanic male youths are more likely to be employed than females.

Youths of all backgrounds tend to have much higher unemployment rates than older workers, and their rate of unemployment is more sensitive to business cycles. White youths have the lowest unemployment level, while blacks have the highest rate of unemployment, which tends to be less sensitive to changes in the economy than either the white or

Hispanic rates. Unemployment rates for Hispanics fluctuate between the two others. During upturns in the economy, the rate of unemployment declines more sharply for Hispanic youths, while during downturns, it rises much more rapidly than for either whites or blacks.

In 1988, the unemployment rate for youths ages 16-19 was 12.7 percent for whites. For blacks it was 32.4 percent, and for Hispanics, 19.4 percent.

In the third quarter of 1990, the median weekly earnings for full-time male workers ages 16-24 were $283 for whites, $255 for blacks, and $238 for Hispanics. Among female youths, the earnings were $250 for whites and $225 for blacks and Hispanics.

✸ WOMEN'S EMPLOYMENT

During the past decade, the number of Hispanic women in the work force increased more rapidly than any other major population group, and by the end of the decade their rate of participation nearly equaled those of women in other groups. The distinctiveness of Hispanic women in employment has been largely erased. Between 1978 and 1988, Hispanic female participation in the work force more than doubled, from 1.7 million to 3.6 million. In 1988, 56.6 percent of Hispanic women were in the work force, compared with 66.2 percent of white women and 63.8 percent of blacks. The lower rate for Hispanic women can be attributed largely to their younger age and higher number of children than black and white women.

Hispanic women in 1988 formed 6.5 percent of the civilian labor force. Of the total of 3.6 million Hispanic women workers, 58.5 percent were of Mexican origin, 10.4 percent were Puerto Rican, 6.6 percent were of Cuban origin, and the other 24.5 percent were of other Hispanic backgrounds. By ethnicity, 53.9 percent of women of Mexican origin, compared with 54.9 percent of Cuban origin and 41.4 percent of Puerto Rican origin, were employed.

In March 1988, 41.1 percent of working Hispanic women were employed in technical, sales, and administrative support occupations, rates not much different from those of other women. At that same date, there were sharper differences in occupations of high and low pay and status. In the higher-status managerial and professional jobs, 15.7 percent of Hispanic women found employment, versus 25.3 percent of all women. Meanwhile, 16.6 percent of Hispanic women worked as lower-paid operators, fabricators, and laborers, compared with only 8.8 percent of all women. There were very few Hispanic women in extractive occupations, in mechanic and repairer jobs, or in most construction trades.

In the fourth quarter of 1990, the median weekly earnings of Hispanic women was $283, compared with $313 for black women and $361 for white women. Because of sharp increases in the work force, Hispanic women in the 1990s are about as likely to be employed in wage labor as other women. But their incomes remain substantially below those of women in the other major groups.

Government Programs

The federal government committed itself to eliminating discrimination in employment when it passed the Fair Employment Practices Act in 1941. The act created a monitoring mechanism in the Fair Employment Practices Commission (FEPC), which went out of existence in 1945. Despite its ongoing commitment, the federal government made little systematic effort to address fair employment practices again until the Kennedy administration.

The Manpower Development and Training Act (MDTA), passed in 1962, initially offered vocational training for unemployed adult workers displaced by automation, and later it was expanded to include youth training programs. The government effort increased with the enactment of the Economic Opportunity Act (EOA) of 1964, the flagship of the War on Poverty. Among the programs included in the act aimed at the poor, including Hispanics, were the Neighborhood Youth Corp, the Job Corps, the Community Action Program, and VISTA. The EOA also had a section dealing specifically with migrant and seasonal farm workers.

The War on Poverty held a philosophical position that a culture of poverty existed. Leaders of the New Frontier and Great Society considered it the responsibility of the federal government to take steps to eradicate poverty through a centralized program of training and other forms of direct action. They were convinced that eliminating poverty and discrimination would not succeed if responsibilities remained in the hands of local authorities and employers, or if left to the individual efforts of the poor.

The New Frontier and Great Society were also responding to the needs of their own constituencies among labor, community, black, and Hispanic groups. Part of the EEOC thrust was directed toward Hispanics because of the efforts of the two most important Mexican-American organizations in the country, the American G.I. Forum and the League of United Latin American Citizens (LULAC). Immediately after the EOA was passed, the two initiated an independent program, Jobs for Progress, commonly known as SER (service, employment, redevelopment; in Spanish ser means "to be"). SER began as a voluntary job placement center in Washington, D.C., and through its close ties to the government, soon expanded. By 1966, SER was receiving funds from the

Office of Economic Opportunity, the Department of Health, Education and Welfare, the Department of Labor, and private sources to meet its goals of providing skills training and related services to the Hispanics of the Southwest. In 1970, SER became a categorical program under the Department of Labor. By 1972, it had expanded to thirteen states in the Southwest and Midwest, plus the District of Columbia. SER is a nonprofit corporation whose principal objectives are to assist the disadvantaged, with a priority given to Hispanics and emphasis on manpower and related programs to upgrade educational and vocational skills and open career opportunities. It is closest single link between a Hispanic job training organization and the federal government.

The direction of government action and philosophy has undergone two major changes since the EOA was enacted in 1964. In 1973, the government created the Comprehensive Employment and Training Administration (CETA), an effort to alter the direction of government programs that it felt were gaining too much power. CETA, which was to be the major federal legislation governing employment and training programs for the next decade, offered a decentralized delivery system that gave state and local governments a greater degree of control over the programs, the original intent being to allow the poor, blacks, and Hispanics to have a direct voice in their own affairs.

The direction of CETA was sharply altered in 1983 when the Job Training Partnership Act (JTPA) was initiated. It became an employer-oriented organization in which the demands of local employers were given priority over the specific needs of the unemployed and poor.

Occupations

The occupational distribution of the Hispanic work force is highly overrepresented in manufacturing, operator, and service jobs, including semiskilled and clerical positions. Hispanics are highly underrepresented in managerial, sales, technical, and administrative areas. In 1989, 27 percent of Hispanic men were employed in managerial, sales, technical, and administrative positions, compared with 48 percent of non-Hispanic men. They were twice as likely to be employed in service occupations as non-Hispanics (18 percent versus 9 percent).

In 1989, Hispanic women were more likely than non-Hispanic women to be employed in service occupations (24 percent versus 17 percent), and less likely to work in managerial or professional occupations (15 percent versus 27 percent).

✸INCOME, POVERTY, AND UNEMPLOYMENT

Median family income in 1989 for white families was $35,210; for blacks, $20,210; and for Hispanics, $23,450. Per capita income was $14,060 for whites, $8,750 for blacks, and $8,390 for Hispanics. Among Hispanics, family income was highest among Cuban and lowest among Mexican families. In 1988, non-Hispanics were twice as likely as Hispanics to earn more than $25,000 per year (42.7 percent versus 21.5 percent).

As individual workers, the incomes of Hispanic men and women in the late 1980s and early 1990s were lower than either blacks or whites. Between 1982 and 1988, the income gap between Hispanic and non-Hispanic families increased as median family income for Hispanic families fell from 68 percent to 57 percent of non-Hispanic family incomes.

Between 1978 and 1988, the proportion of Hispanic children living in poverty rose more than 45 percent, and by 1989, 38 percent of Hispanic children were living in poverty. Between 1978 and 1988, the rate of poverty for all whites rose from 8.7 percent to 10.1 percent; for blacks it rose from 30.6 percent to 31.6 percent; and for Hispanics it rose from 21.6 percent to 26.8 percent. During this same period, poverty rates for white children under age 18 rose from 11.3 percent to 14.6 percent; for black children from 41.5 percent to 44.2 percent; and for Hispanic children from 28 percent to 37.9 percent.

The poverty rates for married-couple Hispanic families are higher than for other major groups. Between 1978 and 1988, poverty rates for white families remained constant at 5 percent, fell for blacks from 13 percent to 11 percent, and for Hispanics increased from 13 percent to 16 percent. The median income of Hispanic families below the poverty level fell from $7,238 in 1978 to $6,557 in 1987, controlling for inflation.

In 1987, 70.1 percent of Hispanic female-headed households with children were living in poverty.

In 1988, the unemployment rate for whites was 4.5 percent, compared with 11.4 percent for blacks, and 8.0 percent for Hispanics. By December 1990, the rate for whites rose to 5.3 percent, for blacks to 12.2 percent, and for Hispanics to 9.3 percent. By January 1991, the highest rate of unemployment in the United States was in Puerto Rico, with a rate of 15.1 percent.

Hispanics are more than three times as likely as non-Hispanic Whites to be poor. In 1988, 26.7 percent of Hispanics, versus 10.1 percent of Whites and 31.3 percent of Blacks, lived below the poverty level. Between 1982 and 1988, the number of Hispanic families in poverty increased from 875,000 to 1.1 million. During the 1980s, the number of poor Hispanic families increased by 30 percent, while the number of poor White families declined by 10.3 percent.

Selected Labor Facts

Fact 1

Total Hispanic employment grew by 43 percent between 1980 and 1987. Rates of growth varied, from 48 percent for individuals of Mexican origin, to 24 percent for Puerto Ricans, 27 percent for Cubans, and 44 percent for other Hispanics. The rate of growth was almost three times the rate for other workers.

Fact 2

Eighty percent of Hispanic men are in the labor force, compared with 74 percent for all other U.S. men.

Fact 3

Unemployment for Hispanics fell from 16.5 percent in March 1983 to 8.5 percent in March 1988. It then rose to 9.3 percent in December 1990, compared with 5.3 percent for whites and 12.2 percent for blacks.

Fact 4

Median weekly earnings in the third quarter of 1990 for white men were $492; for white women, $350; for black men, $438; for black women, $302; for Hispanic men, $317; and for Hispanic women, $302. In percentages, white women earned 71 percent of the amount earned by white men; black men earned 89 percent, Hispanic men 64 percent, and black and Hispanic women 61 percent of that amount. The earnings discrepancies between men and women of the same background were 71 percent for whites, 69 percent for blacks, and 95 percent for Hispanics. Of the three groups, income disparities between women and men were greatest among whites, and least among Hispanics.

Fact 5

In 1988, one-third of white and Hispanic union members were women, while 44 percent of black union members were women. Union membership among all women declined from 14.6 percent to 12.6 percent between 1983 and 1988.

Fact 6

In 1988, 6.5 percent of women in the labor force, or 3.6 million women, were of Hispanic origin. Of the total, 58.5 percent were of Mexican origin, 10.4 percent of Puerto Rican origin, 6.6 percent of Cuban origin, and 24.5 percent were of other Hispanic origin. Of all Hispanic women age 16 and over, 53.2 percent were in the labor force in 1988, compared with 56.6 percent for non-Hispanic women.

Fact 7

In 1988, labor force participation for all Hispanics was 67.4 percent, compared with 66.2 percent for whites and 63.8 percent for blacks.

Fact 8

In 1988, the mean family income for non-Hispanic families was $34,563, for those of Mexican origin it was $25,051, for those of Puerto Rican origin it was $21,963, for those of Cuban origin it was $33,350, and for those of Central and South American origin it was $30,641. On a per capita basis, income for non-Hispanics was $13,449; for Mexicans, $6,627; for Puerto Ricans, $7,652; for Cubans, $13,241; for Central and South Americans, $9,342; and for other Hispanics, $9,441.

Fact 9

In March 1989, 9.4 percent of non-Hispanic families were below the poverty line, compared with 23.7 percent of Hispanic families. Among specific groups, the rates were 24.9 percent for Mexicans, 30.8 percent for Puerto Ricans, 16.9 percent for Cubans, 16.6 percent for Central and South Americans, and 20.6 percent for other Hispanic families.

Fact 10

In March 1989 per capita earnings for individuals in non-Hispanic families was $12,701, compared with $7,287 for all individuals in Hispanic families. Among the different Hispanic groups, the amounts were $6,325 for Mexicans, $7,293 for Puerto Ricans, $12,855 for Cubans, $8,855 for Central and South Americans, and $8,925 for other Hispanics. The per capita earnings for Hispanics was 57.3 percent of that of non-Hispanics, 49.8 percent for Mexicans, 57.4 percent for Puerto Ricans, 101.2 for Cubans, 69.7 percent for Central and South Americans, and 70.2 for other Hispanics.

References

Acuña, Rodolfo. *Occupied America: A History of Chicanos.* 3d ed. New York: Harper and Row, 1988.

Bean, Frank D., and Marta Tienda. *The Hispanic Population of the United States.* New York: Russell Sage Foundation, 1988.

Cattan, Peter. "The Growing Presence of Hispanics in the U.S. Work Force." *Monthly Labor Review,* 111, no. 8 (August 1988): 9-14.

McHugh, Kevin E. "Hispanic Migration and Population Redistribution in the United States." *Professional Geographer* 41, no. 4 (November 1989): 429-39.

Miranda, Leticia, and Julia Teresa Quiroz. *The Decade of the Hispanic: An Economic Retrospective*. Washington, D.C.: National Council of La Raza, 1990.

Portes, Alejandro, and Robert L. Bach. *Latin Journey: Cuban and Mexican Immigrants in the United States*. Berkeley: University of California Press, 1985.

Santos, Richard. *Hispanic Youth: Emerging Workers*. New York: Praeger, 1987.

U.S. Bureau of the Census. *Statistical Abstract of the United States: 1990*. 110th ed. Washington, D.C.: GPO, 1990.

U.S. Department of Labor. *Women of Hispanic Origin in the Labor Force*. Washington, D.C.: U.S. Department of Labor Women's Bureau.

Valdés, Dennis Nodín. *Al Norte: Agricultural Workers in the Great Lakes Region, 1917-1970*. Austin: University of Texas Press, 1991. Labor Tables.

Dennis Valdez

Women

✳ Traditional Attitudes Regarding Hispanic Female Roles ✳ Hispanics and Women's Liberation ✳ Current Hispanic Women's Issues ✳ Selected Outstanding Hispanic Women

One of the most important things to remember about Hispanic women is how diverse they are. To consider them all alike is to take away from their identity and simplify their complex world. So when we say "Hispanic women," we must also keep in mind the diversity within that group.

Hispanic women make up approximately 4.5 percent of the U.S. population. Within that group are several subgroups, including Mexican Americans, Puerto Ricans, Cubans, and natives of the specific regions of Central and South America. Each subgroup can trace specific cultural traditions to their region of origin. For example, the Caribbean influence on Puerto Rican and Cuban women in the United States is different from the Mexican influence on Mexican-American women.

Along with cultural differences, there are also important language differences among the Hispanic community. A common myth is that all Hispanics speak Spanish. Some speak only English, some speak Spanish and English, others speak only Spanish. Class status levels among Hispanic women are as varied as in the mainstream society: working class, middle class, upper class, white collar, blue collar. Depending on the individual, her values may represent her class, not her culture.

Another important difference among Hispanic women is educational level. A large proportion have had no formal education. Then there are those who have had formal education but have not completed high school; this is a large segment of the population, reflecting the less than 50 percent high school graduation rate among Hispanics. The attitudes and values expressed by these women are influenced by their education.

So, the differences that define Hispanic women can be understood as the same differences that define all individuals: cultural traditions, language, class, edu-

cation, religious affiliation and race. The diversity we see in the general population we also see in the subgroups of Hispanics. What influences and makes Hispanic women who they are is the focus of this chapter.

✳TRADITIONAL ATTITUDES REGARDING HISPANIC FEMALE ROLES

The traditional cultural stereotype of the Hispanic female is based on a dualistic perspective of the sexes and a strong belief in appropriate roles for each gender. Traditional attitudes regarding female roles are also informed by the assumption that there are "natural" gender roles, and any deviation is deemed inappropriate. Hence, females and males are strongly encouraged to accept the prescribed gender roles. These include submissive behavior for females and aggressive behavior for males. The wife is expected to accept the husband's role as absolute authority. The woman is characterized as self-sacrificing to the needs of others and confined to the home. She is to be nurturing to husband and children. A woman's primary function is to bear and raise her husband's children. Training for these roles begins early. In childhood, girls are expected to help with the housework and care for the other children. Boys are given more freedom than girls and expected to learn what roles each will assume as adults.

The most traditional role of the female is to be wife and mother. Her domain becomes the home, the private realm, and not the public realm. The male is expected to take on the responsibilities for providing for the family and engaging in the public realm. He is the ultimate authority in the family. Among the roles of children, a daughter must always be responsive to the males in the family. A female is the responsibility first of her father and then her husband. Self-auton-

Poster advertising a Hispanic women's conference in Texas in 1987.

has a specifically defined role that is subordinate to the male role.

Where do these traditional gender attitudes come from? They are the product of the influences of Spain, the Arab-Semitic traditions, the Catholic church, and the indigenous cultures of Central and South America. Each tradition had its own concept of the appropriate role for women within its community. Spanish culture was heavily influenced by the Romans, who gave Spain its Latin language base as well as its legal system based on a patriarchal tradition. (Patriarchy is an organizational system that traces its authority in a male line of descent.) During the Diaspora, many Jews immigrated to Spain. Their influence on Spanish culture included a recognition of Hebrew codes that consigned women to a subservient position in the society and in the family. Nurturance and selflessness were assigned to the female gender role as the most appropriate and venerated behavior.

With the influx of the Moors around 700 A.D., Spanish culture was again heavily influenced. The

omy and independence are considered inappropriate for a female and are labeled selfish. The quality of selflessness is the highest, most treasured quality in a female. It is the female who is traditionally allowed to be emotional. The male is expected to remain a stoic individual and is commonly discouraged from expressing his emotions. Traditionally, it is the female who is expected to uphold and defend the moral code of the community. She is expected to follow the strictly defined code more vehemently than the male. This is also true for religion. Religious rituals and beliefs are the responsibility of the female. She is the spiritual and moral leader of the family.

All of these traditionally defined roles for women are based on the concept of *la familia*, the family. In traditional Hispanic families, la familia represents more than just the nuclear family. Also included is the extended family: grandparents, aunts and uncles, cousins, and even second cousins and *compadres* (the relationship between a child's parents and godparents). La familia can extend to include a neighborhood and individuals not related by marriage or blood. Within this concept of family, a female

Traditional roles for women still hold a great deal of influence in the community. A beauty queen for the Fiestas Patrias celebration, Houston. (Photo by Curtis Dowell. Courtesy of the *Texas Catholic Herald*.)

Arab culture with its Moslem basis also assigned a subservient position to women. Modern Arab states continue as strong patriarchal societies with specific codes for the behavior of women. Those codes, mostly found in the Koran, served to reinforce an already hierarchical system designating women to an unequal and lower status within Spanish culture.

As the Spaniards moved on to conquer the New World, Spanish culture mixed with the indigenous cultures of Mexico. The Aztecs were a patriarchal society whose gods were mostly male deities. There are, however, hints of very powerful fertility and earth goddesses who were precursors to the male deities. These matriarchal goddesses include Tonantsi, a "good mother" symbol who is reflected in the Catholic Guadalupe. The good mother deity came to represent the position of women within the community as nurturing and subservient. The combined influences of Spanish, Arab, Jewish, and Aztec patriarchy served to reinforce the culture that developed in Mexico and eventually moved to the Southwest. These traditional patriarchal attitudes toward gender roles have been one of the distinctive differentiators of Hispanic culture from the mainstream culture.

Although the Hispanic communities have a strong investment in traditional gender roles and attitudes toward them, throughout history those stereotypes of Hispanic women as passive and subservient family members have been completely inaccurate. It is true that in the codes of the legal system, the status of women was not equal to that of males. However, in many Hispanic families, the power rests with the mother and not the father. Studies of Hispanic families acknowledge a strong matricentric tradition. What this means is that the family revolves around the mother and her wishes, with the father becoming a passive member of the family. The power within a matriarchal system rests with the female head of the family. The legal patriarchal hierarchy is replaced with an informal matriarchal one. So while the state may recognize the male as head of the family, the true head is the female.

The split between the public and private realm is reflected in the power balance termed *marianismo/machismo* (Meier, 1981, 207-208). *Marianismo* defines the role of the woman as limited to the private sphere but allows her superior moral and spiritual power over the man. *Machismo* is the role that encourages the man to exert his superiority in the public sphere but at the same time calls for a childlike relationship with his wife, who is cast in the role of nurturing, forgiving mother. It is this assigned dualism that represents the status of women in the Hispanic society.

Officially, Hispanic communities are patriarchal, and yet these communities have allowed women to gain power in the public realm, subverting traditional gender roles. For example, Puerto Rico is considered a male-centered society, yet San Juan had a female mayor, Felisa Rincón de Gautier. During the Mexican Revolution of 1910, women played an important role and became national heroes. The first acknowledged Mexican poet was Sor Juana Inés de la Cruz, a woman. Traditional gender attitudes, which informed women of the importance of passive, nurturing behavior, did not stop women from seeking power in and outside the family.

The question still remains, Are assigned gender roles for women in the Hispanic community operative? The answer depends on the individual. Although the Hispanic culture has a legal and linguistic history of required subservience for women, exceptions have always existed in the public realm. And as for the family, studies indicate a strong matriarchy within many families, but exceptions to the matriarchy also exist. Despite a strong patriarchal tradition, women have broken those patterns in the past and continue to break traditional conceptions.

Traditional attitudes regarding Hispanic female roles are becoming a part of the past. Specific divisions between appropriate roles for men and women are disappearing.

✳HISPANICS AND WOMEN'S LIBERATION

Rigid acceptance of traditional gender roles has diminished in the Hispanic population of the United States. The change, however, does not necessarily mean that Hispanic women have become feminist or that males in the community accept the changes in gender roles. What has occurred is a loosening of rigid attitudes toward traditional roles for both males and females. This phenomenon, of course, has not occurred without resistance.

Studies indicate that changes have occurred for many reasons, including economic necessity, educational and employment opportunities, an increase in the Hispanic urban community, and increased assimilation into the mainstream culture (Zambrana, 1982). These and other factors have contributed to the modification and resistance of traditional gender roles. Economic necessity has traditionally sent the Hispanic woman into the paid work force. A population that consistently ranks as one of the lowest-paid, and highest-poverty communities requires the financial assistance of the female head of the house. Researchers have investigated the changes that occur in a traditional household when the female enters the paid work force. What they have found is that a change does occur; however, the change may not necessarily be easily recognizable or immediate (Padilla, 1984).

One common assumption about the Hispanic community is the impression of a clear disparity in authority between the male head of the household and the female. Several studies show this not to be necessarily true (Cromwell & Ruiz, 1979; Canino, 1982; Zinn, 1979). The assumed domination of the male in a marital relationship is not the obvious pattern. While complete parity may not exist, marital relationships are substantially more equal then previously reported. Studies also indicate that traditional marital patterns with traditional gender roles are more likely to be challenged by second-generation U.S. citizens than by their parents (Canino, 1982, 30).

Other factors contributing to changing attitudes toward traditional roles for women include the increased urbanization of the Hispanic community. Urbanization means more contact with the majority population. Included in the contact is familiarity with the less rigid gender-role demands upon non-Hispanic females. Thus, the realization by Hispanics that women are demanding equal opportunities is a product of urbanization. The American women's movement and heightened consciousness about forms of oppression has politicized some Hispanic women who have become active in women's organizations. Nevertheless, the contact between Hispanic women and feminists has been limited. Few Hispanic women become members of feminist organizations. The reasons for the limited participation include racism within those organizations and the sense by Hispanics that the underlying assumption of feminism is an attempt to destroy the concept of family.

Hispanic women who have become interested in the women's movement have often found themselves accused of "selling out" their culture—*vendidas*. The women's movement is seen by the Hispanic community as destructive to the common good of the family. The movement also carries assumptions about the importance of independence and self-autonomy, a direct challenge to traditional Hispanic attitudes concerning the importance of relationships to family and community. As critics of the women's movement, some Hispanic women argue, such as Margarita Melville in *Twice a Minority: Mexican American Women* and Marta Cotera in her writing that the feminist movement is alienating to Hispanic women because of its devaluation of traditional values. What has emerged from Hispanic women's experience with feminism is an acknowledgment by Hispanic feminists of pride in their traditional heritage but with a realistic attitude toward its limitations, as well as an acknowledgment of the limitations of feminism. One

criticism of feminism is its inability to acknowledge cultural differences. It was the Afro-American feminists who first discussed this limitation in feminism and created the space for development of Hispanic feminism.

Hispanic feminism is different from mainstream feminism because it tries to accommodate cultural traditions and spiritual issues and not just critique patriarchy. The issues that Hispanic feminism attempts to address include economic and educational needs and child care, as well as how those issues are affected in the context of Hispanic cultural traditions. While the women's movement has focused attention on the issues concerning gender inequality, traditional gender roles were already in the process of being challenged and questioned. The women's movement, however, provided the example and the language with which Hispanic women could challenge traditional attitudes toward women's roles.

One of the harsh realities that comes with change is the accompanying high level of stress. Tension and discomfort within families increase with change. Marital strife seems to be a product of the renegotiation of gender roles. Children are also given confused signals as to appropriate and inappropriate behavior. Clearly, the women's movement does not provide all the answers. If anything, feminism has created more questions than answers.

While economic necessity sent Hispanic women into the work force originally, women now have more options as to their roles in society. They may opt for a traditional role or a nontraditional one, or even a combination of the two, spending a certain period of their time in traditional roles and then moving on to the work force.

Employment opportunities for Hispanic women depend on educational opportunities. The educational attainment level of the overall Hispanic population is seriously inadequate. With fewer than half graduating from high school, Hispanic elementary and secondary schoolchildren have one of the lowest retention rates for any population group in the United States. Hispanic females are more likely to drop out of school than Hispanic males. However, those who do remain in high school often earn better grades than their male counterparts. The retention rate of Hispanic females in college is even more discouraging, with Hispanic males more likely than females to complete a college program.

Hispanic females are starting to become aware of the direct correlation between educational levels and employment opportunities. The more education a woman has, the more options for job opportunities are available; hence Hispanic women are seeking more educational opportunities in greater numbers.

A workshop at the 1980 California Governor's Chicana Issues Conference.

This encouraging information is qualified, however, because while the numbers do show more Hispanic women entering educational programs, they also still show that fewer than half of Hispanics receive a high school diploma.

Another factor in the changing attitudes toward traditional gender roles is the contact with mainstream U.S. society. Anglo-American attitudes toward women are different and considered more liberal than those of Hispanics. As Hispanic women enter the work force and continue to be exposed to U.S. societal attitudes toward gender roles, traditional Hispanic assumptions will be questioned and challenged.

Hispanic women have made little impact thus far on many women's organizations. For example, the National Organization for Women (NOW) does not have a very active Hispanic women's political caucus. Other women's organizations attempt to address Hispanic women's issues by setting up caucuses and task forces. For example, the National Women's Studies Association (NWSA) has a Chicana/Latina task force and a women of color caucus in an attempt to incorporate within the power structure Hispanic women's issues and voices. The success of these cau-

cuses and task forces in influencing the power structure of organizations has been marginal. Because Hispanic women's organizations are set up separately from the mainstream, they quickly become marginal to current debates and are left unrecognized as a valuable resource. The old discussion of whether to attempt to become part of the mainstream leadership or set up one's own organization has been a continual strategic problem. Resistant to traditional leadership and yet unable to fully merge with a nationally recognized organization, Hispanic women are struggling to move from the margin to the center of women's organizations.

Hispanic women's organizations seem to have a greater impact when they are part of a larger organization. For example, there is an active women's caucus in the Hispanic National Bar Association. Hispanic women are brought together because of a common interest, in this example, the practice of law. The common ground allows for a concerted effort to organize around an issue instead of an identity. Hispanic women have come to recognize the diversity of opinions and interests among Hispanics. Building an organization solely on the basis of Hispanic identity has proved impossible. Building one on issues of concern has proved more successful. For example, there are strong and active Hispanic women's caucuses or interest groups in such organizations as the American Psychological Association, the Hispanic National Bar Association, the League of United Latin American Citizens, the Modern Language Association, the National Association of Chicano Studies, the National Council of La Raza, the National Women's Caucus, the National Women's Studies Association, and many others. While one may wish for a powerful national Hispanic women's association, such an association would be in constant turmoil as to what agenda to follow, what values to represent, and what interests to pursue, because of the diversity of opinion and interests among Hispanic women. Hence, successful Hispanic women's organizations must be centered around specific issues, not identity.

Clearly, the women's movement has contributed a great deal to change and has challenged traditional Hispanic gender roles. At the same time, many women are fearful of the term "feminist" and claim no allegiance to such a movement. Many issues that face Hispanic women, however, are feminist issues; they are just not called that.

✵CURRENT HISPANIC WOMEN'S ISSUES

Hispanic women's issues are many and as diverse as the communities from which the women come. There are some general issues, however, that many Hispanic women are concerned about, including education, employment, health, and alien status and politics. While this is surely not an exhaustive list, it does include some of the major concerns of Hispanic women.

Education

As previously pointed out, fewer than half of Hispanics graduate from high school, and in certain communities the dropout rate is almost 75 percent. Also, most Hispanic parents of adolescents do not possess a college degree. In five states with some of the highest concentrations of Hispanics, only 7 percent of Hispanics hold college degrees. There are very few educated role models for adolescent girls. The pattern these girls see consistently is that of a woman who has quit school. Among Hispanic women, who are becoming single heads of household in ever-increasing numbers, few even have high school degrees. In addition, of those who do graduate from high school, fewer than half enroll in college. And the majority of those who do attempt higher education enter two-year colleges. For Hispanic girls, low aspirations are the norm conveyed to them. The pattern that emerges is that of an undereducated, un-

derskilled population of women who are fast becoming single parents. However, as mentioned earlier, Hispanic women are beginning to recognize the necessity for education in order to find employment opportunities and are beginning to return to school.

Employment

Employment has become one of the most important issues Hispanic women face. Now that many of the traditional roles for women have been challenged, they face the stresses of seeking and keeping employment. In 1981, among Hispanic women over age 20, approximately 50 percent were employed. That number has consistently grown, and Hispanic women are more likely to be employed in service industries or clerical work than in other areas. Hispanic women are also more likely to earn a great deal less than most of the population. The U.S. Bureau of the Census (1985) reports that Hispanic men earn approximately 75 percent of what the Anglo male population earns. Anglo women earn approximately 72 percent of what Anglo men earn. And Hispanic women earn 62 percent of what the Anglo males earn. Another pattern emerges: Hispanic women are consistently underemployed and underpaid. These employment patterns show the status of Hispanic women in the economic realm. They are some of the lowest-paid workers in the country.

Single Heads of Household and Child Care

Hispanic women are becoming single heads of household in ever-increasing numbers. As women assume the roles of traditional heads of household, child care becomes a necessary issue. Faced with the limited availability of affordable child care, Hispanic women may find themselves unable to afford to work. They stay at home to care for their children and find themselves unable to meet monetary needs. Unable to find affordable child care, they turn to the state for assistance.

One response of many Hispanics to the shortage of affordable child care is to turn to the extended family. Many Hispanic children are cared for by their grandmothers or aunts. The ability to turn to members of the family is one of the strengths of Hispanic culture. The closeness of Hispanic families allows a woman to turn to her mother or sister or some family member in times of need. For many Hispanic women, however, this closeness is a double-edged sword. Along with the closeness comes a sense of not having any privacy, as well as feeling suffocated by the abundance of nurturing. Common among Hispanic women is an inability to acknowledge individuality. These women only know themselves in relation to their parents, their children, their husband. Once they decide to assert their individuality, however, they find themselves faced with emotional stress.

For many Hispanic women, issues of survival for themselves and their children continue to be the most immediate concern. Undereducated, underemployed, and with a very high reproductive rate compared with other groups in the nation, these women face the harsh issue of day-to-day survival.

Health Issues

Health issues of Hispanic women have only recently begun to be explored by the medical establishment. Already documented, however, are several common ailments. For example, evidence indicates that Hispanic women, because of their traditional cultural diet, are at high risk for diabetes.

Another issue is the ability to pay for health services. Many Hispanic women are underinsured or have no health insurance. Many hold jobs that provide very limited or no health benefits, like housekeeping and farm work. As with the rest of the population, the inability to receive affordable health care is quickly reaching crisis levels.

Illegal Aliens

There exists a truly invisible Hispanic woman— the illegal alien. Without immigration papers, usually with no formal education and no skills in English, the Hispanic woman who is not a citizen or legal alien in the United States is silenced and invisible. Estimates vary as to the number of illegal aliens. They continue to be the most exploited members of the Hispanic community.

Many of these women work in the fields as migrant workers. Farmers are able to pay substandard wages and not fear government reprisal because these workers hold no legal rights in the United States and hence will not report them. These women also work in service industries, as unskilled laborers and as housekeepers. Because of their illegal status and limited English, an underground community exists in the midst of U.S. society.

Religion

A cultural and personal concern for Hispanic women is religion. While most Hispanic women are Catholic, many are beginning to question much of the traditional attitudes the church has about women. As Catholic dogma is very clear as to the status of women—subservience to man and God—women are beginning to test the actual limits of dogma. Admittedly, few Hispanic women actively voice their opposition to the dictates of the Catholic church; a

more quiet revolution is actually occurring. For example, the Catholic church does not condone artificial forms of birth control, yet more and more Hispanic women continue to seek birth control.

Traditionally, the woman's position in the Catholic church has been to serve the needs of the community. Women have not been allowed to participate in the Mass except as members of the congregation. If a woman wanted a more active role in the church, she became a nun and lived in a world separate from all males and laypersons. The leadership and power within the church was reserved only for priests. However, in the past thirty years the church has encouraged a more active role for women. Clearly, a change has occurred in the status of women within the traditional ceremony, allowing both male and female lay persons to participate in the Mass. In its own ranks, the church still continues the practice of limiting and designating certain duties to either the priest or the nun. The most exalted positions within the Catholic church—priest, bishop, cardinal, pope—continue to be reserved only for men. The leadership of the church continues to remain selely the domain of men.

Politics

In the political realm, Hispanic women continue to be underrepresented, if not ignored. No research is available that reveals the voting patterns of Hispanic women. What is now becoming more readily available is the voting patterns for Hispanic communities. Unclear is whether or not Hispanic women differ from Hispanic men in their political participation. Politically, Hispanic women have yet to make an impact, but this may be changing. The surgeon general of the United States, Antonia Novello, is a Hispanic woman, as is the U.S. treasurer, Catalina Villalpando. There is one Hispanic woman in Congress, Ileana Ros-Lehtinen of Florida. Hispanic women politicians are more active at the city and county level than at the highest levels of government. The pattern may suggest that as Hispanic women continue to gain more experience in politics at the local levels they will then move on to the next levels, the state and national political arenas.

Hispanic women have many diverse concerns, as do all women. The fear, however, is that Hispanic women will continue to be invisible politically. This may change with continued growth in the community, the recognition of Hispanic women by politicians, businesses, and researchers, and the demands that Hispanic women themselves will make. The tradition of subservience, silence, passivity will need to be changed if Hispanic women are to make any impact on mainstream society.

✳SELECTED OUTSTANDING HISPANIC WOMEN

The first Cuban-American congresswoman is Ileana Ros-Lehtinen of Florida. Elected to Congress in 1989, she is a Republican and a member of the Foreign Affairs Committee. She has been a Florida state representative and state senator. At present, she is the only Hispanic woman in Congress.

As mentioned earlier, Antonia Novello, a Puerto Rican, is the surgeon general of the United States under the Bush administration. In a highly visible position, Novello is a strong role model. Catalina Villalpando, a Texan, is the treasurer of the United States. Some of our outstanding leadership comes at the local level. For example, Gloria Molina is a member of the Los Angeles Board of Supervisors, and Sally Hernandez-Pinero is deputy mayor of finance and economic development for the City of New York. Lena Guerrero is the chair of the Texas Railroad Commission, one of the country's most powerful commissions. The president of the Hispanic National Bar Association is Dolores Atencio from Denver. The founder and president of what is clearly becoming a very important group, Hispanics for Free Trade, is Elaine Coronado. Peggy M. Ventura is a member of the Colorado Reapportionment Commission. These are individuals, whose work affects many people's lives, not just Hispanics'.

Listed below are a few of the outstanding Hispanic women in the United States.

Deborah Aguiar Vélez

See Chapter 11

Norma Alarcón

See Chapter 16

Lupe Anguiano (1929-)

Born on March 12, 1929, in La Junta, Colorado, Anguiano received her M.A. degree from Antioch University in 1978. She taught at Our Lady of Victory Missionary Sisters from 1949 to 1965. She was the East Los Angeles coordinator of the Los Angeles Federation of Neighborhood Centers, 1965-66; a presidential appointee to the U.S. Office of Education, 1967-69; the Southwest regional director for the National Association for the Advancement of Colored People, Legal Defense and Educational Fund, 1969; a civil rights officer for the U.S. Department of Health, Education and Welfare, 1970-72; the Southwest regional director for the National Conference of Catholic Bishops, 1973-77; and president of the National Women's Program Development in 1977-78. She is also the founder and, since 1979, president of Na-

tional Women's Employment and Education, Inc., and president/consultant of Lupe and Associates since 1982. She is the author of *Women's Employment and Education Model Program* (1982) and the editor and publisher of *Comunidad Newsletter* (1975-77) and *Women's Employment Newsletter* (1978-80). Her many honors include being named one of the *Ladies" Home Journal*"s 100 Most Important Women (1988) and receiving the Soroptimist International of Auburn (Tacoma, Washington) Women Helping Women Award (1985).

Polly Baca-Barragán (1941-)

Born in a small town near Greeley, Colorado, Baca-Barragán received a degree in political science form Colorado State University. She went on to work as an editor for two union publications. In 1974, she was elected to the Colorado House of Representatives and in 1978 to the state senate. She was the first Hispanic woman to be elected to those offices. She remains active in politics working on behalf of Mexican Americans and dealing with housing issues.

Mary Helen Barro

See Chapter 25

Teresa Bernárdez (1931-)

Born on June 11, 1931, in Buenos Aires, Argentina, Bernárdez received her B.A. degree from Liceo No. 1 de Señoritas in 1948 and her degree in medicine form the School of Medicine, University of Buenos Aires, in 1956. Her internship was at *Hospital de Clinicas* (University Hospital) in Argentina, and her residency was in psychiatry at the Menninger School of Psychiatry, Topeka State Hospital, Topeka, Kansas. She was a staff psychiatrist at the Menninger Memorial Hospital, 1960-65; a staff psychiatrist at the Menninger Foundation, Department of Psychotherapy, 1965-71; a professor in the Department of Psychiatry at Michigan State University, 1971-89; and has taught at Tavistock Clinic, Adult Psychiatry Department, London, England (1977-78) and the Mary Ingraham Bunting Institute, Radcliffe College (1984-85). She has been a consultant to many national and international groups and has done a great deal of research and publishing on the subject of women. Her awards and honors include the Distinguished Faculty Award, Michigan State University Faculty Women's Association (1982), the first Leadership Workshop Award from the American Medical Women's Association (1977), and the Peace Award from the Pawlowski Foundation (1974).

Teresa Bernárdez, M.D.

Gloria Bonilla Santiago

See Chapter 11

Vikki Car

See Chapter 25

Lynda Córdoba Carter

See Chapter 25

Margarita Hortensia Colmenares (1957-)

Born on July 20, 1957, in Sacramento, California, Colmenares was educated at Stanford University, where she received her B.S. degree in civil engineering in 1981. She has worked for Chevron as an environmental affairs air quality specialist, lead engineer on the Subsurface Recovery Project, compliance specialist in marketing operations, foreign training representative, recruiting coordinator, and field construction engineer. She has been the national president of the Society of Hispanic Professional Engineers since 1989 and a member of the board of directors of the Hispanic Women's Network of Texas. Her honors include Leadership America, Training Program Participant (1990); National Hispana Leadership Initiative, Training Program Participant (1989); Hispanic Engineer Magazine Community Service Award (1989); and Hispanic Role Model of the Year, Society of Hispanic Professional Engineers (1989).

Gilda Cruz-Romo

See Chapter 25

Margarita Fernández Olmos

See Chapter 16

Beatriz Angela Ginorio (1947-)

Born on January 30, 1947, in Hato Rey, Puerto Rico, Ginorio received her B.A. and M.A. degrees in psychology from the University of Puerto Rico (1968 and 1971) and her Ph.D. degree in social psychology from Fordham the University (1979). She has taught at the University of Puerto Rico (1970-71), the University of Illinois (1976-78), Bowling Green State University (1978-80), and the University of Washington (1981-82). She was a counselor in the Special Services Program (1981-83), served as director of the Women's Information Center (1983-87), and is currently the director of the Northwest Center for Research on Women (1987) at the University of Washington. She has published extensively and is active in the American Psychological Association and the Mexican American Women's National Association. She is the first Puerto Rican to direct a center for research on women in the United States. She has been recognized by the campus chapter of the Business and Professional Women with a Woman of the Year award (1986) and by the Mexican American Women's National Association, Seattle Chapter, with a Certificate of Appreciation (1987).

Maria Elena Girone (1939-)

Born on March 31, 1939, in Puerto Rico, Girone was educated at the Universidad de Puerto Rico, where she received a B.A. degree in psychology (1964) and a Master's degree in social work (1967). She has taught at the Puerto Rico University and is currently the national executive director of the Puerto Rican Family Institute. She is on the executive committee of the National Puerto Rican Coalition and has been recognized for her outstanding work by the New York City Hispanic Heritage (1986), the Institute Cultura (1988), and the National Coalition of Hispanics Health and Human Services Organizations (1990).

Elsa Gómez

See Chapter 25

Deena J. González (1952-)

Born on August 25, 1952, in Hatch, New Mexico, González received her B.A degree from New Mexico State University (1974) and her M.A. degree (1976) and Ph.D. degree (1985) from the University of California, Berkeley. She was a professor of history and Chicano studies at Pomona College (1983-91), acting chair of Chicano studies (1990), and is currently visiting associate professor in history and women's studies at the University of New Mexico. She has received grants from Hewlett Packard and the National Endowment for the Humanities, and her publications include a *The Spanish-Mexican Women of Santa Fe* (1993) and *On Their Own* (1988). She has served on numerous committees for universities and other organizations and currently serves on advisory and editorial boards for *Signs*, Women of the West Museum, and Program in Collegiate Scholars in History at the University of Florida.

Lucía Parsons González (1852-1942)

Born in a small town south of Fort Worth, Texas, González grew up to become a labor leader. During the early 1880s, she joined the Chicago Working Women's Union and led marches for women's rights and an eight-hour workday. Her husband, Albert Parsons, was executed for being part of the Haymarket riot, a labor demonstration. After his execution, González continued to be active in the radical labor movement and the women's movement and was one of the founders of the International Labor Defense and the Industrial Workers of the World. Even through her eighties, González was an active figure in the International Labor Defense. She died at ninety as a result of a fire that destroyed her home.

Suzanna Guzman

See Chapter 25

Carolina Herrera

See Chapter 25

Dolores Huerta

See Chapter 25

Mari-Luci Jaramillo (1928-)

Born in Las Vegas, New Mexico, Jaramillo received her A.B. (1955), M.A. (1959), and Ph.D. (1970) degrees from New Mexico Highlands University, Las Vegas. She was a professor education at the University of New Mexico (1972-77). She became a well-known speaker and educational researcher. President Jimmy Carter appointed her U.S. ambassador to Honduras in 1977.

Olga Mapula (1938-)

Born on January 30, 1938, in Williams, Arizona, Mapula received her B.A. degree from Texas Western College (1958) and her M.A. degree from the University of Texas at El Paso (1973). She was an El Paso public school teacher (1958-60), field representative for the Social Security Administration (1960-71), lecturer for the University of Texas at El Paso (1973-75), program evaluator for the Bilingual Consortium (1975-78), consultant for Educational Consulting

(1979-86), and marketing director for KXCR/ETCOM, Inc. (1983-85). At present she is president of The Communications Group sits on the board of directors for the El Paso Chamber of Commerce, the Minority Business Council, and the Private Industry Council. She is director of the El Paso Certified Development Corporation, Hispanic Women's Network of Texas, and the Hispanic Leadership Institute. She is vice president of the University of Texas, El Paso, Alumni Fund for Excellence and a trustee for the El Paso Community College. She has been recognized for her outstanding work by El Paso Women in Education/ Employment (1986), Hispanic Women in Communications (1988), and Texas Teachers of English to Speakers of Other Languages (1989) and was a nominee to the Texas Women's Hall of Fame (1987).

Vilma Martínez

See Chapter 9

Antonia Coello Novello

See Chapter 25

Ellen Ochoa

See Chapter 25

Graciela Olivárez (1928-)

Born near Phoenix, Arizona, Olivárez worked in the radio industry before she was encouraged to enter the University of Notre Dame Law School, graduating in 1970 and receiving her juris doctor degree in 1978. Active in the civil rights movement in the Southwest, she was appointed director of planning for New Mexico (1975-77). President Jimmy Carter appointed her director of the Community Services Administration in Washington, D.C. (1977-80). In 1980, she became a senior consultant for the United Way of America.

Katherine D. Ortega

See Chapter 25

Vilma Ortiz

See Chapter 9

Gaudalupe C. Quintanilla

See Chapter 25

Tey Diana Rebolledo (1937-)

Born on April 29, 1937, in Las Vegas, New Mexico, Rebolledo received her B.A. degree from Connecticut College (1959), her M.A. degree from the University of New Mexico (1962), and her Ph.D. from the University of Arizona (1979). She has taught at the University of North Carolina, Chapel Hill (1977-78), and the University of Nevada, Reno (1978-84). She has been a professor at the University of New Mexico since 1984. She is editor of *Las mujeres hablan: An Anthology of Nuevo Mexicana Writers* (1988) and author of numerous articles. She serves on the editorial boards of El Norte Publication, and Arte Publico Press. She was designated an eminent scholar by the New Mexico Commission on Higher Education (1989). She is a member of the Group Project of the University of New Mexico in India, Fulbright Foundation (1988); fellow of the Aspen Institute (1987); and recipient of a research grant from the National Endowment for the Humanities (1984-87).

Eliana Rivero

See Chapter 16

Emyré Barrios Robinson (1926-)

Born on March 23, 1926, in El Paso, Texas, Robinson received her B.A. degree in Spanish from the University of Houston (1971). She was a data services manager and later business manager for Kentron International (1976-80). In 1980, she became founder

Emyré Barrios Robinson

and president of Barrios Technology, Inc. She is chair of the Texas Space Commission (1990); president of Armand Bayou Nature Center (1989-90); a member of the University of Houston Development Board (1986-90) and the University of Houston, Clear Lake, Development and Advisory Council (1985-90); a member of the board of directors of the Bay Area Bank and Trust (1985-90); and a member of the board of trustees of the United Way, Gulf Coast (1985-90). She has been recognized for her outstanding work by the Small Business Administration, Texas Executive Women, NASA, and the Houston Hispanic Chamber of Commerce.

Elizabeth Rodríguez (1953-)

Born on March 18, 1953, in San Benito, Texas, Rodríguez was educated at the University of New Mexico, where she received her B.S. (1975) and M.A. (1976) degrees in mathematics and her Ph. D. degree (1980) in program management and development/experimental statistics. She was a mathematician and program manager for the Pacific Missile Test Center (1980-88) and an instructor for Oxnard Community College (1981-84). Currently, she is a research analyst for RAM/suitability for the Office of the Secretary of Defense/Director of Operational Test and Evaluation. A member and leader of numerous organizations and author of numerous articles, Rodríguez has been honored for her work by the Pacific Missile Test Center, *Gente* magazine, and Ventura County, California, Commission for Women.

Gloria G. Rodríguez

See Chapter 25

Ileana Ros-Lehtinen

See Chapter 9

Vicki L. Ruiz (1955-)

Born on May 21, 1955, in Atlanta, Georgia, Ruiz received her B.S. degree from Florida State University (1977) and her A.M degree (1978) and Ph.D. degree (1982) from Stanford University. She was director of the Institute of Oral History at the University of Texas from 1982 to 1985 and has taught at the University of California, Davis since 1985. She is active and a leader in the Organization of American Historians, the Immigration History Society, and the American Studies Association. She is an editorial board member of the *NWSA Journal*; author of *Cannery Women, Cannery Lives: Mexican Women, Unionization and the California Food Processing Industry, 1930-1950* (1984); and co-editor of *Women on the U.S.-Mexico Border* (1977), *Western Women* (1988), and *Unequal Sisters* (1990).

Virginia Korrol Sánchez (19?-)

Born in New York City, Sánchez received her B.A. degree from Brooklyn College, City University of New York (1960), and her M.A. degree (1972) and Ph.D. degree (1981) from the State University of New York, Stony Brook. She taught in the public schools of Chicago and is currently a professor of Puerto Rican Studies at Brooklyn College, City University of New York. She is author of *From Colonia to Community: History of Puerto Ricans in New York City: 1917-1948* (1983); coeditor of *The Puerto Rican Struggle: Essays on Survival in the U.S.* (1984); coauthor of *Restoring Women to History: Women in the History of Africa, Asia, Latin America and the Caribbean and the Middle East*; and author of numerous articles on the history of Puerto Rican women and Latinos in the United States.

Cristina Saralegui

See Chapter 25

María-Luisa Urdaneta (1931-)

Born on October 2, 1931, in Cali, Colombia, Urdaneta received her professional nursing degree from Methodist Hospital, Dallas, Texas (1956), her R.N. degree from Baylor University (1958), her B.A. degree in psychology (1965) and M.A. degree in sociology (1969) from the University of Texas, Austin, and her M.A. degree in anthropology (1974) and Ph.D. degree in anthropology (1976) from Southern Methodist University, Dallas. She was a staff anesthetist at Methodist Hospital of Dallas (1958-59) and Brackenridge Hospital (1960-69 and 1972-74); a research associate at the University of Texas Health Science Center at San Antonio (1974-75); and since 1975 has been a professor at the University of Texas, San Antonio. Author of numerous articles on Mexican Americans and health, Urdaneta has been recognized by the San Antonio Women's Hall of Fame, the Texas Diabetes Council, the National Institutes of Health, the Mexican-American Business and Professional Women's Club of San Antonio, and the National Chicano Research Network.

Paquita Vivó (19?-)

Born in San Juan, Puerto Rico, Vivó was educated at the University of Puerto Rico (1953-55). She was assistant to the under secretary of the commonwealth Department of State (1955-60); staff writer and researcher for the Puerto Rico News Service (1960-62); public affairs officer for the Organization of American States (1962-80); and independent consultant of Public Relations, Public Affairs (1970-80). She has been president of ISLA, Inc., since 1980 and president of the Institute for Puerto Rican Affairs, Inc., since 1988. She has been president, treasurer, and secretary of the National Conference of Puerto Rican Women (1972-89); member of the boards for the National Urban Coalition (1980-86) and the National Puerto Rican Coalition (1976-79); and member of the Women's Research and Education Institution and the Council for Puerto Rico-U.S. Affairs. She is author of *The Puerto Ricans: An Annotated Bibliography*, selected by the American Library Association as one of the outstanding reference books of 1974. Her awards include the Center for Women Policy Studies, Wise Women Award (1989); the National Urban Coalition, Distinguished Community Service Award (1986); the National Conference of Puerto Rican Women, Isabel Award (1988); and the National Council of Negro Women, International Women of Distinction Award.

Carmen Delgado Votaw (19?-)

Born in Humacao, Puerto Rico, Votaw was educated at The American University in Washington, D.C., where she received her B.A. degree. She was vice president and member of the board of directors of the Overseas Education Fund of the League of Women Voters (1964-81). She has served as Federal Programs Specialist, Office of the Commonwealth of Puerto Rico, Washington, D.C. (1972-76); cochair of the National Advisory Committee on Women (1977-79); U.S. representative to the Inter American Commission of Women and its Executive Committee (1977-81); president of the Inter American Commission of Women of the Organization of American States (1978-80); vice president of ISLA, Inc. (1981-84); administrative assistant to Congressman Jaime B. Fuster (1985-91); and is currently director of the Washington office of Girl Scouts U.S.A. She is author of *Puerto Rican Women: Some Biographical Profiles* (1978) and numerous articles. She has received numerous awards and honors, including the National Council of Hispanic Women Award for Outstanding Achievement (1991); was profiled in the *Maryland Women's History Resource Packet* (1987 and 1990); and received an honorary doctorate of humanities from Hood College, Frederick, Maryland (1982).

Olga Jiménez de Wagenheim

See Chapter 16

Maxine Baca Zinn (1942-)

Born on June 11, 1942, in Santa Fe, New Mexico, Zinn was educated in sociology at California State College (B.A., 1966), the University of New Mexico (M.A., 1970), and the University of Oregon, where she

Carmen Delgado Votaw, Director, Washington Office, Girls Scouts, USA.

received her Ph.D. degree in 1978. She has taught women's studies at the University of Delaware (1988-89) and has been a professor at the University of Michigan, Flint, since 1975. She is the author of numerous articles on the Hispanic family and is an associate editor of the *Social Science Journal*. She was a recipient of a Ford Foundation fellowship (1973-75) and is acknowledged as an outstanding sociology scholar.

References

Acosta-Belén, Edna, ed. *The Puerto Rican Woman*. 2d ed. New York: Praeger, 1986.

Canino, Gloria. "Transactional Family Patterns: A Preliminary Exploration of Puerto Rican Family Adolescents." In *Work, Family, and Health*, edited by Ruth E. Zambrana, New York: Hispanic Research Center, Fordham University, 1982, 27-36.

Chacón, Maria A., Elizabeth G. Cohen, Margaret Camarena, Judith Gonzales, and Sharon Strover. *Chicanas in Postsecondary Education*. Stanford, Calif.: Center for Research on Women, Stanford University, 1982.

Cotera, Martha P. *Latina Sourcebook: Bibliography of Mexican American, Cuban, Puerto Rican and Other Hispanic Women Materials in the USA*. Austin: Information Systems Development, 1982.

———. *The Chicana Feminist*. Austin, Tex.: Information Systems Development, 1977.

———. *Diosa y Hembra: The History and Heritage of Chicanas in the United States*. Austin, Tex.: Information Systems Development, 1976.

Cromwell, R. F., and R. A. Ruiz. "The Myth of Macho Dominance in Decision Making Within Mexican and Chicano Families." *Hispanic Journal of Behavioral Science* 1, no. 4 (1979): 355-75.

Elsasser, Nan; Kyule Mackenzie, and Yvonne Tixier y Vigil. *Las Mujeres: Conversations from a Hispanic Community*. Old Westbury, N.Y.: Feminist Press, 1980.

McKenna, Teresa Flora and Ida Ortiz, eds. *The Broken Web: The Education Experience of Hispanic American Women*. Berkeley, Calif.: Floricanto Press and The Tomás Rivera Center, 1988.

Meier, Matt S., and Feliciano Rivera. *Dictionary of Mexican American History*. Westport, Conn.: Greenwood Press, 1981.

Melville, Margarita, ed. *Twice a Minority: Mexican American Women*. St. Louis Mo.: Mosby, 1980.

Mirandé, Alfredo, and Evangelina Enriquez. *La Chicana: The Mexican American Woman*. Chicago: University of Chicago Press, 1979.

Mora, Magdalena, and Adelaida R.Del Castillo. *Mexican Women in the United States: Struggles Past and Present*. Occasional paper, no. 2. Los Angeles: Chicano Studies Research Center Publications, University of California, 1980.

Padilla, Amado M., and Kathryn J. Lindholm. "Hispanic Behavioral Science Research: Recommendations for Future Research." *Hispanic Journal of Behavioral Sciences* 6, no. 1 (1984): 13-32.

Rodríguez, Clara E., Virginia Sanchez Korrol, and José Oscar Alers, eds. *The Puerto Rican Struggle: Essays on Survival in the U.S.* New York: Puerto Rican Migration Research Consortium, 1980.

Tomás Rivera Center. *The Changing Profile of Mexican America: A Sourcebook for Policy Making*. Claremont, Calif.: Tomás Rivera Center, 1985.

Zambrana, Ruth E., ed. *Work, Family, and Health: Latina Women in Transition*. New York: Hispanic Research Center, Fordham University, 1982.

———. "Latina Women in Transition." In *Work, Family, and Health*, ix-xiii. New York: Hispanic Research Center, Fordham University, 1982.

Zavella, Patricia. *Women's Work and Chicano Families: Cannery Workers of the Santa Clara Valley*. Ithaca, N.Y.: Cornell University Press, 1987.

Zinn, Maxine Baca. "Chicano Family Research: Conceptual Distortions and Alternative Directions." *Journal of Ethnic Studies* 7, no. 3 (1979): 59-71.

María González

Religion

★ The Beginnings ★ Instruments of Religious Conversion
★ Our Lady of Guadalupe and the Saints ★ Florida ★ New Mexico ★ Texas ★ Arizona
★ California ★ The Anglo Conquest ★ Developing a Pastoral Approach ★ A Search for Parity
★ Protestantism and Hispanics ★ Popular Religiosity ★ Beyond Orthodoxy

Hispanics are an eminently religious people. Throughout the centuries, regardless of the accessibility of priests or places of worship, or the availability of religious instruction, they have maintained their faith through the nuturing of their families and villages. Often misunderstood and chastised as ignorant, retrograde, or pagan, they have clung to the symbols of a deep spirituality received from their elders. Religious expression is apparent in the exchanges of everyday life—in the readiness with which Hispanics add the expressions *Gracias a Dios* (Thanks be to God) or *Si Dios quiere* (God willing) and the ever-present invocations to God, the Virgin, and the saints. That the manner of religious expression for U.S. Hispanics is fundamentally Christian and Catholic is natural; Catholicism is still the religion of choice of Hispanics everywhere. The most recent surveys reveal that 75 percent of U.S. Hispanics consider themselves Catholic, 19 percent Protestant, and 5 percent "other" (Jewish, Jehovah's Witnesses, Mormon, to name a few).

Two hundred fifty years before the Pilgrims landed at Plymouth Rock, Hispanics brought Christianity to present-day Florida and the Southwest. This period of Christianity on U.S. soil is largely ignored by mainstream church historians. A 1989 five-volume work on this subject commissioned by the U.S. Conference of Catholic Bishops devotes only nine pages to Hispanics. It places them exclusively in the context of an "immigrant" church. As Moisés Sandoval explains in *On the Move*, a history of the Hispanic church in the United States, "there is great ignorance about Hispanics in the Church, extending not only to their past and current religious contributions but even to their very existence." Hispanic religious

contributions are worthy of examination, however, if prejudice is to be dispelled.

★THE BEGINNINGS

Catholicism, the religious affiliation of the majority of U.S. Hispanics, came to the New World with Christopher Columbus in 1492. The Spanish conquerors, imbued with the religious ardor of their day, were not content with seizing and claiming kingdoms and treasures in the name of the Spanish sovereigns; they also wanted to win over the inhabitants of the newly discovered territories to Christianity. This was a natural development, for Spain had just fought for seven centuries a religious crusade against the Moors on its own soil. Throughout the first two centuries of the European presence in the Americas, Spain was the most zealous daughter of the Roman church.

Uniformity of religious belief, in this case Catholicism, was one of the main pillars on which the Spanish Empire rested. At the time of the discovery of the Americas, Spain was preoccupied with uniting into one nation and under one monarch the various medieval kingdoms into which the Iberian Peninsula was divided. Roughly twenty years before, through the marriage of Isabella of Castile and Ferdinand of Aragon, all but the southern, Muslim-occupied territories came under the royal couple's joint reign. Religious diversity, which provided for the more or less peaceful, if not totally tolerant, coexistence of Christians, Muslims, and Jews, seemed ill-advised to the monarchs; they were already having a difficult enough time coping with the behind-the-scenes machinations of noblemen who resented surrendering

A Catholic charismatic prayer meeting. (Courtesy of the *Texas Catholic Herald*.)

their prerogatives as feudal overlords to a centralized government.

The significance of the year 1492 goes far beyond the fateful encounter with the Americas; it constitutes the boundary between religious plurality and uniformity for Spain. Following that date, Spain tolerated no religion other than Catholicism on its soil or in the vast lands it set forth to bring beneath its imperial mantle. In January 1492, Isabella and Ferdinand captured Granada, the last Moorish stronghold in Iberia. This put an end to the seven-hundred-year-long Reconquest, which had begun shortly after 711 when the Moors invaded all but the extreme northern regions of Spain. In April, the monarchs gave notice to the Jews that they had until July to repudiate their faith or leave Spain. An estimated 140,000 chose the road to exile. Thenceforth, only the Cross would follow the sword of the Spanish soldiers, both to the European battlefields, where the Spanish Hapsburg kings fought their religious wars against Protestants, and to the remote jungles and deserts of the newly discovered regions of the Americas and Asia.

Father Virgilio Elizondo points out in his book *Galilean Journey* (1985, 23-24) that in matters of religion the attitudes of the Spanish conquistador and his English counterpart were worlds apart. Early in the period of conquest and discovery, theologians like Father Francisco Vitoria, a Spanish Dominican, settled the question as to whether Indians were human. Indians, they determined, were made in God's image and likeness and were endowed with an immortal soul. Converting them to Christianity became a sacred mandate for the Spaniards. According to Elizondo, the Spanish conquerors were not concerned about their own personal salvation, of which they felt assured. Whenever they sought royal permission and support for their enterprises, they listed the evangelization of the native populations as a goal. In Bernal Díaz del Castillo's account of Hernán Cortés's conquest of Mexico, he states that after each village and town surrendered to the conquistadors, the Spaniards immediately took time to destroy the pagan idols and temples and in their place erected crosses and shrines in honor of the Virgin Mary. To Cortés and most Spaniards of his day, the conquest was not merely a political and economic enterprise but a religious crusade.

Their English counterparts, on the other hand, coming from the austerity of Protestant Europe, were obsessed with achieving their own salvation and gave no thought to the spiritual well-being of the American native. From their standpoint, the natives were less than human, unworthy of the Christian promise, children of the Devil. They were not to be evangelized, but rather destroyed; thus, the expression popular during the conquest of the American Far West, "The only good Indian is a dead Indian."

✳INSTRUMENTS OF RELIGIOUS CONVERSION

Conversion of the Indians facilitated interbreeding of the Spanish and the Indians. The Spaniards, Elizondo (1985, 24) explains, contrary to the early English colonists, considered sexual relations with the native women as something natural. The conquistadors took them as mistresses, concubines, and wives and accepted both their legitimate and illegitimate children, producing almost from the outset a generation of Christian mestizos.

On a less fortunate note, converting the Indians mandated the development of systems and strategies that would render them receptive to Christian teachings or force them into accepting them. In the name of evangelization, the unscrupulous or overzealous committed abuses never intended by either the Crown or the church. From the first, the Indians were exploited, enslaved or forced into some sort of servitude. The church consistently censured these ex-

The Franciscan method of teaching the Indians by pictures. (From an engraving based on Fray Diego Valdés, o.F.M., in his *Rhetorica Christiana*, Rome, 1579.)

cesses; the Spanish Crown attempted to prevent and remedy them, as the passing of the *Leyes de Indias* (Laws of the Indies) makes evident. This body of laws, among other things, recognized the natives as subjects of the Crown and forbade their forced conversion and enslavement. Unfortunately, the Spanish monarchs and their courts were an ocean away, and more often than not the letter of the law was executed rather than its intent.

The first approach to the orderly evangelization of the natives, the *encomienda*, further opened the door to the inhumane excesses that would characterize the colonization of the New World. The encomienda entrusted a group of Indians to a colonist, known as the *encomendero* (trustee), who was responsible for providing for the material needs and religious instruction of his charges. In exchange for his paternalism, the encomendero was entitled to work the Indians. The provisions of the laws that set down in detail the responsibilities of the encomendero and regulated the conditions under which the Indians would labor were largely ignored. The *repartimiento*, a variation of the encomienda, offered no relief to the sufferings of the newly conquered peoples. It merely placed colonial authorities instead of individuals in charge of the natives. The latter, when not forced to work in Crown-owned mines, farms, or other projects, were apportioned out to private citizens as laborers. In either case, whether as part of an encomienda or a repartimiento, the Indians were brutalized, starved, and often worked to death. Whole populations were wiped out in the West Indies, where the encomiendas and the repartimientos were first imposed. Preeminent among the voices that rose to the defense of human rights for the Indians was Father Bartolomé de las Casas (1474-1566), a Spanish-born Dominican priest and historian. To his protests and pleas can be attributed the above-mentioned Laws of the Indies enacted by the Crown in 1476.

A vastly more humane instrument of evangelization, and the one most widely utilized in the Spanish territories now encompassed by the United States, was the mission, a temporary institution established and run by priests who resided among or in proximity to native populations. The missionary usually came right on the heels of the conquistador and built his rudimentary chapel and convent at a reasonable distance from the military garrison, once the

Bartolomé de las Casas (1474-1566).

area was somewhat pacified. Instead of force, it was the missionary's works of mercy and his teachings that often brought about the evangelization of the natives. The vulnerability of the unarmed, nonthreatening padre was often his greatest strength. Missionaries could succeed where the conquistadors failed. Such was the case in the Sonora region of northern Mexico (southern Arizona today) and in the peninsula of Baja California, where the hostility of the natives prevented the soldiers from making inroads. After several failed attempts, the Mexican viceroy entrusted the Jesuits with this conquest, which they performed successfully with no other weapon than the Cross.

The mission, in most cases, served as a center for religious instruction and a beachhead from which the padre could set out to scout for other promising mission sites, where another beachhead in the evangelization process could be established. Missions, therefore, as was the case in Florida and the Southwest, tended to stretch out over a territory much like the links of a chain. This arrangement, in turn, facilitated the logistics of supplying and defending them. The Texas and California missions established by the Franciscan friars were rather ambitious institutions. Some were villages unto themselves. The Indians learned Christian doctrine and a variety of skills—farming, animal husbandry, weaving, metalwork, leather craft, carpentry, and masonry—aimed at bringing about economic self-sufficiency to populations that once depended on collecting, hunting, or fishing for their sustenance. These missions became very wealthy, supplying not merely their own residents but the garrisons and townships in the immediate area.

The missions were secularized during the first part of the nineteenth century, either for political reasons or because their original aims had been achieved. By this time and because in most cases their residents had fused with the people of the surrounding townships and farms, missions became the nuclei for modern-day parishes. It is not uncommon for the descendants of the first Indian neophytes baptized within mission walls to still flock to the same old church buildings generation after generation.

In light of this, the assertion that missions and missionaries served the purposes of the empire cannot be denied. The missions contributed to the

The San Juan Capistrano Mission in San Antonio, Texas. (Photo by Silvia Novo Pena. Courtesy of the *Texas Catholic Herald*.)

pacification of the Indians, and in so doing facilitated the process of colonization. They fostered the development of townships in their immediate vicinity. Furthermore, by Christianizing and Hispanicizing the Indians, the missionaries transformed entire populations into loyal subjects of the Spanish kings and obedient children of the Roman church.

One of the services offered by the church, which served to both Cristianize and Hispanicize the native and mestizo populations, was formal education. In townships and missions, the clergy was expected to establish schools, both for boys and girls, to teach the children to read and write and learn the catechism. The curriculum sometimes included Indian languages. As early as 1534, archbishop of Mexico Juan de Zumárraga had a school built at Tlatelolco, the first in the Americas. Countless Indian children spent their mornings reading, writing, and singing and their afternoons involved in religious instruction. Zumárraga, an indefatigable worker for the education of the Indians, published numerous books on the subject, paying special attention to the education of girls.

✳ OUR LADY OF GUADALUPE AND THE SAINTS

The spiritual conquest of Mexico served as the first chapter in the spiritual conquest of the Hispanic territories now encompassed by the United States, Florida and Louisiana being the exceptions. As Carey McWilliams aptly underscores in his book *North from Mexico* (1968, 54-55), the Spanish-speaking colonists who settled Texas and the Southwest were, but for rare exceptions, mestizos, second generation and beyond, born of Spanish fathers and Mexican Indian mothers; the balance was constituted by Christianized Mexican Indians (the ductile Tlaxcalans, in particular), blacks, and mulattoes. The Catholic religiosity of the Mexican mestizo would come to predominate in this area even after the final invasion of northern Mexico by the United States in 1846. This religiosity continues to be reaffirmed by the various waves of Mexican immigrants that have entered the United States since the late nineteenth century.

A providential event that contributed to the conversion of the native population of Mexico and Central America to Roman Catholicism was the alleged miraculous apparition of the Virgin Mary in Tepeyac in the environs of Moctezuma's vanquished capital of Tenochtitlán shortly after the conquest of the Aztec Empire by Hernán Cortés in 1521. In the early morning hours of December 9, 1531, Juan Diego, a converted Indian, was on his way to mass when he was surprised by the sound of beautiful singing voices coming from a hill. As he approached the site, he saw a woman enveloped by a brilliant aura. She identified herself as the Virgin Mary. In the course of several apparitions, she requested that Juan Diego inform Archbishop Zumárraga of what he had seen and heard and that she wished for a temple to be built on the hill at Tepeyac so that she could communicate all her love and compassion, help and defend all the inhabitants of the land, and remedy their misery, pain, and suffering. The archbishop refused to believe Juan Diego's story. Finally, so that he could prove his veracity, the Virgin performed a miracle. She instructed Diego to gather roses from a bush that would not normally bloom that time of year and take them to the archbishop. When the humble messenger unfolded his cloak before Zumárraga, so as to put before him the roses the Lady was sending, the image of the Virgin Mary appeared imprinted on the cloth.

Detractors have claimed that the clergy perpetrated a hoax on the credulous natives in order to speed up their conversion. It was too much of a coincidence that the apparition took place on a site dedicated to the cult of the Aztec mother goddess Tonantzin. The image, however, displayed to this day in the basilica of Our Lady of Guadalupe in Mexico City, has not disintegrated in over four centuries, even though it is imprinted on a highly perishable cloth made of agave fibers. Furthermore, scientific testing has failed to explain the origin of the image or its durability.

News of the miracle spread throughout the colony, bringing about mass conversions. To the natives, the fact that the Virgin had chosen to appear before one of the oppressed and the vanquished, that she had adopted the physical appearance of a brown woman, and that she communicated in Nahuatl, the language of the Indians, established a bond between them and Christianity. The fact that her body blocked the face of the sun, the focal point of the native religions, established the precedence of the new faith brought by the Spaniards over the old faith of the Aztecs.

Noted Mexican writer Carlos Fuentes observed in a 1992 presentation at the University of Houston that mestizo artisans invariably portrayed Christ as a broken, bleeding god suffering on the Cross. The Virgin of Guadalupe, on the other hand, appears surrounded by flowers, rays of sunlight, and all of nature triumphant. As he explained it, the first Indian converts identified the death of their old gods with Christ. He was a god who was willing to be destroyed to save his people. The Virgin, on the other hand, surrounded by all the symbols of a joyous nature, brought the hope for a new beginning.

The colorful liturgy of Catholicism and its doc-

The Image of Our Lady of Guadalupe on tour from Mexico at Our Lady of Guadalupe Church in Houston, Texas, 1992. (Photo by Curtis Dowell. Courtesy of the *Texas Catholic Herald*.)

trine of the veneration of saints further paved the way for native conversions. The Mexican Indians were accustomed to paying tribute to a wide variety of deities. Each clan, each site, each day, week, and month was the purvey of a god or goddess whose favor was sought to ensure the happy outcome of events. They felt quite at home with the feast days assigned by the church calendar to holy men and women of the past, who were also named patrons for townships and villages, professions and trades and protectors for individuals. By the same token, elaborate priestly vestments, music, incense, candles, ornate sacred vessels, and other external aspects of the Catholic church must have appeared to the Indians as echoes of their past devotions.

✳ FLORIDA

The first chapter of the Christian saga in present-day Florida began shortly after the Easter season—*la Pascua Florida*—of 1513 with the arrival of Juan Ponce de León. Although no priest is known to have accompanied this expedition, the customs of the day presupposed that there was an act of thanksgiving to

God for the safe arrival of the conquistadors. Ponce de León returned in 1526 as military escort for a contingent of secular and regular priests. He was commissioned by the Crown to establish mission posts for the dual purpose of affirming Spain's presence in the newly discovered territories and spreading the gospel. Finding armed resistance from the Indians of the Gulf Coast area where they landed, the Spaniards retreated to Cuba, Ponce de León dying en route from wounds he sustained.

After several failed attempts, Spain abandoned all efforts to colonize Florida until 1564, when a handful of French soldiers, some of them Protestant Huguenots, founded Fort Caroline on the Saint John's River near present-day Saint Augustine. Pedro Mendez Avilés, a man known for his zeal and cruelty, was dispatched by the government to protect its claims against the intruders and to destroy the fort. Carried away by the religious fanaticism typical of the day, Mendez Avilés ordered the non-Catholic French soldiers put to the sword even after they had surrendered. Three years later, the Spanish garrison that held the little fort, by then renamed San Mateo, was subjected to the same fate at the hands of the Frenchman Dominique Gourges.

The establishment of Saint Augustine in 1565 by Mendez Avilés was pivotal to the evangelization efforts. Using Saint Augustine as a base, the handful of diocesan priests who first accompanied Mendez Avilés—Jesuits from the order's province of Andalusia after 1566 and Franciscans after 1587—sailed north along the Atlantic coast, establishing and operating missions among the Indians. The diocesan priests also ministered to the white settlers in garrisons and outposts. Time and conditions permitting, they also saw to the spiritual welfare of neighboring Indian tribes. By 1647, a chain of missions and forts spanned from Saint Augustine in the south to Fort San Felipe on Parris Island, South Carolina.

Beginning in 1607, the Franciscans, with Father Francisco Prieto in the role of pioneer, ventured into northwestern Florida to do missionary work among the Apalache Indians. Their dedication bore fruit, and by 1655 the friars could claim 26,000 converts. Their missions in the Gulf and northwestern areas of Florida stretched from the Suwannee River in the south to the Apalachicola River in the northwest.

The state of the church in Florida in 1674 was recorded by Bishop Gabriel Díaz Vara Calderón of Santiago de Cuba, who, at the insistance of Queen Mariana, made an episcopal visit there (Gannon p. 92). Upon his return, after confirming 13,152 Christianized Indians and Spaniards and traveling hundreds of leagues to visit every one of the thirty-six missions in the province, Bishop Calderón gave a detailed account of his observations in a letter to the pious Spanish queen. His assessment was that in spite of the hardships and the indifference and sometimes cruelty of the civil authorities, the missionaries had succeeded. The missions, although poor, served as firm bulwarks of the faith upon which the empire rested.

Less than fifty years later, beginning with the outbreak in 1702 of the War of Spanish Succession, which pitted France and Spain against England, the network of Florida missions was laid to waste. When in 1763 at the end of the war Spain ceded Florida to France according to the terms of the Treaty of Paris, only two parish churches and a handful of mission buildings still stood.

❋NEW MEXICO

As in Florida, the early expeditions or *entradas* into New Mexico from Mexico were of little consequence to the efforts of evangelization. From 1536, when Alvar Núñez Cabeza de Vaca, after years of captivity among the Karankawa Indians of Texas,

heard of the big Zuni pueblos of New Mexico and mistook them for the legendary Seven Cities of Gold, until 1598, when Juan de Oñate led his group of settlers northward along the banks of the Rio Grande, New Mexico remained virtually unaffected by religious campaigns elsewhere. Heroes, cowards, martyrs, and scoundrels crossed from Mexico into the northern frontier, with or without permission from the Crown, leaving behind nothing but their failed hopes, a few relics, the carcasses of their beasts, their fallen comrades, and their rusting swords.

The course of religious history took a turn with Oñate's entrada of 1598. Oñate, a silver miner and the wealthiest man in Mexico, like Ponce de León in Florida, had a mandate from the Crown to Christianize the native people of New Mexico, among which his settlers were to dwell. Consequently, he took—in addition to his eighty-three oxcarts of goods, seven thousand head of stock, and four hundred soldiers—a handful of priests and a plan that called for the creation of seven mission districts, each to be headed by a Franciscan friar. By 1630, twenty-five missions had been founded among the various settled tribes known collectively as the Pueblos.

As would be the case wherever sword and Cross ventured jointly, a conflict soon developed between the priests and the civil and military authorities. Abuse and exploitation of the natives were the order of the day. The military, sent to establish an orderly government among the Indians, stole from them, did them all sorts of violence, and raped the women.

The Pueblos were an agricultural people. They raised corn, beans, and a variety of foodstuffs. As the newcomers saw their own supplies dwindle, they robbed the Pueblos of their stores. Oñate, an irascible man who had little patience with either the settlers or the Pueblos, ordered the removal of grain from the Indians, even when it meant destroying villages and injuring the defenders.

The clergy protested. They described the excesses and the sufferings of the Pueblos at the hands of the Hispanic contingent in official reports to the civil and ecclesiastic authorities in Mexico. Fray Francisco de Zamora, to give an example, wrote that the depredations of the Hispanics against the Pueblos were a discredit to Christian teaching (Kessell, p. 195). He said that the natives were "stabbed and knifed when things were taken from them" and that the women were often raped by the soldiers. Echoing the feelings of other friars, he recommended that New Mexico be abandoned, so that the Pueblos might live in peace and the Word of God not be further dishonored.

Needless to say, Oñate's supporters countered these reports to the authorities with accusations of sloth on the part of the clergy and recommendations that the colony not be abandoned. They made these arguments hypocritically in the name of Christian evangelization. A later report to the viceroy that the conversion of seven thousand Indians had been accomplished was instrumental in saving the colony, pointing to the fact that religious accomplishments were vital to determining the success or failure of the colonizing enterprise. The viceroy made provisions to ensure against any further injustices and ill treatment of the natives. These included replacing Oñate as governor with Pedro de Peralta in 1609 and limiting the largest military garrison to fifty married soldiers.

The Pueblos were not willing converts to Christianity. They had their own cults to ancestors and to various natural forces that had to be propitiated to ensure abundant crops. They worshiped the sun and the mother earth and believed in life after death. Their ceremonial life was rich and colorful. To give in to the missionaries, as they saw it, could result in famine and many other calamities. Conversions were seldom totally sincere, and apostasy was quite common. Those who were outwardly Christianized more than likely practiced the old rituals secretly. For these infractions they were routinely punished by the friars. The troublemakers were sold into slavery along with Apaches caught raiding the settlements. The yearly trade caravan from Santa Fe to Mexico City led them tethered like cattle, a human chain of captives to be sold in the marketplace along with the buffalo hides and wool of the New Mexican Hispanos.

The excesses of the civilian population and the unbending zeal of the Franciscan friars brought about the Pueblo rebellion of 1680. Fanning the fires of religious discontent, Popé, a Pueblo chieftain from Taos, organized the villages against the Hispanics. An initial bloody rampage forced fifteen hundred settlers and Christianized Indians to retreat South to Isleta, near present-day El Paso. Upriver, Popé and his men ransacked the churches of the hated religion, burning vestments, defacing statues, and destroying sacred vessels and ornaments. Furthermore, in an effort to remove all traces of Christianity, they rubbed themselves with a solution made out of yucca to erase the waters of baptism from their bodies.

The Cross and the sword, however, did not concede defeat. On September 13, 1893, a well-armed detachment of soldiers headed by Diego de Vargas, a deeply religious man, arrived outside Santa Fe after an almost bloodless campaign to retake New Mexico. Popé, seen as the devil incarnate, was dead. Under his reign the Pueblos had suffered almost as much as under the Hispanics. The Pueblo delegation that had met with Vargas initially argued that if it surrendered, their people would be subjected to forced labor, put to work in encomiendas as slaves, and be made to rebuild the churches. Vargas assured them that the people who had abused them would not return. He further gave them one hour to abjure their pagan beliefs, to pledge their allegiance to the Spanish king, and to be willing to adopt Christianity. The alternative was destruction. The Pueblos acceded. On December 16, a vanguard of soldiers and priests, which was part of a long column of more than eight hundred colonists and eighteen supply wagons, arrived at the outskirts of Santa Fe. The priests entered the city singing hymns while the sullen Indians watched. Christianity was permanently implanted on New Mexican soil, even though it would never succeed in eradicating the ancient Pueblo beliefs.

✴ TEXAS

Twenty expeditions are known to have entered Texas before the threat of French encroachment forced the Spanish Crown to think of making good its territorial claims over the region.

In 1685, Robert Cavalier, sieur de la Salle, established Fort Saint Louis on Matagorda Bay. The Spanish, having word of this development ordered the colony found and destroyed. Four consecutive expeditions by Alonso de León searched the upper Gulf Coast of Texas before the ruins of the French fort were found. In the course of the fourth expedition, a Franciscan from the College of Querétaro, Father Damián Massenet, was invited by an Indian chief whom he met near the Guadalupe River to visit his people. He indicated that they dwelled further east. The Indian's invitation, according to some accounts, came from the tradition among his people of a lady in blue who had appeared to their ancestors and had recommended they go seek priests that would bring the true faith to them.

The story of the lady in blue first surfaced among the Jumano Indians near Isleta. In 1639, fifty Jumanos appeared before missionaries in Isleta, requesting instruction in the Christian faith so that they could eventually be baptized. After some investigation, it was determined that the lady in blue was Sor María de Jesús, a cloistered nun who had never gone beyond the confines of her convent in Agreda, Spain. A mystic, she was so well known for her piety that on occasion King Philip IV visited and consulted her. Sor María is said to have experienced in her mystical trances the phenomenon of bilocation, whereby she found herself in the New World teaching religion to the Indians.

Father Massenet was enthusiastic in responding to the Indian chief. For years the competing

Franciscan colleges of Querétaro and Zacatecas, in Mexico, had sought the opportunity of opening Texas as a new mission field, but the Crown had only lent a deaf ear to their pleas. No missions had been allowed north of the Rio Grande. The implications of La Salle's failed expedition changed the political picture. The expedition pointed to the fact that the French, who already had claimed the valley of the Mississippi River, were harboring imperial designs for Texas. Consequently, in 1690 Alonso de León was sent at the head of a fifth expedition into Texas. He was accompanied by Father Massenet and three other Franciscans sent to establish missions in the easternmost region of Texas and evangelize the Hasinai Indians (incorrectly labeled "Tejas" by the first explorers). The underlying purpose was to buttress Spanish claims to the territory. The Franciscans founded two missions: San Francisco de los Tejas and El Santísimo Nombre de María. The missions were short-lived. Constant bickering between the friars and the military authorities over the treatment of the Indians, poor crops, the inability to make a settled people out of the nomadic eastern Texas tribes, and the easing of tensions with France brought about their closing in 1593.

In 1714, a French trader, Louis Juchereau de St. Denis, appeared at the San Juan Bautista mission on the southern bank of the Rio Grande. That a foreigner could openly enter Mexico through the back door instilled fear in the Spanish authorities. Once again they decided to establish missions along the eastern Texas border as a buffer against the French. "By this means similar incursions will be prevented and, what is more important, these Indians will obtain instruction in our Holy Catholic Faith and the spiritual welfare of their souls," the viceroy wrote in 1715, outlining the plan for resettlement of eastern Texas (Castiñeda, Vol.1, p. 428).

The following year, Captain Domingo Ramón, commandant of the San Juan Bautista presidio, led the expedition aimed at founding the new missions. Twenty-five soldiers and their families, eleven Franciscans, from both the Colleges of Querétaro and Zacatecas, and one thousand head of cattle traveled to eastern Texas. Among the missionaries was a leading figure who would come to be known as the Father of Texas Missions, Fray Antonio Margil de Jesús. Already sixty years of age when he joined the expedition, Margil had previously established missions in Guatemala, founded the Franciscan College of Zacatecas, and helped establish its rival institution in Querétaro. Years later, Margil would be the founder of Mission San José y San Miguel de Aguayo in San Antonio, Texas, which is reputedly the best example of Spanish missionary architecture in the

United States. In a flurry of activity fired by evangelical zeal, Margil and his brethren built six missions among the Hasinai between July 1716 and the early part of 1717. Once the task was completed, it became evident that the logistics of supplying eastern Texas called for the establishment of another outpost midway between the Rio Grande and this distant frontier.

A proposal made by Father Antonio de Olivares, who had long strived to establish a mission on the San Antonio River, paved the way for the new foundation. Over twenty years before, Father Olivares swam across the Rio Grande into Texas and ambled north to the site occupied today by the city of San Antonio. The good friar was overcome with excitement by the sight of thousands of Indians congregated on the banks of San Pedro Springs. Having assumed these to be permanent Indian settlements, Fray Olivares set off on a campaign to establish missions in their midst, projecting a plentiful harvest of converts to the faith. He returned years later with Captain Diego Ramón on a journey of exploration geared to whetting the appetite of the Crown on behalf of his missionary project. In the course of this expedition, the river was given the name San Antonio de Padua. In December 1716, Olivares's proposal was approved with additions that provided for a presidio and a township to house the relatives of the garrison soldiers. In 1718, Mission San Antonio de Valero, the fateful Alamo of Texas revolutionary history, was founded, together with the presidio and the township.

The height of missionary activity in Texas followed the inspection tour of the royal visitor the Marquis de Aguayo in 1720. After assessing the situation in Texas, Aguayo granted permission to build Mission San José in San Antonio and the Presidio La Bahía near the mouth of the San Antonio River on Matagorda Bay. From San José, missionaries would subsequently set off to evangelize the Lipan Apache Indians, who eventually made peace with the Hispanic population. In the environs of La Bahía, missions were founded to attempt the conversion of the Karankawa and the Apache.

Missions in Texas were never truly successful. The Apache, for instance, are said to have assisted in the building process to please the friars, but they were never willing to give up their nomadic life and their horse-thieving ways. Time and again they made promises of settling down "next season" or "after the hunt," but they never remained for long. Like migratory birds, their sojourns were brief. As to the other Indians, mission life was never too attractive. At its peak, Mission San José had no more than fourteen hundred native dwellers. Their lack of success notwithstanding, some of the missions became wealthy in terms of arable lands and herds, awakening the greed of the authorities. By the time of Mexican independence in 1821, they all had been secularized, their lands and herds had been forfeited, and their buildings had fallen into disrepair. The settled areas of Texas at the time, however—Nacogdoches, San Antonio, and La Bahía (Goliad)—owed their existence to the efforts of the old friars.

✳ ARIZONA

The name of Jesuit Father Eusebio Kino, a German-educated Italian, pervades the history of evangelization in southern Arizona. Kino, a cartographer, among other things, had labored in the missions of Baja California, which he succeeded in proving was a peninsula rather than an island.

In 1687, he was sent to the northern Sonoran Desert to work in the conversion of the region known as Pimería Alta. In the course of the next twenty-four years, until his death in 1711, Kino established twenty-nine missions, using the Mission Nuestra Señora de los Dolores in Sonora as his base of operations. Three of these missions—Guevavi, Tumacacori, and San Xavier de Bac—were located within the borders of the modern state of Arizona.

Kino was first and foremost a diplomat. He succeeded where others failed in winning the goodwill of Indian chieftains. Kino's mediation succeeded in bringing peace to the region in 1695, when war broke out among the Indian tribes divided over the issue of loyalty to the Spanish newcomers. As a missionary, Kino developed in the people a desire for conversion. In the course of developing a mission, and before settling down to the task of religious instruction, he routinely introduced cattle ranching to the Indians. Then, after convincing the chieftains of the advantages of Christianity, he would have them travel to the Jesuit superior to request missionaries for their people. Unfortunately, there were never enough missionaries to satisfy the demands. The Hispanic settlers, on the other hand, were always eager to dismantle the missions. They wanted control of the herds and wanted Indian labor in the form of repartimientos to support work in the mines.

A second Pima uprising in 1751 and the expulsion of the Jesuits from all Spanish territories left little of Father Kino's work intact. The Franciscans who were entrusted with the Arizona missions were largely confined to Tumacacori and San Xavier. The Pimas for the most part returned to their ancient pagan ways.

✳ CALIFORNIA

The last mission territory to be opened in the northern frontier of Mexico was California. On July 1, 1769, more than two hundred years after the Portuguese Juan Rodríguez Cabrillo, sailing under the flag of Spain, first discovered it, Franciscan Father Junípero Serra celebrated a solemn mass of thanksgiving on the shores of the Bay of San Diego. Months before, four expeditions, two by sea and two by land, had left Baja California for San Diego for the purpose of initiating the missionary process.

The original force behind this effort was Don José de Gálvez, visitor general for King Charles III, a man as visionary and driven by faith as Fray Junípero. As part of his duties, Gálvez visited in 1767 a handful of desolate missions in the rugged peninsula of Baja California. Built by the Jesuits, upon their expulsion these missions were entrusted to the Franciscans. Gálvez had a plan for Father Serra. Worried about the activities of Russian fur trappers who traveled into North America through the Bering Straits, the Spanish Crown began to look with interest at long-neglected California. Gálvez's proposal to Serra, the president of the Baja California missions, was a plan to establish a series of missions along the coast of northern California.

Junípero Serra (1713-84) was born on the island of Mallorca, off the southern coast of Spain. Shunning the opportunity for further training as a theologian, for which he was eminently qualified, he offered himself for mission work and was sent to Mexico in 1747. From that date forward, Serra tirelessly traveled through Mexico giving himself completely to the task of evangelization and, as a result, putting his health at serious risk. Needless to say, José Gálvez's mission plan was earmarked for the indefatigable padre, and during the late spring of 1769, the visitor general and Serra, undertaking the task of stevedores, personally packed and loaded on board a ship bound for San Diego chalices, vestments, altar cloths, and other items for the churches soon to be built in the northern California frontier.

July 16, 1769, marks the foundation of the first California mission, San Diego de Alcalá, on a hill overlooking the beautiful bay of the same name. Fifty-four years later, in 1823, the last of a chain of twenty-one missions, San Francisco Solano, was established north of the city of San Francisco. The missions were joined by the Camino Real, or Royal Road. They achieved, as nowhere else, great prosperity, with some of the missions owning over a dozen cattle ranches. Vineyards, orchards, vast fields of grain dotted the landscape surrounding the mission buildings. Within their confines life was orderly, the ringing of bells dividing the day into work, rest, instructional, and devotional periods. Artisans and craftsmen brought from Mexico taught the residents a wealth of skills. Additionally, the missions operated schools and hospitals. The role that the missions played in the development of California cannot be overexaggerated. The development of a population from the fusion of the Hispanic mestizo settlers that came from Mexico and the native populations, the founding of townships and villages, and the emergence of a prosperous agricultural and cattle industry are primarily owed to the missions.

✳THE ANGLO CONQUEST

By the time of the Treaty of Guadalupe Hidalgo in 1848, the mission system had disappeared, but the faith was kept alive by the people. Secular priests belonging to the northern dioceses of Mexico ministered to the needs of the faithful as well as they could, considering the vast distances they had to travel and the sparseness of their numbers. In distant villages and ranches, months and years would pass without a visit from a priest. In northern New Mexico, the Brotherhood of the Penitentes (Fraternidad Piadosa de Nuestro Padre Jesús Nazareno—the Pious Fraternity of Our Father Jesús the Nazarene) filled in the spiritual vacuum. These penitential organizations, which, according to some historians, have their roots in the Third Order of St. Francis, a lay arm of the Franciscans, practiced scourging and a rigorous piety centered on the sufferings of Christ. In the absence of clergy, they organized liturgies for the different feasts in the church calendar and taught religion to the young.

Although originally Rome had intended for the bishops of northern Mexico to continue administering the affairs of the church in what had now become the southwestern frontier of the United States, the North American bishops protested, voicing the displeasure of their government and probably their own jealousy. Political expediency forced the Vatican to bow before the pressures of the new rulers and appoint foreign bishops to each newly erected diocese or vicariate. The effects of this decision are still felt in our day. Texas, which fell under the diocese of Coahuila, was made a missionary vicariate under Rome in 1841. In 1847, the diocese of Galveston (now Galveston-Houston) was erected by the Vatican. It encompassed the entire state and its first bishop was Jean Marie Odin, a native of Lyon, France. The spiritual needs of the thousands of European Catholic immigrants that poured into Texas became the primary concern of the local church. Neglect of the Hispanic faithful became the norm.

The fate of the church in Texas was repeated in New Mexico, Arizona, Colorado, and California. Vicariates and dioceses were erected in all conquered territories, and with rare exceptions non-Hispanic bishops were apointed to head them. The new bishops and vicars, in turn, brought in almost exclusively European priests and congregations of religious men and women. The disdain that the newcomers felt toward the native population was reflected in the myth that its clergy were worthless and lazy. Underlying this assumption was the fear of the authorities that Hispanic priests were by virtue of their place in the community natural leaders who could induce their flocks to rebellion. Their fears materialized in the person of Father Antonio José Martínez of Taos, New Mexico.

Father Martínez (1793-1868), a native of Río Arriba County, New Mexico, was ordained to the priesthood after being widowed and fathering a daughter. His defense of the rights of Hispanic clergy before the unreasonable demands of French-born bishop Jean Baptiste Lamy of Santa Fe and his resistance to the suppression of the Penitente brotherhood led to his excommunication. Lamy's attitude toward the Hispanic faithful was typical of the church leaders sent to the conquered territories at the bequest of the U.S. bishops. The religious traditions of the people were shunned. The beautiful old adobe churches were allowed to decay. Plaster religious images replaced the colorful hand-carved cottonwood santos. Popular Hispanic religiosity was attacked as superstitious or pagan. To be Catholic you first had to be American, you had to pray in English, you had to give up your traditional religious practices.

By the end of the nineteenth century, Father Moisés Sandoval states, Hispanic Americans in the Southwest had no institutional voice in the church. The native Hispanic priests who had been their spokesmen in midcentury had all been purged or had died of old age. The Hispanic laity returned to their homespun religious traditions, which had served them well throughout the centuries.

Ironically enough, during this same period a Hispanic priest was working on behalf of the destitute Irish Catholic immigrants who were arriving in droves to this country. Cuban-born Father Félix Varela (1778-1853) was a political exile living in New York when Catholicism was the faith of a minority. The plight of the poor Irish, who would become the backbone of the church in the United States, was a catalyst that drove this intellectual into active social ministry. His acts of charity on behalf of the Irish and the sensitive and intelligent manner in which he defended and promoted Catholicism—he established the second Catholic newspaper in the United

States—have served to bolster the cause for his canonization.

✺DEVELOPING A PASTORAL APPROACH

Although the original attitude of the English-speaking conquerors of the Mexican Southwest was that Hispanics would eventually disappear, migrations from Mexico, Cuba, and Puerto Rico in the latter part of the nineteenth century and the early years of the twentieth mandated a new approach on the part of the church. The church now saw herself as an instrument in the process of integrating Hispanics into the mainstream. For this purpose, national parishes were established for Hispanics, an approach utilized with other ethnic groups, such as the Polish, the Italians, and the Germans. Contrary to other nationalities, however, native Hispanic priests who could supply leadership and role models for their own people were seldom available. One of the salient reasons for this absence was the failure by church authorities to promote vocations among Hispanics, who, because of prevalent social and economic conditions, could seldom meet the educational standards required by seminaries and novitiates. The gap was filled by Spanish-speaking priests of other national origins. In Texas, two religious orders, the Oblates of Mary Immaculate and the Claretians, were invited in by the different bishops specifically to minister to Hispanics.

In the meantime, Hispanics grew in number and began to settle in areas other than the Southwest. Waves of migration came from Mexico and, after 1917, when its people were granted U.S. citizenship, from Puerto Rico. By the 1920s, it was evident that more than a diocesan approach was needed to serve this population. In 1923, the U.S. bishops established an immigration office in El Paso, Texas, aimed at ministering to the large number of Mexicans fleeing the revolution, which had begun in 1910. In 1944, Archbishop Robert E. Lucey of San Antonio held a seminar for the Spanish-speaking to discuss the needs of the Hispanic faithful. In 1945, the Bishops Committee for the Spanish-speaking was created to establish programs, both of a social and a pastoral nature, in Texas, California, Colorado, and Santa Fe. One of its goals was to put an end to prejudice and discrimination against Hispanics in the church. The catalyst for these measures was the increasing proselytism of Hispanics by Protestant churches.

✺A SEARCH FOR PARITY

Although in the 1950s and 1960s the number of Hispanic priests and nuns increased, they were often not allowed to work with their own people. Archbishop Patrick Flores, the highest-ranking Hispanic in the U.S. Catholic church today, likes to recall how as a young priest assigned to a predominantly Hispanic parish in Houston, Texas, he was forbidden by his pastor the use of Spanish except in the confessional.

The reforms imposed on the church by the Second Vatican Council in the early 1960s, particularly those calling for the use of the vernacular rather than Latin in the celebration of the Mass, and the activism among minority groups in the period that followed brought to a head the silent struggle of Hispanic Catholics. Demands that the Mass and the sacraments be offered in Spanish mounted. In 1967, Henry Casso of San Antonio was named executive director of the Bishops Committee for the Spanish-speaking, a position occupied by Anglos from its inception. In 1969, Hispanic priests organized Priests Associated for Religious, Educational and Social Rights (PADRES), and in 1971 Hispanic sisters followed suit with the creation of Las Hermanas, an organization representing twenty religious orders. The same year saw the creation in San Antonio of the Mexican American Cultural Center (MACC), a Hispanic pastoral institute aimed at training clergy and lay leaders to serve the spiritual needs of Hispanics. The moving force behind MACC was Father Virgilio Elizondo, a native of San Antonio and a leading Hispanic theologian. Hispanic offices at the regional and diocesan level were also established about this time. Finally, in 1974, the U.S. bishops, at the instance of PADRES, created the Secretariat for Hispanic Affairs as a permanent office within the U.S. Catholic Conference. The secretariat is charged with assisting and advising the bishops.

Three Encuentros, or national meetings, of delegates representing Hispanic Catholics from throughout the land have been held in the nation's capital, in 1972, 1977, and 1985. The Encuentros served to voice the needs and expectations of Hispanic Catholics and were instrumental in promulgating the U.S. bishops'' pastoral letter, "The Hispanic Presence: Challenge and Commitment" (1983), and a national plan for Hispanic ministry approved by the bishops in 1987.

The first Hispanic to be ordained bishop was Patrick Flores, the son of poor migrant workers from Ganado, Texas. Flores was ordained on May 5, 1970, and named auxiliary bishop of San Antonio and later installed as bishop of El Paso, Texas. With his appointment in 1979 to the archdiocese of San Antonio, which heads the ecclesiastical province of Texas, he became the first and to date the only Hispanic to be installed as an archbishop in this country. Since 1971, the Vatican has appointed more Hispanics as auxiliary bishops, but only infrequently as full bishops to U.S. dioceses. Their numbers, however, fail to reflect demographic reality. Although population projections indicate that by the year 2000 the majority of U.S. Catholics will be Hispanic, as of 1992 only 19 out of more than 360 bishops and only 1 out of some 45 archbishops in the United States were Hispanic—of these, two were Cubans, two Puerto Ricans, one Ecuadorian, one Venezuelan, two Spaniards, and two Mexicans. The balance were U.S.-born Hispanics.

In 1991, the Missionary Catechists of Divine Providence, the only religious order of Mexican-American women, was granted total independence by the Vatican. Having begun as an organization for lay catechists in Houston, Texas, in the 1930s, the missionary catechists are dedicated to foment leadership among Hispanics in different dioceses of the Southwest.

✳PROTESTANTISM AND HISPANICS

Latin America was missionary territory for the nineteenth-century U.S. Protestant churches. As the Latin American nations gained their independence from Catholic Spain, Protestant England's traditional foe, English-speaking missionaries, aware of the anticlericalism present in the independence movements south of the border decided that the time had come for the spiritual conquest of the region. Proselytism of Hispanics born in the United States was now a goal of the Protestant ministers who traveled south to the lands newly conquered from Mexico. Those who converted were valuable as Spanish-speaking leaders who could be sent to the promising mission fields of Mexico. A case in point was Alejo Hernández, a former Catholic priest who had converted to the Methodist faith and was ordained deacon in Corpus Christi, Texas, in 1871. Shortly after his ordination, he had to abandon the work he had begun in Texas among his own people to become a missionary in Mexico City. As in the case of the Catholic church after the U.S. takeover of Texas and the Southwest, the Protestant churches assumed that the native Hispanic population would disappear in time. Ministering to U.S. Hispanics also helped Anglo missionaries to learn the ways and the language of the people south of the border, whose conversion was their ultimate goal.

The level of preparation for Hispanic ministers was lower than that of their Anglo counterparts. A system of patronage developed in Texas and the Southwest whereby Hispanic congregations and ministers were made to depend upon their more enlightened and wealthier Anglo counterparts. According to Methodist Church Historian Edwin E. Sylvester, the essential patterns and structures of Hispanic-Ameri-

can Protestantism in this region were fixed in the second half of the nineteenth century (Sandoval, p.192). Anglos controlled the churches and their institutions. Hispanic churches were not encouraged to develop self-determination, but to assimilate and accommodate to the customs and the institutional interests of the conquering culture. Hispanic leaders were trained out of expediency rather than out of respect for the values that their culture could bring to the churches.

In 1898, after the end of the Spanish-American War, Protestant missionaries descended upon Cuba and Puerto Rico, where they achieved a modicum of success. Some were born in Cuba or Puerto Rico and had converted as exiles in the United States. Catholicism was seen by many as the faith of the old oppressive order and Protestantism as a more enlightened faith.

Conversion, however, implied relinquishing traditional values. Cuban-born Protestant theologian and church historian Justo González explains in his book *Mañana* (1990, 59) that for Hispanics to become Protestant entailed a surrender of their identity similar to that expected of Hispanic Catholics in the United States. Becoming Protestant required Americanization, partly because Catholicism was so ingrained in Hispanic culture. As González points out, when these Cuban and Puerto Rican Protestants migrated to the United States, they had a sense of alienation from both the Anglos and their own compatriots.

The seeds planted during the first part of the twentieth century began to root and by the 1930s a Spanish-speaking Protestant clergy was emerging. For Methodists and Presbyterians, a big stumbling block, then as now, was the integration of Hispanics into national conferences of their respective churches. Hispanics, wishing to preserve their cultural and linguistic identities, often fear being absorbed by the non-Hispanic majority in the conferences. One of the most successful of the mainstream Hispanic churches has been the Rio Grande Conference, which includes Hispanic Methodists in Texas and New Mexico. Its roots date back to the early 1930s when Alfredo Náñez, the first Hispanic to receive his B.D. degree from Southern Methodist University, and Francisco Ramos were selected as presiding elders of the Texas American Conference. In 1939, it became the Rio Grande Conference, a powerful group of churches that has chosen, in spite all pressures, to remain independent. Under similar historical circumstances, the Latin American Conference of Southern California opted to merge with the Anglo conferences, a move that has resulted in declining membership. The less structured nature of the Southern

Baptists and the Pentecostals, whereby each congregation retains partial or total autonomy, has contributed to their increasing Hispanic membership, the only mainstream churches to experience such growth.

Pentecostalism, a brand of evangelical Christianity that is sweeping Central and South America, is growing in leaps and bounds among U.S. Hispanics. Its popularity seems to rest in the small-community atmosphere of the individual churches, which allows Hispanics a feeling of belonging. More particularly, because Pentecotalism does not dismantle for Hispanics the building blocks of their religious expression, Hispanic converts to Pentecostalism find in their new church room to express their religiosity. According to a study done in Chile by Lalive d'Epinay, although Pentecostalism disallows Catholic traditions such as processions and other external religious manifestations, it provides the convert with a highly emotional form of worship (Sandoval, p. 187). The place that the saints and the Virgin occupied as protectors, intercessors, and healers of suffering humanity is now replaced with the healing powers of the Holy Spirit. Catholic clerical authority finds its counterpart in the authority that those who have received the baptism of the Holy Spirit acquire. Interestingly enough, the charismatic renewal movement in the Roman Catholic church, which like the Pentecostals stresses the worship of the third person of the Trinity (God the Holy Spirit), is most popular among Hispanics.

During the period of brown power activism in the 1960s, Hispanic Protestants tended to remain on the sidelines. But it must be noted that two of the early leaders of the Chicano movement were Reies Tijerina, a Pentecostal minister who fought for the rights of New Mexicans to their ancestral land grants, and Rudolfo "Corky" González, a Presbyterian leader. González, a former boxer who had served time for his political involvement in the struggle for Mexican-American rights, was an early Chicano literary figure, having authored the important epic poem "Yo soy Joaquin."

✳ POPULAR RELIGIOSITY

Hispanics who live in the territories occupied by the United States in the nineteenth century and those who migrated from Mexico and the other Spanish-American countries have succeeded in preserving the religious traditions of their forefathers. Perhaps because of the almost universal scarcity of priests in the Spanish-speaking Americas, the family and the home have always been at the center of Hispanic religiosity. This religiosity is not necessarily derived from

Feast of the Crowning of Mary, Sacred Heart Cathedral, Houston, 1987. (Photo by Curtis Dowell. Courtesy of the *Texas Catholic Herald*.)

the teachings of childhood catechisms nor the homilies of parish priests. It is formed by assimilating and adapting the private religious practices that individuals observe within their extended family, which includes not only relatives, but friends and neighbors as well.

The religious instruction of the children, rosaries, novenas, *promesas* or *mandas* (the practice of making sacrificial offerings for some specific purpose), and the wearing of scapulars and medals occur or are promoted in the home usually at the behest of the grandmother or some other elderly female figure. For Hispanics, religion is often the concern of the women, who must look out for the spiritual well-being and even the salvation of their menfolk. In this context, it should be noted that in some cultures, particularly among Hispanics of Mexican origin, the *quinceañera* (fifteenth birthday) celebration, which marks the coming of age of the young girls, involves a mass or prayer service with a sermon that usually reminds the young woman of her future responsibilities as a Christian wife and mother.

Within the Hispanic household it is not unusual to

find a place that functions as an altar. In creating the altar, the Hispanic woman tries to gather within the confines of her private domain symbols of the spiritual forces on which she depends for assistance in fulfilling her primary responsibility as caretaker of a family. The home altar might be nothing more than a religious picture before which candles are lit in a wordless form of prayer; it can be a statuette of a saint, of Christ or the Virgin on a table or a television set accompanied by a vase filled with flowers; or it can be elaborate, attempting to approximate an altar within a church, with a profusion of religious images, hand-embroidered cloths, candles, incense, holy water, and other objects of the Roman Catholic worship.

Veneration of the Virgin Mary in her different aspects is foremost for most Hispanic groups: Our Lady of Guadalupe and Our Lady of San Juan de los Lagos for the Mexicans, Our Lady of Providencia for the Puerto Ricans, La Caridad del Cobre for the Cubans, and Altagracia for the Dominicans, to name a few. Veneration of Our Lady of Sorrows (Dolores) is prevalent among all groups, particularly among women, who as mothers identify with the Virgin suffering for her son. The degree of identification with this aspect of the Virgin is manifest in a tradition observed by some Mexican Americans that involves visitation of a local image of the Virgin on Good Friday to offer condolences for the death of Christ. Another tradition that reveals the intimacy of the people with their celestial Mother is observed on February 2, the feast of the Purification of Mary. For Mexican Americans this is the day when the Holy Infant first sits up—"El Asentamiento del Niño." A *madrina* (godmother) is selected for the Child. She thus strengthens her bonds through godparenting with Our Lady. The madrina, often a young girl, dresses a doll-like image of the Infant with new clothes and helps him sit up. This feast concludes for the Mexicans the Christmas season, which begins with the apparition of Our Lady of Guadalupe on December 12.

The special meaning of the Virgin for Hispanics cannot be stressed enough. For the males she is the understanding mother who forgives and intercedes for her errant sons; for the women she sympathizes with the earthly travails of a mother, sister, or daughter. Even Protestants are not immune to the appeal of this veneration. Justo González, the Protestant historian, recounts how in his seminary days some of the students, wanting to ingratiate themselves with their teacher, began to mock the cult of Our Lady of Guadalupe. The old professor, a Mexican, stopped them with the admonition that they were free to tear down Roman Catholic dogma, but they should be careful of being disrespectful toward "mi virgencita" (my little Virgin).

Adoration of particular images of Christ is traditional among certain national groups: for Guatemalans there is El Cristo Negro de Esquipulas (The Black Christ of Esquipulas); for Colombians, El Señor de los Milagros (The Lord of Miracles); and for Salvadorans, Cristo El Salvador (Christ the Savior). Additionally, the cult of the Sacred Heart of Jesus, representing the suffering aspect of Christ's human love for people, is universally popular. As noted previously, these cults invariably center on a bleeding, wounded representation of Jesus. It is not unusual for theologians or priests to bemoan Hispanics'' stress on the dead rather than on the resurrected Christ.

Hispanics worship Jesus as a child, frequently under the name El Santo Niño de Atocha (The Holy Child of Atocha). This traditional cult dates back to the time of the Reconquest of Spain, when allegedly a child brought a basket of bread to Christian captives held in a Moslem prison. The child revealed himself to them as Jesus, who had come to bring them the bread of Holy Communion. Theorists claim that the fear of the early explorers and settlers of falling captive to the Indians is responsible for the popularity of the Niño de Atocha in the Americas. Similar reasons are adduced for the popularity of El Niño Perdido (Jesus lost and found in the temple by his parents).

According to Father Virgilio Elizondo, in a 1990 speech at Peabody University, the most popular saint among U.S. Hispanics is Martin of Porres, a seventeenth-century Dominican lay brother who was the illegitimate son of a black woman and a Spaniard. Martin chose to perform the most menial tasks at his convent and to personally feed and heal the poor.

The veneration of different Franciscan saints was propagated by the early missionaries, a great many of whom were members of the Franciscan order. Saint Francis of Assisi, founder of this order, and his close friend Saint Anthony of Padua have been popular since colonial days. Veneration of Saint Joseph dates back to the days of exploration and colonization, because he is the patron saint of expeditions. The same can be said about Saint Christopher, protector of travelers. Among Cuban Americans, the veneration of Saint Lazarus and Saint Barbara are very popular and more than likely related to the phenomenon of religious syncretism evident in Santería. *Velorios de santos*, celebrations on the eve of either saint's feast day, are often held in the homes of devotees.

Processions, pilgrimages, and other external manifestations are an important element of religious expression for Hispanics. In the United States, the feast

Annual mass on the feast day of Our Lady of Guadalupe, Houston, Texas. (Courtesy of the *Texas Catholic Herald*.)

of the patron saint of a national group or a town still calls for a solemn mass followed by different forms of merriment. Processions sometimes are held, but seldom do they go beyond the grounds of the church. Exceptions to this rule are the processions of Our Lady of Guadalupe in the Southwest and of La Caridad del Cobre in the Miami area.

Pilgrimages to the shrine of Our Lady of Guadalupe in Mexico City are routinely organized wherever large groups of Mexican Americans reside. Of great interest are the pilgrimages to the shrine of Our Lady of San Juan de los Lagos in Jalisco, Mexico, which dates back to colonial times and is popular among people in northern Mexico and the U.S. Southwest. The subject of this veneration is an image of the Immaculate Conception that since the early 1600s has been said to possess healing powers. Today a large shrine to the Virgin in the Texas border town of San Juan attracts many pilgrimages from within the United States. The shrine to La Caridad del Cobre facing Biscayne Bay in Coral Gables, Florida, built with funds collected among Cuban exiles in the 1960s, attracts Cuban-American pilgrims from throughout the United States.

An integral part of many pilgrimages is the fulfill-

ing of vows made by the faithful. This may involve making the final part of the journey on one's knees. Among Mexican Americans and some Central Americans, the tradition of the ex voto (gifts presented to a saint as a show of gratitude for a favor conceded) still remains. Colonial ex votos were often primitive drawings on tin or wood depicting the miracle performed by the saint and often included a written explanation. Modern ex votos can be photographs, bridal wreaths, baby shoes, letters of gratitude, and, in many cases, the traditional *milagrito* (a charm made out of tin, gold, or silver and shaped in the form of an arm, a leg, a baby, or a house, for instance). More graphic ex votos are crutches, leg braces, eyeglasses, and other devices that through supernatural intercession the presenter was able to discard. Both the magnificent shrine in San Juan, Texas, and the quaint Sanctuary of Chimayo in Chimayo, New Mexico, where the soil behind the chapel is said to have curative powers, are excellent examples of churches where this practice flourishes.

Mexican Americans have preserved to this day the traditional *posada*, a novena that ends on Christmas eve and dates back to colonial days. For nine nights a different neighborhood family serves as host for the

The celebration of the feast day of Our Lady of Caridad del Cobre, the patron of Cubans, in Houston, 1986. (Photo by Curtis Dowell. Courtesy of the *Texas Catholic Herald*.)

posada. The "pilgrims," reenacting Mary and Joseph's search for lodging, knock at the designated home, singing a traditional hymn and asking for shelter, but are refused repeatedly. Finally, an innkeeper allows them into a home, a rosary is said, and refreshments are served. The *Pastorela*, a folk play dating to the colonial period that reenacts the adoration of the shepherds, is still presented in some Mexican-American communities during this season.

In northern New Mexico, in spite of periods of persecution, the *penitentes* continue to observe their Holy Week traditions. The brothers, all laymen, gather in the "moradas," or secret meeting places. They still practice some sort of corporal punishment, if not the extreme forms of flagellation and crucifixion observed up through the nineteenth century. After commemoration of the death of Christ on Good Friday, "tinieblas" is observed. In the completely dark morada, fearful sounds meant to instill in the faithful a contemplation of the horrors of hell are made with traditional wood and metal noisemakers.

Mexican Americans as a whole reflect, less severely perhaps, the spirit of the penitentes. Without question, Ash Wednesday draws the biggest crowds of faithful to Catholic churches in Mexican-American neighborhoods. According to Virgilio Elizondo's, 1990 speech at Peabody University, this penitential tendency reveals the feelings of inferiority of the Indian and the mestizo before the Spanish conquistador. At the opposite end of the spectrum is December 12, the feast of Our Lady of Guadalupe, which also draws multitudes to the churches. The faithful come to this feast to rejoice in their new hope, according to Elizondo. Symbols of this joy and this hope are the flowers with which they shower the Virgin and the traditional singing of "Las Mañanitas" (Morning Songs) by mariachi groups at the break of dawn.

✳ BEYOND ORTHODOXY

In spite of all precautions by church authorities, pagan or non-Christian cults have always coexisted with orthodox practices. Herb shops known as "yerberías" by Mexican Americans and "botánicas" by people of Hispanic-Caribbean descent offer not only medicinal plants but also a variety of products

A Christmas *posada* sponsored by the Club Sembradores de la Amistad in Houston in 1988. (Photo by Curtis Dowell. Courtesy of the *Texas Catholic Herald*.)

used or recommended by spiritualists and faith healers.

Yerberos are herb specialists who know the medicinal qualities of plants and utilize them to cure physical ailments. They claim that the roots, leaves, and seeds of many herbs can offset snakebites, infertility, arthritis, kidney stones, and any other conceivable illness.

The *curandero* is also a folk healer, but one who can cure ailments of a physical and a spiritual nature.

He can also remedy just about any human condition by utilizing the forces of good and evil. To bring about the desired results, the *curandero* uses, among other things, medicinal plants, eggs, candles, spells, perfumes, prayers, incense, holy water, and religious images. The curandero can, to name a few gifts, remove a spell that renders a person physically ill, make an unfaithful husband return to his wife, cure a child of "ojo" (the effects of someone's covetousness) or "susto" (fright), help someone have good luck in business or gambling, prevent or terminate pregnancies, and prepare amulets, oils, ointments, and charms. A curandero who does evil is technically a witch, a *brujo* or *bruja*. He uses the tools of his trade to do harm to others. Most curanderos, however, practice both white and black magic.

Spiritism and spiritualism sometimes coexist with curanderismo. Spiritism is a pseudoscience developed in Europe in the last century by Alan Kardec. By the 1860s it had reached Latin America. Spiritists invoke the spirits of the dead through mediums. They seek through these communications to give guidance, advice, and revelations of a supernatural nature. Spiritists may pride themselves in having access to the spirits of famous persons, such as Napoleon, Moctezuma, or Cleopatra, or they may "work" through ordinary spirits—a black slave, a great-grandmother, a fisherman. The services performed by a spirit relate to characteristics it allegedly had while alive. In this context it should be noted that Pancho Villa, the Mexican bandit and revolutionary, is a favorite among U.S. Hispanic spiritists. Villa, who was known for his hot temper, is called upon to chase away all evil spirits.

Diversity in Hispanic evangelism. (Photo by Curtis Dowell. Courtesy of the *Texas Catholic Herald*.)

Spiritualism is a cult developed in Mexico, also during the nineteenth century. Spiritualists, unlike spiritists, are usually practicing Catholics. They consider themselves vehicles or "cajas" (boxes) for great religious figures and utilize these powers to heal. Among Mexican Americans, spiritualists often serve as channels for two late spiritualists: Don Pedrito Jaramillo, a curandero from Falfurrias, Texas, and the Niño Fidencio, from a village outside Monterrey, Nuevo León, Mexico. Today there is a popular movement of canonization of these healers by the Catholic church. Others have created separate cults. In the case of Fidencio, his devotees display images of Our Lady of Guadalupe and the Sacred Heart of Jesus bearing the healer's face where the face of Mary or Jesus would normally appear.

Santeros and *babalaos* are the curanderos and brujos of Caribbean Hispanics. They are the spiritual healers, advisers, and witches of the cults brought from the western coast of Africa by the Yoruba slaves, who were imported in large numbers to Cuba and Puerto Rico during the last century. Today Miami, Tampa, New York, and San Juan, Puerto Rico, are centers of this religious cult. Santería in the United States has spread beyond the Cuban and Puerto Rican communities to people of other national origins. It is already influencing and being influenced by Mexican-American curanderismo. Santería merges elements from different Yoruba cults and Catholicism. African slaves, often forced to accept baptism by their masters, continued to worship their African gods under the external cult of the Christian saints. A less complex form of Santería is practiced by people from the Dominican Republic. This cult is a modified form of the Haitian voodoo.

Santería is a cult of the *orishas* (deities), who control the forces of nature. The most popular of these gods are portrayed on candles and icons labeled Las Siete Potencias (the Seven Powerful Spirits). Ruling over all of these spiritual forces is Olofin, God the Creator. His son, Obatala, takes the form of Our Lady of Mercy, although he is also worshiped in his male aspect as Christ, and in some Mexican-American areas as Our Lady of San Juan. Obatala is vengeful, powerful, and indifferent, and his devotees wear white. Chango, the god of war, the god of the snake, storm, and thunder, takes the form of Saint Barbara. Her color is red, the color of blood. Babalu-aye, the god of healing, is Saint Lazarus, portrayed as a leper on crutches, often accompanied by two dogs. Ogun is John the Baptist, a wild man of the forest who controls things made out of iron. Ochun, Our Lady of la Caridad del Cobre, is the goddess of love. Yemaya rules the waters. She is Our Lady of Regla. Orula, St. Francis of Assisi, can see the future.

The babalaos are the diviners of Ifa, a system they learn after many years of study. Their powers come from the god Orula. They use the so called Rosary of Ifa (sixteen cowrie shells, mango seeds, or pieces of coconut shell) to determine which god or orisha is affecting a person's life. The babalao casts the shells or seeds and determines which of the possible 16 x 16 patterns they follow. Each pattern asks for a verse the babalao recites by rote and then interprets for the client. The babalao further determines what sacrifice must be offered to the orisha to appease him or win his favor and performs it. The client must pay him for both the divination and the sacrifice. The sacrifice varies. Different gods like different gifts in terms of food, perfumes, ornaments, and so forth. Before reaching most of these gods, however, one must appeal to Elegua, who under the guise of Saint Christopher, rules road crossings. Some of the saints demand animal sacrifices. In the case of Obatala, for example, because his favorite color is white, it must be a white hen or dove.

Santeros are the devotees of the different gods. After rigorous initiation, they become the son or daughter of the orisha and are endowed with special faculties. The orisha lives in a container within the santero's house (in the United States it is usually an expensive soup tureen in the orisha's favorite color). The santero wears the orisha's color, builds him elaborate altars, and celebrates his feast day with great fanfare and at great expense. The priests and priestesses of Santería are charged with directing the liturgy.

There are three "reglas," or ways to practice Santería. The one described above is the regla of Obatala, the most widespread. The regla Lucumi is similar to the regla Obatala, although there is less syncretism between African and Christian saints. The third way is the regla Mayombera or Palo Mayombé, which intermingles Congolese rites with spiritism or the cult of the dead. It is similar to Haitian voodoo in that it works more with the *ngangas* (the spirits of the dead) than with the orishas or deities. The practitioners (*mayomberos*) are feared as powerful magicians. They can exorcise evil spirits, cast spells, make amulets. A client may chose to consult a babalao to determine the nature of his problem and go to a mayombero for the cure or solution.

A cult incorrectly connected with Santería is Nañiguismo. Nañigos are members of the Sociedad Abakúa, a secret society that combines religious elements of the Carabalí (Efik people from the coast of Calabar in southern Nigeria) and Freemasonry. Nañiguismo has its roots in the early days of slavery. Encouraged by the church, slaves grouped themselves into cabildos (religious brotherhoods dedicated to promoting the veneration of a saint). The cabildos helped slaves from the same African nations to maintain their ties unbeknownst to their white masters. The Sociedad Abakúa developed from a cabildo formed by the Carabalí. Nañiguismo, as it is commonly known, has survived to this date, thanks to its elaborate secret rules and rituals.

References

Bolton, Herbert Eugene. *Rim of Christendom: A Biography of Fray Eusebio Kino.* Tucson: University of Arizona Press, 1984.

Castañeda, Carlos. *Our Catholic Heritage in Texas.* 7 vols. Austin: Von Boeckmann-Jones, 1936-1941.

Diaz del Castillo, Bernal. *La verdadera historia de la conquista de la Nueva España.* México City: Porrúa, 1966.

Elizondo, Virgilio. *Galilean Journey: The Mexican American Promise.* Maryknoll, N.Y.: Orbis Books, 1985.

Gannon, Michael V. *The Cross in the Sand: The Early Catholic Church in Florida, 1513-1870.* Gainesville: University Presses of Florida, 1983.

González, Justo. *Mañana: Christian Theology from a Hispanic Perspective.* Nashville, Tenn.: Abingdon Press, 1990.

Goodpasture, H. McKennie. *Cross and Sword: An Eyewitness History of Christianity in Latin America.* Maryknoll, N.Y: Orbis Books, 1989.

Kessell, John L. *Kiva. Cross and Crown: The Pecos Indians and New Mexico, 1540-1840.* Albuquerque: University of New Mexico Press, 1987.

McWilliams, Carey. *North From Mexico: The Spanish-Speaking People of the United States.* Westport, Conn.: Greenwood Press, 1968.

Macklin, June, and Margarite B. Melville, eds. "All the Good and Bad in this World," 127-148. In *Twice a Minority: Mexican American Women.* St. Louis, Mo.: Mosby, 1980.

Mirandé, Alfredo. *The Chicano Experience: An Alternative Perspective.* Notre Dame, Ind.: University of Notre Dame Press, 1985.

Palou, Fr. Francisco. *Vida de Fr. Junípero Serra y Misiones de la California Septentrional.* Mexico City: Editorial Porrúa, 1975.

Pena, Silvia Novo, and Robert Flores, eds. *Interiors: Secular Aspects of Religion.* Houston, Tex.: Houston Public Libraries, 1982.

Pollak-Eltz. *Cultos afroamericanos.* Caracas: Universidad Católica Andrés Bello, 1977.

Sandoval, Moisés. *On the Move: A History of the Hispanic Church in the United States.* Maryknoll, N.Y.: Orbis Books, 1990.

Steele, Thomas J. *Santos and Saints: The Religious Folk Art of Hispanic New Mexico.* Santa Fe, N.Mex.: Ancient City Press, 1974.

Terrell, John Upton. *Pueblos, Gods and Spaniards.* New York: Dial Press, 1973.

Silvia Novo Pena

Organizations

Almost from the first moment that Hispanics found themselves within the political, social, and economic context of a larger Anglo-American society, they began to form organizations for mutual protection and defense of their language and culture. Since the mid-nineteent century, Hispanic organizations have been many and varied, reflecting their specific ethnicity, social class, religion, and place of origin. It has only been recently that broad national organizations that transcend these differentiating factors have been formed, as a national Hispanic consciousness is emerging within the borders of the United States.

When such areas as California came under Anglo-American domination, organizations such as the Junta Patriótica Mexicana (Mexican Patriotic Group) in San Francisco sprang up to encourage Mexican patriotism, defend the rights of Mexicans, and even raise funds for social causes in Mexico, including relief for the victims of the French intervention of 1862. Later in the century, such Mexican revolutionaries as the Flores Magón brothers formed chapters of the Partido Liberal Mexicano (Liberal Mexican party) in the Southwest to support the cause against dictator Porfirio Díaz, while Cuban, Dominican, and Puerto Rican patriots were developing political organizations in New York, Philadelphia, New Orleans, Tampa, and Key West to support the independence of their island nations from Spain.

All the Hispanic immigrant groups—in this way similar to European immigrants—formed mutual aid societies, often called *mutualistas*, to pool their resources in order to offer the members low-cost health care, insurance, funerals, low-interest loans, and other types of economic assistance. While originating as an institution to provide economic security, the mutualista, in fact, became the second most important institution in the community after the church. The immigrants workers" resources were strong enough to either buy, rent, or construct a building that usually housed a hall and/or theater and became a principal gathering place for the members and the community. The mutualista became the site of theatrical performances, dances, and other healthy and safe entertainment for the youth, as well as a place for political organizing and fund-raising for various causes. In many ways, the mutual aid societies provided the foundation for the labor and civil rights organizations that followed years later.

There were many mutual aid societies, and their history is varied and intriguing. In general, among Mexican immigrants, the societies were usually created by a group of immigrants originating from the same town or region in Mexico, and more than likely, from the same social class, usually laborers. They often baptized their societies with names honoring their favorite heroes—Sociedad Benito Juárez, Sociedad Coahotemoc, Sociedad Hidalgo, or, simply, Unión Benéfica Mexicana (Mexican Benefit Society).

The same practice was also common among Puerto Ricans and Cubans, and a network of associated societies arose, called The Brotherhood. In New York and Tampa, Spaniards tenaciously held to their *patria chica* (home regions), founding such organizations as the Casa Galicia (Galician House), Calpe Americano (Alicante in America), Círculo Valenciano (Valencian Circle), and the Centro Asturiano (Asturian Center). In both cities, the Cubans and Puerto Ricans were organized in separate organizations. But in Tampa, in the heart of the Jim Crow South, Afro-Cubans were not admitted to either the Círculo Cubano (Cuban Circle) or the Spanish societies. They therefore formed their own organization under the names of the two revolutionary heroes who transcended racism: Sociedad Martí-Maceo.

Despite the regionalism and classism, there were several societies in cosmopolitan New York that brought various Hispanic nationalities together, such as the Ateneo Hispano (Hispanic Atheneum)

A march by the Council of Puerto Rican Organizations from the Lower East Side of New York City over the Brooklyn Bridge to protest the poor conditions of public schools in the Puerto Rican community. (Historic Archive of the Department of Puerto Rican Community Affairs in the United States. Courtesy of the Center for Puerto Rican Studies Library and Archives, Hunter College, CUNY).

A celebration of the Three Kings sponsored by the Puerto Rican Workers Mutual Aid Society, New York City. (Jesús Colón Papers. Courtesy of the Center for Puerto Rican Studies Library and Archives, Hunter College, CUNY).

and the Sociedad Hispana La Amistad (The Friendship Hispanic Society). In truth, the various Hispanic nationalities interrelated freely and organized together at other institutions, such as churches, theaters, and labor unions. And because Hispanics were predominantly working-class people and Catholic, there was a plethora of organizations related to the church and workplace. In particular, Puerto Rican and Cuban cigar-rollers in Tampa and New York were prime movers in union and socialist organizing, as were many of the expatriates from the Spanish Civil War during the 1930s and 1940s.

While a more politically active type of mutualism, as practiced by such groups as the Alianza Hispano-Americana (Hispanic-American Alliance), founded in Tucson during 1894, multiplied itself in chapters throughout the Southwest, there were very few openly political organizations until Mexican-American veterans returning from World War I became active in the American Legion and founded the Order of the Sons of America in 1921 and the Knights of America and the League of United Latin American Citizens (LULAC) in 1929. From then on (and reinforced by the veterans returning from World War II and their organizations, such as the American G.I. Forum, founded in 1947), Mexican Americans and other Hispanics became politically active to protect their rights as U.S. citizens. From the postwar period to the present, numerous political organizations have been formed, such as the Mexican American Political Association (1959) and the Political Association of Spanish-Speaking Organizations (1960), as well as separate political parties, such as the Raza Unida party (1970), and Hispanic Democratic and Republican organizations. Today, there is also a National Association of Hispanic Elected Officials and a Hispanic Congressional Caucus, which is duplicated in various state legislatures as well. (For specific and detailed information on Hispanic religious, labor, and political groups, refer, respectively, to Chapters 14, 12, and 9.)

In addition, there are myriad other Hispanic social, health, and professional groups. In almost all the major communities of Hispanics throughout the United States, there are Puerto Rican, Cuban, Mexican-American, Hispanic, and inter-American chambers of commerce, bar associations, medical associations, organizations of accountants and engineers, and associations of professors and teachers, many of which are united in their national organizations, such as the National Hispanic Chamber of Commerce, the National Association for Bilingual Education, and the National Association for Chicano Studies. There are myriad social service and civil rights

A parade organized by the Tucson's Alianza Hispano-Americana. (Courtesy of the Arizona Historical Society.)

groups, as well as such national research and lobbyist entities as the National Council of La Raza.

Primary Hispanic Organizations: Associations of Broad or National Scope

American G.I. Forum
3317 Manor Road
Austin, TX 78723
(512)477-3222

Established in 1948, the American G.I. Forum has 540 affiliate organizations and 20,000 members in chapters in every state. The forum is one of the major advocacy organizations for Hispanics in the United States. Its special programs include the Business Development Center, Education Foundation, Veteran's Outreach Program, and National Economic Development Program (SER-Jobs for Progress). The forum also is associated with the American G.I. Women Forum, which has a membership of 6,000 active in social and educational programs. The forum publishes a monthly bulletin, *The Forumeer.*

Asociación Nacional Pro Personas Mayores
(National Association of Hispanic Elderly)
3325 Wilshire Boulevard, Suite 800
Los Angeles, CA 90010-1724
(213)487-1922

Founded in 1975, the Asociación Nacional Pro Personas Mayores has 3,100 members and 13 affiliates. The association is an advocacy organization for the Hispanic elderly and the low-income elderly. It administers a nationwide employment program and provides technical assistance to community groups and professionals in the field of aging. It operates the National Hispanic Research Center, which conducts gerontological studies and issues bilingual reports. It also publishes the *Legislative Bulletin* quarterly.

ASPIRA Association, Inc.
1112 Sixteenth Street, NW, Suite 340
Washington, DC 20036
(202)835-3600

Founded in 1969, ASPIRA (hope) is a grass roots organization working to provide leadership development and educational assistance to Hispanics. AS-

PIRA offers educational counseling for high school and college students, a forum for group discussions, workshops, tutoring, and assistance in applying for college and financial aid. It establishes high school clubs and sponsors the National Health Careers Program, the ASPIRA Public Policy Research Program, and the Institute for Policy Research. ASPIRA publishes a quarterly, *Aspira News*, and reports.

Comisión Femenil Mexicana Nacional, Inc.
(National Mexican Women's Commission)
379 South Loma Drive
Los Angeles, CA 90017
(213)484-1515

Founded in 1970, the Comisión Femenil Mexicana Nacional has some 5,000 members in 23 affiliate chapters. The organization advocates Hispanic women's rights and works to advance Hispanic women politically, economically, socially, and educationally. It administers the Chicana Service Center, which provides job skills training; the Centro de Niños (The Children's Center), which provides bilingual child development programs; and Casa Victoria (Victory House), which is a group home for teens. Its standing committees include Development, Education, Health and Welfare, Legislative, Reproductive Rights, and Teen Pregnancy. The commission publishes *La Mujer* (The Woman) semiannually.

Congressional Hispanic Caucus
H2-557
Washington, DC 20515
(202)226-3430

Founded in 1957, the Congressional Hispanic Caucus is a legislative service organization dedicated to improving the condition of Hispanics through the legislative process. The caucus monitors the executive and judicial branches of government and seeks to strengthen the role of Hispanics at all levels of government. It publishes the *Legislative Review*, a monthly.

Cuban American Legal Defense and Education Fund
2119 South Webster Street
Fort Wayne, IN 46804
(219)745-5421

Founded in 1980, the Cuban American Legal Defense and Education Fund advocates equal treatment for Hispanics in education, employment, housing, politics, and justice. It strives to end negative stereotyping of Hispanics and to educate the public about their plight in the United States. It publishes a monthly *Hispanic Newsletter*. (*See* National League of Cuban American Community-Based Centers.)

Cuban American National Foundation
1000 Thomas Jefferson Street, NW
Washington, DC 20007
(202)265-2822

Founded in 1981, the Cuban American National Foundation has three affiliates. It produces and disseminates research on the economic, political, and social issues affecting Cubans in the United States and in Cuba. The organization supports the concept

President Ronald Reagan presents the Medal of Freedom to Dr. Héctor García (far right), founder of the American G.I. Forum.

of a free and democratic Cuba. The foundation advocates Cuban civil rights and attempts to affect public opinion on Cubans and Cuban issues. It publishes *Boletín informativo* (Informative Bulletin) and *Cuban Update*.

Cuban American National Council
300 Southwest Twelfth Ave.
Miami, FL 33130-2038
(305)642-3484

Founded in 1972, the Cuban American National Council is a private nonprofit social service agency that researches the economic, social, and educational needs of Cubans Americans and assists them in their adjustment to American society. The council administers a network of programs in the three above-named areas and also fosters multiethnic cooperation. It publishes a quarterly, the *Council Letter*.

Consortium of National Hispanic Organizations
1030 Fifteenth Street, NW, Suite 1053
Washington, DC 20005
(202)371-2100

Founded in 1976, the Consortium of National Hispanic Organizations has 26 organizational members, which have come together to discuss and share information on issues affecting the Hispanic community. The consortium sponsors seminars and symposia. Its committees include Civic Education, Health, Housing, Immigration, International Issues, Labor, and Press and Media. The consortium issues reports and sponsors an annual convention.

Hispanic Academy of Media Arts and Sciences
Box 291774
Los Angeles, CA 90029
(818)954-2720

The Hispanic Academy of Media Arts and Sciences advocates the fair and equal representation of Hispanics in film and television, monitors how they are portrayed, and works for access to employment at all levels in television and film. The organization sponsors an annual awards event that highlights the contributions of Hispanics to the industry.

Hispanics in Philanthropy
116 New Montgomery Street
San Francisco, CA 94105-3607
(415)788-2982

Founded in 1981, Hispanics in Philanthropy has three affiliates. The organization is a volunteer association of Hispanic trustees and staff members of grant-making foundations and corporate contributions programs. The association shares information and advocates causes in the Council on Foundations and in the world of philanthropy. It offers workshops and training to organizations providing grant-seeking training services to the Hispanic community. It publishes a quarterly newsletter.

National IMAGE, Inc.
930 W. Seventh Ave., Suite 117-121
Denver, CO 80204
(303)534-6534

Founded in 1972, IMAGE has 3,000 members in 52 chapters. IMAGE works to increase employment opportunities for Hispanics and to seek equality with other groups in status and achievement. Its Project Cambio (change) provides scholarships for Hispanic women pursuing a career change or reentry to the work force. It publishes *National IMAGE*.

Las Hermanas-United States of America
(The Sisters-USA)
P.O. Box 15792
San Antonio, TX 78212
(512)434-0947

Founded in 1971, Las Hermanas has 1,000 members, mostly Catholic nuns, in twelve regional chapters and forty affiliate groups. Las Hermanas advocates the needs of Hispanics in the church and the society, with the specific goal of engaging Hispanic women in active ministry among Hispanics. It conducts leadership training, workshops, and retreats. It publishes *Informes*, a quarterly newsletter.

Hispanic Association of Colleges and Universities
411 Southwest Twenty-fourth Street
San Antonio, TX 78207-4617
(512)433-1501

Founded in 1986, the Hispanic Association of Colleges and Universities has 34 institutional members, whose purpose is to bring together colleges and universities with corporations, government agencies, and individuals to promote the development of member institutions and improve the quality and accessibility of postsecondary education for Hispanics.

League of United Latin American Citizens
400 First Street, NW, Suite 721
Washington, D.C. 20001
(202)628-8516

Founded in 1929, LULAC has 110,000 members in 12 regional and 43 state groups. LULAC is concerned with seeking full social, political, economic, and educational rights for Hispanics in the United States. LULAC supports the fifteen LULAC National Education Service Centers, offers employment and training programs, conducts research on postsecondary education, and sponsors Hispanics Organized for Political Education, which encourages voter registration and political awareness. LULAC publishes the *HOPE Voter's Guide*, reports, and the monthly *LULAC National Reporter*.

Los P.A.D.R.E.S.

(The Fathers)
2216 East 108th Street
Los Angeles, CA 90059
(213)569-5951

Founded in 1969, Los PADRES has 500 members, mostly Hispanic Catholic priests, brothers, and deacons. The acronym stands for Padres Asociados para Derechos Religiosos, Educativos y Sociales (Fathers Associated for Religious, Educational, and Social Rights). Its purpose is to develop the critical conscience whereby poor people see themselves as masters of their own destiny and capable of bringing about structural change. It promotes a supportive ministry and advocates Hispanic issues and rights in the church. It publishes a quarterly newsletter, *Los P.A.D.R.E.S.*

Mexican American Legal Defense and Education Fund

634 South Spring Street
Los Angeles, CA 90014
(213)625-2512

Founded in 1968, the Mexican American Legal Defense and Education Fund (MALDEF) currently has six affiliate offices, in San Francisco, Los Angeles, Sacramento, San Antonio, Chicago, and Washington, D.C. MALDEF is in the forefront of protecting Mexican-American civil rights. It has been responsible for civil rights class-action litigation affecting Hispanics. Litigation departments are maintained in the areas of education, employment, immigration, and voting rights. It maintains a law school scholarship and other programs to assist students in entering the legal profession. MALDEF publishes two triquarterly newsletters, *Leadership Program Newsletter* and *MALDEF Newsletter*.

Movimiento Familiar Cristiano

(Christian Family Movement)
2610 John Ralston Road
Houston, TX 77013
(713)451-2248

Founded in 1969, the Movimiento Familiar Cristiano has 5,000 members in 42 regional groups. The organization is made up of husbands and wives working together to improve the quality of life in the Spanish-speaking communities of the United States. The program involves a cycle of four years of study of family life. The organization also sponsors retreats.

The organization publishes manuals and brochures and the monthly *MFC-USA Bulletin*.

Mujeres Activas en Letras y Cambio Social

(Women Active in Letters and Social Change)
c/o Ethnic Studies Program
Santa Clara University
Santa Clara, CA 95953
(408)554-4511

Founded in 1982, Mujeres Activas en Letras y Cambio Social (MALCS) has 90 members, with seven regional groups. The organization is made up of Hispanic women in higher education who foster research and writing on Hispanic women. MALCS seeks to fight race, class, and gender oppression at universities and to develop strategies for social change. It publishes a triquarterly newsletter, *Noticiera de MALCS*.

National Association for Chicano Studies

c/o Devón Peña
14 East Cuche LaPoundre
Colorado Springs, CO 80903
(719)389-6642

Founded in 1971, the National Association for Chicano Studies has over 300 members in 6 regional groups made up mostly of Mexican-American college professors. The organization fosters research and exchange of ideas on Chicano subjects and sponsors an annual convention as well as conventions of regional groups. The organization publishes its annual proceedings, which are made up mostly of formal papers read at the convention.

National Association of Hispanic Journalists

National Press Building, Suite 634
Washington, D.C. 20045
(202)662-7145 or (202)662-7168

The National Association of Hispanic Journalists (NAHJ) has source 500 members and various state and regional affiliates. It seeks to enhance opportunities for Hispanic journalists and works to seek balanced and fair portrayal of Hispanics by the media. It provides support for Hispanic journalists to maintain their identity as they work within the non-Hispanic media. The organization has various programs to encourage Hispanic students to go into journalism, including its annual essay contest, whose winners are awarded scholarships. NAHJ publishes a newsletter.

National Association of Hispanic Publications

P.O. Box 2285
Orlando, FL 32802
(407)425-9911

Founded in 1982, the National Association of Hispanic Publications has 25 chapters made up of senior-level staff from more than 100 Hispanic newspapers, magazines, and newsletters from throughout the United States. The organization functions to research Hispanic media, to promote Hispanic publications, to encourage advertisers to use these publications, and to encourage Hispanics to enter the field. It publishes the *Hispanic Media Directory* and the quarterly *Hispanic Print*.

National Association of Latino Elected and Appointed Officials

708 G Street, SE
Washington, D.C. 20003
(202)546-2536

Founded in 1975, the National Association of Latino Elected and Appointed Officials (NALEO) has 3,000 members made up of Hispanic elected officials and people who support them, including both individuals and corporate members. NALEO is a comprehensive advocacy and leadership network dedicated to the advancement of Hispanic people. It also serves as a clearinghouse on citizenship information and compiles Hispanic voting statistics. It maintains data bases on Hispanic businesses in the minority procurement program, on citizenship services providers, and on Hispanic elected officials. NALEO has various quarterly and annual publications, including directories and rosters.

National Caucus of Hispanic School Board Members

24 East Cody Drive
Phoenix, AZ 85040
(602)243-4804

Founded in 1975, the membership of the National Caucus of Hispanic School Board Members is made up of board members and others interested in the education of Hispanic students. The organization is an educational advocacy group as well as a caucus of the National School Boards Association.

National Coalition of Hispanic Health & Human Services Organizations

1501 Sixteenth Street, NW
Washington, DC 20036
(202)387-5000

Founded in 1974, the National Coalition of Hispanic Health & Human Services Organizations has 507 members. It conducts research and functions as an advocate for Hispanic health and social services needs. It publishes *Roadrunner* and *Reporter*, both six times a year, and *COSSMHO Aids Update* monthly.

National Concilio of America

41 Sutter, Suite 1067
San Francisco, CA 94104
(415)550-0785

Founded in 1977, the National Concilio of America (NCA) has 13 member organizations representing a network of over 100 community-based organizations. Its purposes include cultivating leaders that will interact with local voluntary and philanthropic institutions, train staff in the technical skills required for administration, conduct needs assessments, review demographic and marketing data, develop long-range plans for Hispanic communities, and identify existing financial resources. The NCA publishes two quarterlies, *Executive Brief* and *Horizontes*, a newsletter.

National Conference of Puerto Rican Women

5 Thomas Circle
Washington, DC 20005
(202)387-4716

Established in 1972, the National Conference of Puerto Rican Women has 4,500 members in 15 chapters. The organization strives to ensure the participation of Puerto Rican women in the mainstream of social, political, and economic life in the United States, works for equal rights for all Hispanic women, and offers leadership development. It publishes the quarterly *Ecos Nacionales* (National Echoes).

National Congress for Puerto Rican Rights

160 West Lippincott Street
Philadelphia, PA 19133
(215)426-8723

Founded in 1981, the National Congress for Puerto Rican Rights has 3,000 members and 5 affiliates. The congress is an advocate for the civil and human rights of Puerto Ricans in education, labor, voting, housing, women's issues, media, health, and justice and for the end to the government's intervention in the affairs of Latin America and the Caribbean. It publishes the quarterly *Unidad Borinqueña* (Puerto Rican Unity) and the biennial *Status Report on Puerto Ricans in the U.S.*

National Congress of Puerto Rican Veterans

140 Broadway
New York, NY 10015
(212)658-5340

Founded in 1967, the National Congress of Puerto Rican Veterans has 8,000 members. It functions as a support group for Puerto Rican veterans by assisting them in obtaining equal treatment and fair access to services provided to all veterans.

Brooklyn Chapter of the Liga Puertorriqueña e Hispana (Puerto Rican and Hispanic League), circa 1927. (Jesús Colón Papers. Courtesy of the Center for Puerto Rican Studies Library and Archives, Hunter College, CUNY).

National Council of Hispanic Women

P.O. Box 23266
L'Enfant Plaza Station
Washington, DC 20013
(703)768-3596 or (703)486-8112

Made up of 175 Hispanic women, universities, and corporations interested in strengthening the role of Hispanic women in society, the organization encourages Hispanic women to take part in decision making in government and business. It publishes the quarterly *NCHW Newsletter*.

National Council of La Raza

810 First Street, NE, No. 300
Washington, DC 20002-4205
(202)289-1380

Founded in 1968, the National Council of La Raza has 75 organizational members; it serves as an umbrella organization working for civil rights and economic opportunities for Hispanics. It provides technical assistance to Hispanic community-based organizations in comprehensive community development. It conducts research and serves as an advocate for Hispanic causes. It also offers private sector resource development training, board of directors training, and proposal writing training. It publishes a variety of newsletters and reports.

National Council of Puerto Rican Volunteers

c/o Mrs. Pedro G. Valdés
541 South Sixth Avenue
Mt. Vernon, NY 10550
(914)665-1287

Founded in 1964, the National Council of Puerto Rican Volunteers has 10,000 members. It aims to organize groups of Puerto Rican and Spanish-speaking volunteers to help bridge the language barriers that prevent many Puerto Ricans from taking advantage of facilities in existence for their welfare and improvement. It furnishes public and private service organizations with bilingual volunteers.

National Hispanic Corporate Council

P.O. Box 61421
Phoenix, AZ 85082-1412
(602)257-5515

Founded in 1985, the National Hispanic Corporate Council has 43 members, who are executives of Fortune 500 companies. The goals include exchanging information, ideas, and research that will assist corporate America in focusing on the Hispanic community and the market it represents. The council publishes a newsletter.

National Hispanic Council on Aging

2713 Ontario Road, NW, No. 200
Washington, DC 20009
(202)745-2521

Founded in 1980, the National Hispanic Council on Aging has 3,000 members and 4 chapters. The council is an advocate for the Hispanic aging and develops and disseminates information, educational materials, research, and policy analysis regarding Hispanic elderly. The council is affiliated with the American Society on Aging and the Gerontological Society of America. It publishes a quarterly newsletter, *Noticias*.

National League of Cuban American Community-Based Centers

2119 S. Webster Street
Fort Wayne, IN 46802
(219)745-5421

The National League of Cuban American Community-Based Centers was founded in 1980 to establish linkages among Cuban American community centers and to open new centers wherever needed. The league assesses the needs of minority communities in relation to education, training, manpower development, and health care. It promotes awareness among Hispanics of employment opportunities. The league publishes a monthly *Hispanic Newsletter*.

National Puerto Rican Forum

31 East Thirty-second Street, Fourth Floor
New York, NY 10016
(212)685-2311

Founded in 1957, the National Puerto Rican Forum is concerned with the overall improvement of Puerto Rican and Hispanic communities throughout the United States. It designs and implements programs in job counseling, training and placement, and the teaching of English. It sponsors career services and a job placement program at the national level. It publishes occasional reports.

The Puerto Rican Family Institute, Inc.
116 West Fourteenth Street
New York, NY 10011
(212)924-6320

Founded in 1960 for the preservation of the health, well-being, and integrity of Puerto Rican and Hispanic families in the United States, The Puerto Rican Family Institute's programs include social work and educational services to migrants and newly arrived immigrants, child-placement, prevention programs, and health clinics. Its services are also administered by a branch office in Río Piedras, Puerto Rico.

Puerto Rican Legal Defense and Education Fund, Inc.
99 Hudson Street, Fourteenth Floor
New York, NY 10013
(212)219-3360

The Puerto Rican Legal Defense and Education Fund was established in 1972 to protect and further the rights of Puerto Ricans and other Hispanics, especially against discrimination in housing, education, employment, health, and political participation. It also maintains placement services for Hispanic lawyers. It publishes a newsletter, *Civil Rights Litigation*.

Secretariat for Hispanic Affairs
National Council of Bishops
3211 Fourth Street, NE
Washington, DC 20017-1194
(202)541-3150

Founded in 1945, the Secretariat for Hispanic Affairs has 140 diocesan directors as members. It offers consultation services operated by the Catholic Bishops of the United States to assist those dioceses with large Hispanic populations in developing a far-reaching and effective response to the pastoral needs of Hispanics in the United States. It conducts and disseminates research and provides liaisons with other institutions and agencies. It publishes the quarterly *En Marcha* (On the March).

SER-Jobs for Progress
1355 River Bend Drive, Suite 240
Dallas, TX 75247
(214)631-3999

Founded in 1964, SER is a voluntary community-based organization with 111 affiliate programs in 83 cities. It is a national network of organizations that develop programs for the full utilization of Hispanics in the economy, including a wide range of job-training and educational programs. SER is sponsored by and affiliated with the League of United Latin American Citizens and the American G.I. Forum *see* American G.I. Forum). It publishes the quarterly *SER America*.

Southwest Voter Registration Education Project
403 East Commerce Street, Suite 220
San Antonio, TX 78205
(512)222-0224

Founded in 1975, the Southwest Voter Registration Education Project is made up of church, civic, labor, and fraternal groups that organize coalitions to register minority voters in the Southwest and 13 western states. It conducts nonpartisan voter education projects and research on Hispanic and native American political organization participation in the Southwest. It seeks reapportionment of gerrymandered counties and cities. It publishes the *National Hispanic Voter Registration Campaign* and research studies. Regional planning committees publish newsletters.

REFORMA: The National Association to Promote Library Services to the Spanish-Speaking
American Library Association
50 Huron Street
Chicago, IL 60611
(916)323-4400

Founded in 1971, REFORMA has 700 members in 8 affiliates. REFORMA works for the improvement of the full range of library services to Hispanics of the United States. REFORMA advocates the creation of library collections in Spanish, the recruitment of bilingual and bicultural library personnel, and the development of specialized services for the Hispanic community. REFORMA offers scholarships for graduate library study. It is affiliated with the American Library Association. REFORMA publishes the quarterly *Reforma Newsletter*.

United Farm Workers of America
P.O. Box 62 - La Paz
Keene, CA 93531
(805)822-5571

Founded in 1962, the United Farm Workers of America, a labor union, currently has a membership of over 100,000. The main goal is to enhance the living conditions of farm workers through collective bargaining with agricultural producers. It issues two publications, *El Malcriado* (monthly) and *Food and Justice* (monthly).

Poster for the Spanish-Speaking Coalition Conference of October, 1971. Mexican American and Puerto Rican groups came together to agree upon unified goals.

U.S. Hispanic Chamber of Commerce

2000 Massachusetts Ave. NW, No. 860
Washington, DC 20036-3307
(202)862-3939

Founded in 1979, the U.S. Hispanic Chamber of Commerce has 40,000 members and 20 affiliates interested in the development and promotion of Hispanic businesses and the promotion of the business leadership in the Hispanic community. It promotes a positive image for Hispanics and encourages corporate involvement with Hispanic companies. It conducts business-related workshops, conferences, and management training seminars; compiles statistics; reports on business achievements and vendor programs of major corporations; and sponsors competitions and bestows awards. Its publications include a periodic *National Hispanic Business Directory* and two quarterly newsletters, *Legislative Update* and *Networking*.

References

Furtaw, Julia C., ed. *Hispanic Americans Information Directory 1992-93*. Detroit, Mich.: Gale Research, 1992.

Schorr, Edward Alan. *Hispanic Resource Directory*. Juneau, Alaska: Denali Press, 1988.

Zavaler, Angela E., ed. *Anvario Hispano-Hispanic Yearbook*. McLean, Virginia: T.I.Y.M. Publishing Comapny, 1991.

Nicolás Kanellos

16

Scholarship

The biographies in this chapter are of scholars not covered in other chapters of this almanac, such as the ones on science, law and politics, and other chapters where scholars are studied or mentioned. Scholars that have become university presidents are included in the chapter on prominent Hispanics. Primarily, the scholars here have made their careers in the humanities and social sciences and have been pioneers in Hispanic studies, a field of scholarship that did not exist two decades ago. Many of them were involved in the civil rights movement of the late 1960s and were among the first scholars to research the history and culture of Hispanics in the United States. They were actively involved in creating the intellectual and structural bases for the creation of Mexican-American, Puerto Rican, and Cuban studies departments and centers, as well as bilingual education programs at universities throughout the country. Many of them took as their models and mentors such early pioneer scholars as María Teresa Babín, Arthur León Campa, Carlos Castañeda, Luis Leal, Américo Paredes, and George I. Sánchez, who were among the extremely few Hispanic researchers in academia during the 1940s, 1950s, and early 1960s. Today, most of them are tenured associate and full professors, continuing their efforts to broaden the curriculum so that Hispanic history and culture are not only taught but also attain their rightful place as a substantial part of the cultural identity of the United States as a whole. In addition, many of the social scientists are working toward alleviating many of the social and educational problems that continue to afflict Hispanics in American society. As a group, their research is contributing to the information about Hispanics that appears today in textbooks at every curricular level, from preschool to graduate school, and to the policies and practices of government at every level as well.

Edna Acosta-Belén (1948-)
Literature

Born on January 14, 1948, in Hormigueros, Puerto Rico, Acosta-Belén received her B.A. and M.A. degrees from the State University of New York, Albany, in 1969 and 1971, respectively, and her Ph.D. degree from Columbia University in 1977. She has been a National Endowment for the Humanities summer fellow at the University of Massachusetts (1982) and Princeton University (1978) and a visiting fellow at Yale University (1979-80). From 1972 to the present, she ascended the ranks from instructor to full professor with joint appointments in the Department of Latin American and Caribbean Studies and the Department of Women's Studies. From 1989 to the present, she has served as the director of the Center for Latin American and Caribbean Studies and, from 1983 to 1986 and again from 1988 to 1989, as chair of the Department for Latin American and Caribbean Studies. From 1987 to 1991, she was the cofounding associate director of the Institute for Research on Women. Acosta-Belén is the recipient of numerous awards, including the New York State Chapter of the National Organization of Women's Making Waves Award (1991), the Chancellor's Award for Excellence in Teaching (1989), and the President's Award for Excellence in Teaching (1988). Her books include *In the Shadow of the Giant: Colonialism, Migration and Puerto Rican Culture* (1992), the coedited *Integrating Latin American and Caribbean Women into the Curriculum and Research: Perspectives and Sources* (1991), *The Hispanic Experience in the United States* (1988), and *The Puerto Rican Woman: Perspectives on Culture, History and Society* (1979, 1986).

Rodolfo Acuña (1932-)
History

Born on May 18, 1932, in Los Angeles, California, Acuña received his B.A. and M.A. degrees from Los

Angeles State College in 1957 and 1962, respectively, and his Ph.D. degree from the University of Southern California in 1962. He began his teaching career in 1962, at Mount St. Mary's as an instructor and has risen to the rank of full professor at California State University, Northridge. He is the founder of the Chicano studies department at Northridge and the author of the standard Chicano history textbook, *Occupied America: the Chicano's Struggle towards Liberation* (1972, 1981, 1987). Acuña is a dynamic speaker and teacher as well as an assiduous researcher whose articles have been published far and wide.

Norma Alarcón (19?-)
Chicano Studies

Born in Mexico, Alarcón received her B.A., M.A., and Ph.D. degrees in Spanish from Indiana University in 1970, 1972, and 1983, respectively. From 1983 to 1987, she was an assistant professor at Purdue University. From 1987 to the present she has been a member of the Chicano studies department at the University of California, Berkeley. In 1991, she was promoted to associate professor with tenure. Alarcón has been an outstanding editor and promoter of Hispanic women's literature. From 1981 to the present, she has been the founding editor of Third Woman Press, and from 1975 to the present, a contributing editor of *The Americas Review*. She is the author of *La poética feminista de Rosario Castellanos* (1992) and various articles on feminist literary theory, especially as relates to women of color.

Fernando Alegría (1918-)
Literature

Born on September 26, 1918, in Santiago, Chile, Alegría received his early education in Chile, his M.A. degree from Bowling Green State University in 1941 and his Ph.D. degree in Spanish from the University of California, Berkeley in 1947. After receiving his doctorate, he made his entire career at Stanford University, where he ascended the ranks to full professor with a chair, and finally professor emeritus, which is his current status. Alegría has been a pioneer in the study of Latin American literature, in which his books have concentrated on narrative, and he has also been a distinguished novelist, essayist, and poet, recognized in both the Spanish- and English-speaking world. His book *Historia de la novela hispanoamericana* (*History of the Spanish American Novel*, 1965) has gone through various editions and served as a standard text of Latin American literature. He has received a Guggenheim Fellowship and has won numerous other awards and distinctions. Alegría was also one of the first and most influential

scholars to acknowledge and promote Hispanic literature of the United States in academia.

Rodolfo Alvarez (1936-)
Sociology

Born on October 23, 1936, in San Antonio, Texas, Alvarez received his B.A. degree in 1961 from San Francisco State University and his M.A. and Ph.D. degrees from the University of Washington in 1964 and 1966, respectively. He served as an assistant professor at Yale University from 1966 to 1972, after which he moved to the University of California, Los Angeles, as an associate professor; in 1980 he became a full professor. From 1972 to 1974, he served as the director of the Chicano Studies Research Center at UCLA, and from 1973 to 1975 he served as the founding director of the Spanish-Speaking Mental Health Research Center. Alvarez has been active in his profession and in the community, serving on numerous boards and committees, including the board of the Mexican American Legal Defense and Education Fund (1975 to 1979), the presidency of the ACLU of Southern California (1980 to 1981), and the presidency of the Society for the Study of Social Problems (1985-86). He has coedited various books, including *Racism, Elitism, Professionalism: Barriers to Community Mental Health* (1976) and *Discrimination in Organizations* (1979).

María Teresa Babín (1910-)
Literature

Born in Ponce, Puerto Rico, in 1910, Babín received her early education in Ponce, her M.A. degree from the University of Puerto Rico in 1939, and her Ph.D. degree from Columbia University in 1951. She served for many years as the director of the Spanish-language program of the Puerto Rican Department of Public Instruction and the Hispanic Studies Program at the University of Puerto Rico at Mayagüez. During the 1970s, Babín finished her career as a pioneer in Puerto Rican studies at the City College of New York, where she taught some of the first courses in Puerto Rican literature and culture. Her best-known and most important book is her pioneering history and overview of Puerto Rican culture, *Panorama de la cultura puertorriqueña* (1958). Another pioneering work by Babín is the anthology that she cowrote with Stan Steiner, *Borinquen: An Anthology of Puerto Rican Literature* (1974), which is one of only two anthologies of Puerto Rican literature in the English language and which includes works by Puerto Rican (Nuyorican) writers of the United States. Babín's other books include *Introducción a la cultura hispánica* (*Introduction to Hispanic Culture,* 1949), *El mundo poético de García Lorca* (*The Poetic World of*

García Lorca, 1954), and *García Lorca: Vida y obra* (*García Lorca: His Life and Works,* 1955. Babín is also a creative writer, the author of local-color essays, *Fantasía Boricua: Estampas de mi tierra* (*Puerto Rican Fantasy: Scenes from My Land,* 1956, 1957); a play, *La hora colmada* (*The Over-Filled Hour,* 1960); and a book of poems, *Las voces de tu voz* (*The Voices of Your Voice,* 1962).

Maxine Baca-Zinn (1942-)
Sociology

Born on June 11, 1942, in Santa Fe, New Mexico, Baca-Zinn received her B.A. degree from California State College in 1966, her M.A. degree from the University of New Mexico in 1970, and her Ph.D. degree from the University of Oregon in 1978. Since 1975 to the present, Zinn has developed her career at the University of Michigan, Flint. In 1988-89, she served as a visiting professor in the Women's Studies Program at the University of Delaware. Baca-Zinn is currently the associate editor of the *Social Science Journal.*

Frank Bonilla (192?-)
Political Science

Frank Bonilla received his B.B.A. from City College of New York in 1949, his M.A. in sociology from New York University in 1954, and his Ph.D. from the Department of Social Relations, Harvard University in 1959. From 1960 to 1963, Bonilla was a member of the American Universities Field Staff on a contract to be carried out on behalf of UNESCO, investigating the relations between social development and education in Argentina, Chile, Mexico, and Brazil. In 1963, he became an associate professor of Political Science at Massachusetts Institute of Technology; in 1967, he was promoted to full professor. In 1969, he became a professor of Political Science at Stanford University. Since 1973, he has served as a full professor of Political Science at the City University of New York and the Director of the Center for Puerto Rican Studies. Bonilla is a pioneer in Puerto Rican Studies and is known for helping develop some of the most important scholars in the field and for administering the leading program in the field. His awards include the 1986 Ralph C. Guzmán Award from CUNY. He is the author of numerous articles, books, and monographs, including *The Failure of Elites,* (1970) and *Industry and Idleness,* (1986). He coauthored *Labor Migration unde Capitalism* (1979).

Gloria Bonilla-Santiago
Social Work

Bonilla-Santiago received her B.A. degree in political science from Glassboro State College in New Jersey in 1976, her M.S.W. degree from Rutgers University in 1978, her M.A. degree in philosophy from the City University of New York in 1986, and her Ph.D. degree in sociology from the City University of New York in 1986. Bonilla-Santiago is a member of the Graduate School of Social Work at Rutgers University, chairperson of the Hispanic Women's Task Force of New Jersey, and director of the Hispanic Women's Leadership Institute at the Graduate School of Social Work. In 1992, she received the Warren I. Sussman Excellence in Teaching Award at Rutgers. She is the author of numerous reports, articles, book chapters, monographs, and two books: *Hispanic Women Leaders Breaking Ground and Barriers* (1993) and *Organizing Puerto Rican Migrant Farmworkers: The Experience of Puerto Ricans in New Jersey* (1988). She is also the coauthor (with Diane Tegler) of *Notable Hispanic American Women* (1992) In addition to her academic career, Bonilla-Santiago has been instrumental in passing legislation for Hispanic women in New Jersey.

Juan Bruce-Novoa (1944-)
Literature

Born on June 20, 1944, in San José, Costa Rica, Bruce-Novoa received his Ph.D. degree from the University of Colorado in 1974. He has taught Chicano literature at Yale University, Trinity University, and, since 1990, at the University of California, Irvine, as a full professor. Bruce-Novoa is a leading scholar in literary theory as applied to Chicano literature. His books include *Chicano Authors: Inquiry by Interview* (1980), *Chicano Poetry: A Response to Chaos* (1982), and *Retrospace* (1990). Bruce-Novoa has been particularly active in developing a following among European scholars for Hispanic literature of the United States by participating in the organization of conferences in Germany, France, and Spain.

Pastora San Juan Cafferty (1940-)
Social Work

Born on July 24, 1940, in Cienfuegos, Las Villas, Cuba, Cafferty received her B.A. degree in English from St. Bernard College and her M.A. and Ph.D. degrees in American literature and cultural history from George Washington University in 1966 and 1971, respectively. Cafferty served as assistant to the secretary of the U.S. Department of Transportation and the U.S. Department of Housing and Urban Development from 1967 to 1969 and from 1969 to 1970, respectively. Since 1971, Cafferty has been a professor in the School of Social Service Administration of the University of Chicago. Included among her honors are the following: Doctor in Humane Letters, Columbia College (1987), White House Fellow (1969), Smithsonian Research Fellow (1966), Woman of the Year, Operation PUSH (1975), and Award of Achievement, U.S. Girl Scouts (1987). Cafferty has cowritten various books: *Hispanics in the USA: A New Social Agenda*, with William McCready (1985); *The Dilemma of Immigration in America: Beyond the Golden Door*, with Barry Chiswick et al. (1983); *The Politics of Language: The Dilemma of Bilingual Education for Puerto Ricans*, with Carmen Martínez (1981); and others.

Albert Michael Camarillo.

Albert Michael Camarillo (1948-)
History

Born on February 9, 1948, in Compton, California, Camarillo received his B.A. and his Ph.D. degrees from the University of California, Los Angeles, in 1970 and 1975, respectively. Camarillo developed his career at Stanford University, where he has risen in rank to full professor. From 1983 to 1988, he served as the executive director of the important Inter-University Program for Latino Research. From 1980 to 1985, Camarillo served as the director of the Stanford Center for Chicano Research. In 1988, he received the Lloyd W. Dinklespiel Award for Outstanding Service to Undergraduate Education at Stanford. He is the author of *Chicanos in a Changing Society* (1979), *Chicanos in California* (1984), and various coedited books.

Arthur León Campa (1905-78)
Folklore, Literature

Born on February 20, 1905, in Guaymas, Sonora, Mexico, of American parents (his father was a Methodist missionary killed by Francisco Villa during the revolution), Campa was raised in El Paso, Texas. He received his B.A. and M.A. degrees from the University of New Mexico in 1928 and 1930, respectively, and his Ph.D. degree in Spanish from Columbia University in 1940. From 1933 to 1942 Campa rose from instructor to full professor at the University of New Mexico. From 1942 to 1945, he served in World War II as a combat intelligence officer, suffering a back injury and winning a Bronze Star. After the war, he returned to the University of New Mexico. During the postwar years he served as a State Department lecturer in Spain (1953) and as a cultural affairs officer at the U.S. embassy in Lima, Peru. During the 1960s he served as a language training coordinator for the Peace Corps and as a director of Peace Corps Training Projects in Peru, Ecuador, and Venezuela.

Included among his many fellowships are the Guggenheim and the Rockefeller. He was named to the national academies of scholars in Argentina, Brazil, Chile, Mexico, Peru, and Spain. Campa also served as the regional editor for *Western Folklore* and on various other editorial boards. He won many awards for his numerous books, most of which were pioneering collections and analyses of Hispanic folklore of the Southwest. His last, all-embracing vision

Arthur León Campa.

is represented by his book *Hispanic Culture in the Southwest* (1978).

Antonia I. Castañeda (1942-)
History

Born into a migrant labor family in Texas, Castañeda's family moved to the state of Washington while following the crops. In 1966, she received her B.A. degree in Spanish and in education from Western Washington State University; she received her M.A. degree in Latin American studies from the University of Washington in 1970 and her Ph.D. degree in American history from Stanford University in 1990. She has been the recipient of various fellowships, including the Ford (1976), the Whiting (1980), the American Association of University Women (1981), and the University of California, San Diego, chancellor's fellowship (1990). From 1971 to the present, she has taught Chicano, Latin American, and Women's history at various universities and colleges, including the University of Washington, Stanford University, Foothills Community College, University of California, Davis, Sacramento City College, and Pomona College. In 1991, she began as an assistant professor with a joint appointment in the Departments of Women's Studies and Chicano Studies at the University of California, Santa Barbara. Castañeda is the author of numerous research articles and papers and the coeditor of the important historical anthology *Chicano Literature: Text and Context* (1972).

Carlos Eduardo Castañeda (1896-1958)
History

Born in 1896 in Ciudad Camargo, Chihuahua, Mexico, Castañeda moved with his family to Brownsville, Texas, in 1906, where he received his early education, graduating valedictorian from Brownsville High School in 1916. After high school, his scholarship studies at the University of Texas were interrupted by his service in World War I. He received his B.A. and M.A. degrees from the University of Texas in 1921 and 1923, respectively. In 1923, he was appointed associate professor at William and Mary College in Virginia. He returned to the University of Texas in 1927 as a librarian and received his Ph.D. degree in history there in 1932. Castañeda is best known for his *Our Catholic Heritage in Texas*, a six-volume history of Texas from 1519 to 1836 and a history of the Catholic church in Texas from 1836. Castañeda worked on the voluminous history book from 1936 to 1950. It was in 1939 that he joined the faculty of the history department at the University of Texas, and in 1946 he became full professor. Over the course of his career, he served at various times as editor of the *Hispanic American Historical Review, The Americas Review,*

and *The Handbook of Latin American Studies*. Over all, Castañeda produced twelve books and more than eighty articles on Mexican and Southwest history.

Carlos E. Cortés (1934-)
History

Born on April 6, 1934, in Oakland, California, Cortés received his B.A. degree in communications and public policy from the University of California, Berkeley, in 1956, his M.S. degree in journalism from Columbia University in 1957, his M.A. degree in Portuguese and Spanish from the University of New Mexico in 1956, and his Ph.D. degree in history from the University of New Mexico in 1969. Since 1961, Cortés has developed his teaching and research career at the University of California, Riverside; since 1968, he has been a full professor there. Cortés has lectured widely throughout the United States, Latin America, Europe, and Asia. His honors include numerous fellowships and honors, including the 1980 Distinguished California Humanist Award, conferred by the California Council for the Humanities, and the 1974 Herring Award, conferred by the Pacific Coast Council on Latin American Studies. His books include *Three Perspectives on Ethnicity: Blacks, Chi-*

Carlos E. Cortés.

canos and Native Americans, Understanding You and Them, Gaucho Politics in Brazil (1974), and *A Filmic Approach to the Study of Historical Dilemmas.*

Rodolfo J. Cortina (1946-)
Literature

Born on February 23, 1946, in Cuba, Cortina received his B.A. degree in Spanish and economics from Texas A&I University in 1966 and his M.A. and Ph.D. degrees from Case Western Reserve University in 1968 and 1972, respectively. In 1971, he began his career as an assistant professor of Spanish at the University of Wisconsin, Milwaukee, and was promoted to associate professor in 1977. In 1986, he moved to Florida International University as an associate professor and was promoted to full professor in 1989. At the University of Wisconsin, Milwaukee, he served in various administrative positions, including chair of the Department of Spanish, director of the Spanish-Speaking Outreach Institute, and chair of the Latin American Studies Program. At Florida International University from 1985 to 1989, he was the director of the Center for Multilingual and Multicultural Studies, and from 1989 to the present, the director of Hispanic Research Programs. Cortina

Rodolfo J. Cortina.

is the recipient of various awards, including the Jaycees Outstanding Young Man of America (1979), the Special Award of the Governor of Wisconsin (1980), and the Five Year Service Award at Florida International University (1991). He has coedited various anthologies of scholarly articles and is the editor of *Cuban American Theater* (1992). He is the author of *El lenguaje poético de Federico García Lorca (The Poetic Language of Federico García Lorca,* 1985) and *Blasco Ibáñez y la novela evocativa (Blasco Ibánez and the Evocative Novel,* 1973).

Rodolfo de la Garza (1942-)
Political Science

Born on August 17, 1942, in Tucson, Arizona, De la Garza received his B.S. and M.A. degrees in marketing from the University of Arizona in 1964 and 1967, respectively, and his Ph.D. degree in Latin American Studies from Arizona in 1972. He also studied foreign trade and political research at the American Institute of Foreign Trade and at the University of Michigan Inter-University Consortium for Political Research in 1965 and 1971. From 1974 to 1980, he served as an assistant dean and, from 1978 to 1980, as director of the Southwest Studies Program at Colorado College. From 1981 to 1985 and again in 1987, he served as the director of the Center for Mexican American Studies at the University of Texas. Since 1983, he has been the codirector of the Inter-University Project of the Ford Foundation at the University of Texas, where he is a full professor. Among his many awards are the following: (University of Texas) Dean's Award for Outstanding Classroom Performance, 1987-88; University of Colorado Outstanding Faculty Award, 1980; Western Political Science Association Best Paper on Chicano Politics, 1979. De la Garza has been a productive researcher and author on Hispanic political topics and has served on the editorial boards of the *Western Political Science Quarterly,* the *Social Science Quarterly,* the *Journal of Politics,* and the *Hispanic Journal of Behavioral Science.* He is also the editor of two books: *The Mexican American Experience: An Interdisciplinary Anthology* (1985) and *Ignored Voices: Latinos and Public Opinion Poles in the United States* (1986).

Jorge I. Domínguez (1945-)
Government

Born on June 2, 1945, in Havana, Cuba, Domínguez received his B.A. degree from Yale University in 1967, and his M.A. and Ph.D. degrees from Harvard University in 1968 and 1972, respectively. From 1972 on, Domínguez developed his teaching career at Harvard University, ascending the ranks to his current position of full professor, which he achieved in 1979.

Domínguez is a member of the editorial boards of *Political Science Quarterly, Mexican Studies, Journal of Inter-American Studies and World Affairs,* and *Cuban Studies,* for which he has served as coeditor since 1990. Domínguez's books include *To Make a World Safe for Revolution* (1989), *U.S. Interests in the Caribbean and in Central America* (1982), *Cuba: Internal and International Affairs* (1982), and *Insurrection or Loyalty: The Breakdown of the Spanish American Empire* (1980).

José B. Fernández (1948-)
History and Literature

Born on August 20, 1948, in Sagua la Grande, Cuba, Fernández received his B.A., M.A., and Ph.D. degrees in Spanish and history from Florida State University in Tallahassee in 1970, 1971, and 1973, respectively. From 1973 to 1976, he served as an assistant professor and, from 1976 to 1979, as associate professor at the University of Colorado at Colorado Springs, where he also served as chairman of the Department of Foreign Languages. From 1981 to the present, he has been a professor of history and foreign languages at the University of Central Florida in Orlando. Fernández has been a Fulbright Lecturer in Argentina (1984) and has received various other awards, including the University of Colorado (Colorado Springs) Outstanding Teaching Award (1977) and the Chancellor's Award (1979). Fernández is the author of numerous articles and books, including *Alvar Núñez Cabeza de Vaca: The Forgotten Chronicler* (1975), *Indice bibliográfico de autores cubanos* (*Bibliographic Index of Cuban Authors,* 1983), and (with Nasario García) *Nuevos Horizontes: Cuentos chicanos, puertorriqueños y cubanos* (*New Horizons: Chicano, Puerto Rican and Cuban Stories,* 1982).

Margarita Fernández Olmos (1949-)
Literature

Born in 1949 in New York City, Fernández Olmos received her B.A. degree from Montclair State College in New Jersey in 1970 and her M.A. and Ph.D. degrees in Spanish from New York University in 1972 and 1979, respectively. Following her graduate studies, Fernández Olmos was able to develop her career at Brooklyn College of the City University of New York, where she rose to he present rank of full professor. Fernández Olmos has written extensively on Latin American and U.S. Hispanic literature, with a special interest in women's literature. Her books include *La cuéntistica de Juan Bosch* (*The Short Story Art of Juan Bosch,* 1982), *Sobre la literatura puertorriqueña de aquí y de allá: aproximaciones feministas* (*On Puerto Rican Literature from the Mainland and the Island: Feminist Approaches,* 1989), and two

Margarita Fernández Olmos.

coedited anthologies of Latin American women's literature: (with Doris Meyer) *Contemporary Women Authors of Latin America: New Translations and Introductory Essays* (1983) and (with Lizabeth Paravisini-Gebert) *El placer de la palabra: literatura erótica femenina de América Latina* (*The Pleasure of the Word: Erotic Women's Literature of Latin America,* 1991).

Juan Flores (?-)
Literature, Sociology

Born in New York City, Flores received his B.A. degree in German from Queens College in 1964 and his M.A. and Ph.D. degrees in German from Yale University in 1966 and 1968, respectively. He began his career as an assistant professor of German at Stanford University in 1968, but in 1975 redirected his career toward Puerto Rican studies when he became the research director and consultant for the Center for Puerto Rican Studies at Hunter College, CUNY. From 1981 to 1989, he worked as an associate professor in the Department of Sociology of Queens College, CUNY; from 1990 to the present, he has been a member of the graduate faculty in the sociology program of the Graduate Center of CUNY. Flores is a distinguished researcher whose books have won important awards. His *Insularismo e ideología burguesa: Nueva lectura de Antonio S. Pedreira* (*Insularism and Bourgeois Ideology: A New Reading of Antonio S. Pedreira,* 1980) won the prestigious international Casa de las Americas prize. His other books include *Divided Borders: Essays on Puerto Rican Identity* (1992) and (with Jean Franco and George Yúdice) *On Edge: The Crisis in Contemporary Latin American Culture* (1992). His introduction and edition of Jesús Colón's *A Puerto Rican in New York* (1984) won the American Book Award.

Juan Gómez-Quiñones (1940-)
History

Born in 1940 in Parral, Chihuahua, Mexico, Gómez immigrated to the United States with his family as a young child and became a naturalized citizen. He received his B.A. degree in English, his M.A. degree in Latin American Studies, and his Ph.D. degree in history from the University of California, Los Angeles in 1962, 1974, and 1972, respectively. He is a full professor of history at the University of California, Los Angeles, where he has developed his entire career and served for many years as the director of the Chicano Research Center. He is a cofounder/codirector of the Mexican American Legal Defense and Education Fund and is a board member of the Los Angeles Urban Coalition. He is the author of numerous articles and books, including *Sembradores: Ricardo Flores Magón y El Partido Liberal: A Eulogy and a Critique* (1973).

Deena J. González (1952-)
History

See Chapter 13

Erlinda González-Berry (1942-)
Literature

The native New Mexican received her B.A., M.A., and Ph.D. degrees from the University of New Mexico in 1964, 1971, and 1978, respectively. In 1974, she began as an assistant professor in Earlham College in Indiana, moved to New Mexico State University in 1978, and then to the University of New Mexico in 1979, where she has risen in rank to her present full professorship. González-Berry is an outstanding teacher and researcher. In 1984, she received the University of New Mexico President's Award as Outstanding Teacher of the Year and, in 1991, the Outstanding Teacher of the Year Award from the "His-

Erlinda González-Berry.

panics at UNM." González has published numerous articles on Chicano literature and is the editor of two books: *Pasó por Aquí: Four Centuries of New Mexican Hispanic Literature* (1989) and (with Tey Diana Rebolledo and Teresa Márquez) *Las mujeres hablan: An Anthology of Nuevomexicana Writings* (1988).

Richard A. Griswold del Castillo (1942-)
History

Born on October 26, 1942, in Los Angeles, California, Griswold received his B.A., M.A., and Ph.D. degrees from the University of California, Los Angeles, in 1968, 1969, and 1974, respectively. From 1974 to the present, he has developed his career at San Diego State University, where he is currently a full professor and chair of the Mexican American Studies. From 1985 through 1988, he was the recipient of the San Diego State Outstanding Faculty Award. Among his many publications are the following books: *The Treaty of Guadalupe Hidalgo* (1990), *La Familia Chicana: Chicano Families in the Urban Southwest, 1848 to the Present* (1984), and *The Los Angeles Barrio, 1850-1890: A Social History* (1980).

Ramón Gutiérrez (1951-)
History

Born on April 19, 1951, in Albuquerque, New Mexico, Gutiérrez obtained his B.A. degree from the University of New Mexico in 1973 and his M.A. and Ph.D. degrees from the University of Wisconsin in 1976 and 1980, respectively. From 1980 to 1982, he served as an assistant professor at Pomona College and from 1982 to the present he has been an associate professor at the University of California, San Diego. His honors include a prestigious MacArthur Fellowship, 1983-88, as well as the Best Book Award for 1991 from the American Historical Association, Pacific Coast Branch, the Best Article Award from the AHA Conference on Latin American History in 1986, and the Hubert Herring Prize for the Best Dissertation in Latin American Studies in 1981. Gutiérrez has won numerous fellowships, including the Fulbright, Danforth, and National Defense Education Act. Gutiérrez is the author of numerous ground-breaking articles in Latin American and Chicano history and a book, *When Jesus Came the Corn Mothers Went Away: Marriage, Sexuality and Power in New Mexico, 1500-1846.*

José Manuel Hernández (1925-)
History

Born on February 18, 1925, in Cuba, Hernández received his law degree from the University of Havana in 1947 and his M.A. and Ph.D. degress in history from Georgetown University in 1969 and 1976, respectively. From 1973 to 1980, he served as assistant dean of the School of Languages and Linguistics at Georgetown University, and since 1980, as associate dean. From 1984 to 1987, he served as the director of the Latin American Studies Program at Georgetown. Included in his many honors is the Georgetown University Vicennial Medal. His published scholarship includes the book *ACU, los primeros cincuenta años* (*ACU, the First Fifty Years,* 1981).

María Herrera-Sobek (?-)
Literature

Born in Mexico, Herrera-Sobek received her B.A. degree in chemistry from California State University, Northridge, in 1974, her M.A. degree in Latin American studies from the University of California, Irvine, and her Ph.D. degree from the University of California, Los Angeles, in 1975. From 1975 to the present, she has developed her entire career at the University of California, Irvine, rising in rank from assistant to full professor as of 1987. Included among her honors are the Orange County Book of the Year Award (1980), the Hispanic Woman of the Year Award from the League of United Latin American Citizens, Orange County (1981), and the Educator of the Year Award given by the Mexican-American Educators Association, Orange County chapter (1990). Herrera-Sobek has published numerous articles, edited various anthologies, and written the following books: *The Bracero Experience: Elitelore versus Folklore* (1979), *The Mexican Corrido: A Feminist Analysis* (1990), and *Northward Bound: The Mexican Immigrant Experience in Corridos and Canciones* (1993).

Olga Jiménez-Wagenheim (1941-)
History

Born in Camuy, Puerto Rico, on September 24, 1941, Jiménez received her B.A. degree from the Inter-American University in Puerto Rico in 1970, her M.A. degree from the State University of New York at Buffalo in 1971, and her Ph.D. degree from Rutgers University in 1981. After achieving the Ph.D. degree, she has developed her university career at Rutgers University, where she has served as an associate professor since 1986. Her honors include the Hispanic Association for Higher Education Scholarly Achievement Award (1989) and the Hispanic Women's Task Force of New Jersey Award (1988). Jiménez's books include *Puerto Rico's Revolt for Independence: El Grito de Lares* (1985), *El grito de Lares: Sus causas y sus hombres* (*The Shout of Lares: Its Causes and Its Men,* 1984) and her coedited *The Puerto Ricans: A Documentary History* (1973).

Olga Jiménez-Wagenheim.

Luis Leal (1907-)
Literature

Born on September 17, 1907, in Linares, Mexico, Leal received his B.A. degree from Northwestern University in 1940 and his A.M. and Ph.D. degrees from the University of Chicago in 1941 and 1951. Leal is one of the most productive, most respected, and most honored scholars of Latin American and Chicano literature, a true pioneer in both disciplines. In his long career, he has taught at the University of Chicago, the University of Mississippi, Emory University, the University of Illinois, where he has been professor emeritus since 1976, and the University of California, Santa Barbara, where he has served as a visiting professor and acting director of Chicano studies since 1980. He is the author of some sixteen books, including his important *El cuento hispanoamericano* (*The Spanish American Short Story,* 1967) and his *Breve historia de la literatura hispanoamericana* (*Brief History of Spanish American Literature,* 1971). He has also edited some twenty-one anthologies and other books, besides publishing

Luis Leal.

scores of articles. In 1978, a conference was held and a book published in his praise: *Homenaje a Luis Leal* (*Homage to Luis Leal*), edited by Donald W. Bleznick and Juan O. Valencia.

Francisco A. Lomelí (1947-)
Literature

Born on April 13, 1947, in Sombrerete, Zacatecas, Mexico, Lomelí received his B.A. and M.A. degrees from San Diego State University in 1971 and 1974, respectively, and his Ph.D. degree from the University of New Mexico in 1978. Since 1978, he has ascended the ranks at the University of California, Santa Barbara, where he became a full professor in 1989. Lomelí has won numerous fellowships, including the Rotary International (1983), Fulbright (1969), Ford (1974), and Rockefeller (1989). He is the author of numerous articles of literary criticism and the editor of various reference works: *Dictionary of Literary Biography: Chicano Writers* (1989), *Chicano Literature: A Reference Guide* (1985), and *Aztlán: Essays on the Chicano Homeland* (1989). Lomelí also serves on the editorial board of various journals, including *The*

Americas Review, *The Bilingual Review*, *Discurso Literario*, and *The Latino Studies Journal*.

Roberto Márquez (1942-)
Latin American Studies

Born on July 14, 1942, in New York City, Márquez received his B.A. in comparitive literature from Brandeis University in 1964, and his M.A. and Ph.D. degrees in romance languages and literatures from Harvard University in 1970 and 1975, respectively. From 1970 to 1986, he taught at Hampshire College in Hispanic American and Caribbean literatures, where in 1983 he was named the first incumbent of the Harold F. Johnson Professorial Chair. From 1986 to 1989, he was the Robinson Professor at George Mason University and, from 1989 to the present, the William F. Kenan Professor of Latin American studies at Mount Holyoke College. Márquez is the author of numerous articles, anthologies of Latin American poetry, which he also translates, and the book, *The Third World: The Dialectic of Culture* (1978). He is also the founder and editor of *Caliban: A Journal of New World Thought and Writing* (1975-1982).

Oscar Martínez (1943-)
History

Born in Mexico on March 4, 1943, Martínez received his B.A. degree from California State University in Los Angeles in 1969, his M.A. degree from Stanford in 1970, and his Ph.D. degree from the University of California, Los Angeles, in 1975. From 1975 to 1988, he ascended the ranks from assistant to full professor at the University of Texas at El Paso. From 1975 to 1988, he served as the director of the Institute for Oral History at UTEP. In 1988, he became a full professor at the University of Arizona. He has served as president of the Association of Borderland Scholars and is a member of various editorial boards, including the *Journal of Borderland Studies*, the *Latin American Research Review*, and the *Journal of the Southwest*. He has won two book awards, 1978 and 1988, from the Border Region Library Association. His books include *Border Boom Town* (1978), *Fragments of the Mexican Revolution* (1983), *Across Boundaries* (1986), and *Troublesome Border* (1988).

Alfredo Matilla (1937-)
Puerto Rican Studies

Born in Valencia, Spain, on July 31, 1937, Matilla was raised in Puerto Rico. He received his B.A. from the University of Puerto Rico in 1959, his M.A. and Ph.D. from New York University in 1961 and 1967, respectively. From 1965 to 1968, he served as an assistant professor of Spanish at Goucher College; in 1968 he moved to Rutgers University as an associate professor, and then in 1980 to Brooklyn College. Since 1982, he has taught at the State University of New York, Buffalo, and was named full professor of Puerto Rican studies/American studies in 1988. Matilla is the author of various books and articles primarily on Puerto Rican and Nuyorican literature. With Iván Silén, he edited a ground-breaking anthology in bilingual format, *The Puerto Rican Poets/Los poetas puertorriquenos*, 1972. He is also a respected poet, author of *Catálogo de locos* (*Catalog of Insane People*, 1977), and translations.

Carmelo Mesa-Lago (1934-)
Economics

Born on August 11, 1934, in Havana, Cuba, Mesa-Lago received his LL.M. degree in civil law from the University of Havana in 1965, his LL.D. degree from the University of Madrid in 1958, his M.A. degree in economics from the University of Miami in 1965, and his Ph.D. degree in labor economics from Cornell University in 1968. From 1967 on, Mesa-Lago developed his career at the University of Pittsburgh, beginning as an assistant professor in economics and rising to the rank of full professor in 1980. During his tenure there, he also served as the director of the Center for Latin American Studies (1974 to 1986). He has lectured and taught in Europe and Latin America as well and has held prestigious fellowships, including the Ford, Rockefeller, and Tinker. Mesa-Lago has also served as the president of the Latin American Studies Association (1980) and as regional advisor for the United Nations on Social Security and Development (1983-84). Included among his many honors is the Alexander von Humbolt Senior Research Award on Social Security (1990-92), the Bicentennial Medallion of the University of Pittsburgh (1987), and the Hoover Institution Prize for Best Article on Latin America (1986). Included among his many books are *Cuba after the Cold War* (1993), *Health Care for the Poor in Latin America and the Caribbean: Problems, Cases and Solutions* (1992), *Social Security and Prospects for Equity in Latin America* (1991), and *Portfolio Performance of Selected Social Security Institutes in Latin America* (1991), to name just some of the most recent.

Raúl Moncarraz (?-)
Economics

Born in Cuba, Moncarraz received his B.S. degree in business administration from Florida Atlantic University in 1965 and his M.B.A. and Ph.D. degrees in economics from Florida State University in 1966 and 1969, respectively. From 1969 to 1972, he rose from an assistant professorship to associate professor

Raúl Moncarraz.

at Louisiana State University. From 1972 to the present, he has taught at Florida International University, where he became a full professor and chairman of the Department of Economics in 1988. Among his many honors is a Gold Medal from the Consulate of Venezuela in Miami (1984) and various scholarships and fellowships. Moncarraz is the author of numerous publications on development issues in Central America and the Caribbean and on labor market issues.

Sonia Nieto (1943-)
Children's Literature and Bilingual Education

Nieto received her B.S. degree in Education from St. John's University in 1965, her M.A. degree in Spanish from New York University in 1966, and her Ed.D. degree in curriculum with minors in bilingual and multicultural education from the University of Massachusetts, Amherst, in 1979. From 1972 to 1975, Nieto was and instructor and deputy chairperson of the Department of Puerto Rican Studies, Brooklyn College; from 1979 to 1980, the LAU Coordinator for the Massachusetts Department of Education; and in 1980, she began her career at the University of Massachusetts, rising to her present rank of associate professor and program director of Cultural Diversity and Curriculum Reform in 1988. Nieto received the Human and Civil Rights Award from the Massachusetts Teachers Association in 1988 and the Outstanding Accomplishment in Higher Education Award from the Hispanic Caucus of the American Association of Higher Education in 1991. Nieto is an expert on Hispanic and culturally diverse children's literature, which is reflected in her many articles, book chapters, lectures, and papers. She is the author of *Affirming Diversity: The Sociopolitical Context of Multicultural Education* (1992) and coauthor (with Roberto Márquez) of *Puerto Rican Literature and*

Sonia Nieto.

Society: A Curriculum for the Secondary School (1986).

Julián Olivares (1940-)
Literature

Born on December 6, 1940, in San Antonio, Texas, Olivares received his B.A. degree from California State University at Los Angeles in 1968 and his M.A.

Julián Olivares.

and Ph.D. degrees from the University of Texas in 1974 and 1977, respectively. He served as an assistant professor at Bridgewater State College from 1978 to 1981, when he relocated to the University of Houston. In 1986, he became an associate professor of Spanish at the University of Houston, where he also has served since 1981 as the editor of the prestigious *The Americas Review* and senior editor of Arte Publico Press. Olivares is a respected scholar in two fields: Golden Age Spanish literature and Chicano literature. He has won numerous fellowships, including the Ford (1975), National Endowment for the Humanities (1984), and National Research Council/Ford (1985). As editor of *The Americas Review*, he has won two unprecedented Citations of Achievement from the Council of Literary Magazines and Presses. His books include *Tras el espejo la musa escribe: Lírica femenina del Siglo de Oro* (*Behind the Looking Glass the Muse Writes: Women's Lyrics of the Golden Age*, 1992) and *The Love Poetry of Francisco de Quevedo* (1983). His edited books include *Hispanic Short Fiction* (1992), *International Studies in Honor of Tomás Rivera* (1985), and all of the works of Tomás Rivera (in four separate volumes).

Vilma Ortiz (?-)
Social Psychology

Ortiz received her B.A. degree in psychology from the City College of New York in 1976 and her M.A. and Ph.D. degrees in social psychology from New York University in 1979 and 1981, respectively. From 1981 to 1985, she has had three postdoctoral fellowships at Fordham University, the University of Michigan, and the University of Wisconsin, respectively. From 1985 to 1987, she served as a visiting scholar at the Educational Testing Service in Princeton, New Jersey. She began her teaching career in 1988 as an assistant professor in the Department of Sociology, University of California, Los Angeles, where she has been an associate professor since 1990. Since 1990, Ortiz has been the director of the Interdepartmental Program in Chicana and Chicano Studies at UCLA. Ortiz's specialties are urban poverty and social welfare policy, race and ethnicity, Puerto Rican migration, and Hispanic women, among other research interests that form the bases of her numerous articles and book chapters.

Gustavo Pérez-Firmat (1949-)
Literature

Born on March 7, 1949, in Havana, Cuba, Pérez-Firmat received his B.A. degree in English and M.A. degree in Spanish from the University of Miami in 1972 and 1973, respectively. He received his Ph.D. degree in comparative literature from the University of Michigan in 1979. Since 1979, he has developed his career at Duke University, where he has risen in rank from assistant to full professor in Spanish and in the Graduate Literature Program. Pérez-Firmat has created a dual career as a literary historian and critic and as a creative writer. His academic books include *Idle Fictions: The Hispanic Vanguard Novel, 1926-1934*(1982), *Literature and Liminality: Festive Readings in the Hispanic Tradition* (1986), *The Cuban Condition: Translation and Identity in Modern Cuban Literature* (1989), and *The Cuban-American Way* (1993). His creative books include two collections of his poems: *Triple Crown: Chicano, Puerto Rican and Cuban American Poetry* (1987) and *Equivocaciones* (*Mistakes*, 1989). He is also the author of numerous articles and poems for journals and magazines.

Harry Pachón (1945-)
Political Science

Born on June 4, 1945, in Miami, Florida, Pachón received his B.A. and his M.A. degrees from California State University in Los Angeles in 1967 and 1968, respectively, and his Ph.D. degree from the Claremont Graduate School in 1973. He served as an assistant professor at Michigan State University from 1974 to 1976 and as an administrative assistant at the United States House of Representatives from 1977 to 1981. From 1981 to 1986, he was an associate professor at the City University of New York, and since 1986, the Kenan Professor of Political Science at Pitzer College. Pachón is a founding board member of the National Association of Latino Elected and Appointed Officials (since 1981), and since 1983, he has served as its national director. Pachón has been a fellow of the National Endowment for the Humanities and has published research articles and two books: *Hispanics in the U.S.* (1985) and *Mexican Americans* (1975).

Amado Manuel Padilla (1942-)
Psychology

Born on October 14, 1942, in Albuquerque, New Mexico, Padilla received his B.A. degree in 1964 from New Mexico Highlands University, his M.S. degree in 1966 from Oklahoma State University, and his Ph.D. degree in 1969 from the University of New Mexico. He was an assistant professor at the State University of New York from 1967 to 1971 and at the University of California, Santa Barbara, from 1971 to 1974. He moved to the University of California, Los Angeles, in 1974, where he rose to the rank of full professor. From 1988 to the present, he has been a full professor at Stanford University. Padilla has been a Fulbright Scholar and is the recipient of the American Educational Research Association Distin-

guished Scholar Award (1987). His books include *Crossing Cultures in Therapy* (1980), *Chicano Ethnicity* (1987), *Foreign Language Education: Issues and Strategies* (1990), and *Bilingual Education: Issues and Strategies* (1990).

Américo Paredes (1915-)
Folklore

Born on September 3, 1915, in Brownsville, Texas, Paredes received his B.A., M.A., and Ph.D. degrees from the University of Texas in 1951, 1953, and 1956, respectively. After working at a variety of jobs, including journalist, and serving in the armed forces, Paredes received an advanced education later in life and became one of the most distinguished Hispanic scholars in U.S. history. Paredes has taught at the University of Texas from 1951 on and is currently professor emeritus of English and anthropology there. He has been instrumental in the development of the field of folklore in academia as well as in the field of Mexican American studies. He has served as president of the American Folklore Society and been recognized for his leadership internationally. In the United States, he was awarded one of the nation's highest awards for a humanist, the Charles Frankel Prize given by the National Endowment for the Arts (1989), and in Mexico, the highest award given a foreigner by the Mexican government, the Aguila Azteca (the Aztec Eagle) medal (1991). Besides publishing numerous research articles, he is the author of *With a Pistol in His Hand: A Border Ballad and Its Hero* (1958), *Folktales of Mexico* (1970), *A Texas Mexican Cancionero* (1976), and *Uncle Remus con chile* (*Uncle Remus with Chile*, 1992). He is also the author of a novel, *George Washington Gomez* (1990) and a book of poems, *Between Two Worlds* (1991).

Guadalupe C. Quintanilla (1937-)
Language

See Chapter 25

Tey Diana Rebolledo (1937-)
Literature

See Chapter 13

Eliana Rivero (1940-)
Literature

Born in Cuba in 1940, Rivero immigrated to the United States in 1961. She received her Ph.D. degree in Spanish from the University of Miami in 1968, and from that time on has developed her career at the University of Arizona, where she is currently a full professor in the Spanish department. Her specialties are Latin American and U.S. Hispanic literatures and women's literature and feminist criticism. Rivero is the author of *El gran amor de Pablo Neruda: estudio crítico de su poesía* (*The Great Love of Pablo Neruda: A Critical Study of His Poetry*, 1971) and numerous articles. She is also the coeditor (with Tey Diana Rebolledo) of *Infinite Divisions: An Anthology of Chicana Literature* (1993). Rivero is also a respected poet whose books include *De cal y arena* (*Of Lime and Sand*, 1975) and *Cuerpos breves* (*Brief Bodies*, 1977).

Sergio G. Roca (1961-)
Economics

Born in Cuba, Roca received his B.A. degree in economics from Drew University in 1965 and his Ph.D. degree from Rutgers University in 1975. From 1971 to the present, he has developed his career at Adelphi University; he has been a full professor there since 1984. In 1988, he received the Adelphi University Merit Award for Scholarship. He is the author of numerous articles and two books: *Socialist Cuba: Past Interpretations and Future Challenges* (1988) and *Cuban Economic Policy and Ideology: The Ten Million Ton Sugar Harvest* (1976).

Clara Rodríguez (1944-)
Sociology

Born on March 29, 1944, Rodríguez received her B.A. degree in sociology from the City College of New York in 1965, her M.A. degree in Latin American studies from Cornell University in 1969, and her Ph.D. degree in sociology and urban and regional studies from Washington University in St. Louis in 1973. From 1974 to 1976, Rodríguez served as chair of the Department of Puerto Rican Studies at Lehman College, CUNY; from 1976 to "98, she was dean of general studies at Fordham University, after which she took leaves of absence and visiting fellowships at the Massachusetts Institute of Technology and Yale University. From 1981 to the present, she has been a full professor at Fordham University. Rodríguez has presented numerous lectures and papers and published many articles on the sociology of race, ethnicity, and gender, especially as relates to Puerto Ricans. Her books include *Puerto Ricans: Born in the USA* (1989, 1991), *The Ethnic Queue in the United States: The Case of Puerto Ricans* (1974), and two coedited books: (with Virginia Sánchez Korrol and Oscar Alers) *The Puerto Rican Struggle: Essays on Survival in the U.S.* (1979) and (with Edwin Meléndez and Janice Barry-Figueroa) *Hispanics in the Labor Force: Issues and Policies* (1991).

Ricardo Romo.

Ricardo Romo (1943-)
History

Born on June 23, 1943, in San Antonio, Texas, Romo received his B.A. degree from the University of Texas in 1967, his M.A. degree from Loyola University of Los Angeles in 1970, and his Ph.D. degree from the University of California, Los Angeles, in 1975. From 1974 to 1980, he was an assistant professor at the University of California, San Diego, and from 1980 to the present, a full professor at the University of Texas at Austin. Since 1988, he has also been the director of the Tomás Rivera Center, a research institute in San Antonio. He has been a member of the board of editors of *Social Science Quarterly* since 1982 and has been the managing editor of the Mexican American Monograph Series at the University of Texas since 1981. Romo has received various fellowships during his career and he is the author of *East Los Angeles: A History of a Barrio* (1983) and coeditor of *The Mexican American Experience: An Interdisciplinary Anthology* (1985) and *New Directions in Chicano Scholarship* (1978).

Ramón Eduardo Ruiz (1921-)
History, Literature

Ruiz received his Ph.D. degree in history from the University of California, Berkeley, in 1954. He began his career as an assistant professor at the University of Oregon in 1956-57 and Southern Methodist University in 1957-58. He moved to Smith College in 1958 as an assistant professor and was promoted to associate professor in 1961 and to full professor of Latin American History in 1963. Since 1970, he has been a full professor at the University of California, San Diego. Among his many awards are the 1981 Hubert C. Herring Prize from the Pacific Coast Council on Latin

Ramón Eduardo Ruiz.

American Studies for his *The Great Rebellion, Mexico, 1905-1924* (1980) and various fellowships, including the Fulbright. Included among his thirteen books are *Triumphs and Tragedy: A History of the Mexican People* (1991), *The People of Sonora and Yankee Capitalists* (1988), and *Labor and Ambivalent Revolutionaries: Mexico, 1905-1924* (1976).

Vicki L. Ruiz (1955-)
History

See Chapter 13

Julián Samora (1920-)
Sociology

Born on March 1, 1920, in Pagosa Springs, Colorado, Samora received his B.A. degree from Adams State College in 1942, his M.S. degree from Colorado State University in 1974, and his Ph.D. degree from Washington University in 1953. From 1955 to 1957, he was an assistant professor at the University of Colorado Medical School, associate professor at Michigan State University from 1957 to 1959, and a full professor at the University of Notre Dame from 1959 to 1985, when he became professor emeritus. Samora

is one of the pioneer Hispanic sociologists and has trained a whole generation of important sociologists whose ranks include the noted Mexican sociologist Jorge Bustamante. Among his many awards is the White House Hispanic Heritage Award (1985) and the Mexican government's highest award given to a foreigner, the Aguila Azteca (Aztec Eagle) medal (1991). Included among his books are *A History of the Mexican-American People* (1977) and *Gunpowder Justice: A Reassessment of the Texas Rangers* (1979). In 1991, a research center at the Michigan State University was named in his honor.

José Sánchez-Boudy (1928-)
Literature

See Chapter 17

Virginia Sánchez-Korrol (1936-)
History

See Chapter 13

Saskia Sassen (1947-)
Economics and Sociology

Born on January 5, 1947, in The Hague, Netherlands, Sassen received first-year certificates from the University of Buenos Aires, Argentina, and the Universitá degli Studi in Rome in 1966 and 1968, respectively. She received her M.A. degree in sociology and her Ph.D. degree in economics and sociology from the University of Notre Dame in 1968 and 1971, respectively. From 1974 to 1975, she was a postdoctoral fellow at the Harvard Center for International Affairs, and she climbed the ranks at the City University of New York from assistant to full professor from 1976 to 1985. Since 1985, she has been a full professor of urban planning in the Department of Architecture at Columbia University. Sassen has been a consultant and member of policy groups on Hispanic social and political issues for the Ford Foundation, the Rockefeller Foundation, the Inter-University Group in Latino Research, the Russell Sage Foundation, and on women's and other issues for the United Nations. In 1986, Sassen was awarded the American Institute of Certified Planners National Award. She is the author of *The Mobility of Labor and Capital* (1988) and *The Global City: New York, London, Tokyo* (1990), as well as numerous research articles.

George I. Sánchez (1906-1972)
Educational Administration, Educational Psychology

Born on October 4, 1906, in Albuquerque, New Mexico, to parents with long histories in the territory, Sánchez became a teacher while he was still a student at the University of New Mexico, which he attended only during the summer months. He graduated from the University of New Mexico in 1930 with a B.A. degree in Spanish. After that he received an M.S. degree in educational psychology at the University of Texas and then his Ed.D. in educational administration from the University of California, Berkeley, in 1934. During the next thirty-five years Sánchez became the foremost expert on the education of Hispanic children and a tireless and effective civil rights leader on their behalf. He also became an expert on Latin American education and a pioneer in bilingual, bicultural education. Among his many writings are *Mexico: A Revolution by Education* (1936) and *Forgotten People* (1940), the latter a work that documents the educational neglect of Mexican-American children in New Mexico during the 1930s. After working in the state of New Mexico educational administration, Sánchez joined the faculty of the University of Texas in 1940, and in 1941, became the president of the League of United Latin American Citizens. From then on, he used LULAC as a forum to struggle against the practices that were inhibiting the civil and educational rights of Hispanics. In 1951 he founded a national organization to bring together all of the civil rights-oriented Hispanic organizations and focus their efforts, the American Council of Spanish-Speaking People. It was this council that experienced early civil rights legal victories and prepared the way from many of the gains made during the 1960s and for the later emergence of the Mexican American Legal Defense and Education Fund. Because of his many pioneering studies, articles, and books, as well as the very important role he played in preparing the ground for the Hispanic civil rights and educational movements, George I. Sánchez has been the subject of numerous books, articles, and homages, and there is many a school named in his honor today.

Rosaura Sánchez (1941-)
Linguistics, Literature

Born on December 6, 1941, in San Angelo, Texas, Sánchez received her B.A. degree in Spanish and English in 1963, her M.A. degree in Spanish in 1969, and her Ph.D. degree in romance linguistics in 1974 from the University of Texas. Since 1972, Sánchez has developed her entire teaching career in the literature department at the University of California, San Diego, where she serves as a full professor. Sánchez is the author of *Chicano Discourse*, a fundamental book for the understanding of Mexican-American Spanish and English patterns. She is also the author of numerous articles in linguistics and literature, as well as the author of short stories. Sánchez's work in linguistics has involved both the theoretical and the applied; she has been a pioneer in the teaching of spanish to Spanish-speakers. In her literary studies, she has also concentrated on literary theory and feminist theory, as well as conducted critical studies of works by such writers a s Gina Valdez, Arturo Islas, and Rolando Hinojosa.

José Sánchez-Boudy (1928-)
Literature

See Chapter 17

Adljiza Sosa-Riddell (1937-)
Political Science

See Chapter 13

References

Martínez, Julio A. *Chicano Scholars and Writers. A Bio-Bibliographic Directory.* Metuchen, N.J.: Scarecrow Press, 1979.

Meier, Matt S. and Feliciano Rivera. *Dictionary of Mexican American History.* Westport, Conn.: Greenwood Press, 1981.

Unterberger, Amy L., ed. *Who's Who among Hispanic Americans 1991-92.* Detroit, Mich.: Gale Research, 1991.

Nicolás Kanellos

Literature

✸ The Colonial Period ✸ The Nineteenth Century ✸ The Early Twentieth Century
✸ World War II to the Present ✸ Outstanding Hispanic Literary Figures

Hispanic literature of the United States is the literature written by Americans of Hispanic descent. It includes the Spanish-language literature of what became the U.S. Southwest before this territory was incorporated through war and annexation. It thus incorporates a broad geographic and historical space, and even includes the writings of early explorers of the North American continent as well as Spanish-speaking immigrants and exiles who made the United States their home. It is a literature that reflects the diverse ethnic and national origins of Hispanics in the United States, and thus includes writers of South and Central American, Caribbean, and Spanish descent, as well as writers of Afro-Hispanic and Indo-Hispanic literatures; it may also include writers of Sephardic (exiled Spanish Jews) origins who identified themselves as Hispanic, should their works be brought to light in the future. Finally, Hispanic literature of the United States is a literature that also reflects the linguistic diversity of the people and has been written and published in both Spanish and English and even bilingually.

✸ THE COLONIAL PERIOD

The roots of Hispanic literature were planted north of the Rio Grande quite some time before the landing of the Mayflower at Plymouth Rock. Juan de Oñate's 1598 colonizing expedition up from central Mexico into what is today New Mexico is doubly important as the beginning of a written and oral literary tradition in a European language, Spanish. The written tradition is represented by the landmark epic poem *La conquista de la Nueva México* (*The Conquest of the New Mexico*), by one of the soldiers on the expedition, Gaspar Pérez de Villagrá. The oral Spanish literary tradition was introduced with the improvised dramas, songs, ballads, and poetic recita-

tions of the soldiers, colonists, and missionaries, some of which have survived in New Mexico and the Southwest to this date.

The Northeast of what is today the United States, on the other hand, can point to its earliest written and oral expression in Spanish with the founding of the colony of Sephardic Jews in New Amsterdam in 1654. Both the Northeast and Southwest can boast an unbroken literary tradition in Spanish that predates the American Revolutionary War. Much of this early literary patrimony from the colonial period has been lost or has not been collected and studied; the same can be said of all periods of the literature except for contemporary Hispanic literature in the United States. A missionary and colonial literature of historical chronicles, diaries, and letters and an oral literature developed in the Southwest until the Mexican-American War of 1846-48.

✸ THE NINETEENTH CENTURY

Following the Mexican-American War and up to 1910, the foundation was really laid for the creation of a true Mexican-American literature, a U.S. Hispanic literature, with the resident population of the Southwest adapting to the new U.S. political and social framework. It was the period when many Spanish-language newspapers begin publishing throughout the Southwest and when they and the creative literature they contained became an alternative to Anglo-American information and cultural flow. During this period the important commercial centers of San Francisco and Los Angeles supported numerous newspapers, which, besides fulfilling their commercial and informational functions, also published short stories, poetry, essays, and even serialized novels, such *Las aventuras de Joaquín Murieta* (The Adventures of Joaquín Murieta), a novel of the legendary California social bandit, published in 1881 by the Santa Barbara newspaper *La gaceta*. Among the more important newspapers in California were Los Angeles's *El clamor público* (*The Public Clamor*) and *La estrella de Los Angeles* (*The Los Angeles Star*), issued in the 1850s, and *La crónica* (*The Chronicle*), from the 1870s to the 1890s, and San Francisco's *La voz del Nuevo Mundo* (*The Voice of the New World*), *La sociedad* (*Society*), *La cronista* (*The Chronicles*), and *La República* (*The Republic*), issued during the last four decades of the century. In New Mexico, *El clarín mexicano* (*The Mexican Clarion*) and *El fronterizo* (*The Frontier*), in the 1870s, *El nuevomexicano* (*The New Mexican*), from the 1850s to the turn of the century, and *El defensor del pueblo* (*The People's Defender*), in the 1890s, were important. Among Texas's contributions during this period were San Antonio's *El bejareño* (*The Bejar County*) during the 1850s, El Paso's *Las dos Américas* (*The Two Americas*) in the 1890s, and *El clarín del norte* (*The Northern Clarion*) in the 1900s. These were but a few of the literally hundreds of newspapers that provided for the cultural enrichment and entertainment of the Mexican-American communities while they provided information, helped to solidify the community, and defended the rights of Mexican Americans in the face of the growing influence of Anglo-American culture.

During the latter part of the nineteenth century various literary authors were published in book form. In southern California, Pilar Ruiz de Burton through her English-language novels, such as *The Squatter and the Don* (1881), attacked the passage of wealth and power from the hands of the Californians into those of the Anglo newcomers. Also in 1881, New Mexican Manuel M. Salazar published a novel of romantic adventure, *La historia de un caminante, o Gervacio y Aurora* (*The History of a Traveler on Foot, or Gervacio and Aurora*), which creates a colorful picture of the pastoral life in New Mexico at this time. Another New Mexican, Eusebio Chacón (1869-1948) published two short novels in 1892 that are celebrated today: *El hijo de la tempestad* (*Child of the Storm*) and *Tras la tormenta la calma* (*The Calm after the Storm*). New Mexican Miguel Antonio Otero (1859-1944) issued a three-volume autobiography, *My Life on the Frontier* (1935), in English, in which he covers his life from age 5 until just after his term as governor of New Mexico ended in 1906.

At this time poetry was primarily lyric, amorous, and pastoral and appeared regularly in the newspapers, with very few authors ever collecting their works in books. Among the most frequently appearing poets were the Texan E. Montalván in *El bejareño*, Felipe Maximiliano Chacón and Julio Flores in New Mexico papers, and Dantés in Santa Bar-

Miguel Antonio Otero (Miguel A. Otero Collection, Special Collections, General Library, University of New Mexico, Neg. No. 000-021-0004).

bara's *La gaceta* (*The Gazette*). One of the most interesting poets of the turn of the century was Sara Estela Ramírez, who published her poems and some speeches in Laredo's *La crónica* (*The Chronicle*) and *El demócrata* (*The Democrat*) and in her own literary periodicals, *La corregidora* (*The Corrector*) and *Aurora*, between the years 1904 and 1910. In her life and in her literary works, Ramírez was an activist for the Mexican Liberal Party in its movement to overthrow dictator Porfirio Díaz, and for workers'' and women's rights. But much work needs to be done in collecting and analyzing Ramírez's works and the thousands upon thousands of other poems that were published throughout the Southwest during the nineteenth century.

On the other hand, the late nineteenth century is the period when the Mexican *corrido*, (a folk ballad related to the *romance* introduced by the Spanish colonists and missionaries) came into maturity and proliferated throughout the Southwest. In particular, the border ballad, which chronicled the adventures of social bandits, like Joaquín Murieta, Aniceto Pizaña, and even Billy the Kid, became a popular anvil on which was forged a Mexican-American identity. The corrido increased its popularity in the twentieth century and became a living historical and poetic document that records the history of the great Mexican immigrations and labor struggles between the two world wars.

During the nineteenth century, the New York area sustained various Hispanic literary activities and cultural institutions. Again the newspapers came to play a key role in providing a forum for literary creation for a community that at that time was made up principally of Spaniards and Cubans. Such newspapers as *El menasajero semanal* (*The Weekly Messenger*) and the weekly *El mercurio de Nueva York* (*The New York Mercury*), during the late 1820s and the 1830s published news of the homeland, political commentary and poetry, short stories, essays, and even excerpts of plays. Two other early newspapers were *La crónica* (*The Chronicle*) and *La voz de América* (*The Voice of America*), appearing in the 1850s and 1860s, respectively. Among the poets publishing at this time were Miguel Teurbe Tolón (1820-58), who was born in the United States, educated in Cuba, and

Title page of *El hijo de la tempestad* by Eusebio Chacón (Special Collections, General Library, University of New Mexico).

Eusebio Chacón (Miguel A. Otero Collection, Special Collections, General Library, University of New Mexico, Neg. No. 000-021-0168)

became a conspirator for Cuban independence from Spain. One of the few books of poetry in Spanish was published in 1828: *Poesías de un mexicano* (*Poems by a Mexican*), by Anastacio Ochoa y Acuña.

But it was not until the late nineteenth century that newspaper, magazine, and book publishing really began to expand, because of increased immigration and the political and cultural activity related to the Cuban, Puerto Rican, and Dominican independence movements and the Spanish-American War. In this regard, the most noteworthy institution was the Cuban newspaper *La patria*, in whose pages could be found essays by the leading Cuban and Puerto Rican patriots. Furthermore, numerous essays, letters, diaries, poems, short stories, and literary creations by some of Puerto Rico's most important literary and patriotic figures were written in New York while they worked for the revolution. Included among these were Eugenio María de Hostos, Ramón Emeterio Betances, Lola Rodríguez de Tió, and Sotero Figueroa. Active as well in literature and political organizing were the revolutionary leaders Francisco González "Pachín" Marín, a Puerto Rican, and the

Cuban José Martí. Marín, a typesetter by trade and an important figure in Puerto Rican poetry for his break with romanticism, left us an important essay, "Nueva York por dentro; una faz de su vida bohemia" ("New York on the Inside; One Side of Its Bohemian Life"), in which he sketches New York from the perspective of a disillusioned immigrant; this is perhaps the earliest document in Spanish that takes this point of view and can be perhaps considered the beginning of Hispanic immigrant literature. Martí was an international literary figure in his own right, and his writings are still studied today in Latin American literature classes throughout the world; he has left us a legacy of many essays and other writings that relate directly to his life in New York and elsewhere in the United States.

Also of importance as the most widely circulated weekly was *Las novedades* (1893-1918, *The News*), whose theater, music, and literary critic was the famed Dominican writer Pedro Henríquez Ureña. An early Puerto Rican contribution was *La gaceta ilustrada* (*The Illustrated Gazette*), edited in the 1890s by writer Francisco Amy. Many of the Spanish-language literary books published in New York were also related to the Cuban independence struggle, such as Luis García Pérez's *El grito de Yara* (1879, *The Shout at Yara*) and Desiderio Fajardo Ortiz's *La fuga de Evangelina* (1898, *The Escape of Evangelina*), the story of Cuban heroine Evangelina Cossío's escape from incarceration by the Spaniards and her trip to freedom and the organizing effort in New York.

✸THE EARLY TWENTIETH CENTURY

The Southwest

The turn of the century brought record immigration from Mexico to the Southwest and Midwest because of the Mexican Revolution of 1910. During the period from 1910 until World War II, immigrant workers and upper-class and educated professionals from Mexico interacted with the Mexican-origin residents of the Southwest, who had been somewhat cut off from the evolution of Mexican culture inside Mexico. During this period Hispanic newspaper and book publishing flourished throughout the Southwest. Both San Antonio and Los Angeles supported Spanish-language daily newspapers that serve diverse readerships made up of regional groups from the Southwest, immigrant laborers, and political refugees from the revolution. The educated, political refugees played a key role in publishing, and in light of their upper social class, they created an ideology of a Mexican community in exile, or "México de afuera" (Mexico on the outside).

In the offices of San Antonio's *La prensa* (*The Press*) and Los Angeles's *La opinión* (*The Opinion*) and *El heraldo de México* (*The Mexican Herald*), some of the most talented writers from Mexico, Spain, and Latin America, such as Miguel Arce, Esteban Escalante, Gabriel Navarro, Teodoro Torres, and Daniel Venegas, earned their living as reporters, columnists and critics. These and many others wrote hundreds of books of poetry, essays, and novels, many of which were published in book form and marketed by the newspapers themselves via mail and in their own bookstores. Besides the publishing houses related to these large dailies, there were many other smaller companies, such as Laredo Publishing Company, Los Angeles's Spanish American Printing, and San Diego's Imprenta Bolaños Cacho Hnos.

The largest and most productive publishers resided in San Antonio. Leading the list was the publishing house founded by the owner, of *La prensa* and Los Angeles's *La opinión*, Ignacio Lozano. The Casa Editorial Lozano was by far the largest publishing establishment ever owned by a Hispanic in the United States. Among the San Antonio publishers were the Viola Novelty Company, probably a subsidiary of P. Viola, publisher of the satiric newspapers *El*

Cuban literary and patriotic figure, José Martí.

vacilón (*The Joker*) and *El fandango* (*The Fandango*), active from 1916 until at least 1927; the Whitt Company; and the Librería Española, which still exists today as a bookstore. Many of the novels produced by these houses were part of the genre known as "novels of the Mexican Revolution"; the stories were set within the context of the revolution and often commented on historical events and personalities. In the United States, the refugees who wrote these novels were very conservative and quite often attacked the revolution and Mexican politicians, which they saw as the reason for their exile. Included among these were Miguel Bolaños Cacho's *Sembradores de viento* (1928, *Sewers of the Wind*), Brígido Caro's *Plutarco Elías Calles: dictador volchevique de México* (1924, *Plutarco Elías Calles: Bolshevik Dictator of Mexico*), and Lázaro Gutiérrez de Lara's *Los bribones rebeldes* (1932, *The Rebel Rogues*). Many were the authors of this very popular genre, including Miguel Arce, Conrado Espinosa, Alfredo González, Esteban Maqueo Castellanos, Manuel Mateos, Ramón Puente, and Teodoro Torres. The most famous has become Mariano Azuela, author of the masterpiece that is one of the foundations of modern Mexican literature, *Los de abajo* (*The Underdogs*), which was first published in 1915 in a serialized version in *El Paso's* newspaper El paso del norte (*The Northern Pass*) and was issued later by the same newspaper in book form.

Although most of the novels published during these years gravitated toward the political and counterrevolutionary, there were others of a more sentimental nature and even some titles that can be considered forerunners of the Chicano novel of the 1960s in their identification with the working-class Mexicans of the Southwest, their use of popular dialects, and their political stance in regard to U.S. government and society. The prime example of this new sensibility is newspaperman Daniel Venegas's *Las aventuras de Don Chipote o Cuando los pericos mamen* (1928, *The Adventures of Don Chipote or When Parakeets May Suckle Their Young*), a humorous picaresque account of a Mexican immigrant, Don Chipote, who travels through the Southwest working here and there at menial tasks and running into one misadventure after the other, suffering at the hands of rogues, the authorities, and his bosses while in search of the mythic streets of gold that the United States is supposed to offer immigrants. *Don Chipote* is a novel of immigration, a picaresque novel, and a novel of protest all wrapped into one, and furthermore, it is the one clear forerunner of today's Chicano literature.

One of the most important literary genres that developed in the newspapers at this time was *la crónica*, (chronicle). It was a short satirical column that was full of local color, current topics, and observation of social habits. It owed its origins to Addison and Steele in England and José Mariano de Lara in Spain, but was cultivated extensively throughout Mexico and Latin America. In the Southwest it came to function and serve purposes never before thought of in Mexico or Spain. From Los Angeles to San Antonio, Mexican moralists satirized the customs and behavior of the colony whose very existence was seen as threatened by the dominant Anglo-Saxon culture. It was the *cronista*"s (cronicler's) job to enforce the ideology of "México de afuera" and battle the influence of Anglo-American culture and the erosion of the Spanish language caused by the influence of speaking English. The cronistas, using such pseudonyms as El Malcriado (The Spoiled Brat—Daniel Venegas), Kaskabel (Rattler—Benjamín Padilla), Az.T.K. (Aztec), and Chicote (The Whip), were literally whipping and stinging the community into conformity, commenting on or simply poking fun at the common folks" mixing of Spanish and English and Mexican women's adapting American dress and more liberalized customs, such as cutting their hair short, raising the hemlines, and smoking.

First and foremost behind the ideology of the crónica writers and the owners of the newspapers was the goal of returning to the homeland; as soon as the hostilities of the revolution ended, the immigrants were supposed to return to Mexico with their culture intact. Quite often the target of their humorous attacks were stereotyped country bumpkins, like Don Chipote, who were having a hard time getting around in the modern American city. They also poked fun at the Mexican immigrants to the United States who became impressed with the wealth, modern technology, efficiency, and informality of American culture, to the extent that they considered everything American superior and everything Mexican inferior. In some of his chronicles, Jorge Ulica satirized women who made much to do about throwing American-style surprise parties and celebrating Thanksgiving, and criticized their taking advantage of greater independence and power at the expense of men's machismo. The cronistas quite often drew from popular jokes, anecdotes, and oral tradition to create these tales. Two of the most popular cronistas, who saw their columns syndicated throughout the Southwest, were the aforementioned Benjamín Padilla, an expatriate newspaperman from Guadalajara, and Julio Arce, who was also a political refugee from Guadalajara and used the pseudonym Jorge Ulica for his "Crónicas Diabólicas" (Diabolical Chronicles). So popular was this type of satire that entire weekly newspapers, usually of no more than eight pages in length, were dedicated to it. Daniel Venegas's weekly

The cover of Daniel Venegas's satirical newspaper, *El Malcriado*.

Fray Angelico Chávez. A Franciscan monk, Chávez's poetry books are principally made up of poems to Christ and the Virgin Mary: *Clothed with the Sun* (1939), *New Mexico Triptych* (1940), *Eleven Lady Lyrics and Other Poems* (1945), *The Single Rose* (1948), and *Selected Poems with an Apologia* (1969). From the 1930s to the 1950s there appeared a number of short story writers who succeeded in publishing their works in mainstream English-language magazines. Most of these, such as Texas's Josefina Escajeda and Jovita González, based their works on folktales, oral tradition, and the picturesque customs of Mexicans in the Southwest. Robert Hernán Torres, who published some of his stories in *Esquire* magazine, focused his works on the cruelty and senselessness of the revolution in Mexico. Another prose writer in English who experienced relative success was Josephina Niggli: she focused many of her novels and short stories on life in Mexico after the revolution. Despite the significance of Chávez, Paredes, Niggli, and the others, it was not until the 1960s that there was a significant resurgence of Mexican-American literary activity, except that by the end of that decade it was called Chicano literature.

El Malcriado (*The Brat*) and P. Viola's *El vacilón* (*The Joker*) are prime examples of these.

Much of this literary activity in the Mexican-American Southwest came to an abrupt halt with the Great Depression and the repatriation, forced or voluntary, of a large segment of that society back to Mexico. Some writers during the depression, like Américo Paredes, began to write in both Spanish and English and to express a very pronounced and politicized Mexican-American sensibility. His English novel *George Washington Gómez* was written from 1936 to 1940 (but not published until 1990), and during the 1930s and 1940s he was a frequent contributor of poetry in Spanish, English, and bilingual format to newspapers in Texas, including *La prensa*. In 1937, he published a collection of poems, *Cantos de adolescencia* (*Songs of Adolescence*), at age 22, but it was not until 1991 that his collected poems were issued, under the title *Between Two Worlds*, a collection containing works selected from his writings from the late 1930s to the 1950s.

Another very important literary figure who emerged during the depression and began to publish poetry and tales based on New Mexican folklore was

Fray Angélico Chávez (Special Collections, General Library, University of New Mexico).

The Northeast

In New York, the period from the turn of the century up into the Great Depression was also one of increased immigration and interaction of various Hispanic groups. It was a period of increased Puerto Rican migration, facilitated by the Jones Act, which declared Puerto Ricans to be citizens of the United States, and later of immigration of Spanish workers and refugees from the Spanish Civil War. Artistic and literary creation in the Hispanic community quite often supported the Puerto Rican nationalist movement and the movement to reestablish the Spanish republic. At the turn of the century, Cuban and Spanish writers and newspapers still dominated the scene. The first decade of the century witnessed the founding of *La prensa* (*The Press*), whose heritage continues today in *El diario-La prensa* (*The Daily-The Press*), born of a merger in 1963. Also publishing during the decade were *Sangre latina* (*Latin Blood*), out of Columbia University, *Revista Pan-Americana* (*Pan American Review*), and *La paz y el trabajo* (*Peace and Work*), a monthly review of commerce, literature, science, and the arts. Even places as far away as Buffalo began to support their own publications, such as *La hacienda* (*The State*), founded in 1906.

Spanish-language literary publishing did not begin to expand until the late teens and early twenties. By far the most interesting volume that has come down to us from the teens is an early example of the immigrant novel. Somewhat similar in theme to *Don Chipote*, Venezuelan author Alirio Díaz Guerra's *Lucas Guevara* (1917) is the story of a young man who comes to the city seeking his fortune, but is ultimately disillusioned. While *Lucas Guevara* was probably self-published at the New York Printing Company, there were Spanish-language publishing houses functioning during the teens in New York. One of the most important and long-lived houses, Spanish American Publishing Company, began issuing titles at this time and continued well into the 1950s. It too was an early publisher of books on the theme of Hispanics in New York, such as Puerto Rican playwright Javier Lara's *En la metrópoli del dólar* (*In the Metropolis of the Dollar*), circa 1919. *Las novedades* newspaper also published books, including Pedro Henríquez Ureña's *El nacimiento de Dionisos* (1916, *The Birth of Dionysus*).

Although during the 1920s the Spanish American Publishing Company, Carlos López Press, The Phos Press, and others were issuing occasional literary titles, it was not until the late twenties and early thirties that there was an intensification of activity. To begin with, various specialized newspapers began to appear. Probably as an outgrowth of the very active theatrical movement that was taking place in

Cover of the first issue of *Gráfico* newspaper.

Manhattan and Brooklyn, *Gráfico* (*Graphic*) began publishing in 1927 as a theater and entertainment weekly newspaper under the editorship of the prolific writer Alberto O'Farrill, who was also a playwright and a leading comic actor in Cuban blackface farces (*teatro bufo cubano*). As was also the custom in the Southwest, *Gráfico* and the other newspapers and magazines published numerous poems, short stories, literary essays, and crónicas by the leading New York Hispanic writers. Among the most notable cronistas were those unknown writers using the pseudonyms Maquiavelo (Machiavelli) and Samurai; O'Farrill himself was an important contributor to the tradition, signing his columns "Ofa." As in the Southwest, these cronistas labored in their writings to solidify the Hispanic community, which in New York was even more diverse than in the Southwest, drawing from many ethnic and national backgrounds. They too were protecting the purity of Hispanic culture against the dangers of assimilation, as they voiced the political and social concerns of the community and corrected and satirized current habits. While in the Southwest the cronistas promoted a "México de afuera," in New York they often attempted to create a

"Trópico en Manhattan" (A Tropical [or Caribbean] Culture in Manhattan).

Unlike in the Southwest, there were no massive repatriations and deportations disrupting the cultural life in the Hispanic community during the Great Depression. In fact, New York continued to receive large waves of Hispanics during the depression and World War II: refugees from the Spanish Civil War, workers for the service and manufacturing industries flown in from Puerto Rico during World War II in the largest airborne migration in history, and Hispanics from the Southwest. Newspapers were founded that reflected this renewed interest in Spanish, Puerto Rican, and working-class culture: *Vida obrera* (1930, *Worker's Life*), *Alma boricua* (1934-35, *Puerto Rican Soul), España libre* (1943, *Free Spain*), and *Cultura proletaria* (1943, *Proletariat Culture*). The pages of these newspapers are valuable sources of an important body of testimonial literature that reflected the life of the immigrant. They frequently took the form of autobiographical sketches, anecdotes, and stories, quite often in a homey, straightforward language that was also replete with pathos and artistic sensibility. Despite the many sources available in print, a large part of Puerto Rican, Cuban, Dominican, and Spanish literature in New York is an oral literature, a folk literature, completely consistent with and emerging from the working-class nature of the immigrants. For the Caribbean peoples there is an immense repository of lyric and narrative poetry that is to be found in their songs, such as the *décimas, plenas,* and *sones,* and in the popular recorded music of such lyrical geniuses as Rafael Hernández, Pedro Flores, and Ramito, whose compositions began appearing on recordings in the 1930s and continue to influence Puerto Rican culture on the island and in New York to the present. Of course, the compositions of Hernández and Flores have influenced Hispanic popular music around the world.

As the Puerto Rican community grew in the late 1920s and into World War II, Puerto Rican literature began to gain a larger profile in New York, but within a decidedly political context. It also seems that the literature with the most impact for the Puerto Rican community was the dramatic literature, if published books are a measure. Poet Gonzalo O'Neill (1867-1942) was a businessman who during the 1920s and 1930s was at the hub of Puerto Rican and Hispanic cultural life, not only as a writer, but as a cultural entrepreneur, investing his money in the theater and protecting and offering support to other writers. O'Neill began his literary training and career in Puerto Rico as a teenager in association with a magazine, *El palenque de la juventud (The Young People's Arena)*, which featured the works of some of the most important writers in Puerto Rico, such as Luis Muñoz Rivera, Lola Rodríguez de Tió, Vicente Palés, and many other notables. O'Neill's first published book was a dramatic dialogue in verse, more appropriate for reading aloud than staging: *La indiana borinqueña* (1922, *The Puerto Rican Indians*). Here O'Neill revealed himself to be intensely patriotic and interested in Puerto Rican independence from the United States. His second published book was the three-act play *Moncho Reyes*, named after the central character, issued by Spanish American Publishing in 1923. In 1924, O'Neill published a book of nationalistic poetry, *Sonoras bagatelas o sicilianas (Sonorous Bagatelles or Sicilian Verses)*, for which Manuel Quevedo Baez stated in the prologue that "Gonzalo is a spontaneous and ingenuous poet. . .. He is a poet of creole stock, passionate, tender, and as melancholic as Gautier Benítez" (Gautier Benítez was Puerto Rico's greatest poet to date). Although all of his plays, even *La indiana borinqueña*, enjoyed stage productions, it was his third play, *Bajo una sola bandera* (1928, *Under Only One Flag*), that went on to critical acclaim and various productions on stages in New York as well as in Puerto Rico. *Bajo una sola bandera* examines the political options facing Puerto Rico, as personified by down-to-earth flesh-and-blood characters. (See Chapter 19 for a more extensive study of O'Neill's plays.) A glowing review in San Juan's *La democracia* (*Democracy*) on April 16, 1929, marveled at O'Neill's conserving perfect Spanish and his Puerto Rican identity, despite having lived in the United States for forty years. O'Neill certainly continued to write, although the remainder of his work is unknown or has been lost. Newspapers report that another play of his, *Amoríos borincanos* (*Puerto Rican Loves*), was produced for the stage in 1938.

Following the example of Gonzalo O'Neill, there were many other Puerto Ricans who wrote for the stage and even published some of their works from the late 1920s to the 1940s, such as Alberto M. González, Juan Nadal de Santa Coloma, José Enamorado Cuesta, Frank Martínez, and Erasmo Vando. But one poet-playwright stands out among the rest as a politically committed woman, although the major portion of her work has been lost: Franca de Armiño (probably a pseudonym). Franca de Armiño wrote three works that have been lost and are inaccessible today: *Luz de tienieblas* (*Light of Darkness*), a book of poems on various themes; *Aspectos de la vida* (*Aspects of Life*), philosophical essays; and *Tragedia puertorriqueña* (*Puerto Rican Tragedy*), a comedy of social criticism. Her one published and available play, *Los hipócritas: comedia dramática social* (*The Hypocrits: A Social Drama*), self-published in 1937 at the Modernistic Editorial

Company, is a major work that demands critical attention. Dedicated to "the oppressed and all those who work for ideas of social renovation," the work is set in Spain during the time of the republic and is openly anti-Fascist and revolutionary, calling for a rebellion of workers. *Los hipócritas*, which begins with the 1929 stock market crash, deals with a daughter's refusal to marry her father's choice, the son of a duke. Rather, she is romantically involved with a son of the working class, Gerónimo, whom her father calls a Communist and who has led her into atheism. The plot is complicated, with Gerónimo organizing workers for a strike, a Fascist dictatorship developing in Spain, and a corrupt priest trying to arrange for Gloria to become a nun so that the church will receive her dowry. The play ends with Gloria and Gerónimo together, the traitors unmasked, and the workers'' strike prevailing over police, who attack them brutally. While full of propaganda and stereotyped characters, *Los hipócritas* is a gripping and entertaining play that reflects the tenor of the times, as far as the Great Depression, labor organizing, and the Spanish Civil War are concerned.

A cigar roller who settled in New York in 1916, Bernardo Vega reconstructed life in the Puerto Rican community during the period between the two great wars. Written in 1940, his *Memorias de Bernardo Vega* was published in 1977, and its translation was published in English as *The Memoirs of Bernardo Vega* in 1984. Valuable as both a literary and a historical document, Vega's memoirs make mention of numerous literary figures, such as poet Alfonso Dieppa, whose works were either not published or are lost to us. Vega is an important forerunner of the Nuyorican writers of the 1960s because he wrote about New York as a person who was there to stay, with no intention to return to live in Puerto Rico.

The literature of this period is also represented by a newspaper columnist who wrote in English and was very active in the Communist party: Jesús Colón, author of columns for the *Daily Worker*. Colón's was a heroic intellectual battle against the oppression of workers and racial discrimination; he nevertheless wrote about and supported Puerto Rican culture and literature, even to the extent of founding a small publishing company that has the distinction of issuing some of the first works of the great Puerto Rican novelist and short story writer José Luis González. In 1961, Colón selected some of the autobiographical sketches that had appeared in newspapers and published them in book form in *A Puerto Rican in New York*, which was perhaps the one literary and historical document that was accessible to young Nuyorican writers and helped to form their literary and social awareness, as well as stimulate their production of literature. Colón, a black Puerto Rican, had created a document that, tempered with his political ideology, presented insight into Puerto Rican minority status in the United States, rather than just immigrant or ethnic status. In this it was quite different from all that had preceded it.

✳ WORLD WAR II TO THE PRESENT

Chicano Literature

Scholars consider the year 1943 as the beginning of a new period in Mexican-American history and culture. This is the year when the so-called Zoot Suit Riots occurred in the Los Angeles area; they mark a stage in the cultural development of the Mexican American in which there was a consciousness of not belonging to either Mexico or the United States, and there was an attempt to assert a separate independent identity, just as the zoot-suiters in their own subculture were doing by adopting their style of dress, speech, and music (zoot-suiters were Mexican-American youth who used as symbols of their subculture the baggy pants and long, feathered, wide-brimmed hat that made up a zoot suit.) Then, too, Mexican-

Lola Rodríguez de Tió (Archives, Arte Público Press).

American veterans serving in and returning from World War II, where they proportionately suffered more casualties and won more medals for valor than any other group in U.S. society, now felt that they had earned their rights as citizens of the United States and were prepared to assert that citizenship and to reform the political and economic system so that they could participate equitably. Thus the quest for identity in modern American society was initiated, and by the 1960s, a younger generation made up of the children of the veterans, not only took up this pursuit of democracy and equity in the civil rights movements but also explored the question of identity in all of the arts, paramount of which was literature.

Because of the interruption caused by the depression, repatriation, and World War II, and the decreased production of literature that ensued during the 1940s and 1950s, the renewed literary and artistic productivity that occurred during the 1960s has often been considered to be a Chicano renaissance. In reality it was an awakening that accompanied the younger generation's greater access to college and its participation in the civil rights movements, the farmworker labor struggle and the protest movement against the Vietnam War. For Chicano literature the decade of the 1960s was characterized by a questioning of all the commonly accepted truths in the society, foremost of which was the question of equality. The first writers of Chicano literature in the 1960s committed their literary voices to the political, economic, and educational struggles. Their works were frequently used to inspire social and political action, quite often with poets reading their verses at organizing meetings, at boycotts, and before and after protest marches. Of necessity many of the first writers to gain prominence in the movement were the poets who could tap into an oral tradition of recitation and declamation, such as Abelardo Delgado, Ricardo Sánchez, and Alurista (Alberto Urista), and create works to be performed orally before groups of students and workers, in order to inspire them and raise their level of consciousness.

The most important literary work in this period that was used at the grass roots level as well as by university students to provide a sense of history, mission, and Chicano identity was an epic poem written by an ex-boxer in Denver, Colorado: Rodolfo "Corky" González's *I Am Joaquín/Yo Soy Joaquín* (1964). The short, bilingual pamphlet edition of the poem was literally passed from hand to hand in the communities, was read from at rallies, dramatized by street theaters, and even produced as a slide show on film with a dramatic reading by none other than Luis Valdez, the leading Chicano director and playwright. The influence and social impact of *I Am Joaquín* and

poems such as "Stupid America," by Abelardo Delgado, which was published and reprinted in community and movement newspapers throughout the Southwest, then cut out of those papers and passed hand to hand, is inestimable. "Stupid America" was included as well in Abelardo's landmark collection, *Chicano: 25 Pieces of a Chicano Mind* (1969). This period was one of euphoria, power, and influence for the Chicano poet, who was sought after, almost as a priest, to give his blessings in the form of readings at all cultural and Chicano movement events.

The 1960s was an era of intense grass roots organizing and cultural fermentation, and along with this occurred a renewed interest in publishing small community and workers'' newspapers and magazines, such as the California farm workers'' *El Malcriado* (*The Brat*) and Houston's *Papel Chicano* (*Chicano Newspaper*), which were now quite often published bilingually. During the late 1960s and early 1970s, literary magazines proliferated, from the academic, such as Berkeley's *El grito* (*The Shout* [for independence]), to the grass roots type printed on newsprint and available for twenty-five cents, such as San Antonio's *Caracol* (*Shell*), to the artsy, streetwise, avant-garde, and irreverent, such as Los Angeles's *Con Safos* (*Safety Zone*).

In 1967 appeared the most influential Chicano literary magazine, *El grito*, which initiated the careers of some of the most prominent names in Chicano literature and, along with the publishing house Editorial Quinto Sol, which it established in 1968, began to delineate the canon that is the official identity of Chicano literature by publishing those works that best exemplified Chicano culture, language, themes, and styles. The very name of the publishing house emphasized its Mexican/Aztec identity, as well as the Spanish language; the "quinto sol" (fifth sun), referred to Aztec belief in a period of cultural flowering that would take place some time in the future, in a fifth age that conveniently coincided with the rise of Chicano culture. Included in its 1968 anthology, *El espejo/The Mirror*, edited by the owners of Quinto Sol, Octavio Romano and Herminio Ríos, were such writers as Alurista, Tomás Rivera, and Miguel Méndez, who are still models of Chicano literature. *El espejo* recognized the linguistic diversity and the erosion of Spanish literacy among the young by accompanying works originally written in Spanish with an English translation; it even included Miguel Méndez's original Yaqui-language version of his short story "Tata Casehue." In *El espejo* and in later books that Quinto Sol published, there was a definite insistence on working-class and rural culture and language, as exemplified in the works of Tomás Rivera, Rolando Hinojosa, and most of the other authors published in book form. Also, there was not only a tolerance but a promotion of works written bilingually and in *caló*, the code of street culture, switching between both English and Spanish and various social dialects of each one in the same literary piece, as in the poems of Alurista and the plays of Carlos Morton.

In 1970, Quinto Sol reinforced its leadership in creating the concept of Chicano literature by instituting the national award for Chicano literature, Premio Quinto Sol (Fifth Sun Award), which carried with it a one-thousand-dollar prize and publication of the winning manuscript. The first three years of prizes went to books that today are still seen as exemplary Chicano novels and, in fact, are still among the best-selling Chicano literary texts: Tomás Rivera's *...y no se lo tragó la tierra/...And the Earth Did Not Part* (1971), Rudolfo Anaya's *Bless Me, Ultima* (1972), and Rolando Hinojosa's *Estampas del valle y otras obras/Sketches of the Valley and Other Works*. Rivera's outwardly simple but inwardly complex novel is much in the line of experimental Latin American fiction, demanding that the reader take part in unraveling the story and in coming to his own conclusions about the identity and relationships of the characters, as well as the meaning. Drawing upon his own life as a migrant worker from Texas, Rivera constructed a novel in the straightforward but poetic language of migrant workers in which a nameless central character attempts to find himself by reconstructing the over-heard conversations and stories as well as events that took place during a metaphorical year, which really represents his whole life. It is the story of a sensitive boy who is trying to understand the hardship that surrounds his family and community of migrant workers; his path is first one of rejection of them only to embrace them and their culture dearly as his own at the end of the book. In many ways, *...y no se lo tragó la tierra* came to be the most influential book in the Chicano search for identity.

Rivera, who became a very successful university professor and administrator—he rose to the position of chancellor of the University of California, Riverside, before his death in 1984—wrote and published other stories, essays, and poems. Through his essays, such as "Chicano Literature: Fiesta of the Living" (1979) and "Into the Labyrinth: The Chicano in Liter-

(L.to R.) Abelardo Delgado, Ron Arias and Rolando Hinojosa at the Second National Latino Book Fair and Writers Festival, Houston, Texas, 1980 (Archives, Arte Público Press).

When
love to be?
when
leaves warmly cover
protectingly from
sun and snow and wind
and feet
everyone will walk toward me
not away
when
love to be
comes
now, no one listens

I've been ready for so long

since many times
of leaves covering
warmly to protect
yet dying
from sun and snow and wind
and feet

I've been ready for so long

when
love to be?
when
everyone will walk toward me
and stay

The original manuscript of the Tomás Rivera poem, "When love to be?" Archives, Arte Público Press).

which has also kept his first novel in print and has recently published *Tomás Rivera: The Complete Works* (1990). In 1987, *. . . y no se lo tragó la tierra* was given a liberal translation into Texan dialect under the title *This Migrant Earth* (1987) by Rolando Hinojosa; the translation that accompanies the Arte Público bilingual edition was done by poet Evangelina Vigil-Piñón. By any accounts, Tomás Rivera remains the most outstanding and influential figure in the literature of Mexican peoples in the United States, and he deserves a place in the canon of Spanish-language literature in the world.

Rudolfo Anaya's *Bless Me, Ultima* is a straightforward novel about a boy's coming of age. Written in a poetic and clear English, it has reached more readers, especially non-Chicano readers, than any other Chicano literary work. In *Bless Me, Ultima*, again we have the search for identity, but this time the central character, Antonio, must decide between the more Spanish heritage of the plainsman-rancher or the more Indian heritage of the farmer; he is guided and inspired in his attempts to understand good and evil and his role in life by a larger than life folk healer, Ultima, who passes on many of her secrets and insights about life to Antonio. Anaya puts to good use his knowledge of the countryside of New Mexico, its romance and picturesque qualities, in fashioning this novel full of mystery and references to the symbols and folk knowledge of American Indian, Asian, and Spanish culture.

Anaya went on to become celebrated in his home state and to head the creative writing program at the University of New Mexico. His subsequent novels, all dealing with Chicano/Indian culture in New Mexico, have not been as well received by the critics: *Heart of Aztlán* (1976), *Tortuga* (1979, Tortoise), *The Silence of the Llano* (1982), and *Lord of the Dawn: The Legend of Quetzalcoatl* (1987). As can be seen from these titles, Anaya is a promoter of the concept of Aztlán, the mythical place of origin of the Aztec, supposedly located in what has become the five states of the Southwest. He and numerous other Chicano writers have derived both poetic inspiration and a sense of mission in reviving the cultural glories of Mexico's indigenous past. For Anaya and especially for poets and playwrights such as Alurista and Luis Valdez, the Aztec and Mayan past has been a source of imagery, symbols, and myths that have enriched their works.

Rolando Hinojosa is the most prolific and probably the most bilingually talented of the novelists, with original creations in both English and Spanish published in the United States and abroad. His Quinto Sol Award-winning *Estampas del valle y otras obras/Sketches of the Valley and Other Works* is a mosaic of

ature" (1971), and his personal and scholarly activities, he was one of the prime movers in the promotion of Chicano authors, in the creation of the concept of Chicano literature, and in the creation of Chicano literature and culture as legitimate academic areas in the college curriculum. In 1989, his stories were collected and published under the title *The Harvest*, which was also the title of one of his stories, and in 1990 his poems were collected and published under the title *The Searchers*, both by Arte Público Press, the picturesque character types, folk customs, and speech of the bilingual community in the small towns along Texas's Rio Grande valley. His sketches and insights at times reminiscent of the local color of the *crónicas* of the 1920s, Hinojosa's art is one of the most sophisticated contributions to Chicano literature.

Estampas was just the beginning phase of a continuing novel that has become a broad epic of the history and culture of the Mexican Americans and Anglos of

The cover of Rudolfo Anaya's best-selling novel, *Bless Me, Ultima* (Archives, Arte Público Press).

Evangelina Vigil-Piñón, reciting at the Third National Hispanic Book Fair, Houston, 1987 (Photo: Julián Olivares. Archives, Arte Público Press).

the valley, centered in the fictitious Belken County and around two fictitious characters and a narrator—Rafa Buenrostro, Jehú Malacara, and P. Galindo—all of whom may be partial alter egos of Hinojosa himself. What is especially intriguing about Hinojosa's continuing novel, which he calls the Klail City Death Trip Series, is his experimentation with various forms of narration—derived from Spanish, Mexican, English, and American literary history—in the respective installments of the novel. *Klail City y sus alrededores* (1976, *Klail City and Surroundings*) owes much to the picaresque novel, *Korean Love Songs* (1980) is narrative poetry, *Mi querido Rafa* (1981, *Dear Rafe*) is part epistolary novel and part reportage, *Rites and Witnesses* (1982) is mainly a novel in dialogue, *Partners in Crime* (1985) is a detective novel, *Claros varones de Belken* (1986, *Fair Gentlemen of Belken*) is a composite, and *Becky and Her Friends* (1990) continues the novel in the style of reportage, but with a new unnamed narrator, P. Galindo having died.

While there have been translations by others of his works, Hinojosa has penned and published re-creations in English and Spanish of all of these books,

A vendor at the First National Latino Book Fair in 1979 in Chicago (Archives, Arte Público Press).

except for the English titles *Korean Love Songs*, *Rites and Witnesses*, and *Partners in Crime*. *Mi querido Rafa* is especially important because it represents the first novel to experiment with bilingual narration and demands of the reader a good knowledge of both English and Spanish and their south Texas dialects.

Because of his many awards—including the international award for Latin American fiction given in Cuba, Premio Casa de las Americas, 1976—his academic background and doctorate in Spanish, and the positive response to his sophisticated art from critics and university professors, in particular, Hinojosa is one of the few Hispanic writers in the country to teach in creative writing programs at a high level. In holding the distinguished title Ellen Clayton Garwood Professor of English and Creative Writing at the University of Texas, Hinojosa is the most recognized and highest-ranking Chicano/Hispanic author in academia.

It was not until 1975 that the Quinto Sol Award was given to a woman, Estela Portillo Trambley, for her short story collection *Rain of Scorpions*, and it marked the ascendancy of women's voices in Chicano literature, which had been too dominated by males. And Portillo Trambley's strong feminist and

irreverent stories did much both to sensitize the publishing powers in Chicano literature and to encourage a new generation of women writers to persevere in getting their works published; their works were soon to change the character of Chicano literature in the 1980s. In nine finely crafted stories and a novella Portillo Trambley presents a series of female characters who draw from an inner strength and impose their personalities on the world around them. In the novella that gives title to the collection, a fat and unattractive central character overcomes her own dreams of beauty and the set roles that society has for her to prevail as a woman who from behind the scenes controls and determines the action around her. She has chosen her life and how to live it; it will not be imposed upon her by others. In the most feminist of the short stories, "If It Weren't for the Honeysuckle," the eldest of three women being oppressed and enslaved by a drunk and irrational male succeeds in poisoning him and in freeing the women. In this as in the other stories, as well as in her books to follow— *The Day of the Swallows* (1971), the collection of plays *Sor Juana* (1983, *Sister Juana*), and the novel *Trini* (1986)—Portillo Trambley has created strong women who prevail in a male-dominated world. Her latest work, *Trini*, is the story of a Tarahumara woman who leaves her Indian life behind and, after numerous tragedies and betrayals, crosses the border to give birth to her child in the United States, where she is able to control her life for herself and even become a landowner. In all of her work Portillo Trambley has demonstrated an uncompromising pursuit for equality and liberation for women.

By the end of the 1970s most of the literary magazines and Chicano literary presses had disappeared, including Editorial Quinto Sol and *El grito*. Fortunately, since 1973 a new Hispanic magazine, *Revista Chicano-Riqueña* (*Chicano-Rican Review*), edited by Nicolás Kanellos and Luis Dávila in Gary, Indiana, had been operating and making greater incursions into academia than any other Hispanic literary publication. In 1979, Kanellos founded Arte Público Press as an outgrowth of the magazine and relocated both to Houston, Texas, just in time to carry on where Quinto Sol had left off and to assume the leadership in publishing the works of a blossoming Hispanic women's literary movement. During the 1980s, Arte Público published books of poetry by San Antonio poets Evangelina Vigil and Angela de Hoyos, Chicago poets and prose writers Ana Castillo and Sandra

Helena María Viramontes, 1986 (Photo by Georgia McInnis. Archives, Arte Público Press).

Cisneros, San Francisco Bay Area novelist and poet Lucha Corpi, Los Angeles short story writer and former editor of the magazine *ChismeArte* Helena María Viramontes, and New Mexico novelist and playwright Denise Chávez, who were to produce some of the best-selling and most highly reviewed Chicano books of the decade.

Along with Arte Público and *Revista Chicano-Riqueña*, which in 1987 became *The Americas Review* and was edited by Julián Olivares and Evangelina Vigil, another magazine/book publisher was founded in Indiana in 1980 and relocated to the University of California, Berkeley, in 1985: *Third Woman*, directed by Norma Alarcón. Around the same time, another Hispanic book publisher with an academic base, *Bilingual Review Press*, also relocated, from Binghamton, New York, to the Southwest, to Arizona State University in Tempe. Supported by these three establishments and various other presses that were occasionally issuing women's titles, this first full-blown generation of Chicana writers flourished, finding a welcome space for their books in the academic curriculum, not only in Chicano literature courses but also in women's studies programs and American

Ana Castillo, 1979. (Archives, Arte Público Press).

Luis Dávila, Co-Editor of *Revista Chicano-Riqueña* at the First National Latino Book Fair, University of Illinois-Chicago Circle in 1979 (Archives, Arte Público Press).

literature courses. The majority of the women were more educated than the 1960s and 1970s writers; most of them were college graduates—two of its representatives, Denise Chavez and Sandra Cisneros, had even obtained master's degrees in creative writing—and they were mostly dominant in English, thus the Spanish language was no barrier to their works" entering literature courses and becoming accessible to broader circles of the reading public. As a whole, they were thoroughly versed in the mainstream feminist movement while preserving their own Chicana identities and culture and developing their literature from it.

At the close of the decade, mainstream textbook publishers were finally responding to the reform movements occurring in academia and to the new demographic statistics relating to the public school markets in the most populous states, which convincingly showed overwhelming Hispanic enrollments then and into the next century. As a result, most of the textbook publishers have begun to desperately search out and include Hispanic writers. In 1990, the nation's largest textbook publisher, Harcourt Brace Jovanovich, in fact, even went so far as to issue a high

school English anthology titled *Mexican American Literature*, which includes selections of works from the colonial period to the present in its more than seven hundred pages. Some of the most successful writers in being chosen for the general American literature textbooks and for such canonizing texts as *The Norton Anthology of American Literature* include Pat Mora and Denise Chávez. Mora is the author of three books of poetry, her first two winning the Southwest Book Award: *Chants* (1984), *Borders* (1986), and *Communion* (1991). Drawing upon the desert landscape and a Mexican Indian sensibility, *Chants* is a richly textured exploration, in beautiful whispered tones, of the desert as a woman and of women as holders of the strength and endurance of the desert. In *Borders,* Mora, an El Paso native, continues in the same vein, drawing upon folk customs and the insight of healers as she explores all types of borders: the political and cultural ones between the United States and Mexico, the borders between the sexes, and so forth. Her latest book, *Communion,* is about communion with other women, other peoples of the earth, as she expands her vision to Asia and Africa.

Denise Chávez is a talented actress and a prolific playwright, but it is as a novelist that she has gained a deserved place in Chicano and American literature as a whole. For Chávez, as for Rolando Hinojosa, literature is very much the art of writing about lives, about individuals, and about the stories they have to tell. Both of her novels, *The Last of the Menu Girls* (1986) and *Face of an Angel* (1993), present series of lives and characters talking for themselves within a loose biographic structure. In the case of her first novel, the unifying structure is the life of Rocío Esquivel, who, through a series of interconnected stories gains maturity by rebelling against the social roles created for her. *Face of an Angel*, on the other hand, centers on the life of a waitress and the unfortunate and tragicomic amorous relationships that she has with men; in the midst of the narration are brought in various types of unlikely elements, such as a manual on how to become a good waitress that the protagonist is writing. Both Mora and Chávez have won attention from the world that was previously off-limits to Chicano writers: the pages of the *New York*

Pat Mora, 1986 (Archives, Arte Público Press).

Times Book Review and the Norton anthologies, important fellowships, and awards.

While women were ascending in the world of Chicano literature, so was a younger generation of male writers who were the products of creative writing programs at universities, through which they gained access to opportunities for study, travel, and publishing never before had by Chicanos (nor Chicanas). To date, theirs is the only Chicano poetry that has begun to become part of the American literary establishment. Of this new cadre of American poets who no longer speak or write in Spanish and no longer derive sustenance from the oral tradition, recitation, and political action, the most famous and prolific is Gary Soto, currently a tenured associate professor in creative writing and ethnic studies at the University of California, Berkeley. He is the winner of numerous prestigious awards, including the Academy of American Poets Prize (1975), the *Discovery*-Nation Award (1975), a Guggenheim Fellowship (1979), an American Book Award, and many other prizes. His poetry is finely crafted, down-to-earth, and rigorous, mostly inspired by the life of the common working man in the fields and factories.

Quite often, as in his book *The Elements of San*

The cover of Rudolfo Anaya's *Cuentos: Tales from the Hispanic Southwest* (Archives, Arte Público Press).

Joaquin, published, as are most of his other poetry books, by the prestigious University of Pittsburgh Press poetry series, his work is a recollection of growing up in Fresno. While dealing with very real and concrete pictures of life in a particular time and setting, such as his youth in the agricultural San Joaquin Valley, Soto frequently approaches his subject from a classical frame of reference. For instance, in the second section of the book, the Valley is envisioned according to the four universal elements of the Greek philosophers: earth, air, water, and fire. He takes these elements and transforms them into the particular sights, smells, and labors of the Valley.

Among Soto's other books of poetry are *The Tale of Sunlight* (1978), *Where Sparrows Work Hard* (1981), *Black Hair* (1985), and *Who Will Know?* (1990). In 1985, Soto also began publishing autobiographical prose essays, which have met with a great deal of success, his first three books winning an American Book Award: *Living Up the Street* (1985), *Small Faces* (1986), and *Lesser Evils: Ten Quartets* (1988).

Among other writers who have made it into university creative writing programs as professors are Arizonan Alberto Rios and Californians Ernesto Trejo

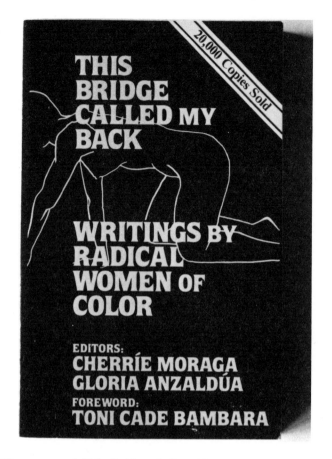

The cover of *This Bridge Called My Back*, a groundbreaking anthology of feminist literature (Archives, Arte Público Press).

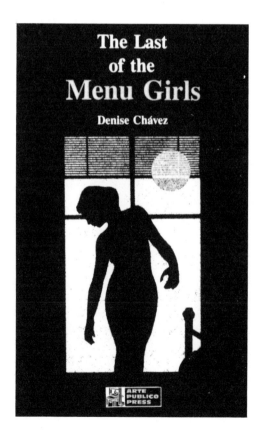

The cover of Denise Chávez's *The Last of the Menu Girls* (Archives, Arte Público Press).

and Lorna Dee Cervantes. Cervantes did not follow the usual trek through master of fine arts programs in creative writing for entrance into her career. She was very much a product of the 1970s and the Chicano literary movement of those days, in which she began reading her poetry in public at a theater festival in 1974, published her first works in *Revista Chicano-Riqueña* in 1975, and shortly thereafter founded and edited a literary magazine, *Mango*, which was free-form and experimental and not limited to publishing Chicanos. By 1981, her first book of poems, *Emplumada* (*Plumed*), was published by the University of Pittsburgh Press. Despite many publications in magazines and success as a performer of poetry, it was not until 1986 that she finished her B.A. degree. In 1990, she earned a Ph.D. in the history of consciousness at the University of California, Santa Cruz. She currently teaches creative writing at the University of Colorado.

Perhaps better than anyone yet, Lorna Dee Cervantes has described the pain of separation from the tongue and culture of family in such poems as "Refugee Ship" and "Oaxaca, 1974." Her work also

Gary Soto and Evangelina Vigil-Piñón at the Third National Hispanic Book Fair and Writers Festival in Houston, Texas, 1987 (Archives, Arte Público Press).

deals with the dehumanizing landscape and the dehumanization that is caused by racism and sexism. Today she is still very much a hard-driving poet who takes risks and is not afraid to deal with taboo topics and violence, whether it be racist, sexist, or psychological, as can be seen in her book *From the Cables of Genocide* (1991).

Today, as greater opportunities in academia have opened up for both Hispanic students and writers, the larger commercial world of publishing is beginning to open its doors to a few more Chicano writers. Under the leadership of writer-scholars, like Tomás Rivera and Rolando Hinojosa, and publishers like Arte Público Press and Bilingual Review Press, Chicano literature has created a firm and lasting base for itself in academia. The larger society of readers and commercial publishing represent the new frontier for the 1990s. A strong beginning is represented by the publication in 1991 of Victor Villaseñor's generational family saga, "the Chicano *Roots*," entitled *Rain of Gold*, which is currently under development as a five-part television miniseries by the Corporation for Public Broadcasting. In 1975, Villaseñor's novel *Macho* was published but barely promoted by Bantam

Books; in 1991, it was reprinted by Arte Público Press and made into a feature film for commercial release. In 1990, the commercial publisher Chronicle Books issued two books of poetry by Chicanos, Gary Soto and Francisco Alarcón, and Random House in 1991 issued two books by Sandra Cisneros. Finally, in 1991 the long-awaited filming of *Bless Me, Ultima* began, with Luis Valdez as director.

Nuyorican Literature

In 1898, Puerto Rico became a colony of the United States; since 1917, Puerto Ricans have been citizens of the United States. Since that latter date, Puerto Ricans have never really been immigrants to the United States, but migrants. Puerto Ricans on the island and those on the continent, despite graphic separation, hold in common their ethnicity, history, and their religious and cultural traits and practices. They also both deal with the confrontation of two languages and cultures. Thus, whether they reside in the continental United States or on the island of Puerto Rico, Puerto Ricans are one people. That is true whether they prefer the Spanish language or

(Central figures) Ricardo Sánchez, Alejandro Morales, critic Salvador Rodríguez del Pino and Victor Villaseñor at a book fair in Mexico City in 1979.

English, whether they were born on the island or not. The island experience and the experience on the continent are two sides of the same coin. Thus, most attempted divisions of the people are for vested interests, whether political or prejudicial.

Puerto Rican culture today is the product of the powerful political, economic, and social forces that descend on small native populations and attempt to evangelize, assimilate, decimate, or otherwise transform them. In the case of Puerto Rico, in 1493 Christopher Columbus initiated the process that forever would make the island's people a blend of the cultures and races of Europe, Africa, and the Americas. It was this act of "discovery" that also resulted in Puerto Rico's becoming a colony in the Spanish Empire until 1898, when it passed into the possession of the next empire to dominate the hemisphere: the United States. It is therefore a land that has been and still is subject to overseas rule—politically and economically, as well as artistically.

Despite being an island geographically cut off from the rest of Latin America and despite being ruled as a colony and not enjoying complete self-determination, Puerto Rican literature has been rich, for it has developed out of the many cultures and experiences that make up its peoples. From the middle of the nineteenth century, it first assumed a creole, Hispanic-American identity, emphasizing the new speech and customs and history of people in this hemisphere as opposed to the Spanish in Europe—Puerto Rico and Cuba were among the very last remnants of Spain's colonial empire, the rest of Spanish America having gained its independence at the beginning of the century. After 1898, Puerto Rico emphasized its Latin American, Spanish-speaking identity as separate from the Anglo-American United States. While the reaction of Puerto Rican artists to the Spanish identity and tastes was to create a nationalism or an ethnic identity based on *mestizaje*, a blending of the cultures and the values of the New World, the reaction to the powerful presence of the United States has come as an insistence on the use of the Spanish language itself and on the relationship to Latin America and its cultures and arts.

At the turn of the century, the island's literature was developing along the lines of Latin American modernism, which was heavily influenced by French, peninsular Spanish, and Latin American models. As was the case in Mexico, Peru, Argentina, and Cuba, the artists and writers of Puerto Rico turned to the indigenous people of the island, their folklore, and national models in an effort to discover the true identity of the national culture. The mestizo highlander, or *jíbaro*, and the black and mulatto became cultural types that related Puerto Rico to the other island cultures of the Caribbean and thus created a space that was identifiable as home, while it challenged the imposition of the English language—which was done officially under U.S. military rule of the island—and the purported benefits of Yankee customs and economic power.

Although he was one of Puerto Rico's master poets, Luis Llorens Torres (1878-1944) was a European-educated intellectual who adapted the verse forms of the plaintive mountain songs (*décimas*) and folk speech of the jíbaros in poems that took pride in rural life and its values rather than in the sophistication and modern advances of the city. His jíbaros were always skeptical and unmoved by the bragging and showing off of Americanized Puerto Ricans who believed in Yankee ingenuity and progress. Puerto Rico's greatest and most universally studied poet, Luis Palés Matos (1898-1959), was the first Puerto Rican literary figure to achieve a lasting impact on the evolution of Latin American literature, principally through the development of a poetic style that was inspired by the rhythms and language of Africa and the black Caribbean. His landmark book, *Tun tun de pasa y griferia* (1937), whose onomatopoic title has no translation, openly claimed a black African heritage and presence for the cultural makeup of Puerto Rico. But the primitivism, vigor, and freedom of his black verses was only a point of departure for his critical stance toward Europe and the United States. In Palés Matos's master poem, "La plena de menéalo" ("The Dance of Shake It"), Puerto Rico is personified by a seductive *mulata* who sweats rum as she erotically dances close to, but just out of reach of, a drooling Uncle Sam.

Two figures are essential in recognition of the transition of Puerto Rican literature from the island to the continent: Julia de Burgos (1914-1953) and René Marqués (1919-1979). The former cultivated beautiful, sensuous verses, odes to her beloved countryside, only to die tragically on the streets of New York. Her lyricism served the parallel desires for personal as well as national liberation. René Marqués, the most widely known Puerto Rican playwright, spent time in New York as well, and was able to capture the true meaning of the dislocation of the native populations from Puerto Rico and their relocation to foreign lands and values. Even more moving than John Steinbeck's *Grapes of Wrath* is the plight of the family of displaced mountain folk in Marqués's *La carreta* (*The Oxcart*), which was first produced on stage in New York in 1953 and then published in Spanish in 1961 and in English in 1969. *La carreta*, which dramatizes the tragic life of this family as they are forced to move from their farm to a San Juan slum and then to New York, ends with an appeal to Puerto Ricans not to leave their homeland and to return to the island and the values of the countryside.

To a great extent, today's major Puerto Rican writers on the island still draw upon Marqués's spirit, style, and message in their attempt to preserve the integrity of the Puerto Rican culture and in their call for the political independence of the island. Prose writers like José Luis González, Pedro Juan Soto, Luis Rafael Sánchez, and Jaime Carrero satirize the complacency of the Americanized middle class, which would like Puerto Rico to become a U.S. state. They also develop the themes of Puerto Rico's past as Edenic and the jíbaro as a child of nature, with his intense code of honor and decency. Most of today's island novelists, while romanticizing the island's past, have, however, also created a one-dimensional image of Puerto Ricans in New York, only focusing on the tragedy of the rootlessness, poverty, and op-

Julia de Burgos.

José Luis González (Archives, Arte Público Press).

civil rights movements of the 1960s, young Puerto Rican writers and intellectuals began using the term *Nuyorican* as a point of departure in affirming their own cultural existence and history as divergent from that of the island of Puerto Rico and that of mainstream America, much as the Chicanos were doing. A literary and artistic flowering in the New York Puerto Rican community ensued in the late 1960s and early 1970s as a result of greater access to education for Puerto Ricans raised in the United States and as a result of the ethnic consciousness movement. Although the term "Nuyorican" was first applied to literature by playwright-novelist Jaime Carrero in his poem "Neo-Rican Jetliner/Jet neorriqueño" in the late 1960s when he resided in New York, and the term finds some stylistic and thematic development in his plays *Noo Jall* (a blending of the Spanish pronunciation of "New York" and the word "jail") and "Pipo Subway no sabe reír" (Pipo Subway Doesn't Know How to Laugh), it was a group of poet-playwrights associated with the Nuyorican Poets" Café in the lower East Side of New York who later really defined and exemplified Nuyorican literature in their works. Included in the group were Miguel Alagarín, Lucky Cienfuegos, Tato

pression of the second-class citizens who seem to be lost in the labyrinth of the monster city.

Puerto Rican writing in New York dates back to the end of the nineteenth century, and writing in English begins about the time that Jesús Colón was writing his columns for the *Daily Worker*. This seems to be a rather appropriate beginning, given that most of the Puerto Rican writers in English that followed identify with the working class. Unlike the writers of the island, who largely are members of an elite, educated class and many of whom are employed as university professors, the New York writers, who came to be known as Nuyoricans, are products of parents transplanted to the metropolis to work in the service and manufacturing industries. These writers are predominantly bilingual in their poetry and English-dominant in their prose; they hail from a folk and popular tradition heavily influenced by roving bards, reciters, storytellers, salsa music composers, and the popular culture and commercial environment of New York City.

Thus Nuyoricans are typically the children of working-class Puerto Rican migrants to the city; they are generally bilingual and bicultural, and so is their literature. During the search for ethnic roots and the

Luis Rafael Sánchez (Archives, Arte Público Press).

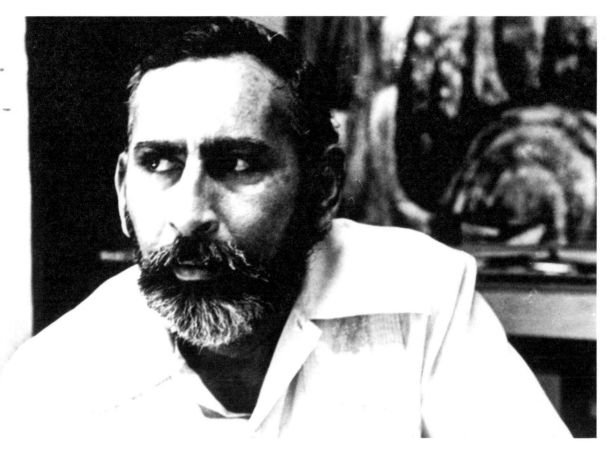

Pedro Juan Soto (Archives, Arte Público Press).

Laviera, and Miguel Piñero. Two members of the group, Cienfuegos and Piñero, were ex-convicts who had begun their writing careers while incarcerated and associating with Afro-American convict-writers; they chose to concentrate on prison life, street life, and the culture of poverty and to protest the oppression of their peoples through their poetry and dramas. Algarín, a university professor and owner and operator of the Nuyorican Poets'' Café, contributed more of a spirit of the avant-garde for the collective and managed to draw into the circle such well-known poets as Alan Ginsberg. Tato Laviera, a virtuoso bilingual poet and performer of poetry (*declamador*), contributed a lyricism and a folk and popular culture tradition that derived from the island experience and the Afro-Caribbean culture but was cultivated specifically in and for New York City.

It was Miguel Piñero's work (and life), however, that became most celebrated, his prison drama, *Short Eyes*, having won an Obie and the New York Drama Critics Award for Best American Play in the 1973-74 season. His success, coupled with that of the autobiography of fellow Nuyorican writer and ex-convict Piri Thomas and that of poet Pedro Pietri, who developed the image of a street urchin always high on marijuana, resulted in Nuyorican literature and theater's often being associated with crime, drugs, abnormal sexuality, and generally negative behavior. Thus, many writers who in fact were affirming Puerto Rican working-class culture did not want to become identified with the movement. Still others wanted to hold onto their ties with the island and saw no reason to emphasize differences, but, rather, wanted to stress similarities. What exacerbated the situation was that the commercial publishing establishment in the early 1970s was quick to take advantage of the literary fervor in the Puerto Rican community by issuing a series of ethnic autobiographies that insisted on the criminality, abnormality, and drug culture of New York Puerto Ricans. Included in this array of mostly paperbacks was, of course, Piri Thomas's *Down These Mean Streets* (1967, issued in paper in 1974), Thomas's *Seven Long Times* (1974), Thomas's *Stories from El Barrio* (1978, issued in paper in 1980), Lefty Barreto's *Nobody's Hero* (1976), and a religious variation on the theme: Nicky Cruz's *Run Nicky Run*. So well worn was this type of supposed autobiography that it generated a satire by another Nuyorican writer, Ed Vega, who comments in the introduction to his novel *The Comeback* (1985) as follows:

Jesús Colón ca. 1950s. (Archives, Centro de Estudios Puertorriqueños, Hunter College).

nervous breakdown and is treated for the classical symptoms of an identity crisis. Throughout the novel are satirized all types of characters that populate the barrio as well as popular culture, such as Puerto Rican revolutionaries, psychiatrists, and a Howard Cosell-type sportscaster. In his interrelated collection of stories told by fictitious narrator Ernesto Mendoza, *Mendoza's Dreams* (1987), Vega surveys the human comedy of everyday barrio life and relates tales of success in small ways in reaching for the American Dream. In his collection *Casualty Report* (1991), he shows us the inverse: the physical, psychological, and moral death of many who live within the poverty and deprivation of the Puerto Rican barrio, as well as in the larger ghetto of a racist society.

More than anything else, the first generation of Nuyorican writers was one that was dominated by poets, many of whom had come out of an oral tradition and had honed their art through public readings; thus the creation of the Nuyorican Poets" Café was a natural outcome of the need to create a specific space for the performance of poetry. Among the consummate performers of Nuyorican poetry were Victor Hernández Cruz, Tato Laviera, Miguel Piñero, and

I started thinking about writing a book, a novel. And then it hit me. I was going to be expected to write one of those great American immigrant stories, like *Studs Lonigan*, *Call It Sleep*, or *Father....* Or maybe I'd have to write something like *Manchild in the Promised Land* or a Piri Thomas" *Down These Mean Streets....* I never shot dope nor had sexual relations with men, didn't for that matter, have sexual relations of any significant importance with women until I was about nineteen.... And I never stole anything.... Aside from fist fights, I've never shot anyone, although I've felt like it. It seems pretty far-fetched to me that I would ever want to do permanent physical harm to anyone. It is equally repulsive for me to write an autobiographical novel about being an immigrant. In fact, I don't like ethnic literature, except when the language is so good that you forget about the ethnic writing it.

The Comeback is the story of a confused college professor who creates for himself the identity of a Puerto Rican-Eskimo ice hockey player; he suffers a

Bernardo Vega in 1948 (Archives, Centro de Estudios Puertorriqueños, Hunter College).

Miguel Algarín. Like his fellow poets, Cruz's initiation into poetry was through popular music and street culture; his first poems have been often considered to be jazz poetry in a bilingual mode, except that English dominated in the bilingualism and thus opened the way for his first book to be published by a mainstream publishing house: *Snaps: Poems* (Random House, 1969). It was quite a feat for a twenty-year-old from an impoverished background. Already announced in *Snaps* were the themes and styles that would dominate and flourish in his subsequent books. In all of Hernández Cruz's poetry of sound, music and performance are central. He always experiments with bilingualism as oral poetry [and written symbols of oral speech,] and he searches for identity through these sounds and symbols. Thus, his next two books are odysseys that take the reader back to Puerto Rico and primordial Indian and African music and poetry (*Mainland*, 1973) and across the United States and back to New York, where the poet finds the city transformed by its Caribbean peoples into their very own cultural home (*Tropicalization*, 1976). *By Lingual Wholes* (1982) is a consuming and total exploration of the various linguistic possibilities in the repertoire of a bilingual poet, and *Rhythm, Content and Flavor* (1989) is a summary of his entire career.

Tato Laviera has said in a 1980 interview with the author of this chapter, "I am the grandson of slaves transplanted from Africa to the Caribbean, a man of the New World come to dominate and revitalize two old world languages." And, indeed, Laviera's bilingualism and linguistic inventiveness have risen to the level of virtuosity. Laviera is the inheritor of the Spanish oral tradition, with all of its classical formulas, and the African oral tradition, with its wedding to music and spirituality; in his works he brings both the Spanish and English languages together as well as the islands of Puerto Rico and Manhattan—a constant duality that is always just in the background. His first book, *La Carreta Made a U-Turn* (1979) was published by Arte Público Press, which has become the leading publisher of Nuyorican literature, despite its location in Houston. *La Carreta Made a U-Turn* uses René Marqués's *Oxcart* as a point of departure and redirects back to the heart of New York, instead of back to the island, as Marqués had desired; Laviera is stating that Puerto Rico can be found here too. His second book, *Enclave* (1981) is a celebration of diverse heroic personalities, both real and imagined: Luis Palés Matos and salsa composers, the neighborhood gossip and John Lennon, Miriam Makeba and Tito Madera Smith, the latter being a fictional, hip offspring of a jíbara and a southern American black. *AmeRícan* (1986) and *Mainstream Ethics* (1988) are surveys of the lives of the poor and

Sandra María Esteves, 1979 (Archives, Arte Público Press).

marginalized in the United States and a challenge for the country to live up to its promises of equality and democracy.

One of the few women's voices to be heard in this generation is a very strong and well-defined one, that of Sandra María Esteves, who from her teen years has been very active in the women's struggle, Afro-American liberation, the Puerto Rican independence movement, and, foremost, the performance of poetry. In 1973, she joined El Grupo, a New York-based

Second National Latino Book Fair and Writers Festival, Houston Public Library Plaza, 1980 (Archives, Arte Público Press).

touring collective of musicians, performing artists, and poets and the cultural wing of the Puerto Rican Socialist party. By 1980, she had published her first collection of poetry, *Yerba Buena*, which is a search for identity of a colonized Hispanic woman of color in the United States, the daughter of immigrants from the Caribbean. All three of her books, *Yerba Buena*, *Tropical Rains: A Bilingual Downpour* (1984), and *Mockingbird Bluestown Mambo* (1990), affirm that womanhood is what gives unity to all of the diverse characterizations of her life.

The most productive and recognized Nuyorican novelist is Nicholasa Mohr. Her works, *Nilda* (1973), *El Bronx Remembered* (1975), *In Nueva York* (1977), *Felita* (1979), and *Going Home* (1986) were all published in hardback and paperback by major commercial publishing houses and are all still in print, three of them having been reissued by Arte Público Press. Her books have entered the mainstream as have no other books by Hispanic authors of the United States. They have won such awards as the New York Times Outstanding Book of the Year, the *School Library Journal* Best Children's Book, and many others, including a decree honoring her by the state legislature

of New York. Her best-loved novel, *Nilda*, traces the coming of age of a young Puerto Rican girl in the Bronx during World War II. Unlike many other such novels of development, Nilda gains awareness of the plight of her people and her own individual problems by examining the racial and economic oppression that surrounds her and her family, in a manner that can be compared to Tomás Rivera's central character in . . . *y no se lo tragó la tierra*.

In two of her other books, *In Nueva York* and *El Bronx Remembered*, Mohr examines through a series of stories and novellas various Puerto Rican neighborhoods and draws sustenance from the common folks'' power to survive and still produce art, folklore, and strong families in the face of oppression and marginalization. *Rituals of Survival: A Woman's Portfolio* (1985), in five stories and a novella, portrays six strong women who take control of their lives, most of them by liberating themselves from husbands, fathers, or families that attempt to keep them confined in narrowly defined female roles. *Rituals* is the book that the mainstream houses would not publish, wanting to keep Mohr confined to what they saw as immi-

(L. to R.) Nicholasa Mohr, Publisher Nicolás Kanellos and Ed Vega on the occasion of their reading at the Bookstop in Houston, Texas, in 1985 (Archives, Arte Público Press).

grant literature and children's literature, as in her *Felita* and *Going Home.*

While not banding together with groups and collectives, Mohr has been one of the most influential of the Nuyorican writers out of sheer productivity and accomplishment. She has also led the way to greater acceptance of Nuyorican and Hispanic writers in creative writing workshops, such as the Millay Colony, in Poets, Editors and Novelists (PEN), and on the funding panels of the National Endowment for the Arts and the New York State Council on the Arts.

Another Nuyorican writer who has not participated in nor benefitted from collective work is Judith Ortiz Cofer, who grew up in Paterson, New Jersey, and has lived much of her adult life in Georgia and Florida. Cofer is one of the few Nuyorican products of the creative writing programs, and much of her early poetry was disseminated through establishment small presses in the South that may have been intrigued by the exoticism of her Puerto Rican subjects, packaged in finely crafted verses, with a magic and mystery that is similar to that of Pat Mora's poetry.

Her first book of poems, *Reaching for the Mainland* (1987), is a chronicle of the displaced person's strug-

gle to find a goal, a home, a language, and a history. In *Terms of Survival* (1987), she explores the psychology and social attitudes of the Puerto Rican dialect and how it controls male and female roles; in particular she carries on a dialogue with her father throughout the poems of the book. In 1989, Cofer published a highly reviewed novel of immigration, *Line of the Sun*, through the University of Georgia Press and in 1990 an even more highly reviewed book, made up of a collection of autobiographical essays, in the style of Virginia Wolf, *Silent Dancing: A Remembrance of Growing Up Puerto Rican*, through Arte Público Press.

In 1988, Cofer and five other writers discussed earlier—Nicholas Mohr, Tato Laviera, Rolando Hinojosa, Alberto Ríos, and Lorna Dee Cervantes— were featured reading and performing their works in a historic documentary, *Growing Up Hispanic*, directed by Jesús Treviño, presented on national television by the Corporation for Public Broadcasting. The future of Hispanic literature in the United States promises to be very fruitful, and more and more segments of the population are getting the message.

Cuban-American Literature

As mentioned previously, Cuban culture and literature in the United States dates back to the nineteenth century when writer-philosopher José Martí and other patriots plotted from the U.S. mainland for Cuban independence from Spain. During the first half of the twentieth century, Cubans and Spaniards dominated Hispanic arts and media in New York. While Cuban culture was on the ascendancy in New York, its island literature had already joined that of Mexico and Argentina in the leadership of Spanish American letters since the nineteenth century, with such internationally acknowledged masters as Gertrudis Gómez de Avellaneda, José Echeverría, Julián del Casal, and José Martí, and in the twentieth century with such leaders as patriarch Nicolás Guillén, who has taken Spanish American poetry from a markedly Afro-Caribbean to a Pan Hispanic vision in support of universal socialist revolution. Cuban writers who have contributed to the Latin American literary boom include Alejo Carpentier, José Lezama Lima, and Gabriel Cabrera Infante.

It is no wonder then that the inheritors of such a rich and dynamic tradition would contribute so greatly to Hispanic culture in the United States, especially given the fact that their mass immigration took place so recently, beginning in 1959 as refugees from the Cuban Revolution. In contrast, whereas Puerto Rican mass migration really had begun during World War II, when the American economy drew heavily on its island territory for workers, the Cubans came as political refugees from a land that had never been a colony of the United States, although it had been a protectorate and an economic dependent since the Spanish-American War. Most of the Puerto Ricans had come as workers and generally did not have the level of education nor the financial resources and relocation services that the Cubans did. This first mass of Cubans came with an outstanding written tradition well intact. And the Cuban literary aesthetic, unlike the Puerto Rican one, had never been so obsessed with protecting the Spanish language and Hispanic culture while defending itself against Anglo-American culture and language. Numerous writers and intellectuals immigrated to the United States as refugees; many of them were able to adapt to and become part of the U.S. Hispanic and mainstream cultural institutions.

Today, after three decades of new Cuban culture in New York, New Jersey, Miami, and dispersed throughout the United States—in contrast to the older Cuban communities in New York City and Tampa—a Cuban-American literary and artistic presence has developed. Younger writers are no longer preoccupied with exile, with eyes cast only on the island past; instead they are looking forward to participating in the English-language mainstream or serving the intellectual and cultural needs of the U.S. Cuban and Hispanic communities. Thus there has developed a definite separation of purpose and aesthetics between the younger writers—Roberto Fernández, Iván Acosta, Virgil Suárez, and Oscar Hijuelos, for instance—and the older writers of exile—Lydia Cabrera, Matías Montes Huidobro, José Sánchez Boudy, and so on. Also, there continues to be an influx of exiled writers, disaffected with Cuban communism, like Heberto Padilla, who must be viewed differently from the earlier generation of exiles who have already created for themselves a solid niche within Hispanic and mainstream institutions such as publishing houses and universities.

What we have seen during the last decades is first a literature that almost exclusively attacked the Cuban Revolution and Marxism. The novel of exile became another weapon in the struggle. Following the first antirevolutionary novel, *Enterrado vivo* (*Buried Alive*), published in Mexico in 1960 by Andrés Rivero Collado, were a host of others published in the United States and abroad by minor writers, such as Emilio Fernández Camus, Orlando Núñez, Manuel Cobo Souza, Raúl A. Fowler, Luis Ricardo Alonso, and many others. When they were not openly propagandistic and rhetorical, they were nostalgic for the homeland to the point of idealization. Poetry and drama followed the same course, for the most part. Later, political verse would come to form a special genre of its own, what has been called by critic Hortensia Ruiz del Viso "poesía del presidio político" (political prisoner poetry), as in the works of Angel Cuadra, Heberto Padilla, and Armando Valladares, who resides in Spain but is quite active in the United States.

A key figure in providing a new direction for Cuban literature in the United States has been

Virgil Suárez, 1991 (Archives, Arte Público Press).

José Sánchez-Boudy.

Celedonio González, who, beginning with *Los primos* (1971, *The Cousins*), changed his focus to concentrate on Cuban life and culture in the United States. Later, in *Los cuatro embajadores* (1973, *The Four Ambassadors*) and *El espesor del pellejo de un gato ya cadáver* (1978, *The Thickness of the Skin on a Cat Already a Corpse*), he not only examined culture shock and conflict between Cubans and Americans, but he also treated a very taboo topic: criticism of the economic system of the United States, especially in its exploitation of Cuban workers. González presents us with Cubans who do not yet see themselves as Americans but who are also conscious that Cuba is no longer theirs.

Ironically, one of the most important writers in forging a Cuban-American literature and in breaking new ground in his use of the English language is a professor of Spanish, Roberto Fernández. Through his novels, Fernández not only touches upon all the taboo subjects in the Cuban community of Miami— the counterrevolutionary movement in the United States, racism, acculturation, and assimilation—but also helps the community to take them in a less serious vein and to laugh at itself. In his two open-form mosaiclike novels, *La vida es un special* (1982,

Life Is on Special) and *La montaña rusa* (1985, *The Roller Coaster*), Fernández presents a biting but loving satire of a community transformed by the materialism and popular culture of the United States, but somewhat paralyzed by the nostalgia and political obsession with a Communist Cuba. In 1988, Fernández continued the community saga in English, with the publication of *Raining Backwards*, which has become his most known and highly regarded novel. Here as in his other works, the hilarious parade of characters, language styles—with quite a bit of bilingual humor—and diverse social events are aimed at encouraging the community to take stock of its present circumstances and reckon with a future here in the United States.

One of the most influential literary magazines of Cuban literature in the United States has been *Linden Lane*, which is published in Spanish. Published by writer Heberto Padilla and edited by poet Belkis Cuza Malé, who is a professor at Princeton University, the magazine has created a forum for the whole Cuban writing community, both the generation of exile and the new Cuban-American generation. In 1990, the magazine formally announced the advent of a Cuban-American literature with its publication of an anthology containing works in both English and Spanish and entitled *Los atrevidos: Cuban American Literature*, edited by Miami poet Carolina Hospital, also an editor of *Linden Lane*. In 1991, Arte Público Press published an anthology that also proclaimed a Cuban-American identity, *Cuban American Theater*, edited by critic Rodolfo Cortina. Both collections draw upon writers dispersed throughout the United States, not just from the Miami and New York communities.

Among the new generation of Cuban-American writers growing up in the United States, there are a few who have gone through creative writing programs at universities and who thus have had access to mainstream publishing opportunities. A graduate of the important writing program at Louisiana State University, Virgil Suárez has had two novels published, *Latin Jazz* (1989) by Morrow and *The Cutter* (1991) by Ballantine Books. His third book, a very fine collection of short stories, *Welcome to the Oasis*, was not accepted by commercial publishers who prefer novels; it was published in 1991 by Arte Público Press. *Latin Jazz* is a somewhat different type of ethnic biographical novel, portraying a whole Cuban family, instead of just one individual; in alternate chapters devoted to each of the family members, Suárez provides their respective histories, hopes, and desires as they wait for a missing family member to arrive in Miami with the Mariel boat-lift.

Probably the most important of the Cuban-American writers to come out of the creative writing schools is Oscar Hijuelos, who is not the son of refugees from the Cuban Revolution, but of earlier immigrants to New York. Nevertheless, Hijuelos's first offering, *Our House in the Last World* (1983), is a typical ethnic autobiography and may be seen as a symbol of Cuban assimilation in that it is one of the few novels that negatively portray the island culture, as personified by an alcoholic and machistic father, while it develops the tried-and-true theme of the American dream in the United States. His novel *The Mambo Kings Play Songs of Love* (1990) made history; it is the first novel by a Hispanic writer of the United States to win the Pulitzer Prize. It is also the first time that a major publishing house, Simon and Shuster, has ever invested heavily in a novel by a Hispanic writer, bringing it out at the top of its list and promoting the book very heavily. *The Mambo Kings* is the story of two musician brothers during the heyday of the mambo and during the time when at least one Cuban had captured the attention of the United States: Desi Arnaz on the "I Love Lucy" show. The novel thus has a historical background that lends it a very rich texture; it allows us to see a portion of American popular culture history through the eyes of two performers very wrapped up in the euphoria of the times and then the waning of interest in things Latin in the United States. The story of the tragic ending of the duo is very touching, but offers hope for the potential of Hispanic culture to influence the mainstream. In fact, Hijuelo's book and the recognition that it has won offer the hope of opening the door to mainstream publishing for other U.S. Hispanic writers.

✳OUTSTANDING HISPANIC LITERARY FIGURES

Miguel Algarín (1941-)

A native of Santurce, Puerto Rico, Miguel Algarín grew up in a hardworking family that loved music and the arts and gave to their children an early appreciation of opera and classical music; Miguel's father taught him to play the violin. The Algaríns moved to New York City in the early 1950s and settled in Spanish Harlem for a while, and then moved to Queens. Miguel Alagarín began his higher education at City College and finished his B.A. degree at the University of Wisconsin in 1963; in 1965, he graduated with a master's degree in English from the Pennsylvania State University. After teaching English literature at Brooklyn College and New York University for a time, Algarín went on to teach at Rutgers, where he is an associate professor in the English department.

Miguel Algarín is the founder and proprietor of the Puerto Rican Poets'' Café, which is dedicated to the support of writers performing their art orally. It was especially important as a gathering place of young writers during the early 1970s when Nuyorican literature was being defined. Algarín played an important leadership role in that definition by also compiling, with Miguel Piñero, an important anthology, *Nuyorican Poetry: An Anthology of Puerto Rican Words and Feelings* (1975). He also founded a short-lived publishing house, the Nuyroican Press, which only issued one book, his own *Mongo Affair* (1978). One year later, he took part in the launching of Arte Público Press, which became the leading publisher of Nuyorican literature.

Algarín has written plays, screenplays, and short stories, but is principally known as a poet. His books include *Mongo Affair, On Call* (1980), *Body Bee Calling from the 21st Century* (1982), and *Time's Now/Ya es tiempo* (1985). Algarín's poetry runs the gamut from jazz-salsa poetry to the mystical and avant-garde. He is one of the foremost experimenters with English-Spanish bilingualism and has even penned trilingual

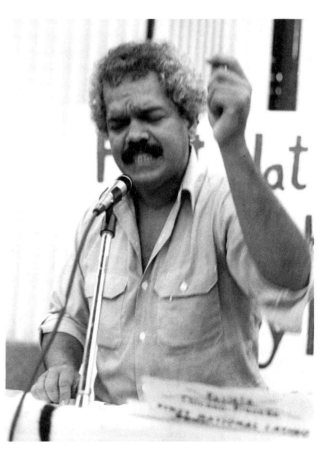

Miguel Algarín reciting his poetry at the First National Latino Book Fair, Chicago, 1979 (Archives, Arte Público Press).

works that incorporate the French language. In 1976, Algarín published translations of the poetry of Chilean Nobel Prize winner Pablo Neruda, under the title *Canción de gesta/A Song of Protest.*

Iván Acosta

See Chapter 19

Alurista (Alberto Baltazar Urista) (1947-)

Alurista is considered one of the pioneers of Chicano literature. He was one of the first poets to support the Chicano movement through his poetry, a writer and signer of important manifestoes of the movement, a founder of the Moviemiento Estudiantil de Aztlán (MECHA, Chicano Student Movement of Aztlán) in 1967, and one of the first to establish the concept of Aztlán in literature, which forecasts a return to the glories of Aztec civilization by the Chicanos in the mythic homeland of the Aztecs, what is today roughly the five states of the Southwest.

Born in Mexico City on August 8, 1947, Alberto Baltazar Urista spent his early years in the states of Morelos and Guerrero. At age 13 he immigrated to the United States with his family, which settled in San Diego, California. He began writing poetry at an early age and was a restless and widely-read student. He began Chapman College in 1965 and transferred to and graduated from San Diego State University in 1970 with a B.A. degree in psychology. He later obtained an M.A. degree from that institution and a Ph.D. degree in literature from the University of California, San Diego, in 1983. Around 1966, he began writing poetry seriously for publication and assumed the pen name Alurista, which is virtually the only name he uses now.

Alurista is a consummate reader and performer of his poetry, which has led to many travels to fulfill invitations nationally and internationally to read his works. He was the founder and coeditor, with his wife, Xelina, of the literary magazine *Maize* and the publishing house associated with it; both ceased to exist after he began his present employment as professor of Spanish at California State University, San Luis Obispo, in 1987. Alurista is a prolific and talented poet, a pioneer of bilingualism in Chicano poetry. Throughout his career his study of the Nahuatl and Mayan languages and mythology have enriched his poetic works and inspired his promotion of the ideology of Aztlán. But it is his bilingualism that has opened new frontiers in poetry, with his free experimentation in combining the sounds, meanings, and graphic representations of Spanish and English in the same poem, quite often achieving surprising and beautiful effects.

Alurista has published the following books of po-

Alurista, 1980 (Archives, Arte Público Press).

etry: *Floricanto en Aztlán* (1971), *Nationchild Plumaroja, 1967-1972* (1972), *Timespace Huracán: Poems, 1972-1975* (1976), *A'nque* (1979), *Spik in Glyph?* (1981), and *Return: Poems Collected and New* (1982).

Rudolfo A. Anaya (1937-)

Rudolfo A. Anaya was born in the village of Pastura, New Mexico, in surroundings similar to those celebrated in his famous novel about growing up in the rural culture of new Mexico: *Bless Me, Ultima.* He attended public schools in Santa Rosa and Albuquerque and earned both his B.A. (1963) and his M.A. (1968) degrees in English from the University of New Mexico. In 1972, he also earned an M.A. degree in guidance and counseling from the same university. From 1963 to 1970, he taught in the public schools, but in 1974 he became a member of the English department of the University of New Mexico. With the success of his writing career, Anaya has risen to become the head of the creative writing program at the University of New Mexico. Included among his many awards are the following: an honorary doctorate from the University of Albuquerque, the New Mexico Governor's Award for Excellence, the President's National Salute to American Poets and Writers in 1980, and the Premio Quinto Sol in 1972 for his novel *Bless Me Ultima*. Anaya is also a fellow of the National Endowment for the Arts and the Kellogg Foundation through whose auspices he has been able to travel to China and other countries for study.

Anaya is very much a believer and promoter of a return to pre-Columbian literature and thought through the reflowering of Aztec civilization in Aztlán, the mythic homeland of the Aztecs, which corresponds to the five states of today's Southwest. He sees his role in literature as that of the shaman; his task as a storyteller is to heal and reestablish balance and harmony. These ideas are present throughout his works, but are most successfully represented in his prize-winning novel *Bless Me, Ultima*, in which the folk healer Ultima works to reestablish harmony and social order in the life of the Mares family and to bring psychological well-being to Antonio, the protagonist, who is struggling to understand the roles of good and evil in life. Anaya's other books are *Heart of Aztlán* (1976), *Tortuga* (1979), *The Silence of the Llano* (1982), *The Legend of La Llorona* (1984), *The Adventures of Juan Chicaspatas* (1985), *A Chicano in China* (1986), *The Farolitas of Christmas* (1987), *Lord of the Dawn: The Legend of Quetzalcoatl* (1987). He is also the author of plays and screenplays and has coedited three literary anthologies: with Simon Ortiz, *Ceremony of Brotherhood, 1680-1980* (1980); with José Griego y Maestas, *Cuentos: Tales from the Hispanic Southwest* (1980); and with Antonio Márquez, *Cuentos Chicanos* (1980, *Chicano Stories*).

Angélico Chávez (1910-)

Fray Angélico Chávez is one of the most renowned religious poets in the United States. The author of some nineteen books, Chávez is also a historian of his order, the Franciscan brothers, and of the Catholic church in New Mexico. Born on April 10, 1910, in Wagon Mound, New Mexico, he was named Manuel Chávez by his parents. Chávez was raised in Mora and attended St. Francis Seminary in Cincinnati, Ohio, and colleges in the Midwest. In 1937, he became the first New Mexican to become a Franciscan friar. From the time of his ordination at age 27 until age 62, he served as a pastor in several towns and Indian pueblos of New Mexico.

What unifies Chávez's large output as a poet and historian is his interest in New Mexico's past, the work of his order in New Mexico, and his own Catholicism. Beginning as essentially a religious poet, he later took an interest in historical fiction and, finally, in the history of the region itself, as in his most famous historical essay, *My Penitente Land: Reflections on Spanish New Mexico* (1974). Other historical writings by Chávez also were intended to provide an accurate understanding of Hispanic New Mexico; these include *Our Lady of the Conquest* (1948), *Origins of New Mexico Families in the Spanish Colonial Period* (1954), *Coronado's Friars* (1968), *But Time and Chance: The Story of Padre Martínez of Taos, 1793-1867* (1981), and other edited books.

His works of historical fiction include *New Mexico Triptych: Being Three Panels and Three Accounts: 1. The Angel's New Wing, 2. The Penitente Thief, 3. Hunchback Madonna* (1940), *La Conquistadora: The Autobiography of an Ancient Statue* (1954), *From an Altar Screen/ El retablo: Tales from New Mexico* (1957), and *The Lady from Toledo* (1960).

Chávez's reputation as a creative writer rests upon an important body of poetic works that include *Clothed with the Sun* (1939), *Eleven Lady Lyrics, and Other Poems* (1945), *The Single Rose; the Rose Unica and Commentary of Fray Manuel de Santa Clara* (1948), and *The Virgin of Port Lligat* (1959). Although Chávez's poetry and all of his works are grounded in New Mexico Catholicism, his poems are not local-color pieces celebrating New Mexico's picturesque landscape; instead they depict Chávez's inner life. In *The Single Rose*, Chávez was so intent on communicating the poems'' inner religious meaning that he included commentary in the book, which studies the rose as an allegorical figure for human and divine love. Chávez's last poetry collection was *Selected Poems, With an Apologia* (1969), which brought together some of his most successful poems along with an apologia that announced that he would no longer publish poetry, due to changing fashions in poetry and his loss of excitement in writing verse.

Denise Chávez (1948-)

Denise Chávez is a novelist, playwright, and poet who, through her writings, has brought to life entire populations of memorable characters of the Southwest, both Mexican-American and Anglo-American. Born on August 15, 1948, in Las Cruces, New Mexico, Chávez was raised principally by her mother, Delfina, a teacher, because her father had abandoned the family while she was still young. After attending schools and colleges in Las Cruces, Chávez obtained a master's degree in theater arts from Trinity University in San Antonio, Texas, in 1974, and a master's degree in creative writing from the University of New Mexico in Albuquerque in 1984. During her career she has taught and been a writer in residence at numerous institutions in New Mexico and elsewhere. In 1988, she became a professor in the drama department of the University of Houston.

Denise Chávez has won numerous awards and fellowships, including Best Play award for *The Wait* from New Mexico State University in 1970, the Steele Jones Fiction Award in 1986 for her story "The Last of the Menu Girls," two fellowships from the National Endowment for the Arts in 1981 and 1982, a Rockefeller Foundation Fellowship in 1984, and the Creative Writing Arts Fellowship from the Cultural Arts Council of Houston in 1990.

As a playwright, Chávez has written and seen produced numerous unpublished plays, including *Novitiates* (1971), *Elevators* (1972), *The Mask of November* (1977), *Nacimiento* (1979, *Birth*), *Santa Fe Charm* (1980), *Sí, Hay Posada* (1980, *Yes, There Is Room*), *El Santero de Córdova* (1981, *The Saintmaker of Córdova*), *Hecho en México* (1982, *Made in Mexico*) (with Nita Luna) *The Green Madonna* (1982), *La Morenita* (1983, *The Little Brown Girl*), *Francis!* (1983), *How Junior Got Throwed in the Joint* (1981), *Plaza* (1984), *Novena Narrativa* (1986, *A Narrative Novena*), *The Step* (1987), *Language of Vision* (1987), and *The Last of the Menu Girls* (1990). She has also seen three of her children's plays produced on stage: *The Adobe Rabbit* (1979), *El Más Pequeño de Mis Hijos* (1983, *The Smallest of My Children*), and *The Flying Tortilla Man* (1975), which was also published

Denise Chávez, 1989 (Photo by Georgia McInnis. Archives, Arte Público Press).

in a high school textbook, *Mexican American Literature*, edited by Charles Tatum (1990). Chávez has also edited an anthology of plays, *Plays by Hispanic Women of the United States* (1991).

Despite Chávez's high productivity as a playwright, it is her published works of fiction that have contributed most to her national reputation. Chávez has published short stories in magazines and has two novels in print, *The Last of the Menu Girls* (1986) and *Face of an Angel* (1993). The first of these is a series of stories centering on the coming of age of Rocío Esquivel that come together to form a novel. As Rocío compares her own life to that of her mother and as she encounters a wide range of characters in her neighborhood and at work, she begins to formulate her own identity. By the end of the book, we realize that we have been participating in the making of a novelist, and that what we have been reading is the product of Rocío's creative and psychological exploration. While still centering on the life of a female central character and her development, *Face of an Angel* is completely different from her first novel. It is unrestrained, bawdy, irreverent, and hilariously funny as it explores some of the major themes of the women's liberation movement as represented in the life of a waitress, who is an author in her own right (of a manual on waitressing, which is included in the novel). Soveida Dosamantes, it seems, is one of those people who are destined to repeat over and over the same mistakes in their choice of a male partner. The novel thus consists of her experiences with a number of lazy, good-for-nothing men who are irresistible to her. But *Face of an Angel* is also populated with a host of other humorous and tragic figures that represent a cross section of life in the Southwest.

Lorna Dee Cervantes (1954–)

Of Mexican and Amerindian ancestry, Lorna Dee Cervantes was born into a very economically deprived family, but she discovered the world of books at a very early age. Born on August 6, 1954, in the Mission District of San Francisco, at age 5 she moved with her mother and brother to San Jose to live with her grandmother when her parents separated. Lorna began writing poetry when she was six years old; poems written when she was fourteen were eventually published in a magazine after Cervantes had established her career as a writer. Cervantes later attended college, but did not finish her B.A. degree from California State University until after she had initiated her writing career; in 1990 she obtained a Ph.D. degree from the University of California, Santa Cruz, where she studied philosophy and aesthetics. She then went on to teach creative writing at the University of Colorado in Denver.

Lorna Dee Cervantes, 1990 (Photo by Georgia McInnis. Archives, Arte Público Press).

Emplumada (1981, *Plumed*), Cervantes's first collection of poems, is made up of works published in literary magazines throughout the Southwest. The book's popularity has made it the best-selling title in the University of Pittsburgh's prestigious poetry series. *Emplumada* presents a young woman coming of age, discovering the gap that exists in life between one's hopes and desires and what life eventually offers in reality. The predominant themes include culture conflict, oppression of women and minorities, and alienation from one's roots. Cervantes's poetry is very well crafted and has the distinction of using highly lyrical language while at the same time being direct and powerful. The same can be said of her second book, *From the Cables of Genocide*, which is very much the work of a mature poet dealing with the great themes of life, death, social conflict, and poverty.

Judith Ortiz Cofer (1952-)

Judith Ortiz was born in Puerto Rico in 1952 into a family that was destined to move back and forth between Puerto Rico and Paterson, New Jersey. Her father, Jesús Ortiz Lugo, was a navy man, first as-

signed to the Brooklyn Navy Yard and then other points around the world. In Puertro Rico, the young Judith attended San José Catholic School in San Germán, and in Paterson she went to public schools at first and then to Saint Joseph's Catholic School. In 1968, after her father had retired from the navy with a nervous breakdown, the family moved to Augusta, Georgia, where she attended high school and Augusta College. She met John Cofer at the college and they were married. After graduation and the birth of her daughter, they moved to West Palm Beach, Florida, and she earned an M.A. degree at Florida Alantic University. She was also awarded a scholarship to do graduate work at Oxford University by the English-Speaking Union of America. Included among many other awards were fellowships from the Florida Arts Council (1980), the Bread Loaf Writers Conference (1981), and the National Endowment for the Arts (1989).

While teaching English in south Florida colleges, Ortiz Cofer began writing poetry, and her works were soon appearing in such magazines as the *New Mexico Humanities Review*, *Kansas Quarterly*, *Prairie Schooner*, *Revista Chicano-Riqueña*, *Southern Humanities Review*, *Southern Poetry Review*, and elsewhere. Her collections of poetry include four chapbooks—*Latin Women Pray* (1980), *Among the Ancestors* (1981), *The Native Dancer* (1981), *Peregrina* (1986)—and two full-length books—*Reaching for the Mainland* (1987) and *Terms of Survival* (1987). Her well-crafted poetry reflects her struggle as a writer to create a history for herself out of the cultural ambiguity of a childhood spent traveling back and forth between the United States and Puerto Rico. Through her poetry she also explores from a feminist perspective her relationship with her father, mother, and grandmother, while also considering the different expectations for the males and females in Anglo-American and Hispanic cultures. In particular, her

Judith Ortiz Cofer, 1989 (Archives, Arte Público Press).

book of autobiographical essays, *Silent Dancing: A Remembrance of a Puerto Rican Childhood* (1990), pursues this question. Her novel *The Line of the Sun* (1990) is based on her family's gradual immigration to the United States and chronicles the years from the Great Depression to the 1960s.

Jesús Colón (1901-74)

Jesús Colón's writings are considered to be landmarks in the development of Puerto Rican literature in the continental United States because he is one of the first writers to become well known through his use of English, because of his identification with the working class, and because of his ideas on race. These three factors in the essays that he was already writing in the 1940s and 1950s make him a clear forerunner of the Nuyorican writers who began to appear two decades later.

Colón was born into a working-class family in Cayey, Puerto Rico. At age 16, he stowed away on a ship that landed in Brooklyn. In New York, he worked in a series of jobs that exposed him to the exploitation and abuse of lower-class and unskilled workers. He became involved in literary and journalistic endeavors while working as a laborer, trying to establish a newspaper and writing translations of English-language poetry. As he strived to develop his literary and journalistic career, he encountered racial prejudice, mainly because of his skin color, for Colón was of Afro-Puerto Rican heritage. Despite discrimination, Colón became active in community and political activities. He became a columnist for the *Daily Worker*, the publication of the national office of the Communist party, as an outgrowth of these activities and his literary interests. Colón also founded and operated a publishing house, Hispanic Publishers (Editorial Hispánica), which published history and literary books, as well as political information in Spanish. In 1952 and 1969, he ran for public office on the Communist party ticket, but was unsuccessful.

A selection of Colón's newspaper columns and essays was collected and published in 1961 in book form under the title *A Puerto Rican in New York and Other Sketches*. In this work, Colón's major themes are (1) the creation and development of a political consciousness, (2) his own literary development and worth, (3) advocacy for the working-class poor, and (4) the injustices of capitalist society in which racial and class discrimination is all too frequent and individual worth does not seem to exist. The collection as a whole is richly expressive of a socially conscious and humanistic point of view.

Victor Hernández Cruz, 1980 (Archives, Arte Público Press).

Victor Hernández Cruz (1949-)

Victor Hernández Cruz is the Nuyorican poet most recognized and acclaimed by the mainstream. Born on February 6, 1949, in Aguas Buenas, Puerto Rico, he moved with his family to New York's Spanish Harlem at age 5. Cruz attended Benjamin Franklin High School, where he began writing poetry. In the years following graduation, his poetry began to appear in

Evergreen Review, New York Review of Books, Ramparts, Down Here, and in small magazines. In 1973, Cruz left New York and took up residence in San Francisco, where he worked for the U.S. Postal Service. In 1989, he moved back to Puerto Rico, where he currently resides.

Victor Hernández Cruz's poetry books include *Papo Got His Gun* (1966), *Snaps* (1969), *Mainland* (1973), *Tropicalization* (1976), *By Lingual Wholes* (1982), and *Rhythm, Content and Flavor* (1989). Classifying his poetry as Afro-Latin, Cruz has developed as a consummate bilingual poet and experimenter who consistently explores the relationship of music to poetry in a multiracial, multicultural context. Cruz has often been considered a jazz poet or an Afro-American poet. The April 1981 issue of *Life* magazine included Cruz among a handful of outstanding American poets.

Abelardo Delgado (1931-)

Abelardo "Lalo" Delgado is one of the most renowned and prolific Chicano poets, a pioneer of bilingualism in Hispanic poetry and a consummate oral performer of his works. Delgado was born in the small town of La Boquilla de Conchos in northern

Abelardo Delgado, 1979 (Archives, Arte Público Press).

Mexico on November 27, 1931. At age 12 he and his mother immigrated to El Paso, Texas. In El Paso, he lived in a poor Mexican barrio until 1969. Despite early problems in school with the English language, Delgado excelled as a student, and by graduation in 1950 from Bowie High School, he had become vice president of the National Honor Society chapter there. He went on to college while working at a variety of jobs and graduated from the University of Texas, El Paso, in 1962. Since that time he has earned his living as a counselor for migrant workers and as a teacher in Texas and later in Colorado. During the late 1960s and throughout most of the 1970s, Delgado was also one of the most popular speakers and poetry readers in the Southwest, which translated into a life of frequent tours and engagements. This was the height of the Chicano movement, and Delgado was one of its most celebrated animators and poet laureates.

Besides writing numerous poems, essays, and stories that have been published in literary magazines and anthologies nationwide, Delgado is the author of some fourteen books and chapbooks; many of these were published through his own small printing operation known as Barrio Press. Delgado's first book, *Chicano: 25 Pieces of a Chicano Mind* (1969), is his best known, containing many of the poems that were performed personally in the heat of the protest movement and that subsequently received widespread distribution through small community newspapers and hand-to-hand circulation throughout the Southwest. Poems such as his "Stupid America" not only embodied the values of life in the barrio but also called for the types of social reform that became anthems for the Chicano movement. Other noteworthy titles include *It's Cold: 52 Cold-Thought Poems of Abelardo* (1974), *Here Lies Lalo: 25 Deaths of Abelardo* (1979), and his book of essays, *Letters to Louise* (1982), which ponder the feminist movement and the social roles of women and men and was awarded the Premio Quinto Sol, the national award for Chicano literature. In all, Delgado is a remarkably agile bilingual poet, an outstanding satirist and humorist, an undaunted and militant protester and pacifist, and a warmhearted and loving narrator and chronicler of the life and tradition of his people.

Roberto Fernández (1951-)

Roberto Fernández is in the vanguard of Cuban-American literature, having made the transition from the literature of exile to a literature very much of the culture and social conditions of Cubans in the United States, and having made the transition from producing works in Spanish to writing in English. Born in Sagua la Grande, Cuba, on September 24,

Roberto Fernández, 1989 (Archives, Arte Público Press).

1951, just eight years before the Cuban Revolution, he went into exile with his family at age 11. His family settled in southern Florida, not in the Cuban community of Miami but in areas where Anglo-American culture was dominant. This led to periods of adjustment to what seemed like a hostile environment to the young boy, an impression that accounts for some of the culture conflict that is narrated in his writings. The Fernández family nevertheless maintained close ties with the Miami community, and this too became subject matter for the writer. Fernández became interested in writing as an adolescent, and this interest led him to college and graduate school. In 1978, he completed a Ph.D. degree in linguistics at Florida State University; by that time he had already published two collections of stories, *Cuentos sin rumbo* (1975, *Directionless Tales*) and *El jardín de la luna* (1976, *The Garden of the Moon*). At this point he also began his career as an academic, teaching linguistics and Hispanic literature at Florida State University in Tallahassee.

Roberto Fernández is the author of three open-formed novels that have created for him the reputation of being a satirist and humorist of the Miami Cuban community. In all three, he is also a master at capturing the nuances of Cuban dialect in Spanish and English. *La vida es un special* (1982, *Life Is on Special*), *La montaña rusa* (1985, *The Roller Coaster*), and *Raining Backwards* (1988) are all mosaics made up of monologues, dialogues, letters, phone conversations, speeches, and other types of oral performance that, in the composite, make up a continuing tale of the development of the exile community and its younger generations of increasingly acculturated Cuban Americans. Through the pages of these books the author charts the goings-on at social clubs and coming-out parties, follows counterrevolutionary guerrilla movements in the Florida swamps and the emergence of a Cuban pope, plots a mystery novel, discusses a poetry and art contest, and gives many other episodic bits and pieces that create a broad and epic spectrum of a dynamic community caught between two cultures, two sets of values, two languages, and two political systems. *Raining Backwards*, Fernández's first book to be published in English, became somewhat of a small press hit, receiving outstanding reviews from coast to coast in major newspapers and magazines (*The New York Times, USA Today, San Francisco Chronicle,* to name a few), and was optioned to become a feature film.

Lionel G. García (1935-)

Lionel G. García is a novelist who has created some of the most memorable characters in Chicano literature in a style that is well steeped in the traditions of Texas tall-tale and Mexican-American folk narrative. Born in San Diego, Texas, in 1935, García grew up in an environment in which Mexican Americans were the majority population in his small town and on the ranches where he worked and played. His father was a paint-and-body man and his mother was a teacher, so García lived a middle-class background; he did so well in school that he was one of the very few Mexican Americans admitted to Texas A&M University, where he majored in biology, but was also encouraged by one of his English professors to write. After graduating he attempted to become a full-time writer but was unsuccessful in getting his works published. He served in the army, and after being discharged honorably, he returned to Texas A&M and graduated from that institution in 1969 as a doctor of veterinary science. Since then he has developed a successful career as a veterinarian.

Throughout this time he has continued to write. In the early 1980s, he once again attempted to publish, and he found that there were many more opportunities at hand. In 1983, he won the PEN Southwest Discovery Award for his novel in progress, *Leaving Home*, which was published in 1985. This and his second novel, *A Shroud in the Family* (1987), draw

Lionel G. García, 1989 (Archives, Arte Público Press).

heavily on his family experiences and small-town background. In part, *A Shroud in the Family* also demythologizes the "great" Texas heroes, such as Sam Houston and Jim Bowie, who have become symbols of Anglo-Texans" defeat of and superiority over Mexicans; this was García's contribution to the Texas sesquicentennial celebrations. His novel *Hardscrub* (1989) is a departure from his former works; it is a realistically drawn chronicle of the life of an Anglo child in an abusive family relationship. García has also published short stories in magazines, newspapers, and anthologies.

Celedonio González (1923-)

Celedonio Gonzalez has been known as "el cronista de la diáspora" (the chronicler of the Cuban diaspora or flight from Cuba). Of all of the Cuban exile novelists, he is the one who has turned his attention most to the trials, tribulations, and successes of the Cuban refugees and their children in the United States. Born on September 9, 1923, in the small town of La Esperanza in central Cuba, González began his education in the neighboring city of Santa Clara at a Catholic school and later graduated from a Protestant high school in the city of Cárdenas. Upon returning to La Esperanza he began working in his family's farming enterprises, which he eventually came to manage. He was a supporter of progressive causes and of Castro's revolution, but by 1960 he had become disillusioned with the revolution and was imprisoned for two months as a counterrevolutionary. Upon release, he immigrated to the United States with his wife and children. In Miami he eked out a living at a number of odd jobs. In 1965, he and his family resettled in Chicago in search of a better living.

It was there that he began writing, but it was not until his return to Miami at age 41 that he wrote his first successful novel, *Los primos* (1971, *The Cousins*), a mirror of Cuban life in Miami during the 1960s. The same year, his short stories depicting the loneliness of Cuban exile life in the United States, *La soledad es una amiga que vendrá* (*Solitude Is a Friend Who Will Come*), were published in book form. His novel *Los cuatro embajadores* (1973, *The Four Ambassadors*) criticizes American capitalism and the dehumanization in American life. His greatest work to date is his *El espesor del pellejo de un gato ya cadáver* (1978, *The Thickness of Skin of a Dead Cat*), a call for Cubans to give up their dreams of returning to the island of their birth and to make the best of life in the United States. González's short stories also deal with life in the United States from the vantage point, quite often, of the Cuban laboring classes and small-scale shopkeepers.

Oscar Hijuelos (1951-)

Oscar Hijuelos is the first Hispanic writer to win the Pulitzer Prize for Fiction (1990). Born on August 24, 1951, to Cuban-American working-class parents in New York City, Hijuelos was educated in public schools and obtained a B.A. degree in 1975 and an M.A. degree in 1976, both in English, from City College of the City University of New York. While at City College he studied creative writing with and was guided by the noted novelist Donald Barthelme. Hijuelos is one of the few Hispanic writers to have formally studied creative writing and to have broken into the Anglo-dominated creative writing circles, participating in prestigious workshops such as the Breadloaf Writers Conference and benefiting from highly competitive fellowships, such as the American Academy in Rome Fellowship from the American Academy and the Institute for Arts and Letters (1985), the National Endowment for the Arts Fellowship (1985), and the Guggenheim Fellowship (1990).

Hijuelos is the author of various short stories and two novels, *Our House in the Last World* (1983) and *The Mambo Kings Play Songs of Love* (1989), the latter winning the Pulitzer Prize. His first novel follows in the tradition of ethnic autobiography and the novel of immigration, as it chronicles the life and maladjustment of a Cuban immigrant family in the United States during the 1940s. *The Mambo Kings Play Songs of Love*, more than just a story of immigration, examines a period in time when Hispanic culture was highly visible in the United States and was able to influence American popular culture: the 1950s during the height of the mambo craze and the overwhelming success of Desi Arnaz's television show, "I Love Lucy." Written in a poetic but almost documentary style, the novel follows two brothers who are musicians trying to ride the crest of the Latin music wave. While providing a picture of one segment of American life never seen before in English-language fiction, the novel also indicts, as does *Our House in the Last World*, womanizing and alcoholism as particularly Cuban flaws.

Rolando Hinojosa (1929-)

Rolando Hinojosa is the most prolific and bilingual of the Hispanic novelists of the United States. Not only has he created memorable Mexican-American and Anglo characters, but he has completely populated a fictional county in the lower Rio Grande Valley of Texas through his continuing generational narrative that he calls the Klail City Death Trip Series.

Born in Mercedes, Texas, on January 21, 1929, to a Mexican-American father and a bilingual Anglo-American mother, his paternal ancestors arrived in the lower Rio Grande Valley in 1749 as part of the José Escandón expedition. Hinojosa was educated at first in Mexican schools in Mercedes and later in the segregated public schools of the area where all his classmates were Mexican Americans. He only began integrated classes in junior high. It was in high school that Hinojosa began to write, with his first pieces in English published in an annual literary magazine, *Creative Bits*. Hinojosa left the valley in 1946 when he graduated from college, but the language, culture, and history of the area form the substance of all his novels. The ensuing years saw a stretch in the army, studies at the University of Texas, reactivation into the army to fight in the Korean War (an experience that informs his poetic narrative *Korean Love Songs*), graduation form the University of Texas in 1954 with a degree in Spanish, and back to Brownsville as a teacher, among a variety of other jobs, and finally on to graduate school. In 1969 he obtained his Ph.D. degree in Spanish from the University of Illinois and returned to teach at Texas colleges. Hinojosa has remained in academia in a variety of positions at several universities; today he serves as Ellen Clayton Garwood Professor of English and Creative Writing at the University of Texas.

Although he has continued writing throughout his life, Rolando Hinojosa did not publish a book until his *Estampas del Valle y otras obras* (which he recreated in English and published as *The Valley* in 1983) was published in 1973. The book won the national award for Chicano literature, Premio Quinto Sol. From that time on he has become the most prolific Chicano novelist, publishing one novel after another

Rolando Hinojosa, 1987 (Archives, Arte Público Press).

in his generational narrative that centers around the lives of two of his alter egos, Rafa Buenrostro and Jehú Malacara, in individual installments that vary in form from poetry and dialogue to the picaresque novel and the detective novel. His titles in English alone include *Korean Love Songs* (1980), *Rites and Witnesses* (1982), *Dear Rafe* (1985), *Partners in Crime: A Rafe Buenrostro Mystery* (1985), *Claros varones de Belken/Fair Gentlemen of Belken County* (1986, bilingual edition), *Klail City* (1987), and *Becky and Her Friends* (1989). His original Spanish version of *Klail City*, entitled *Klail City y sus alrededores* (1976), won an international award for fiction, Premio Casa de las Américas, from Cuba in 1976; it was issued there under this title and a year later a version was published in the United States under the title *Generaciones y semblanzas*. The book was also published in German two years later. Hinojosa has also published short stories and essays widely, as well as installments of a satirical running commentary on life and current events in the United States, known as "The Mexican American Devil's Dictionary," supposedly created by another of his alter egos who is also one of the narrators of the Klail City Death Trip Series: P. Galindo (meaning "right on target" in Spanish).

Hinojosa has been hailed as a master satirist, an acute observer of the human comedy, a Chicano William Faulkner for his creation of the history and people of Belken County, a faithful recorder of the customs and dialects in Spanish and English of both Anglos and Mexicans in the lower Rio Grande Valley. Hinojosa is one of the best-loved and most highly regarded Hispanic writers; he is totally committed to the novelistic world that he has created and that has helped us to understand Mexican-American life so well.

Tato Laviera (1950-)

Jesús Abraham "Tato" Laviera is the best-selling Hispanic poet of the United States, and he bears the distinction of still having all his books in print. Born in Santurce, Puerto Rico, on September 5, 1950, he migrated to New York at age 10 with his family, which settled in a poor area of the lower East Side. After finding himself in an alien society and with practically no English, Laviera was able to adjust and eventually graduate high school as an honor student. Despite having no other degrees, his intelligence, aggressiveness, and thorough knowledge of his community led to his developing a career in the administration of social service agencies. After the publication of his first book *La Carreta Made a U-Turn* (1979), Laviera gave up administrative work to dedicate his time to writing. Since 1980, his career has

Tato Laviera, 1990 (Photo by Georgia McInnis. Archives, Arte Público Press).

included not only writing but touring nationally as a performer of his poetry, directing plays, and producing cultural events. In 1980, he was received by President Jimmy Carter at the White House gathering of American poets. In 1981, his second book, *Enclave*, was the recipient of the American Book Award of the Before Columbus Foundation.

All Tato Laviera's books have been well received by critics, most of whom place him within the context of Afro-Caribbean poetry and U.S. Hispanic bilingualism. *La Carreta Made a U-Turn* is bilingual, jazz- or salsa-poetry that presents the reader with a slice of life drawn from the Puerto Rican community of the lower East Side. As such, it examines both oppression of the migrant community and its alienation through such popular culture forms as soap operas; it probes crime and drug addiction while affirming the spiritual and social values of the community and the place of art, poetry, and music in what many may consider to be the unlikeliest of social environments. Laviera, here as in the rest of his books, acknowledges and supports the existence of a true Puerto and Latino culture within the heart of the metropolis and within the very belly of the United States. He further affirms that there is no need to return to a homeland on an island or south of the border, for Latinos have made their home here and are transforming not only mainstream culture in the United States, but throughout the hemisphere.

In *Enclave*, Laviera celebrates such cultural heroes, both real and imagined, as Alicia Alonso, Suni Paz, John Lennon, Miriam Makeba, the fictitious half-southern black, half-Puerto Rican Tito Madera Smith, the barrio gossip Juana Bochisme, and the neighborhood tough Esquina Dude. As in *La Carreta Made a U-Turn*, Laviera acknowledges his debt to Afro-Caribbean music and poetry in his eulogies of salsa composer Rafael Cortijo, the famed poetry reciter Juan Boria, and master poets Luis Palés Matos and Nicolás Guillén. *AmeRícan* (1986), published on the occasion of the centennial celebration of the Statue of Liberty, is a poetic reconsideration of immigrant life in New York City and the United States. *Mainstream Ethics* (1988) proposes transforming the United States from a Eurocentric culture to one that is ethnically and racially pluralistic in its official identity. *Continental* (1992), published during the Columbus quincentenary, extends these themes and imperatives to the whole hemisphere.

Despite Laviera's outstanding publishing record, the sophistication of his vision, and his artistic bilingualism, he is an oral poet, a consummate performer of his poetry, which slowly but surely is constituting a living epic of the Hispanic peoples of the United States. Even Laviera's written and published poems have been created out of a process that attempts to recreate as much as possible the oral performance. For Laviera, part of that oral tradition and performance are the structures, spirit, and rhythms of popular and folk music, especially those drawn from Afro-Puerto Rican music.

Julio Matas

See Chapter 19

Nicholasa Mohr (1935-)

To date, Nicholasa Mohr is the only U.S. Hispanic woman to have developed a long career as a creative writer for the major publishing houses. Since 1973, her books for such publishers as Dell/Dial, Harper & Row, and Bantam Books, in both the adult and children's literature categories, have won numerous awards and outstanding reviews. Part and parcel of her work is the experience of growing up a female, a Hispanic, and a minority in New York City.

Born on November 1, 1935, in New York City, Nicholasa Mohr was raised in Spanish Harlem. Educated in New York City schools, she finally escaped poverty after graduating from the Pratt Center for Contemporary Printmaking in 1969. From that date until the publication of her first book, *Nilda* (1973), Mohr developed a successful career as a graphic artist. *Nilda*, a novel that traces the life of a young Puerto Rican girl confronting prejudice and coming of age during World War II, won the Jane Addams Children's Book Award and was selected by *School Library Journal* as a Best Book of the Year. After *Nilda*"s success, Mohr was able to produce numerous stories, scripts, and the following titles: *El Bronx Remembered* (1975), *In Nueva York* (1977), *Felita* (1979), *Rituals of Survival: A Woman's Portfolio* (1985), and *Going Home* (1986). Selections from all these story collections have been reprinted widely in a variety of anthologies and textbooks.

Mohr's works have been praised for depicting the life of Puerto Ricans in New York with empathy, realism, and humor. In her stories for children, Mohr has been able to deal with the most serious and tragic of subjects, from the death of a loved one to incest, in a sensitive and humane way. Mohr has been able to contribute to the world of commercial publishing—where stereotypes have reigned supreme—some of the most honest and memorable depictions of Puerto Ricans in the United States. In this and in her crusade

Nicholasa Mohr, 1990 (Archives, Arte Público Press).

to open the doors of publishing and the literary world to Hispanics, Nicholasa Mohr is a true pioneer.

Matías Montes Huidobro

See Chapter 19

Cherríe Moraga (1952-)

The works of Cherríe Moraga have opened up the world of Chicano literature to the life and aesthetics of feminism and gay women. Moraga's works are well known in both feminist and Hispanic circles for their battles against sexism, classism, and racism. Born in Whittier, California, on September 25, 1952, to a Mexican-American mother and an Anglo father, Moraga was educated in public schools in the Los Angeles area, after which she graduated from college with a B.A. degree in English in 1974. While working as a teacher she discovered her interest in writing, and in 1977 moved to the San Francisco Bay Area, where she became acquainted with the Anglo lesbian literary movement. In part to fulfill the requirements for a master's degree at San Francisco State University, Moraga collaborated with Gloria Anzaldúa in compiling the first anthology of writings by women of color, *This Bridge Called My Back: Writings by Radical Women of Color* (1981), which has become the most famous and best-selling anthology of its kind and has inspired a movement of Hispanic feminist and lesbian writers. In her writings here and in other books, Moraga explains that her understanding of racial and class oppression suffered by Chicanas only came as she experienced the prejudice against lesbians. In 1983, Moraga edited another ground-breaking anthology with Alma Gómez and Mariana Romo-Carmona, *Cuentos: Stories by Latinas. Cuentos* attempts to establish a poetics or a canon of Hispanic feminist creativity, a canon where there is room for, and indeed, respect for, the insights of lesbianism. In 1983, Moraga published a collection of her own essays and poems dating back to 1976, *Loving in the War Years: (lo que nunca pasó por sus labios)*, in which she explores the dialectical relationship between sexuality and cultural identity. Her conclusion here, as elsewhere, is that women must be put first. Moraga is also a playwright whose work *Giving Up the Ghost* was produced in 1984 and published in 1986. Her latest produced play, *The Shadow of a Man*, was published in 1991. To date, Moraga remains one of the most militant and controversial of the Hispanic literary figures.

Alejandro Morales (1944-)

Alejandro Morales is one of the leading Chicano novelists, having published substantial novels in

Alejandro Morales, 1991 (Archives, Arte Público Press).

both Spanish and English in the United States and Mexico and having created through them a better understanding of Mexican-American history, at least as seen from the vantage point of working-class culture. Born in Montebello, California, on October 14, 1944, Morales grew up in East Los Angeles and received his B.A. degree from California Sate University, Los Angeles. He went on to complete an M.A. degree (1973) and a Ph.D. degree (1975) in Spanish at Rutgers University in New Jersey. Today Morales is a full professor in the Spanish and Portuguese department at the University of California, Irvine.

Morales is at once a recorder of the Chicano experience, basing many of his narratives on historical research, and he is also an imaginative interpreter of that experience by creating memorable and dynamic characters and language. His first books were written in Spanish and published in Mexico, due to the lack of opportunity here in the United States. *Caras viejas y vino nuevo* (1975, translated as *Old Faces and New Wine*, 1981), examines the conflict of generations in a barrio family. *La verdad sin voz* (1979, translated as *Death of an Anglo*, 1988) is a continuation of the earlier novel, but is created against the backdrop of actual occurrences of Chicano-Anglo conflict in the town of Mathis, Texas. The novel also includes autobiographical elements in the form of a section that deals with racism in academia, which comes to a head when a Chicano professor goes up for tenure. *Reto en el paraíso* (1983, *Challenge in Paradise*) is based on more than a hundred years of Mexican-American history and myth, as it centers on a basic comparison of the decline of the famed Coronel family of Californios and the rise of the Irish immigrant Lifford family. The novel charts the transfer of power and wealth from the native inhabitants of California to the gold-and land-hungry immigrants empowered by Manifest Destiny. *The Brick People* (1988) traces the development of two families connected with the Simons Brick Factory, one of the largest enterprises of its type in the country. Again, Morales uses the technique of comparing the lives of two families, those of the owners of the factory and those of an immigrant laborer's family. Morales's novel *The Rag Doll Plagues* (1991), while still incorporating a historical structure, follows the development of a plague and a Spanish-Mexican doctor who is forever caught in mortal battle with this plague in three time periods and locations: colonial Mexico, contemporary Southern California, and the future in a country made up of Mexico and California united together.

In all, Morales is a meticulous researcher and a creator of novelistic circumstances that are symbolic of Mexican-American history and cultural development. His novels have an epic sweep that are cinematic and highly literary.

Alberto O'Farrill

See Chapter 19

Josephina Niggli (1910-)

Josephina Niggli demonstrated many of the sensibilities that would develop into a full-blown literary movement in the 1960s and 1970s. Born on July 13, 1910, in Monterrey, Mexico, she came to the United States with her parents in 1913 during the Mexican Revolution. Educated in American schools, she attended a Catholic high school in San Antonio, received her B.A. degree from Incarnate Word College (1931), and an M.A. degree from the University of North Carolina (1937). During her adolescence she began her writing career, publishing short stories and poems in such magazines as *Ladies" Home Journal* and *Mexican Life*. By age 18, she had published her first collection of poetry, *Mexican Silhouettes* (1928). She later received training in playwriting and had various of her plays produced and some screenplays made into Hollywood films. The following plays have been published in anthologies: *Soldadera* (1938), *This Is Villa* (1939), *Red Velvet Goat* (1938),

Sunday Costs Five Pesos (1939), *Miracle at Blaise* (1942), *The Ring of General Macías* (1943), and *This Bull Ate Nutmeg* (1945). In 1945, the University of North Carolina Press published her novel *Mexican Village*. The press had already published her collection of *Mexican Folk Plays* in 1938; from 1942 on, Niggli embarked upon a career as an instructor and later professor of radio, television, theater arts, and speech at the University of North Carolina. Today she is still a professor emeritus of that institution. While working as a professor at the University of North Carolina, Niggli also published another novel, *Step Down, Elder Brother* (1947), so successful that it was distributed by the Book-of-the-Month Club. In 1964, she published a young adult book, *A Miracle for Mexico*.

Niggli's writings reveal a thorough knowledge of Mexican customs, traditions, and history. Some of her works also analyze the role of women in Mexican life, especially from her bicultural perspective. All of her work together that is set in Mexico can been seen as a mosaic of Mexican life and character types; her depiction of the Mexican Revolution is realistic and epic in nature, acquainting her readers with the struggles that would bring about the birth of modern Mexico.

Gustavo O'Neill

See Chapter 19

Américo Paredes

See Chapter 16

Pedro Pietri (1943-)

Pedro Pietri is famous for the literary persona of street urchin or skid-row bum that he has created for himself. His works are characterized by the consistent perspective of the underclass in language, philosophy, and creative and psychological freedom. Pietri was born in Ponce, Puerto Rico, on March 21, 1943, just two years before his family migrated to New York. He was orphaned of both parents while still a child and raised by his grandmother. Pietri attended public schools in New York City and served in the army from 1966 to 1968. Other than his having taught writing occasionally and participated in workshops, very little else is known about this intentionally mysterious and unconventional figure.

Pietri has published collections of poems and poetry chapbooks: *The Blue and the Gray* (1975), *Invisible Poetry* (1979), *Out of Order* (1980), *Uptown Train* (1980), *An Alternate* (1980), and *Traffic Violations* (1983). Nevertheless, it was his first book of poetry, *Puerto Rican Obituary* (1971), that brought him his greatest fame and a host of imitators. In 1973, a live performance by him of poems from this book was recorded and distributed by Folkways Records. In 1980, Pietri's short story *Lost in the Museum of Natural History* was published in bilingual format in Puerto Rico. Pietri has also had numerous unpublished, but produced, plays and one published collection, *The Masses Are Asses* (1984). Always a master of the incongruous and surprising, Pietri has created unlikely but humorous narrative situations in both his poetry and plays, such as that in his poem "Suicide Note from a Cockroach in a Low Income Housing Project" and in a dialogue between a character and her own feces in his play *Appearing in Person Tonight —Your Mother*. Pietri's work is one of a total break with conventions, both literary and social, and it is subversive in its open rejection of established society and its hypocrisies.

Miguel Piñero

See Chapter 19

Dolores Prida

See Chapter 19

Album cover of a live poetry recital by Pedro Pietri.

Tomás Rivera

See Chapter 16

Ricardo Sánchez (1941-)

Ricardo Sánchez is one of the most prolific Chicano poets, one of the first creators of a bilingual literary style, and one of the first to be identified with the Chicano movement. Born the youngest of thirteen children on March 21, 1941, he was raised in the notorious Barrio del Diablo (Devil's Neighborhood) in El Paso, Texas. He became a high school dropout, an army enlistee, and later a repeat offender sentenced to prison terms in Soledad Prison in California and Ramsey Prison Farm Number One in Texas; at these prisons he began his literary career before his last parole in 1969. Much of his early life experience of oppressive poverty and overwhelming racism, as well as his suffering in prisons and his self-education and rise to a level of political and social consciousness, is chronicled in his poetry, which although very lyrical, is the most autobiographical of all the Hispanic poets'. Once his writing career was established and Sánchez began to publish his works with both mainstream and alternative literary presses, he assumed various visiting appointments as a professor or writer in residence at various universities. He was a founder of the short-lived Mictla Publications in El Paso, editor of various special issues of literary magazines, such as *De Colores* and *Wood/Ibis*, a columnist for the *San Antonio Express*, a bookseller, and a migrant worker counselor, and he is still an active performer of his poetry on tours in the United States and abroad.

Sánchez's poetry is characterized by an unbridled linguistic inventiveness that not only calls upon both English and Spanish lexicon but also is a source of neologisms and surprising combinations of the sounds and symbols of both languages in single works. His work can be virile and violent at one moment and delicate and sentimental at the next, as he follows the formulas and dictates of a poetry written for oral performance. His is often the exaggerated gesture and emotion of the *declamador* (poetic orator), whose works are performed to inspire a protest rally, inaugurate a mural, celebrate a patriotic holiday, or eulogize the dead. Most of all, Sanchez is the autobiographical poet who casts himself as a Chicano Everyman participating in the epic history of his people through his poetry. His bilingual facility and immense vocabulary and inventiveness are legendary in Chicano literature.

Besides publishing hundreds of poems in magazines and anthologies, Sánchez is author of the following collections: *Canto y grito mi liberación (y lloro mis desmadrazgos)* (1971, I *Sing and Shout for My*

Ricardo Sánchez, 1987 (Archives, Arte Público Press).

Liberation (and Cry for My Insults), Hechizospells: Poetry/Stories/Vignettes/ Articles/Notes on the Human Condition of Chicanos & Pícaros, Words & Hopes within Soulmind (1976), *Milhuas Blues and Gritos Norteños* (1980), *Amsterdam cantos y poemas pistos* (1983), and *Selected Poems* (1985).

Gustavo Solano

See Chapter 19

Gary Soto, 1991 (Photo by M.L. Marinelli. Publicity Department, Chronicle Books).

Gary Soto (1952-)

In academic and creative writing circles, Soto is considered the most outstanding Chicano poet; he is certainly the most widely known Hispanic poet in the Anglo-American poetry establishment, as represented by creative writing departments, magazines, and workshops. Born to Mexican-American parents in Fresno, California, on April 12, 1952, Soto was raised in the environs of the San Joaquin Valley and attended Fresno City College and California State University in Fresno, where he came under the guidance of poet Philip Levine and his creative writing career was born. Soto graduated magna cum laude from California State University in 1975, and in 1976 he earned an M.F.A. degree in creative writing from the University of California, Irvine. In 1977, he began teaching at the University of California, Berkeley; today he is a tenured associate professor in the English and Ethnic Studies departments of the University of California, Berkeley.

Soto has more prestigious awards than any other Hispanic poet in the United States, including the

Academy of American Poets Prize in 1975, the *Discovery*-Nation Award in 1975, the United States Award of the International Poetry Forum in 1976, the Bess Hopkins Prize from *Poetry* magazine in 1977, the Guggenheim Fellowship in 1979, the National Association Fellowship in 1981, the Levinson Award from *Poetry* magazine in 1984, and the American Book Award from the Before Columbus Foundation in 1984.

Soto's books of poetry include the following: *The Elements of San Joaquin* (1977), *Father Is a Pillow Tied to a Broom* (1980), *Where Sparrows Work Hard* (1981), *Black Hair* (1985), and *Who Will Know Us?* (1990). Soto has also published three collections of autobiographical essays and stories: *Living Up the Street: Narrative Recollections* (1985), *Small Faces* (1986), and *Lesser Evils: Ten Quartets* (1988). His most recent book is a young adult novel, *Baseball in April* (1990).

All of Soto's works are highly autobiographical and characterized by a highly polished craft. In his poetry and prose, there is also a great attention paid to narration and characterization; whether he is writing a poem or an essay, Soto is always cognizant of telling a story. Critics have always stated that Soto has something important and human to say, and it is poignantly said in well-crafted writing. While writing from his particular ethnic stance and worldview, he also maintains that there are certain values, experiences, and feelings that are universal.

Piri Thomas (1928-)

Piri Thomas is one of the most widely known cultivators of ethnic autobiography; his *Down These Mean Streets* (1976) was so successful as a powerful chronicle of growing up in the barrio that it spawned a host of Puerto Rican imitators. Piri (John Peter) Thomas was born on September 30, 1928, in New York City, to a Puerto Rican mother and a Cuban father. Thomas grew up during the Great Depression, facing both poverty and racism in New York's East Harlem. American society perceived Thomas as black, while his family perceived him as Puerto Rican and encouraged his identity with the island that he had never seen. However, out on the streets and later in prison, he began to identify and take pride in an Afro-American identity, even becoming a Black Muslim for a while. Thomas entered a life of theft, gang violence, and criminality in adolescence, and he met his inevitable fate of imprisonment. After serving seven years of a fifteen-year term, he was paroled at age 28. While in prison he had obtained his high school equivalency diploma and also had begun to learn to express himself in writing; he also developed a sense of dignity

and self-respect. After returning to his old neighborhood and then to his family, who now lived in Long Island, he worked at a variety of jobs, but eventually developed his career as a writer.

All of Thomas's literary works are highly autobiographical, dealing mostly with his upbringing in the poverty, racism, and culture conflict of the barrio. In addition to his well-known *Down These Mean Streets*, Thomas also wrote a sequel, *Saviour, Saviour Hold My Hand* (1972), and a book on his seven-year imprisonment, *Seven Long Times* (1974). He has also had published a collection of stories, *Stories from el Barrio* (1978). In addition, Thomas has written numerous published articles and essays and has written plays that have been produced on stage. Thomas's work is important for having been one of the first to break through to the mainstream, with all of his books having been issued by major publishers, and *Down These Mean Streets* was so highly reviewed that it projected Thomas into the television talk-show circuit and instant celebrity. A powerful and charming speaker, Thomas became an important spokesperson for the Puerto Rican community. In his books and in his public presentations he became identified with the search for identity, and to many readers and critics of the time this became the most important characteristic of Hispanic literature in the United States.

Omar Torres

See Chapter 19

Estela Portillo Trambley (1936-)

Estela Portillo Trambley is one of the first women writers to successfully publish prose in the early male-dominated stages of the Chicano literary movement. Born in El Paso, Texas, on January 16, 1936, she was raised and educated in El Paso, where she attended high school and the University of Texas, El Paso, for her B.A. degree (1957) and her M.A. degree (1977). After graduation from college, she became a high school English teacher and administrator. Since 1979, she has been affiliated with the Department of Special Services of the El Paso Public Schools. From 1970 to 1975, she served as dramatist in residence at El Paso Community College.

Estela Portillo Trambley was the first woman to win the national award for Chicano literature, Premio Quinto Sol, in 1973, for her collection of short stories and novela *Rain of Scorpions and Other Writings*, which was published in 1975. Besides stories and plays published in magazines and anthologies, Portillo Trambley has written a collection of plays, *Sor Juana and Other Plays* (1981), and a novel, *Trini*

(1983). In both her prose and drama, Portillo Trambley develops strong women who resist the social roles that have been predetermined for them because of their sex. In her fiction, women command center stage and achieve a level of self-determination and control over social and cultural circumstances. The culmination of her pursuit of strong women is represented in her exploration of the life of the eighteenth-century poet and essayist Sor Juan Inés de la Cruz in her play *Sor Juana*. The protagonist of her novel, *Trini*, is a fictional character who struggles against poverty and adversity to make her way in life; she eventually leaves Mexico and crosses the border illegally to find the power over her own life for which she has been searching.

Luis Valdez

See Chapter 19

Sabine Ulibarrí (1919-)

Short story writer, poet, and essayist Sabine Ulibarrí has had one of the longest and most productive literary careers in Chicano literature. He is a well-known and highly respected chronicler of the way things once were in his beloved New Mexico. Born on September 21, 1919, in the small village of Tierra Amarilla, New Mexico, he was raised on a ranch by his parents, both of whom were college graduates. Besides learning the ways of rural life and the rugged countryside, Ulibarrí also experienced firsthand the folk culture of the area, which included not only the full repository of oral literature but also a strong connection to the language and oral literature of Spain and the Spanish-speaking Americas. His early love for the Spanish language and Hispanic literature took Ulibarrí to college and eventually to a Ph.D. degree in Spanish. Over the years he taught at every level, from elementary school to graduate school, except during World War II, when he flew thirty-five combat missions as an air force gunner. Today he is a professor emeritus of the University of New Mexico, where he spent most of his academic career as a student and professor.

Among Ulibarrí's awards are the following: Governor's Award for Excellence in Literature (1988), Distinguished Alumni Award and Regents'' Medal of Merit, University of New Mexico (1989), and the White House Hispanic Heritage Award (1989). Ulibarrí has had published two books of poems, *Al cielo se sube a pie* (1966, *You Reach Heaven on Foot*) and *Amor y Ecuador* (1966, *Love and Ecuador*), and the following collections of short stories in bilingual format: *Tierra Amarilla: Stories of New Mexico/ Tierra Amarilla: Cuentos de Nuevo México* (1971), *Mi abuela fumaba puros y otros cuentos de Tierra Amarilla/ My Grandma Smoked Cigars and Other Stories of Tierra Amarilla* (1977), *Primeros encuentros/First Encounters* (1982), *El gobernador Glu Glu* (1988, *Governor Glu Glu*), and *El Cóndor and Other Stories* (1989).

In all of his work, Ulibarrí preserves a style, narrative technique, and language that owes much to the oral folk tradition. Through his works he has been able to capture the ethos and the spirit of rural New Mexico before the coming of the Anglo. His works memorialize myths and legends and such distinctive characters of the past as cowboys, sheriffs, folk healers, penitents, and just the common everyday folk. Quite often writing two versions of the same story, in English and Spanish, in all of modern Chicano literature his works are among the most direct and accessible to broad audiences.

Sabine Ulibarrí, 1989 (Archives, Arte Público Press).

Ed Vega (1936-)

Ed Vega is a Puerto Rican fiction writer who bases many of his works on life in New York City's Spanish Harlem. Edgardo Vega Yunqué was born in Ponce, Puerto Rico, on May 20, 1936, where he lived with his

Ed Vega, 1991 (Archives, Arte Público Press).

family until they moved to the Bronx, New York, in 1949. He was raised in a devout Baptist home, his father having been a minister of that faith; today, Vega and his wife and children have adopted the Buddhist faith. As a child, books were very accessible at home, and he began both his education and writing at an early age in Spanish in Puerto Rico. After moving to New York and going through the public education system of the city, he served in the air force and studied at Santa Monica College in California under the G.I. Bill. In 1963, Vega almost graduated as a Phi Beta Kappa from New York University with a major in political science; he was short three hours of credit and did not actually graduate until 1969. He did not return to finish until that date because he had become disillusioned after personally experiencing racism at the university. After leaving there in 1963, he worked in a variety of social service programs. In 1969, he returned to academic life as a lecturer for Hunter College and thereafter assumed various other lecturing and assistant professor positions at other colleges. From 1977 to 1982, he worked at such community-based education programs as ASPIRA of New

Jersey. From 1982 to the present, he has been a full-time writer.

Vega is one of the most prolific Hispanic prose writers, although much of his work remains unpublished. In 1977, his short stories began to be published by Hispanic magazines, such as *Nuestro*, *Maize* and *Revista Chicano-Riqueña*. In 1985, his novel *The Comeback*, a rollicking satire of ethnic autobiography and the identity crisis, as personified by a half-Puerto Rican, half-Eskimo ice hockey player who becomes involved in an underground revolutionary movement for Puerto Rican independence, was published. In 1987, a collection of interconnected short stories, *Mendoza's Dreams*, narrated by a warmhearted observer of the human comedy, Alberto Mendoza, was published. An additional common thread holding these barrio stories together is their charting of various Puerto Ricans on the road to success in the United States; thus, once again we have a Puerto Rican interpretation of the American dream. Vega's third book, *Casualty Report* (1991), is just the opposite; for the most part the collection of stories included here chronicle the death of dreams, as characters faced with racism, poverty, and crime succumb to despair in many forms: violence, alcohol and drug abuse, withdrawal, and resignation.

Daniel Venegas (? -)

Daniel Venegas was a harbinger of today's Chicano writers not only in openly proclaiming a Chicano identity and pursuing working-class language but also in generating a style and a literary attitude that would come to typify the Chicano novels of the late 1960s and the 1970s. Very little is known of his life. Born and raised in Mexico, his level of formal education is uncertain. In Los Angeles, he maintained an active life in the world of Mexican journalism and the theater during the 1920s and 1930s. There he founded and edited a weekly satirical newspaper, *El malcriado* (*The Brat*), from 1924 into the 1930s. He was the director of a popular vaudeville theatrical company and the author of numerous plays, short stories, and one novel that relates to the language, customs, and values of working-class Mexican immigrants, who at that time were known as *chicanos*.

All of his theatrical works have been lost, only one issue of *El malcriado* has been located (this containing two short stories by Venegas), and his novel, *Las aventuras de Don Chipote o Cuando los pericos mamen* (1928, *The Adventures of Don Chipote or When Parakeets Suckle Their Young*), was rediscovered and reissued in 1985. *Don Chipote* is the humorous tale of the trials and tribulations of one Don Chipote, who immigrates to the United States from Mexico believing naively that he can shovel up the gold from the streets and send it back to his family. The novel becomes a picaresque story of Chipote's struggle to survive in the alien environment while facing oppression and exploitation from foremen and representatives of industry and the legal authorities and while serving as a target for con men and other underworld characters bent on fleecing him. The satirical tale ends with a moral that warns Mexicans not to come to the United States in search of riches. What is important about *Don Chipote* is the identification of the author-narrator with Chicanos and his having as ideal readers the Chicanos themselves. Not only does it imply that a good portion of those workers knew how to read, but also that those workers, like the author himself, were capable of producing literature and art.

Victor Villaseñor (1940-)

Victor Villaseñor is a novelist and screenwriter who has brought Chicano literature to the widest of audiences through his novel of immigration, *Macho!*, issued in 1973 by the world's largest paperback publisher, Bantam Books; through the epic saga of his own family in *Rain of Gold* (1991); and through the

Victor Villaseñor, 1991 (Photo by Tony Bullard. Archives, Arte Público Press).

television screenplay *The Ballad of Gregorio Cortez*, the miniseries *Rain of Gold*, and the feature film, *Macho*. Born on May 11, 1940, in Carlsbad, California, the son of Mexican immigrants, Villaseñor was raised on a ranch in Oceanside and experienced great difficulty with the educational system, having started school as a Spanish-speaker and dyslexic. He dropped out of high school and worked on the ranch and in the fields and as a construction worker. After attempting college at the University of San Diego for a brief period, he again dropped out and went to live in Mexico, where he discovered the world of books and learned to take pride in his identity and cultural heritage. From then on he read extensively and taught himself the art of writing fiction. During years of work in California as a construction worker, he completed nine novels and sixty-five short stories, all of which were rejected for publication, except for *Macho!*, which launched his professional writing career. His second publishing venture was the nonfiction narrative of the life and trial of a serial killer, *Jury: The People versus Juan Corona* (1977). Negative experiences with stereotyping and discrimination of Hispanics in the commercial publishing world led Villaseñor to publish his most important literary effort with a small, not-for-profit Hispanic press, Arte Público Press of Houston.

Macho! tells the tale of a young Mexican Indian's illegal entry into the United States to find work, along the classic lines of the novel of immigration; however, it departs from the model in that, upon return to his hometown in central Mexico, the protagonist has been forever changed, unable to accept the traditional social code, especially as it concerns *machismo*. *Rain of Gold*, on the other hand, is the nonfiction saga of various generations of Villaseñor's own family and how they experienced the Mexican Revolution and eventually immigrated to establish themselves in California. The saga is narrated in a style full of spiritualism and respect for myths and oral tradition, derived not only from Villaseñor's growing up in the bosom of his extended working-class family but also from the years of interviews and research that he did in preparing the book. The popularity of *Rain of Gold* has brought to millions of Americans the family stories of the social, economic, and political struggles that have resulted in Mexican immigration to the United States, where new stories of racism, discrimination, and the triumph over some of these barriers continue to develop in the epic of Mexican-American life.

References

Kanellos, Nicolás. *Biographical Dictionary of Hispanic Literature in the United States*. Westport, Conn.: Greenwood Press, 1989.

Lomelí, Francisco, and Julio A. Martínez, eds. *Chicano Literature: A Reference Guide*. Westport, Conn.: Greenwood Press, 1985.

———, and Carl F. Shirley, eds. *Chicano Writers: First Series*. Detroit, Mich.: Gale Research, 1989.

Tatum, Charles M. *Chicano Literature*. Boston: Twayne, 1982.

Nicolás Kanellos

Art

Hispanic-American art from its beginnings in the seventeenth century until the present is the focus of this chapter. What is Hispanic art? What are its sources? When and where did it begin? What are its characteristics? How has it changed over time? What forces altered or determined its direction? How does it differ from the art of other groups of people? These and related questions are examined in order to provide a historical framework for the art of Hispanics in the United States.

Hispanic-American art is art produced by American artists who have a Hispanic background. "Hispanic" in this context refers to individuals whose antecedents are traced to Spanish America, where most of the people speak Spanish and their culture is related to that of Spain, the American Indians, or the African slaves introduced by Europeans. The development of these cultures was determined greatly by a long history of exploration, settlement, and control of the area by Spain.

Each region in Spanish America developed its own variant of Hispanic culture because of local conditions, resources, and people. Mountains, jungles, and other natural barriers isolated settlements and affected communications between them. The cultural differences were also the result of differences in the size of the indigenous populations and their level of civilization at the time of European contact. Finally, the history of the areas determined how the peoples of Spanish America developed as nations following their independence from Spain in the early nineteenth century.

The Spaniards encountered highly developed civilizations in central and southern Mexico, Guatemala, and the Andean region now divided into the countries of Ecuador, Bolivia, and Peru. The large populations in these regions served the needs of the colonial empire established by Spain in Latin America. In the Caribbean basin and other coastal areas of Central and South America, where the population was smaller, the Spaniards brought in slaves from Africa.

The result is that Hispanic-American cultures have been tempered by European, indigenous, and African peoples. There is no single Hispanic-American culture because Hispanic Americans trace their antecedents to Spanish America, where each country has its own individual culture and history, influenced by African, indigenous, and/or European peoples.

✳ THE SOURCES OF HISPANIC ART

The sources of Hispanic art in the United States are found primarily in Mexico and the Caribbean basin as well as in the regions where most Hispanics reside (Texas, Colorado, New Mexico, Arizona, California, New York, and Florida). The countries or territories to the immediate south of the United States—Mexico, Puerto Rico, and Cuba—have had a greater influence on the art of Hispanic Americans than others because of their geographical proximity and the result of wars between Spain, Mexico, and the United States in the nineteenth century. There are fewer people from other parts of Latin America, and as a result, their impact on Hispanic art in the United States has not been as great.

Mexico, the largest country south of the border, is

the place of origin for the vast majority of Hispanics in the United States, who identify themselves as Mexican Americans, Hispanos (Spanish Americans), or Chicanos. They are found primarily in the Southwest, Pacific Southwest and Pacific Northwest, and Great Lakes regions. They are related to the people of Mexico and share their history, religion, and culture. They identify with Mexican history, which began with the Indian civilizations of the pre-Columbian epoch and continued through the colonial period under Spanish rule, which lasted three centuries. The modern period began in 1821 with Mexican independence from Spain and the rise of a civilization that combines Indian and Spanish roots. Thus, the over-riding Spanish influence in the northern territory was tempered by the Mexican experience, which began with Mexican independence and continued into the twentieth century with constant immigration caused by economic necessity and the Mexican Revolution of 1910. Anglo-American influence began in the middle of the nineteenth century and has continued unabated throughout the area.

Continued American expansion toward the end of the nineteenth century led to the acquisition of Puerto Rico following the war between the United States and Spain in 1898. By 1917, Puerto Ricans were made citizens of the United States and thus were able to travel freely and to settle in the United States without any immigration restrictions. Cubans have lived in the United States since the nineteenth century, but extensive Cuban immigration began after the takeover of Cuba by Fidel Castro and his partisans in 1959 and the failed Bay of Pigs invasion of 1962. They and other Hispanic-American groups from all over Latin America have continued to immigrate to the United States. Thus, the largest groups of Hispanics in the northeastern and southeastern parts of the United States are from Puerto Rico, Cuba, and other nations in the Caribbean area, and to a lesser extent from the rest of Latin America.

✳EXPLORATION, SETTLEMENT, AND HISTORY OF HISPANICS IN THE UNITED STATES

Spanish presence in the area now encompassed by the states of Florida, Texas, and California began in the early sixteenth century. The first explorations were carried out by Spaniards based in the Caribbean region following the discovery of the New World in 1492 and later by Spaniards from Mexico (named New Spain by the Spaniards) after the fall of the Aztec Empire in 1521. The Spaniards were seeking a northern passage to the South Sea (Pacific Ocean) that would lead them to the fabled cities of the Far East.

The newly discovered lands were not immediately settled because the Spaniards were busy exploring, conquering, and consolidating their holdings in Central and South America as well as in the far western reaches of the Pacific Ocean.

By the end of the sixteenth century, the settlements in New Spain had reached what is today the state of New Mexico. Other parts to the east and west of this vast area were settled over the next several centuries, largely as the result of competition between the Spanish, French, Dutch, English, and the Russians. Most of New Mexico was settled toward the end of the seventeenth century but was temporarily lost following the Pueblo Indian revolt of 1682. The Spaniards resettled the area in 1692. In the meantime, French incursions into the Gulf Coast of Texas prompted the Spaniards to establish settlements in eastern Texas in 1690. Their reinforcement in 1715 and the establishment of other settlements in central Texas (San Antonio) firmed up the territory for the Spaniards. Similar incursions in California by the Russians stimulated the Spaniards to settle that territory in the 1770s from San Diego to San Francisco. The entire area from Florida to California formed the northern reaches of the Spanish Empire from the late fifteenth century to the beginning of the nineteenth century.

Spain lost most of its colonies when Mexico and other Spanish-American countries declared and gained their independence in the early nineteenth century. Following Mexican independence in 1821, the southern border of the new nation included most of the Yucatán Peninsula southward to the Pacific Ocean, limited by the border with Guatemala. Its northern border stretched from Texas to California and included the area now encompassed by those states along with New Mexico, Arizona, and parts of Colorado, Utah, and Nevada. The loss of the northern territories began with Texas independence in 1836 and continued when Texas joined the United States ten years later. This led to war between Mexico and the United States and the subsequent loss of the northern territory in 1848.

In summary, the earliest Hispanics were the New Spaniards who settled in New Mexico, Arizona, Texas, and California during the seventeenth and eighteenth centuries, when the area was claimed by Spain. Other Hispanics began to arrive in the nineteenth and twentieth centuries. Most arrived as a result of conquest (New Spaniards and Mexicans in the Southwest in the middle of the nineteenth century and Puerto Rico at the turn of the century) or upheavals in their countries in this century (Mexicans following their revolution and on up to the present, and Cubans since the 1960s).

What brings these disparate groups together? How do they differ? What distinguishes one from the other?

✸NEW SPANIARDS AND MEXICANS: 1599 TO 1848

The Missions

The missions built from Texas to California in the seventeenth and eighteenth centuries were intended to serve as Christianizing outposts as well as economic, social, and political units. The Franciscan friars in charge of the northernmost missions were sometimes the sole Europeans along the frontier. The missions, therefore, had to serve the many assigned functions and be relatively independent, self-contained units.

The northern missions are related to the architectural complexes built by the friars in central New Spain in the sixteenth century. These complexes, known as *conventos*, always included a single-nave church and the various units associated with it, such as the sacristy (a small room next to the altar for storage of religious vestments), the friars'' quarters, the cloister, the refectory or dining room, the kitchen, and other areas. The friars also included a large open space in front of the church, known as the *atrio* (atrium), with small chapels called *posas* at each of the four corners and a cross in the center. The posas were used for religious processions and the cross was used to teach the Indians about the new religion.

The seventeenth- and eighteenth-century missions in the Indian pueblos of New Mexico follow the same arrangement used in the conventos of central New Spain. Examples are found in New Mexico at the Indian pueblos of Laguna (San José, about 1700) and Acoma (San Esteban del Rey, 1629-1641).

By the eighteenth and early nineteenth centuries, the standard arrangements seen in the sixteenth-century conventos were no longer strictly followed in the northern territories. They varied from region to region. The church no longer seemed to be the focal point of the complex, since the various units were not clustered around it as in central New Spain, nor did they have the standard east-west orientation of the earlier churches. Most churches had Latin cross plans, which also correspond to examples found in central New Spain. Examples are seen in the churches of Nuestra Señora de la Purísima Concepción (1755) in San Antonio, Texas, San Xavier del Bac (1783-97), south of Tucson, Arizona, San Juan Capistrano (1796-1806) in California, and San Francisco de Assís (1813-15) in Ranchos de Taos, New Mexico.

Figure 18.1. Bell wall, San Juan Capistrano Mission, 1760-87. San Antonio, Texas. (Photograph by Jacinto Quirarte).

The facades of the mission churches also followed examples seen in the churches of central New Spain. The early convento churches have a vertical extension of the facade sometimes used as a belfry (*espadaña*), as in the churches of the Indian pueblos of Laguna and Picuris, New Mexico, and in the San Francisco de la Espada church in San Antonio. Another type of belfry is the bellwall (*campanario*), a wall with one or more openings for bells. A campanario was added to one of the walls of the nave of the San Juan Capistrano church in San Antonio (Figure 18.1). Another was built as an independent tower or wall adjacent to the facade but not part of it as in the churches of the San Diego, San Gabriel, and Santa Inés missions in California.

The bell towers of the later colonial period and a dome over the crossing of the nave and transept are seen in the San José and Concepción churches in San Antonio, and the San Xavier church in Arizona. Bell towers but not the domes are seen in the Acoma and Ranchos de Taos churches in New Mexico, and the

Santa Barbara, Carmel, San Buenaventura, and San Luis Rey churches in California.

Although the missions of the Southwest have *espadañas*, campanarios, bell towers, and domes, each region or mission field has its own characteristics due to the local conditions and the time that the building programs began. The style of the New Mexico missions, built in adobe, remained unchanged over a period of several hundred years. The others differ only slightly, owing to the differences in style (baroque in Texas and Arizona and neoclassical in California) and distance from the central part of New Spain.

The primary function of the mission churches and chapels was to provide an area for religious celebratons carried out on a daily, weekly, and annual basis. The images on the exterior portal facades and the altarpieces placed inside these sacred areas were meant to be viewed and experienced for their religious meaning, with the devout using them for veneration and supplication purposes. Thus, purpose and function were related to the religious content and meaning the images conveyed, rather than their being created for purely artistic or aesthetic reasons.

The best examples of portal facades with figural and architectural sculptures are found in the mission churches of San José y San Miguel de Aguayo (1768-82) in San Antonio and San Xavier del Bac (1783-97) near Tucson. Figural sculptures are placed in niches framed by columnar supports, known as *estipites*, at San Xavier and on pedestals placed within niche-pilasters at San José. The pilaster is so named because it functions as a background for the sculptures.

San José and San Miguel de Aguayo

The architectural frame of the San José church portal has a single bay that spans its two stories. The entablature of the first story establishes its width and the niche-pilasters provide its outer frame. Inner pilasters extend up to the entablature beyond the jambs of the doorway, which has a mixtilineo arch. The second-story bay, narrower than the first, has an entablature with supporting pilasters and a choir window, which are in line with the inner dimensions of the main doorway. The pedestals with sculptures are in line with the inner pilasters of the first story. Mixtilineo brackets provide the frame for the ensemble and a transition to the cornice topped by a stone cross.

Figural sculptures are on each side of the doorway, and above it under the cornice of the entablature. The same arrangement is seen around the choir window of the second story (Figure 18.2).

The main doorway is flanked by sculptures of Saint Joachim on the left and Saint Anne on the right

(Figures 18.3 and 18.4). A sculpture of Our Lady of Guadalupe is seen over the doorway. There is a sculpture of Saint Dominic on the left side of the choir window and one of Saint Francis on the right. A sculpture of Saint Joseph holding the Christ Child is seen above the choir window. The arrangement of the sculptures by threes at each level of the portal is in keeping with other similar ones found throughout New Spain. There is no other example like this one in the mission churches of New Mexico, Arizona, or California. The closest to this arrangement is found at San Xavier, where the sculptures are located in niches on each side of the door and choir window. However, there are no sculptures along the central axis.

San Xavier del Bac

The estipite columns and the entablatures of the San Xavier portal are arranged in a rectangular grid (Figure 18.5). This is contrasted by the third story, framed by the curvilinear frame known as a reretted cornice. There is a sculpture of Saint Francis of Assisi in the central part of the cornice, known as a cham-

Figure 18.2. Facade, San José y San Miguel de Aguayo Mission, 1768-82. San Antonio, Texas. (Photograph by Kathy Vargas).

Figure 18.3. *Saint Joachim* portal sculpture (left side of the doorway), 1768-82, San José y San Miguel de Aguayo Mission. San Antonio, Texas. (Photograph by Kathy Vargas).

fered center. The sculptures on either side of the doorway are Saint Catherine of Siena on the left and Saint Lucy on the right (Figure 18.6). The sculptures on the second story are Saint Barbara on the left and Saint Cecilia on the right. These are much smaller in relation to their surrounding spaces than those at San José.

Other Mission Church Portals

The few sculptures that may have been placed in the portal niches of the California mission churches have long since disappeared. As an example, the three sculptures on the portal of the Santa Barbara church are modern replacements of those that were destroyed by an earthquake in 1925. The sculptures of the San Luis Rey church have disappeared. Those that were undoubtedly on the portal of the San Juan Capistrano church were destroyed by the earthquake of 1812. And finally, the sculpture in a niche on the portal of the San Gabriel church is a modern addition.

The mission churches of New Mexico did not have figural or architectural sculptures on the facades,

owing to the use of adobe, which does not lend itself to this type of decoration. The primary focus in these churches was on the interior walls used for paintings and individual panels hung as pictures. Every church had an altar screen, known as a *reredos* in New Mexico (and *retablo* in Mexico), on the back wall of the sanctuary and numerous freestanding sculptures of holy images, known as *santos* (literally, saints), placed in front of it on altar tables.

Architectural Polychromy

Some of the mission churches also had painted decorations on the exterior surfaces to enhance their appearance, particularly in those cases where it was too expensive to add architectural and figural sculptures on the portals. A good example of this practice is seen on the facade of Nuestra Señora de la Purísima Concepción de Acuña Mission (1755) in San Antonio (Figure 18.7). All the windows and the portal and tower bases and the belfries were painted to simulate stone masonry frames and belfry arches. Simulated masonry was also painted on each side of the portal to

Figure 18.4. *Saint Anne* portal sculpture (right side of the doorway), 1768-82, San José y San Miguel de Aguayo Mission. San Antonio, Texas. (Photograph by Kathy Vargas)

Figure 18.5. Facade, 1783-97, San Xavier del Bac Mission. Tuscon, Arizona. (Photograph by Jacinto Quirarte).

original or date from the mission period. Those seen in some of the churches may not be from that period but are recent additions. Others that are from the mission period, as in the case of the San Antonio missions, are no longer in their original locations because the altarpieces in which they were placed disappeared in the nineteenth century.

Most of the sculptures and paintings of the altarpieces in Texas and California were probably brought in from central New Spain where they were produced. Some wood sculptures originally located in altarpieces or altar areas of the Texas mission churches are now placed on pedestals (altars), in museum exhibitions, or in storage. There are also isolated sculptures and paintings in the California mission churches and museums. Some are placed in modern altarpieces.

Only the church of San Xavier del Bac and others in New Mexico have their original altar screens in place. Those at San Xavier cover the altar area and the transepts (the arms of a Latin cross). The apostles are represented in the nave and chancel (the area in front of the altar at the crossing of the transepts and

give the illusion of tower bases. Simulated fluted pilasters were painted near the corners of each side of the belfry towers. Finally, a sun and a moon were painted on the upper part of the portal with the letters "AE" (Ave María). Other examples are found at San José mission church, where a quatrefoil pattern was painted over the entire facade along with simulated block frames on the tower base windows and zig-zags on the dome (Figure 18.8). Examples of architectural painting in California are seen in the mission churches of Santa Clara de Assís (1822-23) and Santa Inés.

The use of colors on the facades of the Texas and California churches reflects the interest in creating dramatic effects of light and color seen in the churches of central Mexico (New Spain), where glazed tiles were used on domes and, on occasion, on facades as well. The best example of this practice is seen at the church of San Francisco Acatepec, Puebla.

Altarpieces

Few of the mission churches in Texas and California have sculptures or paintings on canvas that are

Figure 18.6. *Saint Lucy*. Portal sculpture (right side of the doorway), 1783-97, San Xavier del Bac Mission. Tucson, Arizona. (Photograph by Jacinto Quirarte).

Figure 18.7. Main Portal, 1755, Nuestra Señora de la Purísma Concepción de Acúna Mission. San Antonio, Texas. (Photograph by Kathy Vargas).

the nave). The focus is on man's salvation (entrance to the chancel), and within the chancel are references to the missionary work of Saint Francis Xavier, the birth of the Virgin Mary, the earthly experience of Adam's offspring, and God the Father giving his benediction.

The altarpieces of the New Mexico mission churches were painted by local artisans in a folk art style. The sculptures made of wood and painted in different colors were also done by local craftsmen. Some mission altar screens are now found in museums in Santa Fe (Museum of New Mexico) and Colorado Springs, Colorado (Taylor Museum).

Alteration and Restoration of the Mission Churches

Many of the original churches have been altered over the years as a result of neglect and, in some cases, restorations carried out in the nineteenth and twentieth centuries. In the nineteenth century, some of the New Mexico churches were altered when Victorian-style decorations were added to the adobe structures. Most of these additions were removed in the twentieth century and efforts made to restore the

churches to their original configurations. Unfortunately, the need to continually maintain the adobe surfaces because of the fragile nature of the material has led to unintended changes in the details of the structures.

More durable materials were used in Texas and Arizona, and to some extent in California. It is on the portal facades of these structures that figural and architectural sculptures are more apt to be found than on the adobe churches of New Mexico. However, these sculptures have suffered as a result of abandonment and vandalism in the nineteenth century. This began when the missions were secularized a few years after Mexico gained its independence from Spain in 1821. Political turmoil and war between Texas and Mexico eventually led to the partial destruction of some of the sculptures found on these facades. Some of them have been restored in the twentieth century.

New Mexico Santeros

The relatively isolated New Mexicans developed a folk art independent of academic models far to the

Figure 18.8. Polychromy (reconstruction, 1948), south tower, 1768-82, San José y San Miguel de Aguayo Mission. San Antonio, Texas. (Photograph by Kathy Vargas).

south during the first half of the nineteenth century. That style, generally dated from 1810 to 1850, is characterized by the work of holy image makers known as *santeros* (literally makers of saint images—sculptures and paintings). The paintings on panels were called *retablos*; the sculptures were called *bultos*. However, they were not totally isolated. Works by masters from the metropolitan cities were available in such places as the church at Pecos Pueblo and the church of Our Lady of Guadalupe in Santa Fe. In addition, the earlier paintings and sculptures produced in New Mexico during the eighteenth century are derivative of academic styles.

The Laguna Santero

The unique style of painting and sculpture in New Mexico began with the work of the anonymous Laguna santero who worked there from 1796 to 1808. The design of his altar screens and paintings indicate that he may have been from the provinces of Mexico. His work is clearly derived from Mexican provincial sources, specifically paintings and engravings, but is simplified to such an extent (all the forms are flattened out) that the figures appear weightless. The facial expressions are neutral in contrast to the more animated baroque examples from central New Spain. The baroque image and its variety of poses and expressions was meant to accentuate the ecstasy or other states of the saintly or holy person portrayed. The expression of religious piety in the works by the Laguna santero are closer to the images of medieval Europe.

A good example of the santero's work is the Laguna altar screen, dated 1800 to 1808. It has three bays on the first story and a single one on the second story. Solomonic columns frame each of the side bays and solomonic balusters top the two outer columns on the second story. (Other santeros painted altar screens in a similar style, that is, they emphasized the architectural frame for the images as in the examples found in central New Spain.) Altar screens attributed to the Laguna santero are found in Pojoaque (about 1796-1800), Santa Fe (around 1796 and 1798), Zia and Santa Ana (both about 1798), and Acoma (1802). The altar screens have three bays and usually two stories.

The Laguna santero had several followers, among them Molleno, who may have worked in the santero's workshop. Among Molleno's works is the altar screen at the church in Rio Chiquito (1828). Another santero, known as the Quill Pen Santero, was a follower of Molleno. These two artists, like the Laguna santero, emphasized the linear treatment of all forms and details.

José Aragón

José Aragón differed from the other santeros because he could read and write, and this ability was reflected in his work. He used engravings as models for his paintings, signed them, and even included lengthy prayers in them. While his work can be considered folk in style, it has a relationship to academic sources. It is sophisticated in its definition of form and the proportions of the human figure.

A good example of Aragón's *reredos* (altar screen) paintings is the one of Our Lady of Guadalupe, now in the Taylor Museum in Colorado Springs. The iconographic program is clearly based on the well-known conventional sources, but Aragón emphasized the formal rather than the narrative qualities of the image. There is a fine linearity that permeates all of the narrative panels and the spaces between them as well as the frame that contains them all. The Virgin is represented in the center, and her appearance to Juan Diego and the events subsequent to it are depicted in the four corners of the painting. Christ is seen in the top center, and the church that the Virgin ordered built in her honor is seen at the bottom center.

The Truchas Master

Another of the anonymous santeros working in the first quarter of the nineteenth century was initially identified as the Dot-Dash Painter, then later as don Antonio Fresques, and more recently as the Truchas Master. Works by this artist are dated between 1790 and 1830.

The *reredos* painting of Our Lady of Guadalupe, now in the Taylor Museum in Colorado Springs is also a good example of the Truchas Master's work. This painting is unlike most representations of the Virgin, which are based on the original in the basilica of Guadalupe near Mexico City. The artist ignored the standard proportions of the slender figure of the Virgin and did away with all semblance of naturalism in the depiction of her downward gaze. The eyes are simple crescent shapes and each iris is indicated by a black dot. The other features are defined with an equal economy of means. The figure and the slender form of the original have been transformed into a schematic rendition in which there is an emphasis on the colors and the vigorous line used to outline all forms.

José Rafael Aragón

José Rafael Aragón was born in 1796 or 1797 and died in 1862. His earliest dated altar screen (1825) is found in the pueblo church of San Lorenzo de Picuris.

Other works are in Chimayo, Taos, Talpa, and the Cordoba/Santa Cruz area.

Aragón was the major artist from around 1820 to 1860, and his *reredos* panel paintings, altar screens, and sculptures are the finest examples of the local folk art style.

Aragón took all the abstracting tendencies of his predecessors and created even finer examples of this type of art. His work is known for his bold use of line and pure color, and although he used late baroque models, his work was not dependent on them. Typical of his mature work is the altar screen originally in the chapel of Our Lady of Talpa (near Taos) and now in the Taylor Museum in Colorado Springs. It was completed in 1838. The style is softer than his earlier works. The faces tend to be round instead of elongated ovals, and the figures are relatively static in presentation.

A fine example of Aragón's sculpture is a *bulto* (religious sculpture) from the Talpa chapel, now in the Taylor Museum collection of Our Lady of Talpa. She is crowned and holds the Christ Child in her left arm. As in the retablo and altar screen paintings, the artist created a fine balance between the decorative and figural elements in the sculpture.

✳HISPANICS AND MEXICAN AMERICANS: 1848 TO THE PRESENT

1848 to 1920

There is little information on the art of Hispanos (Spanish Americans) and Mexican Americans dating from the period immediately following 1848, when the northernmost territories of Mexico became part of the United States. The process of bringing the entire area into the economic, political, and cultural life of the United States was begun at this time and continued during the remainder of the nineteenth century and the first two decades of the twentieth. The area became known as the Southwest and Pacific Southwest of the United States. Its incorporation into the country's economic system was hastened by the building of railroads in the area. Cultural changes were eventually brought about by the people who began to go into the area from the eastern seaboard and other parts of the country.

Modernization in Mexico and the United States during the last decades of the nineteenth century led to a period of consolidation on both sides of the border. There were no great movements of people in either direction. On the American side, the modernization affected various regions of the area during the second half of the nineteenth century. The most apparent changes took place in New Mexico, where new churches were built on American and European models, and the old ones were changed with the addition of wood siding, pointed spires, and a general refurbishing consistent with the eclectic tastes of the nineteenth century. Plaster saints and inexpensive religious prints were also introduced into the area. The latter supplanted the retablo painting tradition but the former did not stop the production of bultos. A few of the artists who continued to produce santos were "discovered" in the twentieth century.

Santos and Santeros

The production of santos in New Mexico declined in number and in style, as well as technical quality, after the 1850s. The changes were the result of a change in patronage of the church, first under the Spanish Crown and later Mexico, and the importation of plaster saints and inexpensive prints after 1848. The few santos produced for Spanish Americans in the isolated communities of northern New Mexico are the work of less technically proficient artists. Santos were made for the oratories and *moradas* (meeting houses) and were used by the Penitente Brotherhood for the first time in 1833, when they were condemned by the Mexican church. The Penitentes eventually became the first of many groups of Hispanics who sought to retain the integrity of their culture against the attacks of Protestant Americans and the Catholic church in the 1850s. Although the Penitentes had been condemned by the Mexican Catholic church, their persecution by American Catholics and Protestants in the mid-1850s eventually led to their activities becoming more and more secretive. The Penitentes provided the patronage as well as the selection of certain subjects that were an essential part of their religious observances and practices. The subjects most often represented were the death figures and the suffering Christ of the Passion.

Miguel Herrera (1835-1905)

Miguel Herrera, a resident of Arroyo Hondo in Taos County, was among the several santeros serving the needs of the Penitentes and others in the area. He worked in the 1870s, 1880s, and possibly later as a bulto maker. (No retablos are known to have been produced by him, but this is not surprising, since religious prints were readily available.) The tall figures with attention paid only to the head and hands were meant to be dressed in fabric clothing. His santos are noted for small seashell ears set too low on the head. Much of his work was done for the moradas of the Penitentes. A fine example of his work is the *Christ in the Holy Sepulchre*, in the Taylor Museum

(Colorado Springs) collection. It is life-size and its knees, shoulders, neck, and jaw are articulated.

José Benito Ortega (1858-1941)

José Benito Ortega traveled from town to town, a true itinerant artist, to seek out potential patrons. He was one of several such artists serving the needs of the Hispanos in northern New Mexico. When Ortega received an order, he stayed in the town until he finished the work. He also made death figures for use in the moradas. His santo figures are very simple and stylized with sharply defined Spanish features and painted in bright colors.

An example of Ortega's work is *San Isidro Labrador (Saint Isidore the Farmer)* in the Denver Art Museum, made of wood and gesso, and painted (Figure 18.9). The work is modeled on the traditional representations of this saint in the tin paintings of northern Mexico, in which the size of the figures is based on their importance rather than on how they would appear in nature. The saint towers over all the other figures in the group. The winged angel behind the plow is slightly less than half the size of Saint Isidor! The oxen are also less than half the size of the angel, thereby creating a pronounced distortion of scale in the work.

Figure 18.9. José Benito Ortega. *Saint Isidore the Farmer,* 1880s-1907. Denver Art Museum.

Traditional Arts from 1920 to the Present

By the 1920s, the Hispanic communities in various parts of the Southwest had begun to change as a result of American cultural dominance in the area and the increased immigration from Mexico following the political and economic chaos caused by the Mexican Revolution of 1910. The most immediate changes occurred in northern New Mexico following World War I, when the traditional arts of santo making were brought to an end as a result of economic changes in the area. They were revived but in different form and to serve other than religious purposes. However, the traditional arts were strengthened in other parts of the Southwest by the new arrivals from Mexico. Their strong devotion to the saints and Our Lady of Guadalupe, to whom they prayed for salvation and assistance in resolving problems, especially in time of crisis, led to the creation of private oratories, known as yard shrines and home altars. The latter have inspired contemporary Chicano artists who call themselves *altaristas* (altar makers). The former have inspired contemporary santeros in New Mexico. Both are expressions of the Hispanic experience in the Southwest and Pacific Southwest.

The new emphasis on santo making was created by a number of American artists who began to arrive in Santa Fe and Taos in the 1920s. The craftsmen were encouraged to continue making furniture and other domestic products as well as sculptures that were similar to the traditional santos of the nineteenth century. Unlike the earlier pieces, however, the new santos were not painted in different colors, nor were they intended for chapels or churches. They were produced for collectors and tourists who acquired such objects as mementos of a trip through the area. Another change was seen in the production of the santos. Entire families were now involved in making santos, in contrast to the production of works by single artists in the past.

The revival of santo making took place primarily in the small community of Cordoba, New Mexico. However, the impetus for it can be found in Santa Fe, where the needed mechanisms were instituted starting in 1919 with the "revival" of the Santa Fe Fiesta and culminating in 1929 with the incorporation of the Spanish Colonial Arts Society, which had an impact on the making of santos in northern New Mexico. An annual fiesta exhibition was adopted in the late 1920s in which the works of Hispanic craftsmen were included. These exhibitions were variously called Spanish Colonial Handicrafts, Spanish Fair, and

Spanish Arts and Crafts Exhibition. In 1929, the Spanish Arts Shop was established by the Spanish Colonial Arts Society in Sena Plaza, Santa Fe. During the time it lasted, through the early 1930s, it served as an impetus to some of the santeros, such as José Dolores López and others, who began to concentrate on the production of objects that were acceptable to Anglo patrons. As patrons, the Anglos determined questions of quality and originality of craftsmanship. Santos were no longer produced on the basis of the Hispanics'' own understanding of their heritage.

José Dolores López (1868-1937)

One of the most important of the new santeros was José Dolores López, whose works date from about 1929 to 1937, the year of his death. He was primarily a furniture maker from 1917 to about 1929. He also did carpentry work—window and door frames, roof beams and corbels, crosses for grave markers, coffins, and chests—and small wooden figures, primarily for relaxation and as gifts for neighbors and relatives. He began to carve birds and animals as well as santos after 1929 because he could no longer earn a living from his fields and livestock and his carpentry work.

This new endeavor coincided with the emerging interest in Hispanic culture and handicrafts generated by a few Anglo artists. They were interested in revitalizing Hispanic "traditional," "colonial," and "Spanish" crafts. These external factors created new markets for Hispanic crafts and competition between artists. At the same time, the new patrons taught the Hispanic artists to be "selective" in their work, that is, to produce objects for the non-Hispanic market.

López made several changes in his work during the period of transition from an older Hispanic tradition to the new one created by Anglo patrons. The furniture he produced in painted and unpainted versions was changed exclusively to the latter because the painted pieces were too "gaudy" for Anglo patrons. He then turned to making unpainted santos at the prodding of Frank Applegate, who was in charge of arts and crafts for the Spanish Colonial Arts Society. Another reason for the change had to do with the success of the image carvings by Celso Gallegos, who was awarded several prizes for his work in 1926 and 1927. Gallegos, a santero from Agua Fria who was slightly older than José Dolores López, carved sacred images and animals in stone and wood and, like López, served as *sacristan* (caretaker) for his church.

Figure 18.10. José Dolores López. *Expulsion from the Garden of Eden.*

He was among the last of the pious santeros. Both santeros were deeply religious.

The santos by López demonstrate an interest in narrative content. This differs from the emphasis on local prototypes of favored saints and other religious figures represented in the traditional santos. López used several sources for his images, among them an old book of French drawings that he displayed with pride to visitors. He was also influenced by the work of José Rafael Aragón, which he saw in the Cordova church in the course of his work as a sacristan of the sanctuary. He is known to have overpainted and repaired several worn traditional images during that period.

Among the subjects López portrayed in his work are Saint Anthony, Saint Peter, Saint Michael with the dragon, a *nacimiento* (nativity) in which all the appropriate figures are included, a *muerte* (death cart), and Adam and Eve, in which the Garden of Eden and the Tree of Life with the Serpent are included. The latter is a formal extension of earlier trees with birds made by the artist. A good example of the Adam and Eve theme is the piece in the Taylor Museum (Colorado Springs) collection titled *Adam and Eve in the Garden of Eden*. It is made up of three separate units that can be moved around to create different arrangements. The figures of Adam and Eve are placed on a long, narrow base, which allows a frontal presentation of the two figures. Behind them is a stylized representation of the garden, composed of vertical plants inserted onto a similar base, which is used as a backdrop for Adam and Eve. To the side is the Tree of Life with the forbidden fruit and the Serpent. "The Tree of Life of the Good and the Bad" is inscribed on its base in English and Spanish. López made other elaborate santos, such as *The Expulsion from the Garden of Eden* (Figure 18.10), in the collections of the Museum of International Folk Art, Santa Fe; *Michael the Archangel and the Dragon*, in the Taylor Museum (Colorado Springs; *The Expulsion from Paradise*, in the collections of the Museum of International Folk Art, Santa Fe; and in the same museum, the *Flight into Egypt*.

Patrocino Barela (1908-1964)

The work of Patrocino Barela, a Taos wood-carver, was supported by the Federal Art Project (FAP), part of the Works Progress Administration, from 1936 to 1943. He began to carve santos in 1931, and his work was later exhibited nationally under the auspices of the FAP. His benefactors had an even greater impact on his work than was the case with the López family. Barela broke away from the santero tradition and began to carve figurative works that have an overall organic quality usually suggested by the grain of the woods he used for his works.

A good example of Barela's work is *Saint George*, in the National Museum of American Art in Washington, D.C. It was carved from a single piece of cedar. The helmetlike nose and brow of the saint form one continuous shape that is echoed by the figure's crown, just as the V-neck of the tunic mirrors the shape created by the position of the figure's legs. The saint's expression is characterized by a stern projecting chin and the gentle slit of the mouth, set off to one side. Through a dynamic series of directions and counterdirections—created by the play between positive and negative form and space—Barela adroitly depicted the slaying of the dragon.

George López (1925-)

The increased markets and competition between artists led to an increase in the number of people making santos in the 1930s. The children of José Dolores López began to make santos at this time. Among them was George López, who began carving objects in 1925 but was not able to devote full time to it until 1932. Eventually, his work became more widely known than that of the other Cordova santeros. By the 1960s, he was considered the best of the santeros.

Outdoor Shrines and Home Altars

The yard shrines or private oratories found in the barrios of the Southwest are similar to the folk art produced in New Mexico in terms of genesis, purpose, function, and meaning. These private oratories are called *capillas* (chapels) in San Antonio, *nichos* (niches) in Tucson, and *grutas* (grottoes) in Los Angeles. They express the deeply held religious beliefs of the people who made them. In their genesis they are related to the *exvotos* of northern New Mexico painted in the nineteenth century. Both are responses to a time of crisis experienced by individuals who promised to paint an image (exvoto) as an offering or as a testament of their salvation or to build a shrine (oratory) for similar reasons, if their prayers were answered. The words in Spanish for these acts of devotion and thanksgiving are *promesa* (promise) and *manda* (gift, offering).

The exvoto paintings and the shrines testify to relief from an illness, a malady, financial problems, accidents, robberies, pursuit by enemies or the police, and so on. The nature of the problem determined the manner of supplication: through prayer at the time and place of the natural or man-made catastrophe or in a formal setting, such as a church, for a long-standing illness, or prayer coupled with the use of milagros placed on the saint selected for the occasion. Milagros are small sculptures made of various metals (brass, tin, nickel, silver, or gold) into numerous configurations (natural and man-made objects) that can be used to point to the problem. All the body parts are represented, as are the human figure, animals, automobiles, houses, and so forth. The images were used for relief from some illness, such as an arthritic arm, leg, or other part of the body, or a financial problem, such as an outstanding debt or a pending mortgage on a house.

Milagros have been used traditionally in Latin American and some European countries where Catholicism is practiced. Parishioners routinely place milagros on favored saints found in the chapels. Devout parishioners continue to use milagros in some of the mission churches of the Indian pueblos, such as San Xavier del Bac. Mexican Americans use milagros in the shrines and home altars, which are usually comprised of a small sacred image on a shelf or framed for placement on a wall.

San Antonio

As of the early 1980s, there were over 175 oratories in the west side of San Antonio. Some were built as early as the 1940s. Many of them have deteriorated because the younger residents have not maintained them when the owners or builders died. Some have suffered from vandalism. Enough remain, however, to demonstrate the survival of a strong tradition of religious folk art.

The oratories are made of concrete, wood, mirror fragments, tile, brick, stone, pebbles, aluminum, plexiglass, seashells, cement, or other materials. The sacred images placed inside them can be lighted with Christmas lights, plain light bulbs, or even neon light. In most cases, the oratory was built from scratch by the person who made the promise; in other cases, the individual embellished a ready-made oratory available in west-side shops that also sell figurines and flowerpots. In both cases, the individuals placed the sacred image of the saint to whom it was dedicated along with other sacred images inside the shrine. These were decorated with plants, flowers (real, paper, or plastic), candles, seashells, and assorted Christmas decorations.

The shrines vary in size from relatively small constructions (no more than one foot in height) to highly elaborate structures (twelve feet in height, nine feet wide, and eight feet in depth), in which the sacred image was placed. The two most popular images used, were Our Lady of Guadalupe and Our Lady of San Juan de los Lagos. Oratories for the latter were modeled on the miraculous statue in the town of San Juan de los Lagos in the state of Jalisco, Mexico.

A good example of the shrines in San Antonio is the one dedicated to Our Lady of San Juan, built in the mid-1950s by Ramiro Rocha as a manda (offering) to the Virgin. The shrine had a statue of Our Lady in the front central part of the niche, and statues in the corners in the back—the Sacred Heart, left, and San Martín de Porres, right. An electric light was suspended directly above the Virgin. The niche was protected by a glass door. Rocha built the shrine on the property of Elia González, who paid for the materials (the reason is unknown, since Rocha is deceased). González, who allowed her mother, María Garza, to live there, maintained the shrine by looking after it and repainting and cleaning it. González was also responsible for the neon that spelled out the name of the Virgin as follows: "San Juanita de los Lagos," with "viva" in front of it. The shrine was, therefore, appropriately identified by its makers and its location as the Garza/González/Rocha shrine. The property was later sold, and the shrine was destroyed.

Tucson

The private oratories in Tucson, Arizona, are called *nichos* by the residents of the barrio. Most of them have representations of Our Lady of Guadalupe in them. Some of the yard shrines are as elaborate as the shrines of San Antonio. Most were built of brick or stone, and on occasion embellished with tiles added to enhance the appearance of the image placed inside the shrine.

There is an unusual example in which holy images are placed inside a square niche and on a shelf above it (Figure 18.11). The shrine was built out of a discarded refrigerator in 1957 on Theodora Sánchez's front lawn by her husband as a fulfillment of a promise made to Saint Dymphna, the patron saint of lunatics. This was in response to their prayers to the saint to save their son's girlfriend, who went crazy when she visited his grave five years after his death in Korea in the early 1950s. When she got well, they fulfilled their promise to build the shrine.

Framed pictures of Our Lady of Guadalupe are propped up in each corner of the lower niche, in which the statue of Saint Dymphna is placed. On the top shelf there is a statue of Saint Francis Xavier lying in a glass box. This shrine is reminiscent of the work *Christ in the Holy Sepulchre*, by Miguel Herrera, in the Taylor Museum (Colorado Springs) collection.

Austin

In Austin, the yard shrines differ from the small oratories constructed inside the home, appropriately called home altars by those who study them, and *altares* (altars) or *altarcitos* (little altars) by those

Figure 18.11. Theodora Sánchez. *Nicho* (Yard Shrine), dedicated to Saint Dymphna. 1957. Tucson, Arizona. (Photograph by Jacinto Quirarte).

who build them. The former are "public" and the result of a manda (offering), the latter are "private" and are not tied down to a specific promise given in a time of "need." Both serve a religious function and can be equally complex. Home altars, however, are probably found over a wider area.

The most frequently used image in the Austin home altars is Our Lady of Guadalupe, although other sacred images are also used. The altars include votive candles, flowers, milagros (small sculptures), family photographs, ceramic birds, shells, stones, stuffed animals, bottles full of buttons, ribbons, tea cups, and even photographs of John Kennedy and Bobby Kennedy (both martyred) and other political figures. The altars, therefore, provide the focus for religious as well secular concerns.

✱HISPANIC-AMERICAN ARTISTS: 1920s THROUGH THE 1950s

Throughout the period from World War I through the 1950s, most Hispano (Spanish-American), Mexican-American, and other Hispanic-American artists

were part of mainstream art in the United States. Their work was part of the figurative and regionalist traditions that dominated such art in the 1920s through the 1940s. Among the noted artists whose works are characteristic of the period are the Mexican-American artists Octavio Medellín, Antonio García, José Aceves, and Edward Chávez. Other important Hispanic artists of the period are Francisco Luis Mora, born in Uruguay, and Carlos López, born in Cuba. Among the Spanish-born artists are José Moya del Pino and Xavier González. The latter two are also associated with Mexico, González through immigration before entering the United States, and Moya del Pino through the subjects and style of his work.

The Mexican-American artists were primarily found in the Southwest, and other Hispanics lived in the Great Lakes and northeastern regions. Medellin, García, and Aceves were based in Texas; Chavez in New Mexico, Colorado, and New York; López in Michigan; and Mora in New York and Connecticut. González was initially based in Texas and later in Louisiana, and Moya del Pino in California.

Mexican-American Artists

The subject matter of most of the works by Mexican-American and other Hispanic artists was primarily American, particularly in the murals they painted in the 1930s under the auspices of the Works Progress Art Project (WPAP). However, some of the Mexican-American artists focused on their Mexican as well as American background in their work, as in the case of García and Medellín.

Antonio García (1901-)
and
Octavio Medellín (1907-)

Antonio García used the Spanish Conquest of Mexico as a theme in a work titled *Aztec Advance* (1929), and a Mexican national and religious icon in a mural titled *Our Lady of Guadalupe* (1946-47). Medellín dealt with the entire scope of Mexican history, from pre-Columbian times to the revolution to the 1940s with a sculpture titled *History of Mexico* (1949), and treated the pre-Columbian Maya and Toltec in a series of prints titled *Xtol: Dance of the Ancient Maya People* (1962), based on research he carried out in Yucatán in 1938 (Figure 18.12).

Antonio García, born in Monterrey, Mexico, in 1901, moved with his family to San Diego, Texas, around 1911. He studied at the Chicago Art Institute from 1927 to 1930 and taught art at Del Mar College, Corpus Christi, Texas, from 1950 to 1970. He is retired and continues to reside in Corpus Christi.

Octavio Medellín, born in Matehuala, Mexico, in 1907, moved to San Antonio, Texas, in 1920, where he studied painting under José Arpa and drawing under Xavier González at the San Antonio School of Art from 1921 to 1928; he studied at the Chicago Art Institute in 1928. He traveled the Gulf Coast of Mexico from 1929 to 1931 and the Yucatán in 1938. He taught at North Texas State College (now the University of North Texas), Denton, from 1938 to 1942, and at Southern Methodist University, Dallas, from 1945 to 1966. In 1969 he opened his own art school in Dallas. He is retired and lives in Bandera, Texas.

José Aceves (1909-)

José Aceves painted murals (framed oil paintings) for the post offices in Borger and Mart, Texas (both in 1939). The mural in Borger, titled *Big City News*, deals with the mail service's delivering news to the most remote and isolated regions of the country. The mural in Mart, titled *McLennan Looking for a Home*, focuses on the arrival in 1841 of Neil McLennan and his family in the Bosque River Valley, eight miles east of Waco, Texas. The latter is typical of the idealized portrayals of the pioneers in the Southwest seen in

Figure 18.12. Octavio Medellín. *Xtol* print. (Photograph courtesy of the artist).

post office murals of that period. Aceves was influenced by the muralist Edward Holsag in the development of the western subject matter in the Mart painting.

Aceves was born in Chihuahua, Mexico, in 1909, and moved with his family to El Paso in 1915 as a result of the chaos created by the Mexican Revolution. He studied art at the Museum of Fine Arts in Dallas and at the Chicago Art Institute in the 1930s.

Edward Chávez (1917-)

Edward Chávez painted murals for post offices and other government buildings from 1939 to 1943 in Denver, Colorado, Geneva, Nebraska, Center, Texas, and Fort Warren, Wyoming. His murals deal with a direct portrayal of life and industry in each of the areas where he received commissions for his work. He turned to abstraction in the 1950s and 1960s.

For the Denver Center High School panels, titled *The Pioneers* (1939), Chávez focused on the daily chores of tending the oxen on the wagon trail and chopping down trees. He chose the actual building of a sod house as the subject for his Geneva, Nebraska, mural, *Building a Sod House* (1941). He portrayed the early method of hauling logs in the lumber industry around Center, Texas, for that city's post office mural, *Logging Scene* (1941). He focused on the Indians and the first white men in Wyoming for the mural in Fort Warren, *Indians of the Plains* (1943). All his works were painted with oil on canvas except for the one in Wyoming, which was painted with egg tempera on plywood.

The large wall of Chávez's mural in the Fort Warren Service Club measures eighteen feet high by forty feet wide (Figure 18.13). It has double doors in the lower center and stairs on each side that break up the rectangular format of the mural. A large Indian in the central part of the mural over the doors kneels on one leg, holds a peace pipe in one hand, and gestures with the other. There are numerous scenes in which hunting and other everyday activities of the Indians are depicted in two horizontal registers to the left and right of the large Indian. American soldiers standing by a tent are seen on the lowermost panel on the left, and Indians are standing by a tepee on the right.

Edward Chávez was born in New Mexico in 1917 and now lives in Woodstock, New York. Although he studied at the Colorado Springs Fine Arts Center, he considers himself to be largely self-taught as an artist. He taught at the Art Students League, New York City, 1954 and 1955-1958; Colorado College, Colorado Springs, 1959; Syracuse University in New York, 1960-1961, and Dutchess Community College, Poughkeepsie, New York, 1963. He was appointed artist in

Figure 18.13. Edward Chávez. *Indians of the Plains*. 1943. Egg Tempera on Plywood. 18' high x 40' wide. Service Club, Fort Warren, Wyoming. (Photograph courtesy of the artist).

residence at the Huntington Fine Arts Gallery in West Virginia in 1967.

Other Mexican-American Artists

From the 1940s through the 1950s, other Mexican-American artists continued to reflect regional concerns in their work in a figurative or realistic style. Others worked in the abstract and nonfigurative styles of the same period. There was an emphasis on regionalism in the landscapes of the New Mexican artist Margaret Herrera Chávez and the Texas bluebonnet painter Porfirio Salinas. Other regionalists, such as Pedro Cervantes of New Mexico, painted still lifes.

Herrera Chávez was born in Las Vegas, New Mexico, in 1912. Salinas, born in Bastrop, Texas in 1912, was raised in San Antonio, where he died in 1973. Cervantes, born in Wilcox, Arizona, in 1915, has spent most of his life in Clovis, New Mexico.

Chelo González Amezcua, a contemporary of Antonio García and Octavio Medellín, devoted the last ten to twenty years of her life to her art and poetry. Most of her work was based on a highly personal ichnography in which there are depictions of numerous birds and exotic places and personages. Amezcua was born in Ciudad Acuña, Mexico, in 1903, but lived most of her life in Del Rio, Texas, where she died in 1975.

Other Hispanic-American Artists

The murals painted by other Hispanic artists in the 1930s were similar to those painted by Aceves, Chávez, and other Mexican-American artists. The subjects portrayed invariably dealt with the history, industry, identity, or landscape of the city or region for which they were painted.

Francisco Luis Mora (1874-1940)

Francisco Luis Mora painted murals for the Orpheum Theatre in Los Angeles, the reading room of the Lynn Public Library in Lynn, Massachusetts, the central building of the Red Cross in Washington, D.C., and in Clarksville, Tennessee (1938). Among his earliest public works was a large decoration for the Missouri State Building for the Saint Louis Fair of 1904, for which he received a Bronze Medal.

The Clarksville mural deals with the settlement of the area by Moses Renfroe and his family, who arrived there in April 1779, and modern Tennessee, its resources, and its industries. The subjects were depicted in two panels. The first focuses on the first settlement of the area. A group of settlers is seen on the top of a bank overlooking the Red River. Colonel Donaldson, who had brought them there, is shown in conversation with the elder Renfroe. Most of the settlers were later killed by the Indians in the area. The second panel focuses on the many resources of modern Tennessee—tobacco, corn, cotton, lumber, and marble—and its mills and factories. According to the artist, the first panel deals with "sacrifice," the second with "a sense of achievement."

Mora was born in Montevideo, Uruguay, in 1874, and his family immigrated to the United States in 1880. He studied with his father, a sculptor, and at the Museum of Fine Arts School in Boston and at the Art Students League in New York. He taught painting and drawing for many years at the Chare School and the Art Students League in New York. He died in New York City in 1940.

José Moya del Pino (1891-1969)

Throughout the 1930s, Moya del Pino painted murals under the auspices of the WPAP and for private corporations. In 1933, he painted murals and did the decorations, in Aztec and Mayan motifs, for the rathskeller of the Aztec Brewery in San Diego, California. In the mid 1930s, he worked on the WPAP-sponsored murals painted in San Francisco's Coit Tower. He also painted murals in Stockton (1936), Redwood City (1937), and Lancaster, California (1937), and Alpine, Texas (1940).

As in the case of the other muralists, Moya del Pino focused on the industries and landscapes of the cities where his works were placed. The Redwood City mural, *Flower Farming and Vegetable Raising*, deals with the important activities of the county—agriculture, horticulture, industry, maritime trade, and leisure. The Lancaster mural, *Hauling Water Pipe Through Antelope Valley*, focuses on the characteristic view of this desert valley with a long mule team hauling a wagon filled with water pipe for irrigation. The Alpine, Texas, mural, *View of Alpine*, emphasizes the vast landscape, with placement of the town of Alpine in the middle distance, and in the foreground, students with their books, cattle, horses, and a cattleman reading his farm journal.

In 1988, Moya del Pino's murals and decorations in the rathskeller of the Aztec Brewery in San Diego were threatened with destruction when the brewery was targeted for demolition to make way for the construction of a ten-million-dollar concrete ware-house. The brewery had been closed for over thirty years. When Salvador Roberto Torres, a leading Chicano activist from the Barrio de la Logan, learned of the demolition, he sought to have the murals saved.

José Moya del Pino, born in Cordova, Spain, in 1891, studied art in his native country and settled in San Francisco, California, in 1928. He died in Ross, outside San Francisco, in 1969. Most of his work was done in California.

Xavier González (1898-19?)

In 1930, Xavier González won third prize in a national competition for murals on the subject "The Dynamic of Man's Creative Power." The winning entries were installed in the Los Angeles Museum. He later painted murals for the post offices in Hammond and Covington, Louisiana (1936 and 1939), the federal courtroom in Huntsville, Alabama (1937), and the post offices in Kilgore and Mission, Texas (1941 and 1942).

Typical of González's work is the mural for the Huntsville federal courtroom, titled *Tennessee Valley Authority*. The five figures in the painting symbolize, according to the artist, "a community devoted to the activities of a well-organized society." The figures are independent of each other but were drawn to the same scale. The arrangement of the figures creates a circular motion on the frontal plane. Each figure represents an aspect of human endeavor in the scientific, agricultural, economic, or artistic sphere and the social organization needed to coordinate these spheres. A standing woman in the center with a basket of fruit represents youth and fertility, and a man on the upper right represents work. A young man holding a plant of corn below him represents "scientific agriculture." A woman making pottery on the upper left represents artistic endeavor, and the woman holding a child in the lower center of the painting represents motherhood. They are placed within a landscape that is characteristic of Huntsville.

Xavier González was born in Almeira, Spain, in 1898, and received his art training at the Chicago Art Institute. He taught art in San Antonio, Texas, in the early 1920s and at Newcomb College, Tulane University, from 1929 to 1943. He presently lives in Newark, New Jersey.

Carlos López (1908-1953)

Carlos López painted murals under the WPAP from 1937 to 1942. His first mural was painted in Dwight, Illinois (1937), followed by three others in the Michigan cities of Plymouth (1938), Paw Paw (1940), and Birmingham (1942).

The Dwight mural, *The Stage at Dawn*, depicts a

Wells Fargo stagecoach being harnessed for its journey to the western boundaries of the United States. The Plymouth mural, *Plymouth Trail*, represents a passenger coach arriving in Plymouth around the mid-1860s. The focus is on the transportation link between Indiana and Illinois and the east. The Paw Paw mural, *Bounty*, depicts the agricultural industries (fruit and vegetables) and recreations of the people of Paw Paw (grape festival with square dancing, and an ice-skating scene).

Throughout the 1940s, López received numerous commissions from several federal agencies and from private companies to portray various aspects of American life: American industries at war for the War Department, a pictorial record of the war for *Life* magazine, the amphibious training activities for the navy, and the project Michigan on Canvas, for the J. L. Hudson Company. After World War II, López's work turned toward fantasy and symbol, conveyed by figures that always appear to stand alone, lonely and sad.

López, born in Havana, Cuba, in 1908, spent his early years in Spain and lived in South America before immigrating to the United States when he was eleven years old. He studied at the Art Institute of Chicago and the Detroit Art Academy and taught art at the University of Michigan from 1945 until his death in 1953.

Rufino Silva (1919-)

The work of Rufino Silva, a Chicago-based artist, belongs to the Chicago school of social realism in a surrealistic vein. His work is similar to that of Jack Levine, but less trenchant.

Silva was born in Humacao, Puerto Rico, in 1919. He studied at the Chicago Art Institute from 1938 to 1942 on a fellowship from the Puerto Rican government. He taught at the Layton School of Art, Milwaukee, from 1946 to 1947 and studied abroad for four years, 1947-51, in Europe and South America on grants from the art institute. He returned to Chicago in 1952 and joined the faculty. He retired in the 1970s.

✳HISPANIC-AMERICAN ARTISTS: 1960s AND 1970s

In the 1960s, the art of Mexican-American and other Hispanic-American artists continued to reflect the many current styles of art, from figurative to abstract, to pop, op, and funk, to destructive and all the others. Some of the artists who had painted murals in the 1930s and 1940s turned to abstraction, as in the case of Edward Chávez. However, he continued to make references in his abstract works to his background by using Mexican place-names, such as Xochimilco in one of his paintings.

Among the Mexican-American and Chicano artists who matured in the 1960s are Michael Ponce de León of New York, Eugenio Quesada of Phoenix, Arizona, Peter Rodríguez of San Francisco, Melesio Casas of San Antonio, Texas, Manuel Neri of San Francisco, Ernesto Palomino of Fresno, California, and Luis Jiménez of Hondo, New Mexico. Puerto Rican artists who matured during the same period include New York-based artists Olga Albizu, Pedro Villarini, Rafael Montañez-Ortiz (Ralph Ortiz), and Rafael Ferrer. There were many other artists from Latin America working in New York and other U.S. cities at the time, but their work falls outside the confines of this study because their formative years as artists were spent in their country of origin. Their presence, however, has not gone unnoticed by Hispanic-American and other American artists. Some remained in the United States for many years and then returned to their native countries. Others stayed to continue their careers.

Among those who stayed and attained national and international status for their work is the Argentine printmaker Mauricio Lasansky, who immigrated to the United States in 1943 and taught printmaking at Iowa State University, Ames. He influenced generations of American printmakers through his teaching and his work. He was born in Buenos Aires in 1914 and became a U.S. citizen in 1952. Marisol Escobar, born to Venezuelan parents in Paris in 1930, has resided in New York City since 1960. She became internationally famous in the 1960s with her sculptures of well-known personalities, such as Lyndon Baines Johnson and John Wayne. Fernando Botero, known for his paintings of overblown figures used in satirical contexts, arrived in New York City in 1960. He was born in Medellín, Colombia, and now resides in New York City and Paris.

Mexican-American Artists

Michael Ponce de León (1922-)

The work of New York printmaker Michael Ponce de León was in keeping with the new styles of the 1960s. He used a raised surface (relief) and objects to create works that were expressive of his feelings toward words, places, conditions, and events.

Ponce de León was born in Miami, Florida, in 1922 and spent his early years in Mexico City. He joined the U.S. Air Force during World War II. After working as a cartoonist in New York in the 1940s and early 1950s, he turned to printmaking in the late 1950s. He has taught printmaking at the Pratt Graphic Center in New York.

Peter Rodríguez (1926-)
and
Eugenio Quesada (1927-)

Peter Rodríguez of California and Eugenio Quesada of Arizona spent several years in Mexico, and their work reflects that experience. Rodríguez used Mexican place-names in some of his abstract works, such as *Tlalpan*. In recent years, he has concentrated on making altars that have a closer relationship to his background as a Chicano in northern California. Quesada's drawings of Mexican-American children are similar in form and subject to the paintings and drawings of Mexican artists such as Raúl Anguiano.

Rodríguez was born in Stockton, California, in 1926 and received all his schooling in that city. As founder of the Mexican Museum in San Francisco in 1972, he has had a great impact on the development of the Chicano art movement in the San Francisco Bay area.

Quesada, born in Wickenburg, Arizona, in 1927, studied at Mesa Community College and Arizona State University, where he received a bachelor of arts degree. He taught at Santa Paula High School, California, in 1954, Glendale Community College, Arizona, in 1972, and has taught at Arizona State University since 1972.

Manuel Neri (1930-)

Manuel Neri of the San Francisco Bay area was at the forefront of the art movements of the 1960s, especially funk art. Although his work was based primarily on the human figure defined in plaster and selective polychromy, he referred to pre-Columbian architectural forms, such as the pyramid, in other works.

Neri, born in Sanger, California, in 1930, received all his early schooling in Los Angeles. He studied ceramics from 1949 to 1953 at San Francisco City College, the University of California, and the Bray Foundation in Helena, Montana. He also studied at the Oakland School of Art and Crafts from 1955 to 1957 and at the California School of Art, now the San Francisco Art Institute, from 1957 to 1959. He has taught at the University of California, Davis, for many years.

Chicano Artists

Melesio Casas (1929-)

Melesio Casas of San Antonio, Texas, was among the pioneers of the Chicano art movement. Although he began to include references to the United Farm Workers" eagle logo and pre-Columbian motifs in his work as early as 1970, the way in which these were used reflects the pop art style of the early 1960s. Typical of these works is the 1970 painting *Brownies of the Southwest*.

Casas was born in El Paso, Texas, in 1929. He attended Texas Western University, where he received his bachelor of arts degree in 1956, and the University of the Americas in Mexico City, where he received his master of fine arts degree in 1958. As a teacher and an artist at San Antonio College for almost thirty years, he had a strong impact on the training and education of many Chicano artists in San Antonio. He is retired and presently lives in southern Italy.

Ernesto Palomino (1933-)

Ernesto Palomino was among the first of the Chicano muralists to use pre-Columbian and Mexican as well as Chicano motifs in murals, such as the one he painted in Fresno, California, in 1971. Before he began work as a muralist, Palomino made constructions of various materials that were characteristic of the works being produced in the San Francisco Bay area in the mid-1960s.

Palomino, born in Fresno, California, in 1933, has spent most of his life in that city as an artist, and has been a professor at Fresno State University since 1970. He attended the San Francisco Art Institute, 1954, Fresno City College, 1957, and San Francisco State University, 1960-65.

Luis Jiménez (1940-)

Luis Jiménez, of El Paso, Texas, is primarily known for his sculptures made of resin epoxy coated with fiberglass. Jiménez paraphrased Mexican art, American Western art, and used pre-Columbian concepts in his works of the late 1960s and early 1970s. Since then, he has concentrated on the Southwest for a series of sculptures and colored-pencil drawings. Among the early works are *Man on Fire* (1969-1970), *The End of the Trail* (1971), *The American Dream* (1967-1969), and *Indians to Rockets* (1972).

Jiménez initially selected the many post office murals found all over the country as a source for the imagery in the *Indian to Rockets* project. The murals in the Southwest invariably deal with the history of the region or its industries. What struck the artist most was the emphasis in all of these murals on the notion of progress, exemplified by the machine. Starting in the early 1970s, he did studies on the history of the Southwest that were eventually used for a series of sculptures on that subject, titled *Progress I*, *Progress II*, and so on.

Toward the end of the 1970s, Jiménez began to concentrate more specifically on regional subjects in which the Chicano, the Anglo, and others were represented in their natural surroundings. A good example of these works is the drawing of a man and woman dancing while an onlooker watches, titled *Honky Tonk* (1981-86).

Jiménez was born in El Paso, Texas, in 1940. He attended the University of Texas, Austin, where he received his bachelor of fine arts degree in 1964. He received a fellowship from the National University of Mexico. Shortly afterward, he moved to New York, where he worked and exhibited in several galleries. He now resides in Hondo, New Mexico.

Puerto Rican Artists

Olga Albizu (1924-)

Olga Albizu is an abstract painter who became widely known for her paintings for RCA record covers for the music of Stan Getz in the late 1950s. Albizu was born in Ponce, Puerto Rico, in 1924 and has lived in the United States since 1956. She first arrived in New York City in 1948 with a University of Puerto Rico fellowship for postgraduate study. She studied with the well-known abstract expressionist Hans Hoffmann at the Art Students League, 1948-51, and that experience is evident in her work. She also studied in Paris and Florence in 1951.

Rafael Ferrer (1933-)

In the 1960s, Rafael Ferrer was at the forefront of the movement in New York City that dealt with temporary installations and other ephemeral works and deemphasized "the object" as a work of art. He experimented with a variety of media and methods, from assemblages, constructions, and freestanding sculpture to lengths of chain-link fence, blocks of ice, bales of hay, and masses of dry leaves used to create environments for indoor and outdoor exhibitions. These temporary installations were related to the nonobject events of conceptual art of the early 1970s.

In the early 1970s, Ferrer began to focus on imaginary voyages and the apparatus used to carry them out—maps, kayaks, tents, and boats—in works assembled or constructed of steel, wood, and other materials.

Ferrer was born in Santurce, Puerto Rico, in 1933. He studied at the Shunton Military Academy, Virginia, from 1948 to 1951 and at Syracuse University, New York, from 1951 to 1952. He abandoned his studies at Syracuse to study art in Puerto Rico, where he was introduced to the work of the surrealists by the Spanish painter E. F. Granell. From then on he spent part of the year in Puerto Rico and part in the United States until 1966, when he settled in Philadelphia.

Pedro Villarini (1933-)

Pedro Villarini defines all the motifs in his paintings with great precision. There is a stillness and an air of calm in his painting *La Fortaleza* (1968). The peaceful effect is enhanced by the horizontal directions established by the fortress wall and the buildings in the middle ground, and by the clouds in the sky. They are balanced by the turret of the fortress on the left side of the painting.

Villarini was born in 1933 in Hato Ray, Puerto Rico, and has lived in New York City since 1947. He is a self-taught painter.

Ralph Ortiz (1934-)

The work of Rafael Montañez-Ortiz (Ralph Ortiz), was part of the European and American movement known as destructive art. His best-known piece, *Piano Destruction Concert*, was performed on BBC television in 1966 and later presented on national and local television in the United States (Figure 18.14). The extreme gestures in Ortiz's work have their source in the work of the European Dadaists, who

Figure 18.14. Ralph Ortiz. *Piano Destruction Concert Duncan Terrace.* Destruction in Art Symposium, September 1966, London. (Photograph courtesy of the artist).

emerged during World War I. In one of their events, they invited viewers to use an ax placed next to a small exhibit to destroy the art. This was only one of many antiart gestures of the Dadaists. Ortiz focused on the violence itself in order to emphasize its pervasive presence in our lives. This was unlike the "happenings" of Claes Oldemburg, Allan Kaprow, and others, which were essentially formalist events.

Ortiz also used pre-Columbian references in a series he called Archaeological Finds, in order to focus on his non-European roots and the destruction wrought by the first Europeans who arrived in the Americas. A typical piece in this series is an upholstered chair that was torn apart—destroyed—and titled *Tlazolteotl* (1963, a manifestation of the Aztec earth goddess).

Ortiz was born in New York City in 1934. He studied at the High School of Art and Design, the Brooklyn Museum of Art, and the Pratt Institute, where he received a bachelor of science degree and a master of fine arts degree in 1964. He received the doctorate of fine arts and fine arts higher education degrees from Columbia University in 1967. He taught at New York University, 1968, and was an adjunct professor at Hostos Community College, in the Bronx in 1970.

✳ HISPANIC-AMERICAN ARTISTS: 1970s TO THE PRESENT

Chicano Artists

There were many Chicano artists who matured in the 1970s and 1980s. Some were muralists or public artists, others were not. There were many easel painters, sculptors, printmakers, and poster artists who were also interested in the Chicano movement as a source of their work. Some of them started as muralists and then turned to painting easel pictures, making altars, or creating other nonmural work.

The greatest number of Hispanic artists are found in California, followed by Texas and then the other states where Mexican Americans and Chicanos reside. Many have received recognition for their work through regional, national, and international exhibitions that have focused on their background as Mexican Americans, Chicanos, or Hispanics. In the late 1960s and early 1970s, exhibitions of Chicano art were strictly local and regional events. By the late 1970s, major exhibitions that included all Hispanic groups were being organized and presented in the United States and abroad.

Los Angeles, California

In Los Angeles, there were numerous muralists as well as easel painters, sculptors, and printmakers. Those who painted murals in the 1970s concentrated more and more on nonmural work by the 1980s. Among the artists who did both are Carlos Almaraz, Gilbert Sánchez Luján (Magú), Frank Romero, John Valadez, and Gronk. Almaraz, Sánchez Luján (Magú), and Romero were members of the group called Los Four. The other member was Beto de la Rocha. They focused on Mexican icons and the Chicano political movement in their work. Gronk was a member of ASCO (nausea) along with Willie Herrón, Harry Gamboa, and Patssi Valdez. They were conceptual and performance artists as well as muralists in the 1970s.

Gilbert Sánchez Luján (Magú) (1940-)

Sánchez Luján is known for his pastel paintings and painted wood sculptures that deal with barrio life in southern California. In some of the wood sculptures, he combines brightly colored cactus and palm trees in tableaus that include smartly dressed figures with dog faces! Their activities on the street, at the beach, or elsewhere in the barrio strike a responsive chord in the viewer who reacts to the humor in the scenes. A good example of his work is the sculpture *Hot Dog Meets La Fufu con su Poochie* (1986). The wood cutouts of the two figures, the dog, the plants, and the small fence were painted in different colors and constructed to create a whimsical street scene with two young people in the barrio reacting to each other.

Luján was born in French Camp (Stockton), California, in 1940. He attended East Los Angeles Junior College and Long Beach State College, where he received his bachelor of arts degree. He received his master of fine arts degree at the University of California, Irvine, and made a commitment to Chicano art at this time. He joined Almaraz and Romero to form the exhibiting group known as Los Four. Their first show went up at Irvine in 1974. He taught ethnic studies at Fresno City College, 1976-81, and then returned to Los Angeles, where he taught at the Municipal Art Center at Barnsdall Park.

Carlos Almaraz (1941-)

Carlos Almaraz was deeply involved with the Chicano movement in the 1970s, doing volunteer work with the United Farmworkers Union from 1972 to 1974, and graphic designs for the Teatro Campesino, which was formed to promote the farm worker cause. He was also a counselor and program director for the All Nations Neighborhood Center, helping "hard core" youth from 1974 to 1976. He also painted murals in East Los Angeles during the same period until 1978. Since the 1980s, he has concentrated on painting nonmural works of art that focus on his background as a Chicano. A good example of his nonmural work is the painting *Europe and the Jaguar* (1982), in which the two major strands of Mexican and Mexican-American or Chicano culture—the European and the indigenous—are woven into a complex pictorial statement. A woman and a jaguar walking hand in hand are in front of a backdrop full of isolated motifs—a house, a train, a quarter moon, human heads in profile—painted in an explosive style. A man between them on a lower level stands calmly smoking a cigarette. The backdrop seems to be full of multicolored sparks that give the surface a luminous effect. Almaraz was born in Mexico City in 1941. His family moved to Chicago when he was one year old, and to California when he was eight. He attended Loyola University in New Orleans, California State University, Los Angeles, East Los Angeles College, and Los Angeles Community College. He also attended the New School of Social Research and the Art Students League in New York City. Almaraz received his master of fine arts degree from the Otis Art Institute in 1974. He exhibited as a member of Los Four in 1974 at the University of California, Irvine and the Los Angeles County Museum.

Rupert García (1941-)

The precisely defined flat areas that are characteristic of the silk-screen process make the work of Rupert García immediately recognizable. The unvarying fields of color, which are also part of this process, carry over into some of his painting. This aspect of his work is so strong that a design he provided for a mural in Chicano Park, San Diego, retained the look of a silk-screen print. The pylon mural, actually painted by Víctor Ochoa and the Barrio Renovation Team, focuses on *Los Tres Grandes* (Diego Rivera, José Clemente Orozco, and David Alfaro Siqueiros) and *Frida Kahlo* (1978).

García was born in French Camp, California, in 1941. He attended Stockton College and San Francisco State University, where he received his bachelor of arts degree, in painting in 1968 and a master of arts degree in printmaking (silk-screen) in 1970. He pursued his doctoral studies in art education at the University of California, Berkeley, from 1973 to 1975, and received another master of arts degree, in the history of modern art, in 1981. He taught at San Francisco State University, 1969-81; the San Francisco Art Institute, 1973-80; the University of Califor-

nia, Berkeley, 1979-present; Mills College, 1981; Washington State University, 1984; and the Mexican Museum, San Francisco, 1986.

Frank Romero (1941-)

Frank Romero, another member of the Los Four, has often focused on street scenes in his paintings, in which automobiles are prominently displayed. Sometimes he makes a statement about barrio life in Los Angeles. He works in various media other than painting and drawing—photography, graphics, ceramics, and textile design. A good example of his work is the painting *The Closing of Whittier Boulevard* (1984). The night scene includes a bird's-eye view of a street corner in East Los Angeles where the police have set up barricades to stop the flow of traffic. The two streets leading up to the corner are filled with cars with their lights illuminating the police behind the barricades, who are holding billy clubs. The toylike appearance of the figures and the cars gives the entire scene an eerie effect.

Romero was born in East Los Angeles in 1941. He attended the Otis Art Institute and California State University, Los Angeles, where he met Carlos Almaraz in the 1960s. He met Gilbert Luján and Beto de la Rocha in 1969 during a sojourn in New York (1968-69) during which he stayed with his friend Almaraz. Throughout the early 1970s, he was involved in the Chicano movement.

Yolanda López (1942-)

López used Our Lady of Guadalupe in a series of works that emphasize Chicano culture and identity. She substituted human figures and an Aztec deity for Our Lady of Guadalupe in several works, including her grandmother, Tonantzin (Our Mother), a small sculpture of Coatlicue (Serpents her Skirt), an Indian woman nursing her child, and the artist herself. Her self-portraits include a performance piece and a painting. In the former, the artist was photographed moving toward the viewer armed with paint brushes and wearing blue shorts, a sleeveless undershirt with stars painted on it, and sneakers. In the latter, the artist is shown appropriating the attributes of Our Lady of Guadalupe and her pre-Columbian counterpart. She runs toward the observer with an expression of triumph while holding a serpent in one hand and a mantle with a star-studded blue field in the other.

López was born in San Diego in 1942. She received her master of fine arts degree from the University of California, San Diego, 1978. She is currently a visiting lecturer in painting at the California College of Arts and Crafts.

Amalia Mesa-Baines (1943-)

Although the altar installations by Amalia Mesa-Baines are not directly religious in content, their format has allowed her to attain a spiritual sensibility that is in tune with her personal and cultural life. She has used these altars to pay homage to ancestors and Mexican historical figures in the arts, religion, and the cinema, such as Frida Kahlo, Sor Juana de la Cruz, and Dolores del Rio.

Mesa-Baines uses Mexican symbols in her altars, such as *calaveras* (skulls), *corazones* (hearts), crosses, and images of the Virgin in her many manifestations. She also cuts her own paper (*papel picado*), makes the altar cloths and paper flowers, and builds the *nichos* and the *retablo* boxes with the help of a carpenter.

One of her major works, *Altar for San Juana Inés de la Cruz* (1981), a mixed-media construction, was shown in the Made in Aztlán exhibition at the Centro Cultural de la Raza in San Diego in 1986.

Mesa-Baines first exhibited an altar in the annual show at the Galería de la Raza in 1976 and later at the San Francisco Museum of Art in 1980. She has since exhibited altars in several national and international exhibitions. Mesa-Baines received her doctor of philosophy in psychology with an emphasis on culture and identity.

Ester Hernández (1944-)

Ester Hernández has used her painting and graphic work to make statements about Chicano culture and the economic forces that have had a negative impact on one segment of it: the farm-working communities in California. One of the most controversial works by Hernández is a print that was published on the cover of *En frecuencia*, a guide for public radio in Santa Rosa, California. The primary focus of the image was on Our Lady of Guadalupe, but instead of using the traditional image of the Virgin, she used a woman in a karate stance to make a statement about the liberation of Chicanas.

Hernández was born in Dinuba, California, in 1944 to farm-worker parents. She moved to the San Francisco Bay area in 1971 to continue her studies. She met and worked with other Chicano artists, among them Malaquías Montoya, and became involved with Mujeres Muralistas (Women Muralists). She teaches at an art center for the developmentally disabled in San Francisco.

Patricia Rodríguez (1944-)

Patricia Rodríguez was one of the leading muralists in the Bay Area in the 1970s. In 1972, she organized the group known as Mujeres Muralistas, and with them painted murals from 1972 to 1977. Its members were Consuelo Méndez, Irene Pérez, and Graciela Carrillo. In 1980, she began working on box constructions, inspired by the traditional *nichos* that serve a religious function for the Chicano family. She focused on religious prejudice, cultural identity, and the world around her. The boxes or nichos, made with found and handmade objects, are based on Catholic traditions as well as on the myths, legends, and magic of Mexican culture dating all the way back to the Aztecs and the Mayans.

Rodríguez was born in Marfa, Texas, in 1944. She was raised by her grandparents, and at age 11 lived with her parents, who worked as migrants throughout the Southwest. At age 13, in the 1950s, she attended public schools in California. She later attended junior college and the San Francisco Art Institute on a scholarship. She taught at the University of California from 1975 to 1980.

Judy Baca (1946-)

Judy Baca is one of the pioneers of the mural movement in Los Angeles. She founded the first city of Los Angeles mural program in 1974, and in 1976 she cofounded the Social and Public Art Resource Center (SPARC) in Venice, California, where she served as artistic director throughout the 1970s and 1980s. Her best-known work is *The Great Wall of Los Angeles*. Painted over five summers, the half-mile long mural employed 40 ethnic scholars, 450 multicultural neighborhood youth, 40 assisting artists, and over 100 support staff (Figure 18.15).

She is currently working on a mural program that addresses issues of war, peace, cooperation, interdependence, and spiritual growth. It is titled *World Wall: A Vision of the Future Without Fear* and consists of seven portable panels that measure ten feet by thirty feet each.

Baca was born in Los Angeles in 1946. She attended California State University, Northridge, where she received her bachelor of arts degree in 1969. She also did work toward a master of art education degree and completed an intensive mural techniques course in Cuernavaca, Mexico.

Carmen Lomas Garza (1948-)

Carmen Lomas Garza, a painter and printmaker, uses her Chicano background as the primary focus of her work. Her images, based on recollections of her childhood in south Texas, are used to heal the wounds she suffered as a result of racism and discrimination.

One of Lomas Garza's most widely known series is the one based on the game Lotería (The Lottery) (Figure 18.16). In the work, titled *Lotería—Tabla Llena*, she consciously used an exaggerated perspective, reminiscent of the works of native artists, be-

Figure 18.15. Judy Baca. *The Great Wall of Los Angeles*. "350 Mexicans Deported and Dustbowl Refugees." Detail of the Great Wall of Los Angeles. 1980. Mural program was begun in 1976. (Photograph by Jacinto Quirarte).

cause it allowed her to present all the thematic elements (motifs) in the work in as clear a fashion as possible. The large table was presented as if seen from above, and everything else—the figures, the animals, furniture, plants, and trees—was represented as if seen head-on. The only exception is the walkway at the bottom of the print, also shown as if seen from above.

Garza was born in Kingsville, Texas, in 1948. She attended Texas A&I University in Kingsville, where she received her bachelor of arts degree in 1972. She attended Antioch Graduate School of Education, Juarez Lincoln Extension (Austin), where she received her master of arts degree in 1973. She received another master of arts degree from San Francisco State University in 1980. She currently resides in San Francisco.

San Francisco, California

In San Francisco since the 1960s, artists have focused on social, political, cultural, and feminist issues in their nonmural works. Malaquías Montoya and Rupert García were two of the most active politcal artists in the Bay Area. Their comments against American involvement in the internal affairs of Latin American countries appeared repeatedly in their silk-screen prints, posters, and paintings of the 1970s and 1980s. Many women artists dealt with cultural and feminist issues during the same time. Yolanda López focused on the family and Our Lady of Guadalupe in her drawings, paintings, and installations of the late 1970s. Amalia Mesa Baines dealt with similar issues in her altar installations. Ester Hernández dealt with feminist and environmental issues in her prints and paintings. Patricia Rodríguez, a muralist in the 1970s, turned to cultural issues in the 1980s, with boxes that have their genesis in the home altars found in many Chicano homes. Carmen Lomas Garza focused on her childhood in south Texas in her prints and paintings of the 1970s and 1980s.

San Diego, California

Many Chicano artists in San Diego were at the forefront of the Chicano mural movement. Their struggle to create Chicano Park in the Barrio de la

Figure 18.16. Carmen Lomas Garza. *Lotería—Table Llena,* 1974. (Photograph courtesy of the artist).

Logan and the Centro Cultural in Balboa Park has been recounted in numerous local, national, and international publications. The story has even been told in an hour-long video that has been telecast over National Public Television. Among the pioneers of that struggle were Salvador Roberto Torres, Víctor Ochoa, David Avalos, and others who were members of the group called Toltecas en Aztlán, initially, and later Congreso de Artistas Chicanos en Aztlan. (See the section later in this chapter on Chicano murals for more information.)

Víctor Ochoa (1948-)

Víctor Ochoa, who is one of the pioneers of the Chicano art movement in San Diego, has concentrated primarily on mural painting. A good example of his work is the mural *Gerónimo* (1981) on one part of the wall of the Centro Cultural in Balboa Park (Figure 18.17). It is a gigantic depiction of the late-nineteenth-century Apache warrior Gerónimo. It is a faithful rendition of a well-known photograph of the Apache leader. Ochoa saw him as a freedom fighter, with whom he identified as a Chicano fighting for his rights in his community. This is in contrast to the

view of Gerónimo in traditional American history as a renegade. The other figures on either side are also rendered from photographs. There is a potter on the left and a woman in a skeletal costume on the right. Behind her is a view of Chicano Park with the kiosk where celebrations take place (Figure 18.18). The Coronado Bridge is seen in the background.

San Antonio, Texas

Although Chicano murals were painted in San Antonio, most of the artists in that city concentrated on nonmural work as painters, sculptors, printmakers, and photographers. Among the best-known Chicano artists in San Antonio are César Martínez, Rudy Treviño, Jesse Treviño, and Adán Hernandez.

César Martínez (1944-)

In the late 1970s, César Martínez dealt with specific Chicano motifs other than the usual Huelga eagle and the Chicano triface. He was fascinated with the pachuco (zoot-suiter) as an important icon in Chicano culture. As a teenager in the 1950s and 1960s, he saw individuals who adopted the dress of the pachucos. He also included other figures in his works

Figure 18.17. Víctor Ochoa. *Gerónimo,* 1981. Centro Cultural de la Raza, Balboa Park, San Diego, CA. (Photograph by Jacinto Quirarte).

that he classified as *batos locos* (pachucos) and *mujeres* (women). Since he did not have any other visual information, other than his memory and photographs (snapshots and high school annual pictures), he used them as sources for some of his paintings. He was interested in these types as individuals rather than as a social phenomenon. An example of these works is *La Pareja* (*The Couple*), (1979, shown in Figure 18.19).

Aside from these Chicano subjects, Martínez also did a painting of Our Lady of Guadalupe under the guise of Leonardo's Mona Lisa; it was a bizarre juxtaposition of motifs. The work, titled *Mona Lupe,* demonstrates the power that each of its sources has to evoke emotions and to function within several levels of meaning. First of all, there is the antiart posture first articulated by Marcel Duchamp in his work of 1919 titled *L.H.O.O.Q.* (a reproduction of Leonardo's Mona Lisa with a mustache and beard added in pencil), and second, there is the entire realm of Chicano identity, exemplified by the religious, national, and political icon of Our Lady of Guadalupe. Martínez was born in Laredo, Texas, in 1944. He attended Texas A&I University in Kingsville, where he re-

ceived his bachelor of science degree in 1968. He resides in San Antonio.

Rudy Treviño (1945-)

Rudy Treviño worked in an abstract style in the 1960s and in a more figurative one in the 1970s and 1980s in which he used pre-Columbian, Mexican, and Chicano subjects. An example of Chicano ichnography is his work titled "George Zapata." (Fig. 59) The work refers to the Mexican revolutionary hero, Emiliano Zapata and to the American revolutionary hero, George Washington, both of which are components of Chicano culture and identity.

Jesse Treviño (1946-)

Jesse Treviño used everyday scenes and places in the barrio for works that have been included in photorealism exhibitions in San Antonio and elsewhere. An example of the very matter-of-fact portrayals of the barrio is the painting *La Panaderia (The Bakery),* shown in (Figure 18.20).

Treviño was born in Monterrey, Mexico, in 1946. His family moved to San Antonio in 1948. He attended

Figure 18.18. Víctor Ochoa. *Chicano Park,* 1981. Centro Cultural de la Raza, Balboa Park, San Diego, CA. (Photograph by Jacinto Quirarte).

the Art Students League in New York City on an art scholarship and studied portrait painting under William Draper, 1965-66. He attended Our Lady of the Lake University in San Antonio, where he received his bachelor of arts degree in 1974. He attended the University of Texas, San Antonio where he received his master of fine arts degree in 1979.

Brownsville, Texas

George Trúan (1944-)

George Trúan used the altar format in the late 1970s in a series of works he called Altares Chicanos. Among those works is *Self-Portrait,* which includes a statue of Our Lady of Guadalupe in the center of the tabletop with a backdrop filled with numerous photographs of the artist taken at different ages. Next to the image of Our Lady of Guadalupe is a photograph of John Kennedy, and above that, a print of the Santo Niño de Atocha (The Christ Child of Atocha). Flowers were placed in vases on the left and right sides of the tabletop.

Trúan was born in Kingsville, Texas, in 1944. He attended Texas A&I University in Kingsville, where

he received his bachelor of arts degree in 1968 and his master of arts degree in 1974. He resides in Brownsville, Texas, where he is an art professor at Southmost College.

Santa Fe, New Mexico

The artists in Santa Fe are unique because they have been able to build on the santero (mission caretaker) tradition as well as the Chicano muralist movement that was central to Chicano art in the 1970s and 1980s. No other region where Chicanos reside has santeros. (For more information on the Chicano murals in Santa Fe, see the section on Chicano murals later in this chapter.)

The resurgence of the santo-(saint)making tradition dates from the 1960s when New Mexico artists looked to their own past for inspiration for their work. They ignored the work of the López family and other twentieth-century santeros and turned to the use of colors to make the pieces closer to the traditional ones produced in the nineteenth century. Among the well-known new santeros are Luis Tapia of Santa Fe and Félix A. López of Española.

Figure 18.19. Cesar Martinez. *La Pareja,* 1979. (Photograph courtesy of the artist).

Félix A. López (1942-)
and
Luis Tapia (1950-)

Typical of the new works are the sculptures of Saint Michael by Félix López and Luis Tapia. *San Miguel* (1984) by López, in a private collection, shows the saint with his sword in one hand and the scales in the other. This is the traditional image of the saint. The other way in which Saint Michael was portrayed is seen in the elaborate image of *St. Michael and the Dragon* by Tapia in the collection of the Museum of International Folk Art, Santa Fe. These and other pieces by these santeros are generally larger than the unpainted santos made in Cordova and are meant to be taken more seriously as images related to the Hispanic tradition in New Mexico.

López was born in Gilman, Colorado, in 1942. He attended New Mexico Highlands University, where he received his bachelor's degree with a major in Spanish and a minor in German in 1965. He taught high school in Corcoran and Orange, California, in the late 1960s. He continued his studies and received his master's degree in Spanish literature in 1972 from the University of New Mexico, Albuquerque. He began making santos in 1977.

Tapia was born in Santa Fe, New Mexico, in 1950. He attended New Mexico State University for a year and began making santos around 1970 when he became aware of the Hispanic issues related to the civil rights movement. Unlike the earlier santeros, he began to use bright colors for the figures; this was shocking to viewers in the early 1970s. He also paints altar screens in the old style.

Chicago, Illinois

As in other regions where Hispanics are found, Chicago is home to numerous Chicano artists who painted murals during the late 1960s through the 1970s and part of the 1980s and now devote their energies to producing portable objects or nonmural art. Some have turned to painting, printmaking, or sculpture. (See the section on Chicano murals later in this chapter for more information on the murals of the Chicago area.)

José Gonzalez (1933-)

José González of Chicago, Illinois, is a multitalented painter, photographer, and arts administrator who has been at the forefront of the muralist movement in that city since the early 1970s. He has also worked with the publication *Revista Chicano Riqueña,* now *The Americas Review,* published in Houston, Texas, by Nicolás Kanellos. Among the designs by González for *The Americas Review* is the one titled *Barrio murals* (1976, Figure 18.21). The cover design is a photo collage composed of the many murals painted in Chicago in the early 1970s.

González, born in Iturbide, Nuevo León, Mexico, in 1933, has lived most of his life in the United States. He studied and received a diploma from the Chicago Academy of Fine Arts in the mid-1950s and continued his studies at several institutions in the 1960s: the Instituto Allende, San Miguel Allende, Mexico; the University of Chicago; the School of the Art Institute of Chicago, where he received his bachelor of fine arts degree in 1970; and the University of Notre Dame, where he received his master of fine arts degree in 1971. He devoted all his energies to the Chicano movement throughout the 1970s and 1980s as a muralist, organizer of exhibitions, and founder of organizations, such as Movimiento Artístico Chicano (MArCh) and others.

Marcos Raya (1948-)

One of the most prolific painters of murals and easel pictures is Marcos Raya, who was a full participant in the Chicano mural movement in Chicago and

Figure 18.20. Jesse Treviño. *Panadería*, late 1970s. (Photograph courtesy of the artist).

in recent years has also made altars with secular subjects, such as *Frida and Her Nurse* (1987).

Raya's murals deal with political issues in Chicago and abroad, with particular emphasis on Central America. This is seen in his panel for the mural program *Stop World War III* (1980) (Figure 18.22), in which six other artists participated. The mural project was initiated by the Chicago Mural group under the leadership of John Weber. The block-long mural includes different panels framed in accordance with a series of curvilinear formats. Raya's work is seen on the upper left of the mural. The motifs include the fallen statue of a Central American dictator and a group of figures above it holding banners and flags with the image of Che Guevara and references to El Salvador and Guatemala.

Raya was born in Irapuato, Guanajuato, Mexico, and moved to Chicago in 1964. He studied drawing and painting for two years with Allan Thiekler.

Other Hispanic-American Artists

Puerto Ricans in the United States, Cuban Americans, and non-Mexican Hispanics are found primarily in New York, New Jersey, Miami, and Chicago.

Their work is varied and represents the many styles that are found in the United States, Europe, and Latin America. It is difficult, therefore, to distinguish their work as being distinctively Puerto Rican, Cuban, and so forth. A few of the better-known artists and their works are discussed below.

Rafael Colón-Morales (1941-)

Rafael Colón-Morales was a member of Borinquen 12, an artists'' group formed to find venues for their work. The artists did not have a unifying goal in their work other than a practical aim to have their art exhibited, and the group no longer exists. Colón-Morales's early work was primarily geometric abstraction. His later works bear a resemblance to the Cuban surrealist painter Wifredo Lam, with crescent shapes and spiked projections within a dense thicket of forms. An example is *Apestosito* (*Stinker*) (1969).

Colón-Morales was born in 1941 in Trujillo Alto, Puerto Rico. He has lived in New York since 1970.

Luis Cruz Azaceta (1942-)

The Cuban-American artist Luis Cruz Azaceta, like other Hispanic artists in New York, has been

Figure 18.21. José González. *Barrio Murals.* 1976. Cover design for *Revista Chicano-Riqueña.* (Photograph courtesy of the artist).

concerned with the brutalizing effects of violence in his work, in which cartoonlike characters are often presented as victims. According to Azaceta, "My art takes the form of violence, destruction, cruelty, injustice, humor, absurdity and obscenity, as a revolt against our condition and man's evil instincts. I want my paintings and drawings to be an outcry, to awaken man's deepest feelings. Feelings of love, nobility and brotherhood."

Azaceta, born in Havana, Cuba, in 1942, arrived in the United States in 1960 and settled in Hoboken, New Jersey. He began to take life-drawing lessons at an adult center in Queens in the mid-1960s. While working nights as a clerk in the library of New York University, he enrolled in the School of Visual Arts in 1966 and received the equivalent of a bachelor of arts degree in 1969. He has taught at the University of California, Davis (1980), Louisiana State University, Baton Rouge (1982), the University of California, Berkeley (1983), and Cooper Union, New York (1984). He lives in Queens, New York.

Jorge Soto (1947-)

Jorge Soto of New York, became identified with the Taller Boricua (Puerto Rican Workshop), established in the barrio, where he distinguished himself as an artist. Like many self-taught artists, Soto defines his forms with very elaborate linear patterns. A good example is an untitled work on canvas painted in acrylic and ink. The two meticulously defined nude figures, a female and a male, are armless and shown standing in a frontal position on a green field with a few tropical plants around their legs. He is concerned with recovering an African and Taino Indian aesthetic in his works.

Soto was born in New York City in 1947.

Carlos Alfonso (1950-)

Carlos Alfonso, a Miami-based Cuban-American artist, draws his images from the Afro-Cuban religious tradition. Among the motifs he uses is the knife, which stands for protection against the evil eye. The knife through the tongue is intended to keep evil quiet. He uses such motifs for their connotations as well as for formal reasons. His paintings include numerous references to the human figure presented in simplified configurations that recall the jungle paintings (1943) of Wifredo Lam. They are shown within a flattened-out visual field full of crescent shapes that can be used to define large mouths with toothy grins, tongues, large leaves, and eye masks.

Alfonso was born in Cuba in 1950. He studied painting, sculpture, and printmaking at the Academia de Bellas Artes San Alejandro in Havana (1969-1973) and art history at the University of Havana (1974-1977). He began a teaching career at the Academia San Alejandro as instructor in art history (1971-1973), and then taught studio courses in art schools of the Ministry of Culture (1973 and 1980). He immigrated to the United States in 1980 for ideological and professional reasons.

Arnaldo Roche Rabell (1955-)

Arnaldo Roche Rabell, a Chicago-based Puerto Rican artist, has a unique style of painting in which the figures and their surroundings are almost overwhelmed by a densely painted surface. An overall furlike effect is the result of the paint being applied and then scratched with a sharp instrument. Rubbings and projections are the two methods he uses in his work. He lays a piece of canvas or paper over a model or an object that has been smeared with paint. He then rubs it and elaborates upon the distorted image. His projections of face-only self-portraits are presented in frontal view.

Roche was born in Puerto Rico in 1955. He studied

Figure 18.22. Marcos Raya. *Stop World War III.* (Photograph courtesy of the artist). Mural. Chicago, IL.

architecture but gave it up for painting. He studied at the Chicago Art Institute, where he received a bachelor of fine arts degree and later a master of fine arts degree in 1984. He continues to live much of the year in Chicago.

✸CHICANO MURALS

Although there is great diversity in the works of the Chicano muralists, they shared a desire to paint walls in the barrios where large numbers of Hispanics reside. Their aim was to provide images that were acceptable to that community. Finally, they all had an affinity for the Mexican muralists of the 1920s through the 1950s.

Chicano murals are found over a vast area in the barrios of the Southwest, Pacific Southwest, Northwest, and the Great Lakes region. The number of murals in each community varies from just a few in some cities, like Houston, Texas, to the many hundreds in Los Angeles, California. Only a few of the most representative murals are included in this discussion because of limited space. The intent is to give the reader an understanding of the form, content, and meaning of the murals rather than a full survey of all

the murals that were painted from the late 1960s through the early 1990s. The murals selected for discussion are among the most complex in thematic and formal terms. They are not the best, nor do they represent all the regions, but they span the decade of the 1970s, the period of greatest activity in the mural movement. Many of the artists have since worked on easel paintings and other portable works.

Diagrams of the murals are provided in the text, where appropriate, with captions listing the motifs used by the artists. The murals are discussed in chronological order as follows:

1. *History and Heroes*, by Congreso de Artistas Chicanos en Aztlán and Toltecas en Aztlán. 1973, Chicano Park, San Diego, California.
2. *Black and White Mural*, by Willie Herron and Gronk. 1973 and 1978, Los Angeles, California.
3. *History of the Mexican American Worker*, by Vicente Mendoza, José Nario, and Raymond Patlán. 1974-1975, Blue Island, Illinois.
4. *La Raza Cosmica* (*The Cosmic Race*), Raúl Valdez. 1977, Austin, Texas.
5. *En la lucha . . . ponte trucha*, (*In the struggle . . . Beware*), by Rogelio Cárdenas. 1978, Hayward, California.

6. *Multicultural Mural*, by Gilberto Garduño and others. 1980, Santa Fe, New Mexico.

San Diego, California

Some of the earliest murals were painted in the San Diego area known as Chicano Park, in the Barrio de la Logan, and at the Centro Cultural de la Raza in Balboa Park, near downtown. Although murals were painted in other barrios of the city, it is in these two places that most of the murals were painted by local artists as well as by those who came in from other parts of California over a period of ten years in the 1970s.

Chicano Park exemplifies the mural movement, in which the community, artists" groups, students, and others were involved in efforts to give the area cohesiveness, direction, and meaning. The story behind the movement, which began in earnest in 1970 in the Barrio de la Logan (named after the street that runs through it), was reported in the local press and in several books.

The Barrio de la Logan was first altered when a freeway was built through its center in a north-south direction in the early 1960s. By 1969, the completion of the Coronado Bridge, running in an east-west direction, fragmented it further. Many residents lost their homes as a result of such massive construction. In spite of these changes, Salvador Roberto Torres, a former resident and a graduate of the Oakland School of Arts and Crafts, returned to the barrio in 1968 and began planning the concept he had been formulating to turn the area under the bridge into a Chicano park. The plan was to make it a green corridor all the way to the waterfront and thereby open up the area to the sky and the bay for the people. In order to achieve this, the refuse dump under the bridge had to be cleaned up and murals painted along the way. The waterfront itself also had to be cleaned up.

By early 1970, Torres, along with other Chicano artists who called themselves Toltecas en Aztlán, began to discuss ideas regarding the bridge, the community, and their role as artists in it. This led to the discussion of murals in Chicano Park. Among those involved in the planning were Guillermo Aranda, Mario Acevedo, Víctor Ochoa, Tomás Castañeda, and Salvador Barajas.

While Torres and others were continuing with their plans to revitalize the barrio, an event that was to activate the entire community took place in April 1970. The California Highway Patrol moved in with a bulldozer to clear the topsoil under the bridge for the construction of a parking lot for thirty patrol cars. In addition, Chicano artists found out that the highway patrol had plans for a small brick building once used by the bridge engineer, which they wanted for themselves. The response was immediate. Artists, students, families, and children occupied the Ford Building in Balboa Park to emphasize the need for a Chicano cultural center. The area under the bridge was eventually turned over to the community piece by piece, and an abandoned water tank in Balboa Park was turned over to the group for a cultural center in 1971.

Chicano Park has more than eighteen concrete pillars, which have been painted on both sides since 1973. The area is bounded by the approaches to the bay bridge (completed in 1969) connecting Coronado Island to the mainland and Interstate Highway 5, and the freeway running perpendicular to it. Over thirty individual panels were painted during the 1970s and early 1980s by artists from San Diego and other California cities. The pillars supporting the bridge approaches are T-shaped and of varying heights. Almost all the pillars on the various ramps between National and Logan Avenues have been painted.

History and Heroes, Congreso de Artistas Chicanos en Aztlán and Toltecas en Aztlán. 1973.

The *History and Heroes* painting program began on the easternmost side of the area on two of the off-ramps flanking Logan Avenue. The triangular-shaped ramps were painted during the months of March and April 1973 by artists and people from the community. Both murals were coordinated by Congreso de Artistas en Aztlán and Toltecas en Aztlán. Among the artists who worked on both panels were Guillermo Aranda, Víctor Ochoa, Abraham Quevedo, Salvador Barajas, Arturo Román, Guillermo Rosete, Mario Acevedo, Tomas Castañeda, and Salvador Roberto Torres.

The off-ramp mural on the west side of Logan Avenue is typical of what was painted in the early 1970s in the Chicano barrios everywhere. It includes references to all three Mexican epochs (pre-Columbian, colonial, and modern) and recent Chicano history. In addition, there are references to contemporary events, such as space travel and civil rights demonstrations. It is immediately apparent that the entire mural was painted by several different artists. There are sharp lines of demarcation, with panels having little or no relation to others on either side, and the themes are not fully articulated.

To make the description and discussion of the mural easier to follow, a diagram in which all the motifs and themes are numbered and identified in the caption is included. Also listed are the names of the artists and the portions each one painted.

The people represented along the upper portion of the mural, numbered from 1 to 17, represent historical as well as contemporary figures and are the work of several artists. The first four heads were painted by Guillermo Aranda: Pablo Picasso (1), included because he died when the mural was being painted; Jose Clemente Orozco (2) and David Alfaro Siqueiros (4), two of the Mexican muralists most admired by the Chicano artists; and *La Niña Cosmica*, or the Cosmic Child (3), a reference to the people of Mexican descent and their future.

Carlos Santana (5), the rock music star, and Che Guevara (6), the Cuban-based Communist leader, were painted by an unknown artist, possibly Guillermo Rosete.

Víctor Ochoa painted César Chávez (7), the head of the United Farmworkers Union, and Joaquín Murrieta (10), a folk hero and bandit in nineteenth-century California. Chávez was a key figure in the Chicano movement for equal rights along economic, political, and educational lines.

The next heads were painted by Salvador Barajas. Rubén Salazar (8), a well-known newspaperman, was accidentally killed by police during the National Chicano Moratorium demonstration against the Vietnam War that took place in East Los Angeles on August 29, 1970. Salazar was considered the first martyr of the Chicano movement. Ramón Ortiz (9), born in Santa Fe, New Mexico (1813-1896), was a diplomat and priest who worked for better U.S.-Mexican relations during the 1840s. He was also appointed to oversee the removal of those New Mexicans who wished to live in Mexico after the war between Mexico and the United States. The next heads represent heroes of Mexican history: Miguel Hidalgo y Costilla (11) and José Guadalupe Morelos (13), heroes of the War of Independence (1810-1821); Benito Juárez (14), the leading figure during the War of Reform of the 1850s and in the struggle against the French occupation of the 1860s; and the key figures of the Mexican Revolution of 1910: Venustiano Carranza (12), Francisco Villa (15), Rojas (16), and Emiliano Zapata (17).

There are panels from the extreme left to right beneath the heads appearing on the upper register. The first one on the left (18), painted by Guillermo Aranda and Guillermo Rosete, is a reference to the conquest of Mexico by the Spaniards. Skeletal figures wearing Spanish helmets are engulfed by flames and a jaguar is shown in their midst. The jaguar refers to the pre-Columbian peoples of Mexico. The flames, a paraphrase of José Clemente Orozco's murals in Mexico and the United States, refer to destruction as well as regeneration or rebirth. The skeletal figures are also a reference to Mexican art in general and to the work of José Guadalupe Posada in particular.

The next set of panels, also painted by Guillermo Aranda, focus on the future, the present, and the past. The first panel (19) deals with outer space with some celestial bodies, and the present—the Chicano struggle for economic parity with other Americans—directly below it with the inclusion of the United Farmworkers'' eagle symbol. The pyramid (20) refers to the ancient past of Mexico, with which Chicanos identify.

The next two panels, painted by Arturo Román, focus on Chicano identity and the struggle to save the Barrio de la Logan from destruction by local and state authorities. Our Lady of Guadalupe (21), a reference to Mexican and Chicano identity, has religious as well as political meaning. The demonstration by barrio residents (22) includes banners of Our Lady of Guadalupe and United Farmworkers flags. The stylized rainbow and workers in the fields above the demonstration scene were painted by Guillermo Rosete.

The Olmec collosal head (23) was painted by Víctor Ochoa, and the two *soldaderas* (female soldiers of the Mexican Revolution) (24) were painted by Arturo Román. The final two motifs, the man on horseback and the flag (25 and 26) were painted by Guillermo Rosete and Sal Barajas. The man on horseback started out as a portrait of Francisco Villa carrying a Mexican flag and was later changed to a member of the Brown Berets, a paramilitary group of young Chicano militants, and the triface motif in the center of the flag is a reference to the mestizo, part Spanish, part Indian.

Los Angeles

Hundreds of murals were painted in Los Angeles over an extremely large area and on every conceivable type of surface (brick, wood, stucco, and concrete) and building (end walls of housing project buildings, in back alleys, concrete stairways, park pavillions, side walls of grocery stores, pharmacies, launderettes, cultural centers, and many structures). Although most were painted in East Los Angeles, some were painted in other parts of the city, such as the Tujunga Wash murals by Judy Baca, miles away from the barrio. The earliest murals date from 1972 and are found in Estrada Courts and at the Mechicano Art Center.

Among the many artists who painted murals in East Los Angeles, starting in 1972, were Leonard Castellanos, who directed the Mechicano Art Center on Whittier Boulevard, and Charles Félix, who was associated with the Goez Gallery and others. Judy Baca, mentioned earlier, founded and headed the arts organization known as SPARC (Social and Public Art Resource Center) for many years. Many of the artists worked as members of groups such as ASCO (Distasteful), Los Dos (The Two) Streetscapers, Los Four (The Four), and others.

Castellanos was committed to finding ways to initiate and implement programs emanating from the Mechicano Art Center and introducing them into the barrio. The murals were part of the center's stated reasons for being. Eventually twenty-five murals were painted in Echo Par and fifteen in Ramona Gardens, a federal housing project of six hundred families.

The most extensive mural project at one location in the barrios of East Los Angeles is found at the Estrada Courts housing complex. The work, under the direction of Charles Félix, was begun in the summer of 1973. Materials for the project were provided by the Los Angeles City Housing Authority and the Los Angeles Fire Department, initially, and also by the Board of Public Works.

The murals designed by Charles Félix and other community artists were painted by youths living in the housing complex and surrounding community. About 125 of the more than 150 youngsters who participated in the project during the first summer were paid by the Los Angeles Housing Authority with funds from the Neighborhood Youth Corps.

There is great variety in the murals of Estrada Courts. The subjects portrayed range from the usual pre-Columbian references to historical and contemporary ones relating to Mexico and the United States. The subjects had to be approved by a group of residents, organized under the name of Residentes Unidos (United Residents). Among the artists who painted murals at the courts are Willie Herron and Gronk, and Mario Torero of San Diego, as well as other members of the San Diego artist's group Congreso de Artistas Chicanos en Aztlán. Nearly sixty panels were painted by 1977. Many others were painted after that date.

Black and White Mural, by Willie Herron and Gronk. 1973 and 1978.

Black and White Mural (Figures 18.23 amd 18.24), by Willie Herron and Gronk has various narratives and is composed of heads and massed figures that were placed in interlocking squares and rectangular units. There are long views of street scenes, as in the upper central part interspersed with other smaller units in which groups of figures are also shown at various eye levels. These are contrasted with individual heads that fill up the square formats and extreme close-ups of only the eyes of a human head presented upside down and right side up to the right of center.

The artists focused on their community, the Chicano movement, and their own lives as well as on their own artwork in the mural. The panels were evenly distributed in terms of space allotted to each artist. Herron painted a baboon (1) on the upper left,

and Gronk painted a head of a long-haired youth (2) next to it. The rest of the panels on this register and most of the next one below it deal with East Los Angeles in general and the National Chicano Moratorium in particular. Herron painted a Los Angeles street scene (5), demonstrators carrying placards (7), and the largest panel, in which the demonstration itself is depicted (8). Gronk presents a helmeted soldier with rifle (3), figures behind bars (4), and women and children who may have sat and stood on the sidelines during the demonstration (6).

The remaining panels on the second through the fourth registers deal with terror, religion, death, Chicano art, portraiture, and the family in the barrio. Herron painted the remaining two panels of the second register from the top, which represent a terror-struck screaming woman (9) and the Catholic Sacred Heart (10). He also painted two panels in the third register, which represent a work performed by members of the artist's group ASCO in the early 1970s, known as the Walking Mural (13), and a self-portrait with his sister based on a photograph taken of them when they were children (15). Herron also painted panels on the fourth register. On the extreme lower left a figure is being pulled by another by the arm (16), and next to it there is a long-haired head in profile with skeletal attributes (17). Toward the right there are demonstrators reacting to tear gas (19), a portrait of Patssi Valdés (20), a member of ASCO (Herron, Gronk, and Harry Gamboa were the other members), and a woman using a telephone (21).

On the extreme left of the third register, Gronk painted a sprawled dead figure (11) seen from above and only from the waist up, and the face of a clown (12) next to it. To the right of center on the same register, he painted two different views of the same set of eyes framed by barbed wire and a crown of thorns (14). On the fourth register, he painted a profile head (18), which has a somber aspect and the young couple (22) seen on the extreme right in the only vertical format used in the mural.

Gronk's young couple embracing each other and Herron's self-portrait with his sister were added in the late 1970s. They worked on the mural for the last time in 1980. The mural remains untitled. (Black and White Mural is used for convenience only).

Chicago and Blue Island, Illinois

In Chicago, most of the artists were grouped around three organizations: The Public Art Workshop, The Chicago Mural Group, and Movimiento Artistico Chicano (Chicano Artistic Movement, MArCH).

The first Hispanic murals were painted in 1968 and 1969 by Mario Castillo, a Mexican-born artist. He

Figure 18.23. Willie Herrón and Gronk. *Black and White Mural,* 1973 and 1978. Estrada Courts, Los Angeles, CA. (Photograph by Jacinto Quirarte).

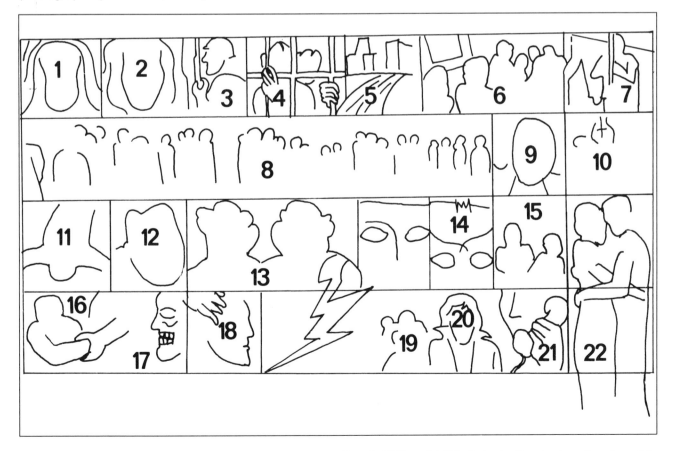

Figure 18.24. Willie Herrón and Gronk. *Black and White Mural,* 1973 and 1978. Estrada Courts, Los Angeles, CA. (Diagram by Jacinto Quirarte).

used pre-Columbian references in both murals, which are essentially nonfigurative works. In the first mural, *Metafísica*, the artist used enamel paints on a brick wall. In the second mural, *Wall of Brotherhood*, he used acrylic paints.

Raymond Patlán was an early muralist who painted on the inside and outside walls of Casa Aztlán (Aztlán House) cultural center. The murals deal with Mexican and Mexican-American history. The first was painted by the artist in the auditorium of Casa Aztlán in 1970-71. Titled *From my Fathers and Yours*, it deals with Mexican history from the time of the Spanish conquest of Mexico to the Revolution of 1910 and with Mexican-American history in the United States. The narrative is carried primarily by the portraits of historical figures, such Moctezuma, Hernán Cortes, Miguel Hidalgo y Costilla, Emiliano Zapata, César Chávez, and Rodolfo "Corky" González. There are thematic references to the War of Independence, the Revolution of 1910, and the Mexican-American worker. The latter is conveyed by three figures in procession wearing hardhats, blue pants, work shoes, no shirts, and holding tools of their trade in the right hand, while the one leading the trio points with his left. The viewer's attention is drawn to a portrait of César Chávez shown in profile and placed in a cartouche.

History of the Mexican American Worker, by Vicente Mendoza, José Nario, and Raymond Patlán. 1974-1975.

One of the most ambitious murals in thematic and formal terms was painted in Blue Island (a suburb of Chicago), Illinois, by Raymond Patlán, Vicente Mendoza, and José Nario in 1974 and 1975. *History of the Mexican American Worker* (Figures 18.25 and 18.26) has allegorical and historical figures, Mexican and Chicano icons, medicine, and a pre-Columbian life-death symbol along the upper register. Farm workers, steelworkers, and meat-packers were represented along the lower register. The discussion of the themes and motifs corresponds to the numbers shown in the diagram.

There is a gigantic figure on the extreme upper left of the mural shown lunging forward (1). Only the upper half of the figure, from the waist up, is represented. Its greatly foreshortened arms and hands hold two cog wheels with interlocking sprocketed gears in which there are representations of Our Lady of Guadalupe (greatly simplified) and the Huelga eagle. The large figure is reminiscent of the many lunging figures in the works of the Mexican muralist David Alfaro Siqueiros.

The next cluster of motifs to the right of the lunging figure is comprised of an open book (2)

flanked by two gigantic figures presented in bust form (head and shoulders only). The two figures presented in frontal view have their arms around each other as evidenced by the hands shown on each figure's shoulder. The man is a blue-collar worker and the woman is his counterpart. The open book has quotes from the writings of Abraham Lincoln and José Vasconcelos, who was the minister of education in Mexico (1921-1924) and the man responsible for the government support that helped initiate the mural movement in Mexico.

To the right of center there is a large hand shown in the open position with fingers spread apart and, directly below it, the other one shown extended toward the viewer (3). These are the hands of Benito Juárez, the president of Mexico who led the fight against French intervention in the 1860s. Right next to him is a three-quarter view of Abraham Lincoln's face.

A profile head next to Lincoln draws the viewer's attention to the last scene on the right side of the mural. It includes a physician on the left side holding a newborn child by the ankles with his left hand and a nurse behind him (5). The physician extends his arm in a gesture of offering to a woman in white on the right side who appears to be reaching for the baby (6). There is an American flag behind the physician and the nurse, and a very large life-death head in the midst of the offering scene.

Mexican-American workers picking grapes in the fields are seen on the extreme left of the lower register (7). A railroad worker and machinist are seen to the immediate right below a man and woman flanking an open book (8). A Mexican flag and the American Bicentennial logo (9) are seen below Benito Juárez. Molten steel spills out of a tilted vat (10), and next to it are the meat-packers (11) and other workers (12) that complete the scene on the right side of the mural.

History of the Mexican American Worker generated controversy even before it was completed. This was not unusual. Opposition to murals led to confrontations all over the Southwest. Opposition, regardless of the reasons for it, was expressed through direct action (vandalism and defacement of murals), pressure through the press or local governments, by petitions, and even by legal action. Such opposition occurred in Santa Barbara, California, Santa Fe, New Mexico, Denver and Pueblo, Colorado, and Houston, Texas.

The Blue Island muralists have the distinction of having been enjoined by the city council of that industrial suburb of Chicago to stop painting under the threat of arrest because they were in violation of a city ordinance that prohibited the use of advertising on public walls. The focus of the controversy was on

Figure 18.25. Raymond Patlán and others. *History of the Mexican American Worker,* 1974-75. Blue Island, IL. (Photograph by Jose Gonzalez).

the Huelga eagle seen in the upper left side of the mural. No arrests were made, but painting stopped pending a decision by U.S. District Court Judge Richard B. Austin. This followed action by the ACLU (American Civil Liberties Union) to keep the city council from prohibiting the artists from working on the mural. Judge Austin ruled in favor of the artists, citing First Amendment rights of freedom of expression. The judge ruled that the mural dealt with ideas rather than advertising and should therefore not be destroyed. This precedent-setting decision established the Blue Island murals as an example of the muralist's freedom to work without outside interference.

The mural was defaced by vandals in May 1975, but the artists continued their work on it in the following two months. The mural was dedicated on July 19, 1975.

Figure 18.26. Raymond Patlán and others. *History of the Mexican American Worker,* 1974-75. Blue Island, IL. (Diagram by Jacinto Quirarte).

La Raza Cósmica, by Raul Valdez. 1977. Austin, Texas.

One of the most elaborate mural programs of the Chicano art movement is found in Austin, Texas. Raúl Valdez and those who assisted him painted on every available surface of the Pan American Center outdoor stage and its adjacent buildings in 1977. Discussion of the mural follows a left-to-right numbering of the ten scenes (even though this is not the thematic order of the mural program). This should be

Figure 18.27. Raúl Valdez and others. *La Raza Cósmica*, 1977. Austin, TX. (Photograph by Jacinto Quirarte).

kept in mind as the historical themes are discussed in chronological order. (Figures 18.27 and 18.28-18.31.)

The focus of the mural program is found on the stage area, with the United Farmworkers eagle dominating the entire central area (6). The long horizontal band in the upper section was painted in the center to create the profile head and wings of the eagle. The suspended sound deflectors directly below and above the stage area function as the stepped wings associated with this emblem. On the stage wall, there are two bodiless hands presented in a welcoming gesture. They float over a large expanse of space whose depth is defined by linear perspective. There is a large celestial body in the center (instead of the head for the implied figure) with outstretched arms.

Various panels on each side are taken up with references to the history of Mexico. To the immediate left side of the stage area there is an elaborate scene of battle between the Spaniards and the Aztecs with a pyramid and temple in the background (5). The entire scene is enveloped by flames. Next to it on the left is the violently gesturing figure of Miguel Hidalgo y Costilla (4). The word *Independencia* (independence) is lettered on a banner seen directly below the half-figure, modeled on the leader of Mexican indepen-

Figure 18.28. Raúl Valdez and others. *La Raza Cósmica*, 1977. Austin, TX. (Diagram by Jacinto Quirarte).

dence painted by José Clemente Orozco in the state government palace stairway in Guadalajara, Jalisco, Mexico.

A figure corresponding to the Mexican Revolution of 1910 is seen to the immediate right of the stage area (7). He is backed up by a woman fighter and other fighters of that conflict. The artist included multiple

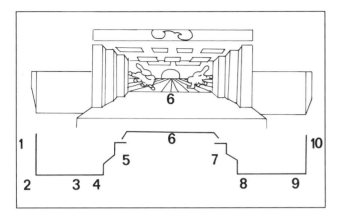

Figure 18.29. Raúl Valdez and others. *La Raza Cósmica*, 1977. Austin, TX. (Diagram by Jacinto Quirarte).

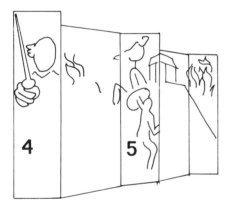

Figure 18.30. Raúl Valdez and others. *La Raza Cósmica*, 1977. Austin, TX. (Diagram by Jacinto Quirarte).

arms for the main figure because the single arm proved insufficient visually to encompass the available space.

References to modern barrio life and culture were

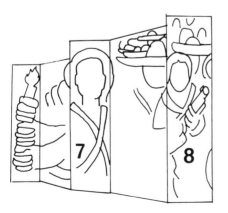

Figure 18.31. Raúl Valdez and others. *La Raza Cósmica*, 1977. Austin, TX. (Diagram by Jacinto Quirarte).

portrayed on the walls of the small building adjacent to the stage on the left side. The artist incorporated two windows right under the flat roof of the end wall in his depiction of the back of a truck with figures seated on the back of it (1). A red 1950s Chevrolet, next to it, was foreshortened to enhance the illusion of a single flat surface for the painting, which actually encompasses the meeting of the two walls at the corner of the building (2). There are folk dancers to the right of the Chevrolet (3). The mural continues all the way around the building to the right of the stage area in a series of violent scenes, some of which are shown with buildings in flames (9 and 10).

Finally, on the rear wall of the stage panel, but on the back, is a representation of a figure with outstretched arms designed by Pedro Rodríguez of San Antonio, Texas. It was based on the New Democracy Freeing Herself figure painted by David Alfaro Siqueiros in the Palace of Fine Arts in Mexico City.

En la lucha . . . ponte trucha by Rogelio Cárdenas. 1978. Hayward, California.

Rogelio Cárdenas and assistants designed and painted a large mural in 1978 on the side of a tortilla factory in Hayward, California (Figures 18.32 and 18.33). It has elements of Chicano culture as well as references to several Latin American countries. The numbers assigned to the various motifs in the mural read from left to right on the top register and then in similar fashion on the lower one.

The mural is dominated by a monumental figure with outstretched arms that paraphrases the New Democracy figure by Alfaro Siqueiros in the Palace of Fine Arts in Mexico City (3). The Cárdenas woman, however, has a triface and long flowing hair. An eagle is enveloped protectively under her hair on the left side (2) and a serpent on the right (4). The serpent bares its fangs as it coils around the chain that contains the two creatures. The chain is behind the woman's neck and above her shoulders and arms. She holds a hammer in her right hand (1) and her left hand turns into a flaming circular shield with a Greek cross superimposed on it (5). The hammer has a United Farmworkers eagle within a circle inscribed on its side. The flags of Mexico, Cuba, Pan-Africa, and Puerto Rico are on the inner circle (running clockwise from the upper right) of the shield. Native American peace symbols are in the center of the cross.

References to Chicano identity and barrio culture are seen along the lower register. In the center over the monumental figure's chest is a representation of Our Lady of Guadalupe painted on the lower part of a Latin cross with the caption "Hayward, Califas" (California) above and the artist's name Rogelio Cárdenas below (7). A lowrider Chevrolet is seen

Figure 18.32. Rogelio Cárdenas. *En la lucha ponte trucha,* 1978. Hayward, CA. (Photograph by Jacinto Quirarte).

under each arm of the woman. The one on the left dates from the late 1940s (6), and the one on the right from the mid-1950s (8). There is a corn plant and a pre-Columbian Indian on the extreme lower right of the mural (9).

There are stencil-like representations of roses on a bordered band all the way across the bottom of the

Figure 18.33. Rogelio Cárdenas. *En la lucha ponte trucha,* 1978. Hayward, CA. (Diagram by Jacinto Quirarte).

mural (10). This is a reference to the roses that miraculously appeared on the *tilma* (vest) of Juan Diego, along with the image of Our Lady of Guadalupe engraved on it, when he appeared before Fray Diego de Zumárraga, bishop of Mexico, in 1531.

The left side of the wall contains several motifs, among them skulls, a large hand, and flames around the actual windows. The title of the mural, its dedication, and the names of those who worked on it are listed on the adjacent wall to the left.

Santa Fe, New Mexico

The mural activity in Santa Fe, New Mexico, was dominated by the Leyba brothers, who painted their first murals in the early 1970s. They and other artists identified themselves under the name of Artes Guadalupanos de Aztlán (Guadalupe Arts of Aztlán). Members of the group were Samuel, Carlos, and Albert Leyba, Gilberto Garduño, Gerónimo Guzmán, and Pancho Hunter.

One of the first murals painted by the Artes group dates from 1971. It was painted on the exterior wall of a building in the barrio used for the Clínica de Gente (The People's Clinic). The mural was later painted

Figure 18.34. Gilberto Garduño and others. *Multicultural Mural,* 1980. Santa Fe, NM. (Photograph by Jacinto Quirarte).

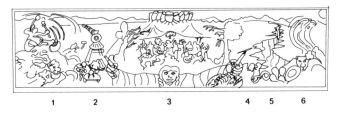

Figure 18.35. Gilberto Garduño and others. *Multicultural Mural,* 1980. Santa Fe, NM. (Diagram by Jacinto Quirarte).

Multicultural Mural, by Gilberto Garduño and others. 1980.

Multicultural Mural (Figures 18.34 and 18.35) was painted on the side of the New Mexico State Records Center in Santa Fe. Its main theme deals with the multicultural history of the state of New Mexico. The numerous figures are presented in different scales and symmetrically arranged within an elaborate landscape. Each thematic section has been numbered from left to right in the mural diagram. Each number from 1 to 6 encompasses an area filled from top to bottom with several motifs and themes.

The scene on the left side of the mural is dominated by a large bull amidst red flowers below and Indians wielding batons above (1). This is the coming together of the Hispanic and Indian cultures. The next scene includes a train in the middle ground shown in foreshortened position (2). The train appears to be moving toward the viewer. In the foreground are workers busily repairing the tracks. Below them are two figures holding onto tools that resemble handlebars. One is an Anglo, the other is an Indian.

The central scene is dominated by the Indian with outstretched arms holding the instruments of tech-

over. It had an Indian figure clothed in white in the center of a long wall. It was presented in cruciform fashion with wings attached to the arms and a United Farmworkers eagle attached to the head. A patient was wheeled into an operating room by a Chicano doctor and an Indian on the left side of the mural. Several patients were depicted on the right side.

nology in each hand (3). In the middle ground are Spanish dancers framed by a gnarled tree on the left and one with foliage on one side only on the right. Spectators are seen on each side of the dancers. The Mount Rushmore-type heads in the background represent the peoples that have settled New Mexico: Indians, Hispanics, Anglos, and Afro-Americans. The males are seen on the left side, the females on the right.

The Mexican national emblem emblazoned on the Mexican flag is seen next to the left hand of the native American figure with outstretched arms (4). A mountain lion peering at the viewer from behind cactus and prickly pears is seen on the lower right side of the mural (6). Three flying figures appear to be reaching for the sun above it. Ravines are seen in the middle ground.

The background of the entire mural is composed of the mountains and high plains that are characteristic of the northern part of New Mexico.

References

Beardsley, J. and J. Livingston. *Hispanic Art in the United States*. New York: Abbeville Press, 1987.

Boyd, E. *Popular Arts of Spanish New Mexico*. Santa Fe: Museum of New Mexico Press, 1974.

Cancel, L. and others. *The Latin American Spirit: Art and Artists in the United States, 1920-1970*. Bronx: The Bronx Museum of the Arts, 1988.

Chicano Art History: A Book of Selected Readings. Ed. Jacinto Quirarte. San Antonio: Research Center for the Arts and Humanities, 1984.

Quirarte, J. *Mexican American Artists*. Austin: University of Texas Press, 1973.

Wroth, W. *Christian Images in Hispanic New Mexico*, The Taylor Museum Collection of *Santos*. Colorado Springs: Colorado Springs Fine Arts Center, 1982.

Jacinto Quirarte

Illustrations

Henry F. Whitey, 1936. W.P.A.); *p. 141:* General Vallejo House (photo by Roger Sturtevant, 1934); *p. 141:* Castillo de San Marcos, St. Augustine; *p. 142:* The Cabildo in New Orleans (courtesy of the U.S. Department of the Interior and the National Park Service); *p. 144:* The Convent of Porta Coeli in San Germán; *p. 144:* The Alamo, San Antonio (courtesy of the Department of the Interior and the National Park Service); *p. 145:* San Francisco de la Espada Mission, San Antonio; *p. 145:* La Bahía Mission (courtesy of the U.S. Department of the Interior and the National Park Service); *p. 146:* Monument honoring the fallen at the Alamo, San Antonio (courtesy of the U.S. Department of the Interior and the National Park Service); *p. 147:* A reconstruction of the San Francisco Mission in East Texas (courtesy of the *Texas Catholic Herald*); *p. 148:* San Miguel Mission, Santa Fe, New Mexico (courtesy of the U.S. Department of the Interior and the National Park Service); *p. 148:* San José y San Miguel Aguayo Mission (photo by Arthur W. Stewart, 1936. W.P.A.).

The Family: *p. 152:* The Lugo Family, circa 1888 (courtesy of Los Angeles County Museum of Natural History); *p. 153:* A child's birthday party in New York City (Justo A. Martí Collection, Center for Puerto Rican Studies Library, Hunter College, CUNY); *p. 154:* United Bronx Parents, Inc. (Records of the United Bronx Parents, Inc. Courtesy of the Center for Puerto Rican Studies Library, Hunter College, CUNY); *p. 154:* A Puerto Rican mine worker and his family, Bingham Canyon, Utah (Historical Archive, Departamento de Asuntos de la Comunidad Puertorriqueña. Courtesy of the Center for Puerto Rican Studies Library, Hunter College, CUNY); *p. 155:* Mexican Mother of the Year, 1969: Mrs. Dolores Venegas, Houston, Texas (courtesy of the *Texas Catholic Herald*); *p. 157:* A Hispanic family attends mass, Houston, Texas (photo by Curtis Dowell. Courtesy of the *Texas Catholic Herald*); *p. 158:* A *posada* rehearsal, Houston, Texas, 1988 (photo by Curtis Dowell. Courtesy of the *Texas Catholic Herald*).

Relations with Spain and Spanish America: *p. 177:* Rally in East Lower Harlem (El Barrio) in Manhattan in support of the independence of Puerto Rico (The Jesús Colón Papers. Courtesy of the Center for Puerto Rican Studies, Hunter College, CUNY; Benigno Giboyeaux for the Estate of Jesús Colón and the Communist Party of the United States of America); *p. 193:* Fidel Castro; *p. 194:* Archbishop Oscar Romero of El Salvador (courtesy of the *Texas Catholic Herald*); *p. 196:* Guerrillas of El Frente Farabundo Martí por la Liberación Nacional (FMLN) in El Salvador; *p. 198:* Demonstrators opposing U.S. military aid to El Salvador in 1980 (courtesy of the *Texas Catholic Herald*).

Population Growth and Distribution: *p. 200:* Senior citizens at the Domino Park in Little Havana, Miami (courtesy of the *Texas Catholic Herald*); *p. 201:* Undocumented workers entering the United States at El Paso, Texas, 1990 (courtesy of the *Texas Catholic Herald*); *p. 201:* A group of Hispanics have just been issued their temporary residence cards, 1991 (photo by Les Fetchko. Courtesy of the *Texas Catholic Herald*); *p. 202:* The drive to legalize undocumented workers in Houston, Texas (photo by Curtis Dowell. Courtesy of the *Texas Catholic Herald*); *p. 203:* A poster for National Migration Week; *p. 204:* Mexican Independence Day Parade, Houston, Texas, 1982 (photo by Curtis Dowell. Courtesy of the *Texas Catholic Herald*); *p. 206:* A mass citizenship swearing in ceremony at Hoffheinz Pavilion of the University of Houston in 1987 (photo by Curtis Dowell. Courtesy of the *Texas Catholic Herald*).

Language: *p. 210:* The Teatro Puerto Rico in October, 1960 (Justo A. Martí Collection. Courtesy of the Center for Puerto Rican Studies Library, Hunter College, CUNY); *p. 214:* Downtown El Paso, Texas (courtesy of the *Texas Catholic Herald*); *p. 218:* A typical Hispanic grocery store in New York City (Justo A. Martí Collection. Courtesy of the Center for Puerto Rican Studies Library, Hunter College, CUNY); *p. 219:* Two scenes from the *Villa Alegre* television series; *p. 220:* A customer buying *La prensa* (Justo A. Martí Collection. Courtesy of the Center for Puerto Rican Studies Library, Hunter College, CUNY); *p. 222:* A voter registration drive in New York City (Justo A. Martí Collection. Courtesy of the Center for Puerto Rican Studies Library, Hunter College, CUNY); *p. 223:* Our Lady of Guadalupe Church in Queen Creek, Arizona (courtesy of the *Texas Catholic Herald*).

Law and Politics: *p. 240:* Four charts on law school enrollment (*Consultant's Digest*, May 1991); *p. 242:* Wilfredo Caraballo; *p. 243:* Antonia Hernández; *p. 244:* Mario G. Obledo; *p. 246:* Table 9.1, Hispanic Judges in State Courts (courtesy of the Hispanic National Bar Association Nationwide Summary of Hispanics in the State Judiciary, 1992); *p. 247:* Judge Reynaldo G. Garza; *p. 249:* Judge Raymond L. Acosta; *p. 249:* Justice John A. Argüelles; *p. 250:* Justice Joseph F. Baca; *p. 251:* Judge José A. Cabranes; *p. 253:* Judge George La Plata; *p. 254:* Judge Federico A. Moreno; *p. 255:* Chief Judge Manuel L. Real; *p. 256:* Justice Dorothy Comstock Riley; *p. 257:* Judge Joseph H. Rodríguez; *p. 257:* Chief Justice Luis D.

Rovirá; *p. 260:* Ben Blaz. Delegate to the U.S. Congress from Guam; *p. 261:* E. (Kika) de la Garza, U.S. Congressman (D-Texas); *p. 261:* Ron de Lugo. Delegate to the U.S. Congress from the U.S. Virgin Islands; *p. 262:* Matthew G. Martínez, U.S. Congressman (D-California); *p. 263:* Solomon *P. Ortiz, U.S. Congressman (D-Texas); p. 263:* Bill Richardson, U.S. Congressman (D-New Mexico); *p. 264:* Ileana Ros-Lehtinen, U.S. Congresswoman (R-Florida); *p. 264:* Edward R. Roybal, U.S. Congressman (D-California); *p. 265:* José E. Serrano, U.S. Congressman (D-New York); *p. 266:* Esteban E. Torres, U.S. Congressman (D-California); *p. 267:* Hispanic Members of the House of Representatives (courtesy of the Congressional Hispanic Caucus); *p. 268:* Herman Badillo, Former U.S. Congressman (D-New York); *p. 273:* Cari M. Domínguez, Director, Office of Federal Contract Compliance Programs; *p. 273:* Manuel Luján, Jr., Secretary of the Interior; *p. 274:* Robert Martínez, Director, Office of National Drug Control Policy, and Former Governor of Florida; *p. 275:* Antonia C. Novello, M.D., M.P.H., Surgeon General, United States Public Health Service; *p. 275:* Catalina Vásquez Villalpando, Treasurer of the United States; *p. 278:* Stephanie González, Secretary of State, New Mexico; *p. 279:* Ygnacio D. Garza, Mayor, Brownsville, Texas; *p. 280:* Gloria Molina, Los Angeles County Supervisor; *p. 281:* Federico Peña, Mayor, Denver (photo by Larry Lazlo); *p. 281:* Louis E. Saavedra, Mayor, Albuquerque; *p. 282:* Xavier L. Suárez, Mayor, Miami.

Education: *p. 287:* Children at recess, the Guadalupe Aztlán alternative school, Houston, 1981 (photo by Curtis Dowell. Courtesy of the *Texas Catholic Herald*); *p. 299:* Mexican fourth-graders at Drachman School (circa 1913) (courtesy of the Arizona Historical Society); *p. 300:* A poster encouraging Hispanics to register to vote; *p. 302:* Children at the Guadalupe Aztlán alternative school, Houston, 1981 (photo by Curtis Dowell. Courtesy of the *Texas Catholic Herald*); *p. 303:* A sixth-grade classroom in the Huelga School, an alternative school set up in St. Patrick's Chapel, Houston (photo by Curtis Dowell. Courtesy of the *Texas Catholic Herald*); *p. 304:* A poster encouraging affirmative action and equal opportunity in education in California; *p. 305:* Dr. Manuel Pacheco, President of the University of Arizona.

Business: *p. 309:* Table 11.1, Hispanic and Nonminority Businesses; *p. 309:* Poster for the 1985 United States Hispanic Chamber of Commerce convention; *p. 310:* Figure 11.1, Origin of U.S. Hispanic Business Owners; *p. 310:* Table 11.2, Number of Businesses, Sales Volume, Number of Employees, and Payroll by Hispanic Origin of Owners (source: United

States Bureau of the Census, 1991); *p. 311:* Table 11.3, Hispanic Businesses by Major Industry Category (source: United States Bureau of the Census, 1991); *p. 311:* Table 11.4, Number and Sales Volume of Hispanic Businesses in the Ten Largest Metropolitan Statistical Areas versus Those in the Entire State (source: United States Bureau of the Census, 1991); *p. 312:* Table 11.5, Number of Employees in Hispanic Businesses (source: United States Bureau of the Census, 1992); *p. 312:* Table 11.6, Sales Volume of Hispanic Businesses (source: United States Bureau of the Census, 1987); *p. 313:* Table 11.7, The Thirty Largest Hispanic Businesses (courtesy of "The 500," 1991); *p. 314:* Table 11.8, Hispanic and Nonminority Business Owners by Age (source: United States Bureau of the Census, 1987); *p. 314:* Table 11.9, Hispanic and Nonminority Business Owners by Years of Education (source: United States Bureau of the Census, 1987); *p. 314:* Table 11.10, Hispanic and Nonminority Business Owners Across Four Characteristics (source: United States Bureau of the Census, 1987); *p. 315:* Table 11.11, Start-up Capital Required for Hispanic and Nonminority Business Owners; *p. 315:* Figure 11.2, Sources of Start-up Capital for Hispanic and Nonminority Business Owners; *p. 316:* Table 11.12, Profit and Loss for Hispanic and Nonminority Businesses (source: United States Bureau of the Census, 1987); *p. 316:* Table 11.13, Minority Employees in Hispanic and Nonminority Businesses (source: United States Bureau of the Census, 1987); *p. 318:* Gilbert Cuéllar, Jr; *p. 319:* Roberto C. Goizueta; *p. 319:* Frederick J. González; *p. 320:* Edgar J. Milán; *p. 322:* Lionel Sosa; *p. 323:* Clifford L. Whitehill.

Labor and Employment: *p. 325:* César Chávez exhorting people to start a new grape boycott in 1986 (courtesy of the *Texas Catholic Herald*); *p. 326:* Mexican women working at a commercial tortilla factory in the 1930s (courtesy of the Library of Congress); *p. 327:* A cotton picker in 1933 (photo by Dorothea Lange. Courtesy of the Library of Congress); *p. 328:* Mexican mine workers in the early 1900s (courtesy of the Arizona Historical Society); *p. 329:* Puerto Rican garment workers in New York City; *p. 329:* A Mexican worker being finger-printed for deportation (courtesy of the Library of Congress); *p. 330:* Southern Pacific railroad workers during World War II in Tucson, Arizona (courtesy of the Arizona Historical Society); *p. 332:* Unemployed workers at a relief office during the Depression (courtesy of the Library of Congress); *p. 332:* A fruit picker in California (courtesy of the *Texas Catholic Herald*); *p. 333:* A parade ending National Farm Workers Week, Union Square, New York, 1975 (courtesy of the *Texas Catholic Herald*); *p. 334:* A United Farm Workers picket line in Coachella,

California, 1973 (courtesy of the *Texas Catholic Herald*); *p. 336:* A scene from the Bracero Program (courtesy of the Library of Congress); *p. 337:* A field worker in the Bracero Program (courtesy of the Library of Congress); *p. 339:* A migrant work camp (courtesy of the Library of Congress); *p. 340:* The interior of a migrant labor shack (courtesy of the *Texas Catholic Herald*).

Women: *p. 354:* Poster advertising a Hispanic women's conference in Texas in 1987; *p. 354:* A beauty queen for the Fiestas Patrias celebration, Houston (photo by Curtis Dowell. Courtesy of the *Texas Catholic Herald*); *p. 357:* A workshop at the 1980 California Governor's Chicana Issues Conference; *p. 361:* Teresa Bernárdez, M.D; *p. 363:* Emyré Barrios Robinson; *p. 365:* Carmen Delgado Votaw, Director, Washington Office, Girls Scouts, USA.

Religion: *p. 368:* A Catholic charismatic prayer meeting (courtesy of the *Texas Catholic Herald*); *p. 369:* The Franciscan method of teaching the Indians by pictures (from an engraving based on Fray Diego Valdés, o.F.M., in his Rhetorica Christiana, Rome, 1579); *p. 369:* Bartolemé de las Casas (1474-1566); *p. 370:* San Juan Capistrano Mission, San Antonio, Texas (photo by Silvia Novo Pena. Courtesy of the *Texas Catholic Herald*); *p. 372:* The Image of Our Lady of Guadalupe (photo by Curtis Dowell. Courtesy of the *Texas Catholic Herald*); *p. 380:* Feast of the Crowning of Mary, Sacred Heart Cathedral, Houston, 1987 (photo by Curtis Dowell. Courtesy of the *Texas Catholic Herald*); *p. 382:* Annual mass on the feast day of Our Lady of Guadalupe, Houston, Texas (courtesy of the *Texas Catholic Herald*); *p. 383:* The celebration of the feast day of Our Lady of Caridad del Cobre, the patron of Cubans, Houston, 1986 (photo by Curtis Dowell. Courtesy of the *Texas Catholic Herald*); *p. 384:* A Christmas posada, Houston, 1988 (photo by Curtis Dowell. Courtesy of the *Texas Catholic Herald*); *p. 385:* Diversity in Hispanic evangelism (photo by Curtis Dowell. Courtesy of the *Texas Catholic Herald*).

Organizations: *p. 388:* A march from the Lower East Side of New York City over the Brooklyn Bridge to protest the poor conditions of public schools in the Puerto Rican community (Historic Archive of the Department of Puerto Rican Community Affairs in the United States. Courtesy of the Center for Puerto Rican Studies Library and Archives, Hunter College, CUNY); *p. 388:* A celebration of the Three Kings (Jesús Colón Papers. Courtesy of the Center for Puerto Rican Studies Library and Archives, Hunter College, CUNY); *p. 389:* A parade organized by the Tucson's Alianza Hispano-Americana (courtesy of the Arizona Historical Society); *p. 390:* President Ronald Reagan presents the Medal of Freedom to Dr. Héctor García; *p. 394:* Brooklyn Chapter of the Liga Puertorriqueña e Hispana (Puerto Rican and Hispanic League), circa 1927 (Jesús Colón Papers. Courtesy of the Center for Puerto Rican Studies Library and Archives, Hunter College, CUNY); *p. 396:* Poster for the Spanish-Speaking Coalition Conference of October, 1971.

Scholarship: *p. 400:* Albert Michael Camarillo; *p. 400:* Arthur León Campa; *p. 401:* Carlos E. Cortés; *p. 402:* Rodolfo J. Cortina; *p. 403:* Margarita Fernández Olmos; *p. 404:* Erlinda González-Berry; *p. 405:* Olga Jiménez-Wagenheim; *p. 406:* Luis Leal; *p. 407:* Raúl Moncarraz; *p. 408:* Sonia Nieto; *p. 408:* Julián Olivares; *p. 410:* Ricardo Romo; *p. 411:* Ramón Eduardo Ruiz.

Literature: *p. 414:* Miguel Antonio Otero (Miguel A. Otero Collection, Special Collections, General Library, University of New Mexico, Neg. No. 000-021-0004); *p. 415:* Eusebio Chacón (Miguel A. Otero Collection, Special Collections, General Library, University of New Mexico, Neg. No. 000-021-0168); *p. 415:* Title page of El hijo de la tempestad by Eusebio Chacón (Special Collections, General Library, University of New Mexico); *p. 416:* Cuban literary and patriotic figure, José Martí; *p. 418:* The cover of Daniel Venegas's satirical newspaper, *El Malcriado*; *p. 418:* Fray Angélico Chávez (Special Collections, General Library, University of New Mexico); *p. 419:* Cover of the first issue of *Gráfico* newspaper; *p. 421:* Lola Rodríguez de Tió (archives, Arte Público Press); *p. 423:* Abelardo Delgado, Ron Arias and Rolando Hinojosa at the Second National Latino Book Fair and Writers Festival, Houston, Texas, 1980 (archives, Arte Público Press); *p. 424:* The original manuscript of the Tomás Rivera poem, "When love to be?" (archives, Arte Público Press); *p. 425:* Evangelina Vigil-Piñón, reciting at the Third National Hispanic Book Fair, Houston, 1987 (photo: Julián Olivares. Archives, Arte Público Press); *p. 425:* The cover of Rudolfo Anaya's best-selling novel, *Bless Me, Ultima* (archives, Arte Público Press); *p. 426:* A vendor at the First National Latino Book Fair, Chicago, 1979 (archives, Arte Público Press); *p. 427:* Ana Castillo, 1979 (archives, Arte Público Press); *p. 427:* Helena María Viramontes, 1986 (photo by Georgia McInnis, Archives, Arte Público Press); *p. 428:* Luis Dávila at the First National Latino Book Fair, 1979 (archives, Arte Público Press); *p. 429:* The cover of Rudolfo Anaya's *Cuentos: Tales from the Hispanic Southwest* (archives, Arte Público Press); *p. 429:* Pat Mora, 1986 (archives, Arte Público Press); *p. 430:* The cover of Denise Chávez's *The Last of the Menu Girls* (archives, Arte Público Press); *p. 430:* The cover of *This Bridge Called My Back* (archives, Arte Público Press); *p. 431:* Gary Soto and Evangelina Vigil-Piñón, Third National Hispanic Book Fair and Writers Festival, Houston, Texas, 1987 (archives, Arte Público Press); *p. 432:* Ricardo Sánchez, Alejandro Morales, critic Salvador Rodríguez del Pino and Victor Villaseñor at a book fair in Mexico City, 1979; *p. 433:* Julia de Burgos; *p. 434:* José Luis González (archives, Arte Público Press); *p. 434:* Luis Rafael Sánchez (archives, Arte Público Press); *p. 435:* Pedro Juan Soto (archives, Arte Público Press); *p. 436:* Jesús Colón ca. 1950s (archives, Centro de Estudios Puertorriqueños, Hunter College); *p. 436:* Bernardo Vega in 1948 (archives, Centro de Estudios Puertorriqueños, Hunter College); *p. 437:* Sandra María Esteves, 1979 (archives, Arte Público Press); *p. 438:* Second National Latino Book Fair and Writers Festival, Houston Public Library Plaza, 1980 (archives, Arte Público Press); *p. 439:* Nicholasa Mohr, Nicolás Kanellos and Ed Vega at the Bookstop, Houston, Texas, 1985 (archives, Arte Público Press); *p. 440:* Virgil Suárez, 1991 (archives, Arte Público Press); *p. 441:* José Sánchez-Boudy; *p. 442:* Miguel Algarín reciting his poetry at the First National Latino Book Fair, Chicago, 1979 (archives, Arte Público Press); *p. 443:* Alurista, 1980 (archives, Arte Público Press); *p. 445:* Denise Chávez, 1989 (photo by Georgia McInnis. Archives, Arte Público Press); *p. 446:* Lorna Dee Cervantes, 1990 (photo by Georgia McInnis. Archives, Arte Público Press); *p. 446:* Judith Ortiz Cofer, 1989 (archives, Arte Público Press); *p. 447:* Victor Hernández Cruz, 1980 (archives, Arte Público Press); *p. 448:* Abelardo Delgado, 1979 (archives, Arte Público Press); *p. 449:* Roberto Fernández, 1989 (archives, Arte Público Press); *p. 450:* Lionel G. García, 1989 (archives, Arte Público Press); *p. 451:* Rolando Hinojosa, 1987 (archives, Arte Público Press); *p. 452:* Tato Laviera, 1990 (photo by Georgia McInnis. Archives, Arte Público Press); *p. 453:* Nicholasa Mohr, 1990 (archives, Arte Público Press); *p. 454:* Alejandro Morales, 1991 (archives, Arte Público Press); *p. 456:* Album cover of a live poetry recital by Pedro Pietri; *p. 457:* Ricardo Sánchez, 1987 (archives, Arte Público Press); *p. 457:* Gary Soto, 1991 (photo by M.L. Marinelli. Publicity Department, Chronicle Books); *p. 459:* Sabine Ulibarrí, 1989 (archives, Arte Público Press); *p. 460:* Ed Vega, 1991 (archives, Arte Público Press); *p. 461:* Victor Villaseñor, 1991 (photo by Tony Bullard. Archives, Arte Público Press).

Art: *p. 465:* Figure 18.1. Bell wall, San Juan Capistrano Mission, 1760-87. San Antonio, Texas (photograph by Jacinto Quirarte); *p. 466:* Figure 18.2. Facade, San José y San Miguel de Aguayo Mission, 1768-82. San Antonio, Texas (photograph by Kathy Vargas); *p. 467:* Figure 18.3. *Saint Joachim* portal sculpture (left side of the doorway), 1768-82, San José y San Miguel de Aguayo Mission. San Antonio, Texas (photograph by Kathy Vargas); *p. 467:* Figure 18.4. *Saint Anne* portal sculpture, 1768-82. San José y San Miguel de Aguayo Mission. San Antonio, Texas (photograph by Kathy Vargas); *p. 468:* Figure 18.5. Facade, 1783-97, San Xavier del Bac Mission. Tuscon, Arizona (photograph by Jacinto Quirarte); *p. 468:* Figure 18.6. *Saint Lucy*. Portal sculpture, 1783-97, San Xavier del Bac Mission. Tucson, Arizona (photograph by Jacinto Quirarte); *p. 469:* Figure 18.7. Main Portal, 1755, Nuestra Señora de la Purísma Concepción de Acúna Mission. San Antonio, Texas (photograph by Kathy Vargas); *p. 469:* Figure 18.8. Polychromy, 1768-82, San José y San Miguel de Aguayo Mission. San Antonio, Texas (photograph by Kathy Vargas); *p. 472:* Figure 18.9. José Benito Ortega. *Saint Isidore the Farmer,* 1880s-1907. Denver Art Museum; *p. 473:* Figure 18.10. José Dolores López. *Expulsion from the Garden of Eden; p. 476:* Figure 18.11. Theodora Sánchez. *Nicho* (Yard Shrine), dedicated to Saint Dymphna. 1957. Tucson, Arizona (photograph by Jacinto Quirarte); *p. 477:* Figure 18.12. Octavio Medellín. *Xtol* print (photograph courtesy of the artist); *p. 478:* Figure 18.13. Edward Chávez. *Indians of the Plains*. 1943. Egg Tempera on Plywood (photograph courtesy of the artist); *p. 482:* Figure 18.14. Rafael Ortiz. *Piano Destruction Concert, Duncan Terrace.* September 1966, London (photograph courtesy of the artist); *p. 486:* Figure 18.15. Judy Baca. Detail of *The Great Wall of Los Angeles.* 1980 (photograph by Jacinto Quirarte); *p. 487:* Figure 18.16. Carmen Lomas Garza. *Lotería—Table Llena,* 1974 (photograph courtesy of the artist); *p. 488:* Figure 18.17. Víctor Ochoa. Gerónimo, 1981, San Diego, CA (photograph by Jacinto Quirarte); *p. 489:* Figure 18.18. Víctor Ochoa. *Chicano Park,* 1981, San Diego, CA (photograph by Jacinto Quirarte); *p. 490:* Figure 18.19. Cesar Martinez. *La Pareja,* 1979 (photograph courtesy of the artist); *p. 491:* Figure 18.20. Jesse Treviño. *Panadería,* late 1970s (photograph courtesy of the artist); *p. 492:* Figure 18.21. José González. *Barrio Murals.* 1976. Cover design for *Revista Chicano-Riqueña* (photograph courtesy of the artist); *p. 493:* Figure 18.22. Marcos Raya. *Stop World War III* (photograph courtesy of the artist). Mural. Chicago, IL; *p. 497:* Figure 18.23. Willie Herrón and Gronk. *Black and White Mural,* 1973 and 1978. Estrada Courts, Los Angeles, CA (photograph by Jacinto Quirarte); *p. 497:* Figure 18.24. Willie Herrón and Gronk. *Black and White Mural,* 1973 and 1978.

Estrada Courts, Los Angeles, CA (diagram by Jacinto Quirarte); *p. 499:* Figure 18.25. Raymond Patlán and others. *History of the Mexican American Worker,* 1974-75. Blue Island, IL (photograph by Jose Gonzalez); *p. 499:* Figure 18.26. Raymond Patlán and others. *History of the Mexican American Worker,* 1974-75. Blue Island, IL (diagram by Jacinto Quirarte); *p. 500:* Figure 18.27. Raúl Valdez and others. *La Raza Cósmica,* 1977. Austin, TX (photograph by Jacinto Quirarte); *p. 500:* Figure 18.28. Raúl Valdez and others. *La Raza Cósmica,* 1977. Austin, TX (diagram by Jacinto Quirarte); *p. 501:* Figure 18.29. Raúl Valdez and others. *La Raza Cósmica,* 1977. Austin, TX (diagram by Jacinto Quirarte); *p. 501:* Figure 18.30. Raúl Valdez and others. *La Raza Cósmica,* 1977. Austin, TX (diagram by Jacinto Quirarte); *p. 501:* Figure 18.31. Raúl Valdez and others. *La Raza Cósmica,* 1977. Austin, TX (diagram by Jacinto Quirarte); *p. 502:* Figure 18.32. Rogelio Cárdenas. *En la lucha ponte trucha,* 1978. Hayward, CA (photograph by Jacinto Quirarte); *p. 502:* Figure 18.33. Rogelio Cárdenas. *En la lucha ponte trucha,* 1978. Hayward, CA (diagram by Jacinto Quirarte); *p. 503:* Figure 18.34. Gilberto Garduño and others. *Multicultural Mural,* 1980. Santa Fe, NM (photograph by Jacinto Quirarte); *p. 503:* Figure 18.35. Gilberto Garduño and others. *Multicultural Mural,* 1980. Santa Fe, NM (diagram by Jacinto Quirarte).

Theater: *p. 507:* Don Antonio F. Coronel, ex-mayor of Los Angeles, and early theater owner and impresario (courtesy of Los Angeles County Museum of Natural History); *p. 507:* Los Angeles's California Theater; *p. 509:* The Mason Theater, Los Angeles; *p. 510:* Actress Rosalinda Meléndez; *p. 512:* The García girls chorus line from the Carpa García Tent show; *p. 513:* Don Fito, the Carpa García *peladito* from the Carpa García tent show; *p. 517:* The cover of a program for the performance of an operetta at the Centro Español in 1919; *p. 518:* Centro Asturiano, with director Manuel Aparicio at the center front of the audience in 1937 (courtesy of the Dorothea Lynch Collection, Special Collections, George Mason University Library); *p. 519:* A scene from *El niño judío* at the Centro Asturiano (courtesy of the Dorothea Lynch Collection, Special Collections, George Mason University Library); *p. 520:* Manuel Aparicio directing a rehearsal of Sinclair Lewis's *It Can't Happen Here* in Spanish at the Centro Asturiano (courtesy of the Dorothea Lynch Collection, Special Collections, George Mason University); *p. 521:* Manuel Aparicio in Jacinto Benavente's *La Malquerida* (courtesy of the Dorothea Lynch Collection, Special Collections, George Mason University Library); *p. 522:* A scene from El Teatro Urbano's *Anti-Bicentennial Special* in 1976; *p. 524:* A scene from El Teatro de la Esperanza's production of Rodrigo Duarte Clark's *Brujerías; p. 524:* New York's Teatro Hispano in 1939; *p. 525:* Poster from La Farándula Panamericana theater group's 1954 production of *Los árboles mueren de pie,* starring Marita Reid; *p. 526:* Postcard photo of the Bronx's Pregones theater company in 1985; *p. 527:* The elaborate costuming of a Miami production of José Zorrilla's *Don Juan Tenorio; p. 529: Romeo and Juliet* in Spanish in Miami; *p. 537:* A scene from the Los Angeles production of Dolores Prida's *Beautiful Señoritas* (archives, Arte Público Press); *p. 539:* Playwright-director Luis Valdez; *p. 540:* Actress-director Carmen Zapata portrays Isabel la Católica in *Moments to Be Remembered.*

Film: *p. 548:* María Montez, an early Hispanic film star; *p. 551:* Henry Darrow as Zorro; *p. 560:* Carmen Miranda; *p. 561:* The late Freddie Prinze; *p. 561:* Erik Estrada, star of "CHiPs"; *p. 563:* The Sharks face off with the Jets in *West Side Story; p. 564:* A scene from *Boulevard Nights; p. 565:* Anthony Quinn in *The Children of Sánchez; p. 567:* Andy García in *The Godfather, Part III; p. 569:* The poster for *El norte; p. 570:* Raúl Juliá as Salvadoran Archbishop Oscar Romero in *Romero; p. 571:* Jimmy Smits; *p. 574:* Director Jesús Salvador Treviño in 1978; *p. 583:* The late Academy-Award-winning cinematographer, Nestor Almendros; *p. 585:* Producer-Director Moctezuma Esparza; *p. 588:* Ricardo Montalbán in the T.V. series, "Fantasy Island"; *p. 589:* Silvia Morales, director-cinematographer; *p. 590:* Rita Moreno receives her second Emmy in 1978; *p. 591:* Edward James Olmos.

Music: *p. 596:* Mexican musicians in the 1890s in California (courtesy of the Huntington Library, San Marino, California); *p. 596:* Xavier Cugat and his orchestra in the 1940s; *p. 597:* Augusto Coen and his Golden Orchestra, ca. 1930s-1940s; *p. 599:* Lidia Mendoza with Marcelo, comic Tin Tan and Juanita Mendoza in Chicago in the 1950s; *p. 600:* A working-class *orquesta,* circa 1930 (courtesy of Thomas Kreneck); *p. 606:* An *orquesta típica* in Houston (courtesy of Thomas Kreneck); *p. 609:* Beto Villa y su Orquesta, circa 1946 (courtesy of Chris Strachwitz); *p. 610:* Alonzo y su Orquesta, circa 1950 (courtesy of Thomas Kreneck); *p. 611:* Octavo García y sus GGs, circa 1952 (courtesy of Octavio García); *p. 612:* An outdoor *salsa* concert in Houston, Texas (courtesy of the Arte Público Press archives); *p. 613:* Celia Cruz at the Hollywood Palladium; *p. 614:* The Joe Cuba Sextet; *p. 615:* A Machito album cover; *p. 616:* A Tito Puente album cover; *p. 616:* Eddie Palmieri.

Media: p. 628: Wanda de Jesús as "Santa Andrade" in NBC's "Santa Barbara"; p. 629: A. Martínez as "Cruz Castillo" in NBC's "Santa Barbara"; p. 630: Henry Darrow as "Cruz Castillo's" father in NBC's "Santa Barbara"; p. 633: Ignacio E. Lozano, Jr., Editor-in-Chief of La Opinión; p. 634: Mónica Lozano-Centanino, Associate Publisher of *La Opinión;* p. 634: José I. Lozano, Publisher of *La Opinión;* p. 635: Marti Buscaglia, Director of Marketing, *La Opinión;* p. 635: Peter W. Davidson, President, *El Diario-La Prensa; p. 636:* Carlos D. Ramírez, Publisher, *El Diario-La Prensa; p. 637:* Phillip V. Sánchez, Publisher, *Noticias del Mundo* and *New York City Tribune;* p. 640: Cover of *Temas* magazine; p. 640: Cover of *Réplica* magazine; p. 641: Cover of *Más* magazine; p. 641: Cover of *La Familia de Hoy* magazine; p. 642: Cover of *Hispanic* magazine; p. 643: Cover of *Hispanic Business* magazine; p. 643: Charlie Erikson, founding editor of Hispanic Link News Service; p. 644: Cover of *Saludos Hispanos* magazine; p. 645: Pedro J. González; p. 646: Pedro J. González's singing group, "Los Madrugadores"; p. 646: Banner headlines in *La Opinión* newspaper announcing the guilty verdict in the Pedro J. González case; p. 648: Table 22.1, Radio Stations Owned and Controlled by Hispanics (sources: National Association of Broadcasters, Department of Minority and Special Services, Minority Telecommunications Development Program of the National Telecommunications and Information Administration, U.S. Department of Commerce); p. 649: McHenry Tichnor, founder of the Tichnor Media Systems; p. 650: Amancio V. Suárez of the Viva America Media Group; p. 656: Gustavo Godoy, Hispanic American Broadcasting Corporation, founder; p. 657: Henry R. Silverman, Telemundo founder; p. 658: Saul P. Steinberg, Telemundo founder; p. 660: Table 22.2, Stations Owned and Operated by the Univisión Spanish-Language Television Group (Late 1991); p. 658: Table 22.3, UHF Affiliates of the Univisión Spanish-Language Television Group (Late 1991); p. 661: Joaquín F. Blaya, president of Univisión; p. 661: Rosita Perú, senior vice president and director of programming, Univisión; p. 662: Univisión news studio; p. 663: Jorge Ramos and María Elena Salinas of "Noticiero Univisión"; p. 664: Table 22.4, Univisión Programming (Mid-1991); p. 665: Cristina Saralegui, host of Univisión's "El Show de Cristina"; p. 665: Don Francisco, host of Univisión's "Sábado Gigante" (Giant Saturday); p. 666: Luca Bentivoglio, host of Univisión's "Desde Hollywood," with Julio Iglesias; p. 666: Table 22.5, Stations Owned and Operated by the Telemundo Spanish-Language Television Group (Late 1991); p. 667: Table 22.6, Stations Affiliated with the Telemundo Spanish-Language Television Group (Late 1991); p. 668: Table 22.7, Telemundo Program-ming (Mid-1991); p. 669: Enrique Gratas, host of Telemundo's "Ocurrió Así"; p. 669: Andrés García and Rudy Rodríguez, of "El Magnate"; p. 670: Table 22.8, Affiliates of the Galavisión Spanish-Language Television Group (Late 1991); p. 671: Table 22.9, Galavisión Programming; p. 672: Laura Fabián, of Telemundo's "El Magnate"; p. 672: María Laria, host of Telemundo's "Cara a Cara"; p. 673: Milagros Mendoza, Host of "Esta Noche con Usted"

Science: p. 678: Dr. Angeles Alvariño de Leira; p. 679: Alberto V. Baez; p. 680: Graciela Candelas; p. 681: Manuel Cardona; p. 682: David Cardús; p. 683: Guillermo B. Cintrón; p. 684: Antonio E. Colás; p. 684: Francisco Dallmeier; p. 685: George Castro; p. 685: José Alberto Fernández-Pol; p. 686: Jorge Fischbarg; p. 687: Celso Ramón García; p. 688: José D. García; p. 690: Teresa Mercado; p. 691: Isabel Pérez-Farfante; p. 693: Pedro A. Sánchez; p. 694: James J. Valdés.

Sports: p. 697: Ramón Ahumada, known as "El Charro Plateado." (photo, circa 1890. Courtesy of the Arizona Historical Society); p. 699: A baseball team of Mexicans and Anglos, Los Angeles, 1870s (courtesy of the Huntington Library, San Marino, California); p. 703: Rod Carew; p. 704: Roberto Clemente; p. 704: Dave Concepción; p. 705: Roberto Durán; p. 706: Sixto Escobar; p. 707: Tom Flores; p. 707: Pancho González, U.S. Men's Singles Lawn Tennis Championship, 1948 (courtesy of the National Archives); p. 708: Keith Hernández; p. 709: Nancy López; p. 710: Amleto Monacelli; p. 711: Anthony Muñoz; p. 712: Jim Plunkett; p. 713: Juan "Chi Chi" Rodríguez; p. 713: Alberto Bauduy Salazar; p. 715: José "Chegüí" Torres (José A. Martí Collection. Courtesy of the Center for Puerto Rican Studies Library, Hunter College, CUNY); p. 715: Lee Treviño.

Prominent Hispanics: p. 717: Michael Jules Aguirre; p. 718: Tomás A. Arciniega; p. 718: Philip Arreola; p. 719: Tony Bonilla; p. 720: Harry Caicedo; p. 720: Vikki Carr; p. 721: Lynda Carter; p. 722: César Chávez; p. 723: José R. Coronado; p. 724: Jaime Escalante; p. 725: Joseph A. Fernández; p. 726: Archbishop Patrick F. Flores; p. 726: Ernesto Galarza; p. 727: Elsa Gómez; p. 728: Carolina Herrera; p. 729: Dolores Fernández Huerta; p. 730: Tania León; p. 731: Modesto A. Maidique; p. 732: Eduardo Mata; p. 733: Julián Nava; p. 734: Miguel A. Nevárez; p. 735: Katherine D. Ortega; p. 735: Manuel Pacheco (photo by Julieta González); p. 735: Guadalupe C. Quintanilla; p. 736: Mario E. Ramírez (photo by Gittings); p. 736: Paul Rodríguez; p. 737: Luis Santeiro; p. 738: Cristina Saralegui; p. 738: Alberto Serrano; p. 739: Roberto Suárez.

Glossary

A

acto – a one-act Chicano theater piece developed out of collective improvisation.

adelantado – the commander of an expedition who would receive, in advance, the title to any lands that he would discover.

agringado – literally "Gringo-ized" or Americanized.

audiencia – a tribunal that ruled over territories.

Aztlán – originally the mythological land of origin of the Mechica nations, to which the Toltecs and the Aztecs belong. Chicanos identify this land of origin as the geographic region of the American Southwest, figuratively their homeland.

B

babalao – a spiritual healer, witch, or advisor, especially in *santería*.

barrio – neighborhood.

batos locos – See *pachuco(s)*.

behareque – thatched huts used by Indians of the Caribbean.

bodega – a small general store.

bohíos – thatched-roofed huts used by the Caribbean Indians.

botánica – a shop that specializes in herbs and folk potions and medicines.

bracero – from *brazo*, arm, literally someone who works with their arms or performs manual labor; originally applied to temporary Mexican agricultural and railroad workers, it is also occasionally used to refer to any unskilled Mexican worker.

bulto – a wooden sculpture in the image of a Catholic saint.

C

cacique – the American Indian village chieftain.

caló – a Mexican-American dialect, often associated with *pachucos*.

canción – song.

capilla – chapel.

carpa – from the Quechua word meaning an "awning of branches;" in Spanish it has come to mean a tent. Circuses and tent theaters have come to be known as *carpas* by extension.

carreta – cart.

caudillo – chief, leader, originally of the rural poor, but today quite often used to refer to any grass-roots political leader.

charrerías – contests of the Mexican cowboys.

charro – a Mexican cowboy of the Jalisco region, maintaining the dress and customs often associated with *mariachis*.

Chicano – derivative of *Mechicano*, the same Nahuatl word that gave origin to the name of Mexico. The term originally meant Mexican immigrant worker in the early twentieth century, but became the name adopted by Mexican Americans, especially during the days of the civil rights and student movements.

chinampa – a man-made island or floating garden, developed by Meso-American Indians as an agricultural technique.

cimarrones – runaway slaves.

colonia – literally a "colony," it refers to the enclave of Hispanic population within a city, much as the term *barrio* is used today.

compadrazgo – godparenthood, usually through the baptism of a child. *Compadrazgo* is the extension of kinship to non-relatives and the strengthening of responsibilities among kin.

compadres – co-parents; godparents.

confianza – trust, the basis of the relationships between individuals in many spheres of social activity, but especially among kin.

conjunto – said of a Texas, northern-Mexico musical style as well as of the ensemble that plays it, usually made up of a guitar, a base guitar, a drum, and a button accordion.

corrido – a Mexican ballad.

criollo – a Creole, that is, someone of Spanish (European) origin born in the New World.

crónica – a local-color newspaper column often satirizing contemporary customs.

cronista – the writer of a *crónica*.

curandero – a folk healer who combines the practices of the Mexican Indians and Spanish folk-healing.

E

encomendero – the owner of the *encomienda*.

encomienda – the system by which a Spaniard held in high esteem by the King and Queen was given ownership of land in the New World and authorized to "protect" the Indians who had occupied the land in exchange for their free labor. This failed attempt at establishing feudal baronies was marked by the exploitation of the Indians.

ex-voto – a gift presented to a saint as a show of gratitude for a favor conceded.

F

familia, la – the greater family, which includes the immediate nuclear household and relatives that are traced on the female and male sides.

finca – farm, ranch.

G

gallego – in Cuban farce, the stock Galician Spaniard, known for his hard head and frugality.

H

hacendados – the owner of a *hacienda*.

hacienda – a large ranch derivative of the *latifundia* system.

hermandad – brotherhood.

I

indigenismo – an emphasis on American Indian and Pre-Colombian origins and identity.

ingenios – plantations, especially of sugar.

Isleños – descendants of the Canary Island settlers in southern Louisiana.

J

jíbaro – originally an American Indian word for "highlander," it is what Puerto Ricans call the rural mountain folk, but has also come to be symbolic of the national identity of Puerto Ricans.

K

kiva – a secret underground ceremonial chamber, especially as used in Pueblo culture for ceremonies and meetings.

L

latifundia – a large estate or ranch originating in ancient Roman civilization.

lectores – professional (hired) readers who would read books, magazines, and newspapers to cigar-rollers as they performed their laborious tasks.

M

macana – a wooden war club.

manda – a sacrificial offering to a saint in order to receive some favor.

maquiladora – a factory on the Mexican side of the border that performs part of the manual assembly of products at the comparatively lower wages offered by the Mexican economy. These products would then be shipped back to the United States for finishing and marketing by the partner company.

Marielito – a Cuban refugee who arrived in the United States as a result of the Mariel boatlift in the 1980s.

mestizo – an individual of mixed Spanish (or European) and American Indian heritage.

milagro – a charm made of tin, gold, or silver, and shaped in the form of an arm, a leg, a baby, or a house, representing the favor (usually of healing) that is desired from a saint.

morada – the meeting house of the *Penitente* lay brotherhood.

mulata – the stock female Mulatto character in Cuban farce.

música norteña – *conjunto* music from the northern region of Mexico (also includes Texas).

mutualista – mutual aid society, an organization that engaged in social activities and provided basic needs for immigrant workers and their families, including insurance and death benefits for members.

N

nacimiento – a nativity.

Nañiguismo – membership in the secret society of Abakúa, which combines elements of the Efik culture of the southern coast of Nigeria and Freemasonry.

negrito – in Cuban farce, the stock character in black face.

nitainos – principal advisors among the Arawak Indians, quite often in charge of the labor force.

nopal – the prickly pear cactus.

norteño – of northern Mexican origin.

Nuyorican – literally "New York-Rican," a term developed colloquially by Puerto Ricans born or raised in New York to distinguish themselves from those identifying solely with the island.

O

orishas – the African deities of *santería*.

orquesta – a Mexican-American musical ensemble that develops its style around the violin.

P

pachuco – the member of a Mexican-American urban youth subculture, which characteristically developed its own style of dress (zoot suit), its own dialect (*caló*), and its own bilingual-bicultural ideology during the 1940s and 1950s.

padrinos – godparents.

parentesco – kinship sentiment.

parientes – blood relatives.

pastorela – the shepherds play; a folk drama reenacted during the Christmas season.

patria – fatherland.

patria chica – the home region within the fatherland.

pelado – literally the "skinned one" or shirtless one, he was the stock underdog, sharp-witted picaresque character of Mexican vaudeville and tent shows.

Penitente – literally "penitent;" it is the name of a religious brotherhood in New Mexico.

piraguas – a narrow, high-prowed canoe used by the Caribbean Indians.

posada – a community Christmas pageant where carolers go door to door asking for shelter in reenactment of Joseph and Mary's search for lodging.

presidio – a fort, especially characteristic of frontier settlements.

promesa – literally a "promise," it is a sacrificial offering to a saint in order to receive some favor.

R

renegado/a – a renegade, someone who denies his or her Mexican identity.

repartimiento – a form of the *encomienda* which vested the rights over the Indians in the civil authorities.

reredo – altar screen.

retablos – paintings on panels behind the altar in a Catholic church.

revista – a vaudeville musical revue.

S

salsa – literally "sauce," it refers to Afro-Caribbean music.

santería – a synchretic religious sect growing out of the original African religion and the Catholicism of slaves.

santerismo – the same as santería.

santero – in the Southwest, a sculptor of wooden saints; in the Caribbean, a devotee of an *orisha* in *santería*.

santos – the sculpted figures representing saints of the Catholic church; used in worship and prayer.

T

Taino (also Nitaino) – a group of sedentary tribes native to the Caribbean.

V

vaquero – cowboy.

vegas – plantations, especially of coffee.

Y

yerberías – shops specializing in medicinal plants, herbs and potions.

yerberos – folk healers and spiritualists who use herbs in their practices.

yuca – manioc root.

Z

zarzuela – a type of Spanish operetta.

zemíes – gods of the Arawak Indians, also the small Taino religious figure made of clay that represented these gods.

General Bibliography

A

Acosta-Belén, Edna, ed. *The Puerto Rican Woman.* New York: Praeger, 1986.

Acuña, Rodolfo. *Occupied America: A History of Chicanos.* New York: Harper & Row, 1981.

Alvarez, Robert R. *Familia: Migration and Adaptation in Alta and Baja California 1850-1975.* Berkeley: University of California Press, 1987.

B

Barrera, Mario. *Race and Class in the Southwest: A Theory of Racial Inequality.* Notre Dame, Ind.: University of Notre Dame Press, 1979.

Bean, Frank D., and Marta Tienda. *The Hispanic Population of the United States.* New York: Russell Sage Foundation, 1988.

Beardsley, John, and Jane Livingston. *Hispanic Art in the United States: Thirty Painters and Sculptors.* New York: Abbeville Press, 1987.

Boswel, T.D., and J.R. Curtis. *The Cuban American Experience.* Totawa, N.J.: Rowan and Allenheld, 1984.

C

Camarillo, Albert. *Chicanos in a Changing Society.* Cambridge, Mass.: Harvard University Press, 1979.

Cotera, Marta P. *Latina Sourcebook: Bibliography of Mexican American, Cuban, Puerto Rican and Other Hispanic Women Materials in the USA.* Austin, Texas: Information Systems Development, 1982.

E

Elías Olivares, Lucia, ed. *Spanish in the U.S. Setting: Beyond the Southwest.* Rosalyn, Va.: National Clearinghouse for Bilingual Education, 1983.

F

Fitzpatrick, Joseph P. *Puerto Rican Americans: The Meaning of Migration to the Mainland.* Englewood Cliffs, N.J.: Prentice Hall, 1987.

Furtaw, Julia C., ed. *Hispanic American Information Directory 1992-1993.* Detroit, Mich.: Gale Research, 1992.

G

García, Mario T. *Mexican Americans.* New Haven, Conn.: Yale University Press, 1989.

H

Hendricks, G.L. *The Dominican Diaspora: From the Dominican Republic to New York City.* New York: Teacher's College Press of Columbia University, 1974.

History Task Force of the Centro de Estudios Puertorriqueños. *Labor Migration under Capitalism: The Puerto Rican Experience.* New York: Monthly Review Press, 1979.

K

Kanellos, Nicolás. *A History of Hispanic Theater in the United States: Origins to 1940.* Austin: University of Texas Press, 1990.

———, ed. *Biographical Dictionary of Hispanic Literature.* Westport, Conn.: Greenwood Press, 1985.

Knight, Franklin W. *The Caribbean.* New York: Oxford University Press, 1990.

L

Llanes, J. *Cuban Americans, Masters of Survival.* Cambridge, Mass.: Harvard University Press, 1982.

Lomeli, Francisco and Julio A. Martínez. *Chicano Literature: A Reference Guide.* Westport, Conn.: Greenwood Press, 1985.

M

McKenna, Teresa Flora and Ida Ortiz, eds. *The Broken Web: The Education Experience of Hispanic American Women.* Berkeley, Calif.: Floricanto Press and the Tomás Rivera Center, 1988.

Meier, Kenneth J. and Joseph Stewart. *The Politics of Hispanic Education.* New York: Russell Sage Foundation, 1987.

Meier, Matt S. and Feliciano Rivera. *Dictionary of Mexican American History.* Westport, Conn.: Greenwood Press, 1981.

Moore, Joan, and Harry Pachón. *Hispanics in the United States.* Englewood Cliffs, N.J.: Prentice Hall, 1985.

Morales, Julio. *Puerto Rican Poverty and Migration: We Just Had to Try Elsewhere.* New York: Praeger, 1986.

P

Pedraza-Bailey, S. *Political and Economic Migrants in America.* Austin: University of Texas Press, 1985.

Portes, Alejandro, and Robert L. Bach. *Latin Journey: Cuban and Mexican Immigrants in the United States.* Berkeley: University of California Press, 1985.

R

Rodríguez, Clara. *Born in the U.S.A.* Boston, Mass.: Unwin Hyman, 1989.

Ryan, Bryan. *Hispanic Writers.* Detroit, Mich.: Gale Research, 1991.

S

Sánchez-Korrol, Virginia. *From Colonia to Community.* Westport, Conn.: Greenwood Press, 1983.

Sandoval, Moisés. *On the Move: A History of the Hispanic Church in the United States.* Maryknoll, N.Y.: Orbis Books, 1990.

Schorr, Edward Allen. *Hispanic Resource Directory.* Juneau, Alaska: Denali Press, 1988.

Shirley, Carl F., ed. *Chicano Writers: First Series.* Detroit, Mich.: Gale Research, 1989.

Suchliki, Jaime. *Cuba: From Columbus to Castro.* Washington, D.C.: Pergammon Press, 1986.

U

United States Commission on Civil Rights. *Puerto Ricans in the Continental United States: An Uncertain Future.* Washington, D.C.: U.S. Commission on Civil Rights, 1976.

Unterburger, Amy L., ed. *Who's Who among Hispanic Americans, 1992-1993.* Detroit, Mich.: Gale Research, 1992.

V

Veciana-Suárez, Ana. *Hispanic Media: Impact and Influence.* Washington, D.C.: The Media Institute, 1990.

Vivó, Paquita, ed. *The Puerto Ricans: An Annotated Bibliography.* New York: R.R. Bowker, 1973.

W

Wagenheim, Kal. *A Survey of Puerto Ricans in the U.S. Mainland in the 1970s.* New York: Praeger, 1975.

Weber, David. *The Mexican Frontier, 1821-1846: The American Southwest under Mexico.* Albuquerque, University of New Mexico Press, 1982.

Index

G

R
973   213371   C.1
K   Kanellos, Nicolas, ed
                    AUTHOR
Reference library of Hispanic
America   TITLE   VOLUME II

Date	Per	Teachers Name	Room

R   C.1
973
K

Kanellos, Nicolas, ed

Reference library of Hispanic
  America, Volume II